VISUAL QUICKPRO GUIDE

AVID XPRESS PRO

FOR WINDOWS AND MACINTOSH

James Monohan

 Peachpit Press

Visual QuickPro Guide
Avid Xpress Pro for Windows and Macintosh
James Monohan

Peachpit Press
1249 Eighth Street
Berkeley, CA 94710
510/524-2178
800/283-9444
510/524-2221 (fax)

Find us on the World Wide Web at: http://www.peachpit.com
To report errors, please send a note to errata@peachpit.com

Peachpit Press is a division of Pearson Education

Editor: Ralph Fairweather
Production Coordinator: Gloria Márquez
Copyeditor: Judy Ziajka
Compositor: Christi Payne and Van Winkle Design Group
Indexer: Palmer Publishing Services
Cover Design: The Visual Group

Notice of rights

Notice of liability

Trademarks

ISBN 0-321-14597-6

9 8 7 6 5 4 3 2 1

Printed and bound in the United States of America

Dedication

For Mom.

Thank You

Ralph Fairweather: editor, mentor, guru. Thanks for going above and beyond the call of duty.

The amazing staff at Peach Pit: Marjorie Baer, Suki Gear, Suzie Lowey, and Judy Ziajka. Thank you for your keen eyes, hard work, patience, and guidance.

The Avid Xpress Pro team, always friendly and able to help out during my head-scratching moments: Rob Gonsalves, Tony Hamwey, Doug Hansel, Dennis Mahoney, and Charlie Russell.

Seth Buncher of the New York Avid Users Group for all the tips.

Matt Smith for his "pro" perspective.

Those who brought me up to speed on music licenses and performance rights societies: Brian Beshears, John Bickerton, and Frank Valentino.

All the AVX plug-in folks (too numerous to mention) who put up with my weekly harassments.

Those who allowed me to use their footage or images in the book: Reid Baker of Ultimatte Corporation, Erin Cristall, Trudy Davies, Alex Garcia, Stephanie Lane, and Dave Schickler.

Dad, Bridget, Andy, and D.

CONTENTS AT A GLANCE

TABLE OF CONTENTS

TABLE OF CONTENTS

Chapter 13: Media and Project Management   573

Chapter 14: Outputting and Exporting   601

Chapter 15: Special Features and Bundled Applications   627

Appendix A: Xpress Pro Help Resources   639

Appendix B: Post Production Extras   643

Index   667

INTRODUCTION

In the late 1980s, the first computer-based nonlinear editing systems emerged, providing revolutionary alternatives to cutting physical film by hand or using linear tape-to-tape editing machines. Avid Technology led the nonlinear revolution with the release of Media Composer in 1989, an editing system that—along with Avid Film Composer—soon became Hollywood's favorite tool for cutting TV shows and films in the 1990s.

The cross-platform Xpress Pro system, intended for editing both DV and uncompressed video and graphics, is the next step up from Xpress DV and the first tier in Avid's new Digital Nonlinear Accelerator (DNA) family. Avid Media Composer Adrenaline is the second tier, for editing a broader range of standard-definition video, and Avid DS Nitris is the top tier, for editing HDTV and standard-definition formats.

All members of the Avid DNA family are compatible with one another and have similar interfaces, so, for example, if you own a postproduction facility, you can buy one copy of Avid Nitris for high-end finishing and multiple copies of Xpress Pro for offline-quality editing of the same project on laptops.

If you have ambitions of becoming a professional editor, owning Xpress Pro or Xpress DV is an entry into the scalable world of Avid products—from a company that in 2002 boasted that 90 percent of all prime-time TV, 85 percent of all feature films, and 80 percent of TV commercials were created using Avid products for postproduction.

Who Should Use This Book

If you have had any experience with some kind of video-editing application, you are ready to use this book to learn Avid Xpress Pro. If you come from the world of tape-to-tape video editing or film editing and have never used any nonlinear editing software, you may want to spend a few days with a very basic program like Pinnacle Studio (Windows) or iMovie (Mac); then, once you've grasped the essential concepts of nonlinear editing, you can move to a more professional-level product like Xpress Pro, with this book as your guide.

How to Use This Book

This book's chapters follow the general chronology of editing a video or film project, from capture and logging, through editing and effects, to final output of a finished program. However, even though you can traverse this book linearly from cover to cover, many readers will prefer to employ it as a reference—you use it when you need it.

For example, when you're working with effects and wonder "How do I apply a transition effect?" look for that topic in either the index or the table of contents; you'll be directed, in this case, to the steps labeled "To apply a transition effect to an edit point."

Most of your task-oriented queries and needs should be answered by the step-by-step instructions that form the core of this book. You'll also encounter the following features:

- ◆ **"About . . ." sections** introduce important concepts, definitions, interface elements, and background information that you need to know before diving into related task steps.

- ◆ **Tips** either provide cool tricks and shortcuts or caution you about potential hang-ups related to the task at hand.

- ◆ **Sidebars** include real-world strategies for using what you are learning, extended tricks of the trade, background information, or additional information about a complicated concept or topic.

A Word about Customized Buttons, Menus, and Keyboard Commands

The step-by-step tasks in this book teach you how to use Xpress Pro by referring to the application's *default layout* of keyboard mappings, buttons, and menu commands. However, Xpress Pro is an extremely customizable program, and you may be using a system in which you or somebody else has reassigned the default keyboard commands, moved buttons, and made other customizations to the interface.

If this is the case, the default keyboard shortcuts and placement of buttons described in the text and shown in the graphics may not always reflect your particular system. For this reason, this book always includes references to the buttons and keyboard commands on the Command palette, because the Command palette itself cannot be customized. If you are ever in doubt about where to find a button or what a keyboard command is, you can always find it on the Command palette.

In fact, many people like to keep the Command palette open as they learn the many often obscure and hidden features buried deep within the Avid interface. For example, to learn about every kind of manipulation you can perform with a 3D effect, open the Command palette and click the 3D tab.

(For more information on using the Command palette, see "Mapping Buttons to the Keyboard and Interface" in Chapter 3.)

Learning Xpress DV with This Book

Although this book is primarily about using Xpress Pro, you can also use it to learn Xpress DV since the two applications are so similar. Some illustrations in this book show some (usually minor) differences between Xpress DV and Xpress Pro windows. If you come across a task that teaches a function that you cannot immediately find in Xpress DV (for example, replace edits), there's a good chance that it is an Xpress Pro–only feature.

The following features are in Xpress Pro 4.0 and not in Xpress DV 3.5:

- **Mojo support:** For more information about the Mojo box, see Appendix B, "Postproduction Extras."

- **Replace edits:** A replace edit is a special kind of edit that does not require In or Out points and allows you to easily replace one Timeline clip with another. (For more information, see "Performing Replace Edits" in Chapter 6.)

- **Extend Edit button:** This button enables you to lengthen a shot, essentially performing a double-roller trim, without entering Trim mode. (For more information, see "Extending Edits" in Chapter 6.)

- **Mixing different resolutions in the same Timeline:** For example, in Xpress Pro you can mix DV video footage with uncompressed titles in the same sequence.

- **24p support:** You can use Xpress Pro to edit 23.986 fps footage (the application supports the Panasonic AG-DVX100 24p camera).

- **24 video and 24 audio Timeline tracks:** Xpress DV allows only 8 video and audio tracks.

INTRODUCTION

- **J-K-L trimming:** Xpress Pro allows you to trim with the Play Reverse, Pause, and Play Forward keys. (For more information, see "Dynamic Trimming with the J-K-L Keys" in Chapter 7.)

- **Clip grouping and ganging:** If you shot a live show with multiple cameras, you can use Xpress Pro to synchronize clips for easy editing between angles. (For more information, see "Grouping Clips and Multicamera Editing" in Chapter 6.)

- **3D effects and 3D tools:** 3D effects give you the ability to move and manipulate images on the Z axis, as well as on the standard X and y axis. ((For more information, see "Working with Xpress 3D Effects" in Chapter 9).

- **Timewarp effects:** Xpress Pro provides some preset motion effects (including speed ramps) on the Effect palette. (For more information, see "Timewarp Motion Effect Presets" in Chapter 9.)

For the most up-to-date information on Xpress DV and how it differs from Xpress Pro, consult the Avid Web site (www.avid.com).

SETTING UP YOUR EDITING SYSTEM

1

Editing with Avid Xpress Pro requires a good deal more than just the software. This chapter covers the Windows and Macintosh computer system requirements for your editing suite, as well as requirements and recommendations for other hardware devices.

Usually, the day you take Xpress Pro out of the box will not be the day you start editing, unless you're a real whiz at this stuff. So allow some time for connecting, testing, and a little head scratching.

Workstation Minimum Requirements

The kind of computer you need to run Xpress Pro successfully depends on whether you're using the Mojo box. Xpress Pro with Mojo requires a faster computer than Xpress Pro alone.

Xpress Pro Software + Mojo Box

Macintosh

◆ **Operating system:** Mac OS X 10.2.6 or higher

◆ **Qualified tower computer:** Dual 1.25-GHz or 1.42-GHz G4 or better with 1 GB of memory

◆ **Qualified laptop computer:** 1-GHz G4 15- or 17-inch PowerBook with 1 GB of memory

Windows

◆ **Operating system:** Windows XP Professional with Service Pack 1

◆ **Qualified tower computer:** HP xw8000 workstation with dual 2.8-GHz Intel Xeon processor, at least 1 GB of memory, nVIDIA Quadro4 980 XGL graphics card, and integrated 1394 port

◆ **Qualified laptop computer:** Dell Latitude C840 notebook with 1.8- to 2.4-GHz Mobile P4 processor, at least 1 GB of memory, integrated graphics, and 1394 port. (Only the 40-GB drive available with this model delivers adequate performance.)

Xpress Pro Software Only

Macintosh

◆ **Operating system:** Mac OS X 10.2.6 or higher

◆ **Qualified tower computer:**

Apple Power Mac: Dual 1.42-GHz G4 processor with nVIDIA GeForce4 Titanium graphics card and integrated FireWire port

Apple Power Mac: Dual 1.25-GHz G4 processor with nVIDIA GeForce4 Titanium graphics card, integrated FireWire port, and 2-MB L3 cache/processor

◆ **Qualified laptop computer:** 1-GHz G4 15- and 17-inch notebooks with integrated graphics and FireWire port

Windows

◆ **Operating system:** Windows XP Professional with Service Pack 1

◆ **Qualified tower computers (all must have at least 512 MB of memory):** HP xw8000 workstation with dual 2.8-GHz Intel Xeon processor, nVIDIA Quadro4 980 XGL graphics card, and integrated 1394 port

◆ **Qualified laptop computer:** Dell Latitude C840 notebook with 1.8- to 2.4-GHz Mobile P4 processor, integrated graphics, and 1394 port. (Only the 40-GB drive available with this model delivers adequate performance.)

✔ Tip

■ See www.avid.com/xpresspro for the latest specification updates.

Video and Audio Hardware Requirements

Your editing suite needs a way to get your media in and out of your computer (a deck, camera, or digital-analog converter) as well as a way to store and play back media once it's on your computer (internal or external hard drives).

FireWire (1394) Connections

Xpress Pro depends upon the FireWire port (also known as the 1394 or iLink port) on the host computer to get video and audio into and out of your system. The Macintosh systems listed here all come with qualified FireWire connections. If your Windows-based system does not come with integrated 1394 ports, or if you want to add a second 1394 bus, the following PCI cards have been qualified by Avid for use with Xpress Pro:

ADS PYRO BasicDV, part number API-310

ADS PYRO 1394DV, part number API-300

ADS PYRO DV 1394, part number API-1394-PCI

SIIG 1394 3-Port PCI, part number NN-400012

SIIG 1394 3-Port PCI i/e, part number NN-440012

VIDEO AND AUDIO HARDWARE REQUIREMENTS

Media Drives

You should have at least two drives connected to your computer, internally or externally.

One drive holds your operating system and editing application, and the other serves as your media drive—the drive to which you capture your source media files. The advantage of this setup is that the same drive will not be unduly taxed by the triple tasks of running your OS, running the Avid application, and playing back media files.

For editing full-resolution DV (which requires only 3.5 MB per second of bandwidth), your media drive should at least be an ATA/IDE drive that spins at 7200 rotations per minute (RPM). You can also use SCSI drives (though often they're overkill for DV) or externally connected FireWire (or IEEE 1394 or iLink) drives.

Decks, Cameras, and Converters

Technically, you don't absolutely need a deck, camera, or converter if all of your media is made available to your system via a storage drive or through a network, but most editors own such a device both to input media and to output the finished movie to tape.

When inputting your video or audio through FireWire (or IEEE 1394 or iLink), all you need to do is connect a FireWire cable from your deck, camera, or converter to the FireWire port on your computer. If you're using a camera, set it to VTR mode.

A digital-analog converter (or a deck or camera that acts as a converter) is useful when you need to capture analog formats such as Hi-8, VHS, or S-VHS; when you want to output your project from Xpress Pro directly to, say, a VCR; or when you don't have a deck or camera and want to watch your movie on an external broadcast monitor. The converter changes the analog signal into a digital signal (DV) or vice versa.

✔ Tips

- For the most current list of decks, cameras, and converters qualified by Avid, consult www.avid.com/xpresspro.

- Read carefully when selecting a deck or camera. Sometimes a deck or camera will support the basics of Xpress Pro, but will not support functions such as Digital Cut.

- The optional Mojo effects accelerator box is also a digital-analog converter. (For more information about the Mojo box, see Appendix B, "PostProduction Extras.")

MEDIA DRIVES

Monitoring Your Audio

You may want to purchase high-quality studio speakers so you can monitor your audio quality while editing. Another option is to use high-quality headphones.

There are two common ways to monitor your audio while editing:

◆ **Through FireWire:** If you have a deck, camera, or converter (including Mojo) connected to your computer via FireWire, then you can hook up your speakers to the analog out ports of the device. This setup will allow you to monitor exactly what is coming out of the FireWire connection, which is what will eventually go out to tape.

You might want to insert a mixer in this chain, between the analog out port and the speakers, to control the levels of the speakers more accurately.

◆ **From a sound card:** While editing, you can have your audio going out from your sound card to your speakers or to a mixer that connects to your speakers. If you go this route, just remember to configure your system's audio output to use your sound card or your Mac's built-in audio controller and designate your sound card as your output in Xpress Pro's Audio Project settings.

✔ Tip

■ When capturing, you may want to connect your speakers directly to your deck or camera so you can hear exactly what was recorded on tape during production and compare it to what is being captured.

Optional Video and Audio Hardware

Following is a list of optional hardware for your Xpress Pro editing suite. The components you choose to acquire depend on your personal and professional needs as an editor.

◆ **Mojo box:** This highly trumpeted external nonlinear accelerator, which connects to your computer via FireWire, is made by Avid specifically for Xpress Pro. The main advantages of Mojo are as follows:

Real-time effects out to external monitor: Without Mojo, you can view real-time effects playback only on your computer monitor, in the Composer window. With Mojo, you can view real-time playback on your external video monitor.

Uncompressed video input and output: With Mojo, you can capture and edit 1:1 uncompressed video along with regular DV25 video and mix both resolutions in the same Timeline.

Analog-digital conversion: Mojo can act as a digital-analog converter. Hence, you can use it to capture or play back composite video or component S-VHS or CYrYb (also known as YUV or CCIR 601) such as input from a BetaSp deck.

(For more information about the Mojo box, see Appendix B.)

◆ **External video monitor:** Most nonlinear editing setups include an external video monitor that sits right next to the computer screen. This monitor is important during editing and output because it allows you see what your movie will look like when eventually played on a television screen.

To connect your external monitor to your computer, you'll typically have a FireWire cable going from the computer to your deck, camera, or converter and then have analog cables (RCA or S-Video cables) going from that device to the monitor.

◆ **Serial port (Mac users) and serial cable (Mac and PC users):** Although FireWire is great for getting audio and video into and out of your computer, it is not the best type of connection for reading timecode information from your DV tapes during capture.

If your deck includes an RS-422 or RS-232 serial port, then you can read timecode more reliably using RS-422 or RS-232 protocols, as long as you have a serial port on your computer. Most PCs come with a serial port, so all you'll need to purchase is a 9-pin-to-9-pin cable to run from your computer to the RS-422 connection on your deck.

If you're a Mac user, you'll need to purchase a USB–serial port adapter or other add-on serial port device for connecting a serial-to-9-pin cable.

Network and Shared Storage Solutions

For those working with multiple Avid systems, Avid offers shared storage solutions that enable multiple editors working on Windows systems to access the same media, which is all stored on one big Avid drive array:

◆ **Avid Unity LANshare EX—Ethernet Only:** This shared storage solution is designed for the same small organizations that are likely to use Xpress Pro. It allows multiple editors to collaborate on the same project, sharing media over an Ethernet network. Perks include an AutoRecover feature for recovering data on any failing drives, file protection, and selective read and write permissions.

◆ **Avid Unity MediaNetwork:** MediaNetwork is like LANshare but is much higher end. It supports more dual-stream and single-stream clients and much more bandwidth, and features more storage capacity and real-time support for up to nine ProTools systems (LANshare does not provide real-time support for ProTools).

✔ Tip

■ None of Avid's other storage-related productivity solutions work with Xpress Pro.

A TOUR OF
YOUR WORKSPACE

2

Xpress Pro is more like a movie-making factory than a simple editing interface; it can take your project from the script breakdown phase to editing and special effects work, all the way through to the final output of your project in the format of your choice.

This chapter provides a brief tour of the Xpress Pro facilities. Experienced editors familiar with past Avid Xpress incarnations may want to skip to Chapter 3.

For those who are fairly new to Xpress Pro or those familiar with only Composer or Symphony, a click on the Tools menu immediately illustrates the fact that Xpress Pro offers a wide variety of self-contained tools for very specific tasks.

The problem is, all of these tools provide ample opportunity for mind-numbing window clutter, especially since Xpress Pro does not anchor its windows anywhere, and you can have several open at any given time. So remember to open a tool only when you need it and to close it when you don't.

That said, Xpress Pro does include a few space-saving features, such as the multitab Project window, the Audio tool toggle feature, customizable toolsets, and the famous SuperBin, all to be detailed in later chapters.

For now, you'll be treated to a general bird's-eye view of the machinery and layout for "the movie factory."

A Glance at the Basic Interface

Selecting Basic from the Toolset menu displays what Xpress Pro considers the principal windows for image and sound editing (**Figure 2.1**).

No matter what stage of editing you're in, the following windows are your mainstays: the Project window, its related bin windows, one or more source windows, the Composer, and the Timeline.

The Project window *A bin window* *The Composer*

Fast menus

A source clip pop-up monitor

The Timeline

Figure 2.1 Xpress Pro basic editing windows.

A GLANCE AT THE BASIC INTERFACE

Folder Bin

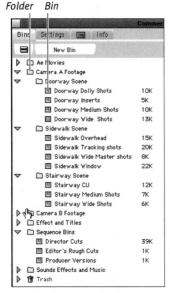

Figure 2.2 This Project window contains several bins and folders as well as a trash can for discarded items.

Figure 2.3 You can customize and then give custom names to multiple versions of settings on the Settings tab.

The Project Window

The Project window is the mother window of your editing session. If you close the Project window, you close your project.

This window contains all of the media and visual effects you can use in your project, as well as your unique user and project settings.

The Project window features four tabs:

◆ **Bins:** This tab contains folders and bins that help organize your project's sequences (the movies you create) as well as anything you could possibly put into a sequence (**Figure 2.2**).

(For more information on using bins, see "Creating Logging Bins" in Chapter 4 and "Organizing with Bins" in Chapter 5.)

The *media objects*—as Xpress Pro calls them—that you can store in bins include master clips, subclips, sequences, custom effects, motion effect clips, precompute files (rendered effects), titles, source files, and even metadata for interactive projects.

(For further information about media objects, see "About Bin Contents: Media Objects" in Chapter 5.)

◆ **Settings:** This tab lists all of your customizable User, Project, and Site settings; the check marks designate which settings are active (**Figure 2.3**).

(For more information on settings, see Chapter 3, "Customizing Your Workspace.")

continues on next page

THE PROJECT WINDOW

◆ 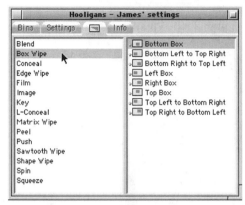 **Effects palette:** The Effects palette contains transition and segment effects: visual effects that you can use in your movie sequence (**Figure 2.4**).

(For more information on how to use the Effects palette, see Chapter 9, "Working with Video Effects.")

◆ **Info:** This tab displays important data about remaining drive space and allocated memory. Click the Hardware or Memory button to see the relevant data (**Figure 2.5**).

(For information on how to set up drive space and memory, see Chapter 1, "Setting Up Your Editing System.")

✔ Tip

■ To tell Xpress Pro which settings to display on the Settings tab, click the Settings tab fast menu (the button that looks like a hamburger) and make a selection from the list that appears.

Figure 2.4 Most effects on the Effects tab (also called the Effects palette) are transition effects.

This drive's capacity is 47.6 GB, with 5.1 GB of free space available.

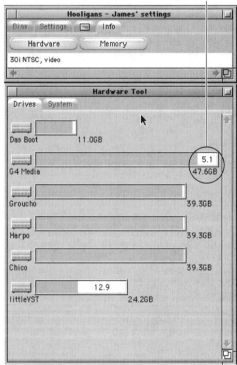

Figure 2.5 Clicking the Hardware button on the Info tab brings up the Hardware tool, which displays information about drive space as well as system information.

The User Profile Routine

After launching an Xpress Pro project, the first thing you should do is click the Settings tab in the Project window and select your personal user profile from the User Profile Selection pop-up menu. Otherwise, Xpress Pro will stick with the default user profile, which contains none of your settings and preferences.

Figure 2.6 You prepare a clip for editing into the Timeline in a source clip pop-up monitor.

Source Clip Monitor

The source clip monitor is where you load and prepare your video and audio clips (or sequences) before you edit them into your main movie sequence.

There are two options for source clip display, depending on how you prefer to organize and configure your workspace. Editors often switch between each mode as they work:

◆ **Independent source monitor:** If the Composer is configured to display one image, double-clicking a clip in a bin opens an independent source pop-up monitor (**Figure 2.6**).

◆ **Source/Record display in the Composer window:** If the Composer is configured to display both a source and a record image, double-clicking a clip in a bin loads a clip into the left (source) side of the Composer (**Figure 2.7**).

Source side   *Record side*

Figure 2.7 In Source/Record mode, the Composer displays source clips on the left side of the window.

To display source clips in independent pop-up monitors:

Do one of the following:

▲ Drag the lower-right corner of the Composer window until the window becomes a square.

The Composer now displays only your sequence's images and sounds, and source clips will be opened in their own, independent source monitor windows (**Figure 2.8**).

▲ On the Settings tab of the Project window, double-click your active Bin setting. In the Bin Settings dialog box that opens, open the Double-Click Loads Object In pop-up menu and choose New Pop-up Monitor (**Figure 2.9**).

Now every time you double-click a clip or sequence, Xpress Pro loads it into an independent source monitor.

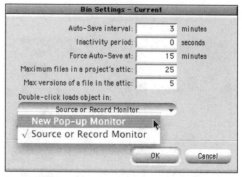

Figure 2.9 If you select New Pop-up Monitor in your Bin settings, a new window opens each time you double-click an object in a bin.

SOURCE CLIP MONITOR

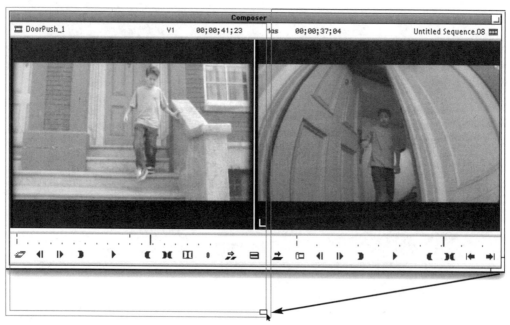

Figure 2.8 In single-monitor (or Basic) display mode, the Composer window displays only what is in the Timeline. To turn a dual-monitor Composer into a single-monitor window, drag the lower right corner to resize it into a square shape.

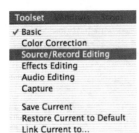

Figure 2.10 You can quickly switch between a single independent source monitor and a dual source/record display using the Toolset menu.

To display source clips in the Composer window:

1. Drag the lower-right corner of the Composer window until the window becomes a rectangle that displays two images.

2. On the Settings tab of the Project window, double-click your active Bin setting. In the Bin Settings dialog box that opens, open the Double-Click Loads Object In pop-up menu and choose Source or Record Monitor.

   The Composer now has two sides: a source side and a record side. Every time you double-click a clip or sequence, Xpress Pro loads it into the source side of the Composer window.

✔ Tip

■ By default, choosing Toolset > Basic configures the Composer for single-monitor display, and choosing Toolset > Source/Record Editing configures the Composer for dual-monitor display (**Figure 2.10**). (For more information on toolsets, see "Using Toolsets" later in this chapter.)

The Composer

The Composer plays the images and sounds of your edited sequence as you create the sequence in the Timeline.

The blue position indicator (the playhead) in the Timeline corresponds to the blue position indicator within the Composer's play bar (the white area underneath the Composer's record monitor; see **Figure 2.11**). Furthermore, marking an In or Out point in the Composer is the same action as marking an In or Out point in the Timeline.

By default, the controls at the bottom of the Composer allow you to play your sequence, mark In and Out points, enter trim mode, and set keyframes. If you prefer, you can change these buttons using the Command palette. (For more information see "Mapping Buttons to the Keyboard and Interface" in Chapter 3.)

In addition, clicking the 🔲 fast menu at the lower left of the Composer opens the Tool palette, to which you can map buttons or menu commands (**Figure 2.12**).

✔ Tip

- For information about the Composer's menus, see "Using the Composer's Menus" in Chapter 6.

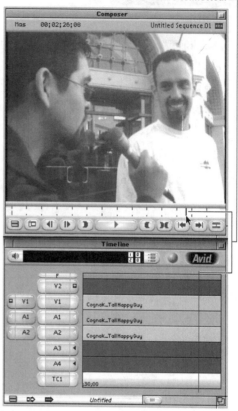

These are connected.

Figure 2.11 When you move the blue playhead in the Composer, the blue playhead in the Timeline follows, and vice versa.

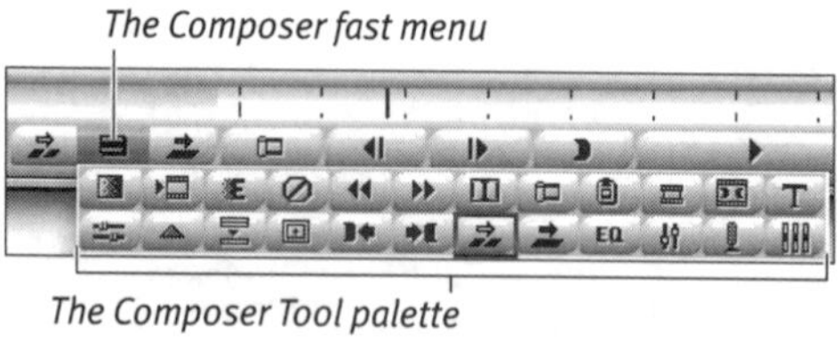

The Composer fast menu

The Composer Tool palette

Figure 2.12 You can map your most frequently used tools onto the Composer Tool palette, which is accessible from the Composer fast menu.

The Timeline

You put together your movie sequence in the Timeline, the window in which Xpress Pro graphically represents your creative work (**Figure 2.13**).

In basic terms, editing in Xpress Pro involves taking media selections from the bins in the Project window and placing them somewhere in the Timeline. (For more information about editing into the Timeline, see Chapter 6, "Making Edits.")

Xpress Pro allows a maximum of 24 tracks (or layers) of video and 24 tracks of audio in the Timeline. If this doesn't sound like enough tracks for you, consider combining video tracks with nesting or audio tracks with mixdowns.

(For more information on nesting, see "Creating Nests" in Chapter 9. For more information on audio mixdowns, see "Mixing Down Audio Tracks" in Chapter 12.)

✔ Tip

■ For information about the Timeline's menus, see "Setting Up and Saving Your Timeline's Display" in Chapter 5.

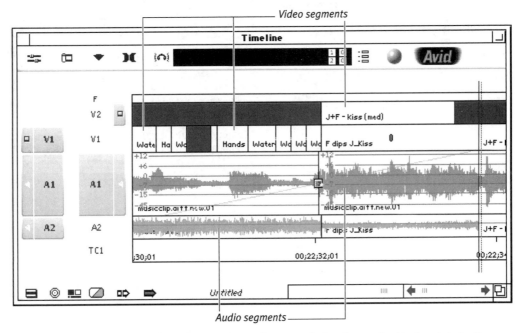

Figure 2.13 Generally, editing involves taking a segment of a source clip (or other media object) and placing it somewhere in the Timeline.

THE TIMELINE

The Clipboard Monitor

The clipboard monitor—almost identical to a source monitor (**Figure 2.14**)—functions as an intermediary in copy, paste, and retrieval operations in the following types of tasks:

◆ Copying a section of a sequence to be used elsewhere in the same sequence or in another sequence

◆ Extracting or lifting material from a sequence to be used elsewhere in the same sequence or in another sequence

Think of the clipboard monitor as a type of source clip monitor used to load something from your sequence as opposed to your bin.

To open the clipboard monitor:

◆ Choose Tools > Clipboard Monitor.

(For more information on how to use the clipboard, see "Creating Subclips and Subsequences" and "Using the Clipboard Monitor" in Chapter 6.)

Copy to Clipboard loads selected tracks only.

Marked material loaded into clipboard

Figure 2.14 After marking a portion of your sequence with In and Out points, select Copy to Clipboard to load the marked portion of your sequence into the clipboard monitor.

The Locators Window

You can use locators to mark particular frames in clips or sequences and add location-specific comments.

Once you add locators to a clip, the Locators window lists those locators with their accompanying comments (**Figure 2.15**).

To open the Locators window:

◆ Choose Tools > Locators.

(For more information on how to use locators, see "Using Locators" in Chapter 6.)

✔ Tip

■ In addition to using locators, you can add comments to clips and segments using the Add Comments option, available in the Composer Clip Name menu. (For more information, see the sidebar "Another Way to Make Comments" in Chapter 6.)

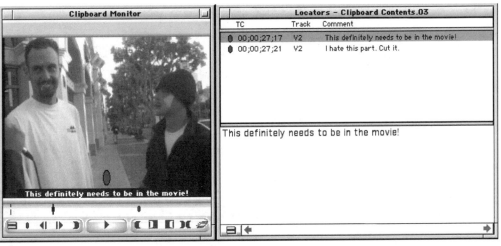

Figure 2.15 Locators are great for adding comments to particular moments in your video. You can view the list of locators in the Locators window.

The Command Palette

The Command palette contains all of Xpress
Pro's mappable command and menu buttons. The palette organizes buttons according to their editing functions (**Figure 2.16**).

You can use the Command palette to map
buttons as well as menu commands to the
keyboard, the Tool palette, the Composer, and
the Timeline; you cannot change the buttons
on source monitors or the clipboard monitor.

In addition, you can work directly from the
Command palette by clicking buttons on
the palette itself.

To open the Command palette:

Do one of the following:

▲ Press Ctrl+3 (Windows) or
Command+3 (Mac).

▲ Choose Tools > Command Palette.

(For more information on using the
Command palette to customize your keyboard and interface, see "Mapping Buttons
to the Keyboard and Interface" in Chapter 3.)

THE COMMAND PALETTE

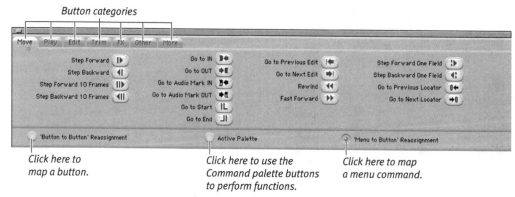

Button categories

Click here to
map a button.

Click here to use the
Command palette buttons
to perform functions.

Click here to map
a menu command.

Figure 2.16 The Command palette allows you to map buttons or menus to the keyboard, the Tool palette,
the Composer, and the Timeline.

Figure 2.17 The Title tool includes dotted title-safe lines so you know what will and won't appear on your broadcast (external) monitor.

The Title Tool

You can use the Title tool to create titles and simple graphics (**Figure 2.17**).

Titles in Xpress Pro can have drop shadows and borders as well as colored backgrounds of varying degrees of transparency. In addition, you can draw simple shapes such as circles, squares, and lines within the title.

If you have particular title treatments that you use over and over again, you can save any title as a template.

To open the Title tool:

1. In the Timeline (or Composer), move the position indicator to the video frame chosen as your background reference image. (Use of a background image is optional.)

2. *Do one of the following:*

   ▲ Choose Clip > New Title.

   ▲ Choose Tools > Title Tool.

   ▲ Click the Title Tool button  on the Composer's fast menu or elsewhere on the interface.

✔ Tip

■ On Windows systems, you can also create titles using the Avid Marquee application (available only in Xpress Pro).

The Audio Tools

Xpress Pro has six audio tools that work together to give you a wide range of control over your audio levels and audio mix.

Audio Tool

The Audio tool is your levels meter (**Figure 2.18**). While recording, editing, or outputting, use this tool to check your audio input or output levels to ensure that they are strong enough to be heard, but are not peaking.

✔ Tips

- To monitor input levels with the Audio tool, click the little O buttons on the top of the window so that they each display I.

- When editing DV, do not let your sound peak over 0 dB on the digital scale. Distortion will occur with any digital audio signal over 0 dB.

To open the Audio tool:

Do one of the following:

▲ Press Ctrl+1 (Windows) or Command+1 (Mac).

▲ Choose Tools > Audio Tool.

(For more information on using the Audio tool, see "Monitoring Your Sound" in Chapter 12.)

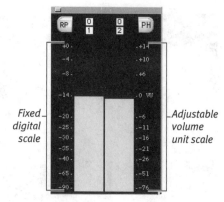

Figure 2.18 The Audio tool displays a fixed digital scale as well as an adjustable volume unit scale. For digital projects (such as DV projects), don't let your audio peak over 0 dB on the digital scale.

Figure 2.19 After selecting Audio Clip Gain in the Timeline fast menu, you can use the Audio Mix tool to gang (or link) two or more tracks together for simultaneous level adjustments.

Graphic audio-level keyframes (or rubber bands)

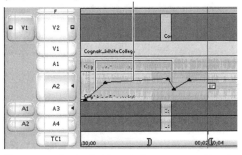

Figure 2.20 The Audio EQ tool allows you to set levels by frequency range.

Click to record audio-level slider actions during playback.

Figure 2.21 After selecting Auto Clip Gain from the Timeline fast menu, you can use the Automation Gain tool to create and manipulate audio-level keyframes within a clip.

Audio Mix Tool

The Audio Mix tool lets you adjust audio levels (the volume) and pan values (left/right speaker settings) for entire audio segments. You can apply such adjustments to one or more segments on one or more tracks at a time (**Figure 2.19**).

To open the Audio Mix tool:

◆ Choose Tools > Audio Mix.

(For more information on the Audio Mix tool, see "Adjusting Audio Levels" in Chapter 12. For more information on panning, see "Panning Audio Tracks and Segments" in Chapter 12.)

Automation Gain Tool

The Automation Gain tool enables you to adjust audio levels within a Timeline segment, creating visible keyframed audio levels (rubber bands) in the Timeline (**Figure 2.20**). The tool also allows you to record level adjustment actions while you play your movie—mixing your movie in real time (**Figure 2.21**).

(For more information on the Automation Gain tool, see "Adjusting Audio Levels" and "Creating and Manipulating Audio-Level Keyframes" in Chapter 12.)

✔ Tips

■ To learn how to create rubber bands without using the Automation Gain tool, see the sidebar "When You Don't Need the Audio Mix and Automation Gain Tools" in Chapter 12.

■ You can also use the Automation Gain tool for panning. See "Panning Audio Tracks and Segments" in Chapter 12.

THE AUDIO TOOLS

Audio EQ Tool

The Audio EQ tool lets you adjust frequencies in the high, mid, and low ranges of an audio segment. You can save EQ effects as templates and apply them to multiple situations (**Figure 2.22**).

To open the Audio EQ tool:

Do one of the following:

▲ Choose Tools > Audio EQ.

▲ Click and hold down the Effect Mode Selector pull-down tab at the top left of the Audio Mix tool, Automation Gain tool, or AudioSuite window. Select Audio EQ Tool.

(For more information on the Audio EQ tool, see "Applying EQ Effects to Audio" in Chapter 12.)

AudioSuite Window

Use the AudioSuite Window to apply audio effects to your audio segments and tracks (**Figure 2.23**).

The plug-ins are courtesy of Digidesign (which is owned by Avid), the maker of Protools, one of the most respected digital audio editing systems in the industry.

In addition to applying them to existing segments, you can apply these plug-ins to create new master clips that contain audio effects.

(For more information, see "Applying AudioSuite Plug-in Effects" in Chapter 12.)

✔ Tip

■ You can purchase additional audio plug-ins not included with your system from Digidesign's Web site.

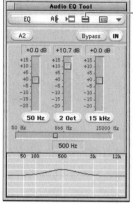

The fast menu lists preset and custom EQ templates.

Figure 2.22 You can manipulate levels and set pan values in the Automation Gain tool. You can also use the tool to record a real-time mix.

Choose your plug-in here.

Figure 2.23 The AudioSuite window.

Figure 2.24 You can save monitor space by toggling between different audio tools from within the same window.

Figure 2.25 You can use the Audio Punch-In tool to quickly add voice-over to your sequence.

To open the AudioSuite plug-in window:

◆ Choose Tools > AudioSuite.

✔ Tip

■ To save space in your interface as you edit, you can toggle among Automation Gain, Audio Mix, Audio EQ, and AudioSuite from within the same window by opening the menu in the upper-left corner of any of these audio tools (**Figure 2.24**).

Audio Punch-In Tool

The Audio Punch-In tool allows you to quickly add narration (voice-over) to your movie (**Figure 2.25**).

The great thing about this tool is that you can record your voice while simultaneously watching your sequence, ensuring that your recording and your movie match.

To open the Audio Punch-In tool:

◆ Choose Tools > Audio Punch-In.

(For more information about the Audio Punch-In tool, see "Recording Audio with the Punch-in Tool" in Chapter 4.)

Toolsets

Clicking through the Tools menu may leave you daunted by the quantity of floating windows in Xpress Pro. To make life a little easier, the application provides the Toolset menu, which offers several default tool/window arrangements designed for particular tasks:

◆ **Basic (Shift+F7):** As discussed earlier in this chapter, this is the traditional arrangement of the Project window, source clip pop-up windows, Timeline, and Composer.

◆ **Color Correction (Shift+F8):** This toolset features a tri-image Composer as well as Xpress Pro's multitab Color Correction window (**Figure 2.26**).

(For more information on color correction, see Chapter 10, "Color Correction.")

◆ **Source/Record (Shift+F9):** As mentioned earlier, this option puts the Composer in dual-display mode.

Three-up Composer —

Color Correction window —

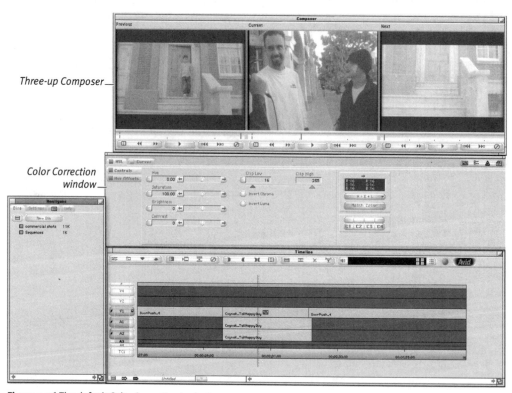

Figure 2.26 The default Color Correction toolset.

◆ **Effects Editing (Shift+F10):** This option adds the Effects Editor window to the Basic toolset arrangement. Use this toolset for editing segment and transition effects.

(For more information on effects editing, see Chapter 9, "Working with Video Effects.")

◆ **Audio Editing (Shift+F11):** Use this arrangement for monitoring, manipulating, and mixing audio levels and frequencies in a sequence (**Figure 2.27**).

(For more information on audio editing, see Chapter 12, "Working with Audio.")

You can switch between audio tools here.

Audio tool

Automation Gain tool

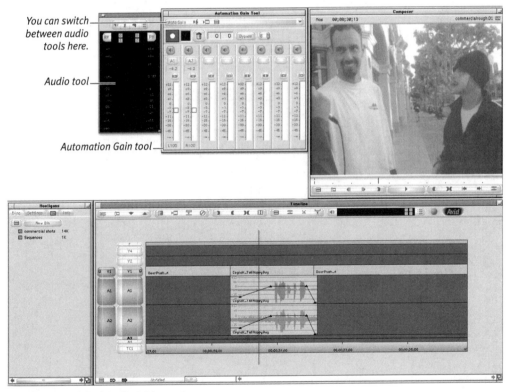

Figure 2.27 The default Audio Editing toolset.

TOOLSETS

◆ **Capture (Shift+F12):** Use this toolset, which features the Capture tool (**Figure 2.28**), for capturing video or audio from your source tapes onto your hard drives.

(For more information on capturing, see Chapter 4, "Capturing and Importing Media.")

Click the Record button to initiate capture.

Name each clip and add comments.

Designate your logging bin and source media drive.

Control your deck or camera.

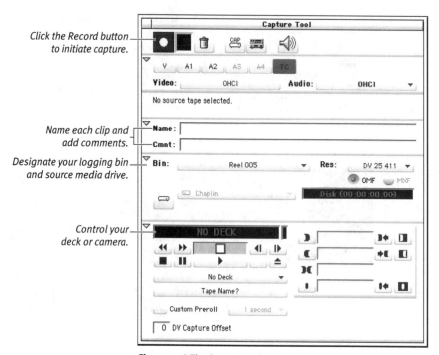

Figure 2.28 The Capture tool.

Figure 2.29 To select something from a fast menu, simply click the fast menu icon. Then select the desired command or item. You don't need to keep the mouse button pressed.

Figure 2.30 The Composer's contextual shortcut menu contains eight shortcuts.

Shortcuts and Fast Menus

Xpress Pro offers three ways to get around the interface and perform commands quickly.

Fast menus

▤ Fast menus (which many Avid editors call the hamburger menu, because of the appearance of the icon) are context-sensitive menus. That means the content of the fast menu is specific to the window or tool in which it is activated. The fast menu usually provides access to display options (such as in the Timeline) or command buttons (such as in the Composer).

To open a fast menu:

◆ Click the fast menu button (the hamburger-like icon) and select an item from the list of options. You don't need to hold down the mouse; the fast menu stays open until you make a selection (**Figure 2.29**).

✔ Tip

■ Clicking the fast menu in the Composer opens the Tool palette, to which you can map buttons and menu options from the Command palette.

Shortcut Menus

Shortcut menus often lead to hidden functions and features that don't appear on any other main menus (**Figure 2.30**).

To open a shortcut menu:

◆ Hold down the mouse in any window and right-click (Windows) or Ctrl+Shift-click (Mac).

A context menu appears, displaying various options specific to that window.

Keyboard Shortcuts

By default, many of Xpress Pro's menu items have keyboard equivalents listed next to them. For example, to create a new bin, you can choose File > New Bin *or* press Ctrl+N (Windows) or Command+N (Mac) (**Figure 2.31**).

Opening a Keyboard window (**Figure 2.32**) from the Settings tab allows you to map buttons as well as menu items to the keyboard.

(For more information on mapping your keyboard, see "Mapping Buttons to the Keyboard and Interface" in Chapter 3.)

Figure 2.31 Xpress Pro lists keyboard shortcuts to the right of menu commands.

The menu command for creating a new bin is mapped to this key.

Figure 2.32 Here, the menu command for creating a new bin is mapped to the B key. If you are unsure what command is mapped to a key, double-click a Keyboard setting on the Settings tab to open a Keyboard window and then hold the pointer over the key. The name of the mapped menu command appears.

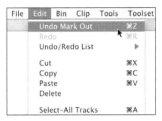

Figure 2.33 Here, since the last action was a Mark Out command, the undo option in the Edit menu is listed as Undo Mark Out.

Figure 2.34 Here, the first recorded action in Xpress Pro's memory is a Splice-In command. Selecting this item will undo the preceding six actions.

Undo

For those times when you make a mistake and want to go back a few steps, Xpress Pro offers two undo features: You can perform the traditional undo or redo of your last action (**Figure 2.33**), or you can use Xpress Pro's Undo/Redo List option and go many steps back in time (**Figure 2.34**).

The Undo/Redo List option is really cool because you can use it to undo or redo a whole sequence of steps in one click, and Xpress Pro displays the name of each action so you know exactly what you're undoing.

✔ Tips

- The Undo/Redo List option lists only editing-related actions in the currently active sequence: actions that you perform in source monitors, the Composer, or the Timeline.

- Closing your current sequence erases the current Undo/Redo list.

To undo the last action performed:

Do one of the following:

▲ Choose Edit > Undo.

▲ Press Ctrl+Z (Windows) or Command+Z (Mac).

To redo an action previously undone:

Do one of the following:

▲ Choose Edit > Redo.

▲ Press Ctrl+R (Windows) or Command+R (Mac).

To select a past action to undo or redo from a history list of actions:

◆ Choose Edit > Undo/Redo List and choose from the list of past actions.

Xpress Pro lists the most recently performed action first and the first action performed last.

Viewing and Emptying the Trash

Xpress Pro provides its own trash can, in the Project window. The trash icon appears only after you select Delete Selected Bins from a Bins tab fast menu.

Bins placed in the trash can are not officially eliminated from your project until you select Empty Trash on the Bins tab.

To make the trash can appear:

1. If the trash is not already visible, select one or more bins on the Bins tab of the Project window.

2. Open the Bins tab fast menu and select Delete Selected Bins (**Figure 2.35**).

   Xpress Pro places the selected bin in a trash can that appears at the bottom of the window. All trashed items have red text (**Figure 2.36**).

Only whole bins can be placed in the Project window's trash can. To place individual objects in the trash, you can create a bin for those items and then drag that bin to the trash.

Figure 2.35 To place bins in the trash can, click the Bins tab's fast menu and choose Delete Selected Bins.

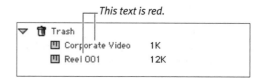

Figure 2.36 You can be sure a bin is in the trash if its name appears in red.

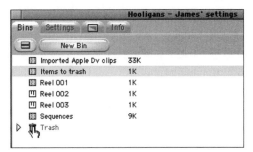

Figure 2.37 The bin named Items to Trash is being dragged to the trash can (this is what the operation looks like just before the mouse is released). The trashed bin will remain in the trash can until you empty the trash.

Figure 2.38 To empty the trash, open the fast menu on the Bins tab of the Project window and select Empty Trash.

To place any object in the Project window's trash:

1. With the trash can visible in the Project window, choose File > New Bin to create a bin for trashed items.

2. In the Project window, drag unwanted objects from other bins into the trash bin you created.

3. Drag the bin containing the unwanted objects onto the trash icon in the Project window (**Figure 2.37**).

   The bin appears in the trash can and can now be deleted by emptying the trash can.

To empty the Xpress Pro trash can:

◆ Click the Project window's fast menu and select Empty Trash (**Figure 2.38**).

✔ Tip

■ You cannot open bins that are in the trash. To open a trashed bin, first drag the bin icon out of the trash.

Information Tools and Utilities

The following tools will help you manage your media files, track timecode and other pertinent information about your files, and troubleshoot your system.

Media Creation Tool

You use the Media Creation dialog box to tell Xpress Pro which media drive to use to store media files and other related data (**Figure 2.39**). You can use this tool to select or filter out particular drives and tell Xpress Pro which drives to use for capturing, title creation, file import, mixdown files, and motion effects.

To open the Media Creation dialog box:

◆ Choose Tools > Media Creation.

(For more information on media creation, see Chapter 4, "Capturing and Importing Media.")

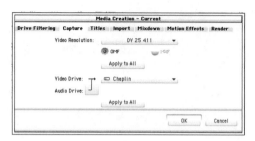

Figure 2.39 On the Capture tab of the Media Creation dialog box, you can tell Xpress Pro to send audio and video to either the same drive (above) or separate drives (below).

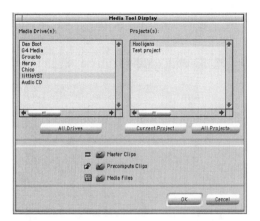

Figure 2.40 Use the Media tool to find and list master clips, precompute clips, and media files. You can display files on selected drives (on the left) or associated with selected project names (on the right).

Media Tool

The Media tool (**Figure 2.40**) lists master clips, precompute files, and media files associated with one or more projects and located on one or more media drives (**Figure 2.41**).

To open the media tool:

◆ Choose Tools > Media Tool.

(For more information on the Media tool, see "Working with Source Media" Chapter 13.)

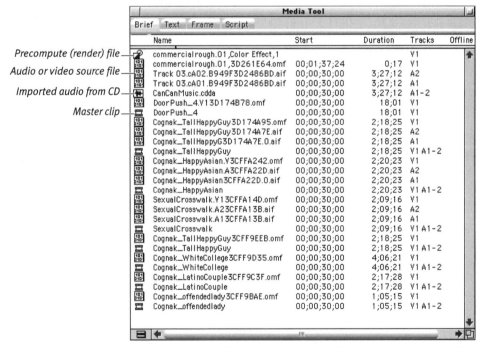

Precompute (render) file
Audio or video source file
Imported audio from CD
Master clip

Figure 2.41 After you click OK in the Media Tool Display window, a window will display all requested files.

The Timecode Window

The Timecode window (**Figure 2.42**) displays the same sequence-related information as the Composer's Tracking Information menu, the difference being that the Timecode window is large and highly visible on your desktop.

The Timecode window can display information timecode numbers, frame numbers or film footage reference numbers for the Timeline position indicator, In to Out point duration, absolute and remaining time duration, and so on. In addition, it can display clip name information, telling you what segment is on what Timeline track.

To open the Timecode window:

◆ Choose Tools > Timecode Window.

By default, the window displays master timecode—timecode for the current position of the playhead in the Timeline.

To display other information in the Timecode window:

1. Click the Timecode window.

2. (Optional) To switch to Frame or Footage display, choose Frame or Footage from the pop-up list that appears.

3. From the pop-up list that appears, select the type of information you want to display (Mas, I/O, and so on; see **Figure 2.43**).

The Timecode window displays that timecode.

✔ Tip

■ For an explanation of the options available in the Timecode window, see the sidebar "Understanding Timecode" in Chapter 4.

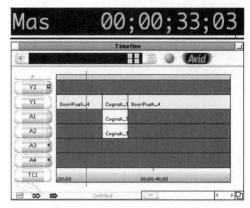

Figure 2.42 In this case, the Timecode window reports that the playhead is at sequence timecode 00;00;33;03. Keep in mind that the start of a sequence doesn't necessarily have to be 00;00;00;00.

Figure 2.43 The Timecode window can display several types of timecode information, such as source and master, drop frame and nondrop frame, as well as clip names.

Figure 2.44 You can use the Xpress Pro Calculator to add, subtract, divide, multiply, and convert timecode and frame numbers.

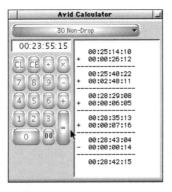

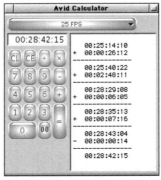

Figure 2.45 Here, timecode calculations are being performed in 30-fps nondrop-frame mode (above) and then converted to 25 fps (below).

The Xpress Pro Calculator

The Xpress Pro Calculator (see **Figure 2.44**) converts timecode and film key numbers between different video and formats. For instance, to convert an NTSC project to a PAL project, you need to know how to translate 29.97 fps timecode into 25 fps timecode.

In addition, the calculator can add, subtract, multiply, and divide video and film durations, and it can convert hours, minutes, and seconds into frames.

To open the Xpress Pro Calculator:

Do one of the following:

▲ Choose Tools > Calculator.

▲ Press Ctrl+2 (Windows) or Command+2 (Mac).

To convert a timecode entry to another format:

1. Make sure the pop-up menu at the top of the Xpress Pro Calculator displays the format from which you are converting.

2. Enter a timecode number or perform a timecode calculation.

3. Click the pop-up menu at the top of the calculator. Choose the format to which you want to convert (**Figure 2.45**).

   Xpress Pro converts your timecode numbers to the new format

✔ Tip

■ You don't need to enter leading zeros, colons, or semicolons when typing timecode. Just type the numbers, and Xpress Pro adds those characters for you.

The Console Window

The Console window (**Figure 2.46**) displays the following types of information:

◆ Loaded Xpress Pro components

◆ Error message logs

◆ System ID and other system information

◆ Duration and other information on sequences, clips, and other objects found in bins or on the Timeline

◆ Information regarding a recent import or recording action

This information is useful for troubleshooting, especially when you're talking to Xpress Pro Customer Support.

Drive name   *Drive ID*   *Total capacity*   *Used space*   *Available space*

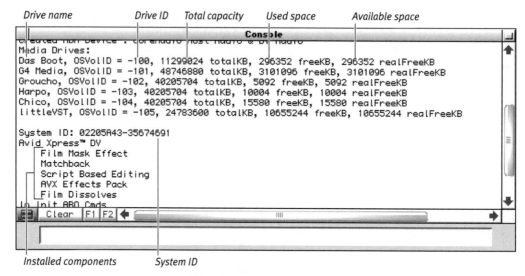

Installed components   *System ID*

Figure 2.46 The Console displays, among other things, information on hard drive identities, free and used drive space, the system ID, and installed Xpress Pro components.

To display system information in the Console window:

1. *Do one of the following:*
   - ▲ Choose Tools > Console.
   - ▲ Press Ctrl+6 (Windows) or Command+6 (Mac).

2. Scroll to the top of the Console window to view the system ID and other system information.

To display Console information on any object in a bin:

1. Choose Tools > Console.

2. Select an object in an open bin.

3. Choose File > Get Bin Info.

   The window displays the total duration of the selected items and the number of items in the bin (**Figure 2.47**).

Refers to objects in the current bin

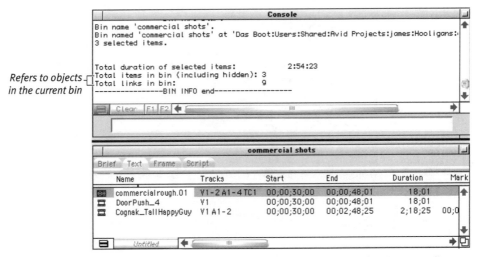

Figure 2.47 This Console reports that the selected bin contains three items, totaling 2 minutes, 54 seconds, and 23 frames of media.

To display Console information on a Timeline segment:

1. Choose Tools > Console.

2. Place the position indicator over a segment in the Timeline.

3. Make sure the Timeline is selected and Choose File > Get Position Info (**Figure 2.48**).

This is the only clip at the position indicator's current location.

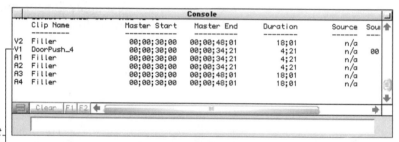

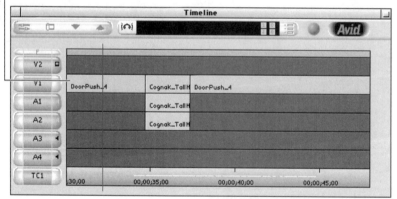

Figure 2.48 In this case, the Console reports that, at the position of the playhead, there is one clip on V1 with a duration of 4 seconds and 21 frames. The rest of the tracks contain black filler.

Available space   Capacity

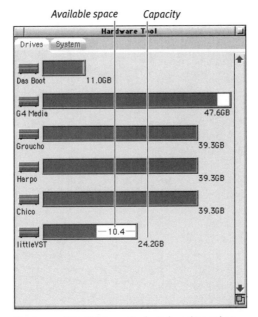

Figure 2.49 This Hardware Tool window shows that the media drives are almost full, except for littleVST, which has 10.4 GB available.

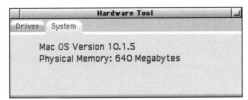

Figure 2.50 The Hardware tool's System tab reports the OS installed on the computer as well as the amount of RAM installed.

The Info Display/Hardware Tool

The Hardware tool displays the same information available by clicking Hardware on the Info tab of the Project window; the tool displays the amount of storage space available on all active hard drives (**Figure 2.49**). It also provides OS and RAM information.

The shaded (pink) areas represent data stored on a drive, and the white areas represent empty space.

To open the Hardware tool:

Do one of the following:

▲ Choose Tools > Hardware.

▲ In the Project window, click the Info tab. Then click the Hardware button.

To view OS and RAM information in the Hardware tool:

◆ In the Hardware tool, click the System tab. Xpress Pro displays the system's OS version number and amount of physical memory (**Figure 2.50**).

CUSTOMIZING YOUR WORKSPACE

3

Everyone has personal workspace preferences, and they often defy default recommendations. Who says you should map Lift and Extract to the Z and X keys? Who says the Timeline always has to be at the bottom of the screen?

Xpress Pro gives you more than enough personal control over the look and layout of tools and windows. By mapping buttons to the keyboard and interface, you can edit in a way that is most intuitive to you and most compatible with your unique approach to editing. Furthermore, thanks to custom toolsets and workspaces, you can group together various tools for different workflow situations, such as editing, color correction, or audio work, and then map the trigger for each particular tool grouping to your keyboard.

Taking the time to create personal settings tailored to your needs will pay off when you get an Xpress Pro job at another location. Simply bring your own customized user profile along on a disk and load it in, and you'll have all of your familiar keyboard shortcuts, color and appearance settings, window arrangements, and favorite buttons instantly at your fingertips.

Understanding User, Project, and Site Settings

The Xpress Pro settings, all found on the Settings tab of the Project window (**Figure 3.1**), are grouped into three categories. Understanding how these groups of settings differ from one another is the key to understanding how Xpress Pro views settings and will help you navigate the myriad customizable features.

- **User settings:** User settings address questions such as "What color do you want your buttons?" and "How are your windows arranged?"

  These settings are linked to the user profile you select in the User Profile Selection pop-up menu at the top of the Settings tab in the Project window. (For more information, see "Creating and Selecting a User Profile" later in this chapter.)

- **Project settings:** Project settings address questions such as "Is the project NTSC or PAL?" and "Are you using drop-frame or nondrop-frame timecode?"

  These settings are tied to a particular project, and you may have different settings for different projects.

- **Site settings:** Site settings address questions such as "Is your DV deck connected via FireWire or through the serial port?" and "Should the system automatically be connected to a LANshare when you launch Xpress Pro?"

  These settings pertain to your editing system's particular hardware and don't change unless you change your overall system setup.

User Profile pop-up menu

Figure 3.1 The Settings tab of the Project window lists User, Project, and Site settings. If you prefer, you can click the Settings tab Fast menu to display only active settings or selected settings. The window shown here displays all settings.

Transferring Your Custom Settings to a Different Xpress Pro Workstation

User settings: If you plan to work on another Xpress Pro editing system, then you should bring your personal user profile folder with you on a disk or over a network. But where do you find your user settings on your current system so you can make a copy?

You can find your user profile folder in the following locations (for Windows users, this is assuming that your program files are stored on drive C; if it's stored elsewhere, substitute that drive letter):

◆ **Windows:** *drive*:\Program Files\Avid\Avid Xpress Pro\Avid Users*user login name*

◆ **Macintosh:** *drive*/Users/Shared/Avid Users/*user login name*

The user settings file itself is named *user name* Settings (Windows) or *user name* Settings.avs (Macintosh). However, when you want to import or copy your personal settings, make sure to import or copy your entire user profile folder, not just the individual file with your user name.

Once you are at the new workstation, copy your user profile folder from the disk or its network location onto the desktop or anywhere else on the new workstation. Open Xpress Pro on the new workstation and choose Import User or User Profile from the User Selection pop-up menu. Find the user profile folder and click Choose. You can now use all of your personal Keyboard settings, window layouts, and so on.

Project settings: When you need to transfer an entire project to another workstation, then you need to bring along your project folder as well as your source media files.

You can find your project folder, which includes two project setting files and all project bin files, in the following locations (for Windows users, this is assuming that your program is stored on drive C; if it's stored elsewhere, substitute that drive letter):

◆ **Windows:** *drive*:\Program Files\Avid\Avid Xpress Pro\Avid Projects*CPU system user name*

◆ **Macintosh:** *drive*/Users/Shared/Avid Projects/*CPU system user name*

(You can find shared project folders—as opposed to private project folders—one level up from the locations described here; in other words, you can access shared folders directly from the Avid Projects folder.)

Site settings: Normally, you do not need to transfer site settings to another workstation because those settings are specific to your particular hardware configuration. Nevertheless, to find your site setting file on your computer, look for a file with the following naming scheme: Site_Settings (Windows) or Site Settings.avs (Macintosh).

You can find your site settings in the following locations (for Windows users, this is assuming that your program is stored on drive C; if it's stored elsewhere, substitute that drive letter):

◆ **Windows:** *drive*:\Program Files\Avid\Avid Xpress Pro\Settings

◆ **Macintosh:** *drive*/Applications/Xpress Pro/Settings/

UNDERSTANDING USER, PROJECT, AND SITE SETTINGS

Creating and Selecting a User Profile

The first time you launch an Xpress Pro XDV system, you should create your own user profile and give it a unique name. Thereafter, you should always switch to your own user profile after launching a project. That way, you are always working with *your* user preferences and not Xpress Pro's default preferences or those of any other editor.

Plus, once you've created a user profile, you can always carry it with you to other workstations. (See the sidebar "Transferring Your Custom Settings to a Different Xpress Pro Workstation" earlier in this chapter.)

To create and select a user profile:

1. In the Project window, select the Settings tab.

2. Click the User Profile pop-up menu and choose Create User Profile (**Figure 3.2**).

3. In the Create User Profile dialog box that appears, give your new profile a unique name, such as *James User Settings* (**Figure 3.3**).

Figure 3.2 You can create multiple profiles by clicking the User Profile pop-up menu and choosing Create User Profile.

Figure 3.3 Give your new user profile a descriptive name.

4. Click OK.

The name of the new user profile now appears in the title bar as well as in the User Profile pop-up menu. The interface will change to reflect your user settings.

Xpress Pro stores your user profile folder, which contains all of your personal user settings, within the Avid Users folder, in a folder named after the system user who is currently logged in to the workstation CPU (**Figure 3.4**). (For the location of this folder, see the sidebar "Transferring Your Custom Settings to a Different Xpress Pro Workstation" earlier in this chapter.)

✔ Tip

■ If the application displays the default user profile when you launch Xpress Pro, switch to your user profile.

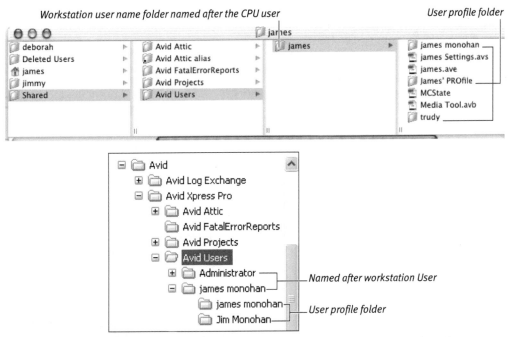

Figure 3.4 Xpress Pro puts your user profile folders in the *CPU user name* folder, which is within the Avid Users folder. Pictured is the Windows (above) and Mac (below) path.

To choose an existing user profile:

Do one of the following:

▲ When you first launch Xpress Pro and the Select Project dialog opens, click on the user profile menu and choose an existing user profile from the list that appears. Then, you can select your project and enter the Xpress Pro interface.

▲ Within the Xpress Pro interface, go to the Project window and click the Settings tab. From the User Profile pop-up menu, choose an existing user profile (**Figure 3.5**).

✔ Tip

■ You can also create or import a user profile in the Select Project dialog, but often it's best to use these options within the Settings tab of the Project window, so you know exactly what settings you're using to create your profile or can immediately see the settings you've just imported.

To import a user profile:

1. (Optional) If importing a user profile from another workstation, mount the drive or disk containing the user profile on your desktop.

2. In the Project window, click the Settings tab.

3. Click the User Profile pop-up menu and choose Import User or User Profile.

4. In the Select User Directory dialog box that appears, navigate to the user profile folder to be imported and select it.

5. Click Choose.

   The User Profile pull-down menu in the Project window now lists the name of the imported user profile. Also, Xpress Pro automatically copies the user folder you imported to the *CPU user name* folder, which is in the Avid Users folder.

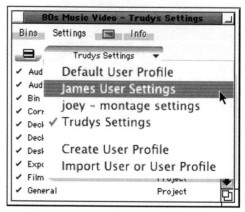

Figure 3.5 To make a user profile active, click the User Profile pop-up menu and select the name of the profile.

✔ Tips

■ Once you have all of your user settings the way you want them, back them up onto a CD or other removable disc, in case your current setup becomes corrupted.

■ If you want, you can import the *workstation user name* folder (found within the Avid Users folder), which contains *all* of the user profile folders created by that CPU user. However, it's less confusing to import only one user profile folder at a time.

Project window Fast menu

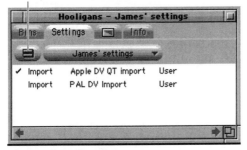

Figure 3.6 After you select Import settings from the Project window's Fast menu, the Settings tab displays only Import settings.

Creating, Naming, and Modifying Settings

Your user profile can include multiple configurations of the same standard settings, such as four different Keyboard settings. Typically, you create different settings for different basic tasks. For instance, you could have Keyboard settings for Capture, for Editing, for Effects, and for Laptop.

To help stay organized, you can give each customized configuration a descriptive name, or category name, in the middle column of the Settings tab. For high productivity and ease of use, you can even link sets of several modified settings together into toolsets by giving careful consideration to the category names you choose. (For more information, see "Linking Toolsets to Your Custom Settings" later in this chapter.)

To view your settings:

1. On the Settings tab of the Project window, open the Fast menu.

2. *Do one of the following:*
   - ▲ To view only currently selected settings (one for each type), choose Active Settings.
   - ▲ To view all possible settings, choose All Settings.
   - ▲ To view a specialized list of settings, such as import settings, choose the appropriate settings category name (**Figure 3.6**).
   - ▲ To view just the minimum group of default settings, choose Base Settings.

✔ Tips

- ■ To make any setting active, click to the left of the setting so that a check mark appears.

- ■ To select and activate multiple settings at once on the Settings tab, Ctrl+click (Windows) or Command+click (Mac).

To create a new custom setting:

1. In the Project window, select the Settings tab.

2. Open the Fast menu and choose All Settings. (If you don't choose All Settings, your new setting will not be visible after you create it.)

3. Select the individual default settings group that you want to modify (for example, Keyboard).

4. *Do one of the following:*

   ▲ From the Edit menu, choose Duplicate (**Figure 3.7**).

   ▲ Press Ctrl+D (Windows) or Command+D (Mac).

   The new duplicated setting now appears on the Settings tab of the Project window, ready for you to modify. Make sure you give it a unique name.

5. Click in the middle (name) column of the Settings tab, to the right of the duplicated setting's standard Xpress Pro name.

6. When a text box appears with a blinking cursor, enter a unique name. For example, you could name one Keyboard setting Capture (**Figure 3.8**), which you can later link to other captured-related settings named Capture.

   The name you gave the setting now appears in the middle column of the Settings tab.

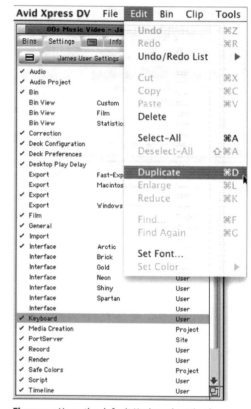

Figure 3.7 Here, the default Keyboard setting has been duplicated by selecting it and choosing Edit > Duplicate from the menu.

*Click the middle column of your
duplicated setting to give the
setting a new custom name.*

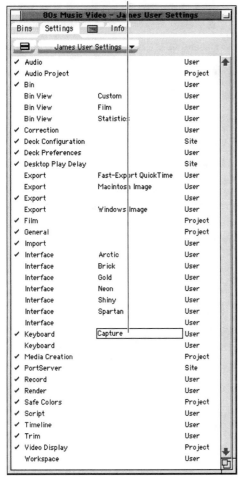

Figure 3.8 You can give your new setting a custom
name in the middle column of the Settings tab.

✔ Tips

■ For best results with creating new
settings, always duplicate an existing
default setting first. This saves time,
because most new settings involve only
minor tweaks to previous settings.

■ By planning ahead and giving a group of
settings the same custom name, you can
use the Link to Named Settings feature
in the Toolset menu's Link Current To
dialog box. (For more information on
how to link settings, see "Linking
Toolsets to Your Custom Settings" later
in this chapter.)

■ To make a newly duplicated setting
active, click to the left of the setting so
that a check mark appears.

To modify the contents of a single setting:

1. Double-click a setting on the Settings tab
of the Project window.

2. In the dialog box that appears, make
changes to the setting.

3. Click OK or Apply or Save (depending on
the dialog) and close the dialog box.

✔ Tips

■ If you modify a user setting within your
user profile, that tweaked setting
remains attached to your user profile.

■ If you modify a project setting, that setting affects only the currently opened
project.

■ If you modify a site setting, the change
pertains only to the particular hardware
connected to your workstation. It affects
all new users and projects on that particular workstation.

Using Toolsets

To get a basic understanding of how toolsets work, go to the Toolset menu and familiarize yourself with Xpress Pro's default toolsets: Basic, Color Correction, Source/Record Editing, Effects Editing, Audio Editing, and Recording.

These toolsets govern the arrangement of Xpress Pro's tools on your computer screen. However, you can change these defaults and save different window arrangements for each toolset (**Figure 3.9**).

To customize your tool layout:

1. From the Toolset menu, select a toolset.

2. Reposition and resize windows and tools according to your preferences.

3. Choose Toolset > Save Current (**Figure 3.10**).

   The next time you access that toolset, Xpress Pro will arrange your tools according to your customized preference.

To restore a toolset to Xpress Pro's default tool arrangement:

1. From the Toolset menu, select the toolset you want to restore.

2. Choose Toolset > Restore Current to Default.

   The toolset now uses the original, default arrangement.

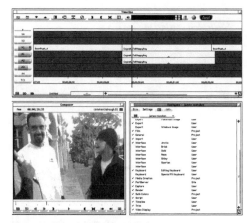

Figure 3.9 You can arrange windows to suit your preference—with the Timeline on top, for instance—and save the configuration to a particular toolset.

Figure 3.10 To save a toolset's current configuration, choose Toolset > Save Current.

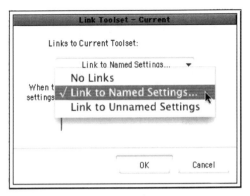

Figure 3.11 To link an active toolset to one or more custom user settings, first choose Link to Current from the Toolset menu and then choose Link to Named Settings in the pop-up menu.

Linking Toolsets to Your Custom Settings

In addition to customizing the layout of the default toolsets, you can link your custom settings on the Settings tab to particular toolsets, so that each toolset uses your own custom Keyboard settings, Timeline View settings, and so on instead of the Xpress Pro defaults.

The key to grouping and linking custom settings to particular toolsets is using a pre-planned custom name strategy, giving the same name to all settings you want to link to a particular toolset.

For example, say you give the same name—Special FX Editing—to a custom Keyboard setting, Timeline setting, and Render setting. Then you link the phrase "Special FX Editing" to the default Effects Editing toolset. Now each time you choose Toolset > Effects Editing, Xpress Pro automatically activates all settings named Special FX Editing, and your FX custom Keyboard, Timeline, and Render settings now override the default settings.

To link a toolset to one or more settings on the Settings tab:

1. From the Toolset menu, select a toolset.

2. Choose Toolset > Link to Current.

3. From the Link Toolset dialog box pop-up menu, choose Link to Named Settings (**Figure 3.11**).

   The Link Toolset - Current dialog box appears.

continues on next page

LINKING TOOLSETS TO YOUR CUSTOM SETTINGS

4. Type the name of the settings to which you want to link your toolset (**Figure 3.12**).

Now whenever you activate the linked toolset, Xpress Pro will activate all of the user settings with the same name in the middle column of the Settings tab (**Figure 3.13**).

✔ Tip

■ You can map a Toolset menu item to a Keyboard setting using the Menu to Button option in the Command palette. (For more information about customizing your keyboard, see "Mapping Buttons to the Keyboard and Interface," later in this chapter.)

To link a toolset to Xpress Pro's default (unnamed) settings:

1. From the Toolset menu, select a toolset.

2. Choose Toolset > Link to Current.

The Link Link Toolset - Current dialog box appears.

3. From the Link Toolset—Current dialog box pop-up menu, choose Link to Unnamed Settings (**Figure 3.14**).

The toolset is now linked to the default, unnamed settings found on the Settings tab.

✔ Tips

■ Unnamed settings are those settings on the Settings tab that don't have a name next to them and are Xpress Pro's default settings. Linking to unnamed settings is a quick, easy way to revert to all default settings for a toolset.

■ When you link to unnamed settings, any links you made to named settings are eliminated.

Figure 3.12 To link named settings with the same name to a toolset, type the shared name of the settings in this dialog box.

Figure 3.13 In this example, the Capture toolset was linked to all customized user settings named Capture.

Figure 3.14 To return a toolset to unnamed, default settings (unlinking it from named settings), select Link to Unnamed Settings.

Active workspace

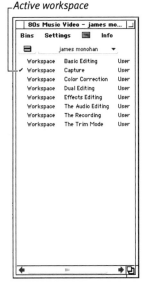

Figure 3.15 Select Workspaces from the Settings tab Fast menu to display all workspaces.

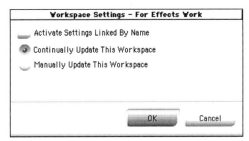

Figure 3.16 The Workspace Settings dialog box tells Xpress Pro how to save your workspace and which (if any) settings should be linked to it.

Using Workspaces

Workspaces are an older version of toolsets. The main difference is that you activate them using the workspace buttons (found on the More tab of the Command palette) rather than the Toolset menu. Most editors find workspaces less intuitive to use than toolsets. However, those who have used Avid software before may feel comfortable continuing to use workspaces.

Workspaces operate just like toolsets. A workspace is a custom arrangement of particular tools and windows that you can connect to user settings that share its name. You can create multiple workspaces for different tasks such as effects editing or capturing. Once created, you can map workspaces to keys on the keyboard.

To create a workspace setting:

1. Open and arrange your tools and windows according to your preferences.

2. On the Settings tab of the Project window, open the Fast menu and select Workspaces.

3. Select a listed workspace or duplicate an existing workspace to create a new one (**Figure 3.15**).

4. Double-click the newly created workspace setting.

   The Workspace Settings dialog box appears (**Figure 3.16**).

   continues on next page

5. *Select one of the following options:*

▲ **Continually Update This Workspace:** Xpress Pro saves the workspace each time you change your tool arrangements.

▲ **Manually Update This Workspace:** With this option selected, a Save Workspace Now button appears, allowing you to save the workspace in its current configuration. Xpress Pro saves changes to your tool arrangements only when you click the Save Workspace Now button (**Figure 3.17**).

6. Click OK.

Xpress Pro updates your workspace tool arrangement according to the changes you made.

To link other settings to a workspace:

1. On the Settings tab of the Project window, create custom settings that have the same name.

2. Give a workspace the same name as the other settings you want to link to it.

3. Double-click the workspace setting to open its dialog box.

4. Select Activate Settings Linked By Name (**Figure 3.18**).

Xpress Pro links all settings that have the same custom name with the workspace of the same name (**Figure 3.19**).

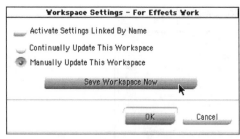

Figure 3.17 You can save your workspace manually to set its window arrangements in stone. With this setting, no matter what rearrangements you make on the fly, the workspace always returns to its original (saved) configuration each time you reactivate it.

Figure 3.18 To link settings with the same custom name in the middle column of the Settings tab to a particular workspace, select Activate Settings Linked By Name in that workspace's settings dialog box.

All custom user settings named Special FX Work will be linked to the workspace named Special FX Work.

Figure 3.19 By selecting Activate Settings Linked By Name in the Workspace settings dialog box, you link all settings of the same name to the workspace of the same name.

Figure 3.20 You can map eight workspace buttons, found on the More tab of the Command palette, to the keyboard or to any button elsewhere in the Xpress Pro interface, such as the Tool palette.

✔ Tips

■ To avoid confusion, you should use either toolsets or workspaces—not both.

■ Some tools, such as the Hardware tool and the Media tool, cannot be assigned to workspaces.

■ Remember that, in addition to Timeline settings, you can create and link Timeline View settings. Timeline View settings include track sizes as well as Sample Plot, Audio Clip Gain, and other settings found on the Timeline Fast menu. (For more information about Timeline View settings, see "Setting Up and Saving Your Timelines Display" in Chapter 5).

To map a workspace to the keyboard:

1. Select Workspaces from the Settings tab Fast menu to list all available workspaces.

2. Open the Command palette by *doing one of the following:*
   ▲ Choose Tools > Command Palette.
   ▲ Press Ctrl+3 (Windows) or Command+3 (Mac).

3. On the Command palette, click the More tab.

   The W1 through W8 buttons represent your workspace settings in the (alphabetical) order that they appear on the Settings tab. The first is W1, the second W2, and so on (**Figure 3.20**).

4. On the Command palette, select 'Button to Button' Reassignment.

5. On the Settings tab of the Project window, double-click a Keyboard setting to open the Keyboard settings window.

   continues on next page

6. To map the first workspace setting listed on the Settings tab, drag the W1 button to an available key in the Keyboard settings window. Map W2, W3, and so on to the remaining workspaces.

(For more information on how to map buttons from the Command palette to the keyboard, see the next section, "Mapping Buttons to the Keyboard and Interface.")

Now, whenever you press W1, for example, Xpress Pro will activate the first workspace listed on the Settings tab.

✔ Tips

■ If you create a new workspace, you need to keep track of how it affects the order of workspaces listed on the Settings tab. This is why workspaces are clunky, because pressing a workspace button may call up a different workspace today than it did yesterday.

■ You should map your workspaces to the same keyboard keys for *all* of your Keyboard settings. Otherwise, you may become confused about how to switch among workspaces, especially if particular Keyboard settings are linked to particular workspaces.

To switch to a different workspace:

Do one of the following:

▲ On the Settings tab of the Project window, select a different workspace setting by clicking to the left of its name, so that a check mark appears.

▲ Press a workspace key mapped to the keyboard (W1, W2, and so on).

Your tool arrangement and settings change according to the new workspace.

To delete a workspace:

1. On the Settings tab of the Project window, select a workspace setting.

2. Press Delete on the keyboard.

Xpress Pro eliminates the workspace.

✔ Tip

■ You cannot delete an active workspace setting, so make sure the workspace you want to delete is not checked on the Settings tab.

Mapping Buttons to the Keyboard and Interface

Everyone's brain and fingers work in different ways; fortunately, with Xpress Pro's mappable keyboard and mappable tool, the application adapts to your quirks and not the other way around.

On the Command palette, you can find all of Xpress Pro's functional command buttons; using this palette, you can map those buttons as well as menu commands to both your keyboard keys and areas of certain tool windows (such as the Composer).

The process of keyboard mapping is very simple: You just drag buttons from the Command palette or any menu choice and drop them on the Keyboard settings window or on the button area of a tool window.

When mapping buttons, you can expand the scope and flexibility of your keyboard command sets by adding the following to your keyboard set:

◆ **Shift+key:** You can create commands in which you hold down the Shift key while pressing another key.

◆ **Modifier keys:** You can add Alt (Windows) or Option and Control (Mac) to the basic keyboard commands.

To open the Command palette:

Do one of the following:

▲ Select Tools > Command Palette.

▲ Press Ctrl+3 (Windows) or Command+3 (Mac).

The Command palette appears, featuring multiple tabs for the multiple button categories.

To open a Keyboard settings window:

◆ On the Settings tab of the Project window, double-click the name of the Keyboard setting you want to configure.

A graphical representation of the keyboard appears.

✔ Tip

■ You can open multiple keyboard sets at once and map them all in one sitting.

To map buttons to a Keyboard setting:

1. Make sure the Command palette and a Keyboard settings window are open.

2. Find the button you want to map by clicking one of the category tabs on the Command palette.

3. Select 'Button to Button' Reassignment at the bottom of the Command palette.

4. Drag the button you want to map onto a key in the Keyboard window.

   The key now displays the graphic for the button you assigned to it (**Figure 3.21**).

5. Close the Keyboard Settings window and the Command palette.

   Your new keyboard button mappings will be in effect whenever that particular Keyboard setting is active on the settings tab.

✔ Tips

- Not all keyboard keys in the Keyboard settings window are mappable. If you click a key on a keyboard map and it depresses, it is mappable; if it doesn't depress, then it can't be mapped.

- To assign a different command to a keyboard key, simply drag the new button (or menu item) on top of the old mapping.

- For information about a particular button on the Command palette, right-click (Windows) or Control+click (Mac) a button and choose What's This? from the context menu.

- To assign a button to a Shift+key command on the keyboard, hold down the Shift key when dragging a button from the Command palette to the Keyboard settings window.

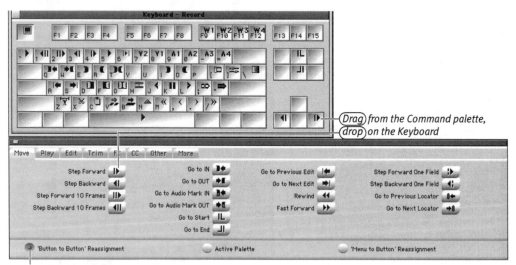

Drag from the Command palette, *drop* on the Keyboard

Select this radio button to map buttons to the keyboard

Figure 3.21 To map a button to a particular keyboard key, simply drag it from the Command palette and drop it on a key in the Keyboard settings dialog box.

To map a menu command to the keyboard:

1. Open the Command palette and a Keyboard settings window.

2. On the Command palette, select 'Menu to Button' Reassignment at the lower right of the window (**Figure 3.22**).

3. Click a button on the keyboard, in the Keyboard settings window.

4. Click a menu title at the top of the screen and choose a menu command.

   The command is mapped to the chosen key on the keyboard (**Figure 3.23**).

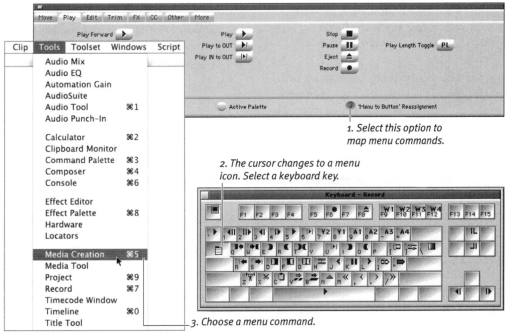

1. Select this option to map menu commands.

2. The cursor changes to a menu icon. Select a keyboard key.

3. Choose a menu command.

Figure 3.22 You can map menu commands to your keyboard by clicking 'Menu to Button' Reassignment, then clicking a key in the Keyboard settings dialog box, and then choosing the menu command you want to map to that key.

MC = Media Creation

Figure 3.23 Xpress Pro abbreviates menu commands in the Keyboard settings window. In this case, MC stands for Media Creation. To find out exactly what an abbreviation means, rest the mouse over the keyboard key in the Keyboard settings window and its name will appear.

To add a modifier key to a button assignment:

1. Map a key to the keyboard using the Command palette and a Keyboard settings window as described in the preceding task.

2. On the Command palette, click the Other tab (**Figure 3.24**).

3. Drag a modifier button, such as Add Option Key, to a key in the Keyboard settings window that already has a button assigned to it.

   Now whenever that key is pressed, a single press of the key will act as if you have also pressed the modifier key. (See the following sidebar, "A Modifier Key Mapping Example," for more information.)

To remove a command from a keyboard key:

1. Select 'Button to Button' Reassignment at the bottom of the Command palette.

2. Click the Other tab of the Command palette.

3. Drag the ☐ Blank key to the key that you want to unassign on the keyboard map.

   The key now appears blank in the Keyboard settings window and has no keyboard command assigned to it.

Figure 3.24 The Other tab contains the Add Option Key and Add Control Key buttons.

A Modifier Key Mapping Example

Adding a modifier key (Alt, Option, or Control) to a keyboard mapping can save you extra finger work. For example, pressing Alt+Next Edit (Windows) or Option+Next Edit (Mac) will jump the Timeline playhead to the next edit point in your sequence regardless of track selections.

But, if you map Alt or Option to the the Next Edit keyboard mapping in your Keyboard settings, then all you need to do is tap that one key to move the playhead to the next edit point regardless of track selection.

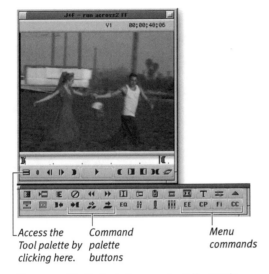

Access the Tool palette by clicking here. *Command palette buttons* *Menu commands*

Figure 3.25 The Tool palette can potentially contain a hundred buttons and menu commands, but it's probably best to use it for only the most essential functions.

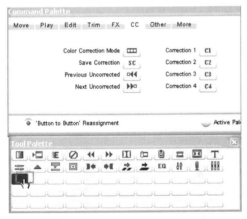

Figure 3.26 With the Command palette open and 'Button to Button' Reassignment or 'Menu to Button Reassignment' selected, you can drag and drop buttons on the Tool palette.

Using the Tool Palette

The Tool palette is a special mappable button window that you can access from the Composer, a source clip monitor, or the clipboard monitor. The Tool palette caters to those who prefer to perform many of their functions using the mouse instead of the keyboard.

You can map as many buttons and menu commands to this floating window as you desire (**Figure 3.25**). Accessing it from the Composer, a source monitor, or the clipboard requires you to map the 🔲 Fast menu button (found on the Other tab of the Command palette) to the bottom of the window.

To open the Tool palette:

1. Open the Fast menu in the Composer, clipboard, or source monitor.

2. To keep the palette open and floating on your desktop, drag the mouse away from the attached window and click the mouse.

   The palette, which you can enlarge to any size, remains open until you close it.

To map buttons and menus to the Tool palette:

1. Open the Tool palette from the Composer, Timeline, clipboard monitor, or source monitor.

2. Choose Tools > Command Palette.

3. On the Command palette, select either 'Button to Button' Reassignment or 'Menu to Button' Reassignment, depending on what you want to do.

4. Drag buttons or assign menu items to the buttons on the Tool palette (**Figure 3.26**).

   The mapped button or menu command appears on the Tool palette whenever you open it. Click the button to perform the mapped function.

Customizing Your Interface Display

Interface settings enable you to control the labels, tool tips, color, shading, and styles of Xpress Pro's buttons and window elements (**Figure 3.27**).

The Settings tab provides six default Interface setting options, but you can also create different color options for different tasks—a color scheme for editing, a color scheme for effects work, and so on—or even for your different moods, using the Appearance tab of the Interface settings dialog. **Table 3.1** summarizes the options on the Appearance tab.

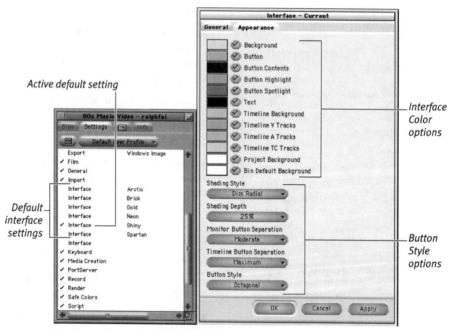

Active default setting

Default interface settings

Interface Color options

Button Style options

Figure 3.27 Xpress Pro includes six default Interface settings that you can use as templates for your own custom versions.

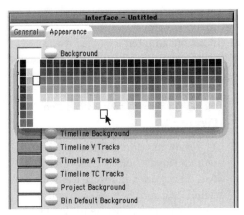

Figure 3.28 Click a rectangular color swatch on the left of the Appearance tab and pick a new color from the color swatch palette.

To customize the color of an interface element:

1. On the Settings tab of the Project window, double-click an Interface setting. In the Interface dialog box, select the Appearance tab.

2. Click the color box to the left of the element you want to change, to open the Xpress Pro color palette.

3. Select a color from the color palette (**Figure 3.28**).

4. Click Apply to preview the result. If you're satisfied, click OK.

   Xpress Pro applies the new color choice throughout the interface.

continues on next page

Table 3.1

Appearance Options	
Background	Sets the color for the general background of windows.
Button	Sets the color for buttons.
Button Contents	Sets the color for the graphic symbols that appear on top of buttons.
Button Highlight	Sets the color of buttons when you select them.
Button Spotlight	Sets the background color of buttons that appear when the cursor passes over them.
Text	Sets the color of text in windows, toolbars, and tool tips.
Timeline Background	Sets the colors of the Timeline's top and bottom toolbars.
Timeline V Tracks	Sets the color of all video clips edited into the Timeline.
Timeline A Tracks	Sets the color of all audio clips edited into the Timeline.
Timeline TC Tracks	Sets the color of timecode tracks in the Timeline.
Project Background	Sets the color of the Project window's background.
Bin Default Background	Sets the background color for newly created bins.
Shading Style	Sets the shading style for buttons and other shaded interface elements. The options are Convex, Dim Radial, Convex Radial, and Bright Radial.
Shading Depth	Sets the depth of the shading set. You can choose a depth in the range 5 to 50 percent.
Monitor Button Separation	Sets the amount of space between your buttons in the Tool palette, Composer, pop-up windows, and elsewhere. The choices are Maximum, Moderate, and None. If you choose None, there will be no spacing or vertical separator lines between buttons.
Timeline Button Separation	Sets the amount of space between buttons on the Timeline. The choices are Maximum, Moderate, and None.
Button Style	Sets the shape of buttons. The choices are Oval, Octagonal, Rounded, Square, Swoosh, and Antique.

CUSTOMIZING YOUR INTERFACE DISPLAY

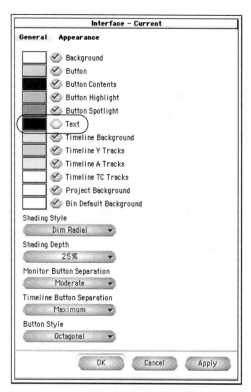

Figure 3.29 Unchecking the Text color option resets the Text color to Xpress Pro's default choice.

✔ Tips

- To restore an interface object to its default color, deactivate its color swatch by removing the check mark that appears to the right of the color box. The interface object returns to its default color (**Figure 3.29**).

- To preview any combination of your color and style choices, click Apply. The styles of any open interface elements will be updated, and then you can continue to make further adjustments, with the settings window still open.

- If you select a background color without selecting a button color, buttons will use the background color.

- You can change the background color of an open bin without changing the background color of the entire interface. To do so, make sure the bin is active and then choose Edit > Set Bin Background.

- You can assign a color to an object in a bin by selecting the object and choosing Edit > Set Clip Color.

The Track Color Alternative

You can also set Timeline track colors from the Timeline Fast menu. First deselect any track color choices on the Appearance tab of your Interface settings (**Figure 3.30**). You can now change the color of individual Timeline tracks by selecting one or more tracks, opening the Timeline Fast menu, choosing Track Color, and picking a color from the palette that appears.

Deselect these options.   *Select this option from the Timeline's Fast menu.*

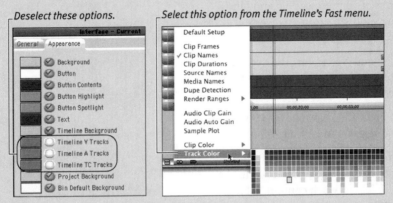

Figure 3.30 You can use the Timeline Fast menu to color-code your video tracks, but only if track color choices are not selected on the Appearance tab of the Interface window.

Saving and Backing Up Your Work

One Xpress Pro project can often represent days or even months of careful editing. Xpress Pro has several options for saving the latest versions of your project file and bins to protect all your work from inadvertent computer catastrophe.

- ◆ When you quit Xpress Pro, the application automatically saves your project in the Avid Projects folder.

- ◆ You can manually save your bins (and anything they contain) at any time.

- ◆ While you edit, the Auto-Save feature saves your bins at regular intervals in the Avid Attic folder, which contains all folders and bins for each of your projects.

To configure your Auto-Save settings:

1. On the Settings tab of the Project window, open your Bin settings.

2. *Modify any of the following settings:*

   ▲ **Auto-Save Interval:** In the Bin settings dialog box, type a number of minutes to tell Xpress Pro how often to save your project.

   ▲ **Inactivity Period:** Enter the number of seconds that you want Xpress Pro to wait after your system becomes inactive before it begins saving. The default value is 0. If you set a value here, Xpress Pro waits for a pause in editing to save your project so it does not interrupt your work.

   ▲ **Force Auto-Save At:** You can specify an interval at which Xpress Pro will forcibly autosave regardless of whether you're in the middle of editing.

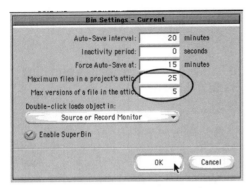

Figure 3.31 As long as you tell Xpress Pro to keep a high number of older files in the Attic, such as 25 or more, you'll be able to travel far back in time if things go wrong.

Figure 3.32 Here, three bins are selected; choose Save All to save them manually.

✔ Tip

- You can find your bin files in your project's folder. (For the location, see the sidebar "Transferring Your Custom Settings to a Different Xpress Pro Workstation" earlier in this chapter.)

▲ **Maximum Files in a Project's Attic:** Specify the number of files to be placed in the Attic folder. Xpress Pro will keep only this number of files in the Attic and discard older files when newer files are saved in the Attic folder.

▲ **Max Versions of a File in the Attic:** Specify the number of versions of the same file to be kept in the Attic. Xpress Pro will keep only a designated number of versions of a file in the Attic.

3. Click OK (**Figure 3.31**).

   Xpress Pro will now automatically save your project and all of its bins and information according to the settings you specified.

✔ Tip

- Keep the Max Files in a Project's Attic value relatively high so you'll have multiple saved files from which to choose.

To save all bins manually:

1. Click the Project window but do not highlight any bins.

2. Choose File > Save All.

   Xpress Pro saves the most current version of all of your bins in your project folder.

To save selected bins manually:

1. In the Project window, select a bin. Ctrl+click (Windows) or Command+click (Mac) any other bins that you want to save.

2. Choose File > Save All (**Figure 3.32**).

   Xpress Pro saves the information contained in the selected bins.

Retrieving Autosaved Versions of Your Work

How do you revert to an earlier version of your project? The simple answer is to find a previous version of your project *bins* in the Avid Attic. After all, bins contain all of your sequences (as well as source clips, titles, and so on).

However, retrieving bins from the Attic is far from a simple, straightforward process. You need to copy the autosaved bins from the Avid Attic to another location before you open them in Xpress Pro. Then, in Xpress Pro, you need to copy what you want to restore—such as the old sequences you need—from the retrieved bins to your current bin.

If things go wrong and you run into trouble, carefully read the following tasks to first find and retrieve a previous version of a bin from the Avid Attic and then restore it into a current project (**Figure 3.33**).

To find your autosaved files and bins in the Avid Attic:

◆ In Windows, go to C:\Program Files\ Avid\Avid Xpress Pro\Avid Users to find the Avid Attic folder (assuming that your program is in drive c; otherwise, substitute the letter for the drive you are using).

◆ In Mac OS, go to *drive*/Users/Shared to find the Avid Attic folder.

Folder that contains backup files for 80s Music Video

Multiple versions of the Reel 005 bin

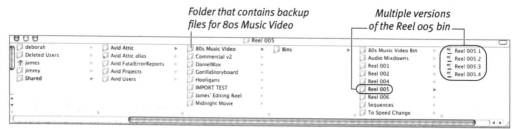

Figure 3.33 Xpress Pro's Auto-Save feature saves backup copies of everything in all of your active bins, in a folder called the Avid Attic.

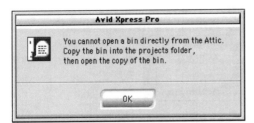

Figure 3.34 If you try to open an old bin directly from the Avid Attic, Xpress Pro presents this dialog box. To open an old bin in Xpress Pro, you need to copy your old bin to your project folder.

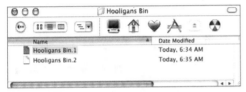

Figure 3.35 To revert to a previous version of your project, go to the Xpress Pro Attic folder, find the bin you want, and sort by Date Modified to find the most recent version.

✔ Tips

- You cannot open a bin straight from the Attic. You have to copy it to somewhere else (such as to your project folder or the desktop). Because of this requirement, keep an alias of the Avid Attic and your project folder on your CPU desktop at all times.

- The bin files have version numbers; the highest number indicates the most recent version of the file. Use the date-modified information for the files to find the specific version of the bin to which you want to revert. If you want to go back in time to 1:30 P.M. today, choose a file that was modified around that time (**Figure 3.35**).

To retrieve saved bin files from the Avid Attic:

1. Quit the Xpress Pro application.

2. Find the Avid Attic folder on your computer in the location described in the preceding task.

3. In the Avid Attic folder, open the Bins folder and then open the folder for your project. In that folder, find the folder with the same title as the bin or bins you want to retrieve.

4. Once you find the right bin folder, find the particular bin files you want by looking at their creation dates.

   Copy the selected backup bin files you want to retrieve to a new location—Xpress Pro does not let you open an old bin directly from the Attic (**Figure 3.34**).

   ▲ In Windows, copy the selected files by dragging them to the desktop or right-clicking them, choosing Copy, going to another location, right-clicking, and choosing Paste.

   ▲ In Mac OS, copy the selected files by Option-dragging them or pressing Command+D (for Duplicate); then drag the copies to the desktop.

   You now have a duplicate copy of your bin files, independent of the copy in the Avid Attic. To open the retrieved bin in Xpress Pro and restore it to your current project, see the next task, "To restore files from the Attic into a current project."

To restore files from the Attic into a current project:

1. Launch the Xpress Pro application again and click the Project window to activate it. Close the current version of the bin you want to restore.

2. Choose File > Open Bin.

3. Navigate to the *copy* of the backup bin file you created in the preceding task and click Open.

   The retrieved bin opens in a new window, and Xpress Pro creates a folder (called Other Bins) for the retrieved bin on the Bins tab of the Project window (**Figure 3.36**).

4. Create a new bin called Temporary Bin. Drag the objects you want to rescue from the retrieved bin to the Temporary Bin folder (**Figure 3.37**).

5. Trash the Other Bins folder from your Project window, by selecting it and pressing the Delete key.

6. Drag the retrieved files from the Temporary Bin folder to any other bin in your Project window. Put the Temporary Bin folder in the trash can in the Project window.

   You can now continue editing using your older sequence version, or whatever it is you retrieved from the Attic.

✔ Tips

- If you try to open an old version of a bin and you get a message that says "Unable to open bin," you probably have another version of that bin open in Xpress Pro. Close that open bin first. Xpress Pro will not allow you to have two versions of the same bin open at once. This is for your own benefit as it avoids confusion.

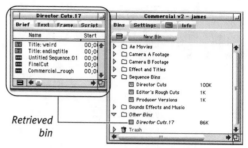

Retrieved bin

Figure 3.36 When you open an old bin from the Avid Attic, a folder called Other Bins is created in your Project window. That folder contains the old, retrieved bin.

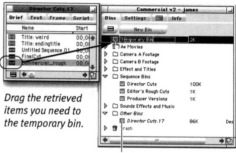

Drag the retrieved items you need to the temporary bin.

Delete this folder.

Figure 3.37 Drag what you want to retrieve from the old, retrieved bin into a temporary bin. Then delete the old, retrieved bin from the Project window (or drag it to the trash). Finally, drag the retrieved objects from the temporary bin to one of your normal bins and trash the temporary bin.

Configuring Other User Settings

The Keyboard settings, Interface settings, and Auto-Save settings discussed earlier in this chapter are the most useful and commonly customized user settings. However, Xpress Pro offers many other settings to help you customize your workflow.

On the Settings tab of the Project window, you can modify any of the following settings:

◆ **Audio:** Using this dialog box, you can control how quickly your audio tools translate your audio changes and what you hear when performing a digital audio scrub. (For more information, see Chapter 12, "Working with Audio.")

◆ **Bin:** Besides Auto-Save settings, covered earlier in this chapter, the Bin settings dialog box includes the Double-Click Loads Objects In pop-up menu (see "Source Clip Monitor" in Chapter 2) and the Enable SuperBin option (see "Using the SuperBin" in Chapter 5).

◆ **Bin View:** These settings determine which information columns are displayed on the Text tab of a bin. (For more information on these settings, see "Working with Information Columns in Text View" in Chapter 5.)

◆ **Capture:** These settings relate to capturing media from your source tapes. (For more information, see Chapter 4, "Capturing and Importing Media").

◆ **Correction Mode:** These settings let you customize the operation of the Color Correction tool. (For more information on these settings, see Chapter 10, "Color Correction.")

continues on next page

◆ **Deck Preferences:** You use the Deck Preferences settings to control the operation of your DV deck or camera. Some settings pertain to logging and recording (or logging and capturing), and some pertain to creation of a digital cut at the end of your edit. (For deck preference settings related to logging and recording, see Chapter 4, "Capturing and Importing Media." For deck preference settings related to creating a digital cut, see Chapter 14, "Outputting and Exporting").

◆ **Export:** You use the Export settings to configure the kinds of files you export. You can export video and audio from Xpress Pro to many different formats: QuickTime movies, still images, Open Media Framework Interchange (OMFI) files, Advanced Authoring Format (AAF) files, QuickTime reference movies, DV streams, and so on. (For more information, see "Exporting Material to Disk" in Chapter 14.)

◆ **Import:** These settings tell Xpress Pro how to import (and convert) incoming files. (For more information, see Chapter 4, "Capturing and Importing Media.")

◆ **Render:** These settings control the sound you hear after rendering as well as the way in which motion effects are created. (For more information, see "Configuring Render-Related Settings" in Chapter 11 and "The Four Motion Effect Render Options" in Chapter 9.)

◆ **Script:** These settings control Xpress Pro's Script Integration feature, which allows you to import a script, break down the script into its shot components (called lining the script), and link clips to the script. (For more information, see "Using Script Integration" in Chapter 15.)

◆ **Timeline:** The Display tab of the Timeline settings controls the way that the Timeline displays clips and tracks in a sequence. The Edit tab contains options for controlling filler frames, flash frames, patching, monitoring, and sync-locking tracks.

(You can further customize your Timeline display by creating Timeline View settings. See "Setting Up and Saving Your Timeline Display" in Chapter 5.)

◆ **Trim:** These settings control the way the play loop operates in Trim mode. You use a play loop to review your fine-tuning of a particular cut point in your sequence. (For more information on the Trim settings, see Chapter 7, "Fine-Tuning Your Edits.")

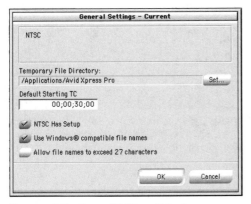

Figure 3.38 The General Settings dialog box.

Configuring Project Settings

Project settings usually configure hardware, file formats, storage locations, and other items that affect the entire project, and they therefore cannot be changed for individual users of the same project.

If you have projects with multiple users, you will want to pay special attention to the project settings and make sure each individual Xpress Pro user understands the standards for the project settings.

The project settings are as follows:

◆ **Audio Project:** These settings provide audio hardware information and allow you to choose the audio format and sampling rate for your project. In addition, there are various other audio-related options to configure. (For more information, see Chapter 4, "Capturing and Importing Media," and Chapter 12, "Working with Audio.")

◆ **Film:** These settings pertain only to projects that originated on film and that will end up on film. These settings ensure that your film's negative cutter will be able to translate your work from Xpress Pro into an accurately cut film negative. (For more information on using film-editing options in Xpress Pro, see Chapter 15, "Special Features and Bundled Applications.")

◆ **General:** These settings are a miscellaneous group of project parameters. You will not want to change most of these settings in the course of your project (**Figure 3.38**).

The General Settings dialog box includes these options:

▲ **Temporary File Directory:** This is where intermediate movie files are stored when you export a movie from Xpress Pro. By default, this folder is in the same location as the Xpress Pro application. If you run out of room on one hard drive, you can put this folder on a different drive.

▲ **Default Starting TC:** Whenever you create a sequence, the first frame of the sequence will be assigned whatever timecode value you enter in the Default Starting TC field. (For more information on creating sequences, see Chapter 5, "Preparing to Edit.")

▲ **Project Format:** You can select only one format per project (NTSC or PAL). To use a different format, you must quit Xpress Pro, relaunch, create a new project, and choose a different format from the Format pull-down menu (**Figure 3.39**).

▲ **Use Windows Compatible File Names:** If you are working on a Windows system or know that at least one of the files you create in Xpress Pro will eventually end up on a Windows platform, definitely leave this option checked.

▲ **Allow File Names to Exceed 27 Characters:** Usually, you will leave this option unchecked. Most applications don't accept such long names.

◆ **Media Creation:** These settings, which are in the same dialog box you get when you choose Tools > Media Creation, tell Xpress Pro which media files will be stored on which drives. (For more information, see Chapter 4, "Capturing and Importing Media.")

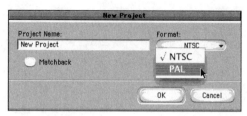

Figure 3.39 You can set your project format only when you create a new project. The two available formats are PAL and NTSC.

◆ **Safe Color:** Use these settings to tell Xpress Pro whether to warn you about violations of three specified safe color limits. You can also set those limits here. (For details on using safe color settings, see Chapter 10, "Color Correction.")

◆ **Video Display:** Use these settings to determine whether or how your sequence plays your real-time effects. (See "Configuring Real-Time Settings" in Chapter 11.)

✔ Tips

■ If you want to mix footage from NTSC and PAL sources in the same project, convert one of the formats to the other before starting to edit in Xpress Pro.

■ You cannot modify the Project Format setting in the General Settings dialog box once you begin a project.

CONFIGURING PROJECT SETTINGS

Configuring Site Settings

Site settings pertain to your particular hardware setup. They include the following:

◆ **Deck Configuration:** These settings are helpful mainly if you have multiple decks or other devices connected to your system. (For information on deck configuration, see Chapter 4, "Capturing and Importing Media.")

◆ **Desktop Play Delay:** When you enable playback of your sequence through FireWire to an external monitor, the audio and video in your Composer window playback may lose sync by a few frames. Use the Desktop Play Delay settings to adjust the offset in the Composer video and your system audio speakers so they play in sync, along with your external monitor.

◆ **Port Server:** These settings control automatic connection to a LANshare if such a network is connected to your system. (For more information, see "Network and Shared Storage Solutions" in Chapter 1.)

CAPTURING & IMPORTING MEDIA

4

Before you can begin editing, you need to get your source media onto your computer and into your Xpress Pro project bins. This process requires either capturing video and audio from source tapes or importing video, audio, stills, and graphics that are already on your drives into the Xpress Pro application.

In this chapter, you'll learn how to configure your deck, camera, or digital-analog converter for capturing your footage, with or without timecode, via a FireWire (IEEE 1394) connection. You'll also learn how to capture audio through your sound card if necessary. Going through the capturing process will take a lot of patience at first, since there are many audio- and video-related settings to configure.

When learning how to import media into Xpress Pro, you'll deal with even more settings as you tell Xpress Pro whether you want to import CCIR 601 or RGB color, square or rectangle pixels, alpha channel information or no alpha channel information, and so on.

Whether capturing or importing source media, the important constant to keep in mind is this: When capturing or importing, Xpress Pro always creates source media using either the Open Media Format Interchange (OMFI) format or Material Exchange Format (MXF); OMFI is the format you'll probably use for 95 percent of your projects. For example, when you import an Apple QuickTime file into Xpress Pro, the application converts the file from Apple QuickTime to the OMFI file format (with the extension ".omf"). The downside to these necessary conversions is the waiting time, but the upside is an efficient workflow between Xpress Pro and other Avid applications such as ProTools and Avid Symphony.

About Capturing Media: An Overview

The Capture tool, the Composer monitor, and a logging bin are all you really need to capture media from your source tapes to your computer. Using the Capture tool, you have three possible strategies for capturing (that is, recording) audio and video:

◆ **Logging shots and batch capturing:** Logging your footage first and then capturing only the sections you want to keep on your drives is the traditional method of bringing footage into a non-linear system.

The advantage of this log-first, capture-second method is that you don't have to sit and watch all of the source footage in real time during the logging process; instead, you can fast-forward to your In and Out points while logging and then take a break while Xpress Pro automatically captures what you have logged.

◆ **Capturing on the fly and then logging shots:** With the capturing-on-the fly strategy, you first capture long runs of footage containing multiple scenes or shots from your source tape and then break the footage into individual subclips for logging after you capture. This method often works best for documentary footage and scripted narrative footage for which the director prefers to shoot long and often keeps the camera rolling between takes. Furthermore, this method is the only one you can use if you capture from a noncontrollable deck such as a consumer VCR or DVD player, where the source tape doesn't provide timecode.

(To learn how to create subclips automatically, see "Creating Subclips with DV Scene Extraction" later in this chapter.)

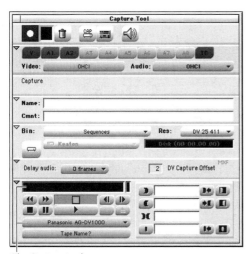

The Capture tool recognizes the deck.

Figure 4.1 When you open the Capture tool, you should see a timecode display in the deck area of the window, meaning that Xpress Pro recognizes your deck or camera.

(For more information about creating subclips manually, see "Creating Subclips and Subsequences" in Chapter 6.)

◆ **Capturing clip by clip:** This method involves setting In and/or Out points and capturing one clip after the next. Use this method if your footage contains timecode breaks that would make batch capturing or capturing on the fly a real headache, or if you have to capture only one or two sections of a tape and need to be precise about the beginning or ending of a shot. See the sidebar "Dealing with Timecode Breaks" later in this chapter for more information.

To open the Capture tool:

Do one of the following:

◆ Choose Tools > Capture.

◆ Press Ctrl+7 (Windows) or Command+7 (Mac).

Xpress Pro opens the Capture tool. If your deck or camera is turned on, connected, and configured properly, timecode numbers appear in the deck control area of the Capture tool (**Figure 4.1**). To proceed with the capturing process, see the next section, "Setting Up Your System for Capture: An Overview."

If Xpress Pro does not recognize your deck for whatever reason, the timecode area reports No Deck. (For information on configuring your deck, see "Setting Up Your Deck or Camera for Capture" later in this chapter.)

✔ Tip

■ You can choose Toolset > Capture to open Xpress Pro's capturing toolset, a default capture-related window arrangement.

ABOUT CAPTURING MEDIA: AN OVERVIEW

Setting Up Your System for Capture: An Overview

The next few sections of this chapter talk you through all of the settings you need to configure before you begin capturing media. The first time you create capture-related settings, the task will be arduous, but after that, preparing for capture should simply be a matter of choosing the right presets.

Before capturing, you'll need to configure the following settings, described in the next few sections of this chapter:

◆ **Hard drive configuration:** Choose the hard drives on which you want to store the Xpress Pro source media files that are created during the capture process.

◆ **Deck or camera configuration:** Tell Xpress Pro which deck or camera you're using to play back your source tapes and how the deck or camera should operate during logging and batch capturing.

Your deck configuration settings also include your video input channel information: Through which pipeline are you getting video into your computer? (Usually, it's FireWire.)

◆ **Video input channel and resolution:** Tell Xpress Pro which video resolution to use for capture and what pipeline you're using for capture. On software-only systems, the resolution options are full-res DV 25 411and single-field DV (15:1s); typically, your channel is FireWire.

◆ **Audio input channel, format, sample rate, and sample size:** Typically you'll choose either FireWire or an analog capture card as your input channel, AIFF or WAV as your format, 32 kHz or 48 kHz as your sample rate, and 16 bit or 24 bit as your sample size.

Change drives in group.

Select drive group.

Figure 4.2 If you have more than one drive available for capturing media, you can include those drives in a drive group. Then if you select Switch to Emptiest Drive When Full in the Capture Settings dialog box, you don't have to worry about switching capture drives when one drive in the group becomes full.

Configuring Your Hard Drives for Capture

The first capture-related settings you should check before using the Capture tool to capture (record) footage are those that relate to choosing your media drives.

You should have more than one hard drive connected to your computer so that you can capture to a designated media drive rather than to the same drive that contains your operating system and Xpress Pro application. If you capture to the drive that contains your OS, performance lapses may occur. Xpress Pro includes a feature for filtering out your system and launch drives to help you avoid this problem.

If you have more than one media drive available, you can create a drive group. If you use a group, you can instruct Xpress Pro to automatically start capturing to another drive in the group if your initial capture drive becomes full.

To choose your capture drives:

◆ Go to the Capture tool's Bin section and *do one of the following:*

▲ To capture video and audio to the same drive, click the drive selection pop-up menu and choose a drive name.

▲ To capture to a group of drives, click the drive selection pop-up menu and choose Change Group. In the dialog box that appears, Shift-click to select the drives you want to belong to the group and then click OK (**Figure 4.2**).

continues on next page

▲ To capture video and audio to different drives or drive groups, click the Single/Dual Drives mode button next to the drive selection pop-up menu, so that two drive selection menus now appear. Choose your video drives from the first menu and your audio drives from the second menu.

Now when you capture video and/or audio with the Capture tool, Xpress Pro will create audio and video source media files (usually OMF files) on your selected drives.

✔ Tip

■ You can also choose your capture drives by opening the Media Creation settings dialog box and clicking the Capture tab. Then choose your capture drives as you would when using the Capture tool (**Figure 4.3**).

To avoid capturing to your system and launch drives:

1. Open your active Media Creation settings by double-clicking the settings name on the Settings tab of the Project window or by choosing Tools > Media Creation.

2. In the Media Creation settings dialog box, click the Drive Filtering tab and select Filter Out System Drive and Filter Out Launch Drive (**Figure 4.4**).

   From now on, Xpress Pro will not capture video or audio to your system drive (the drive containing your operating system) or launch drive (the drive containing the Xpress Pro application).

✔ Tips

■ Selecting Filter Based on Resolution is relevant if you are using Mojo and are capturing 1:1 (uncompressed) video. Xpress Pro will filter out any Avid manufactured drives that don't support such a high resolution.

Choose capture drives here.   *Click this button to apply your drive choice to all other Media Creation tabs.*

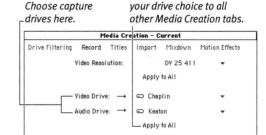

Figure 4.3 You can also designate capture drives in the Media Creation settings dialog box.

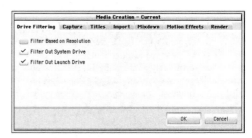

Figure 4.4 If you do not want to capture to the drive that contains your system folder or your Xpress Pro application—and you should especially avoid capturing *video* to those drives—you can filter out those drives in the Media Creation dialog box.

■ In the Media Creation settings dialog box, you can apply your drive selection settings to all other capture and import operations by clicking the Apply to All button.

Choose your buffer here.

Figure 4.5 Use the Capture settings dialog box to set either a file size limit or source clip time limit for capturing. Also use this dialog box to ensure that Xpress Pro always leaves a buffer of extra space on your capture drives.

To set hard drive data limits for capture:

1. On the Settings tab of the Project window, double-click your active (check-marked) Capture settings.

2. In the dialog box that appears, click the Media Files tab (**Figure 4.5**) and set a file size limit *by selecting one of the following:*

   ▲ **Capture to a Single File, 2 GB Limit:** This is the normal option to select, as long as you're not capturing clips that are more than 2 GB in size (for DV, that's just over 9 minutes). For each source clip you capture, Xpress Pro creates a single video and/or audio OMF file on your selected media drive; Xpress Pro will limit the size of the source media file to 2 GB.

   ▲ **Capture to Multiple Files:** Use this method if you plan to capture clips that will result in source media files larger than 2 GB. For each source clip you capture, Xpress Pro creates multiple video and/or audio OMF files across multiple media drive partitions. To determine the time limit for a source clip captured in this manner, enter a number of minutes in the Maximum (Default) Capture Time box. To use this option, you must create a drive group of two or more drives.

3. If you always want to leave a buffer of extra data space on your capture drives, select Switch to Emptiest Drive When Full and choose a number of minutes from the adjacent pop-up menu.

   As long as you have configured two or more drives to be part of a drive group, Xpress Pro will capture to the next available media drive when it reaches the set limit. Leaving a buffer of extra space on your media drive decreases the risk of playback problems.

✔ Tip

■ If you change the default (30 minutes) in the Maximum (Default) Capture Time box, Xpress Pro requires a lot of time to reallocate the number of minutes set for capturing on your drives.

CONFIGURING YOUR HARD DRIVES FOR CAPTURE

Setting Up Your Deck or Camera for Capture

Before launching Xpress Pro, you should turn on your designated capture device and connect it to your computer (usually via FireWire) before configuring your deck, camera, or converter for capture.

✔ Tip

■ If you turn on your deck or camera after you open the Capture tool, Xpress Pro may not immediately recognize your deck. To fix this problem, go to the Capture tool and click the deck selection pull-down menu and click Check Decks. Or if Xpress Pro displays a warning dialog box that says, "The deck configuration doesn't match the decks attached to the system," click Check Decks. Either way, Xpress Pro will automatically search for your deck and bring it online again (**Figure 4.6**).

Deck Configuration Settings

Once you have your playback device connected and turned on, you can use the deck configuration settings and the deck-related Capture settings to tell Xpress Pro the following:

◆ **What type of device is connected to your computer?** Typically, your playback device is a deck (VTR), a camera, a digital-analog converter (which is, in turn, connected to a deck or camera), or the Mojo box (which generally is also connected to a deck or camera).

◆ **What channel are you using for input?** The channel is also known as your video input. To capture anything through a FireWire cable (which is what you'll usually use when capturing DV), the channel you use is typically FireWire—OHCI.

Click here.

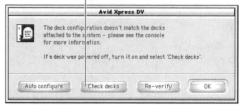

Figure 4.6 If Xpress Pro does not recognize your deck, make sure it's connected and turned on. Then click Check Decks.

Channel setting
Double-click here to
change the setting.

Channel dialog box
Click here to
add a channel.

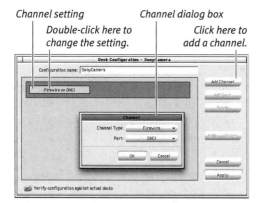

Figure 4.7 To tell Xpress Pro what connection (what channel) you are using to connect a playback device to your computer, click Add Channel in the Deck Configuration dialog box. Create multiple deck configurations for different deck setups.

Select the individual deck rectangle
to delete just the deck setting.

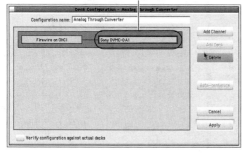

Figure 4.8 To delete a deck setting altogether, select the individual deck rectangle in the Deck Configuration dialog box and click Delete.

✔ Tips

■ You can change the channel information (video input) in the Capture tool by clicking the Video Input pull-down menu and choosing from the list that appears.

■ To change existing settings without deleting them, double-click either a channel or a deck setting (one of the gray rectangles). In the dialog box that appears, make your changes and click OK.

To set the video input channel:

1. Make sure that your camera, deck, converter, or Mojo box is turned on and connected to a FireWire cable, and that the other end of the FireWire cable is plugged into the FireWire connection on your computer.

2. On the Settings tab of the Project window, double-click your active (check-marked) Deck Configuration settings to open the settings dialog box.

3. *Do one of the following:*
   ▲ If no channel (such as FireWire—OHCI) is listed the Deck Configuration dialog box, click Add Channel.
   ▲ If the Deck Configuration dialog box does list a channel—a gray rectangle with the channel name appears on the left—double-click the channel rectangle to open the Channel dialog box and change the channel information.

4. In the Channel dialog box, click the Channel Type pop-up menu and choose a video channel type (for DV capture, choose FireWire). Then click the Port pop-up menu and choose a channel (for FireWire capture, you'll usually use OHCI). Click OK (**Figure 4.7**).

   In the Deck Configuration dialog box, a gray rectangle appears labeled with the name of your channel.

■ To delete your channel setting, click the setting's individual gray rectangle (**Figure 4.8**). Then click the Delete button. To delete both your channel and your deck setting, click the blue area of the large rectangle to select both the channel and deck information. Then click the Delete button.

To tell Xpress Pro what device you're using for capture:

1. On the Settings tab of the Project window, double-click the active (check-marked) Deck Configuration settings.

   The Deck Configuration dialog box appears.

2. In the Deck Configuration dialog box, click Add Deck (note that you must add a channel before you can add a deck).

   A rectangle labeled "New Machine" appears next to your channel setting rectangle. The Deck Settings dialog box opens.

3. At the top of the Deck Settings dialog box, give the deck a name and enter a description in the Description box if you want.

4. To choose the brand of your capture device, click the leftmost Device pop-up menu in the Deck Settings dialog box and choose the brand from the list that appears.

5. To choose a model number for your capture device, click the rightmost Device pop-up menu and choose a specific model number from the list that appears (**Figure 4.9**). If your model number is not listed, then either choose a listed model that is very similar or choose Generic DV Device.

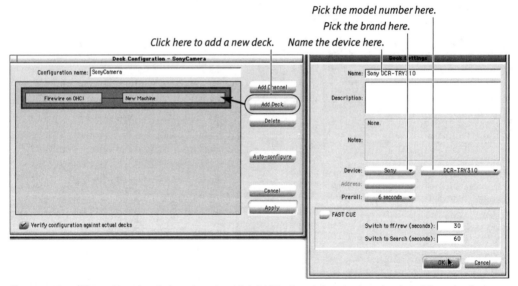

Pick the model number here.
Pick the brand here.
Name the device here.
Click here to add a new deck.

Figure 4.9 To tell Xpress Pro what deck you're using, click Add Deck and choose a brand and model number for your capture device in the Deck Settings dialog box. Give the setting a helpful name and click OK.

Deck configuration
setting name

Name of your deck,
camera, or converter

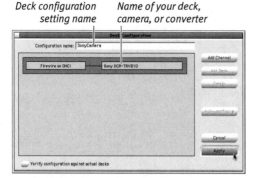

Figure 4.10 Click Apply to save your deck configuration setting.

6. If you are a using a VTR (deck) or camera, you can specify a preroll amount in the Deck Settings dialog box.

   This setting determines how far back the deck rewinds before capturing a logged clip. A healthy number of seconds—6 is recommended for DV—ensures that your deck catches a proper momentum by the time Xpress Pro starts capturing.

7. Click OK.

   The Deck Settings dialog box closes. A deck rectangle labeled with the name of your deck appears in the Deck Configuration dialog box next to the channel rectangle (**Figure 4.10**).

8. In the Deck Configuration dialog box, click Apply.

   In the Capture tool, Xpress Pro now lists the name of your deck right below the deck playback control buttons.

✔ Tips

- To delete your deck setting, click the setting's individual gray rectangle. Then click the Delete button. To delete both your channel and deck setting, click the blue area of the large rectangle to select both the channel and deck information. Then click the Delete button.

- To change existing settings without deleting them, double-click either a channel or deck setting (one of the gray rectangles). In the dialog box that appears, make your changes and click OK.

- You can bypass the Deck Settings dialog box by going to the Capture tool, clicking the pull-down tab right below the Deck playback controls, and selecting Auto-Configure. This option makes Xpress Pro automatically recognize the kind of deck or camera connected to your workstation. However, since Auto-Configure does not recognize all decks or cameras, the manual method is better.

Deck Preferences

After you tell Xpress Pro what device you're using for capture and through what channel the input signal will travel to your computer, you need to specify your deck preference settings to tell the application how you want the device to behave.

The deck preference settings include the following options:

- **When the Deck Contains No Tape, Log As:** When you want to log shots just by the numbers—in other words, without playing a tape in your deck—choose Drop Frame on Non-Drop Frame here to tell Xpress Pro how to notate the timecode. Drop Frame timecode uses semicolons and Non-Drop just uses colons.

    (For more information on logging, see "Logging Clips for Batch Capture" later in this chapter.)

- **Allow Assemble Edit for Digital Cut:** This setting pertains to output to tape (digital cut), not capturing. (For more information about assemble editing, see "Outputting to Tape" in Chapter 14.)

- **Stop Key Pauses Deck:** If you want to pause your deck or camera by pressing the spacebar, select this option. Pausing will not dethread your tape from the deck, which is good if you're doing a lot of capturing back to back. If you want to be able to stop your deck or camera and dethread your tape by pressing the spacebar, deselect this option. In general, you should stop your deck if it's going to be idle for a long period of time.

Setting the Right Preroll

When you log and batch capture or capture clip by clip using In or In and Out points—in other words, when the capture involves an automated operation—preroll becomes important.

Preroll determines how far back Xpress Pro rolls your source tape before playing forward, reading your timecode, and looking for the In point cue to start capturing. You configure your deck's preroll amount in the Deck Settings dialog box, which you can access by clicking the deck name rectangle in the Deck Configuration settings dialog box.

The recommended preroll amounts for various formats are as follows:

- **DV decks and cameras:** 6 seconds
- **Betacam:** 2 or 3 seconds
- **3/4" U-matic:** 5 seconds

If necessary, you can override the preroll amount set in your deck settings, by selecting Custom Preroll in the Capture tool and choosing a preroll time from the adjacent pull-down menu. Usually, you select Custom Preroll only when there is a timecode break problem before your In point and you need to set a preroll value lower than what you specified in your deck settings.

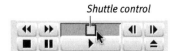

Figure 4.11 The Capture tool's deck controls.

◆ **Shuttle Holds Speed:** If you select this option, after you drag the shuttle control in the Capture window, the deck will continue to shuttle even after you release the mouse (**Figure 4.11**).

◆ **Stop Any Paused Deck When Quitting:** Select this option if you want Xpress Pro to automatically stop your deck after you quit the application, instead of staying in pause mode. Always keep this option selected to save wear and tear on your deck's heads.

◆ **Poll Deck During Digital Cut:** This setting pertains to outputting (digital cut), not capturing. (For more information, see "Outputting to Tape" in Chapter 14.)

◆ **DV Capture Offset:** The number you enter specifies the number of frames by which you want to shift your video or audio behind or in front of the timecode track. This setting is most helpful when you capture your audio and video through FireWire while reading timecode with an RS-422 connection. After performing a series of tests to see how far off the mark your timecode is from the actual frames, you can enter an offset frame amount between –6 and 24 here. (For more details on performing a DV capture offset test, consult the Xpress Pro help menu.)

◆ **Override Recommended Digital Cut Delay and Digital Cut Delay (Frames):** This setting applies to outputting to tape (digital cut), not capturing. (For more information, see "Outputting to Tape" in Chapter 14.)

SETTING UP YOUR DECK OR CAMERA FOR CAPTURE

To set your deck preferences:

1. On the Settings tab of the Project window, double-click the active (check-marked) Deck Preferences settings.

The Deck Preferences dialog box opens (**Figure 4.12**).

2. Make your changes to the deck preferences and click OK.

The Deck Preferences dialog box closes, and you can give the deck preferences a unique name on the Settings tab of the Project window.

Deck-Related Capture Settings

To govern the behavior of your deck or camera during capture, you can configure a few more settings, found on the General tab of the Capture Settings dialog box.

These settings include the following:

♦ **Stop Deck after Capture** or **Pause Deck after Capture:** Select one or the other option to either stop or pause your deck after the capture process finishes.

If you have more immediate capturing to do, choose Pause so you don't dethread the tape. If this is your last capture for awhile, choose Stop to dethread the tape.

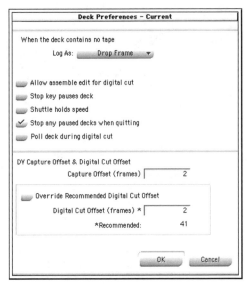

Figure 4.12 Use the Deck Preferences dialog box to tell Xpress Pro how you want your deck to operate during capture or output to tape.

◆ **Preroll Method:** Select the control track Xpress Pro should use when batch-capturing logged clips. The choices are Best Available, Standard Timecode, Best Available Control Track, and Standard Control Track. (For information about preroll, see the sidebar "Setting the Right Preroll" earlier in this chapter.)

▲ **Force Unique Clip Names:** If you want Xpress Pro to create clip names during capture instead of creating unique names yourself, you can select this option to create clip names based on the names of the bins in which the clips are logged and so avoid identical names. So if you capture on the fly by clicking the Record button (or pressing F4) to start and end each clip, without creating names, Xpress Pro will name the clips *BinName*.01, *BinName*.02, and so on in your bin.

◆ **Space Bar Stops Capture:** Select this option if you want to be able to stop the capture process with the spacebar.

◆ **Capture across Timecode Breaks:** If you select this option, Xpress Pro ignores any timecode breaks in your footage during capture. If you deselect this option, Xpress Pro presents an error dialog box whenever it encounters a timecode break.

Caution: You may have major difficulties batch recapturing if you capture across timecode breaks. Choose this option with care. See the sidebar "Dealing with Timecode Breaks" later in this chapter for more information.

◆ **Pause Deck While Logging:** With this option selected, Xpress Pro pauses the deck after you set In and Out points for a clip. Usually, you should keep this option selected because it gives you time to name your clip during the logging process.

Monitoring Your Source Video and Audio during Capture

Usually, when you capture video or audio, you want to see what you're capturing on a real broadcast monitor or hear what you're capturing on speakers or headphones. So when you capture through a deck, camera, or converter, connect video and audio analog cables to the video and audio out ports of your device and connect the other ends of the cables to the inputs on your external broadcast monitor and speakers. Then turn down your computer audio output, so you don't have to listen to the audio delay coming from your computer during capture.

SETTING UP YOUR DECK OR CAMERA FOR CAPTURE

To configure your deck-related Capture settings:

1. On the Settings tab of the Project window, double-click your active (check-marked) Capture settings. In the dialog box that appears, click the General tab.

2. Make your changes and click OK.

   Xpress Pro saves your Capture settings.

Reading Timecode Accurately

Generally, FireWire device control is not the most accurate means of controlling a DV deck. If you want to increase your timecode accuracy, use an RS-422 or RS-232 connection to control your deck and read the timecode information during capture, if your DV deck supports the RS-422 or RS-232 protocol (such as the Sony DSR-25). To connect an RS-422 or RS-232 cable to your computer, you typically need a serial port connection on your CPU.

Most PCs come equipped with serial ports, but most recent Macs do not. However, you can get a serial port for a Mac from a vendor such as (http://www.gefen.com), which sells the Stealth serial port for most Apple CPUs.

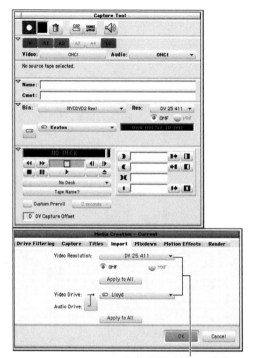

Select the video resolution.

Figure 4.13 You can select your video resolution for capture in one of two places: on the Capture tab of the Media Creation settings dialog box or the Capture tool's Res pop-up menu.

Configuring Your Video Input Resolution

Xpress Pro needs to know what video resolution you want to capture. For DV, a digital format, you usually do not want to deviate from full-resolution DV 25 411 unless you need to save drive space by capturing at single-field resolution (for NTSC or PAL video) of 15:1s.

If you do capture at lower than full-resolution quality (an offline quality), remember that at the end of your project, you'll have to recapture your footage at full resolution.

To select a video resolution for capture:

◆ *Do one of the following:*

▲ Choose Tools > Capture to open the Capture tool and choose a resolution from the Capture tool's Res (resolution) pop-up menu.

▲ Double-click your active (check-marked) Media Creation settings (on the Settings tab of the Project window), click the Capture tab, and choose a resolution from the Video Resolution pop-up menu (**Figure 4.13**).

Xpress Pro will now capture source video at your chosen resolution.

Configuring Your Audio Settings for Capture or Recording

Before you capture a source clip that contains audio or record an audio voice-over with a microphone, you need to give Xpress Pro answers to the following three general questions:

◆ **How are you capturing or recording your audio?** Xpress Pro needs to know your audio input source (source channel). For instance, you can capture your audio through FireWire, through an input on your sound card, or through a microphone input jack.

◆ **At what level do you want to capture or record your audio?** When capturing analog audio, which you can capture using an analog audio capture card, you can use the Input level slider on the Input tab of the Audio Project Settings dialog box to raise or lower the incoming audio level for capture or recording. With digital audio (such as audio playing through FireWire from a DV camera), you cannot adjust the incoming audio level.

◆ **What kind of audio file data do you want Xpress Pro to create?** You need to tell Xpress Pro what sample rate, audio file format, and bit rate you want to use to record your audio. You make these choices on the Main tab of the Audio Project Settings dialog box.

Choose your audio input.

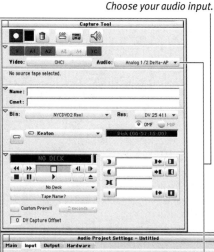

Figure 4.14 You can choose your audio input source in one of two places: on the Input tab of the Audio Project Settings dialog box or the Audio pop-up menu in the Capture tool.

To choose an audio input source:

◆ *Do one of the following:*

▲ On the Settings tab of the Project window, double-click your active (check-marked) Audio Project settings. On the Input tab of the Audio Project Settings dialog box, choose an audio source from the Input Source pop-up menu.

▲ Open the Capture tool. Click the Audio Input pop-up menu and choose an audio input (**Figure 4.14**).

When Xpress Pro captures or records audio, it will expect to receive the audio signal through the chosen audio input source channel.

✔ Tips

■ You cannot simultaneously capture video through OHCI (FireWire) while capturing audio through an audio input channel.

■ If you are capturing DV audio through FireWire, choose OHCI as your audio input source.

CONFIGURING YOUR AUDIO SETTINGS FOR
CAPTURE OR RECORDING

To set your audio file format, sample rate, and sample size:

1. On the Settings tab of the Project window, double-click your active (check-marked) Audio Project settings (**Figure 4.15**).

2. In the Audio Project Settings dialog box that appears, *make a choice for each of the following*:

   ▲ **Sample Rate:** Generally, you should choose the sample rate that matches the sample rate at which your audio was recorded. Most cameras record either 32 kHz (12-bit sample rate) or 48 kHz (16-bit sample rate). Audio CDs use 44.1. Whichever sample rate you choose, you should stick with the same sample rate throughout your project (converting files of different sample rates so that they conform to the one uniform rate).

   ▲ **Audio File Format:** Usually you should choose OMF (AIFF-C)— an Apple Computer format that is popular for both Mac and Windows users—since it is compatible with many third-party applications. Choose OMF (WAVE)—a Microsoft/IBM file format—if all sound work will be done in Windows applications. Choose SDII—a format designed by the makers of ProTools, available only to Macintosh users—if you're working with a sound designer who has an old ProTools system that uses SDII.

   ▲ **Audio File Sample Size:** Choose the bit rate of your audio here. This setting determines the quality of your audio. The default, and the most commonly used bit rate, is 16 bit; 24-bit audio may produce a slightly higher sound quality but is overkill for most projects.

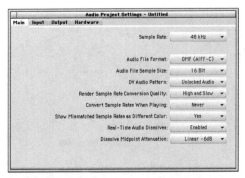

Figure 4.15 You designate your audio format, sample rate, and sample size (as well as other audio-related settings) on the Main tab of the Audio Project Settings dialog box.

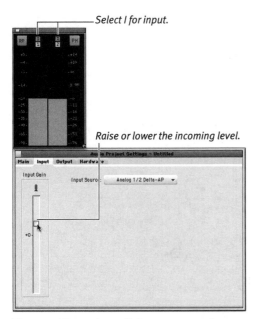

Select I for input.

Raise or lower the incoming level.

Figure 4.16 For analog audio input, you can raise or lower the input gain to receive a healthy signal when capturing or recording audio.

Remember: The 12-bit audio option on your camera refers to the 32-kHz audio sampling rate, not audio file sample size. The 16-bit audio option on your camera refers to the 48-kHz audio sampling rate, not the audio file sample size.

To set the analog audio input level:

1. Choose Tools > Audio Tool to open the Audio tool and click one or both orange In/Out buttons so that they display the letter *I* (for input).

2. On the Settings tab of the Project window, double-click your active (checkmarked) Audio Project settings and click the Input tab.

3. While you play (or speak) your input signal, adjust the Input Gain slider until you get the desired level reading in the Audio tool (**Figure 4.16**).

   When you begin capturing or recording, Xpress Pro maintains the configured input gain level. You should make sure that your audio does not peak in the Audio tool's audio meter. If it does, lower the input gain level.

✔ Tips

- If you need to record voice-over from a microphone, use the Audio Punch-in tool.

- A good way to set your input level is to play a source tape that contains a reference tone. As the tone plays, adjust the audio Input Gain slider until the green bars in the Audio tool audio meter reach the right reference level.

- With DV audio or any other kind of digital audio, you don't need to worry about audio input level.

The DV Audio Pattern Setting

One audio project setting that you usually don't have to worry about is DV Audio Pattern because the default choice, Unlocked Audio, is the right choice for the regular DV format. Switch to Locked Audio only for the DVCAM or DVCPro format.

Controlling Your Deck or Camera

If you connect your deck or camera to your workstation via FireWire or a serial device such as RS-422 or RS-232, then you can control the device remotely using the play controls in the Capture tool (**Figure 4.17**).

You can also control your deck remotely using selected play controls found on the Play tab of the Command palette. These buttons, which you should map to your keyboard, include Play Forward, Play Reverse, Pause, Stop, Step Backward, and Step Forward.

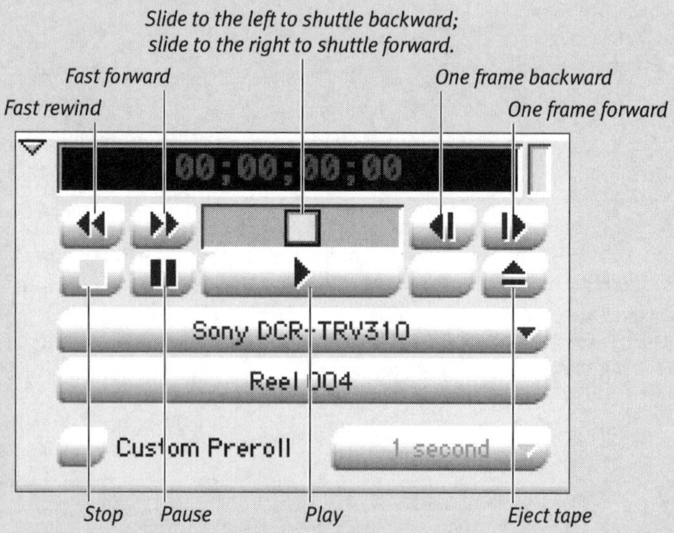

Slide to the left to shuttle backward; slide to the right to shuttle forward.

Fast forward

Fast rewind

One frame backward

One frame forward

Sony DCR-TRV310

Reel 004

Custom Preroll   1 second

Stop   Pause   Play   Eject tape

Figure 4.17 If you can connect your deck or camera to your computer via FireWire or another control connection, then you can operate your deck remotely, using the deck controls in the Capture tool.

Understanding Timecode

Timecode is the means by which you and Xpress Pro keep track of every individual frame in your source footage and your edited sequence. Timecode becomes invaluable in the following types of situations:

◆ **You need to recapture your source media.** If you need to upgrade your project resolution from a less than full-quality resolution (an offline resolution) to a full-quality resolution (an online resolution), or if you need to transfer your project to another type of NLE, or if your source media drive was accidentally erased, then you need to recapture your footage. To erase the old media files and replace them with the new ones without destroying all your hard editing work, Xpress Pro uses your source timecode numbers to batch recapture the new media with the same In and Out points as the old footage.

◆ **You need to re-create your project on a tape-to-tape edit system.** If you plan to re-create your edit on a tape-to-tape machine, that machine will require an edit decision list (EDL), which is a list containing all of the timecode numbers and clip names that represent your edited sequence.

Each video second is composed of multiple frames, and timecode notates each frame as HOURS:MINUTES:SECONDS:FRAMES.

NTSC video uses 29.97 frames per second of video. Because of the idiosyncrasies of the NTSC standard, two types of NTSC timecode are available:

◆ **Drop Frame timecode:** This timecode system, used by most consumer video cameras, discards two timecode reference numbers every minute, except for every tenth minute, to keep the timecode numbers in sync with clock time. This system uses semicolons between hours, minutes, seconds, and frames. For example, you write 0 hours, 3 minutes, 2 seconds, and 21 frames as 00;03;02;21.

◆ **Non Drop Frame timecode:** This type of timecode does not drop any timecode numbers. It use colons between hours, minutes, seconds, and frames. For example, you write 0 hours, 3 minutes, 2 seconds, and 21 frames as 00:03:02:21.

To tell Xpress Pro what kind of NTSC timecode your source footage uses, you generally do not have to do anything. Xpress Pro automatically reads the type of timecode that occurs on your source footage when you capture. However, if you log footage without source tapes, then you need to select Drop Frame or Non-Drop Frame in the top pop-up menu in your deck preference settings.

To tell Xpress Pro what kind of NTSC timecode to use in your sequences, open the General settings dialog box and enter a default starting timecode number, using semicolons for Drop Frame and colons for nondrop frame.

Note that PAL video uses one timecode standard, as it runs at a simple 25 frames per second.

Logging Clips for Batch Capture

The process of logging clips offline, before you capture them, involves playing your deck or camera and logging In and Out point timecodes for the beginning and ending of each clip you want to capture. The logging process also gives you the opportunity to name your clips and add comments to them (in the naming section of the Capture tool or in the bin itself).

To choose which source tracks to log (and capture):

1. Choose Tools > Capture Tool.

   The Capture tool opens.

2. If you want to capture the video track from your source tape, click to select the V button at the top of the Capture tool.

3. If you want to capture audio tracks from your source tape, click to select A1, A2, and so on.

4. If you want to capture the timecode track, keep the TC button selected (**Figure 4.18**).

   When Xpress Pro eventually captures your logged clips, it will capture the tracks you select here (provided you selected Capture the Tracks Logged for Each Clip on the Batch tab of the Capture Settings dialog box).

✔ Tips

- Before logging any clips, double-check to make sure that your capture device is on and connected, Xpress Pro recognizes your capture device in the Capture tool, your logging bin is open, and you designated the name of your logging bin and source tape in the Capture tool.

- If you use a camera for capturing, make sure it is in VTR mode.

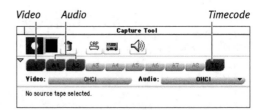

Figure 4.18 Typically, you will capture one video track, two audio tracks, and one Timecode track.

Click here.   *Capture/Log toggle.*

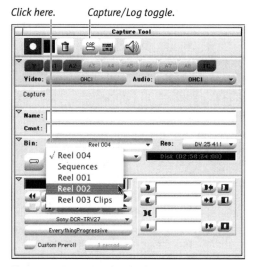

Figure 4.19 To set your logging bin—you can designate only one bin at a time—click the logging bin selection pop-up menu in the Capture tool.

Tape name   *Project name*

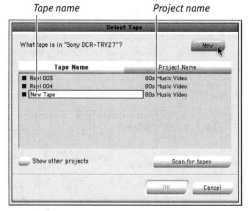

Figure 4.20 If you're working with a source tape you haven't used before, click New in the Select Tape dialog box and type a unique name for your tape.

To log source clips:

1. Put the Capture tool in Log mode by clicking the ⬚ Capture button so it changes to the ⬚ Log mode button.

2. In the Bin section of the Capture tool, choose a logging bin from the Bin pop-up menu (which lists only open bins; see **Figure 4.19**).

   This is where Xpress Pro will send your logged shots.

   You can create a new bin for logging by going to the Bins tab of the Project window and clicking New Bin.

3. Insert a source tape into your deck or camera. When Xpress Pro displays the Source Tape dialog box, *do one of the following*:

   ▲ If this is a new tape, click the New button, give the tape a name, click the Select Tape dialog box's gray area, and click the black square next to the tape's name to select it; then click OK (**Figure 4.20**).

   ▲ If you previously named the current tape, click the black square next to the tape's name to highlight it; then click OK.

4. In the Capture tool, click the Play button or press the spacebar on your keyboard to play your deck or camera.

   As your deck or camera plays, a video image from the tape should appear in the Composer monitor.

   continues on next page

LOGGING CLIPS FOR BATCH CAPTURE

5. When you get to the start of the first clip you want to log, mark an In point *by doing one of the following:*

▲ Press F4.

▲ Press ❱ Mark In (mapped by default to the I key on your keyboard).

The timecode reference for your In point appears at the lower right of the Capture tool (**Figure 4.21**). The deck or camera continues to play.

6. When you get to the end of the first clip, mark an Out point and log the clip *by doing one of the following:*

▲ Press F4.

▲ Press Mark Out 【 (mapped by default to the O key on the keyboard); then click the Log button at the upper left of the Capture tool.

▲ Click the ▣ Mark Out and Log button at the upper left of the Capture tool.

Playback stops, and Xpress Pro logs your clip to the designated logging bin (**Figure 4.22**).

7. If you want to give your clip a unique name now, give it a new name in the bin. Otherwise, continue logging in the Capture tool. Repeat steps 2 through 5 until you've logged all of your clips.

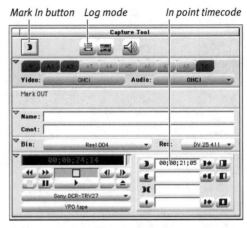

Mark In button   Log mode   In point timecode

Figure 4.21 To log an In point for a clip, press F4, press Mark In, or click the big Mark In button at the upper left of the Capture tool.

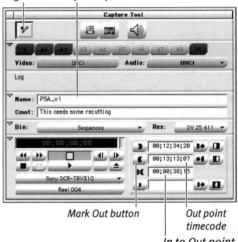

Mark Out and   You can name
Log button   your clip here.

Mark Out button   Out point
                           timecode

                           In to Out point
                           duration

Figure 4.22 You can name your clip in the Capture tool before clicking the Mark Out and Log button, or you can name it later in your bin.

Log Clip Button   Normal Mark Out button

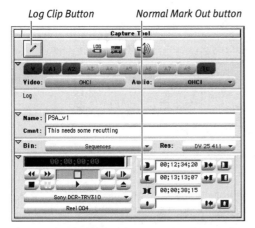

Figure 4.23 One way to make sure you name your clip before you log it to your bin is to click the normal Mark Out button to log your Out point. Xpress Pro will pause your deck (if you select Pause Deck While Logging in the Capture settings). Then you can name the clip before you click the Log Clip button.

Click here.

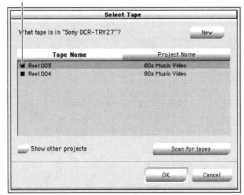

Figure 4.24 To select a source tape in the Select Tape dialog box, click the black square next to a source tape name.

✔ Tips

■ To keep your tape from playing ahead while you name a logged clip, select Pause Deck While Logging on the General tab of the Capture Settings dialog box. With this option selected, Xpress Pro will pause your deck after you log an Out point for a clip.

■ One alternative way to name your clip is to name it in the Capture tool Name box sometime between after you log the previous shot and before you log the shot you're naming (**Figure 4.23**).

■ If you previously named the current source tape, but it was for a different project, in the Select Tape dialog box select Show Other Projects. Then click the Scan for Tapes button until other tapes appear. Click the black square next to a tape's name to select it and then click OK (**Figure 4.24**).

■ Use only letters and numerals for your tape names; do not use other symbols.

■ If you are planning to generate an EDL for import into an edit controller for online editing, find out your controller's tape naming standards beforehand. You may need to make your tape names extremely short.

Logging Using the Keyboard

Why rely on the mouse when you can use your right hand to play through your footage and mark In and Out points?

Remember that you can map any buttons from the Command palette to your keyboard and use them to control your deck and log In and Out points.

These are the most commonly used deck control buttons:

♦ **Mark In** and **Mark Out:** By default these commands are mapped to the I and O keys, but you can map them anywhere from the Edit tab of the Command palette.

♦ **Play Reverse** and **Play Forward:** By default, these commands are mapped to the J and L keys. But you can map them elsewhere from the Play tab of the Command palette. Also, by tapping them between 2 and 5 times, you can play 2X, 3X, 5X, and 8X speed.

♦ **Stop** and **Pause:** You can determine the behavior of the Stop button in the Deck Preferences settings. By default, Pause is mapped to the K key. You can map these buttons from the Play tab of the Command palette.

Dealing with Timecode Breaks

A timecode break is a disruption in the contiguous timecode numbers on your source tape. Usually a timecode break is the fault of your camera operator, caused by recording on the source tape and then starting to record again after playing past the last recorded frame.

Timecode breaks can be a major problem when batch capturing. For one thing, timecode on your tape often starts back at 00;00, so you'll have multiple places on the same tape with the same timecode address.

Also, Xpress Pro will not be able to find your logged In point timecode if a break occurs somewhere between preroll and your In point. For example, if Xpress Pro rewinds six seconds before your In point and starts playing and a timecode break occurs, Xpress will become confused it (as if it hit a bump in the road) and will not reach your In point and start capture.

(For more information on preroll, see the section "Setting Up Your Deck or Camera for Capture" and the sidebar "Setting the Right Preroll" earlier in this chapter.)

Fortunately, you can address timecode breaks in multiple ways:

◆ **You can instruct Xpress Pro to capture across timecode breaks.** Open the Capture Settings dialog box. On the General tab, select Capture Across Timecode Breaks. If you select this choice and Xpress Pro encounters timecode problems during capture, it will start capturing a new clip after the break; this creates two clips out of one clip that has a timecode break in the middle of it.

Note: Xpress Pro assumes that timecode is sequential between breaks. If timecode numbers reset after breaks, this feature will not help you if you need to recapture clips.

◆ **You can capture clip by clip or on the fly.** By capturing clip by clip or on the fly, you can watch for and address timecode problems on a case-by-case basis. In contrast, when batch capturing, you might return to your computer to find out that your capture session aborted due to timecode breaks. (For more information, see the section "About Capturing Clip by Clip" or "Capturing on the Fly" later in this chapter.)

Capturing clip by clip also allows you to set a short preroll time in the Capture tool to avoid a break.

◆ **You can use DV scene extraction.** When working with DV footage that has timecode breaks, you might want to forget logging or capturing individual shots at first. Instead, capture large chunks of footage. Then perform DV scene extraction—which uses time-of-day information instead of timecode—to break the footage into individual shots. (For more information, see "Creating Subclips with DV Scene Extraction" later in this chapter.)

◆ **You can select a better preroll method.** Open the Capture Settings dialog box and on the General tab specify what Xpress Pro should use as the control track. The wisest selection is Best Available Control Track, as it tells Xpress Pro to use whatever works. Unfortunately, this setting does not apply to DV footage, which uses only timecode for its control track.

Batch Capturing Logged Clips

Batch capturing allows you to automatically capture source clips based on the reel names and timecode numbers of your logged clips. In addition, you can batch capture clips based on the timecode numbers of an imported batch list.

Before you pull the batch-capture trigger, however, you need to configure a few batch-related settings. These settings, found on the Batch tab of the Capture Settings dialog box (**Figure 4.25**), include the following:

◆ **Optimize for Disk Space:** Select this option if you want Xpress Pro to capture your clips exactly as logged, adding extra handles (a small amount of extra footage at the beginning and ending of each clip).

◆ **Optimize for Batch Speed:** Select this option if you want Xpress Pro to coalesce any two clips that are close to each other (five or fewer seconds apart on your source tapes).

Use Optimize for Batch Speed only if you have an extreme time crunch. Disk space is more valuable than the few extra minutes you gain by coalescing clips. In addition, separating coalesced clips will take extra time.

◆ **Switch to Emptiest Drive if Current Drive Is Full:** Provided you have more than one media drive selected for capture—in other words, you've created a drive group—choose this option to make Xpress Pro capture to the next available capture drive when the current one becomes full. (To learn about drive groups, see "Configuring Your Hard Drives for Capture" earlier in this chapter.)

Figure 4.25 The Batch tab of the Capture Settings dialog box contains options that determine how Xpress Pro treats logged clips during capture.

Offline Resolutions to Online Resolutions

Batch recapturing is the way to convert your sequence from offline to online quality. For example, you might initially capture and edit your footage using the 15:1s resolution: a single-field resolution.

Here's how full-resolution DV compares to offline resolution DV:

Whereas you can fit 2.1 minutes of full-res DV (DV25 411) with audio into 1 GB of disk space, you can fit 32.1 minutes of 15:1s material into the same amount of space.

For 24p projects, the 15:1s equivalent is 28:1s; you can fit 22.2 minutes of NTSC 28:1s into 1 GB of space, and 19.3 minutes of PAL 28:1s into the same amount of space.

When you finish editing your movie, you can replace all of the offline-resolution media with the full-resolution DV equivalent media, as long as everything was captured with proper timecode.

Usually, you'll first want to select your finished sequence by choosing Bin > Decompose to create an offline version of the sequence. Do not select the Offline Media Items Only option in the Decompose dialog box.

Then you can batch recapture your sequence using DV 25 411 as your resolution.

(For more information on using Decompose, see "Decomposing and Recapturing a Sequence" in Chapter 13.)

◆ **Rewind Tape When Finished:** Select this option if you want Xpress Pro to automatically rewind the tape in your deck or camera after capturing.

◆ **Eject Tape When Finished:** Select this option if you want Xpress Pro to automatically eject your tape from the deck or camera after capturing.

◆ **Log Errors to the Console and Continue Capturing:** Select this option if you do *not* want to Xpress Pro to interrupt capture if any errors occur.

◆ **Capture the Tracks Logged for Each Clip:** Select this option if you want Xpress Pro to capture the tracks (V1, A1, and so on) that you selected in the Capture tool while logging.

◆ **Use the Audio Sample Rate Logged for Each Clip:** Select this option if you want Xpress Pro to capture your audio using the sample rate selected at the time you logged the audio clip.

◆ **Use the Audio Sample Size Logged for Each Clip:** Select this option if you want Xpress Pro to capture your audio using the sample size (bit rate) selected at the time you logged the audio clip.

◆ **Use the Video Compression Logged for Each Clip:** Select this option if you've changed the video resolution in the Capture tool but want Xpress Pro to capture your video according to the resolution selected at the time you logged the video clip. (For more information, see "Configuring Your Video Input Resolution" earlier in this chapter.)

✔ Tip

■ With Optimize for Batch Speed selected, Xpress coalesces only clips that have the same video resolution and audio sample rate.

BATCH CAPTURING LOGGED CLIPS

To configure your batch capture settings:

1. On the Settings tab of the Project window, double-click the active (check-marked) Capture settings.

   The Capture Settings dialog box opens.

2. Click the Batch tab.

   Xpress Pro displays the batch-related settings.

3. Make any necessary adjustments to the settings and click OK.

   The Capture Settings dialog box disappears, and your settings are saved.

To batch capture your logged clips:

1. Open the bin that contains your logged clips.

2. Select the clips you want to capture (use Shift-click to select multiple clips; see **Figure 4.26**).

3. Choose Bin > Batch Capture.

   Xpress Pro opens the Capture tool and the Batch Capture dialog box. The dialog box tells you how many clips you selected.

4. In the Batch Capture dialog box, *choose one or more of the following settings:*

   ▲ **Offline Media Only:** Xpress Pro captures only selected clips that are offline—that is, not attached to any source media. To recapture previously captured media (needed when moving from offline to online quality), do not select this option.

   ▲ **Extend Handles Beyond Master Clip Edges:** Choose this option to add handles (extra footage) to the beginning and ending of your clips. Select this option to be on the safe side with your clips, in case your In and Out points aren't precise.

Selected clips

You can tell these clips need to be captured because their tracks are listed offline.

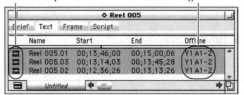

Figure 4.26 To batch capture logged clips, first select them in a bin.

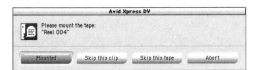

Figure 4.27 When Xpress Pro asks you to mount a source tape, insert the tape into your deck or camera and click Mounted.

5. Click OK.

If you have logged clips from multiple source tapes, a dialog box appears prompting you to mount the first tape for batch capturing (**Figure 4.27**).

6. In the dialog box that appears, *click one of the following:*

▲ **Mounted:** Click this to confirm that the right tape is in your deck or camera. Xpress Pro can begin capturing.

▲ **Skip This Clip**: Click this to skip the first clip in the capturing process. Xpress Pro continues onto the next clip.

▲ **Skip This Tape:** Click this to skip the entire tape and move to capturing clips from the next tape. Xpress Pro prompts you to insert the next tape.

▲ **Abort:** Click this to end the batch-capture process. You can also click Abort during the capture process or click the Trash button in the Capture tool.

The dialog box disappears, and Xpress Pro automatically captures all logged clips. If clips belong to more than one source tape, Xpress Pro may prompt you to insert a new tape to continue capturing.

After batch capture, Xpress Pro displays the message "Batch Capture Complete." Your clips are online now, as opposed to offline.

✔ Tips

■ You must select at least one logged clip before you choose Bin > Batch Capture.

■ Do not select Extend Handles Beyond Master Clip Edges if there are timecode breaks right before or right after your clips.

■ To skip particular clips during capture, click the Trash button in the Capture tool. Then, in the Abort window, click the next clip you want to capture.

■ To end the entire batch capture process, click Abort or click the Trash button in the Capture tool.

Capturing on the Fly

Capturing on the fly is the method you need to use when capturing from a noncontrollable deck. Since you cannot read timecode with a noncontrollable deck, you cannot set In or Out points. Instead, you need to begin and end your capture by clicking the Record button.

Capturing on the fly is not reserved for non-controllable decks, however. In fact, it is also a fast way to capture from a controllable deck, reading proper timecode. But there's one word of caution: it's hard to choose the exact In and Out frame of your captured clip by clicking the Record button. If you want to capture each clip to exact In and Out points, use the log and capture or clip-by-clip capture method, using Mark In and Mark Out to set your In and Out timecode.

To capture on the fly:

1. In the Capture tool, click the Capture/Log Mode button so that it displays "Cap" for the Capture mode.

2. At the top of the Capture tool, select the video and/or audio tracks you want to capture. If you are working with a non-controllable deck, deselect the TC (timecode) button and click the Toggle Source button so that a red line appears through the Deck icon (**Figure 4.28**).

3. If you haven't already done so, insert a source tape into your deck or camera. Choose the name of the tape from the Source Tape dialog box that appears.

4. Play the tape to the approximate place you want to start capturing and play forward.

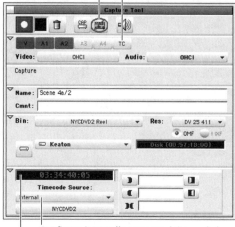

Click to disable deck control. Deselect this.

Configure internally generated timecode here.
Internally generated timecode is mostly useless.

Figure 4.28 When you capture on the fly using a noncontrollable deck, you need to deselect the TC button and click the Toggle Source button to disable the deck controls.

Click this button or press Esc to stop recording.

Deselect this button when capturing from a noncontrollable deck.

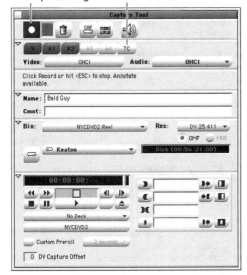

Figure 4.29 Capturing on the fly is the method to use when capturing from a noncontrollable device, such as a consumer VCR or DVD player.

5. Click the Capture button.

The box next to the Capture button begins to flash red as Xpress Pro begins to capture your clip (**Figure 4.29**).

6. At any point, you can type a name for the clip in the Name/Comment area of the Capture tool.

7. To stop capturing, *do one of the following:*

▲ Click the Capture button on the upper left of the Capture tool.

▲ Press the Esc key.

Xpress Pro places your captured clip in the logging bin. If you didn't name it already, you can name it now.

✔ Tips

■ Capturing on the fly is the capture method to use when you want to capture large sections of your footage and then break that footage up into individually named subclips after capture.

■ To abort your capture, click the Trash button in the Capture tool.

■ When capturing on the fly, make sure that there are no timecode numbers at the lower right of the Capture tool. In other words, make sure you delete any previous In and Out marks; otherwise, Xpress Pro may cue the tape to those marks.

■ Remember: when you capture with a noncontrollable deck, you must *deselect* the TC (timecode) button at the top of the Capture tool.

CAPTURING ON THE FLY

Capturing Clip by Clip

Capturing clip by clip involves logging In and/or Out points for one clip and capturing that one clip immediately. One advantage of this method is that you have to set only about one point (the In or the Out point).

You can set an In point and end the capture by clicking the Capture button, or you can set an Out point and being the capture by clicking the Capture button.

Additionally, this method allows you to check for timecode breaks on a clip-by-clip basis. If Xpress Pro tries to capture a clip but can't because of a timecode break (it will display a timecode break warning), or if you visually see the timecode numbers jump or reset during playback, you can select a short custom preroll for an individual clip below the deck controls in the Capture tool. Then Xpress Pro will not rewind the tape as far back as the break.

To capture a clip using an In point, Out point, or both:

1. In the Capture tool, click the Capture/Log Mode button, so it displays "Cap" (for Capture mode).

2. At the top of the Capture tool, select the video and audio tracks you want to capture, as well as the TC button (to capture timecode).

3. Insert and name your tape.

4. Mark your In and/or Out point by *doing one of the following:*

   ▲ To set only an In point, play to the exact point you want to log as your In point and press Mark In (mapped by default to the I key).

   The Capture tool says "Capture from IN" below the video input pop-up menu (**Figure 4.30**).

You can name the clip before capture.

Capture mode   In-point timecode

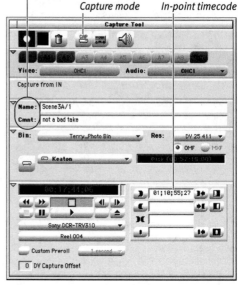

Figure 4.30 Capturing clip by clip using In points may be the most efficient way to capture clips if your shots are not long. It requires setting an In point, pressing the Record button to start capture, and pressing the Record button again to stop capture.

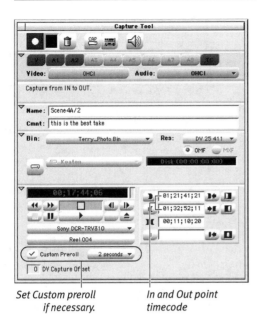

Set Custom preroll if necessary.   *In and Out point timecode*

Figure 4.31 Capturing a clip by setting both In and Out points is helpful when you need to be precise about the beginning and ending of your clip (perhaps to avoid timecode break problems that are both before and after the footage you need).

▲ To set only an Out point, play to the exact point you want to log as your Out point and press Mark Out (mapped by default to the O key).

The Capture tools says "Digitize to OUT" below the video input pop-up menu.

▲ To set both precise In and Out points, play to your In point and press Mark In and play to your Out point and Mark Out.

The Capture tool says "Capture from IN to OUT" below the video source pop-up menu (**Figure 4.31**).

5. To capture your clip, *do one of the following:*

▲ If you set only an In point, click the Capture button at the upper left of the Capture tool. Xpress Pro starts capturing from the In point. When your tape gets to the approximate end point of the clip, click the Capture button again to stop capture.

▲ If you set only an exact Out point, rewind to the approximate In point of the clip, start playback, and click the Capture button. Xpress Pro starts capturing and automatically stops capturing when it gets to your Out point.

▲ If you set both In and Out points, just click the Capture button, and Xpress Pro will automatically capture from your In to your Out point.

The captured clip appears in your designated logging bin. If you didn't name the clip in the Capture tool during capture, you can now name it in the bin.

✔ Tips

■ To end a capture, you can press the Esc key instead of the Capture button.

■ If necessary, set a Custom preroll amount below the deck controls in the Capture tool.

■ You can also capture a clip by setting only an Out point; just use Mark Out instead of Mark In, to set the end of your clip. Rewind to the approximate In point of

CAPTURING CLIP BY CLIP

the clip, play forward, and click Capture when you want to begin capturing.

Capturing Directly to the Timeline

If have been editing your sequence for a while but realize you need to include one more shot in your movie, you can set up your Timeline and Capture tool to capture a clip directly to a specific place in your Timeline. This is an effective technique for last-minute crunch situations.

To capture directly to the Timeline:

1. Load a sequence by dragging a sequence icon from a bin to the Composer monitor or double-clicking a sequence in Source/Record mode.

2. Click Mark In in the Timeline where you want to insert or overwrite the incoming clip.

3. Select the tracks on which you want to place the incoming clip.

4. On the Settings tab of the Project window, double-click your active (check-marked) Capture settings to open the Capture Settings dialog box.

5. On the Edit tab of the Capture Settings dialog box, select Enable Edit to Timeline. Overwrite and Splice-in edit buttons appear at the top of the Capture tool.

6. Enter a handle length (the amount of extra footage you want to capture before and after the In and Out points of your clip) and click OK (**Figure 4.32**).

7. In the Capture tool, enter Capture mode by clicking the Capture/Log Mode button so it displays "Cap" for capture.

Edit tab

Figure 4.32 To capture directly to the Timeline, select Enable Edit to Timeline on the Edit tab of the Capture settings. Entering a handle amount is wise if you plan to use transition effects with the footage.

Click and hold.

The source video will be edited onto Timeline track V2.

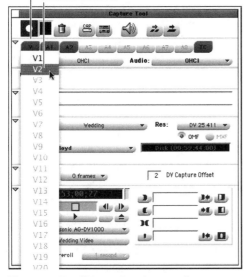

Figure 4.33 To tell Xpress Pro where to edit your captured clip into the Timeline, click and hold on a Capture tool's source track button and choose a Timeline track from the list that appears.

8. Click and hold on the video and audio track buttons at the top of the Capture tool. From the pop-menus that appear, choose the Timeline tracks to which you want to patch the incoming clips (**Figure 4.33**).

9. If you haven't already done so, insert your source tape into the deck or camera and choose the source tape name from the Source Tape dialog box (or create a new name).

10. In the Capture tool, play your source tape and click Mark In and Mark Out to log the In and Out points for your incoming clip.

11. Choose the type of edit to perform by clicking the Splice-in button or the Overwrite button in the Capture tool.

12. To start capturing, click the Record button. Xpress Pro captures your clip and stops capture when it reaches the Out point you marked in the Capture tool. Xpress Pro edits the captured clip into the Timeline and creates a master clip in your bin.

✔ Tips

■ After you capture a clip to the Timeline, name the newly created master clip in your bin.

■ If you are capturing a clip you want to edit onto the end of your sequence, you need to mark only an In point in the Capture tool. During the capture process, you can simply click Record to create your Out point on the fly.

Creating Subclips with DV Scene Extraction

DV scene extraction is an automated method of breaking your footage into individual subclips. Xpress Pro accomplishes this task by using invisible time-of-day (TOD) information that usually exists on DV tapes. The TOD information tells Xpress Pro when you began and stopped recording with your camera by pressing the record button.

You can enable DV scene extraction either before or after you capture a clip. All you need to do is capture a long master clip from your DV source tape. Then when you perform the DV scene extraction, Xpress Pro creates subclips from the master clip, adds locators to the master clip, or both.

The advantage of capturing with this method is that it saves you from having to name and add comments to shots during capture. If you have your deck for only a limited amount of time, it might be a good idea to just get the media on your computer and go through it later.

The drawback to capturing with this method is that you need a lot of hard drive space to capture a long master clip.

Further limitations are as follows:

◆ You must capture video. This method does not work with audio-only footage.

◆ You cannot apply scene extraction to DVCPro-format tapes.

Figure 4.34 To enable DV scene extraction, open your Record Settings dialog box and click the DV Options tab. Select DV Scene Extraction; then select Add Locators, Create Subclips, or Both.

Original master clip

Subclips created by DV scene extraction

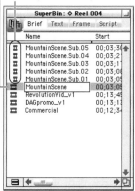

Figure 4.35 If you configure DV scene extraction to create subclips, then Xpress Pro breaks a master clip into multiple subclips, using time-of-day Information.

Master clip

Subclips created from the master clip by DV scene extraction

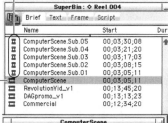

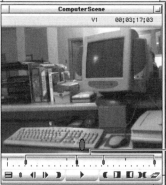

Locators mark TOD information on the master clip.

Figure 4.36 You can configure DV scene extraction to both create subclips from a master clip and add locators on the master clip to mark time-of-day Information.

To preconfigure DV scene extraction before capturing a clip:

1. On the Settings tab of the Project window, double-click your active (check-marked) Capture settings.

2. On the DV Options tab of the Capture Settings dialog box, select DV Scene Extraction (**Figure 4.34**).

3. _Select one of the following options:_
   - ▲ **Add Locators:** Xpress Pro will place locators at the TOD information breaks on your captured master clip.
   - ▲ **Create Subclips:** Xpress Pro will break your captured master clip into subclips that begin at the TOD information breaks on your captured clip (**Figure 4.35**).
   - ▲ **Both:** Xpress Pro will create locators at TOD breaks on your captured master clip and create subclips that begin at the TOD breaks (**Figure 4.36**).

4. Choose a bin to which you want Xpress Pro to send the extracted clips and click OK.

   Now after you capture a new clip, Xpress Pro will add locators to the clip, break it into subclips, or both, based on your settings.

✔ Tip

- DV scene extraction creates subclips that have the same name as the original clip plus the extension .sub.01, .sub.02, and so on. You can rename them.

CREATING SUBCLIPS WITH DV SCENE EXTRACTION

To apply DV scene extraction to an existing clip:

1. Open the bin that contains the clip that you want to affect and select the clip.

2. Choose Bin > Scene Extraction.

3. In the DV Scene Extraction dialog box that appears, *select one of the following*:

   ▲ **Add Locators:** Xpress Pro places locators at the TOD information breaks.

   ▲ **Create Subclips:** Xpress Pro creates subclips that begin at the TOD information breaks.

   ▲ **Both:** Xpress Pro places locators at TOD breaks and also creates subclips that begin at the TOD breaks.

4. In the DV Scene Extraction dialog box, choose the bin where you want to place the subclips (if you choose to create subclips; see **Figure 4.37**).

5. Click OK.

   Xpress Pro creates subclips that have the same name as the original clip plus the extension .sub.01, .sub.02, and so on; or it creates a master clip that has locator marks at TOD information breaks; or it does both.

✔ Tips

■ During the extraction process, Xpress Pro skips non-DV or audio-only clips.

■ During DV scene extraction, you can cancel the procedure by pressing Ctrl+period (Windows) or Command+period (Mac).

Figure 4.37 When applying DV scene extraction to an existing master clip, choose a bin for the new subclips in the DV Scene Extraction dialog box.

Choose the bin for the subclips here.

Recording Audio with the Punch-In Tool

The Audio Punch-In tool is typically used to record voice-over narration with an external microphone. You can record using a microphone connected to your analog sound card, a microphone connected to a digital-analog converter that is connected to the computer via FireWire (OHCI), or the microphone on a DV camcorder connected to your computer via FireWire.

To record audio directly into the Timeline with the Punch-In tool:

1. Load the sequence into which you want to record audio by dragging a sequence icon from a bin to the Composer window.

2. Choose Tools > Audio Punch-In.
   The Audio Punch-In tool opens.

3. In the Audio Punch-In tool, click the Input pop-up menu and choose your audio input (choose OHCI if going through FireWire).

4. Open the Audio tool by choosing Tools > Audio Tool. In the Audio tool, click the two small I/O buttons at the top of the tool so that they display *I* for input.
   Now you can check the levels of your microphone using the Audio tool's input meter.

5. In the Timeline, click Mark In to mark an In point where you want the recording to begin in your sequence. Click Mark Out to mark an Out point where you want the recording to end.

6. In the Audio Punch-In window, choose your audio record channels (Ch1 or Ch2) by clicking the appropriate channel buttons. If you're using a mono mike, click just one channel button.

7. In the Audio Punch-In window, choose a bin in which to store the audio recording from the Target Bin pop-up menu, and from the Track pop-up menu choose the track to which you want to record (choose New Track to create a new track for the audio).

8. Enter a number of seconds in the preroll box to tell Xpress Pro how much of your sequence to play before it starts recording at the In point. Enter a number of seconds in the postroll box to tell Xpress Pro how much of your sequence to play after recording stops at the Out point.

9. (Optional) Enter a handle amount in the Handle box if you want Xpress Pro to record extra amounts before the In and Out points, just to be safe.

continues on next page

10. Click the Record button (**Figure 4.38**).

Xpress Pro backs up before your In point and starts playback. When it reaches the Timeline In point, it starts recording. When it reaches the Out point, it stops recording, and a new audio segment appears in your Timeline.

A new audio segment appears in your target bin.

11. Give the new audio segment a new name.

✔ Tips

■ To abort the punch-in recording process, click the trash can in the Audio Punch-In menu.

■ To ensure smooth performance when recording audio, turn off Timeline Sample Plot (waveform) display by deselecting

Sample Plot in the Timeline Fast menu. (For more information on audio waveforms, see Chapter 12, "Working with Audio.")

■ To ensure smooth performance when recording audio, also turn off your real time effects by clicking the real-time button in the Timeline, so it turns blue. (For more information about real-time effects, see Chapter 11, "Rendering and Real Time.")

■ In the Audio Punch-In tool, you can change your input source by clicking the Input Source pop-up menu and choosing from the list that appears.

■ You can open the Audio tool from within the Audio Punch-In tool by clicking the speaker icon.

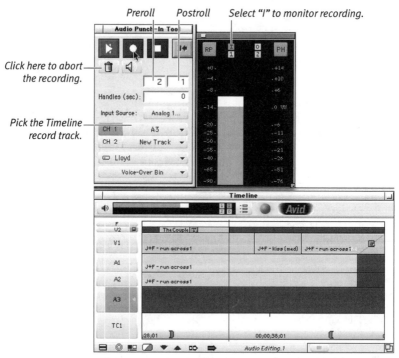

Figure 4.38 To record audio while you watch your movie play, open the Audio Punch-In tool, set In and Out points in the Timeline, select a target track in the Audio Punch-In tool, and click the Record button.

Importing Media into Xpress Pro

Importing media into Xpress Pro is a simple process and follows the same protocols as many graphics applications. However since Xpress pro creates new media files on disk when you import any non-OMFI media, you will need to choose the resolution at which you want Xpress Pro to create the new media, and the drive you want to store it on. If you plan to import a variety of different media, you may want to review and configure your Import settings on the Settings tab of the Project window first. See "Understanding Your Import Settings" later in this chapter for more information.

To import a video clip, audio track, still, or graphic:

1. Click an open bin to select it.

2. Choose File > Import.

3. The Select Files to Import dialog box opens. In the Select Files to Import dialog box, choose the type of file you want to import from the Files of Type (Windows) or Show (Mac) pop-up menu (**Figure 4.39**).

4. In the Select Files to Import dialog box, click the Resolution pop-up menu and choose a resolution for your import (if you are importing a video clip or still) and click the drive menu to select the drive for your import's source media file.

5. (Optional) You can alter your currently active import settings (the import settings checked on the Settings tab of the Project window) directly from within the Import dialog by clicking the Options button. (See "Understanding Your Import Settings" next in this chapter for more information about the many import options.)

continues on next page

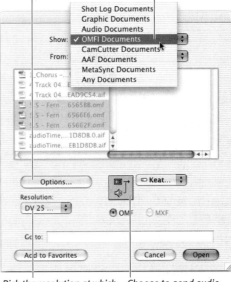

Adjust the current Import settings by clicking here.

Choose the type of file you need to import here.

Pick the resolution at which to import the file (this selection overrides your Media Creation setting).

Choose to send audio and video to the same or separate drives here.

Figure 4.39 In the Select Files to Import dialog box, you can choose a file type to import as well as the media drives to use for new source files that Xpress Pro will create upon import.

6. Navigate to the file you want to import and click Open.

Xpress Pro imports the file and places it in the bin you selected.

✔ Tips

- If you're confident that your import settings are as you want them, then you can simply drag and drop files from your desktop to an open Xpress Pro bin (**Figure 4.40**).

- You don't have to click the Options button and alter your import settings if you select a presaved Import setting on the Settings tab of the Project window before you choose File > Import.

- Usually, an import of a foreign video file will not include the video's timecode track. If that's the case, then Xpress Pro will automatically assign the default starting timecode number (specified in your General settings) to the first frame of the imported video.

- To import an entire sequence from Final Cut Pro into Xpress Pro, the best approach is to use Automatic Duck. (For more information on Automatic Duck, see Appendix B, "Postproduction Extras.")

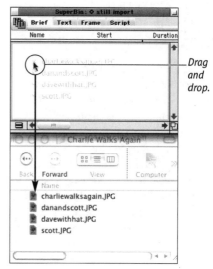

Drag and drop.

Figure 4.40 The easiest way to import a file, provided that your Import settings are already as you want them, is to drag and drop one or more files from your desktop (Windows) or the Finder (Mac) to an open Xpress Pro bin.

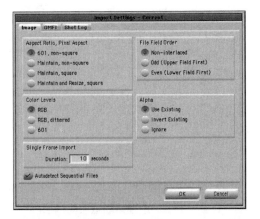

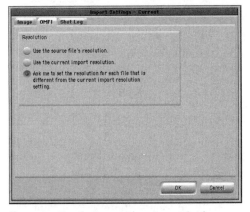

Figure 4.41 Use the Image tab on Import Settings dialog to tell Xpress Pro how to handle any size, pixel aspect ratio, color space and alpha conversions upon import (avove). Review your options on the OMFI tab of the import settings dialog before importing any OMFI media (below).

Understanding Your Import Settings

How Xpress Pro imports moving images, stills, or audio into the application depends on the settings you create in the Import Settings dialog box prior to import. Since there are a variety of images you can import into Xpress Pro, you should create multiple import settings for your most common import preferences.

Before importing anything into Xpress Pro, you need to check your import settings to make sure they're configured for what you want to import.

The **Image** tab of the Import Settings dialog box addresses the following questions that apply to moving images and stills (**Figure 4.41**):

◆ **Do you want to import the image with square pixels or nonsquare pixels? Do you want to resize the image or not?** DV and 601 video use nonsquare (bilinear) pixels, whereas most still and graphic images you use on your computer use square pixels. So when you import an image into Xpress Pro, you need to tell the application how to handle its square or nonsquare pixels, to avoid unwanted distortion. The options are as follows:

601, Non-Square: This is the option to choose for importing other DV clips. You can also select this choice for any image that has DV video's dimensions of 720 x 480 (NTSC) or 720 x 576 (PAL) and has *nonsquare* pixels. If the image has *square* pixels—meaning that it's probably a still image created in a desktop program such as Photoshop—the image needs to have dimensions of 720 x 534 (for NTSC DV), 720 x 540 (for NTSC 601), or 768 x 576 (for standard PAL).

continues on next page

Also select this option if you want to scale up or scale down any image with a 4:3 aspect ratio that is smaller than a full DV frame (so that it fills the DV screen). Do not select this option if your image does not match the 4:3 aspect ratio, or the imported image may look distorted.

Maintain, Non-Square: Use this option to crop any nonsquare images that have a width of more than 480 (NTSC) or 576 (PAL) pixels (such as an image in an NTSC standard frame of 720 x 486). Also use this on nonsquare images that have dimensions smaller than that of DV and that you do not want to scale up or scale down to fill the frame.

Maintain Square: Use this option for icons and titles that you create in a still graphic program using square pixels—those that do not have the square-pixel-compatible dimensions mentioned for the 601, Non-Square option. This options tells Xpress Pro to not scale your image up or down, even if it does not fill the screen.

Maintain and Resize, Square: Use this option if you are importing a square pixel image that does not have the dimensions mentioned for the 601, Non-Square option and that you do want to scale. This option stretches the width or the height to match the width or the height of the DV frame.

◆ **Do you want to import the image with RGB or CCIR 601 color?** If you are importing a video image, choose CCIR 601 color. If you are importing a still image created in an RGB environment, choose RGB. If you are importing a still image that has a gradient, choose RGB Dithered.

◆ **What file field order do you want to use?** Choose Non-Interlaced if you are importing a still. Choose either Lower

Field First or Upper Field First if you are importing video. The choice depends on the type of video you're importing; DV video is always imported using Lower Field First.

◆ **Do you want to use alpha channel information or ignore it?** If you want to include alpha channel information (opacity and transparency information), choose Use Existing or Invert Existing. Otherwise, choose Ignore.

(For more information on alpha channels, see the sidebar "Alpha Channels Explained" in Chapter 9.)

The **OMFI** tab of the Import Settings dialog box presents the following options (**Figure 4.41**):

◆ **Use the Source File's Resolution:** If you select this option, then you are choosing to ignore the resolution set on the Import tab of your Media Creation settings and import the source file at its own resolution. However, this is a misleading choice because Xpress Pro (without Mojo) can import a file only at DV 25 411 or 15:1s.

◆ **Use the Current Import Resolution:** If you select this option, every import uses the resolution you set on the Import tab of the Media Creation settings dialog box.

◆ **Ask Me to Set the Resolution for Each File That Is Different from the Current Import Resolution:** This option is useful to avoid a mistake such as importing a 15:1s file as a DV 25 411 file (which is a useless upgrade). When you select this option, Xpress Pro opens a dialog box if you try to import a file that has a different resolution than the one you set on the Import tab of the Media Creation settings dialog box.

Importing Audio: Special Concerns

The main thing to worry about when importing an audio clip into Xpress Pro is the file's sample rate. For example, audio files on standard CDs use a sample rate of 44.1 kHz. However, editing projects usually use 32-kHz or 48-kHz audio. Hence, when you import a CD file into Xpress Pro, the application asks if you want to convert the file's sample rate to your project's sample rate; generally, you should answer yes.

Before importing or converting any audio files, however, you need to check the following related option in your Audio Project Settings dialog box:

◆ **Render Sample Rate Conversion Quality:** This setting governs the quality of any sample rate conversion you may perform during work on your project, and you should keep High and Slow selected. That said, you might choose Low and Fast when you have hundreds of files to convert and the clock is ticking.

Importing Stills and Graphics: Special Concerns

When you import a still image into Xpress Pro, you need to address two still-related import settings in addition to the other import settings:

◆ **When you import a still, how long do you want the resulting clip to last?** To answer this question, enter a number of seconds in the Single Frame Import Duration box. This tells Xpress Pro how long to make the subclip or sequence that it creates when the program imports a still image.

continues on next page

Importing Stills at Higher than DV Res

Normally, when you import a still image or graphic into Xpress Pro, the application creates a master clip of the same resolution as your project (usually DV resolution). If you want to import and use a still at a higher resolution, you need to use Xpress Pro's Avid Pan & Zoom effect, found in the Image category on the Effect palette.

To use Avid Pan & Zoom, you apply the effect to any clip (which will serve as a placeholder) in your Timeline. Then you open the Effect editor and click the Avid Pan & Zoom's Other Options button at the upper left. This opens a window in which you can navigate to the higher-resolution still that you want to import

(For more information about effects and using the Effect editor, see Chapter 9, "Working with Video Effects.")

◆ **Do you want to combine a group of stills into an image sequence?** If the answer is yes, select Autodetect Sequential Files. If a group of still images in the same folder have sequential names (name.1, name.2, and so on) (**Figure 4.41**), then importing the first of these images will tell Xpress Pro to create a sequence, with the images appearing one after the other in the order that they appear in your folder.

Importing Photoshop and other Multilayer Files

You can import an Adobe Photoshop file—or any multilayered still from another graphic program—into Xpress Pro in several ways. When you import such files, you have two main decisions to make:

◆ **Do you want to include alpha channels?** Alpha channel information is information that you can create in programs such as Photoshop to govern what is opaque and what is transparent in your image. In the Import Settings dialog box (**Figure 4.41**), you can choose whether to ignore this information when you import a still graphic.

If you choose to include alpha channel information in your imports, then Xpress Pro applies Matte Key effects to every layer above the background layer in your imported Photoshop image (**Figure 4.42**).

If you choose to ignore the alpha channel information, then the image will be 100 percent opaque (**Figure 4.43**).

(For more information on alpha channels, see the sidebar "Alpha Channels Explained" in Chapter 9.)

(For more information on the Matte Key effect, see "Using the Matte Key Effect" in Chapter 9.)

continues on next page

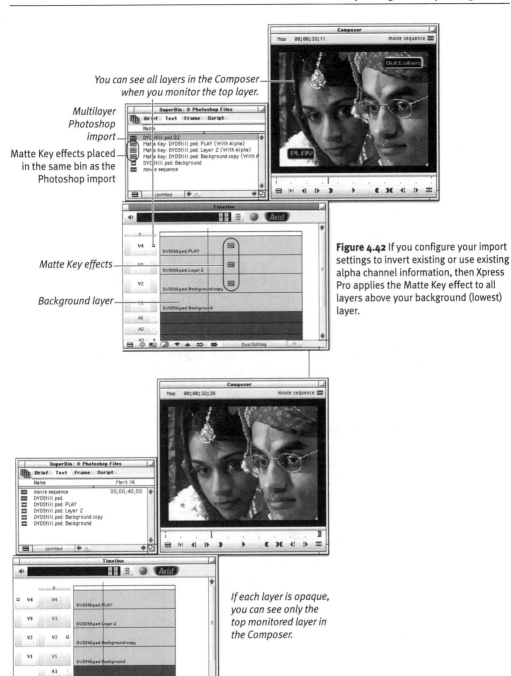

You can see all layers in the Composer when you monitor the top layer.

Multilayer Photoshop import

Matte Key effects placed in the same bin as the Photoshop import

Matte Key effects

Background layer

Figure 4.42 If you configure your import settings to invert existing or use existing alpha channel information, then Xpress Pro applies the Matte Key effect to all layers above your background (lowest) layer.

If each layer is opaque, you can see only the top monitored layer in the Composer.

Figure 4.43 If you configure your import settings to ignore alpha channels, then each of the Photoshop layers that Xpress Pro imports will be totally opaque, which is usually undesirable.

◆ **Do you want to include layers?** When you import a Photoshop file, you can choose to ignore any layers in the image— flattening the image into a simple sub-clip (**Figure 4.44**)—or you can choose to include some or all of the layers in the import.

The cool thing about including layers is that Xpress Pro treats the Photoshop file as a sequence with individual tracks; you can edit and manipulate the layers individually in the Timeline.

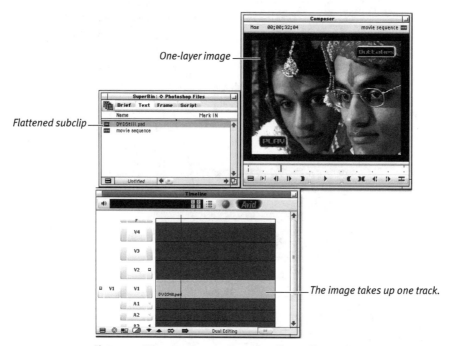

One-layer image

Flattened subclip

The image takes up one track.

Figure 4.44 When you import a Photoshop file as a flattened image, Xpress Pro combines all layers of the image into a one-layer subclip. When edited into the Timeline, the clip takes up only one track.

Figure 4.45 When you import a file that contains layers (such as a Photoshop file), Xpress Pro asks you how to treat the layers. Your choices are to import all of them (Sequence of Layers), none of them (Flattened Image), or some of them (Select Layers).

Figure 4.46 When you click the Select Layers button, Xpress Pro opens the Select Layers dialog box. Select the Photoshop layers you want to include in the import and click OK.

To import a Photoshop file into Xpress Pro:

1. On the Settings tab of the Project window, double-click your active (check-marked) Import and check your alpha channel settings in the Import Settings dialog box.

2. Choose File > Import and point Xpress Pro to the Photoshop file, or drag and drop a Photoshop file into an open bin.

   Xpress Pro displays a dialog box asking you how to treat any layers in the image (**Figure 4.45**).

3. Click Sequence of Layers to import all layers, Flattened Image to combine all layers into one, or Select Layers to import chosen layers.

4. If you choose Select Layers, Xpress Pro opens the Select Layers dialog box, allowing you to select the Photoshop layers you want to import into the application (**Figure 4.46**).

   Xpress Pro imports your Photoshop file as either a subclip (if it's a flattened image) or a sequence (if it contains layers).

Importing Media from Another Xpress Pro Project

If you want to import clips into your project that were captured in another Xpress Pro project, all you have to do is open the relevant bin from the other project and drag and drop clips (or other bin objects) from the foreign bin into one of your current project's bins.

To import source media from another project:

1. Choose File > Open Bin. In the dialog box that appears, choose Bins Documents from the Files of Type (Windows) or Show (Mac) pop-up menu.

2. Navigate to your Avid Projects folder and open your user name folder.

   Your user name folder contains multiple folders, each named after one of your projects.

3. Open the project folder that contains the bin you want to open. Select the bin and click Open (**Figure 4.47**).

   The bin opens in your current Xpress Pro project.

4. In the imported bin's window, select the source media that you want include in your current project (use Shift+click to select multiple clips).

5. Press Ctrl+D (Windows) or Command+D (Mac) to duplicate the selected clips.

6. Drag the clip duplicates into a bin in your current project.

7. Close the foreign bin.

   You can now edit with the source media you copied from your other project.

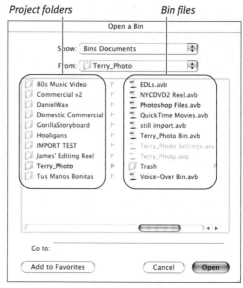

Project folders   Bin files

Figure 4.47 To import shots and other media used in another project, you need to open the bin from the other project that contains the clips you need.

Reconnecting Source Media to Offline Clips: The Batch Import Trick

If your source clips—or any objects in your bin—become disconnected from their source media files, Xpress Pro will mark them "Media Offline." To reconnect the offline clips to their source media files, you need to select them, choose Bin > Batch Import, select Offline Only in the dialog box that appears, and point Xpress Pro to the file in the following Batch Import dialog box.

(For more information on this procedure, see "Relinking Offline Clips to Online Source Media" in Chapter 13.)

Importing Shot Logs

You can create a shot log outside of the Xpress Pro application (perhaps using another NLE) and import the shot log into Xpress Pro. Then you can use the imported log to batch capture source clips.

Before importing your shot log, you need to save it in the Avid Log Exchange (ALE) format using the Avid Log Exchange program. Or you can format and save a shot log as a text document using a word processing application or text editor. Either way, you need your shot log to conform to Avid's specifications. To find out about Avid's Global heading, Column heading, and Log Data heading standards, consult the Xpress Pro help menu.

To tell Xpress Pro how to handle your imported shot log, select the appropriate option on the Shot Log tab of the Import Settings dialog box. Generally, you'll simply select Maintain Events as Logged.

To import a shot log:

1. Choose File > Import.

2. In the Select Files to Import dialog box, click the Files of Type (Windows) or Show (Mac) pop-up tab and *choose one of the following:*

   ▲ **Shot Log Documents:** Choose this option if you created your shot log in Avid Log Exchange and want to import the shot log in the ALE format.

   ▲ **Any Documents:** Choose this option if you created your shot log in a text application and want to import the shot log in the TXT format.

3. Select the shot log and click Open.

   In the bin you selected, Xpress Pro places offline clips that correspond to the shots in your shot log. You can now select the offline clips and capture them by choosing Bin > Batch Capture.

Exchanging Shot Logs and Batch Lists between XPro and FCP: Sebsky Tools

Thanks to a freeware program called Sebsky Tools, you can now edit a video project using both Xpress Pro and Final Cut Pro.

Sebsky Tools allows you to convert FCP batch lists to Avid Log Exchange (ALE) shot logs and vice versa, so you can capture clips in FCP and then recapture them in Xpress Pro, or capture in Xpress Pro and recapture in FCP.

Sebsky Tools also allows you to export actual media files from Xpress Pro, import them into Final Cut Pro, and carry over timecode and source ID (reel name) information.

(For more information about Sebsky Tools, visit www.dharmafilm.com/sebskytools/).

PREPARING TO EDIT

This chapter is dedicated to the two tasks you should always complete before you jump into active editing: organizing your source material and preparing your blank sequence to receive those source clips. Whether you learn now or you learn later the hard way, you'll likely come to understand the following wisdom: the most stress-free editing sessions come to those who organize and plan ahead. You can avoid many headaches and impatient clients down the road if you take the time to clean up the place, sit down, and plan out what you're about to do before you jump into active editing.

Organizing your source material involves working with bins, the SuperBin, folders, and the information columns to arrange, search, sort and sift through your clips, or what Avid calls *media objects,* so that you have all your shots at your fingertips when you need them. Preparing your sequence to receive your clips involves creating and opening a sequence, learning how to load a sequence into the source or record monitor, and setting up your Timeline display preferences for the particular type of editing you plan to do.

You can approach the first task—setting up your media objects in bins—like a painter organizing and mixing the paint colors, and the second task—preparing a blank sequence—like a painter prepping a blank canvas, getting ready for the creative work ahead.

Working with Bins and Folders

Bins are used for organizing all of your *media objects*—your clips, titles, sequences, custom effect templates, and so on (**Figure 5.1**).

Once you have all your media organized into bins, you can use folders to organize all of your bins. Xpress Pro folders look and behave just like folders used in the standard Windows and Mac OS interfaces. You cannot place a bin inside another bin, but you can place folders inside other folders (**Figure 5.2**).

(For more information on media objects, see, "About Media Objects" later in this chapter.)

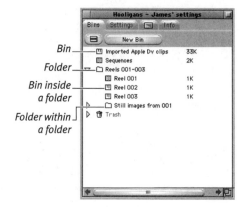

Bin — Imported Apple Dv clips — 33K
Folder — Sequences — 2K
Reels 001-003
Bin inside — Reel 001 — 1K
a folder — Reel 002 — 1K
Reel 003 — 1K
Still images from 001
Folder within — Trash
a folder

Figure 5.2 A folder can contain bins as well as other folders that contain bins.

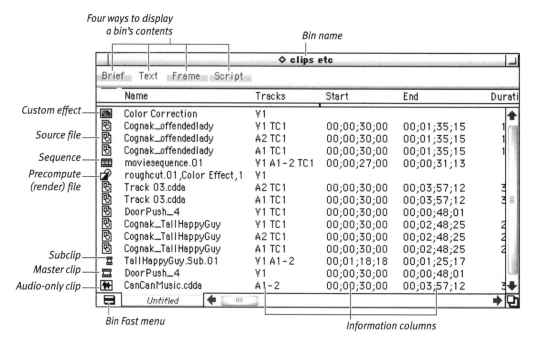

Four ways to display a bin's contents

Bin name

◇ clips etc

Brief   Text   Frame   Script

Name	Tracks	Start	End	Durati
Custom effect — Color Correction	V1			
Source file — Cognak_offendedlady	V1 TC1	00;00;30;00	00;01;35;15	1
Cognak_offendedlady	A2 TC1	00;00;30;00	00;01;35;15	1
Cognak_offendedlady	A1 TC1	00;00;30;00	00;01;35;15	1
Sequence — moviesequence.01	V1 A1-2 TC1	00;00;27;00	00;00;31;13	
Precompute — roughcut.01,Color Effect,1	V1			
(render) file — Track 03.cdda	A2 TC1	00;00;30;00	00;03;57;12	3
Track 03.cdda	A1 TC1	00;00;30;00	00;03;57;12	3
DoorPush_4	V1 TC1	00;00;30;00	00;00;48;01	
Cognak_TallHappyGuy	V1 TC1	00;00;30;00	00;02;48;25	2
Cognak_TallHappyGuy	A2 TC1	00;00;30;00	00;02;48;25	2
Cognak_TallHappyGuy	A1 TC1	00;00;30;00	00;02;48;25	2
Subclip — TallHappyGuy.Sub.01	V1 A1-2	00;01;18;18	00;01;25;17	
Master clip — DoorPush_4	V1	00;00;30;00	00;00;48;01	
Audio-only clip — CanCanMusic.cdda	A1-2	00;00;30;00	00;03;57;12	3

Untitled

Bin Fast menu

Information columns

Figure 5.1 Bins display media object icons and names, along with information columns that detail important data for each object. You can drag bin windows to any location on your screen and resize them as you see fit.

WORKING WITH BINS AND FOLDERS

Click this Fast menu.

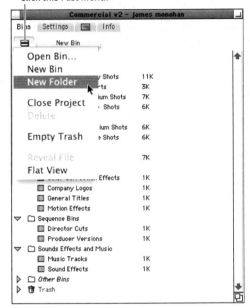

Figure 5.3 To create a folder, click the Bins tab Fast menu and choose New Folder.

- Bins in different folders can have identical names, but bins in the same folder cannot have identical names. An error message will appear if you try to put two identical bins in the same folder.

- To view all project bins in the Project window without displaying any folders, click the Bins tab Fast menu and select Flat View. This approach is useful when you want to quickly see every single bin associated with your project without regard to the folders in which they are organized.

To create a new bin:

1. Click the Bins tab in the Project window and *do one of the following*:
   - ▲ Choose File > New Bin.
   - ▲ At the top of the Bins tab, click the New Bin button.

   Xpress Pro creates a new bin, highlights its name, and opens it in an independent window.

2. Type a name for the bin and press Enter (Windows) or Return (Mac).

   You can now import media objects into the new bin or move media objects from other bins into the new bin.

To create a new folder:

1. Click the Bins tab in the Project window and *do one of the following*:
   - ▲ Click the window's Fast menu and choose New Folder (**Figure 5.3**).
   - ▲ Right-click (Windows) or Ctrl+Shift-click (Mac) in the Project window. Choose New Folder from the pop-up menu.

   Xpress Pro creates a new folder and highlights its name.

2. Type a unique name for the folder and press Enter (Windows) or Return (Mac).

   Xpress Pro creates a new folder in which you can place bins and other folders.

✔ Tips

- To create a new bin, you can also choose New Bin from the Bins tab Fast menu. Another option is to right-click (Windows) or Ctrl+Shift-click (Mac) the Bins tab and choose New Bin from the window that appears.

WORKING WITH BINS AND FOLDERS

Bins and Folders in Action: A Project Example

Folders and bins allow you to organize your media objects in a highly hierarchical fashion. If you have a lot of material or you are working on multiple sequences within the same Xpress Pro project, you can save yourself many headaches by organizing your bins into folders, and those folders into other folders.

In **Figure 5.4**, a project for a TV commercial uses five top-level folders: Camera A Footage, Camera B Footage, Effects and Titles, Sounds Effects and Music, and Sequence Bins.

The organization doesn't end there, however. For example, the Camera A Footage folder contains two more folders: one for the Doorway scene and one for the Stairway scene. The Doorway Scene folder contains four bins for the different types of shots used in the Doorway scene.

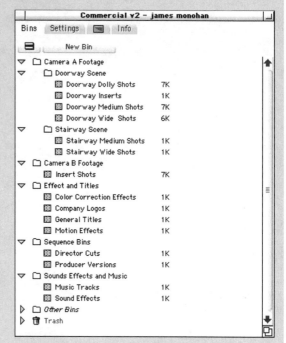

Figure 5.4 An example of a highly organized project.

Devising an organizational hierarchy early in your project saves you time in the long run by allowing you to focus on your creative editing decisions rather than the location of this or that clip.

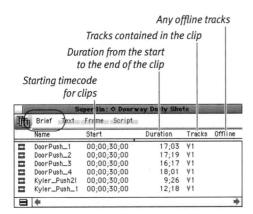

Any offline tracks
Tracks contained in the clip
Duration from the start to the end of the clip
Starting timecode for clips

Figure 5.5 The Brief tab. This mode is useful when logging and recording media from DV tape.

Using the Four Bin Views

You have four options for displaying the media objects you put in bins. You can switch among these modes by clicking one of the four tabs at the top of the bin window.

◆ **Brief:** Brief view lists media objects with small icons and features only a few information columns that are fixed in their positions (**Figure 5.5**).

◆ **Text:** Text view is like a mini-database. This is the only display in which you can see all possible information columns (**Figure 5.6**).

continues on next page

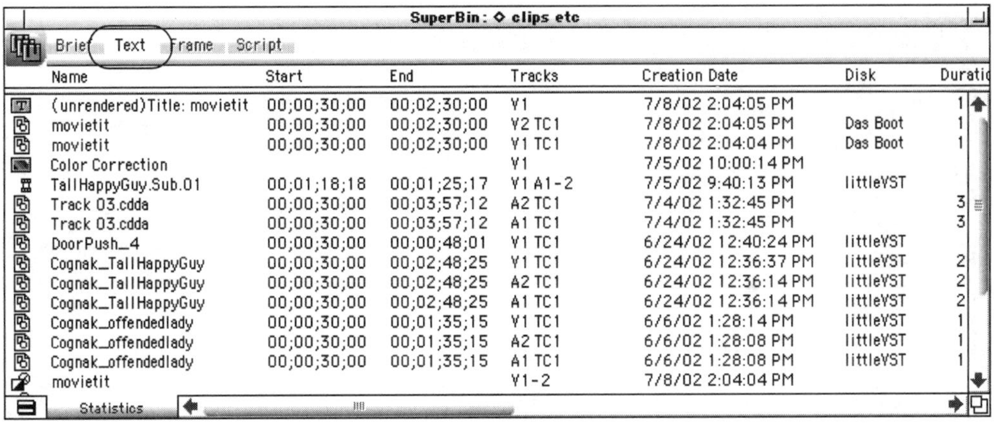

Figure 5.6 Text view. Use this view for finding specific information about clips. You can display, sort, sift and search up to 30 information columns.

WORKING WITH BINS AND FOLDERS

139

- **Frame:** Frame view represents clips, sequences and other bin objects as icons in one of eight different sizes (**Figure 5.7**)

- **Script:** Script view provides a picture icon of your footage, statistical information about each clip, and a large area for notes, comments, dialogue, and action description (**Figure 5.8**).

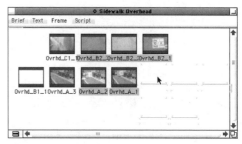

Figure 5.7 In Frame view, each clip displays a representative frame. You can arrange clips in a storyboard, lasso them, and edit them in order into the Timeline.

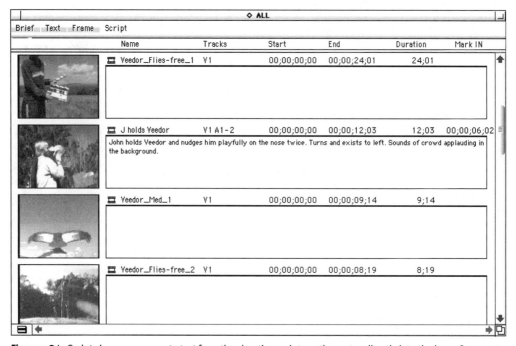

	Name	Tracks	Start	End	Duration	Mark IN
	Veedor_Flies-free_1	V1	00;00;00;00	00;00;24;01	24;01	
	J holds Veedor	V1 A1-2	00;00;00;00	00;00;12;03	12;03	00;00;06;02
	Veedor_Med_1	V1	00;00;00;00	00;00;09;14	9;14	
	Veedor_Flies-free_2	V1	00;00;00;00	00;00;08;19	8;19	

John holds Veedor and nudges him playfully on the nose twice. Turns and exists to left. Sounds of crowd applauding in the background.

Figure 5.8 In Script view, you can paste text from the shooting script or other notes directly into the large Comment field. The only disadvantage is that each clip takes up a lot of room; this may not be the best option for bins that contain a lot of media objects.

Table 5.1

Frame and Script View Keyboard Shortcuts		
OPERATION	SHORTCUT WINDOWS	MAC OS
Enlarge frame	Ctrl+L	Command+L
Reduce frame	Ctrl+K	Command+K
Align frame to grid	Ctrl+T	Command+T
Display clip info	Ctrl+Alt-click	Command-click

Playing and Marking Clips in Frame and Script Views

You can play and mark a master clip, sub-clip, motion effect, or sequence in Frame or Script view without having to load the image into a source window. In Frame and Script views, select one clip. Then use the J-K-L keys to play it just as you would in the source monitor. (For details on the J-K-L keys, see the sidebar "The Power of the J-K-L Keys" in Chapter 6.) While you play the frame, use Mark In and Mark Out to set In and Out points for the clip. You won't see any visual marks appear in the frame, but they're there.

With your clips marked, you can now drag one or more clips directly into the Timeline, without ever using a source monitor.

To choose a bin view:

1. Click the bin once in the Project window to open it.

2. Click one of the four view tabs at the top of the open bin window

(See **Table 5.1** for Frame and Script view shortcuts.)

✔ Tips

■ You can resize your frames in the Frame and Script views to any one of eight standard sizes. Use Edit > Enlarge Frame or Edit > Reduce Frame.

■ If your Frame view bin gets messy, click the bin Fast menu and choose Align to Grid to arrange the frames symmetrically.

■ If you cannot see all of your media objects in Frame view, click the bin Fast menu and choose Fill Window to arrange the frames to fit the bin window.

WORKING WITH BINS AND FOLDERS

Using the SuperBin

Since bin windows are independent windows by default, creating and opening several bins may produce a lot of clutter on your screen. To avoid the mess of multiple bin windows, use the SuperBin.

Although the SuperBin has a grandiose name, it is simply a regular bin window with one added feature: *it can display the contents of any bin.* So one SuperBin window replaces countless independent bin windows.

To use this space-saving feature, you need to first load your independent bins into the SuperBin. Once the bins are loaded, you can display those bins, one at a time, from within the SuperBin window.

To use the SuperBin:

1. On the Settings tab of the Project window, double-click Bin Settings to open the Bin Settings dialog box.

2. In the Bin Settings dialog, select Enable SuperBin (**Figure 5.9**).

   Now that you have enabled the SuperBin function, Xpress Pro lets you load bins into the SuperBin.

3. To load a bin onto the SuperBin, *do one of the following:*
   - ▲ If the bin is closed, on the Bins tab of the Project window, click the bin's icon.
   - ▲ If the bin is already open in its own window, double-click the bin icon on the Bins tab.

   The bin is loaded into the SuperBin.

4. To view a bin loaded in the SuperBin, click the SuperBin button at the upper left of the SuperBin and choose the bin name from the pop-up menu that appears (**Figure 5.10**).

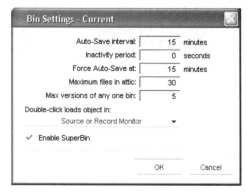

Figure 5.9 To take advantage of the power of the SuperBin, open the Bin Settings dialog box and select Enable SuperBin.

SuperBin icon

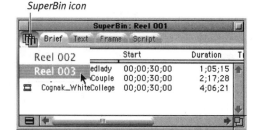

Figure 5.10 To access a bin from the SuperBin, click the SuperBin icon in the upper left of the window and choose the bin name from the list that appears. (The pop-up menu shows only loaded bins.)

✔ Tips

- Only one SuperBin can be open at a time.

- To move a bin out of the SuperBin and into its own window, double-click the bin's icon in the Project window.

- If your desired bin is not listed when you click the SuperBin icon, you haven't loaded it into the SuperBin yet.

- Careful: The SuperBin exists only as long as the current session. Once you close the SuperBin, you will have to reload all of your bins if you want them available again in the SuperBin.

To delete a bin from the SuperBin:

1. In the Bin tab of the Project window, right-click (Windows) or Ctrl+Shift+Click (Mac) the bin you want to delete.

2. Choose Delete Selected Bins from the context menu.

   The bin is deleted from the Bin tab and moved into the Project trash.

USING THE SUPERBIN

About Media Objects

Xpress Pro uses the term *media object* to refer to any of the source media files, titles, or effects that you can keep in a bin.

The following list describes each type of media object. To avoid unwieldy bins, you'll usually want to make some of these types invisible—namely, source files and rendered effects.

(For more information, see the task "To make media objects visible or invisible" later in this chapter.)

◆ **Sequence:** In simplest terms, a sequence is an edited movie. It is a linear ordering of clips and other edited material, arranged to play from left to right, across a timeline.

◆ **Master clip:** Technically speaking, master clips represent the behind-the-scenes source files that Xpress Pro creates on the hard drive when you record or import your video footage. Master clips typically contain one video and two audio tracks and are the most common media object that you will edit into your movie sequence.

◆ **Subclip:** A subclip is portion of a master clip that Xpress Pro treats as its own entity. You can create a subclip by setting In and Out points on a master clip and pressing the ![Make Subclip button] Make Subclip button. (See "Creating Subclips and Subsequences" in Chapter 6.)

◆ **Audio clip:** An audio clip is any clip composed of audio only, such as a music track or a sound effect.

◆ **Title:** A title effect is an effect created with Xpress Pro's Title tool. (For more information, see Chapter 8, "Creating Titles.")

◆ **Motion effect:** A motion effect can be a slow motion, fast motion, strobe motion, or freeze-frame effect.

◆ **Custom effect template:** You can create a custom effect template out of any effect on the Effect palette. In this case, the pictured icon is a custom Picture-in-Picture effect.

◆ **Third-party effect template:** This template is an effect template created from a third-party effect (such as a BorisFX plug-in). These effects always have an icon that looks like a plug.

◆ **Source file:** Usually kept invisible, these objects represent the source media files behind master clips and subclips. Typically, each source file icon represents one component of a clip; hence, a typical DV clip with one video track and two audio tracks has three source files. You can't edit a source file into your movie.

◆ **Source tape:** Usually kept invisible, a source tape icon represents the source tape from which you captured video for the master clips and subclips that appear in your bin.

◆ **Rendered Effects:** Xpress Pro creates a file after rendering an effect (sometimes called a precompute.) Usually, the only reason to make a precompute visible is to delete it.

- ◆ **ITV Enhancement:** This specialized MetaSync-related object represents any enhancement related to an interactive or enhanced project. For example, an ITV enhancement object could be a Web site link embedded in your movie.

- ◆ **Opaque Enhancement:** This object is any MetaSync-related enhancement other than an ITV enhancement.

✔ Tips

- ■ You should usually keep source files and precomputes invisible because they take up a lot of space and you can't edit them into your movie.

- ■ When you delete a clip from a bin, you actually are deleting only the file's reference from your bin. Xpress Pro does not erase that clip's source files from your computer.

- ■ As of Xpress Pro 4.0, ITV enhancement employs only one standard: SMPTE-363M. Avid plans compatibility with other standards in future releases.

Displaying Media Objects

Just because you can display so many types of media objects in your bins doesn't mean that you should. Source media files, for instance, take up a lot of space and do not have much utility since you cannot edit them into your movie. The same applies to rendered effect icons, sometimes called precomputes.

To cut down on the visual mess, you can make certain objects visible or invisible using the Set Bin Display option.

ABOUT MEDIA OBJECTS

To make media objects visible or invisible:

1. With the bin open and selected, *do one of the following:*
   ▲ Click the bin's Fast menu and choose Set Bin Display.
   ▲ Right-click (Windows) or Ctrl+Shift-click (Mac) the bin. In the shortcut menu that appears, choose Set Bin Display.
   The Set Bin Display dialog box appears.

2. In the upper pane of the Set Bin Display dialog box, select the media objects you want to display (**Figure 5.11**).

3. In the bottom pane of the menu, *select one or both of the following:*
   ▲ **Show Clips Created by User**: *Always keep this selected,* unless you want to display only source files, precomputes, and source tapes.
   ▲ **Show Reference Clips**: This function gathers all of the effects, clips, and other objects that are contained in any sequences in your bin. *These include media objects from other bins.*

4. Click OK.
   Xpress Pro displays the selected objects in the bin. This operation applies to only the selected bin.

✔ Tips

■ You can also set the bin display by choosing Bin > Set Bin Display.

■ Selecting Show Reference Clips is helpful toward the end of the editing process when you want an idea of what you are using in a sequence. To avoid confusion, the option works best when your bin contains only one sequence icon.

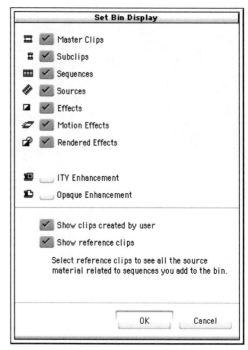

Figure 5.11 In this case, all bin objects are selected for display (except for ITV and Opaque Enhancement). This will result in a very cluttered bin window. Usually, it's best to leave out some objects—like source files and precomputes—while you edit.

■ When you select Show Reference Clips, you should you also select every type of media object. For instance, if you select Show Reference Clips but do not select Master Clips, Xpress Pro will not display master clips even if they are reference clips.

■ Your actual source files are on your media drives in folders called OMFI MediaFiles.

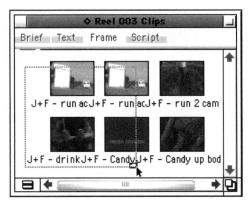

Figure 5.12 Drag to select multiple media objects in a bin. Here, four clips are selected in Frame view. You can then hold Shift and click or lasso additional clips.

Selecting, Moving, and Copying Media Objects

In Xpress Pro, you can easily select media objects that are in bins using typical techniques such as clicking or lassoing. (**Table 5.2** lists the keyboard selection shortcuts.)

Moving and copying objects are trickier operations, however, especially when the SuperBin is involved, so follow the steps in the next tasks carefully.

To select one or more objects in a bin:

Do one of the following:

▲ Click any individual icon or frame. Use Shift-click to select multiple items.

▲ Click and drag to draw a selection marquee around multiple items (**Figure 5.12**).

▲ Choose Edit > Select All to select all objects in a bin. Edit > Deselect All deselects all objects.

Xpress Pro highlights the selected media objects.

✔ Tips

■ Avoid clicking the name field of the icon when you select it as this will open the name for editing rather than selecting the item.

■ You can find out how many objects are in a bin by choosing Bin Info from the bin's Fast menu.

Table 5.2

Bin Selection Keyboard Shortcuts

OPERATION	SHORTCUT WINDOWS	MAC OS
Select All	Ctrl+A	Command+A
Deselect All	Shift+Ctrl+A	Shift+ Command+A
Select Adjacent	Arrow key	Arrow key
Select/Deselect Current and Adjacent	Shift+Arrow key	Shift+Arrow key

To move or copy an object from one bin to another:

Do one of the following:

▲ To move an object, drag it from an open bin window into another open bin window.

▲ To copy an object, Alt-click (Windows) or Option-click (Mac) the media object while you drag it to another open bin window.

The clip appears in the other bin, be it independent or in the SuperBin.

Selecting with the Keyboard

Once you have selected an item in a bin, you can use an arrow key to move to an adjacent item—up, down, left, or right. By holding down the Shift key while pressing an arrow key, you can add to your current selection. If an object is already selected, using Shift-arrow key will deselect it.

A Visual Way to Tag Clips: Use Clip Color

You can use color-coding to mark certain clips so you can visually track them *both in your bins and in the Timeline.*

For instance, color-coding can be helpful when you want to keep track of temporary B-roll shots that you will replace later or particular shots to which you will apply the same color correction and other changes.

After selecting clips in a bin, choose Edit > Set Clip Color. From the menu options, *choose one of the following:*

◆ **Pre-set Colors:** You can choose from seven basic colors.

◆ **Pick:** Use your system's color palette to design a customized color.

◆ **None:** Reset the clip color to black.

To move or copy an object from one bin to another in the SuperBin:

Do one of the following:

▲ To move an object, drag it from the SuperBin into the Project window and drop it onto the icon of the target bin in the Project window (**Figure 5.13**).

▲ To copy an object, Alt-click (Windows) or Option-click (Mac) the object in the SuperBin while you drag the object to the icon of the target bin in the Project window.

The media object appears in the other SuperBin bin.

✔ Tips

■ Copying does not duplicate a media object's source files. It merely duplicates the reference to the source files.

■ To duplicate media objects within the same bin, press Ctrl+D (Windows) or Command+D (Mac).

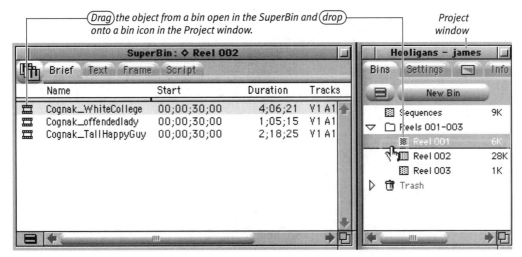

Figure 5.13 Since you can see only one bin at a time in the SuperBin, to move an object from one bin to another bin that's also in the SuperBin, drag the object from the SuperBin to the icon of the target bin in the Project window.

Specialized Selection Commands for Media Objects

Sometimes you cannot easily select media objects by using standard clicking or lassoing or even by selecting or deselecting all objects. Xpress Pro provides four specialized selection commands on the Bin menu (**Figure 5.14**) for use in particular scenarios.

◆ **Reverse Selection:** When you need to select several objects in a bin, this command can save a lot of clicking. First select what you *don't* want to select. Then choose Reverse Selection to select all of the other items (**Figure 5.15**).

◆ **Select Offline Items:** This option selects any clips marked as offline, meaning that Xpress Pro cannot find their source media files. Use this option when you need to find out what clips need to be rerecorded or reimported. To use this function, first click a bin to select it.

◆ **Select Media Relatives:** After selecting a master clip, choose this menu command to select any subclips that were made from that master clip or any sequences that contain that master clip.

◆ **Select Unreferenced Clips:** This option selects any clips not used in a sequence listed in an open bin. Careful: This command selects only clips in sequences that are in open bins. This function is helpful at the end of the editing process to determine what unneeded clips you can erase from your drives. To use this function, first click a bin to select it.

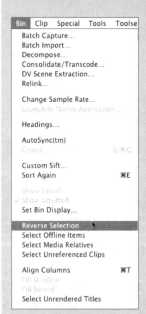

This single clip was selected first, and then Reverse Selection was chosen from the bin menu.

Now all the other clips are selected, as indicated by the highlight in their name field.

Figure 5.14 You can find four specialized bin selection commands in the Bin menu. You can apply one of these commands to one Bin at a time.

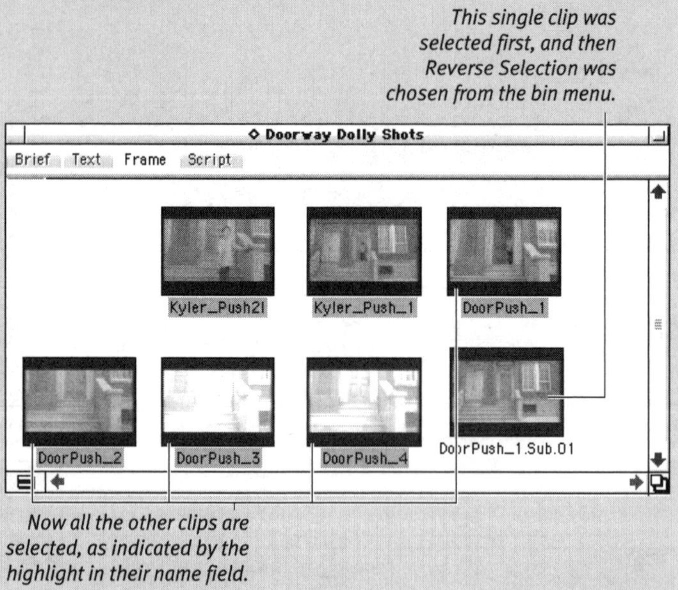

Figure 5.15 Reverse Selection selects the opposite of what you highlight.

Searching for Media Objects

Maybe you need to find a group of clips fast, but your bin is rather disorganized. Custom Sift is like your computer's desktop search engine, but applied to bins.

Sifting allows you to find and display only those bin objects that meet certain criteria or contain certain properties. For the criteria, you can use any information that a bin view displays. For example, in Text view, you can search on any column headings as well as the clip color (**Figure 5.16**).

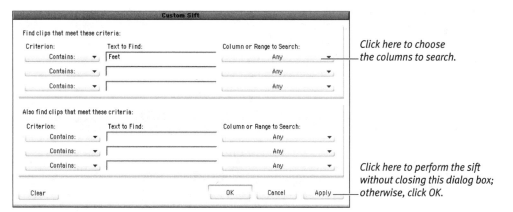

Click here to choose the columns to search.

Click here to perform the sift without closing this dialog box; otherwise, click OK.

Figure 5.16a The Custom Sift dialog box looks for all objects in a bin that contain the word *Feet*.

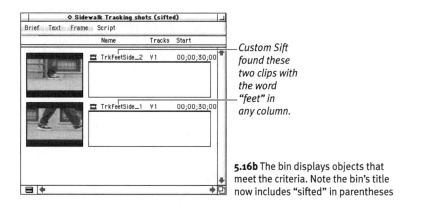

Custom Sift found these two clips with the word "feet" in any column.

5.16b The bin displays objects that meet the criteria. Note the bin's title now includes "sifted" in parentheses

To sift one or more objects:

1. Open the bin you want to sift and *do one of the following*:

▲ Choose Bin > Custom Sift.

▲ From the bin's Fast menu, choose Custom Shift.

2. In the Custom Sift dialog box, type a word or words in the Text to Find box.

3. Click a Column or Range to Search pull-down tab and *choose one of the following*:

▲ **An information column heading name:** For example, if you want to search for the word *Feet* in the names of clips, select Name.

▲ **Any:** Xpress Pro will search all of the information column headings currently displayed in the Text view of the bin.

4. Click a Criterion pull-down tab and *choose one of the following*:

▲ **Contains:** Custom Sift will find all items that contain the words you type in the Text to Find field.

▲ **Begins With:** Custom Sift will find all items that begin with the word you type in the Text to Find field.

▲ **Matches Exactly:** Custom Sift will find—you guessed it—all items that exactly match the word you type in the Text to Find field.

5. Click Apply to see the requested clips listed in the bin, without closing the Custom Sift dialog box. Click OK to both apply the sift criteria and close the dialog. Your bin displays only those clips that meet your criteria.

Searching for Clip Segments in the Timeline

Once you edit source clip segments into the Timeline, you can search for segments by keyword. (For information on how to edit clips into the Timeline, see Chapter 6, "Making Edits.")

You can look for a word in a Timeline segment name by selecting the Timeline, and pressing Ctrl+F (Windows) or Command+F (Mac), selecting Clip Names in the dialog box that appears, and clicking OK. For a Clip Names search to work, however, you must have Clip Names selected in the Timeline Fast menu.

You can also search for any Timeline text. In the Find dialog box, select Timeline text. For a Timeline text search to work, you must first select a text-related Timeline Fast menu item.

✔ Tips

- In Text view, you can sift only *visible* information columns.

- Use the bottom half of the Custom Sift dialog box, the section titled Also Find Clips That Meet These Criteria, to make your bin display additional items.

- You can use Custom Sift with any of the four bin display views.

- Using Custom Sift, you can sift items in a bin by icon color. Enter the color name in the Text to Find box and choose Color as the range to search.

To see the previously sifted view again:

◆ Choose Bin > Show Sifted.

  Xpress Pro displays only those media objects from your previous Sift operation.

To show all media objects:

Do one of the following:

▲ Choose Bin > Show Unsifted. In the dialog box, erase all Text to Find entries and click OK.

▲ Choose Bin > Custom Sift. In the Custom Sift dialog box, click Clear and then click OK.

  Xpress Pro makes all of your bin objects visible again.

Sorting Media Objects in Text View

Performing a Sort operation arranges items in a particular order, usually using one information column as your criterion. The Sort feature is available only in Text view.

For example, you can use Sort if you want to list your clips by name, in ascending alphabetical order, or if you want to list your clips according to increasing or decreasing timecode duration.

You can also perform a multilevel Sort operation, which uses multiple columns for the criteria, with the column on the far left taking precedence.

(For more on information columns, see "Working with Information Columns in Text View" later in this chapter.)

To sort clips in ascending or descending order:

1. In Text view, click the information column that you want to govern your sort (**Figure 5.17**).

2. *Do one of the following:*

   ▲ To sort in ascending order, choose Bin > Sort, or choose Sort from the bin's Fast menu.

   ▲ To sort in descending order, press Alt (Windows) or Option (Mac) and then choose Bin > Sort Reversed, or choose Sort Reversed from the bin's Fast menu.

The objects in your bin are now sorted in ascending or descending order, according to the selected column (**Figure 5.18**). **Table 5.3** lists the Sort keyboard shortcuts.

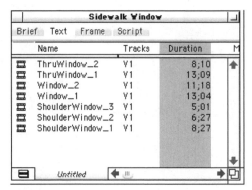

Figure 5.17 Highlight the column you want to use to sort your clips. In this case, it's the Duration column.

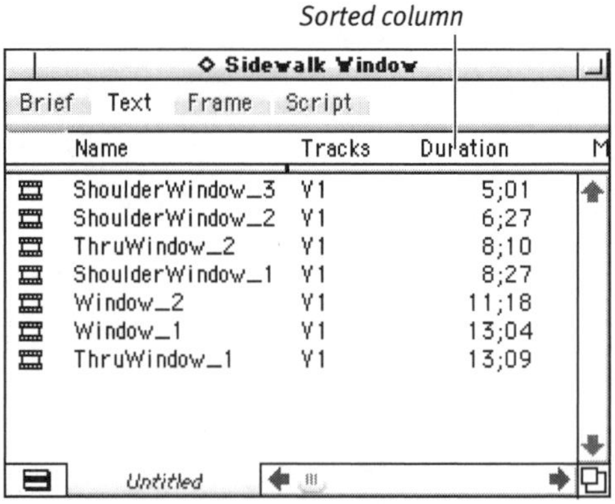

Figure 5.18 After sorting with the Sort command, the clip with the shortest duration appears first and the one with longest duration appears last. For the opposite arrangement, choose Sort Reversed.

Table 5.3

Sort Keyboard Shortcuts

OPERATION	SHORTCUT WINDOWS	MAC OS
Sort	Ctrl+E	Command+E
Sort Reversed	Alt+Ctrl+E	Option+Command+E

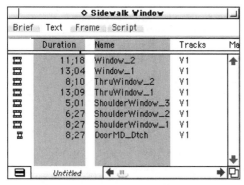

Figure 5.19 In this case, the bin will be sorted using two columns: Duration and Name. Duration will take precedence as a criterion, since it is farthest to the left.

These clips have the same duration.

The names decide the order.

Duration	Name	Tracks	Ma
5;01	ShoulderWindow_3	V1	
6;27	ShoulderWindow_2	V1	
8;10	ThruWindow_2	V1	
8;27	DoorMD_Dtch	V1	
8;27	ShoulderWindow_1	V1	
11;18	Window_2	V1	
13;04	Window_1	V1	
13;09	ThruWindow_1	V1	

Figure 5.20 In this case, a multilevel Sort operation has arranged clips according to Duration and then according to Name. If two or more clips have the same duration, they are then ordered alphabetically by name.

✔ Tips

- You can use a Sort operation to organize the results of a Custom Sift operation.

- If you don't see Sort as an option on the Bin menu, you forgot to first select a column in your bin before opening the menu.

- If you don't see Sort Reversed as an option in the Bin menu, make sure you are pressing and holding Alt (Windows) or Option (Mac) before clicking the menu name.

- When sorting on the Color column, Xpress Pro sorts the items by hue, saturation, and value, in that order.

To perform a multilevel sort using multiple columns:

1. In Text view, click the column you want to use as the primary criterion in the sort order and drag it to the far left.

2. Shift-click one or more additional columns to select them as secondary criteria (**Figure 5.19**).

3. Choose Bin > Sort, or choose Sort from the bin's Fast menu.

   Xpress Pro sorts your clips according to one column. Then, if two cells in the same column have identical data, it solves the ordering problem by using the data in the additional column you selected (**Figure 5.20**).

✔ Tip

- To perform a reverse multilevel Sort operation, hold down Alt (Windows) or Option (Mac) while choosing Bin > Sort.

Working with Information Columns in Text View

Information columns tell you everything from the starting timecode to the creation date of a media object. While a bin's Brief display includes only five information columns, a bin's Text display can contain up to 64 columns, including custom columns (see **Table 5.4**, "Bin Column Headings").

That's a daunting amount of data. However, after you learn how to edit and arrange the data in columns, make some columns invisible, and navigate through columns with simple keystrokes (see **Table 5.5**, "Column Selection Keyboard Shortcuts"), you may feel less overwhelmed.

Table 5.4

Bin Column Headings

COLUMN	INFORMATION
Name	The name of an object.
Audio	The sampling rate of a source clip that contains audio. Typically, this value is 48, 32, or 44.1 kHz.
Audio Format	The audio file format for a source clip that contains audio. Typically, this value is WAVE or AIFF-C.
Audio Sample Size	Indicates the sample size. The two available samples sizes are 16 bit and 24 bit.
Auxiliary Ink	*For film editing only.* Useful for tracking additional information for different film gauges. The choices are the same as for Ink Number.
Auxiliary TC1	The starting auxiliary timecode number as set by choosing Clip > Modify and manually entering auxiliary timecode.
CFPS	Camera frames per second. This is the original frame rate at which your source video or film was recorded.
Cadence	*For film projects.* Indicates the field sequence, which—for NTSC video sourced from 24-fps film—is 3:2. PAL video or film sources uses 2:2 field sequencing.
Cam Roll	*For film editing only.* The roll number for the camera roll source of the clip.
Color	The color for a bin item, selected by choosing Edit > Select Clip Color when a clip is highlighted.
Creation Date	The date the item or clip was recorded or imported.
Drive	The media drive on which you'll find the item's source files.
Duration	The timecode duration of the entire clip.
End	The timecode Out point for the entire clip. This is not the editing Out point; this is the end of the actual recorded clip.
FPS	The frames per second for the individual clip; 29.97 is typical for NTSC, and 25 fps is typical for PAL.
IN-OUT	The timecode duration between the source In and Out points.
Ink Number	*For film editing only.* Indicates a standard ink number format, one that meets your film format as well as your production lab's standards.
KN Duration	*For film editing only.* The duration, in key number amounts, between the start and end of your media.
KN End	*For film editing only.* The ending keyframe number, the code pertaining to the last frame of a clip.
KN Start	*For film editing only.* The starting keyframe number, the code pertaining to the first frame of a clip.
KN IN-OUT	*For film editing only.* The duration, in key numbers, between source In and Out points.
KN Mark IN	*For film editing only.* The key number for the source In mark.
KN Mark OUT	*For film editing only.* The key number for the source Out mark.
KN Start	*For film editing only.* The key number for the start of the source clip.

Table 5.4 *continued*

Bin Column Headings

COLUMN	INFORMATION
Labroll	*For film editing only.* The lab roll number or name.
Lock	Indicates whether an object is locked. You lock an object by selecting it and choosing Clip > Lock Bin Selection. You can do anything you want to a locked object except delete it.
Mark IN	The timecode for the clip's In point.
Mark Out	The timecode for the clip's Out point.
Media File Format	The format for the source media (typically OMF).
Modified Date	The date on which the object was last changed or altered in any way.
Offline	The tracks that do not have source media files online (V1, A1, and/or A2).
Perf	*For film editing only.* Short for perforation; indicates the perforation type of the film.
Pullin	*For film editing only.* Xpress Pro term that combines the terms *pull-down* and *In point*. This column logs the pull-down phase of the start timecode as A, B, X, C, or D. Pullin can be modified before or after recording.
Pullout	*For film editing only.* The opposite of Pullout. This column logs the pull-down phase of the end timecode.
Project	The name of the project in which the item was created.
Scene	The scene number of the clip, typically pertaining to the scene in a movie script.
Shoot Date	The date on which a particular source clip was acquired in production.
Sound TC	For audio that has separate timecode from the video; this column logs the original audio timecode.
Soundroll	The roll number for an audio roll or tape.
Start	The timecode In point for the entire clip. This is not the editing In point; this is the start of the actual clip.
Tape	The name of the source tape (reel) for the individual clip.
Take, not Tale	The take number for the clip. A good column to follow the Scene column.
TC 24/25/25p/30	The starting timecode for a clip shot at 24 fps, 25 fps, 25 fps with pull-down, or 30 fps.
Tale	The take number.
Tape	The tape number for the tape on which you can find the selected source clip.
Tape ID	The tape number for the tape on which you can find the selected source clip.
Tracks	The tracks that make up a clip. A typical recorded clip contains V1 (one video track) and A1 and A2 (two audio tracks).
Video	The video resolution of the clip. For DV, this value typically is DV 25 411.
<Custom heading>	A blank column that you can name as you please.

Table 5.5

Column Selection Keyboard Shortcuts

OPERATION	SHORCUT	
	WINDOWS	MAC OS
Select Cell to Right	Tab	Tab
Select Cell to Left	Shift+Tab	Shift+Tab
Select Cell Above	Enter	Return
Select Cell Below	Shift+Enter	Shift+Return

To edit data in a column cell:

1. In Brief or Text view, click in a column cell to select the information.

2. Type the new information and press Enter (Windows) or Return (Mac).

   The cell's data changes, and the cell directly below it becomes selected (**Figure 5.21**).

To arrange bin information columns:

◆ Click the Text tab, and in Text view click a column title and drag the column to the left or right (**Figure 5.22**).

◆ To align columns, in Text view, choose Bin > Align.

   Xpress Pro eliminates any unnecessary space between information columns.

When you click inside a column cell, the entire row will become highlighted.

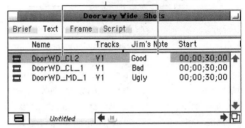

Figure 5.21 To change a column cell's data, click the cell. When it becomes highlighted, you can enter new information.

Drag left or right.

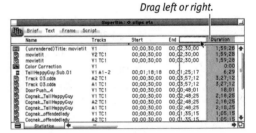

Figure 5.22 To move an information column, click and drag on the column's title.

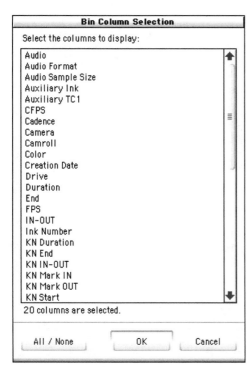

Figure 5.23 Use the Bin Column Selection dialog box to choose the information columns that you want visible in Text view. There are many information columns, many of which you will need only under special circumstances.

To make columns visible or invisible:

1. Click the Text tab, and in Text view, *do one of the following:*

   ▲ From the bin Fast menu, choose Headings.

   ▲ Right-click (Windows) or Ctrl+Shift-click (Mac) in the bin window. In the shortcut menu that appears, choose Headings.

   The Bin Column Selection dialog box appears (**Figure 5.23**).

2. In the Bin Column Selection dialog box, highlight the columns you want to remain visible and click OK.

   The information columns on the Text tab are now updated to reflect your changes.

3. To hide a column, in Bin or Text view, select a column by clicking its heading name. Choose Edit > Delete or press the Delete key.

   The column disappears from view. Don't worry; the information is still there, and you can get the column and its information back by using the Headings dialog box in the bin Fast menu.

√ Tip

- Instead of using Bin > Headings in the Fast menu to change your info column display, you can choose a default or custom Bin View setting. For details, see "Creating Custom Column Arrangements" later in this chapter.

WORKING WITH INFORMATION COLUMNS IN TEXT VIEW

To view obscured columns:

1. If there are columns in Text view that you cannot see, drag the horizontal scroll bar at the bottom of the bin window to the right or left (**Figure 5.24**).

    A black vertical line appears, splitting the bin into two panes. Earlier listed columns are on the left, and later listed columns are on the right.

2. Hold down the mouse over the vertical line until a double arrow appears and drag it to the left or right (**Figure 5.25**).

    Now when you drag the horizontal scroll bar in the bin window to find obscured columns, all of the columns in the left display pane remain fixed and visible, and the scrolling occurs only in the right pane.

To create a custom column:

1. In Bin or Text view, scroll past the last column in the bin.

2. Click a blank column heading space at the top of the bin.

3. When you see a blinking cursor, type a name for the column.

You can now enter data in the cells under your custom column heading (**Figure 5.26**).

Vertical bar marking   These columns were
the display pane   previously out of view.

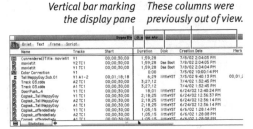

Figure 5.24 Use the scroll bar at the bottom of a bin window to see bin columns that are initially out of view.

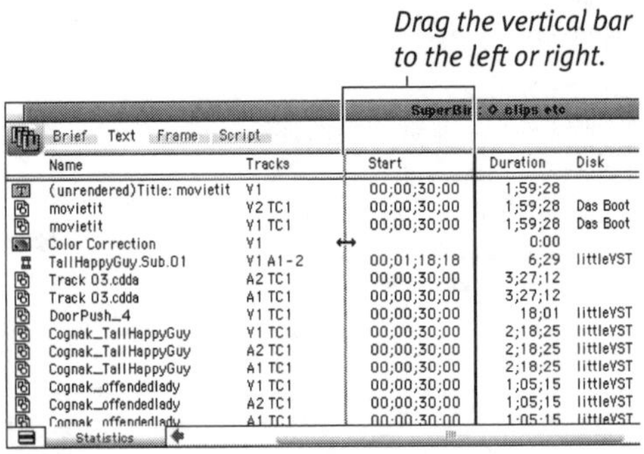

Drag the vertical bar
to the left or right.

Figure 5.25 Adjust your bin's vertical view bar by dragging.

Custom column heading

Figure 5.26 Click an empty column heading area to create your own personal column. You can then type whatever you want in the custom column's cells.

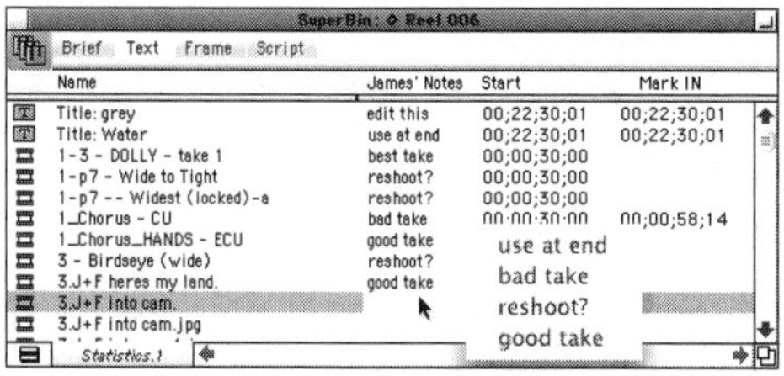

Figure 5.27 To quickly add the same comment you've entered in another custom column cell, Alt-click and hold (Windows) or Option-click and hold (Mac) on a custom column cell and choose a comment from the list that appears.

Viewing Essential Object Info: Click and Hold

One of the quickest ways to get essential information about an object in a bin—faster than sorting the various bin information columns—is to click and hold the mouse for about 3 seconds on a bin object. An information window will appear containing data such as frame rate, video resolution, start and end timecode, and In and Out timecode (**Figure 5.28**).

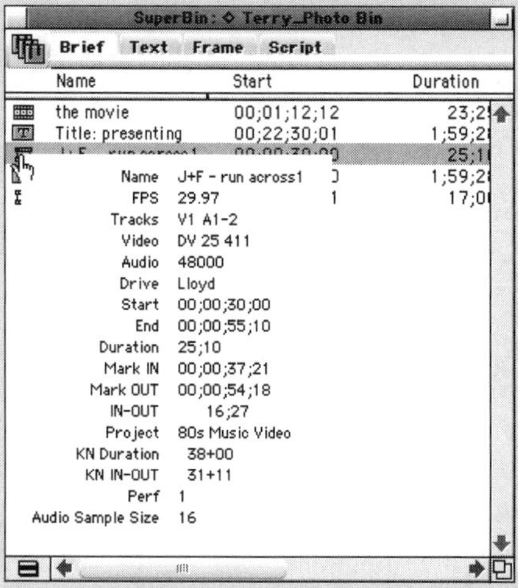

Figure 5.28 To quickly see essential information about a clip or other object in your bin, click the clip and hold for 3 seconds until an info dialog box appears.

✔ Tips

■ To change a custom column heading, Alt-click (Windows) or Option-click (Mac) on the heading.

■ Here's a cool trick for quickly adding common comments to custom column cells: Alt-click-hold (Windows) or Option-click-hold (Mac) on a custom column cell. A pop-up menu appears, from which you can choose one of the comments that you've entered in other cells (**Figure 5.27**).

To copy and paste column data in another column:

1. In Text view, select a column by clicking its heading name and then choose Edit > Duplicate.

2. In the Select dialog box that appears, choose the column to which you want to copy the selected column's data. Click OK.

   Xpress Pro copies the data from the selected column and pastes it in the column you selected.

✔ Tip

■ Use this technique when you want one column's cells (usually a custom column) to include data from another column's cells. For example, if you copy the information from the Name column and paste it into a Custom Comments column, your custom comments will always begin with a clip's name.

Creating Custom Column Arrangements

You may want a different information column display for different situations or different bins. Hence, Xpress Pro lets you save your rearranged column configuration as Bin View settings, which you can apply to any bin at any time.

There are three default Bin View settings to get you started:

◆ **Film:** Information columns useful for cutting a film project.

◆ **Statistics:** Basic information columns, including In and Out points, duration, media start and end timecode, audio sampling rate, and source media drive name.

◆ **Custom:** An empty template for you to customize.

You can change the presets or create your own new settings from scratch. Once you create a new Bin View setting, you can assign it to any open bin.

To create a Bin View setting:

1. In a bin's Text view, configure your information column display using techniques described earlier in this chapter in "Working with Information Columns in Text View."

2. Click the Bin View Name button at the bottom of the bin window and choose Save As from the pop-up menu (**Figure 5.29**).

3. In the View Name dialog box, give the setting a name and click OK (**Figure 5.30**).

   The new setting now appears in the popup menu at the bottom of every bin window as well as on the Settings tab of the Project window.

Click here

Figure 5.29 To save a customized bin view, click the Bin View Name button and select Save As.

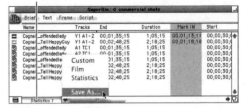

Figure 5.30 Type a name for the bin view in the View Name dialog box. Choose a name that reminds you of the bin view's function.

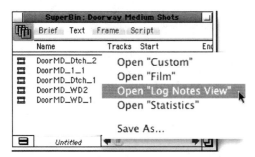

Figure 5.31 You can open a bin setting to modify it by right-clicking (Windows) or Ctrl-clicking (Mac) the Bin View Name button.

✔ Tips

■ It's a good idea to create different Bin View settings for different stages of the editing process, such as Logging, Editing, and Finishing. Choosing your column names carefully at this stage will allow you to create settings that link to specific toolsets (see "Using Toolsets" in Chapter 3 for details).

■ When you modify a default setting, such as Statistics, Xpress Pro displays the default name with a numbered extension (.1) This is Xpress Pro's hint that you should save the adjusted display under a new name.

To select a Bin View setting:

◆ In Text view, click the Bin View Name button at the lower left of the bin window and choose a default or custom setting from the list that appears.

To modify a Bin View setting:

Do one of the following:

▲ On the Settings tab of the Project window, double-click a Bin View setting. Make any changes and click OK.

▲ In a bin window, right-click (Windows) or Ctrl-click (Mac) the Bin View Name button at the lower left of the window. Choose a setting, make any changes, and click OK (**Figure 5.31**).

✔ Tip

■ To see Bin View settings on the Settings tab of the Project window, open the Fast menu and choose Bin Views.

About Sequences and Timelines

In the Avid language of nonlinear editing, the terms *sequence*, *Timeline*, and *Composer* refer to different aspects of the movie or program you are creating. A sequence is the product of your creative editing work; it's a juxtaposition of images and sounds that play in a linear fashion over a certain length of time. A sequence is represented in a bin by a sequence icon, and Xpress Pro projects can contain several sequences, which are often different versions of your movie.

The Timeline, on the other hand, is the interface window where you build your linear sequence by continually arranging and rearranging graphical representations of all your clips, images, and so on. Meanwhile, the Composer window displays the actual movie or program—your sequence's images and sounds—based on the position of the playhead in the Timeline. The Timeline and Composer are tied together by the blue playhead and are often called collectively the Timeline/Composer.

Therefore, in the basic workflow, you load a sequence from a bin into the Timeline and then edit and trim content within the Timeline based on visual and aural feedback from the Composer.

- In Xpress Pro, sequences are limited to 8 tracks of video and 24 tracks of audio.

- You keep sequences in bins along with all other media objects.

- You don't save your work by saving sequences individually. Instead, you save the bins that contain your sequences. (For more information, see "Saving and Backing Up Your Work" in Chapter 3.)

- You can load a sequence into a source monitor (just as you can any other clip) and edit all or portions of it into another sequence.

- You can have only one sequence loaded in the Timeline at a time.

✔ Tip

- You can work around Xpress Pro's 24-track limit by creating video nests, or tracks within tracks.

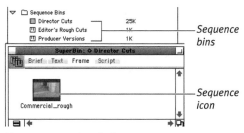

Figure 5.32 Keeping all of your sequences organized in one or more bins helps you keep track of the many different versions in a sequence's life.

Figure 5.33 You can create a new sequence within a bin with the shortcut menu.

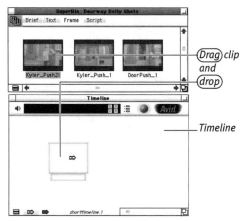

Figure 5.34 If the Timeline is open but empty, you can create a new sequence by opening a bin and dragging a clip into the Timeline window.

Creating, Duplicating, and Deleting Sequences

Creating a new sequence is very easy in Xpress Pro. In fact, you can create as many as you want. Since you can end up with dozens of versions of essentially the same sequence, the key is to give every sequence a unique name when you create it and place it in a bin where you can find it (**Figure 5.32**).

To create a sequence:

1. *Do one of the following:*
   - ▲ Click an open bin to select it and choose Clip > New Sequence.
   - ▲ Right-click (Windows) or Ctrl+Shift-click (Mac) in the Composer, Timeline, or bin window and choose New Sequence from the pop-up menu that appears (**Figure 5.33**).

   A sequence icon appears in your chosen bin.

2. Give the sequence a unique name and click OK.

✔ Tips

- If you don't have a bin open, or if you have multiple bins open, a Select dialog box appears, asking you to choose a bin for your new sequence.

- If the Timeline window is open and empty (without any clips in it), you can create a new sequence by editing a source clip into the empty Timeline. Xpress Pro creates a new sequence icon in the same bin as the edited source clip (**Figure 5.34**).

- The keyboard shortcut for creating a new sequence is Shift+Ctrl+N (Windows) or Shift+Command+N (Mac).

To duplicate a sequence:

Do one of the following:

▲ In the bin where the sequence is located, select the sequence icon and choose Edit > Duplicate.

▲ Load the sequence you want to duplicate into the Composer monitor and click the Clip Name menu in the upper-right corner of the window. Choose Duplicate from the menu that appears.

The duplicated sequence is placed in the bin you selected, and "Copy.01" is appended to the sequence name.

✔ Tips

■ To help you keep track of the creation order of your sequences, develop a consistent sequence naming strategy, such as SequenceName.01, SequenceName.02, and so on.

■ The Select dialog box, which asks you to choose a bin for your sequence, appears only when you have more than one bin open.

To delete a sequence:

1. *Do one of the following:*

   ▲ Select the sequence or sequences in a bin and select Edit > Delete.

   ▲ Select the sequence or sequences and press the Delete key on the keyboard.

2. In the Delete dialog box that appears, make sure Delete 1 (or More) Sequence(s) is checked; then click OK.

   Avid deletes the sequence icon from your bin.

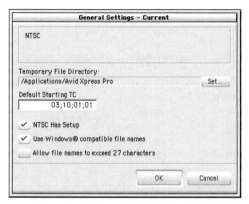

Figure 5.35 You can change the starting timecode for any sequence in the active General Settings dialog, in the Project window.

To set your sequence's starting timecode:

1. On the Settings tab of the Project window, double-click settings labeled General that also have a checkmark next to them, indicating they are the active settings.

   The General Settings—Current dialog box appears.

2. In the Default Starting text box, enter a starting timecode (**Figure 5.35**).

✔ Tips

- You can also change your sequence's starting timecode by opening the bin that contains the sequence, clicking the Brief tab, selecting a cell in the Start column, and typing a new timecode. (In the warning dialog box, click OK.)

- The default starting timecode also determines the starting timecode for imported video clips that do not already contain a readable timecode track.

Recovering a Deleted Sequence

If you mistakenly delete a sequence, you cannot use the Undo function to bring it back. The Undo function works only with edit actions in the Timeline.

But all is not lost. You can find the sequence in the Xpress Pro Attic, under the project name.

CREATING, DUPLICATING, AND DELETING SEQUENCES

Loading a Sequence into the Timeline

The best way to load a sequence in the Timeline/Composer depends on whether your Composer is in Source/Record mode or in a single window. (See the sidebar "Loading a Sequence in Source/Record Mode" below.) However, if you're ever unsure as to how to load a sequence, the fail-safe way is the drag-and-drop method.

Although the Timeline and Composer can display only one sequence at a time, you can have multiple sequences loaded into the Composer window at once. This enables you to quickly toggle back and forth between different sequences (just as you can switch to different bins in the SuperBin).

To load a sequence:

Do one of the following:

▲ If your Composer is a single window, drag a sequence icon from a bin to the Composer. In Source/Record mode, drag the sequence to the right (Record) side of the Composer.

▲ If the Timeline window is empty (not even track buttons are visible), drag a sequence icon to the Timeline.

The Timeline displays the graphical representation of your sequence. You can now play and see your sequence in the Composer window.

Loading a Sequence in Source/Record Mode

If you're one of those people who expect great things to come from double-clicking, this is for you: If the Composer is in Source/Record mode *and* you choose Source or Record Monitor in the Double-Click Loads Objects In pop-up menu in the Bin Settings dialog box, you can load a sequence by double-clicking its icon to load it.

But to avoid confusion when you're not in Source/Record mode, the best way to load a sequence is to drag the sequence icon to the Composer or an empty Timeline.

(For more information on using the Composer as a single monitor or in dual-monitor Source/Record mode, see "The Composer" in Chapter 2.)

Figure 5.36 You can switch to a different, previously loaded sequence by choosing from the Clip Name menu in the upper-right corner of the Composer window.

✔ Tips

■ Dragging a sequence icon into a Timeline that already contains a sequence edits the new sequence into the existing sequence. This is a common mistake when you're trying to load a different sequence into the Composer. You can use Undo to restore the sequence in the Timeline.

■ You can double-click a sequence to load it into a source monitor. Then you can edit all or part of that sequence into the sequence that's displayed in your Timeline.

■ You can use Shift-click to select multiple sequence icons and then load them all at once by dragging them to the Composer.

■ If you prefer to use your keyboard rather than your mouse, you can use the arrow keys to select a sequence in a bin and then press Enter (Windows) or Return (Mac) to load the sequence into the Timeline/Composer.

To activate a previously loaded sequence:

1. Click the Clip Name menu in the upper-right corner of the Composer monitor.

2. From the Clip Name menu that appears, choose a sequence name (**Figure 5.36**).

   The sequence you choose is loaded into both the Timeline and Composer.

✔ Tip

■ To see the sequence names in the order that they were created, hold down Alt (Windows) or Option (Mac) while clicking the Clip Name menu.

Using the Clip Name Menu

You can use the Clip Name menu *at the upper right* of the Composer to switch to a previously loaded sequence, clear the Composer monitor, add comments to a sequence segment, or back up your sequence.

When the Composer is in Source/Record mode, you can use the Clip Name menu *at the upper left* of the Source side of the window to toggle between previously loaded source clips and to add comments or clear the monitor.

The options are as follows:

◆ **Clear Monitor:** Removes the current sequence (or source clip) from the Timeline and clears the image from the Composer window.

◆ **Duplicate:** Copies the currently loaded sequence (or source clip) and asks you to select or create a bin in which to keep the duplicate.

◆ **Add Comments:** After you select a segment in the Timeline, allows you to add long comments to the segment or source track. (See the sidebar "Another Way to Add Comments" in Chapter 6.)

◆ **Clear Menu:** Removes all names from the Clip Name menu. If you've loaded so many sequences or source clips into the Composer that your menu is getting messy or confusing, use this choice to clear them all from the menu and start over.

◆ **Sequence Name:** Loads a previously loaded sequence into the Timeline and Composer (**Figure 5.37**).

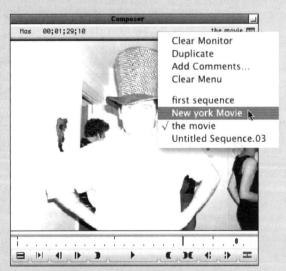

Figure 5.37 You can toggle among previously loaded sequences in the pop-up menu accessed from the upper right of the Composer window.

Figure 5.38 You can get rid of the currently loaded sequence by clicking the upper-right corner of the Composer and selecting Clear Menu.

To clear a sequence from the Composer and Timeline:

◆ Open the Clip Name menu at the upper right of the Composer and choose Clear Monitor (**Figure 5.38**).

The current active sequence is cleared from the Composer and Timeline, and they are both left blank. However, the sequence is still loaded in the Composer, and you can make it active again by selecting it from the Clip Name menu.

To clear all loaded sequences and leave only the current sequence displayed:

◆ Open the Clip Name menu in the upper-right corner of the Composer and choose Clear Menu.

All clip and sequence names are cleared from the Composer and the Clip Name menu, but the active sequence remains active and unchanged.

To find a loaded sequence or clip in a bin:

1. *Do one of the following:*

   ▲ Load the sequence into a single source monitor or into either side of the Source/Record Composer.

   ▲ Load the clip into a source monitor or into the Source side of the Source/Record Composer.

2. On the Other tab of the Command palette, click Find Bin.

LOADING A SEQUENCE INTO THE TIMELINE

Setting Up and Saving Your Timeline Display

Once you start working with a sequence in the Timeline, you may want to modify the window's default setup. Xpress Pro allows you to customize the way the Timeline displays a sequence and then save your preferences as a Timeline View setting.

You can create multiple Timeline View settings for different editing situations. For example, when editing audio, you will probably want your audio tracks displayed as large audio waveforms (Sample Plot), with Audio Auto Gain lines (**Figure 5.39**). In contrast, when working with video effects, you will probably want your audio tracks to be small, without waveform displays.

The Timeline Fast menu display options are as follow:

- **Default Setup:** Returns the Timeline to its default display, with equal track sizes and standard clip names (**Figure 5.40**).

- **Clip Frames:** Displays one thumbnail image for each video clip in the Timeline (**Figure 5.41**).

- **Clip Names:** Displays text names for each video and audio segment in the Timeline.

- **Clip Durations:** Displays one timecode duration for each video and audio segment in the Timeline (**Figure 5.42**).

- **Clip Comments:** Displays clip comments on Timeline segments. (You add a comment by selecting a segment and choosing Add Comments from the Composer window's Clip Name menu.)
  (For more information, see the sidebar "Another Way to Make Comments" in Chapter 6.)

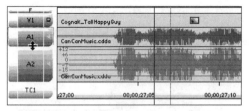

Figure 5.39 Choose Sample Plot in your Timeline View settings to display audio waveforms.

Figure 5.40 The default (Untitled) Timeline view displays tracks of the same size with source clip names.

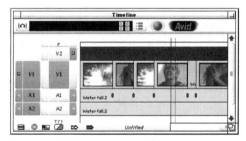

Figure 5.41 With Clip Frames selected, each segment in the Timeline has one thumbnail image.

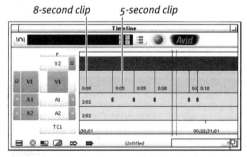

Figure 5.42 Clip durations are displayed on each clip.

The name of the OMF file behind this video segment *The name of the AIF file behind this audio segment*

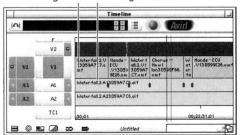

Figure 5.43 With Media Names selected, each segment in the Timeline displays the name of its source media file.

Render range line

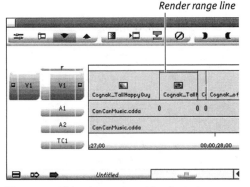

Figure 5.44 All has been selected for displaying Render Ranges, meaning that all segments that need rendering are marked with a colored line.

◆ **Source Names:** Displays source tape names for video and audio segments in the Timeline.

◆ **Media Names:** Displays the names of the original media files for each video and audio clip in the Timeline (**Figure 5.43**).

◆ **Dupe Detection:** Keeps track of any duplicate frames that are found, which are a concern in an online, tape-to-tape session. Colored bars are drawn on top of clips that have duplicate frames. Choose this option if you're planning to generate an Edit Decision List (EDL).

◆ **Render Ranges:** Displays a colored line on segments that will eventually need rendering. Select None to display no render lines, Partial to mark clips that need only partial rendering, and All to mark all clips that need rendering (**Figure 5.44**).

continues on next page

◆ **Audio Clip Gain:** Displays any level adjustments made with the Audio Mix tool, plus audio-level reference lines, ranging from −45 dB to 12 dB (**Figure 5.45**). (For more information, see "Adjusting Audio Levels" in Chapter 12.)

◆ **Audio Auto Gain:** Displays audio keyframes (rubber bands) in the Timeline, along with audio-level reference lines (**Figure 5.46**). (For more information, see "Creating and Manipulating Audio-Level Keyframes" in Chapter 12.)

◆ **Sample Plot:** Displays audio waveforms on audio segments (**Figure 5.47**).

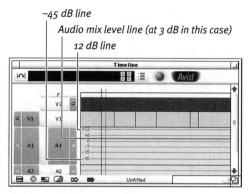

−45 dB line
Audio mix level line (at 3 dB in this case)
12 dB line

Figure 5.45 With Audio Clip Gain selected, Xpress Pro displays audio-level reference lines on audio segments in the Timeline, along with a dark, black line that represents any level change made with the Audio Mix tool.

Audio-level keyframes

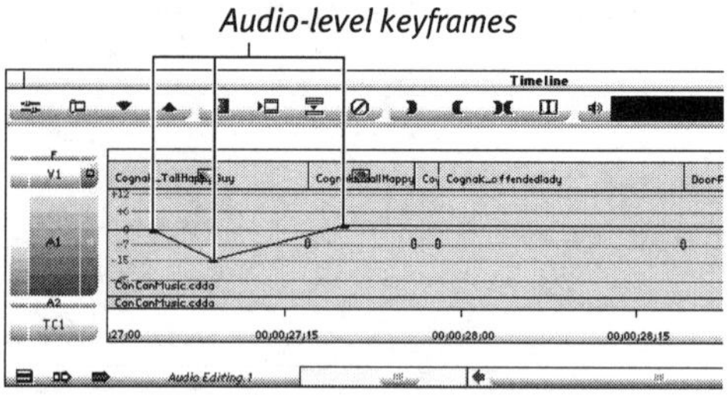

Figure 5.46 Audio Auto Gain is selected, displaying audio keyframe rubber bands on audio segments in the Timeline.

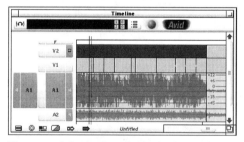

Figure 5.47 Selecting Sample Plot displays audio waveforms on audio segments in the Timeline.

Orange in   *Orange in*
the bin   *the Timeline*

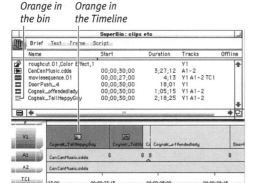

Figure 5.48 Selecting Source in the Clip Color menu gives Timeline segments colors identical to their colors in bins.

Offline tracks
noted in the bin

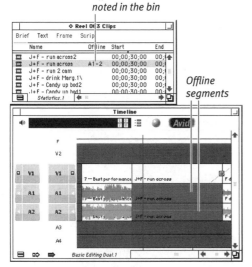

Offline
segments

Figure 5.49 Highlighting offline clips helped the editor see that, although Shot B has online video, its two audio tracks are offline.

◆ **Clip Color:** Choose Source to give Timeline clips (segments) the same color that they've been assigned in bins (**Figure 5.48**). Choose Local if you want to select a segment in the Timeline and choose a color for it (by choosing Clip > Set Local Clip Color) different from its bin color. Choose Offline to highlight clips that are offline (not connected to their source media). The default color for offline clips is red (**Figure 5.49**).

◆ **Track Color:** Lets you choose the color of any enabled tracks. However, your Interface settings will override track colors chosen here. (See the following tips.)

You can save your preferences as a Timeline View setting and keep several Timeline View settings on your Settings tab and even link them to different toolsets or workspaces.

(For more information about using toolsets and workspaces, see Chapter 3, "Customizing Your Workspace.")

✔ Tips

■ You will see your Timeline View settings on the Settings tab only if you open the Fast menu and choose All Settings or Timeline Views.

■ Dupe detection requires FilmScribe and works only for the V1 track. (See "Chapter 13, "Working with Other Applications," for information on FilmScribe.)

continues on next page

- Track colors chosen on the Appearance tab of the Interface settings override any track color choices made in the Timeline View settings. Uncheck track color choices in the Interface settings to use Timeline view color choices (**Figure 5.50**).

- To set individual clip colors in the bins, choose Edit > Set Clip Color.

- With Clip Color > Offline turned on, nests that contain offline clips will be highlighted even if the offline media in question rests many layers deep within the nest.

- To enlarge the size of sample plot waveforms without changing the track size, press Ctrl+Alt+L (Windows) or Command+Option+L (Mac). This command is helpful with loud passages that don't initially display much waveform detail. Pressing Ctrl+Alt+K or Command+Option+K reduces the waveform.

The following Timeline Fast menu display options are most helpful for making temporary display adjustments while you edit, and are usually best left at their default settings when setting up different Timeline Views:

- ◆ **Show Track:** Allows you to choose which tracks to view in the Timeline. There's also an option to hide selected tracks as well as show every track. (Hiding a track does not delete the track from your sequence.)

- ◆ **More Detail/Less Detail:** Similar to using the scale bar or the up and down arrows to zoom in and out of your sequence.

- ◆ **Show Every Frame:** Ensures that you can skip from frame to frame in your sequence by clicking and dragging the position indicator in the Timeline.

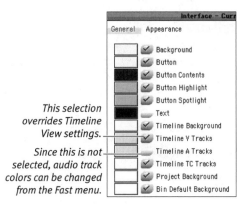

This selection overrides Timeline View settings.

Since this is not selected, audio track colors can be changed from the Fast menu.

Figure 5.50 In the Interface settings dialog box, Timeline V (video) Tracks is checked; the color cannot be changed from the Timeline Fast menu. However, Timeline A (audio) Tracks is not selected and can be changed in the Timeline Fast menu.

SETTING UP AND SAVING YOUR TIMELINE DISPLAY

Selected   The Zoom-in
section   cursor

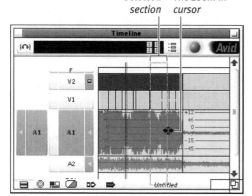

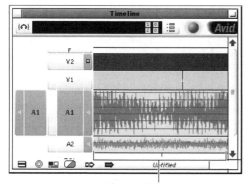

*The Timeline
displays the selection.*

Figure 5.51 When you choose Zoom In (or press Ctrl+M in Windows or Option+M on a Mac), (above), Xpress Pro changes your pointer into a double arrow that you use to select a portion of your sequence you want to examine in detail (below).

◆ **Show Entire Sequence:** Displays your entire sequence no matter what the size of your Timeline window.

◆ **Zoom Back:** Reverses any zooming into your Timeline accomplished by the Zoom In function (see Zoom In).

◆ **Zoom In:** Turns your pointer into a double-arrow icon that you can use to highlight a part of your Timeline that you want to fill the window. In other words, if you highlight a few frames, those few frames will fill the entire Timeline, allowing you to make detailed adjustments (**Figure 5.51**).

To adjust a Timeline Fast menu setting:

1. Click the Timeline Fast menu.

   The Timeline Fast menu opens. Options with check marks are active, and options with no check marks are inactive.

2. Activate or deactivate a Fast menu setting by highlighting it.

   The setting takes effect in the Timeline when you release the menu. The next time you open the Fast menu, a checkmark will appear next to any of the settings that are active.

3. Repeat steps 1 and 2 above until you select all of your desired Fast menu options.

   The Timeline alters its display according to your choices.

SETTING UP AND SAVING YOUR TIMELINE DISPLAY

To save your Timeline configuration as a Timeline View setting:

1. Click the Timeline View menu, at the bottom left of the Timeline.

2. Select Save As (**Figure 5.52**).

3. In the View Name dialog box, give the setting a name (**Figure 5.53**).

   The new name appears at the bottom of the Timeline and the new Timeline View is displayed in the Settings tab of the Project window.

✔ Tips

- To display Timeline View settings in the Project window, choose Timeline Views from the Project window Fast menu.

- The scale and scroll controls of your Timeline are not included in your Timeline View settings.

To activate a saved Timeline view:

◆ Click the Timeline view name at the bottom of the Timeline and select a Timeline view from the list that appears.

✔ Tips

- If you've linked a Timeline view to a different toolset or workspace, you can also switch to that toolset or workspace to activate the Timeline view.

  (For more information about toolsets and workspaces, see "Using Toolsets" and "Using Workspaces" in Chapter 3.)

- A Timeline View setting cannot be activated or changed from the Settings tab of the Project window. However, it can be renamed there.

Click here

Figure 5.52 At the lower left of the Timeline, you can select a Timeline View setting or save a new one.

Figure 5.53 Give your Timeline View setting a name identical to the names of other settings if you want to link settings together in a workspace or toolset.

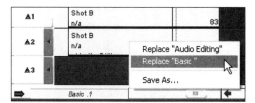

Figure 5.54 To make your current Timeline view replace another Timeline view, hold down Alt (Windows) or Option (Mac) on the View menu and choose from the list that appears.

To replace a saved Timeline View setting:

1. Configure your track size and Fast menu preferences.

2. Press Alt (Windows) or Option (Mac) and open the View menu at the bottom of the Timeline (**Figure 5.54**).

   Every Timeline view name now has the word *Replace* next to it.

3. Choose a Timeline view to replace and click Replace in the dialog box that appears.

   Xpress Pro replaces the old Timeline View setting with the current Timeline View setting. This helps you avoid creating multiple Timeline views that have the same purpose.

✔ Tip

- Note that whenever you alter Timeline View settings, the name of the current Timeline view becomes italicized, with a .1 added to the name. This is Xpress Pro's hint to you that if you like the new adjustment, you should save it under a new name or replace the old version of the setting.

MAKING EDITS

Starting with basic overwrite and splice-in edits, this chapter covers the classic Editing 101 topics as well as advanced techniques—replace edits, fit-to-fill edits, back-timed edits, split edits, clip grouping, and so on—for experienced cutters. This is the meat and potatoes of learning Xpress Pro: actual editing.

You may find yourself leaning toward one of the two editing styles available in Xpress Pro: the keyboard command approach or the drag-and-drop method. Either way you go, you'll find that, as with any NLE, Xpress Pro has its idiosyncrasies. For example, Xpress Pro tracks are not sync-locked by default. Selecting and moving segments in the Timeline requires you to use one of two Segment modes. And black filler frames aren't simply pieces of nothing; they behave like segments.

If you have used other editing applications, you should pay special attention to the sections on patching and targeting tracks; Xpress Pro's approach may be fundamentally different from that of your old NLE. For example, selecting (or targeting) a Timeline video track doesn't mean that the source video will go there; the source video has to be patched to that track as well.

This chapter also shows you how to reshape your initial rough-draft edit without tripping over yourself. Relevant tasks include navigating through the Timeline, moving segments, and deleting unwanted material.

About Editing in Xpress Pro

You've organized your source clips and other media material into bins. You've created a sequence and loaded it into the Timeline. You've customized your Timeline's display by creating one or more Timeline View settings. Now, finally, you're ready to edit.

In very simple terms, editing in any NLE is about deciding what part of a source clip you want to place in your sequence and where in your sequence you want to place it.

There are many ways to achieve the same result in Xpress Pro, but the general steps for performing most edits are as follows:

1. **Load a source clip into a source monitor:** A source clip might be a master clip, a subclip, another sequence, a title, a still image, or a music clip. You can load a source clip into either an independent source monitor or the source (left) side of the Composer in Source/Record mode.

   You can also load a portion of your current sequence into the clipboard, which operates just like a source monitor. (See "Using the Clipboard Monitor" later in this chapter for more information.)

2. **Mark In and/or Out points:** In and Out points in the source window tell Xpress Pro what part of the incoming clip you want to include in your sequence. In and Out points in the Timeline tell Xpress Pro where the source clip will begin or end in your sequence (**Figure 6.1**).

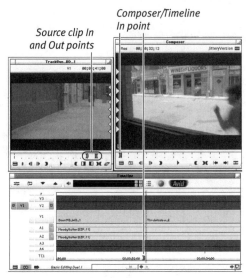

Source clip In and Out points

Composer/Timeline In point

Figure 6.1 Here, In and Out points in the source monitor tell Xpress Pro what piece of the source clip will go into the Timeline. The In point in the TImeline/Composer tells Xpress Pro where to put the source clip in the sequence.

Figure 6.2 Here, the source track V1 is patched to record track V2. This means that the source clip's video will be edited into the Timeline's V2 track.

Figure 6.3 Here, V1, A1, and A2 are all patched to record tracks. However, the V1 record track is the only record track selected (the only one that will receive the edit).

3. **Patch source tracks to record tracks:** The Track Selector panel, often just called the patch panel, tells Xpress Pro which record tracks (the tracks in the Timeline) are targeted to receive the source clip's tracks (a typical source clip has one video track and two audio tracks). See **Figure 6.2**.

4. **Select the record tracks you are targeting:** When you select a record track, you activate it to receive the source clip track that you have patched to it. If a record track is not selected, no media content will be edited to it, even if you have patched a source track to it (**Figure 6.3**).

   (For more information, see "Patching and Selecting Tracks" later in this chapter.)

5. **Perform an overwrite, splice-in, replace, or fit-to-fill edit:** Edits can be performed as three- or four-point edits by clicking one of Xpress Pro's editing buttons or by dragging and dropping your clip onto the Timeline.

   (See the sidebar "Three-Point Editing" later in this chapter.)

Loading Source Clips

Loading your source footage means opening it in one of the following monitors:

- **An independent source monitor:** This is a single, floating window. You can have multiple source monitors open at once (**Figure 6.4**).

- **The source side of the Composer monitor in Source/Record mode:** To enter Source/Record mode, either resize your Composer into a rectangle or choose Toolset > Source/Record Editing (**Figure 6.5**).

- **The clipboard monitor:** You use this monitor to load sections of your currently open sequence or sections of another sequence, which you can then edit into the current Timeline. (For information see "Using the Clipboard Monitor" later in this chapter.)

Figure 6.4 If you want, you can have multiple independent source monitors open at once (if you choose New Pop-Up Monitor from the Double-Click Loads Objects In pop-up menu in the Bin Settings window).

Source clip — Edited clip

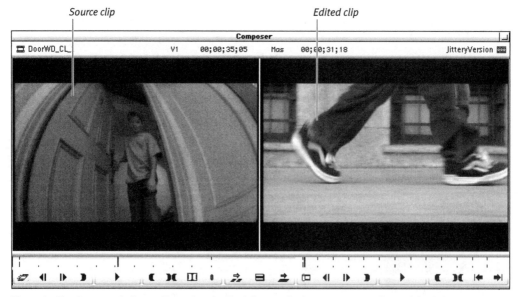

Figure 6.5 The Composer in Source/Record mode. The left pane displays your source clip, and the right pane displays your edited sequence (what's in the Timeline).

The Source/Record Monitor's Advantage

The advantage of using the Composer in Source/Record mode is that, when you're working on the source side of the monitor, you can toggle between previously loaded clips. The source monitor in Source/Record mode operates kind of like the SuperBin (you might call it a SuperSourceMonitor).

To load a previously loaded source clip, just click the name of the clip in the upper-left corner of the Composer monitor and choose from the list that appears (**Figure 6.6**).

An additional benefit of using Source/Record mode is that you can map any button to the Composer toolbar, whereas you cannot change button mapping for an independent source window.

For more information about Source/Record mode, see "Source Clip Monitor" in Chapter 2 and the sidebar "Using the Clip Name Menu" in Chapter 5.

Click here.   *Previously loaded clips*

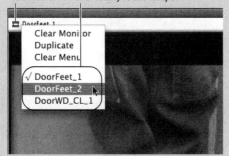

Figure 6.6 To load a different, previously loaded clip into the source monitor in Source/Record mode, click the name of the clip in the upper-left corner or the Composer.

After loading a clip into a source monitor, you can mark In and/or Out points, add locators and comments, or create motion effects. (See "Marking In and Out Points" and "Using Locators" later in this chapter. Also, see "Using Motion Effects" in Chapter 9.)

To load a clip or sequence into a source monitor:

Do one of the following:

- ▲ In a bin window, double-click a source clip.
- ▲ Highlight a clip in a bin and press Enter (Windows) or Return (Mac).
- ▲ In Source/Record monitor mode, drag a source clip from a bin to the source side of the Composer window.

✔ Tips

- In the Bin Settings window, from the Double-Click Loads Objects In pull-down menu, choose New Pop-up Monitor. Double-clicking a source clip will now load it into an independent window, even if you are in Source/Record mode.

- You can load the parent clip for any segment in your Timeline into a source monitor by using the Match Frame button. (See "Using Match Frame" later in this chapter.)

Marking In and Out Points

Marking In and Out points is part of the core craft of video and film editing and involves two critical creative choices: What part of your source clip do you want to edit into the Timeline? Where do you want to edit it to?

Typically, you will prepare an edit by marking *two points* in one monitor—the source monitor or the Timeline/Composer—and *one point* in the other monitor. (See the sidebar "Three-Point Editing" later in this chapter.)

Furthermore, when you make your In/Out-point decisions—either for a source clip or for the Timeline/Composer—your marks are not locked in stone. That's the beauty of nonlinear editing. The computer makes it easy (perhaps too easy!) to go back and adjust your beginnings and endings.

Table 6.1 lists button commands for marking, erasing, and jumping to In and Out points.

To mark In and Out points:

1. *Do one of the following:*
   - ▲ To mark your source clip, select an independent source window or the source side of the Composer in Source/Record mode.
   - ▲ To mark your sequence, select the Timeline, the Composer, or the record side of the Composer in Source/Record mode.

2. Use Xpress Pro's play buttons to find the right frame for either your In or Out point.

   (See "Using the Play Controls" and the sidebar "The Power of the J-K-L Keys" later in this chapter.)

Table 6.1

In and Out Commands	
COMMAND	**FUNCTION**
Mark In	Marks an In point in the selected monitor.
Mark Out	Marks an Out point in the selected monitor.
Mark Clip	Marks In and Out points at the beginning and end of a source clip or Timeline segment.
Clear In Mark	Erases the In mark in the selected monitor.
Clear Out Mark	Erases the Out mark in the selected monitor.
Clear Both Mark	Erases both the In and Out marks in the selected monitor.
Go to In	Jumps the position indicator to the In mark in the selected monitor.
Got to Out	Jumps the position indicator to the Out mark in the selected monitor.
Audio Mark In	Marks an audio In point separate from the video In point.
Audio Mark Out	Marks an audio Out point separate from the video Out point.
Go to Audio Mark In	Jumps the position indicator to the audio In point in the selected monitor.
Go to Audio Mark Out	Jumps the position indicator to the audio Out point in the selected monitor.

The sawtooth bar
identifies the In frame.   Source monitor

Mark In button   Mark Out button

Figure 6.7 By default, Mark In and Mark Out buttons appear on the source and Composer window toolbars. On the Command palette, they appear on the Edit tab.

Alt-drag (Windows) or
Option-drag (Mac).

Figure 6.8 To reposition an In or Out point in a source monitor window, Alt-drag (Windows) or Option-drag (Mac) the In- or Out-point mark.

3. Click Mark In to set an In point or Mark Out to set an Out point.

The Mark In and Mark Out buttons appear in the play bar at the bottom of the relevant monitor. A sawtooth bar appears on the left edge of the image for an In point and on the right edge for an Out point (**Figure 6.7**).

✔ Tips

- You must select the source clip window when marking source clips and select the Composer or Timeline to mark your sequence.

- You can mark In and Out points while a clip plays.

- You can mark separate In and Out points for a clip's audio and video tracks by using Audio Mark In and Audio Mark Out. (For more information, see the sidebar "What Are L-Cuts, J-Cuts, and Split Edits?" later in this chapter.)

To change In and Out points:

Do one of the following:

- ▲ Play to a different In or Out frame and select Mark In and/or Mark Out again.

- ▲ In the play bar at the bottom of the relevant monitor, hold down Alt (Windows) or Option (Mac) and drag either the In or Out marker to a new location (**Figure 6.8**).

To clear In and Out points:

Do one of the following:

▲ Click Clear In Mark to clear the In point or Clear Out Mark to clear the Out point.

▲ Click Clear Both Marks to clear both the In and Out points.

The Mark In and Mark Out buttons disappear from the play bar of the selected monitor.

✔ Tip

■ The Clear In Mark, Clear Out Mark, and Clear Both Marks buttons appear on the Edit tab of the Command palette.

To mark an entire clip or Timeline segment:

Do one of the following:

▲ In a source monitor, click the Mark Clip button.

Xpress Pro places an In mark at the beginning of the clip and an Out mark at the end of the clip.

▲ In the Timeline, place the position indicator over a segment you want to mark and select the track button for the track that contains the segment. Click the Mark Clip button.

Xpress Pro marks a Timeline In point where the segment begins and a Timeline Out point where the segment ends (**Figure 6.9**).

✔ Tip

■ Marking a segment in the Timeline is helpful when you want to replace the marked segment or when you want to edit a clip or title above a marked segment with a matching duration.

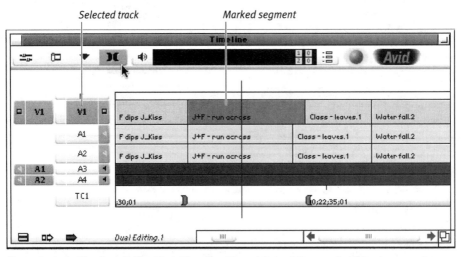

Figure 6.9 In the Timeline, clicking Mark Clip will put In and Out points around whichever segments are underneath your position indicator (on selected tracks). You can use these marks to replace the segment or place a correctly sized segment or title above it.

Three-Point Editing

A three-point edit is the most common type of edit for NLE users. It is named as such because it uses three Mark In/Mark Out points.

In a three-point edit, either two points are marked in a source monitor and one in the Timeline/Composer, or two points are marked in the Timeline/Composer and one in the source monitor.

◆ **Mark In/Mark Out in the source monitor, with Mark In in the Timeline:** When you use this method, you tell Xpress Pro exactly what piece of your source clip you want to edit into your sequence and where you want the source clip to begin in your sequence. The only thing that might be unclear is where the clip will end in your sequence (**Figure 6.10**).

◆ **Mark In in the source monitor, with Mark In/Mark Out in the Timeline:** With this method, you set only the beginning (the In point) of the source clip; you don't care when it will end. In your sequence, however, you specify exactly where you want the source clip to begin and end (**Figure 6.11**).

There's an alternative to these two scenarios, in which you set a lone Out point instead of a lone In point in one monitor, performing what's called a back-timed edit. (For more information, see "Performing Back-Timed Edits" later in this chapter.)

Figure 6.10 Here, the source clip is marked with In and Out points and the Timeline is marked with an In point. This is a very common way of performing a three-point edit.

The title will go here.

Figure 6.11 Here, the source clip is marked with an In point and the Timeline V2 is marked with In and Out points that match the beginning and ending of a clip on V1. The incoming title will be edited on top of the V1 clip (the title's background), matching its length.

Creating Subclips and Subsequences

Essentially, a subclip is a shorter section of a master clip, and a subsequence is a shorter section of a sequence. Xpress Pro lists subclips as separate entities in your bin, and you can use them like any regular master clip. Subsequences behave just like ordinary sequences.

You might want to create subclips in the following circumstances:

◆ If you have long master clips, you will probably want to break them up into shorter subclips, so you don't have to shuttle through so much footage while editing.

◆ If you know you want to use a particular section of your sequence elsewhere in the same sequence or in another sequence, you should create a subclip.

You create a subclip or subsequence by marking In and Out points either in a source monitor or the clipboard monitor. (For more information about the clipboard monitor, see "Using the Clipboard Monitor" later in this chapter.)

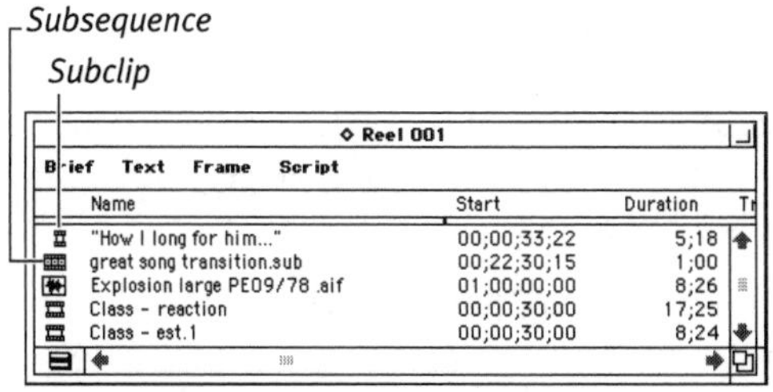

Subsequence

Subclip

Figure 6.12 A subclip created from a master clip has a unique subclip icon. A subsequence has a normal sequence icon. Make sure you give your subclip creations helpful names.

To create a subclip or subsequence:

1. *Do one of the following:*

▲ Load a source clip into a source monitor.

▲ Select ⬚ Copy to Clipboard on the Edit tab of the Command palette to load a section of your Timeline into the clipboard and open the clipboard monitor.

2. Mark In and Out points in the source or clipboard monitor to designate the piece of footage that you want to save as a subclip.

3. Click to select the open bin in which you want to keep your new subclip.

When you create a subclip, Xpress Pro will place it in the most recently selected bin.

4. *Do one of the following:*

▲ On the Edit tab of the Command palette, click Make Subclip.

▲ Press and hold Alt (Windows) or Option (Mac) and drag the picture area of the monitor to a bin.

Xpress Pro creates a subclip or subsequence and places it in the most recently selected bin (**Figure 6.12**).

✔ Tips

■ Creating a subsequence with the clipboard monitor is a great way to take out a section of your main movie sequence and experiment with it. If your experimentation works, overwrite into your main movie sequence. If it doesn't work, keeping the original work intact.

■ Creating a subclip does not create any new source media files. A subclip merely references the source media behind a master clip or sequence.

MARKING IN AND OUT POINTS

Using the Play Controls

Xpress Pro has numerous play controls you can use to play audio and video in a source monitor or the Composer/Timeline. **Table 6.2** summarizes the various play controls found on both the Play and Move tabs of the Command palette.

Xpress Pro's most useful play buttons—Play Reverse, Pause, and Play Forward—are mapped to the J, K, and L keys, conveniently just below the I and O keys, which are used for Mark In and Mark Out. This configuration allows you to quickly play and mark clips with minimal movement in your right hand. (See the sidebar "The Power of the J-K-L Keys" on the next page.)

You can remap the J-K-L keys to any other keys, and you can map play and move buttons (as with any buttons) to the following areas of the interface: the Composer toolbar, the Tool palette, and the Timeline toolbar. You can even use the play buttons directly from the Command palette as long as you select Active Palette at the bottom of the window.

Table 6.2

Play and Move Buttons	
BUTTON	**FUNCTION**
▶ **Play:**	Plays your clip forward at normal speed. Pressing it a second time stops playback.
▶ **Play Forward:**	Plays your clip forward. By tapping it up to five times in succession, you can play up to 8X normal speed.
◀ **Play Reverse:**	Plays your clip in reverse. By tapping it up to five times in succession, you can play up to 8X normal speed.
▮▶ **Step Forward:**	Moves the position indicator one frame forward.
◀▮ **Step Backward:**	Moves the position indicator one frame backward.
▮▮▶ **Step Forward 10 Frames:**	Moves the position indicator 10 frames forward.
◀▮▮ **Step Backward 10 Frames:**	Moves the position indicator 10 frame backward.
▮▮ **Pause:**	Halts playback.
▮◀ **Go to In:**	Jumps the position indicator to the In mark in the selected monitor.
▶▮ **Go to Out:**	Jumps the position indicator to the Out mark in the selected monitor.
▮◀ **Go to Audio Mark In:**	Moves the position indicator to an audio In point.
▶▮ **Go to Audio Mark Out:**	Moves the position indicator to an audio Out point.
▮◀ **Go to Start:**	In the source monitor, jumps the position indicator to the start of the clip. In the Timeline/Composer, jumps to the start of the sequence.
▶▮ **Go to End:**	In the source monitor, jumps the position indicator to the end of the clip. In the Timeline/Composer, jumps to the end of the sequence.
▶▮ **Play to Out:**	No matter where the position indicator is, plays the clip to the Out point and then stops.
▮▶▮ **Play In to Out:**	No matter where the position indicator is, plays the clip from the In point to the Out point.
↕ **Play Loop:**	In the Composer or Timeline, plays from the In to the Out point over and over again until you press the spacebar to stop playback.
▮↕ **Audio Loop Play:**	Lets you preview audio effects or EQ adjustments. (See Chapter 12, "Working with Audio.")
PL **Play Length Toggle:**	With either the Composer or a source monitor selected, when you click Play, plays your clip or sequence for 1 minute and then stops. To turn off this behavior, click this button again.

Figure 6.13 To loop play between In and Out points in a source monitor or the Timeline/Composer, hold down Alt (Windows) or Option (Mac) and click the Audio Play Loop button. Xpress Pro plays between the In/Out marks until you press the spacebar to stop it.

✔ Tips

- If you want to *loop* play between In and Out points in a source monitor or the Timeline/Composer, hold down Alt (Windows) or Option (Mac) and change the Audio Play Loop button (**Figure 6.13**).

- If you click Play in the Timeline and the Composer window merely blinks, another window obscures some portion of the Composer window. Move the Composer window so nothing covers it and click Play again.

The Power of the J-K-L Keys

For many editors, the keys to the kingdom are J, K, and L. Mapping Play Reverse, Pause, and Play Forward to these keys is very convenient because, with Mark In and Mark Out mapped to the I and O keys, you can play and mark clips all with just a few fingers (**Figure 6.14**).

By holding or tapping various combinations of the J-K-L keys, you can easily scrub and shuttle to play your video and hear your audio at various speeds.

- **One frame forward:** Hold down K (Pause) and tap L (Play Forward) once.

- **One frame backward:** Hold down K and tap J (Play Reverse) once.

- **2X, 3X, 5X, 8X speed forward:** Tap the L key two, three, four, or five times in succession.

- **2X, 3X, 5X, 8X speed backward:** Tap the J key two, three, four, or five times in succession.

- **Slow-motion forward:** Hold down the K and L keys.

- **Slow-motion reverse:** Hold down the K and J keys.

When speeding forward or backward, you will always be able to hear your audio while you watch the video image, except when you play at 8X speed. At that speed, the audio drops out.

(For more information on audio scrubbing, see "Scrubbing Audio" in Chapter 12.)

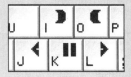

Figure 6.14 The most common keyboard mapping for editors. J, K, and L are mapped to Play Reverse, Pause, and Play Forward. Right above them, I and O are mapped to Mark In and Mark Out.

USING THE PLAY CONTROLS

Manually Scrubbing Through Clips and Sequences

You can navigate through source clips or sequences by dragging the mouse along the source or Composer play bar or in the tracks area of the Timeline.

To hear your audio as you scrub—called a *digital scrub*—hold down the Shift key as you scrub (**Figure 6.15**).

(For more information on scrubbing through audio, see "Scrubbing Audio" in Chapter 12)

✔ Tip

- You can configure your digital scrub settings in the Audio Settings dialog box.

Shift-clicking the Step Forward button scrubs one frame at a time.

Figure 6.15 To digitally scrub through your footage, hold down Shift and drag the position indicator to the left or right, or hold down Shift and click the Step Forward or Step Backward button.

USING THE PLAY CONTROLS

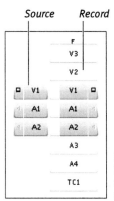

Source   Record

Figure 6.16 In this case, the source clip contains one video track and two audio tracks.

Patching and Selecting Tracks

For those new to the Avid way of editing, using the patch panel at the far left of the Timeline is often the trickiest skill to master.

Patching and selecting tracks in the patch panel tells Xpress Pro two things: which tracks from the source clip or sequence you want to edit in the Timeline, and which record tracks in the Timeline you want to activate to receive those patched source tracks.

◆ **Patching:** When you load a source clip into a source monitor, source patch buttons automatically appear on the source side of the patch panel in the Timeline, corresponding to the number of tracks in the incoming source clip. A typical source clip has one video and two audio tracks (**Figure 6.16**).

◆ **Selecting:** You may not want to activate all patched tracks for every edit, so selecting a source or record track is the second step after patching. This tells Xpress Pro that you definitely want to activate the selected source and record tracks for this particular edit.

(For some patching/selecting strategies, see the sidebar "Make Your Life Easier with Auto-Patching" later in this chapter.)

To patch one or more source tracks to one or more record tracks:

1. Load a clip into a source monitor.

   A certain number of source track buttons appear on the far left of the Timeline, depending on how many tracks the source clip contains (**Figure 6.17**).

2. To patch a source track to a particular record track, *do one of the following:*

   ▲ Hold down the mouse on a source patch button and drag the arrow that appears to the desired record track button (**Figure 6.18**).

   ▲ Hold down the mouse on a source track button and choose a record track from the list that appears (**Figure 6.19**).

   The source track button moves next to its assigned record track button, and the record track button automatically becomes selected.

✔ Tip

■ If you don't want to edit a particular source track into the Timeline, you need to deselect its patch button.

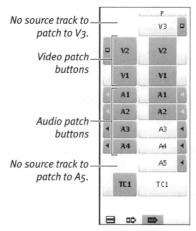

No source track to patch to V3.

Video patch buttons

Audio patch buttons

No source track to patch to A5.

Figure 6.17 Here, a sequence was loaded into the source monitor, and there are more than the typical number of tracks. Patch buttons show that there are two incoming video tracks and four incoming audio tracks.

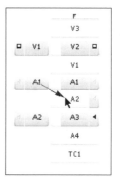 

Figure 6.18 Here, A1 is repatched from the A1 record track to the A2 record track (left). Automatically, the A1 record track button is deselected, and the A2 record track button is selected (right).

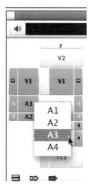

Figure 6.19 You can also patch a source track to a record track by clicking and holding on a patch button and choosing a record track number from the two audio tracks, so their corresponding patch buttons appear in the Timeline.

A Selected Track Minus a Patch Equals Black

If you select a record track with no source button patched to it, Xpress Pro will edit black filler onto that track, which may not be your intention.

For example, if you patch your source video to V2 but keep V1 as well as V2 selected, then the video track will be edited onto V2, *plus* black filler will be edited onto V1.

In this example, if you don't want that black filler in V1, deselect its record button before making the edit (**Figure 6.20**).

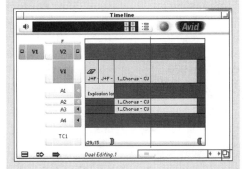

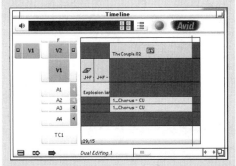

Figure 6.20 Here, an incoming title is patched to V2, and V2 is selected. However, the V1 record track is also selected (above). The result: The edit will overwrite the segment on V1 with black filler (below). The lesson: Be careful about what record tracks you select, even if no source track is patched to them.

To select or deselect a track:

◆ To select a track, click its source track button or record track button.

◆ To deselect a track, click it again.

✔ Tips

■ You can map record track buttons (on the Edit tab of the Command palette) to your keyboard. Pressing a record track button selects or deselects a record track.

■ To select all tracks, press Ctrl+A (Windows) or Command+A (Mac). To deselect all tracks, press Ctrl+Shift+A (Windows) or Command+Shift+A (Mac).

■ You can also select record or source track buttons by dragging a lasso around them with the pointer.

■ You cannot edit deselected source tracks into the Timeline, regardless of the record track selection.

Fast Ways to Select Record Tracks

To select many, but not all, tracks at once, press Ctrl+A (Windows) or Command+A (Mac) to select all of the record tracks. Then you can individually deselect the few you don't need.

Or do the opposite: If all of your record tracks are selected in the Timeline and you need a few or none at all selected, press Shift+Ctrl+A (Windows) or Shift+Command+A (Mac) to deselect all of the record tracks. Then select the few that you need.

Click the Cycle Picture/Sound button (on the Edit tab of the Command palette) to cycle through the following track selections:

◆ All Tracks Selected

◆ Video Tracks Only Selected

◆ Audio Tracks Only Selected

◆ Neither Video nor Audio Tracks Selected

Make Your Life Easier with Auto-Patching

If you want to limit your worries to merely selecting tracks, you can avoid the extra effort of patching by turning on the Auto-Patching feature on the Edit tab of your Timeline settings.

With Auto-Patching enabled, Xpress Pro automatically patches a source track to whatever record track you select. For example, if the video source track is currently patched to the V1 record track, selecting the V2 record track button automatically moves the V1 patch to V2.

For example, using the following approach, the source clips are automatically patched to your selected record tracks, and you don't have to worry about other selected tracks.

1. Load a source clip and mark In and/or Out points.

2. Deselect all tracks.
   Press Ctrl+Shift+A (Windows) or Command+Shift+A (Mac).

3. Select your record tracks.

Click the record track buttons according to where you want to edit your source tracks (or map those buttons to your keyboard and press them).

Xpress Pro automatically patches source tracks to selected record tracks.

The one caveat is this: No matter what you select, the source video track will remain patched to the *first* selected video record track, and the two source audio tracks remain patched to the *first two* selected audio tracks.

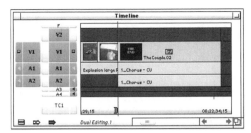

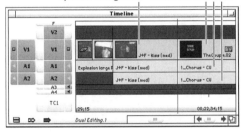

Segments pushed
Spliced-in segment   down the Timeline

Figure 6.21 When you mark a point in the Timeline (above) and select Splice-In everything on selected tracks in the Timeline makes room for the incoming segment (below).

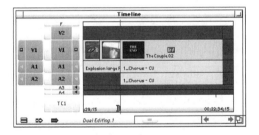

Figure 6.22 When you mark a point in the Timeline (above) and select Overwrite anything in the incoming clip's way is overwritten in the Timeline (below).

Performing Splice-in and Overwrite Edits

Splice-in and overwrite edits are the two most commonly used types of edits used in Xpress Pro to get clips into your sequence.

◆ ⬭ **Splice-in:** Edits a clip or other object into the Timeline *without* replacing or overwriting anything. Instead, it inserts the clip into your sequence, pushing everything to the right of its insertion point, down the Timeline. A splice-in edit adds to the overall duration of the sequence and can therefore affect audio-video sync (**Figure 6.21**).

◆ ⬭ **Overwrite:** Edits a clip into the Timeline and replaces anything in its way by overwriting it. Nothing gets pushed down the Timeline, and the overall duration of the sequence remains unchanged (**Figure 6.22**).

For the typical applications of splice-in and overwrite edits, see the sidebar "Three-Point Editing" earlier in this chapter.

Splice-in and overwrite edits are also used with drag-and-drop editing in Segment modes. See "Drag-and-Drop Edits in Segment Mode" later in this chapter for more information.

To perform a splice-in edit:

1. Load a clip in a source monitor and mark In and/or Out points.

2. Mark In and/or Out points in the Timeline.

3. Patch the source tracks to the desired record tracks.

4. Select the record tracks to which you want to send the source clip.

5. On the Fast menu of the Composer or the Edit tab of Command palette, click the yellow Splice-in button.

   Xpress Pro edits your source tracks onto the patched and selected record tracks by pushing all track material located to the right of the In point down the Timeline, to the right, to make room for the incoming clip.

   (For information on variations in track behavior during this type of edit, see "Working with Audio-Video Sync" later in this chapter.)

✔ Tips

- As with an overwrite edit, if you do not mark an Out point in the source monitor, Xpress Pro uses the end of your clip as the source Out point. With no In point in the source monitor, Xpress Pro uses the beginning of the clip as the source In point.

- If you do not mark an In point in the Timeline when performing an edit, Xpress Pro uses the position indicator's location as the In point.

- The yellow Splice-in button is mapped by default to the left of the Composer Fast menu in Source/Record mode and also appears on the Edit tab of the Command palette.

Laying in a Sound Bed for Dialogue and Narration

Editors often cut scenes with dialogue, interviews, and narration based on where they want the words and sounds of the dialogue to begin and end, rather than on where they want the images to begin.

The idea is to piece together the meaning, pacing, and rhythm of the scene based on the audio before worrying about the images. Constructing your first cut with simple butt cuts based on the audio rather than the video is known as *laying in the sound bed*.

After editing the audio/video source clips into the Timeline as butt cuts, you can switch to Trim mode and use roller trims to determine where the video begins and ends.

This method of creating overlapping edits using Trim mode can be simpler than preoverlapping audio and video in a source monitor with the Audio Mark In and Audio Mark Out commands. The method you use is your choice.

(For more information on Trim mode, see Chapter 7, "Fine-Tuning Your Edits".)

To perform an overwrite edit:

1. Load a clip in a source monitor and mark In and/or Out points.

2. Mark In and/or Out points in the Timeline.

3. Patch the source tracks to the desired record tracks.

4. Select the tracks to which you want to send the source clip.

5. On the Fast menu of the Composer, click the red Overwrite button.

   Xpress Pro edits your source tracks onto the patched/selected record tracks and writes the new incoming clip over anything in the way. With an overwrite edit, nothing moves in the Timeline to make room for the incoming clip, so the sequence duration does not change, and audio-video sync remains unaffected.

✔ Tips

- The red Overwrite button is mapped by default to the right of the Composer Fast menu in Source/Record mode and also appears on the Edit tab of the Command palette.

- As with a splice-in edit, if you do not mark an In point in the Timeline when performing an edit, Xpress Pro uses the position indicator's location as the In point.

- If you do not mark an Out point in the source monitor, Xpress Pro uses the end of your clip as the source Out point. With no In point in the source monitor, Xpress Pro uses the beginning of the clip as the source In point.

- For overwrite and splice-in edits, you typically mark three In and Out points. You use four points only for fit-to-fill edits.

- If you set an In point at the very beginning of the Timeline, a Mark In symbol does not appear in the window, but it's there; you just can't see it!

Performing Lift and Extract Edits

After you edit clips into your sequence, you can move any marked portion of them elsewhere in the Timeline or delete them altogether with a lift or extract edit.

Material that is lifted or extracted is always placed on the clipboard, the monitor that you can then use to reinsert the material elsewhere in your sequence using either a splice-in or overwrite edit.

Typically, you need to mark In and Out points in the Timeline first and then click the Lift or Extract button to remove the marked material and copy it to the clipboard. You can also use lift and extract edits in Segment mode to delete entire clip segments without marking In and Out points in the Timeline.

◆ **Lift:** Clicking this button on the toolbar at the top of the Timeline (or on the Edit tab of the Command palette) deletes a marked Timeline section and leaves black filler (a gap) in its place. You can think of a lift edit as the reverse of an overwrite edit.

Like an overwrite edit, a lift edit does not affect the overall duration of your sequence and therefore will not cause an out-of-sync situation (**Figure 6.23**).

Marked material to be deleted

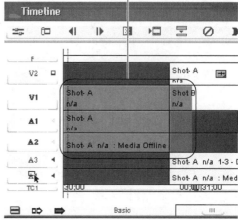

Black filler replacement

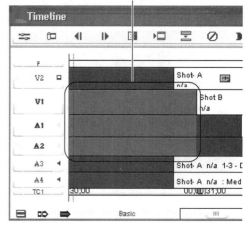

Figure 6.23 When you mark a section of your Timeline with In and Out points (above) and press Lift, the marked section of your sequence is replaced with black filler (below).

Material marked for extraction

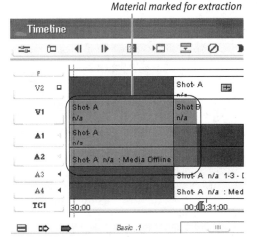

Selected tracks move left to fill the gap.

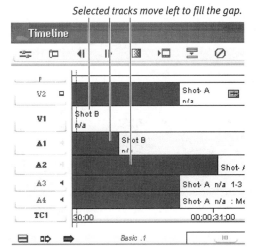

Figure 6.24 When you mark a section of your Timeline with In and Out points (above) and press Extract, the marked section of your sequence is removed and selected tracks push to the left, filling the resulting gap (below).

◆ **Extract:** Clicking this button on the toolbar at the top of the Timeline (or on the Edit tab of the Command palette) deletes a marked Timeline section and causes all material located to the right of the edit on the selected tracks to shift upstream, to the left, to close the remaining gap. An extract edit is essentially the reverse of a splice-in edit.

Like a splice-in edit, an extract edit shortens the overall duration of the sequence, and the subsequent shift of downstream material can cause an unwanted out-of-sync condition (**Figure 6.24**).

See "Working with Audio-Video Sync" later in this chapter for information on how to fix or avoid unwanted out-of-sync conditions.

PERFORMING LIFT AND EXTRACT EDITS

To perform a lift or extract edit:

1. Mark In and Out points in the Timeline/
   Composer at the beginning and end of
   the material you want to lift or extract.

2. Select the tracks you want to affect with
   the lift or extract edit.

3. Click the Lift or Extract button on the
   toolbar at the top of the Timeline
   (**Figure 6.25**).

   A lift edit removes the material from all
   selected tracks, leaving behind a gap with
   black filler. An extract edit removes the
   marked material and moves all downstream clip segments to the left, to close
   up the gap. Both the lift and extract edits
   place the removed material on the clipboard for further editing.

✔ Tip

■ Splice-in, overwrite, lift, and extract edits
can sometimes leave behind a few frames
of lost clips or tiny gaps here and there
that are hard to see in a long sequence.
To find these flash frames in your
Timeline, right-click (Windows) or
Control-click (Mac) in the Timeline and
choose Find Flash Frame from the pop-
up menu (**Figure 6.26**).

To learn how to perform lift and extract
editing in drag-and-drop Segment mode,
see the section "Drag-and-Drop Edits in
Segment Mode," also in this chapter.

Extract   Lift

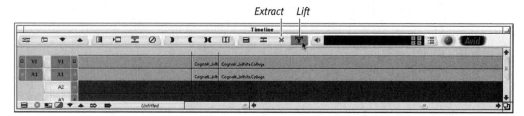

Figure 6.25 By default, the Lift and Extract buttons are mapped to your Timeline toolbar, but you have to size the Timeline to be long in order to see the buttons.

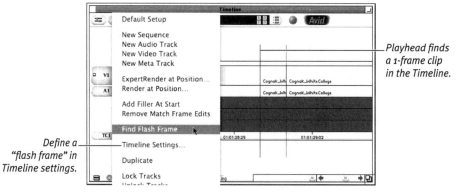

Playhead finds a 1-frame clip in the Timeline.

Define a "flash frame" in Timeline settings.

Figure 6.26 To find flash (potentially unwanted) frames in your Timeline, right-click (Windows) or Ctrl+Shift-click (Mac) in the Timeline and choose Find Flash Frame. The maximum number of frames in a flash frame are defined in your active Timeline settings.

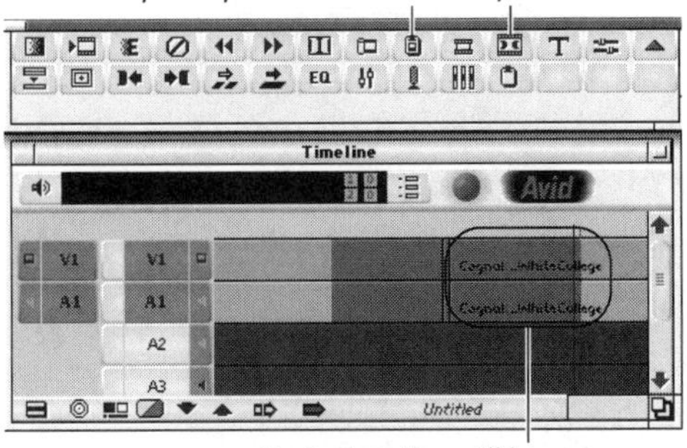

Click "Clipboard Contents"   *The Copy to*
to open clipboard monitor   *Clipboard button*

Marked section will be
loaded in clipboard

Figure 6.27 You can load the marked section of the Timeline into the clipboard monitor by clicking Lift, Extract, or Copy to Clipboard.

Using the Clipboard Monitor

You can think of the clipboard monitor as a specialized source monitor into which you can quickly load material from one or more tracks of a sequence so you can edit it back into that sequence or another sequence, at a new location. In that regard, the clipboard monitor works just like a typical clipboard in any word processing application.

However, the advantage of using a clipboard monitor over a source monitor for loading and editing part of a sequence into another sequence is this: Before you load part of a sequence into the clipboard monitor, you can designate which tracks of the sequence you want to use.

In contrast, if you load a full sequence with many tracks into a typical source monitor, you have to worry about turning particular patch buttons on and off and marking In and Out points before you can edit just the section you want back into a new location.

To load a section of a sequence into the clipboard monitor:

1. In the Timeline, select the tracks containing the material you want to load into the Clipboard, then mark In and Out points at the start and end of the section you want to load.

2. *Do one of the following* (**Figure 6.27**):
   - ▲ Click the Copy to Clipboard button on the top toolbar on the Timeline (or on the Edit tab of the Command palette) to leave the marked material in the Timeline.

continues on next page

USING THE CLIPBOARD MONITOR

▲ Click the Lift button on the top tool-bar on the Timeline (or on the Edit tab of the Command palette) to remove the marked section of the sequence and leave a gap of black filler in its place.

▲ Click the Extract button on the top toolbar on the Timeline (or on the Edit tab of the Command palette) to remove the marked section of the sequence and ripple the remaining segments to the left, to fill the gap.

3. Choose Tools > Clipboard Monitor.

The clipboard monitor opens and contains the material that has been lifted, extracted, or copied. You can treat the material in the clipboard monitor like anything you might load into a source monitor.

Use the Splice-in, Overwrite, or Fit to Fill button to edit the clipboard footage into a sequence.

✔ Tips

■ You can also view the clipboard monitor by clicking the "Clipboard Contents" button, found by default in the Composer Fast menu (the Tool Palette) and in the Edit tab of the Command palette.

■ You can see the tracks that have been loaded in the clipboard by clicking the upper-right corner of the monitor (**Figure 6.28**).

■ If you perform an extract- or lift-style delete operation using the Delete key instead of the Lift or Extract button, nothing will be loaded into the clipboard monitor. This can be useful if you have something already loaded into the clipboard that you want to use, but you want to delete other material in the sequence before you edit the clipboard material back in.

A video and audio track loaded in the clipboard

Figure 6.28 Click on the upper-right corner of the clipboard monitor to check which tracks were loaded.

■ Remember that like almost all commands and buttons in Xpress Pro, the Lift, Extract, and Copy to Clipboard buttons can be mapped to the Tool palette, the Timeline top toolbar, the Composer, or keys on the keyboard.

For more information on copying, lifting, and extracting whole clip segments to the clipboard, see "Drag-and-Drop Edits in Segment Mode" later in this chapter.

Performing Back-Timed Edits

When making standard three-point edits, editors are usually concerned with where a source clip begins in the source monitor and where the head of the clip will start in the Timeline once the edit takes place. However, sometimes the timing of an edit hinges on what frame a source clip *ends* in the source monitor or where that clip's tail frame will *finish* in the Timeline.

Such a back-timed edit is controlled by a single Out point in either the source monitor or Composer/Timeline and typically features one of the two following configurations of a three-point edit:

◆ A single source monitor Out point and an In and Out point in the Timeline

◆ An In and Out point in the source monitor and a single Out point in the Timeline

For instance, you may have a shot of a boy with his hands on his face. As the shot proceeds, his hands go down and he looks up at the camera, dejected. You don't care when this shot begins. You just know that you want the shot to end right when the boy looks up at the camera.

To perform a back-timed edit:

1. Set an Out point for the source clip.

   In the example, this is on the frame when the boy looks up at the camera (**Figure 6.29**).

2. Set an Out point in the Timeline to match the Out point of the source clip.

3. In either the Timeline or the source monitor, set an In point where you want the source clip to start.

4. Patch and select the appropriate tracks and click the Splice-in or Overwrite button.

   The Out point of the source clip now is cut in next to the Out point on the Timeline, and the edit is considered to be back-timed. The In point of the source clip is determined by the In point marked in the Timeline or source monitor.

PERFORMING BACK-TIMED EDITS

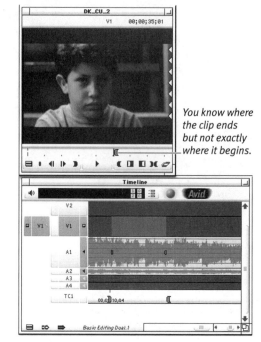

You know where the clip ends but not exactly where it begins.

Figure 6.29 With this back-timed edit, there is an Out point in the source monitor and an In and Out point in the Timeline. In this kind of edit, you care mostly about where the incoming clip will end, and not so much about where it will begin.

*The position indicator is
on the source sync frame.*

*The position
indicator is on
the sequence
sync frame.*

The sync frames line up.

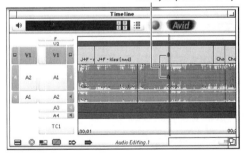

Figure 6.30 A replace edit is an effective way to
perform a sync edit, aligning a frame in your source
monitor with a frame in your sequence. In this case,
no source monitor or Timeline In and Out points are
necessary (above). The replace edit replaces the
segment underneath the Timeline playhead (below).

Performing Replace Edits

A replace edit is a specialized variation
of an overwrite edit that replaces one or
more video or audio clips in the Timeline
with one or more video or audio clips in the
source monitor.

To determine the exact placement of the
new clip segment in the Timeline, a replace
edit matches the frame under the position
indicator (playhead) in the source monitor
with the frame under the position indicator
in the Timeline. Unlike a typical three-point
overwrite edit, a replace edit does not match
up In and Out points.

A replace edit does not require In or Out
points in the source monitor or Timeline.
Xpress Pro simply replaces the existing content of a Timeline segment with new content, without changing the duration of the
Timeline segment (**Figure 6.30**).

A replace edit is also known as a sync edit
because it allows you to match a visual or
audio cue in your source clip with an audio
or video cue in your Timeline.

To perform a replace edit:

1. In the source monitor, play to the frame that you want to sync with a frame in the Timeline and park the position indicator there.

2. In the Timeline, play to the frame that you want to sync with the frame in the source monitor and park the position indicator there.

3. Patch the source track to the record track that contains the segment you want to replace and select the record track button.

4. On the Edit tab of the Command palette, click Replace Edit.

   Xpress Pro edits the source clip into the Timeline by matching the frame under the source monitor position indicator with the frame under the Timeline play-head on the selected record tracks.

Insufficient Content Warning

If you get an "Insufficient content to make this edit" error message when trying to perform a replace edit, you don't have enough media in the source clip to totally replace the content of the clip in the Timeline.

You will have to move the position indicator in the source monitor or In and Out points in the Timeline to make the replace edit.

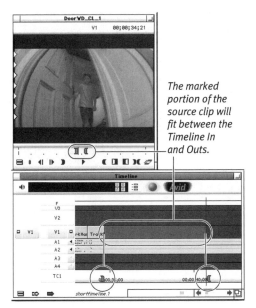

The marked portion of the source clip will fit between the Timeline In and Outs.

Figure 6.31 In a fit-to-fill edit, you mark In and Out points in both the source monitor and the Timeline/Composer. To perform the edit, Xpress Pro applies a motion effect to the incoming source clip.

Performing Fit-to-Fill Edits

A ⬚ fit-to-fill edit changes the playback speed of the source video clip to make it fit into and exactly fill a marked space of fixed duration in the Timeline.

Xpress Pro applies a motion effect to the segment, either speeding it up or slowing it down. Hence, this edit function is a four-point edit and requires you to mark In and Out points in both the source monitor and the Timeline (**Figure 6.31**).

Unfortunately, you cannot use Fit to Fill with audio segments, since motion effects do not apply to audio. Instead, you have to use an AudioSuite plug-in such as Time Compression Expansion to slow down or speed up audio. (See the sidebar "Slowing Down or Speeding Up an Audio or Video Clip" in Chapter 12.)

To perform a fit-to-fill edit:

1. Mark In and Out points in the Timeline and select the record track where you want the source clip to appear.

2. Load a source clip into a source clip monitor and mark In and Out points.

3. Patch the incoming source tracks to the selected record tracks.

4. On the Edit tab of the Command palette, click the Fit to Fill button.

5. In the dialog box that appears, select or create a bin for the required motion effect and click OK (**Figure 6.32**).

   The source clip appears in the Timeline, either sped up or slowed down to fill the designated space.

Figure 6.32
Select a bin, such as the one labeled Motion Effects, in which to store the new motion effect that Fit to Fill creates. Then click OK.

✔ Tips

- If you don't set an In point, Xpress Pro uses the beginning of the clip as the In point; if you don't set an Out point, Xpress Pro uses the end of the clip as the Out point.

- To use Fit to Fill without rendering the resultant motion effect, press Alt (Windows) or Option (Mac) when you click Fit to Fill.

Performing Overlap Edits

A simple edit with an audio-video clip where the audio and video tracks both begin and end at the same edit point is called a butt edit.

On the other hand, an edit where the audio and video tracks of your incoming source clip *do not* begin or end at the same time is called an overlap edit. Overlap edits are most commonly used when you want to hear a character speak before you actually see the person.

You can always create an overlap edit in Trim mode by rolling the video or audio edit point separately, after you've made an initial butt edit. (For more information on trimming, see Chapter 7, "Fine-Tuning Your Edits.")

However, thanks to Audio Mark In and Audio Mark Out (on the Edit tab of the Command palette), you can set up an overlap cut before you actually perform your edit.

The following task presents an example of one possible overlap edit, where the audio of a character talking begins before we see the video image of the character talking.

To perform an overlap edit:

1. From the Tools menu, open the Command palette, click the Edit tab, and click the Active Palette button to activate the Audio Mark In and Audio Mark Out buttons.

2. In the source monitor, click Audio Mark In on the frame where you want the audio dialogue to begin.

3. Click Mark In on the frame where you want the video image to start and Mark Out on the frame where you want the video image to end.

4. (Optional) If you want the audio to end on a different frame than the video, click Audio Mark Out on the frame where you want the audio dialogue to end.

5. In the Timeline, find the frame where you want the incoming image to begin and click Mark In (**Figure 6.33**).

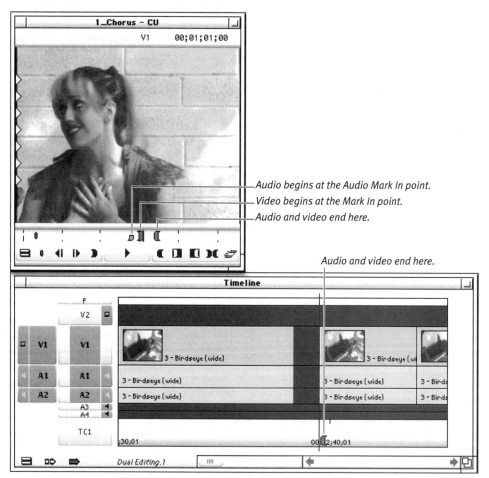

Audio begins at the Audio Mark In point.
Video begins at the Mark In point.
Audio and video end here.

Audio and video end here.

Figure 6.33 In overlap edits, you use Audio Mark In and Audio Mark Out to tell Xpress Pro where to begin and end your incoming audio. You use Mark In and Mark Out to tell Xpress Pro where to begin and end your video.

6. Click Overwrite to perform the edit.

The clip is edited into the Timeline, and its audio begins before its video (**Figure 6.34**). In other words, the character starts speaking before you actually see her.

continues on next page

Source clip's audio starts earlier than its video.   Source clip's video starts later than its audio.

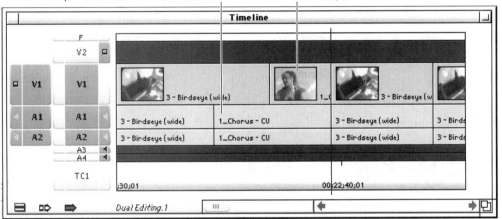

Figure 6.34 The result of an overlap edit is that the incoming video and audio tracks do not start and/or end at the same point.

What Are L-Cuts, J-Cuts, and Split Edits?

L-cuts, J-cuts, and split edits are all terms that have been inherited from the crafts of film and linear tape-to-tape editing. They all refer to specific types of overlap edits where synced audio and video—typically dialogue—begin at different times.

A **J-cut** is any cut where the synced audio begins before the video and we hear a person speak before we see the person. A J-cut is also known as an audio lead-in and is a very common cut in narrative sequences with dialogue.

An **L-cut** is any cut where the synced audio Out point extends past the video and we hear the previous shot's dialogue continue after we cut to the video of the next incoming shot.

A **split edit** is any overlap cut in which the audio and video have different starting points or different ending points. A split-edit clip can begin with a J-cut and end with an L-cut and can also be called simply an overlap edit.

✔ Tips

■ When you use Audio Mark In or Audio Mark Out points in the source monitor or Timeline, regular Mark In and Mark Out points always represent the *video* In and Out points.

■ You can map the Audio Mark In and Audio Mark Out buttons to a more convenient location, such as the source monitor's Fast menu, if you use them often. See Chapter 3, "Customizing Your Workspace," for more information.

■ Xpress Pro always performs an overlap edit by lining up the Mark In or Mark Out points in the source monitor and the Timeline. You cannot use the Audio Mark In or Audio Mark Out points as your timing reference for overlap edits (**Figure 6.35**).

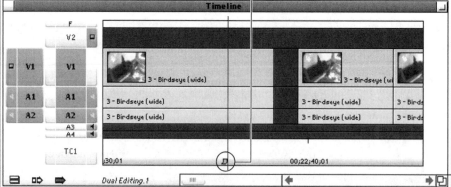

An Audio Mark In point is not sufficient.

Figure 6.35 Xpress Pro will not be able to perform this edit correctly. You must have at least one In or Out point marked in both the source monitor and the Timeline.

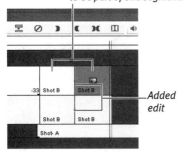

These two segments used to be part of one segment.

Added edit

Figure 6.36 In this case, adding an effect to one part of a shot and not the other required splitting the segment using Add Edit.

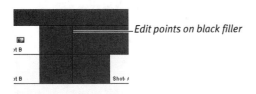

Edit points on black filler

Figure 6.37 Even black filler is susceptible to Add Edit.

Adding Edit Points

Sometimes you need to force an edit point in the Timeline, essentially splitting one segment into two. To do this, use the ⊼ Add Edit button.

The reasons for splitting segments include the following:

◆ You need to add an effect to only part of a segment (**Figure 6.36**).

◆ You need to move part of a segment elsewhere.

After you initially split a clip with Add Edit, an equal sign appears at the new edit point. This means that the two segments are part of a continuous (formerly joined) image. But if you move one of the segments elsewhere, the equal sign disappears.

To create an edit point on a segment:

1. Place the position indicator on the point in the Timeline where you want to split one or more segments.

2. Select the tracks that contain the segments you want to split.

3. On the Timeline toolbar or the Edit tab of the Command palette, click Add Edit. Xpress Pro adds an edit point to all segments on selected tracks. A small equal sign appears at every new Add Edit point.

✔ Tips

■ Remember: Add Edit splits segments on *all* selected tracks, so select only the tracks that contain the segments you want to split.

■ Using Add Edit on black filler creates a cut point on the filler (**Figure 6.37**).

To remove an Add Edit point:

1. Place the position indicator on the Add Edit cut point (any edit point that has an equal sign) and select the track that contains it.

2. *Do one of the following:*

▲ Choose Clip > Remove Match Frame Edit.

▲ Click the 🔲 Trim Mode button to enter Trim mode and then press the Delete key.

The split segment become a single segment again. The edit point disappears.

✔ Tip

■ You cannot remove an Add Edit point that is on an audio segment that has audio-level keyframes.

*Two tracks
selected*   *In point*

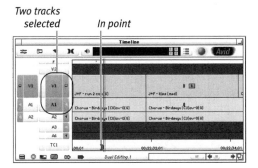

*The heads of both segments
were extended to the left.*

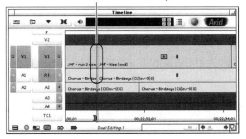

Figure 6.38 To extend the head of one or more segments, first set an In point to the left of an edit point in the Timeline and then select the track containing the segment (above). Click Extend Edit to perform what is essentially a double-roller trim (below).

Extending Edits

If you're coming to Xpress Pro from another application such as Premiere or Final Cut Pro, you may be used to dragging the heads or tails of segments in the Timeline to extend or shorten them. To drag in this way in Xpress Pro requires you to enter Trim mode. In fact, to shorten the head or tail of a segment in Xpress Pro, you must enter Trim mode. (For more information, see the sidebar "Using Trim Mode to Extend or Shorten Segments.")

However, in normal editing mode, you can extend the head or tail of a segment by using the Extend Edit button on the Trim tab of the Command palette.

To extend the head of a segment using Extend Edit:

1. In the Timeline, place the position indicator to the left of the head of a segment, at the point where you want to extend it.

   You can extend more than one segment at a time, but their edit points must be aligned.

2. Select the tracks containing the segments you want to extend.

3. Click Mark In to mark your extension point.

4. Click Extend Edit on the Trim tab of the Command palette.

   Xpress Pro moves the head of the segment back to the In point (**Figure 6.38**). (This is the equivalent of performing a double-roller trim to the left.)

To extend the tail of a segment using Extend Edit:

1. In the Timeline, place the position indicator to the right of the tail of a segment, at the point where you want to extend it.

   You can extend more than one segment at a time, but their edit points must be aligned.

2. Select the tracks containing the segments you want to extend.

3. Click Mark Out to mark your extension point.

4. On the Trim tab of the Command palette, click Active Palette and then click Extend Edit.

   Xpress Pro moves the tail of the segment forward to the Out point. (This is the equivalent of performing a double-roller trim to the right.)

✔ Tip

■ The disadvantage of extending an edit point with Extend Edit versus using Trim mode is that with Extend Edit, you can extend a segment only as far as the next edit point.

Using Trim Mode to Extend or Shorten Edits

You can extend edits while editing normally in the Timeline, but you can both extend *and* shorten segments in Trim mode.

Just remember that Xpress Pro considers black filler to be just as tangible as a video or audio segment, so to extend or shorten a segment that is next to black or another segment without disrupting synchronization, you must use double rollers to trim the edit point.

(For more information on trimming, see Chapter 7, "Fine-Tuning Your Edits.")

Enter the duration here.

Figure 6.39 In this case, the sequence will start with 2 seconds of black.

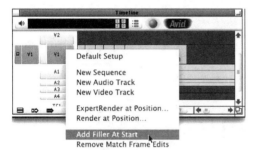

Figure 6.40 The Add Filler at Start option is available on the Timeline context menu (right-click or Ctrl+Shift-click the Timeline).

✔ Tip

■ It does not matter what tracks are patched or selected when you add filler to the start of a sequence. Filler is added to all tracks.

Editing Filler into Your Sequence

Sometimes nothing is actually something, and you may need to edit filler (empty material) into your sequence. Adding filler to a video track means no image (except black) plays on your monitor, while adding filler to an audio track means you hear only silence on that track.

You may want to add filler for the following reasons:

◆ You want to add some empty space to the beginning of your sequence, to provide lead time before your movie starts when it eventually plays on a tape.

◆ You want a placeholder (plus a labeled locator) for a future shot or effect.

◆ You want to fix an audio/video sync problem.

Adding filler to the start of your sequence requires different steps than adding filler elsewhere in your sequence, as you will see in the tasks that follow.

To add filler to the beginning of a sequence:

1. On the Settings tab of the Project window, open the Timeline settings.

2. On the Edit tab of the Timeline Settings dialog box, type a time for Start Filler Duration and click OK (**Figure 6.39**).

   You are now ready to add filler to your Timeline.

3. *Do one of the following:*

   ▲ Select the Timeline window. Choose Clip > Add Filler at Start.

   ▲ Right-click (Windows) or Ctrl+Shift-click (Mac) the Timeline. From the context menu, choose Add Filler at Start (**Figure 6.40**).

To edit filler anywhere in a sequence:

1. With your sequence displayed in the Timeline, choose Clip > Load Filler (**Figure 6.41**).

   A filler source monitor appears containing 2 minutes of black filler (the default amount). The filler behaves just like a regular clip in a source monitor and contains one video track and two silent audio tracks.

2. In the source monitor, use In and Out points to determine the amount of filler you want.

3. In the Timeline, select and patch tracks according to where you want the filler to appear. Mark an In point where you want the filler to begin.

4. Select Overwrite or Splice-in to edit the filler into the sequence (**Figure 6.42**).

✔ Tip

■ Filler cannot be added to the end of a sequence. However, if you want to add a long duration of black to the end of your sequence, a good trick is to add a single frame of a black, blank title to the end of the sequence and then splice in the filler just before that last frame.

Figure 6.41 Choose Clip > Load Filler to load one track of video black filler and two tracks of silent audio into a source monitor.

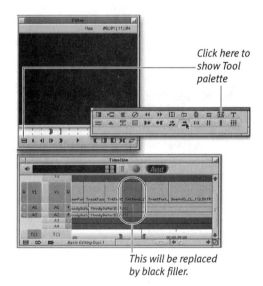

Click here to show Tool palette

This will be replaced by black filler.

Figure 6.42 Here, black filler will be overwritten over the marked section in the Timeline.

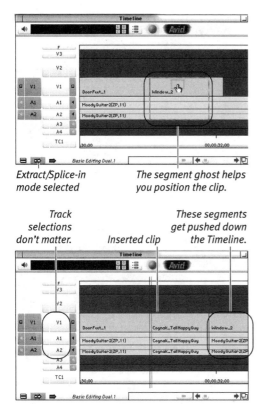

Extract/Splice-in
mode selected

The segment ghost helps
you position the clip.

Track
selections
don't matter.

These segments
get pushed down
the Timeline.

Inserted clip

Figure 6.43 To perform a splice-in drag-and-drop edit, you must first enter Extract/Splice-in mode (above). Then drag and drop a clip from the source monitor to the Timeline (below).

Drag-and-Drop Edits in Segment Mode

Clicking or selecting an editing button is not the only way to perform an edit. You can also drag clips directly from bins or source windows and drop them into the Timeline.

Once you drag a source clip into the Timeline, Xpress Pro calls it a clip segment, or just a segment. If you like, you can reposition the segment while in a Segment mode.

The two Segment modes are Extract/Splice-in and Lift/Overwrite, activated by clicking the Extract/Splice-in and Lift/Overwrite buttons, located by default at the bottom of the Timeline window.

◆ **Extract/Splice-in Segment mode:** Dragging a clip from a bin or source monitor and dropping it into the Timeline results in a splice-in edit (**Figure 6.43**). In the Timeline, selecting and dragging a clip extracts it from its current location and inserts it as a splice-in edit at the location where you drop it.

continues on next page

◆ ⬛⬛ **Lift/Overwrite Segment mode:**
Dragging a clip from a bin or source
monitor and dropping it into the
Timeline results in an overwrite edit. In
the Timeline, selecting and dragging a
clip lifts it from its current location and
inserts it as an overwrite edit at the location where you drop it (**Figure 6.44**).

For a complete description of splice-in and
overwrite edits, see "Performing Splice-in
and Overwrite Edits" earlier in this chapter.

For a complete description of how lift and
extract edits work, see "Performing Lift and
Extract Edits" earlier in this chapter.

To make splice-in or overwrite edits using drag and drop:

1. Mark In and Out points in your source clip.

2. Click the Overwrite or Splice-in Segment
Mode button mapped to the bottom of
the Timeline.

3. Drag your clip from a bin or from a
source monitor to the track in the
Timeline to which you want to edit it.

A ghosted outline of the clip segment
appears in the Timeline, indicating where
Xpress Pro will position the segment
when you drop it. A finger cursor appears,
indicating where the In point of the segment will be placed.

4. Position the segment exactly on the
track where you want it to appear and
release the mouse to drop the segment
onto the track.

The clip segment is edited onto the track,
and the position indicator snaps to the
segment's In point in the Timeline. The
cursor changes from a finger cursor to a
splice-in or overwrite icon, to indicate
the type of edit that you have just made.

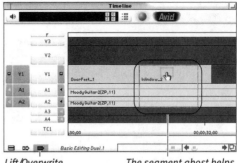

Lift/Overwrite   *The segment ghost helps*
mode selected   *you position the clip.*

The incoming segment
overwrites existing material.

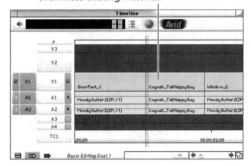

Figure 6.44 In a drag-and-drop overwrite edit, you
must first enter Lift/Overwrite mode (above). Then
drag and drop the a clip into the Timeline (below).

This track will not be
edited into the Timeline.

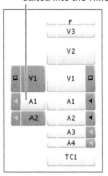

Figure 6.45 For a drag-and-
drop edit, you can disable
certain incoming source tracks
by turning off source patch
buttons before dragging the
clip into the Timeline.

(For more information, see the sidebar
"Drag and Drop: Strategies for Positioning
and Snapping" later in this chapter.)

✔ Tips

- Xpress Pro automatically places you in
  Extract/Splice-in segment mode when
  you drag clips into the Timeline from a
  bin or source monitor, so you don't need
  to click the Splice-in button to perform a
  splice-in edit (unless the red Overwrite
  button is already active).

- If you don't want to include a particular
  source track when you drag and drop a
  segment, load it into a source monitor
  and deselect its source patch button in
  the Timeline patch panel (**Figure 6.45**).

continues on next page

DRAG-AND-DROP EDITS IN SEGMENT MODE

What's So Good about Drag and Drop?

Many people simply prefer to work with one hand on the mouse and the other hand on the
keyboard. However, beyond the ergonomics, there are a few other advantages to drag-and-
drop editing, especially during the rough-in phase of building a sequence.

- **You don't have to worry about patching or selecting record tracks.** Xpress Pro
  ignores all patches and track selections on the record side of the patch panel when you
  drag a clip to the Timeline.

- **You don't have to set In and Out points in the Timeline.** In drag-and-drop editing, you
  can place incoming clips anywhere in the track, without regard to marked In and Out points.

  (For tips on selecting source tracks in Segment mode and for snapping your incoming
  clips to the position indicator or edit points, see the sidebar "Drag and Drop: Strategies for
  Positioning and Snapping" later in this chapter.)

- **You can edit a group of clips simultaneously.** This is a good way to quickly create a
  rough cut after giving your master clips In and Out points.

  (For more information, see the sidebar "Instant Rough Cuts and Storyboard Editing" later
  in this chapter.)

- Xpress Pro allows you to drop a clip that has audio as well as video tracks selected in the source patch panel *only* onto the V1 and A1 + A2 Timeline tracks. If you deselect either the video tracks or audio tracks, you can drop the video-only or audio-only clip segments on any track (**Figure 6.46**).

- Your freedom—or lack of freedom—when positioning clips in the Timeline depends on whether Default Snap to Edit is selected in the Timeline settings. (See the sidebar "Drag and Drop: Strategies for Positioning and Snapping" later in this chapter.)

- You can drag and drop multiple clips into the Timeline with storyboard editing. (See the sidebar, "Instant Rough Cuts and Storyboard Editing" later in this chapter for more information.)

It doesn't matter that the video isn't patched to V2. You can still drop it there.   *The video segment can go on any video track.*

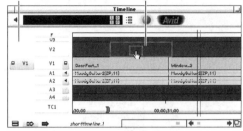

Figure 6.46 If your incoming clip segment is audio only or video only, you can drop it on any track. However, if it contains audio *and* video, Xpress Pro forces you to place the segment on V1, A1, and A2.

Getting Around Xpress Pro's Placement Limitation

If you want to drag and drop a source clip containing both video and audio onto Timeline tracks other than V1, A1, and A2, here's how you do it: Make two edits!

First, load your source clip and deselect its audio source patch buttons in the Timeline. Drag and drop the video portion of the clip onto any track in the Timeline.

Then load the source clip again and deselect its video source patch buttons in the Timeline. Drag and drop the audio portion of the clip on any Timeline track, directly in line with its associated video.

Xpress Pro will never be the wiser.

DRAG-AND-DROP EDITS IN SEGMENT MODE

Drag and Drop: Strategies for Selecting Clips

Whether you need to delete or move one or more segments, you first need to select the segments—and selecting clip segments for drag and drop is not exactly straightforward. There are two principal ways to select one or more segments for drag-and-drop operations:

◆ **The click method:** Click a segment to select it. Select additional segments using Shift-click. Simple, right? But the trick is that you must first select either Extract/Splice-in mode or Lift/Overwrite mode to select segments by clicking.

◆ **The lasso method:** To select segments by lassoing, you must carefully click *above* all of the Timeline tracks, right below the Timeline toolbar (if there is one) and drag *down* and to the *right* (**Figure 6.47**). The tracks containing the segments you lassoed are selected automatically.

(Don't drag right to left instead of left to right, or you'll enter Trim mode and not select anything.)

After you lasso one or more segments, Xpress Pro selects Extract/Splice-in mode by default. If you prefer otherwise, you can choose Lift/Overwrite mode either before or after you lasso one or more segments.

Segment (on A2) will not be selected because it is not entirely lassoed.

Track buttons do not matter when lassoing segments.

Selected segments

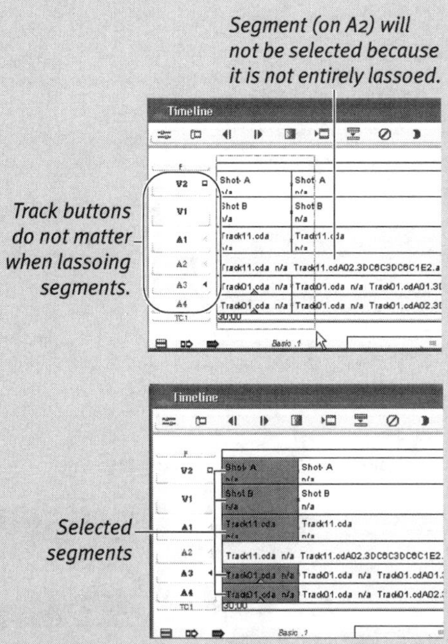

Figure 6.47 To select one or more segments in the Timeline, you can lasso them (above). Only segments completely encircled by the lasso will be selected (below).

Here's a bonus trick when lassoing segments: If you want to lasso one or more segments that are between other segments, hold down Alt (Windows) or Ctrl+Command (Mac), position the cursor right above the segment you want to select, and drag down and to the right (**Figure 6.48**).

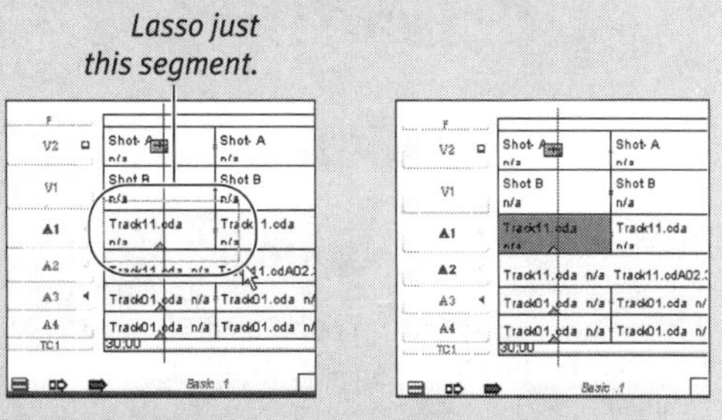

Lasso just this segment.

Figure 6.48 To select one or more segments between tracks, hold down Alt (Windows) or Ctrl+Command (Mac) while you lasso (left). Only the segments you lasso will be selected (right).

DRAG-AND-DROP EDITS IN SEGMENT MODE

Drag and Drop: Strategies for Positioning and Snapping

If you turn on Default Snap to Edit on the Edit tab of your Timeline settings, Xpress Pro will guide your hand when you drag and drop a segment into your sequence, snapping the segment to edit points or the position indicator.

If you enjoy your freedom, however, and desire the flexibility to place your segment anywhere in the Timeline, you can enable Default Snap to Edit only when necessary using the keyboard techniques described later in this sidebar. To use this approach, turn off Default Snap to Edit on the Edit tab of your Timeline Settings. With Snap to Edit deselected in the Timeline settings, you can position your incoming clip anywhere in the Timeline, rather than only next to edit points or the position indicator.

You can still activate Snap to Edit on the fly by holding down Ctrl or Ctrl+Alt (Windows) or Command or Command+Option (Mac) before you release the mouse.

Ctrl (Windows) or Command (Mac): Snaps the head (In point) of your incoming clip to one of the following:

◆ The position indicator (**Figure 6.49**)

◆ Any cut point in the Timeline on any track

◆ The Timeline In point (**Figure 6.50**)

continues on next page

Figure 6.49 Here, a clip is dragged to align with the position indicator. To do this with Default Snap to Edit disabled, hold down Ctrl (Windows) or Command (Mac).

The segment is aligned with the In point.

Figure 6.50 Xpress Pro lets you drag and drop a segment so that its head aligns with the In point. To do this with Default Snap to Edit disabled, hold down Ctrl (Windows) or Command (Mac).

Drag and Drop: Strategies for Positioning and Snapping *(continued)*

Ctrl+Alt (Windows) or Command+Option (Mac): Snaps the tail (Out point) of your incoming clip to one of the following:

- The position indicator

- Any cut point in the Timeline on any track (**Figure 6.51**)

- The Timeline Out point (**Figure 6.52**)

The tail of the segment snaps to the edit point.

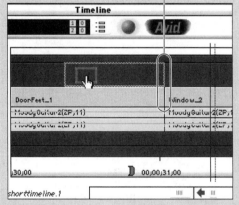

The tail of the incoming clip snaps to the Out point.

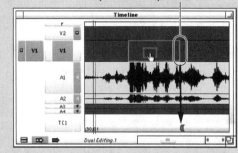

Figure 6.52 To perform a back-timed edit, snapping the tail of your incoming clip to a Timeline Out point when Default Snap to Edit is disabled, hold down Ctrl+Alt (Windows) or Command+Option (Mac) when you drag and drop your clip.

Figure 6.51 By holding down Ctrl+Alt (Windows) or Command+Option (Mac) when Default Snap to Edit is disabled, you can snap a segment's tail to a Timeline edit point.

DRAG-AND-DROP EDITS IN SEGMENT MODE

To reposition a Timeline segment:

1. Select either Lift/Overwrite Segment mode Extract/Splice-in Segment mode on the Edit tab of the Command palette.

2. Click in the Timeline to select the segment you want to move.

3. Drag the selected clip segment to a new location in the Timeline and release the mouse.

   In Lift/Overwrite mode, the clip overwrites anything in its way in its new location, and Xpress Pro leaves black filler behind in its former location. The sequence duration does not change, and sync relationships remain undisturbed.

   In Extract/Splice-in mode, the clip pushes everything to the right, downstream, and inserts itself into its new location. The gap left behind automatically closes, with everything downstream of the old location shifted to the left. Audio-video sync relationships may be affected.

For more information on dragging and dropping clips in the Timeline, see "Locking Tracks" and "Working with Audio-Video Sync" later in this chapter.

✔ Tips

- By default, the Extract/Splice-in and Lift/Overwrite Segment modes are mapped to the lower left of the Timeline. If you do not find them there, you can always find them on the Edit tab of the Command palette.

- You cannot use the Lift and Extract buttons while in a Segment mode.

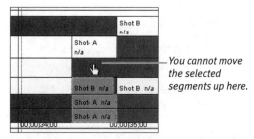

You cannot move the selected segments up here.

Figure 6.53 You cannot move these three clips up one track. Xpress Pro's rule is that you cannot perform a move that overlaps a track that contains what you're moving. The workaround here is to move each clip one at a time.

- Your freedom when positioning segments in the Timeline in a Segment mode depends on whether or not you have Snap to Edit selected in your Timeline settings. See the sidebar "Drag and Drop: Strategies for Positioning and Snapping" earlier in this chapter.

- You can Shift-select and move multiple segments at a time in a Segment mode. However, you cannot move a group of segments to a place that overlaps a track containing one of the segments you're moving (**Figure 6.53**).

- You cannot reposition a segment on a track that is locked. In addition, the result of repositioning segments is affected by whether or not you have Segment Drag Sync Locks enabled.

Instant Rough Cuts and Storyboard Editing

You can impress your clients by creating an instant rough cut at the start of an edit session based on a storyboard that you prearrange in a bin and then drag in its entirety into the Timeline.

First, make sure that all clips that you want to include in your cut are in the same bin.

Then select your bin's Frame View tab and choose Bin > Enlarge Frame to make each clip's representative frame really big.

Next, still in Frame view, arrange all of the clips that you want to use in the order you want them to play in the Timeline.

While you arrange and rearrange the clips, you can play them with the J-K-L keys to review each one. You can even click Mark In and Mark Out to give them In and Out points right there in Frame view, in the bin.

Finally, select some or all of the arranged clips in your bin with the lasso, drag them to the Timeline, and drop them where you want them.

Xpress Pro edits every clip into the sequence according to their order in the bin.

(For more information on working in Frame view, see "Using the Four Bin Views" in Chapter 5.)

To copy or delete clips in Segment mode:

1. Enter a Segment mode by pressing either the red Lift/Overwrite or yellow Extract/Splice-in Segment Mode button at the bottom of the Timeline or on the Edit tab of the Command palette.

2. Click in the Timeline to select the segment you want to copy or delete.

3. Choose Edit > Copy or press the Delete key.

   If you choose Copy, the clip segment is copied to the clipboard.

   If you press Delete, the clip is removed from the Timeline as either a lift (leaves a gap) or extract (closes the gap) edit, and it is not copied to the clipboard.

✔ Tip

- If a segment has audio gain information on it, then selecting the segment and pressing Delete once erases the gain information. Press Delete again to erase the actual segment. (See "Adjusting Audio Levels" in Chapter 12.)

Closing Gaps: The Xpress Pro Way

If you have a gap in your sequence—two segments separated by black filler—you can close the gap in three ways:

- Click the Extract/Splice-in Segment Mode button, select the black filler segment, and press Delete.

- Put In and Out points around the black filler (the gap) and click Extract.

- Enter Trim mode and use a single roller to trim away the black filler. (For more information on Trim mode, see Chapter 7, "Fine-Tuning Your Edits").

Remember: In Xpress Pro, black filler behaves just like a segment.

DRAG-AND-DROP EDITS IN SEGMENT MODE

Cut, Copy, and Paste: Good but Not Great

In word processing applications, you can use the Edit menu's Cut, Copy, and Paste commands to work with typed text. After you select one of Xpress Pro's two Segment mode buttons (Extract/Splice-in or Lift/Overwrite), you can apply the same commands to segments in the Timeline.

- **To copy one or more segments:** After selecting a Segment mode, select the segments and press Ctrl+C (Windows) or Command+C (Mac).

- **To cut (delete) one or more segments:** After selecting a Segment mode, select the segments to be cut and press Ctrl+X (Windows) or Command+X (Mac). Cut material will be copied to the clipboard, just like a lift or extract.

- **To paste the cut or copied segments:** After selecting a Segment mode, place the position indicator wherever you like in the Timeline and press Ctrl+V (Windows) or Command+V (Mac).

The behavior of the Cut and Paste commands depends on the Segment mode you select. For example, using Cut in Extract/Splice-in mode performs an extract deletion edit; using Paste in Extract/Splice-in mode performs a splice-in edit, pushing segments down the Timeline (**Figure 6.54**).

However, for most situations, copying and pasting segment material is best left to a combination of the Lift and Extract buttons and the clipboard monitor.

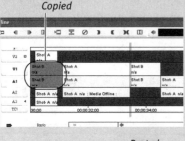

Copied

Pasted

The reason the Copy, Paste, and Cut commands aren't great is that the Paste command will paste only a copied or cut segment to the *same* track in which it originated (**Figure 6.55**).

In contrast, when you use the clipboard monitor, you have more flexibility about where to paste copied or cut material.

(For more information on using the clipboard, see "Using the Clipboard Monitor" earlier in this chapter.)

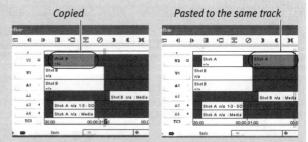

Copied   Pasted to the same track

Figure 6.54 With Extract/Splice-in mode selected, a Paste command pushes material down the Timeline to make room for the copied segment. Pictured is before (above) and after (below) the paste.

Figure 6.55 After you copy a segment with Copy (left), you can paste that segment only to the same track (right).

Drag and Drop: Strategies for Swapping the Order of Segments

Using Extract/Splice-in Segment mode with drag-and-drop editing is a handy way to reverse the order of two shots (**Figure 6.56**).

Just click the Extract/Splice-in Mode button and drag a segment behind or in front of another segment on the same track. Make sure you enable Snap to Edit to snap your segment to adjacent edit points.

Depending on your sync needs, you may or may not want to turn on Segment Drag Sync Locks when performing this procedure.

(For an explanation of Snap to Edit, see the sidebar "Drag and Drop: Strategies for Selecting Clips" earlier in this chapter. For more information on drag sync locks, see "Segment Drag Sync Locks" later in this chapter.)

To be repositioned

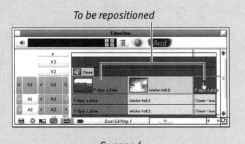

Swapped

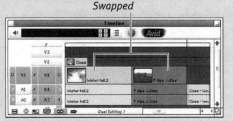

Figure 6.56 Use Extract/Splice-in mode to swap the position of two Timeline segments by dragging one behind the other. Pictured is before (above) and after (below) the swap.

Customizing Your Timeline Settings

Once you edit many source clips into the Timeline and create a rough cut, you can begin the process of reshaping and fine-tuning your work. But before you go too far, you should take a look at the Timeline Settings dialog box, which gives you useful options for fine-tuning your Timeline's display and other common operations while you continue to edit.

On the Display tab of the Timeline Settings window, you can enter or select any of the following:

◆ **Show Toolbar:** Displays the Timeline toolbar, which is yet another place where you can map buttons from the Command palette for easy access. In addition, it includes a master Mute button, an audio level meter, an audio-related Meter menu, and the Toggle Digital Video Out button, which turns real-time playback on and off (**Figure 6.57**).

For more information on the Toggle Video Out button, see Chapter 11, "Rendering and Real Time.")

◆ **Show Marked Region:** Highlights the portion of your sequence that falls between In and Out points on selected tracks in the Timeline (**Figure 6.58**).

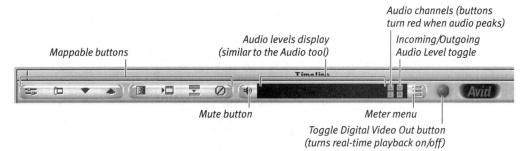

Mappable buttons

Audio levels display (similar to the Audio tool)

Audio channels (buttons turn red when audio peaks)

Incoming/Outgoing Audio Level toggle

Mute button

Meter menu

Toggle Digital Video Out button (turns real-time playback on/off)

Figure 6.57 The Timeline toolbar contains editing buttons that can be mapped to suit your preferences. The toolbar also includes a few display buttons that cannot be changed.

Marked region

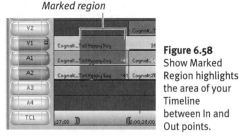

Figure 6.58 Show Marked Region highlights the area of your Timeline between In and Out points.

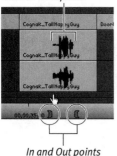

Marked waveforms

In and Out points

Figure 6.59 Selecting Show Marked Waveform increases Xpress Pro's screen drawing speed by displaying only audio waveforms that are between In and Out points.

◆ **Show Marked Waveform:** Displays only audio waveforms that are marked between Timeline In and Out points (**Figure 6.59**). (To turn on audio waveform display, choose Sample Plot from the Timeline Fast menu.)

◆ **Highlight Suggested Render Areas After Playback:** When Xpress Pro is playing back real-time effects in the Timeline, marks ranges where frames could not be played at all, ranges that were difficult to play, and the location of frames that were difficult to play due to disk speed limitations.

(For more information on suggested render areas, see Chapter 11, "Rendering and Real Time.")

On the Edit tab of the Timeline Settings window, you can enter or select the following:

◆ **Start Filler Duration:** Determines the duration of filler inserted at the beginning of your sequence, before your movie begins.

◆ **Find Flash Frames Shorter Than:** Finds unwanted frames. A flash frame is a brief flash of an unwanted image and may be anywhere from 1 to 10 or more frames long. Use this setting to tell Xpress Pro to look for all cuts with fewer frames than the number you enter in the field.

◆ **Auto-Patching:** Specifies that each time you deselect one track and select another track in the Timeline, the newly selected track becomes the patched track automatically. (See the sidebar "Make Your Life Easier with Auto-Patching" earlier in this chapter.)

◆ **Auto-Monitoring:** Tells Xpress Pro to automatically monitor the record track to which a source track is patched.

continues on next page

CUSTOMIZING YOUR TIMELINE SETTINGS

◆ **Segment Drag Sync Locks:** Tells Xpress Pro to keep sync-locked tracks in sync when you drag segments in the Timeline in Splice-in mode (**Figure 6.60**).

(For more information about using segment drag sync locks, see "Segment Drag Sync Locks" later in this chapter.)

◆ **Dupe Detection Handles:** Determines the size of the handles (frames added to the beginning and ending of clips) that are added to check for duplicate frames. This option is used exclusively for internal calculations with the FilmScribe bundle.

To create or modify a timeline setting:

1. Open the Timeline Settings dialog box *by doing one of the following*:
   ▲ On the Settings tab of the Project window, double-click an existing Timeline setting or duplicate an existing setting and rename it.
   ▲ Right-click (Windows) or Shift+ Control-click (Mac) anywhere in the Timeline window and choose Timeline Settings from the pop-up menu.

   The Timeline Settings dialog box opens with two tabs: Display and Edit.

2. Make your changes on either or both tabs and click OK.

   Your changes for the particular Timeline settings that you modified take effect. All other Timeline settings remain unchanged.

✔ Tip

■ You can use Timeline View settings in combination with Timeline settings to further customize and refine your editing environment. (See "Setting Up and Saving Your Timeline Display" in Chapter 5.)

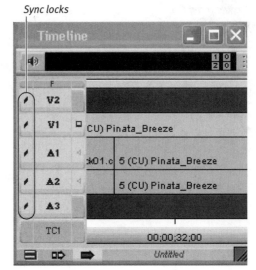

Sync locks

Figure 6.60 To take advantage of Segment Drag Sync Locks, you must sync-lock two or more Timeline tracks.

Moving Around in the Timeline

Reshaping your sequence requires precision; you need to know how to focus in on the minute details of your sequence and zero in on exact edit points and other important frames.

Table 6.2 earlier in this chapter listed all of the buttons that you can use to play your sequence and move through it (buttons found on the Move and Play tabs of the Command palette). In addition to these playback controls, there are several Timeline-only controls to help you view and navigate your sequence with an eye for detail.

Scaling and Zooming

You can zoom in to various levels of detail at the location of the position indicator using the scale slider or Focus button to the left of the horizontal scroll bar at the bottom of the Timeline or the up and down arrows on your keyboard.

To zoom in and out of the Timeline:

Do one of the following:

◆ To show more or less detail in the Timeline, press the keyboard up or down arrow or drag the scale bar to the left or right.

◆ ◎ **Focus:** Clicking this button toggles between zooming almost all the way out of your Timeline and zooming all the way into it.

 Xpress Pro zooms in or out of the Timeline at the location of the position indicator.

Snapping from Cut to Cut

Most NLE editors need the ability to quickly jump from cut to cut in the Timeline. Snapping your position indicator to exact edit points allows you to set In and Out points at the beginning and ending of segments, fine-tune edits, and replace shots precisely.

In Xpress DV, you can use either the mouse or the 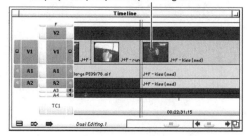 Go to Next Edit and Go to Previous Edit buttons on the Move tab of the Command palette to snap to edit points in your Timeline.

To jump to a cut point on any track:

Do one of the following:

◆ Press Ctrl (Windows) or Command (Mac) and click near a cut (edit point) on any track.

The position indicator jumps to the edit point.

◆ On the keyboard, press Alt (Windows) or Option (Mac) and click the Go to Next Edit or Go to Previous Edit button.

The position indicator jumps from one edit point to the next edit point on any track, regardless of which track is selected. Xpress Pro then deselects all other record tracks and selects only the single track containing the edit point.

✔ Tips

■ A word of caution: When you jump to an edit point, you land on the *first* frame of the segment to the *right* of the playhead. To see the last frame of the previous shot, you need to click the ◀ Step Backward button on the Move tab of the Command palette (**Figure 6.61**).

After you click Go to Next Edit, the Composer displays the first frame of this segment.

Figure 6.61 When the position indicator jumps to a cut point, what you see in the Composer is the first frame of the shot to the right of the indicator. To see the last frame of the previous shot, use Step Backward.

■ When you map Go to Next Edit or Go to Previous Edit to your keyboard, also add the Alt (Windows) or Option (Mac) button (on the Other tab of the Command palette) to the mapping. This way, one click of a button jumps from cut to cut on *any* track, not just the selected one (**Figure 6.62**).

To jump from cut to cut on a single selected track:

1. Deselect all tracks except the one containing the cut points you want to jump to.

2. Click the Go to Next Edit or Go to Previous Edit button.

   The position indicator snaps to cut points on the selected track.

✔ Tip

■ You can quickly deselect all tracks by choosing Edit > Deselect All Tracks or pressing Shift+Alt+A (Windows) or Shift+Command+A (Mac).

Drag this button onto your Go to Next and Previous Edit buttons.

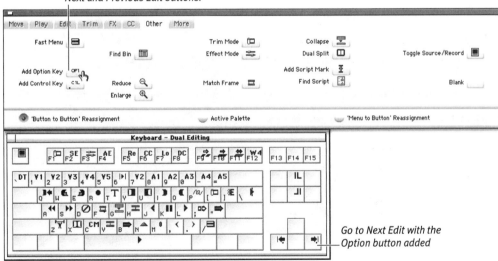

Go to Next Edit with the Option button added

Figure 6.62 Add the Alt (Windows) or Option (Mac) button on the Command palette to the Go to Next Edit or Go to Previous Edit button. That way, pressing one button will skip from edit point to edit point, no matter what track you select.

Moving Around with Timecode

You can move to a specific part of your Timeline (or a source clip) by typing a timecode that corresponds to a particular frame in your sequence. Sometimes, you won't know the exact frame you're looking for, but you'll at least have a ballpark timecode number.

To jump to a specific location using a timecode:

1. With the Timeline or Composer selected, type the timecode using your keyboard's numeric keypad. You don't need to type the colons or semicolons.

   A timecode box appears in the Composer monitor as you type (**Figure 6.63**).

2. Press Enter on the numeric keypad.

   The position indicator jumps to the specified timecode.

✔ Tips

- To jump to a timecode in a source monitor, select the source monitor before you type the value.

- If the timecode you are entering starts with the same hour and minute as your current timecode location, you need to type only the timecode for the seconds and frames, and Xpress Pro will figure out the rest. For example, if you need to jump from 01;01;05;10 to 01;01;07;20, all you have to type is *720*.

Figure 6.63 To jump to a particular frame in a sequence, you can type the frame's timecode and press Enter (Windows) or Return (Mac).

Why Does the Position Indicator Disappear?

You may notice that sometimes when you click the Go to Next Edit or Go to Previous Edit button, the position indicator inexplicably seems to disappear. Well, it didn't really disappear—it just jumped to the end of the sequence.

Why? By default, clicking the Go to Next Edit or Go to Previous Edit button jumps the position indicator only to the edit points that are *common* to all selected tracks. If the selected tracks have no edit points in common, which is often the case, the position indicator jumps to the end or beginning of the sequence, because that's the only edit point shared by all tracks.

To avoid this annoying behavior, press Alt (Windows) or Option (Mac) when clicking Go to Next Edit or Go to Previous Edit, unless you are specifically looking for an edit point common to all selected tracks.

MOVING AROUND IN THE TIMELINE

Toggling Source/Record Modes in the Timeline

In the Timeline, highlighting the ⬛ Toggle Source/Record in Timeline button displays your source clip's tracks in the Timeline. This view may seem like a strange way of looking at things, but it can be helpful when you want to manipulate the source clip (adjust audio levels or add locators) before editing it into the Timeline.

When you display the source clip in the Timeline, the source patch buttons appear on the right instead of the left, and the sequence record buttons appear on the left instead of the right.

In this mode, you can patch any source track to any record track, as you would normally, except from right to left, not left to right (**Figure 6.64**).

The Other Toggle Source/Record Button

Confusingly, Xpress Pro has another Toggle Source/Record button (on the Other tab of the Command palette) that has a slightly different purpose than the button at the bottom of the Timeline. Selecting *that* Toggle Source/Record button toggles between the Composer and the current source monitor window. This button is useful for adding In and Out points to the source clip and then quickly switching to the Composer to add In and Out points to the sequence.

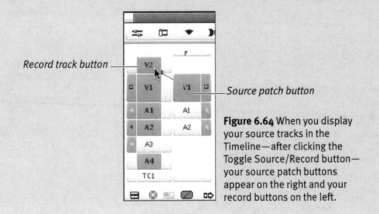

Record track button

Source patch button

Figure 6.64 When you display your source tracks in the Timeline—after clicking the Toggle Source/Record button—your source patch buttons appear on the right and your record buttons on the left.

Adding and Deleting Timeline Tracks

At any time during your editing, you can add or delete video or audio tracks according to the needs of your sequence.

That said, Xpress Pro has its limits: You can create a maximum of only 24 video tracks and 24 audio tracks in Timeline.

By default, Xpress Pro places any new video track above the highest-numbered video track, and any new audio track below the highest-numbered audio track. However, you can control the placement of any new track by pressing the Alt (Windows) or Option (Mac) key when selecting New Video Track or New Audio Track.

To add a track to the Timeline:

Do one of the following:

◆ Select Clip > New Video Track or Clip > New Audio Track.

◆ Right-click (Windows) or Control+Shift-click (Mac) anywhere in the Timeline window. From the context menu, choose New Audio Track or New Video Track (**Figure 6.65**).

◆ Press Ctrl+Y (Windows) or Command+Y (Mac) to create a new video track. Press Ctrl+U (Windows) or Command+U (Mac) to create a new audio track.

Xpress Pro adds a new, empty video or audio track to the Timeline.

✔ Tips

■ For information on track display options, see "Setting Up and Saving Your Timeline Display" in Chapter 5.

■ For information on meta tracks, see Chapter 15, "Special Features and Bundled Applications."

Figure 6.65 To create a new audio or video track, you can right-click (Windows) or Ctrl+Shift-click (Mac) in the Timeline and choose New Video Track or New Audio Track.

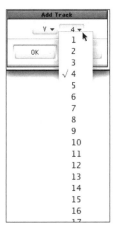

Figure 6.66 In the Add Track dialog box, you can choose the order number for your new audio or video track. You can choose a number in the range 1 to 24.

Figure 6.67 After you select one or more tracks and press Delete, Xpress Pro asks if you know what you're doing.

✔ Tips

- You can select multiple tracks at once by lassoing them in the patch panel.

- If you delete the wrong tracks by mistake, you can get them back using the Edit > Undo/Redo list.

To add a track and choose its ordering:

1. Press Alt (Windows) or Option (Mac). Then choose Clip > New Video Track or Clip > New Audio Track.

   The Add Track dialog box appears.

2. In the first pop-up menu of the Add Track dialog box, change the type of track you want to create, if necessary.

3. In the second pop-up menu of the Add Track dialog box, choose an order number for the new track (**Figure 6.66**).

   Xpress Pro adds the new track to the Timeline in the order you chose (unless the track number you chose is already in use).

✔ Tip

- If the track number you select in the Add Track dialog box already exists, another dialog box pops up asking you to choose Cancel or Insert. Choose Insert to create and insert the track and move the other tracks down one level.

To delete a video or audio track:

1. Select *only* the tracks that you want to delete.

   Be sure that any tracks you want to keep are not selected.

2. *Do one of the following:*
   - ▲ Press the Delete key.
   - ▲ Choose Edit > Delete.

     The Delete Track dialog box appears.

3. In the Delete Track dialog box, confirm that only the tracks you want to delete are selected and click OK (**Figure 6.67**).

   Xpress Pro deletes the selected tracks.

ADDING AND DELETING TIMELINE TRACKS

To adjust the size of one or more tracks:

Do one of the following:

◆ Position the cursor under the record track button in the patch panel and hover until it turns into a double adjustment arrow. Drag the cursor up or down to adjust the size of the track.

◆ Select the record track buttons of the tracks that you want to adjust and tap Ctrl+K (Windows) or Command+K (Mac) to reduce the size of the tracks or Ctrl+L (Windows) or Command+L (Mac) to increase the size of the tracks.

✔ Tip

■ Each track in the Timeline, including the timecode (TC) track, can have a different size.

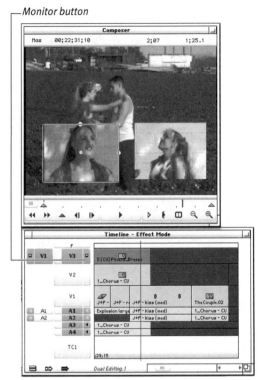

Monitor button

Figure 6.68 Here, V3 is monitored, so every video track below it can be seen in the Composer. Of course, images on the higher tracks will obscure images on the lower tracks.

Monitoring Tracks

When you play or scrub through your Timeline, what you see and hear depends on which monitor buttons you select to the left of the record track buttons. Likewise, to hear source clip tracks, you must keep the source monitor buttons (to the left of the patch buttons) selected.

The rules for monitoring video record tracks are a little different than those for monitoring (hearing) audio record tracks.

◆ **Monitoring a video track:** The Composer plays the track that has the monitor icon, plus all tracks below it (**Figure 6.68**).

◆ **Monitoring an audio track:** Audio track monitor buttons must display either a gold speaker icon or a black track speaker icon for you to hear their associated tracks.

◆ **Monitoring an audio track while scrubbing:** The audio tracks with gold monitor icons are the priority tracks when scrubbing audio. The tracks with the black monitor icons may not be heard when scrubbing in the Timeline if system resources become taxed.

(For more information on scrubbing audio, see "Scrubbing Audio" in Chapter 12.)

To monitor a video track:

Do one of the following:

◆ To monitor a record video track, click the small button to the right of the track's record track button.

   The video track's tiny video track monitor icon appears. The video track with the monitor icon, as well as any track below it, now plays in the Composer.

◆ To monitor any source clip video track, keep the monitor button to the left of the V1 patch button selected at all times.

✔ Tips

■ With no video track monitored, you see only black in the Composer.

■ To turn off monitoring for a track, click the monitor button to make the video track monitor icon disappear.

To monitor an audio track:

Do one of the following:

◆ To monitor an audio Timeline track, click the button to the right of an audio record track's button.

   Either the gold audio track monitor icon or the black audio track monitor icon appears. The gold icon designates tracks that are given priority when scrubbing. (See "Scrubbing Audio" in Chapter 12.)

◆ To monitor a source clip's audio track, keep its monitor button (to the left of the A1 and A2 patch buttons) selected.

✔ Tip

■ By default, odd-numbered audio tracks (A1, A3, and so on) play through the left speaker. Even-numbered audio tracks (A2, A4, and so on) play through the right speaker.

MONITORING TRACKS

Soloing Tracks

When you solo a track, you monitor only that soloed track and temporarily turn off the other tracks.

Soloing a video track enables you to see one video layer without having to see the images from the tracks below or above it and can help you make editing decisions.

Soloing also enhances your playback performance. When sequences become complicated, your Avid system may slow down a bit, but soloing allows you to play tracks unhindered by complexity.

To solo a track:

◆ Ctrl-click (Windows) or Command-click (Mac) a track monitor button.

The background of the track monitor button changes to green. To return to regular monitoring, Ctrl-click or Command-click the button again.

✔ Tip

■ To mute a selected audio track, Alt-click (Windows) or Option-click (Mac) a track solo button.

The Benefit of Auto-Monitoring

With Auto-Monitoring turned on, whenever you patch a source track to a record track, Xpress Pro automatically monitors the record track (**Figure 6.69**). This way, when you edit a source clip into a Timeline track, you can instantly see or hear it play back as part of your sequence.

You can turn on Auto-Monitoring on the Edit tab of the Timeline Settings window. Timeline settings are found on the Settings tab of the Project window.

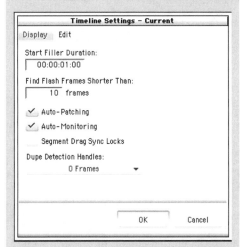

Figure 6.69 You turn on Auto-Monitoring in your Timeline settings. With this choice selected, Xpress Pro monitors the record track to which you patch a source track.

Soloing Multiple Audio Tracks

You can solo only one video track at a time. However, you can solo multiple audio tracks at once. This may help when you want to solo a pair of stereo audio tracks or isolate the mix of sound effects with music, for example, without hearing the dialogue.

Locking Tracks

A track lock prevents you or anyone else from moving or altering a track in any way. Track locks are especially helpful when you want to set your audio editing in stone while you work on the video edits, or vice versa.

Locks also help when a project involves multiple editors; locks can tell your fellow editors that certain parts of your sequence should remain untouched.

To lock and unlock one or more tracks:

1. Select the tracks that you want to lock or unlock.

2. *Do one of the following:*
   - ▲ Right-click (Windows) or Ctrl+Shift-click (Mac) in the Timeline. From the pop-up menu, choose Lock Tracks or Unlock Tracks (**Figure 6.70**).
   - ▲ Choose Clip > Lock Tracks or Unlock Tracks.

   A lock icon appears or disappears to the left of the selected record tracks (**Figure 6.71**). Segments on locked tracks cannot be moved, and you cannot add effects to them.

✔ Tips

- Track locks are different than sync locks. Sync locks make the Timeline behave in a certain way so that audio and video segments do not get out of sync when they are moved. See the next section, "Working with Audio-Video Sync."

- You may notice that you can highlight or unhighlight track lock buttons. A highlighted lock button means that when you unlock that track, a sync lock icon will remain.

Figure 6.70 To lock tracks, select the tracks you want to lock, right-click (Windows) or Ctrl+Shift-click (Mac) and choose Lock Tracks from the menu that appears.

Locked tracks

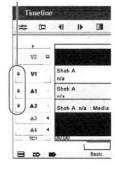

Figure 6.71 You cannot change or move segments on locked tracks.

LOCKING TRACKS

Section marked for extraction

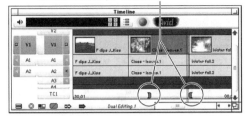

These segments are out of sync after the extraction.

Xpress Pro deletes portions of
these segments to maintain sync.

Figure 6.72 To use Extract, first mark a section of your Timeline with In and Out points (top). Without sync locks enabled, extracting a section of the Timeline might result in an undesirable sync break (middle). With sync locks enabled, Xpress Pro deletes sections of tracks to keep segments aligned (bottom).

Working with Audio-Video Sync

By default, Xpress Pro's Timeline tracks are not sync locked. If you make an editing change that causes segments to move around on a track, Xpress Pro does not assume that a particular video segment needs to remain in sync with a particular audio segment.

Editing procedures that might cause audio and video segments to go out of sync include the following:

◆ A splice-in edit

◆ An extract deletion

(For more information on using Extract, see "Performing Lift and Extract Edits" earlier in this chapter.)

◆ Single-roller trimming of a segment in Trim mode

(For more information, see "Performing Single- and Double-Roller Trims" in Chapter 7.)

Keeping Tracks in Sync with Sync Locks

To tell Xpress Pro that two or more tracks need to remain in sync while you edit, turn on the sync lock buttons to the left of the record track buttons for the tracks you want to synchronize.

When tracks are sync locked, Xpress Pro will do one of the following to any sync-locked tracks, when you move a segment:

◆ Delete portions of sync-locked tracks to maintain sync with the edited track (**Figure 6.72**).

continues on next page

WORKING WITH AUDIO-VIDEO SYNC

◆ Add black filler to a section of the sync-locked track to maintain sync with the edited track (**Figure 6.73**).

✔ Tip

■ Xpress Pro ignores sync locks when you click and drag segments in Extract/Splice-in Segment mode, unless you select Segment Drag Sync Locks in your Timeline settings.

These audio segments are out of sync with their corresponding video.

Spliced-in segment

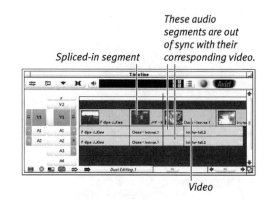

Video

Added black filler

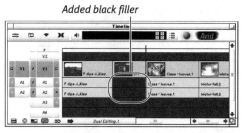

Figure 6.73 (above) When tracks are not sync locked, performing a splice-in edit may move segments out of sync. (below). If you turn on sync locks and you perform a splice-in edit, Xpress Pro adds black filler to keep things in sync.

Out-of-Sync Alerts

Even on tracks that aren't sync-locked, Xpress Pro alerts you when audio and video segments that originally belonged to the same source clip become misaligned (out of sync) in the Timeline.

For example, while editing, you might move an audio segment backward 20 frames. If the audio segment was originally connected to a video segment, then Xpress Pro draws a white line at the bottom of the misaligned segment and displays the number of frames that it is out of sync. In this case, a white line would appear on the audio segment along with the number 20.

An out-of-sync segment is not deadly. Out-of-sync markings are merely a warning. If you wish, you can ignore them.

Figure 6.74 To keep sync-locked tracks in sync when manually repositioning segments in the Timeline, turn on Segment Drag Sync Locks in your Timeline settings.

Segment Drag Sync Locks

Segment Drag Sync Locks, enabled in your Timeline settings (**Figure 6.74**), are useful for maintaining sync when you want to reposition a segment while in Extract/Splice-in mode (**Figure 6.75**).When you enable Segment Drag Sync Locks, Xpress Pro adds black filler to sync-locked tracks after a segment move, preventing a sync break (**Figure 6.76**).

Shot B will be moved in front of Shot A on V1.

Shot A's video was pushed 18 frames to the right when Shot B was moved.

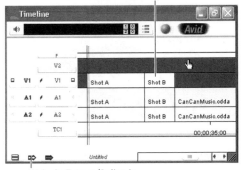

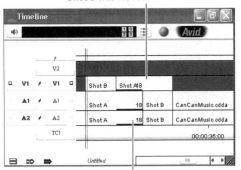

We're in Extract/Splice-in Segment mode.

Shot A's audio and video are now 18 frames out of sync.

Figure 6.75 The Segment Drag Sync Locks feature becomes important when repositioning segments in Extract/Splice-in mode. Here, Segment Drag Sync Locks are disabled (left). After a segment move, a sync problem arises (right).

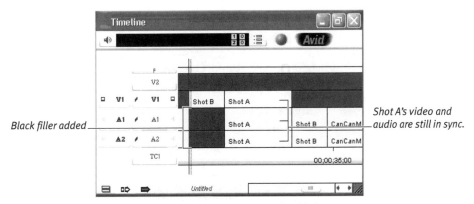

Black filler added

Shot A's video and audio are still in sync.

Figure 6.76 With Segment Drag Sync Locks enabled, Xpress Pro can add black filler on sync-locked tracks, to keep segments in sync after an Extract/Splice-in move.

Sync locks alone do not help you when you drag segments in the Timeline. When you want tracks to remain in sync while you manually reposition segments, you must turn on sync locks for the appropriate tracks and enable Segment Drag Sync Locks in your Timeline settings.

To enable Segment Drag Sync Locks:

1. Open your Timeline settings.

2. Select Segment Drag Sync Locks.

3. Click OK.

✔ Tip

■ When you enable Segment Drag Sync Locks, this setting applies only to clips that are dragged on sync-locked tracks.

Select the track containing the segment you want to match.

Clip loads in source monitor with point marked

Figure 6.77 When you load a master clip into a source monitor using Match Frame, the source clip (the parent clip) displays an In point that corresponds to the start of the clip in the Timeline.

✔ Tips

■ You can use Match Frame on audio segments as well as video segments.

■ If you don't want Xpress Pro to change a source clip's In and Out points when you click Match Frame—it usually marks a new In point—hold down Alt (Windows) or Option (Mac) while clicking the Match Frame button.

Using Match Frame

The ⊡ Match Frame button loads the parent (master) clip of a Timeline clip into a source monitor. The frame position of the playhead in the source monitor matches the frame position of the playhead in the Timeline.

Use the Match Frame feature when you want to do the following:

◆ You want to see or use the source material that comes before the start or after the end of a Timeline segment.

◆ You want to apply a motion effect to a clip and then edit it back into your sequence.

◆ You want to call up a motion or segment effect's original source footage. (For more information on segment and motion effects, see Chapter 9, "Working with Video Effects.")

To use Match Frame:

1. Make sure the position indicator is over the segment in the Timeline that you want to match.

2. Select the track containing the segment to match. For example, if the segment is on V2, select V2.

   (For more information on selecting tracks, see "Patching and Selecting Tracks" earlier in this chapter.)

3. On the Fast menu in the Source monitor or on the Other tab of the Command palette, click the Match Frame button.

   Xpress Pro loads the segment's master clip into a source monitor, marking a source In point that corresponds with the beginning of the segment in the Timeline.

   The frame displayed in the source monitor matches the displayed frame in the Timeline (**Figure 6.77**).

Using Match Frame with Motion Effects

You can use Match Frame to load the parent clips for motion effects by holding down a modifier key when you click Match Frame.

To load a motion effect's original source clip:

1. *Do one of the following:*
   - ▲ Place the position indicator over a motion effect segment in the Timeline.
   - ▲ Load a motion effect clip into a source monitor.

2. Hold down Alt (Windows) or Option (Mac) and click Match Frame.

   Xpress Pro loads the original (unaltered) master clip for the motion effect clip.

✔ Tip

- ■ Clicking Match Frame while over a motion effect without holding down a modifier key simply loads the motion effect source clip into a source monitor (which is different than the *original* master clip, sometimes called the parent clip).

Using Locators

Locators are colored markers that you can add to source clips or the Timeline. Generally, you use locators to do the following:

◆ Add comments to specific frames on clips or segments.

◆ Provide visual sync references for edits.

(For more suggestions for using locators, see the sidebar "When to Use Locators" later in this chapter.)

You can manage all of your locators in the Locators window, where you can keep track of who authored each locator (**Figure 6.78**).

Double-click here to change locator information.

Locators window

Type your comments here.

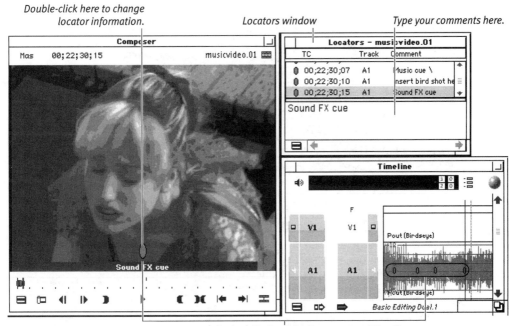

Locators are displayed in both the Composer and Timeline.

Figure 6.78 Use the Locators window to add comments to locators, jump to locators, and keep track of other information attached to locators.

To add a locator to a source clip track or Timeline segment:

1. Select the source monitor or Timeline/ Composer and cue the position indicator to the desired frame.

2. *Do one of the following:*

   ▲ To mark a source clip, make sure the patch button for the track you want to mark is the topmost selected patch button in the Timeline (**Figure 6.79**).

   ▲ To mark a segment in the Timeline, make sure the record track button that contains the segment is the topmost selected record track button in the Timeline.

3. Click one of the Add Locator buttons, located on the More tab of the Command palette.

   Xpress Pro displays a colored locator in your source monitor or Timeline/Composer.

✔ Tips

■ You can add a locator to only one Timeline segment or one source track at a time.

■ You can add one or more locators in real time while your source clip or sequence plays, but you won't see the locators until you pause playback.

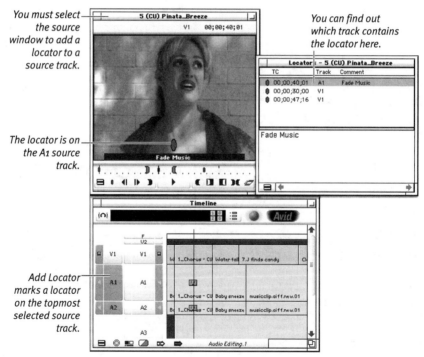

You must select the source window to add a locator to a source track.

You can find out which track contains the locator here.

The locator is on the A1 source track.

Add Locator marks a locator on the topmost selected source track.

Figure 6.79 If you want add a locator to a source clip's audio track, you must deselect the source video patch buttons in the Timeline. You can add a locator only to the topmost selected source track.

USING LOCATORS

To jump from locator to locator:

Do one of the following:

▲ On the Move tab of the Command palette, click Go to Previous Locator or Go to Next Locator.

▲ On the Move tab of the Command palette, click Rewind or Fast Forward.

▲ In the Locators window, double-click a locator listing.

The position indicator jumps to the desired locator.

When to Use Locators

You might use locators when you want to do the following:

◆ Match edits to the beat of music (**Figure 6.80**).

◆ Fix audio and video that has gone out of sync.

◆ Mark a portion of a clip for trimming at a later time.

◆ Add comments to a clip for reviewers, other editors, or EDL lists.

◆ Mark empty places in the Timeline to be filled by particular content.

◆ Build organized lists of particular types of shots (such as cutaway shots).

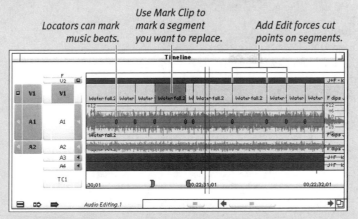

Figure 6.80 Here, locators mark particular beats in a music track. You can jump to each locator using Go to Next Locator and then click Add Edit to create cut points that match the beats. Finally, you can use Mark Clip to mark segments and overwrite them with other footage. Instant music video!

To open the Locators window:

Do one of the following:

- ▲ Choose Tools > Locators.
- ▲ Right-click (Windows) or Shift+ Control-click (Mac) in the Composer or source monitor and choose Locators from the pop-up menu.
- ▲ Park the position indicator on any locator and double-click the oval locator icon in the Composer or pop-up source monitor.

The Locators window opens, with all of the locators and comments listed.

✔ Tip

- ■ You can print the content of your Locators window by choosing File > Print whenever the Locators window is open and active.

Working in the Locators Window

On a multiuser project, locators provide a great means of communication among project personnel. As an editor, you can alert a sound designer to where you need a certain sound effect, or you can ask the director if he or she likes a particular change you made.

You can assign different meanings or different people to individual locator colors and then use the Locators window to keep track of the dates, times, comments, and user identities of each locator.

The features of the Locators window—with its columns and sorting capabilities—may remind you of bin Text tabs.

To add or change a locator comment:

1. *Do one of the following:*
   - ▲ In either the source monitor or the Composer, park the position indicator on a locator and click the locator symbol.
   - ▲ Click a locator listing in the Locators window and press Enter (Windows) or Return (Mac).

   A cursor blinks in the comment area of the window.

2. Type a new comment or change the current one and press Tab (**Figure 6.81**).

   The upper half of the locators window becomes highlighted again, and you can either choose a different locator to modify or return to editing.

✔ Tip

■ You can search for a locator comment in the Timeline by selecting the Timeline, pressing Ctrl+F (Windows) or Command+F (Mac), selecting Locators in the dialog box, entering a keyword, and clicking OK.

To change the color of a Locator:

1. In the Locators window, select a listed locator.

2. From the Locators window Fast menu, choose Locator Color and pick one of the seven color names that appears.

   The locator color changes.

✔ Tip

■ You can assign whatever meaning you want to the locator colors.

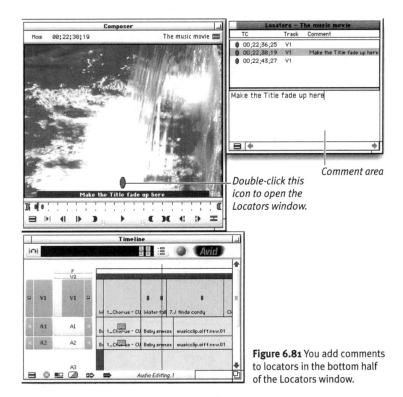

Double-click this icon to open the Locators window.

Comment area

Figure 6.81 You add comments to locators in the bottom half of the Locators window.

To display locators as frames:

◆ In the Locators window, open the Fast menu and select Images.

The window displays a representative frame for each of your locators. You can hide the frames by selecting Images again (**Figure 6.82**). You can double-click a locator frame to jump the play-head to the corresponding locator.

Locator frames provide a visual way to jump to a particular part of your source clip or Timeline.

To display user, date, and time info for locators:

◆ In the Locators window, open the Fast menu and select Details.

The window displays columns listing the names of the users who created the loca-tors and date and time information (**Figure 6.83**).

✔ Tip

■ User, date, and time information can help you determine who made what comment and when.

Representative frame

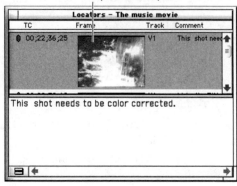

Figure 6.82 To display a representative frame for each locator in the Locators window, select Images from the Locators window Fast menu.

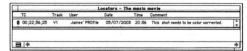

Figure 6.83 Select Details from the Locators window Fast menu to display locator information columns. This tells you who created each locator and when.

Another Way to Add Comments

In addition to using a locator to add comments in the Timeline, you can add comments to individual Timeline segments by clicking the yellow Extract/Splice-in mode arrow or red Lift/Overwrite mode arrow at the bottom of the Timeline, selecting a Timeline segment, and choosing Add Comments from the Composer's Clip Name menu (**Figure 6.84**).

A Comments dialog box opens, allowing you to enter comments for the selected segment (**Figure 6.85**).

To display your segment comments, open the Timeline Fast menu in the lower-left corner of the window and select Clip Comments from the list that appears (**Figure 6.86**).

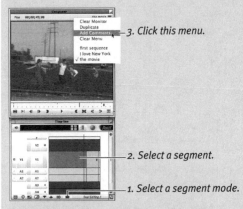

3. Click this menu.

2. Select a segment.

1. Select a segment mode.

Figure 6.84 To add a comment to a segment in the Timeline, click a Segment mode arrow at the bottom of the Timeline, select a segment, click the Composer's upper-right menu, and choose Add Comments.

Figure 6.86: To display clip comments in the Timeline, click on the Timeline fast menu and choose Clip Comments.

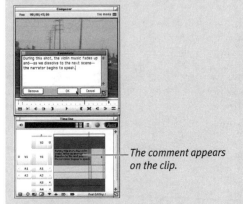

The comment appears on the clip.

Figure 6.85 After you type a comment in the Comments dialog box, the comment appears on the segment in the Timeline if you select Clip Comments in the Timeline Fast menu.

To increase or decrease locator column spacing:

◆ Highlight a locator column, open the Locators Fast menu, and choose Enlarge Track or Reduce Track.

Spacing increases or decreases between the highlighted column and the column next to it.

✔ Tip

■ The keyboard shortcut for Enlarge Track is Ctrl+L (Windows) or Command+L (Mac). The shortcut for Reduce Track is Ctrl+K (Windows) or Command+K (Mac).

To sort locators in ascending or descending order:

Do one of the following:

◆ To sort locators in ascending order (with the first chronological locator listed at the top), choose Sort from the Locators window Fast menu or press Ctrl+E (Windows) or Command+E (Mac).

◆ To sort locators in descending order (with the first chronological locator listed at the bottom), hold down Alt (Windows) or Option (Mac) and choose Sort.

The video image with the green bar is the activated video track.

All of the clips play together.

Figure 6.87 When you load a grouped clip into a source monitor and click Quad Split (on the MCam tab of the Command palette), you can see the clips in the group.

Grouping Clips and Multicamera Editing

If you're editing a multicamera production or a music video, you'll probably want to take advantage of Xpress Pro's ability to group (or *gang*) together up to 18 clips (which may contain up to 18 video and 36 audio tracks) and display either 4 or 9 clips at a time (**Figure 6.87**).

For example, say you group together Shot A and Shot B. When you play the grouped clip, both Shot A and Shot B will start at a sync point that you determine in advance. If you play for 1 minute and stop, you will be 1 minute past Shot A's sync point and 1 minute past shot B's sync point; they roll together simultaneously.

So grouping clips allows you to cut in different angles from different cameras without worrying about the synchronicity of those cameras, as long as they never stop recording during the take. If a camera does stop recording, then you need to create another grouped clip at the start of the next take.

Grouping clips is also helpful for music videos when you have a number of different shots synchronized to the same music track.

To create a grouped clip:

1. Put all of the clips you want to group together in the same bin.

2. In the bin, select all of the clips that you want to group together.

3. Choose Bin > Group Clips.

continues on next page

GROUPING CLIPS AND MULTICAMERA EDITING

4. In the Group Clips dialog box that appears, select one of the sync methods (**Figure 6.88**):

- ▲ **Film TC/Sound TC:** This option is for film projects working in 24 or 25 fps and works if you have matching film and sound timecode.

- ▲ **Inpoints:** Using Mark In, you can pick any point near the beginning of each clip as your sync point. Usually, that point is a slate or light flash filmed by all of the cameras on the set.

- ▲ **Outpoints:** Using Mark Out, you can pick any point near the end of each clip as your sync point. Usually, that point is a tail slate filmed by all of the cameras on the set.

- ▲ **Source Timecode:** This method works only if the clips have matching timecode.

- ▲ **Auxiliary TC1–TC5:** If the clips have matching timecode in the same Auxiliary Timecode column, you can select an auxiliary timecode track, from TC track 1 to TC track 5.

- ▲ **Ink Number:** This method is available for film projects shot at 24 or 25 fps in which the clips have matching ink numbers. This option appears only for film projects.

- ▲ **Auxiliary Ink:** This method is available for film projects shot at 24 or 25 fps in which the clips have matching ink numbers in the same Auxiliary Ink column. This option appears only for film projects.

5. Click OK.

A new, grouped clip appears in the bin, with the name of the first clip in the group, followed by the extension Grp.# (where # represents the number of clips in the group).

Figure 6.88 You can sync together grouped clips by In points, Out points, source timecode, or auxiliary timecode.

If you select this option, Xpress Pro automatically activates whichever audio tracks correspond to the activated video track.

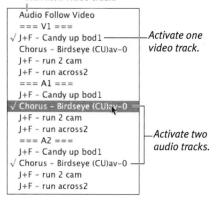

Figure 6.89 To activate a video track and two audio tracks (determining which ones will appear in the Composer once they are edited into the Timeline), click the Group Clip symbol and select the track names.

■ If your group contains more clips than are displayed in the source monitor in Quad or Nine Split view, click Swap Cam Bank on the MCam tab of the Command palette to see the other clips in the source monitor. Click the button again to see the first set of clips.

To edit with a grouped clip:

1. Load the grouped clip into a source monitor as you would any clip.

2. (Optional) To see four grouped clips at once, click Quad Split on the MCam tab of the Command palette. To see nine clips at once, click Nine Split on the MCam tab of the Command palette.

   Xpress Pro displays your clips in the source monitor. The activated clip has a green line underneath it.

3. To activate grouped video and/or audio tracks, *do one of the following:*

   ▲ In Quad or Nine Split view, click the video frame of the video track you want to activate.

   ▲ In Quad Split, Nine Split, or normal view, click the group clip symbol at the top of the source monitor and select one video track for V1, one audio track for A1, and one audio track for A2 from the menu that appears **(Figure 6.89)**.

   ▲ In Quad Split, Nine Split, or normal view, click Previous in Group or Next in Group to activate the next or previous video track.

   Whichever track you activate is the one that will appear in the Timeline/Composer when you edit the grouped clip into your sequence.

✔ Tips

■ Even after you edit part of a grouped clip into the Timeline, you can go back and change the displayed clip. (See the task "To change the grouped clip display for a grouped segment" that follows.)

To change the grouped clip display for a grouped segment:

1. Park the position indicator over a Timeline segment that originated from a grouped clip.

2. Go to the Composer window and click the grouped clip symbol. Choose a different grouped clip track from the list that appears (**Figure 6.90**).

   The Composer displays a different grouped clip angle, and the name of the grouped clip segment changes in the Timeline.

✔ Tips

- If you click the grouped clip symbol at the top of the source monitor and choose Audio Follow Video, then whenever you activate a video track, its corresponding audio tracks automatically become activated. Usually, you should not select this option so that you maintain control over the audio tracks that are activated.

- You can also click M1, M2, M3, and so forth on the MCam tab of the Command palette to activate one of the grouped clips. If you want to use these buttons often, you might want to map them to the keyboard.

Click the grouped clip symbol in the Composer, not in the source monitor.

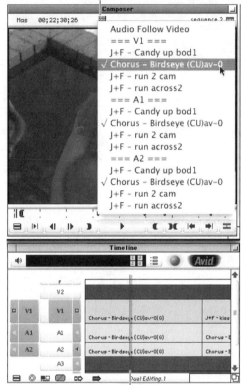

Park the position indicator over the grouped clip segment.

Figure 6.90 Even after you edit part of a grouped clip into the Timeline, you can still toggle it to display a different angle. Use the grouped clip menu in the Composer.

Select to display nothing, if timecode is irrelevant

Displays frame information

For film projects only

Displays timecode information

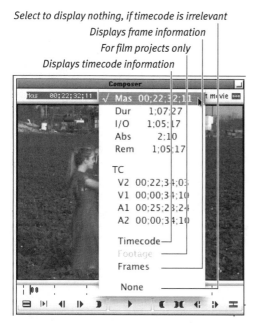

Figure 6.91 Choose from the Tracking Information menu to display timecode information, frame information, and footage information.

Using the Tracking Information Menu

In the single-image Composer monitor (or the record side of the Composer in Source/Record mode), you can use the Tracking Information menu at the upper left of the monitor to display information pertaining to the location of your position indicator in the Timeline (**Figure 6.91**).

Table 6.3 lists all the options available in this menu.

For video projects, the Tracking Information menu can display either the timecode or frame count related to the content of your current sequence. For film projects, the menu can also display footage information, such as key numbers.

✔ Tip

- In Source/Record Display mode (when the Composer shows two monitors), both the source side of the window and the record side include a Tracking Information menu; the menu on the source side pertains to loaded source clips.

Table 6.3

Tracking Information Options

NAME	FUNCTION
Mas	Displays master timecode (or frame numbers or footage reference numbers) for your sequence. The master timecode tells you the location of the position indicator in the Timeline in relation to your sequence's starting timecode.
Dur	Displays the duration of your current sequence from the first frame to the last frame.
I/O	Displays the duration of your sequence that is between Timeline In and Out points.
Abs:	Displays the elapsed duration of your sequence between the beginning of the Timeline and the position indicator.
Rem	Displays the remaining duration of your sequence between the position indicator and the end of the Timeline.
TC	Displays the source timecode (or frame numbers or footage reference numbers) for individual segments on Timeline tracks (V1, A1, and so on) at the location of the position indicator.
Timecode	Displays timecode in the menu.
Footage	For a film project, displays footage reference numbers in the menu.
Frames	Displays frame numbers in the menu.
None	Displays no timecode information, incase it is irrelevant or you find it distracting.

FINE-TUNING YOUR EDITS

Trim mode is especially helpful for finessing dialogue scenes and making matching action cuts seem invisible, by making careful frame-by-frame adjustments to existing Timeline edit points. For example, you can use single-roller or double-roller trims to overlap character A's voice with character B's action or to cut smoothly from a wide shot to a close shot of matching action. Or you can use slip trims to reposition the In and Out points of a Timeline clip segment and slide trims to readjust the positioning of a clip segment in relation to other Timeline material.

Xpress Pro gives you multiple means of performing the same trim techniques, whether you like to click trim buttons, drag rollers on edit points, or stick with the keyboard. Those familiar with past Avid Xpress incarnations will be relieved to know that Trim mode now allows dynamic J-K-L trimming with the Play Reverse, Pause, and Play Forward keys, as its big cousin the Avid Media Composer has done for years. By experimenting, you can discover what best suits your personal philosophy for turning choppy, rough cuts into smooth, invisible cuts.

About Trim Mode

Trim mode allows you to fine-tune the timing of each edit by adding or subtracting frames to the head and tail of individual clips in the Timeline wherever the clips meet at an edit point. When you enter Trim mode, pink rollers appear on one or both sides of any selected edit points, and you add or subtract a few frames from either side of the edit by moving the rollers one way or another.

The type of trim you perform depends on the number of rollers you have added to edit points, the number of edit points on a single track with rollers added, and the overall number of tracks to which you have added rollers. The simplest trim is a single roller at a single edit point on a single track. The most complex trims involve either single rollers or double rollers on multiple edit points on multiple tracks.

Once you have selected one or more edit points with one or more rollers, you move the selected edited pont(s) by either dragging the rollers directly in the Timeline, pressing trim buttons in the Composer, using the J-K-L keys to play the trim to the left or right, or by typing + or − numbers on the numeric keypad.

For instance, if you drag one roller to the right by 10 frames, then 10 frames are added (or subtracted) to *all* edit points with rollers for that particular trim operation (**Figure 7.1**).

Hence, the essence of trimming involves first choosing which edit points to load with single or double rollers and then adding or subtracting frames to one or both sides of edit points to change the timing of the cut.

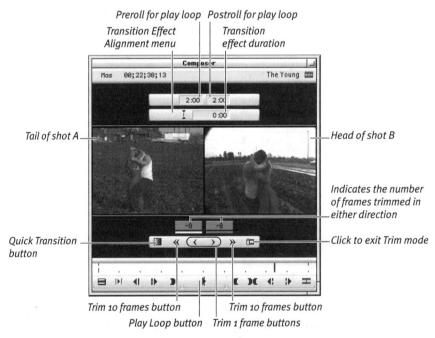

Figure 7.1 When you enter Trim mode, the Composer changes its display. The left image shows the tail of shot A and the right image shows the head of shot B for the topmost selected video edit point.

Click above the Timeline tracks and drag down.

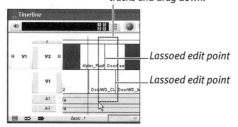

—Lassoed edit point

—Lassoed edit point

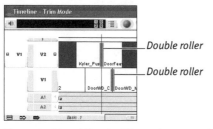

—Double roller

—Double roller

Figure 7.2 (above) To enter Trim mode, you can lasso the edit point you want to trim by clicking above the Timeline and dragging from right to left around the edit point (below) Xpress Pro places double rollers around the lassoed edit point.

Aligned edit points   *Double rollers*

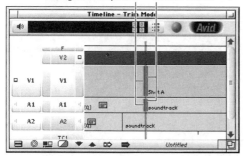

Figure 7.3 When you enter Trim mode, Xpress Pro automatically places double rollers on the edit point closest to the position indicator. If the cut aligns across multiple tracks, then Xpress Pro selects all aligned edit points on the selected track.

To enter and exit Trim mode:

Do any of the following:

▲ To both enter and exit Trim mode, press the 🔲 Trim Mode button (located by default on the Composer and Timeline toolbars).

▲ To enter Trim mode, lasso the edit points you want to trim. In the Timeline, click *above the video tracks* (below the toolbar) and drag down, in a right-to-left motion (**Figure 7.2**).

▲ To exit Trim mode, click the Timecode track area (TC1) at the bottom of the Timeline, press the Escape key on the keyboard, or press the Step Backward or Step Forward key, mapped by default to the Composer window and the left arrow and right arrow keyboard keys.

When you first enter Trim mode, the Composer displays the last frame of the outgoing clip and the first frame of the incoming clip on the topmost selected edit point on a video track.

The position indicator jumps to the nearest edit point on the topmost selected track and by default places double rollers on the edit point, indicating that any trim action will affect both sides of the cut (**Figure 7.3**). See the task "To add or subtract rollers for a trim operation" later in this chapter for information on how to set up a single-roller trim or trims on multiple tracks.

The Composer displays new buttons you can use to trim, review, and keep track of your trimmed edits. When you exit Trim mode, the Composer returns to normal display, and Xpress Pro returns to normal editing mode.

continues on next page

ABOUT TRIM MODE

✔ Tips

- When you enter Trim mode, Xpress Pro disables all Segment mode functionality; so you can no longer click and move segments in the Timeline.

- In dual-monitor Source/Record mode, the Composer monitor images are much larger than in single-image mode. Xpress Pro calls this display Big Trim mode, and many people prefer to work with the larger windows, for improved visual feedback. Single-monitor Basic mode is called Little Trim mode, but the trim functionality is the same in both modes (**Figure 7.4**).

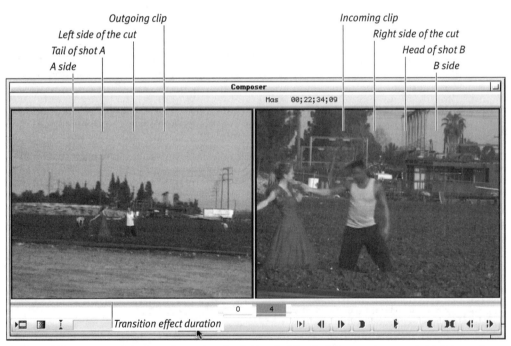

Outgoing clip
Left side of the cut
Tail of shot A
A side

Incoming clip
Right side of the cut
Head of shot B
B side

Figure 7.4 If the Composer is in Source/Record mode, clicking the Trim Mode button places you in Big Trim mode. The functionality is the same, but the images are larger.

About Trim Mode

Understanding Single-Roller and Double-Roller Trims

The key to fast and fluid trimming is an intuitive grasp of how the two basic trim types operate. Double-roller trims are fairly easy to envision, but single-roller trims often take more practice to master.

One good way to practice single- and double-roller trims is to load a single edit point on a single track with rollers, drag the rollers left and right, release, and watch the Timeline update. Once you grasp how single- and double-roller trims operate on a single edit point, trimming multiple edit points on multiple tracks will become much easier.

Double-roller trims: Two pink rollers appear at an edit point—one on each side of the cut—and indicate that as you add frames to one side of the cut, you subtract the same number of frames from the other side. With rollers placed on *both* sides of an edit point, a double-roller trim simultaneously changes the Out point (or tail) of shot A and the In point (or head) of shot B by the same number of frames.

With double-roller trims, the duration of the overall sequence does not change, and no sync relationships are affected.

Single-roller trims: One pink roller appears on one side of an edit point and indicates that you are adding or subtracting frames from *one* side of the cut only, not both. A single-roller trim moves the Out point (tail) or In point (head) of the clip segment that the roller is on and does not affect the clip adjacent to the single roller.

With single-roller trims, you are either shortening or lengthening the duration of the clip, so all clips to the right of the trimmed edit point shift their positions in the Timeline to accommodate the trim. The duration of the overall track or tracks containing the trimmed edit point necessarily changes by the same number of frames as well (**Figure 7.5**).

Hence, single-roller trimming may create sync problems on other tracks, particularly when you trim only the video or only the audio of segments that have synchronous audio and video, such as dialogue and interviews. For information on maintaining sync with single-roller trims, see "Maintaining Sync in Trim Mode" later in this chapter.

Slip and slide trims: Slip and slide trims are variations on single-roller trims; you modify two single rollers on the same track at the same time. Once you understand how a simple single-roller trim works, you will find it easier to understand how the slip and slide variations work. See "Performing a Slip Trim" and "Performing a Slide Trim" later in this chapter for more particular information on these two specialized variations.

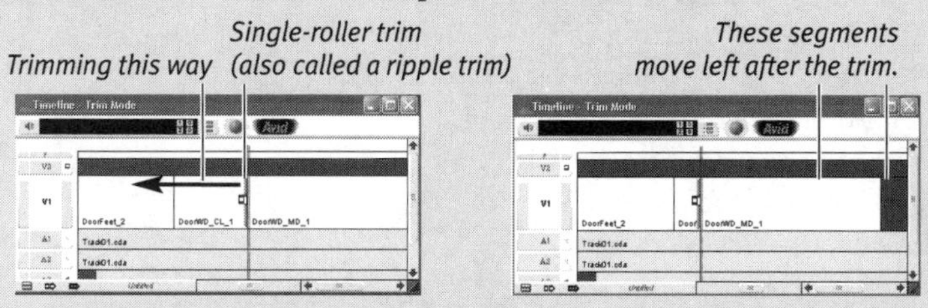

Figure 7.5 Here, the tail of a shot (DoorWD_Cl_1) is trimmed to the left (left). The result (right) is that the following segment and any other segments to the right of the position indicator are pushed to the left. This may present sync issues for the other tracks (unless sync locks are used).

To add or subtract rollers for a trim operation:

1. Click the Trim Mode button or lasso one or more edit points in the Timeline to enter Trim mode and add the default double rollers to one or more edit points.

2. *Do any of the following:*

   ▲ To turn a double-roller selection into a single-roller selection, in the Composer, click the right or left image. To turn a single-roller selection back into a double-roller selection, click near the center vertical line dividing the two images, when the cursor turns into a double-roller icon (**Figure 7.6**).

   ▲ To add or subtract a roller at that edit point, in the Timeline, click the right or left side of any edit point. To add one or more rollers to additional edit points, Shift-click (**Figure 7.7**).

   ▲ To perform a single-roller trim, choose Tools > Command palette, select the Active palette on the Command palette, click the Trim tab, and click the Trim A Side or Trim B Side button. To perform a double-roller trim, instead click the Trim AB Side button.

   ▲ To add or subtract trim rollers to vertically contiguous edit points—edit points that fall on the exact same frame in the Timeline but on different tracks—click one or more Record track selection buttons. For instance, if track V3 has an edit point on the exact same frame in the Timeline as track V1, and the V1 edit point has a single roller, then selecting track V3 in the patch panel will load a matching single roller on the edit point on V3.

Click in the middle. *The cursor must display a double-roller icon.*

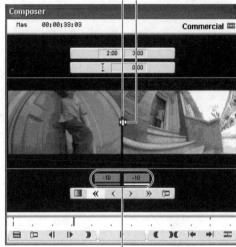

If both boxes are highlighted, then both sides of the cut are selected for trimming.

Figure 7.6 To switch from single-roller to double-roller trimming, hover the cursor in between the two images in the Composer. When the cursor changes to a double-roller icon, click the mouse.

Shift-click here. *Shift-click here.*

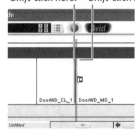

Figure 7.7 Another way to switch to double-roller trimming is to Shift-click both sides of a cut point in the Timeline.

As you add or change single and double rollers in the Timeline, the frame offset counter boxes at the bottom of the Composer window (in Trim mode) are highlighted in purple on the A side, the B side, or both, to reflect your changes.

✔ Tips

■ If you're already in Trim mode and want to mark a different edit point with double rollers, press ▣ Go to Next Edit or ▣ Go to Previous Edit.

■ If you select a number of edit points in Trim mode and then add to that selection, but you later want to return to the original selection, press Alt (Windows) or Option (Mac) and click the ▣ Trim Mode button.

■ You can cycle through single- and double-roller selections by clicking the Cycle Trim Side button (found on the Trim tab of the Command palette).

Become a Lassoing Pro

If you like entering Trim mode by lassoing, you can use a little trick of the trade to make your wrangling life easier; the type of trim Xpress Pro selects depends on what you lasso and the direction of your lasso.

◆ If you lasso a single edit point per track by clicking above the Timeline tracks and dragging from right to left, Xpress Pro selects all encircled edit points with double rollers. You can Shift-click either side of a double roller to turn it into a single roller.

◆ If you want to select edit points between tracks, hold down Alt (Windows) or Control+Option (Mac) and drag a lasso directly on the Timeline tracks (**Figure 7.8**).

◆ If you want to select a clip segment for slipping, drag from right to left, and encircle an entire clip segment. (For more information, see "Performing a Slip Trim" later in this chapter.)

◆ If you want to select a clip segment for sliding, hold down Alt+Shift (Windows) or Option+Shift (Mac), drag right to left, and encircle an entire clip segment. (For more information on sliding in Trim mode, see "Performing a Slide Trim" later in this chapter.)

But here's a warning, edit point wranglers: If you lasso edit points by dragging left to right, you will not enter Trim mode if your lasso completely encircles a clip segment. Instead, you will enter Lift/Overwrite Segment mode (**Figure 7.9**).

This edit point will be selected.

Segment selected after dragging a lasso around it from left to right

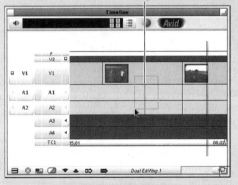

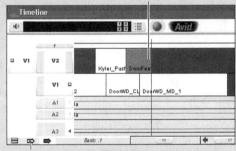

Segment mode selected

Figure 7.8 If you want to select edit points on middle tracks, but not on the track above them, press Alt (Windows) or Control+Option (Mac) and lasso the edit points.

Figure 7.9 If your lasso encircles a segment while dragging left to right, you will enter Lift/Overwrite Segment mode and not Trim mode.

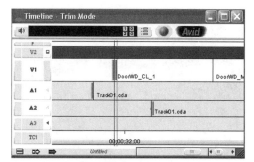

Figure 7.10 Xpress Pro will not let you trim with both double rollers and single rollers. If you press a trim button with the configuration shown here, nothing will happen.

Figure 7.11 Here, typing *+400f* using the numeric keypad causes Xpress Pro to trim 13 seconds and 10 frames to the right.

Performing Single- and Double-Roller Trims

After you enter Trim mode, you set up a particular trim by selecting one or more edit points for trimming, using either a single roller or double rollers. The simplest trims involve a single or double roller on one track, but you can load many rollers on many tracks before you actually perform a trim operation.

The only rule you must remember before actually performing your trim is that you cannot perform double-roller and single-roller trims simultaneously. Any single trim must employ either all double-roller trims or all single-roller trims (**Figure 7.10**).

Once you have set up your rollers, you can perform the trim in any of the following four ways:

◆ **In the Timeline, drag a roller to the right or left:** Dragging an edit point to a new location is an intuitive, hands-on way to control the length of a trim.

◆ **In the Composer, click one of the four trim buttons:** Use the buttons in the Composer to trim to the left or right in 1- or 10-frame increments.

◆ **Use the numeric keypad:** To trim to the right, type the number of frames you want to trim and press Enter (Windows) or Return (Mac) (**Figure 7.11**). To trim to the left, type a minus sign in front of the number.

continues on next page

◆ **Perform dynamic trimming from the keyboard:** To trim an edit point, press Play or Play Reverse to move the edit point, and press Pause to perform the trim. The Play Reverse, Pause, and Play Forward buttons (on the Play tab of the Command palette) are mapped by default to the J, K, and L keys. This method—often referred to as trimming on the fly or dynamic trimming—is preferred among editors because it allows you to see one side of your cut play while you trim. (See the sidebar "Dynamic Trimming with the J-K-L Keys" later in this chapter for more information.)

As you perform one or more trim operations, the Frame Offset counters display the total cumulative number of frames you trimmed. A negative number means that you trimmed to the left; a positive number means that you trimmed to the right (**Figure 7.12**).

✔ Tips

■ For finer control when dragging rollers, hold down Alt (Windows) or Option (Mac) as you drag. For the finest control—trimming frame by frame—zoom all the way into your Timeline before dragging a trim.

■ To snap-align to an edit point on another track, press Ctrl (Windows) or Command (Mac) while dragging a roller (**Figure 7.13**).

16 frames to the left

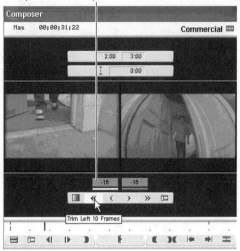

Figure 7.12 Here, the original position of the edit point has been trimmed 16 frames to the left.

V1 snaps to the edit point on A2.

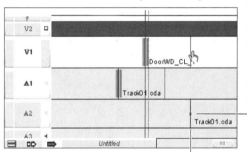

The trim on edit point on A2

Figure 7.13 You can snap to other edit points by holding down Ctrl (Windows) or Command (Mac) while clicking and dragging a trim point.

*Trimming the tail of
this shot to the left*

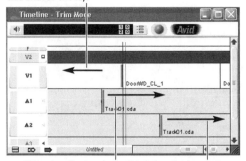

*Trimming the head of   Trimming the head of
this shot to the right   this shot to the right*

Figure 7.14 Xpress Pro lets you single-roller trim in
multiple directions simultaneously. Make sure you
know what you're doing, however, because these
kinds of trims can be confusing.

■ You can perform multiple single-roller
trims in different directions, sometimes
called asynchronous trimming. For
example, you can trim the tail of a segment on one track and simultaneously
trim the head of a segment on another
track (**Figure 7.14**).

■ If you want to enter a trim amount of
more than 99 frames, you must type an *f*
after the number, to tell Xpress Pro that
you are entering frames, not timecode.
For example, to trim 400 frames to the
right, type *+400f.*

Trim Terminology Explained

Over the past 100 years, several distinctly different specialized vocabularies have evolved to name the cut points, trim types, and trim sides that are used in the craft of fine-tuning visual transitions, as we've moved from film editing to tape-to-tape editing to NLE editing. Here's a cheat-sheet to help you keep track of this overlapping trim-related vocabulary and a guide to how the terms are used in this book.

◆ **Cut points = Edit points = Transition points = Straight cuts:** In physical film editing, a cut point is where one piece of film is taped or glued to another piece of film to create an edit. In an NLE (like Xpress Pro) an edit point is where two clip icons are butted together on a Timeline track to create an edit point. A cut or edit point forms a visual transition, but this book uses the term *edit point* rather than *transition*, to avoid confusion with a transition effect, such as a dissolve or wipe, that is applied to an edit point. Sometimes edit points without a dissolve or wipe or other transition effect are referred to as straight cuts or butt cuts.

An edit point is distinguished by two distinct frames on either side where two clips meet: one on the left and one on the right. And that's where the vocabulary fun really begins:

◆ **Tail of Shot A = A side of a trim = Left side of a cut = Outgoing clip or frame:** For single- and double-roller trims, the *left* image in the Composer monitor always displays the A side of a trim, which is the last frame of the clip segment to the left of the edit point and is also known as the outgoing side. This book uses the terms *tail of shot A*, *outgoing frame*, and *A side* interchangeably (see Figure 7.3 for an illustration).

◆ **Head of Shot B = B side of a trim = Right side of a cut = Incoming clip or frame:** For single- and double-roller trims, the *right* image in the Composer monitor always displays the B side of a trim: the first frame of the clip segment to the right of the edit point, also known as the incoming side. This book uses the terms *head of shot B*, *incoming frame*, and *B Side* interchangeably (see Figure 7.3 for an illustration).

Keeping track of the different names of trim types is a little easier:

◆ **Double-roller trims = Roll trims:** A double-roller or roll trim always affects both the A-side frames and B-side frames at the edit point equally. This book uses the term *double-roller trims* (see Figure 7.2 for an illustration). See "Performing Single- and Double-Roller Trims" earlier in this chapter for more information.

◆ **Single-roller trims = Ripple trims:** A single-roller or ripple trim affects only the A side or the B side of an edit point. This book uses the term *single-roller trims* (see Figure 7.5 for an illustration). See "Performing Single- and Double-Roller Trims" earlier in this chapter for more information.

Dynamic Trimming with the J-K-L Keys

Xpress Pro has a mode of trimming that is optimized for people who tend to live in Trim mode all day and like to operate primarily from the keyboard. It's called dynamic trimming, or J-K-L trimming, because you can use the J (Play Forward) and L (Play Reverse) keys to rock back and forth and play one side of a cut, and then use the K (Pause) key to dynamically make the trim as you see and hear the clip play.

Many experienced editors prefer to trim in J-K-L mode and have a hard time trimming without it, once they get the knack of it. However, because you are playing only one side of the cut during the trim, J-K-L trimming takes practice to master. If you are new to trimming, you may want to learn the basics the old-fashioned way first, one button at a time, before learning how to perform dynamic trimming.

The first step in J-K-L trimming is to display the Settings tab in the Project window, open the Trim Settings dialog box, and enable J-K-L Trim on the Features tab (**Figure 7.15**).

To perform J-K-L trims, first select which sides of the cut to trim with a single or double roller using any of the methods described in this chapter. Then you need to choose which side of the cut to play and monitor, by hovering your cursor on either the left or the right purple box in the Composer (the Frame Offset box). The line under the box will become highlighted in green when that side is activated for play. Remember to hover but not click; clicking the purple box will change the side of the cut you are trimming.

Now press J to reverse and L to play forward, and watch the Composer monitor play one side of your cut as you look and listen for that perfect frame. Press K to perform the trim. The Timeline updates to reflect your new trim, and you can press the spacebar to review your trim in Play Loop mode. Press the spacebar again to stop play and to return to Trim mode, to perfect your cut with another trim, or to move on to the next cut.

For even finer control, you can also use the J-K-L keys to play at various speeds, as you can in normal editing mode. (For more information, see the sidebar "The Power of the J-K-L Keys" in Chapter 6.)

Figure 7.15 To trim with the J-K-L (Play Reverse, Pause, and Play Forward) keys, you need to enable J-K-L Trim in your Trim settings.

Maintaining Sync in Trim Mode

Trim operations may or may not disrupt sync relationships between Timeline clip segments. It all depends on the type of trim you perform:

◆ A double-roller trim *cannot* disrupt sync relationships because this type of trim does not reposition any Timeline clip segments.

◆ Single-roller trims, slip trims, and slide trims *can* disrupt sync relationships because these types of trims involve either repositioning one or more Timeline clip segments (single-roller and slide trims) or changing the beginning or ending of a Timeline clip segment (slip trims).

By either using a modifier key during a trim or turning on track sync locks, you can automatically maintain sync relationships while performing a single-roller trim. Unfortunately, Xpress Pro has no automatic way to maintain sync relationships when performing a slip or slide trim; you have to keep track of sync during slips and slides yourself.

To maintain sync during a single-roller trim:

Do one of the following:

◆ While performing a single trim that shortens either the head or tail of a clip segment, hold down Alt (Windows) or Control (Mac).

To maintain sync with other tracks, Xpress Pro overwrites black filler where the trimmed frames used to be (**Figure 7.16**). Unlike in a normal single-roller trim, other clips segments do not move.

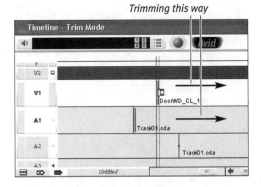

Trimming this way

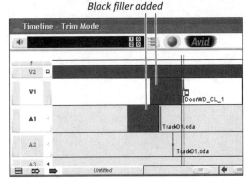

Black filler added

Figure 7.16 Hold down Alt (Windows) or Option (Mac) before you shorten a shot by dragging an edit point (above) to leave black filler in place of the trimmed frames (below).

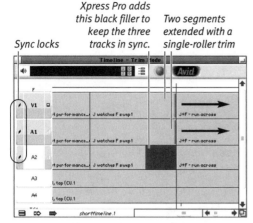

Sync locks *Xpress Pro adds this black filler to keep the three tracks in sync.* *Two segments extended with a single-roller trim*

Figure 7.17 Here, only V1 and A1 are selected for trimming. However, A2 needs to be kept in sync for those tracks. Luckily, the wise editor has sync locks turned on for V1, A1, and A2. When the single-roller trim is performed, Xpress Pro adds black filler to keep A2 in sync.

◆ Enable sync locks for the tracks you want to keep in sync during a single-roller trim.

With sync locks enabled, Xpress Pro will add black filler during a single-roller trim, if necessary, to keep the sync-locked tracks aligned even if they are not all selected for trimming; or Xpress Pro simply won't allow you to perform the trim (**Figure 7.17**).

✔ Tips

■ If you break sync between clip segments, Xpress Pro displays a white sync-break warning below each clip segment that is out of sync. (For more information on sync locks, sync break warnings, and restoring sync, see "Working with Audio-Video Sync" in Chapter 6.)

■ When a clip segment is marked out of sync, you can restore sync by performing a slip, slide, or single-roller trim or entering Segment mode and dragging the out-of-sync clip segment into sync again. (For more information on sync locks, sync break warnings, and restoring sync, see "Working with Audio-Video Sync" in Chapter 6.)

MAINTAINING SYNC IN TRIM MODE

Extend Edit: The Double-Roller Trim Alternative

The Trim tab of the Command palette contains a very handy but little known button called Extend Edit. Clicking this button in normal editing mode—not in Trim mode—lengthens the head or tail of a Timeline segment while simultaneously shortening the adjacent Timeline segment, just like a double-roller trim in Trim mode.

To use Extend Edit, first mark your desired new edit point with an In or an Out point in the Timeline:

♦ Click Mark Out and then Extend Edit if you want to extend the A side of an edit point to the right, lengthening the tail of the clip segment.

♦ Click Mark In and then Extend Edit if you want to extend the B side of an edit point to the left, lengthening the head of the clip segment (**Figure 7.18**).

(For more information on Extend Edit, see "Extending Edits" in Chapter 6.)

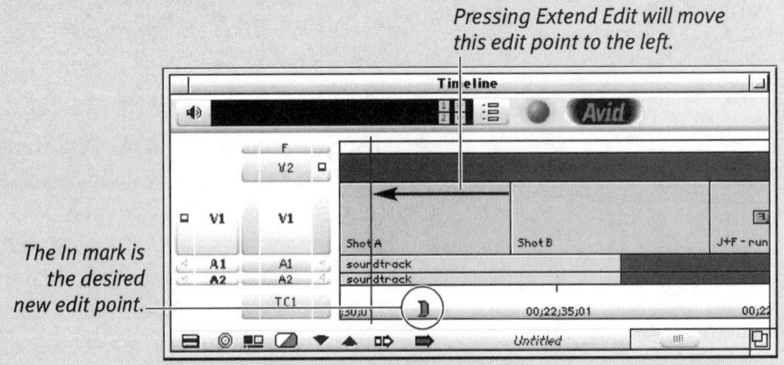

Figure 7.18 To simultaneously extend a clip segment's head backward and shorten the tail of the adjacent clip segment—just as with a double-roller trim—click Mark In where you want the new edit point and then click Extend Edit.

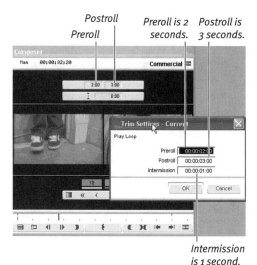

Postroll
Preroll

Preroll is 2 seconds.

Postroll is 3 seconds.

Intermission is 1 second.

Figure 7.19 You can adjust Play Loop Preroll and Postroll in either the Trim Settings dialog box or the Composer window. You can enter an Intermission duration in the Trim Settings dialog box.

Reviewing Your Trim Edits

The best way to review your edit changes in Trim mode is to use the ⬥ Play Loop button. Play Loop backs up a few seconds before the edit point, plays through the edit points, and stops a few seconds after the edit point; then it starts back at the beginning, playing through the edit point again and again until you stop playback with the spacebar.

You designate the preroll and postroll of playback in the Play Loop settings.

To configure your Play Loop settings:

Do one of the following:

1. On the Settings tab of the Project window, double-click your active Trim settings.

2. In the Trim Settings dialog box, set a time duration for Preroll (playback before the edit point), Postroll (playback after the edit point), and Intermission (the pause between loops) (**Figure 7.19**).

3. Click OK.

   or

   Enter Trim mode and go to the top of the Composer.

   Enter a time duration in the top-left box for Preroll and in the right box for Postroll.

To review a trim with Play Loop:

1. After making a trim, press the Play Loop button (mapped by default to the bottom of the Composer window and the spacebar).

   Xpress Pro plays through the edit point you just trimmed, pauses, and begins the playback process all over again.

2. Press Play Loop again to end the transition playback loop.

   Xpress Pro stops playback. You can now perform additional trims.

✔ Tips

- You can map the Play Loop button to the keyboard or interface from the Play tab of the Command palette.

- You can click or select trim buttons while looping around your edit point in Trim mode, but your trimming will not take effect until you stop playback.

Performing a Slip Trim

Slipping uses two single rollers on one clip to simultaneously change both the In and the Out points of the clip in the Timeline, without changing the length or position of the clip relative to the clips on either side of it. If you think a shot begins or ends in the wrong place, but is of the right length and position in the sequence, slipping is a great way to fix the problem very quickly without affecting the overall duration of the sequence.

The easiest way to enter Slip mode is to lasso a segment by dragging the cursor from right to left around the entire segment (**Figure 7.20**).

In Basic Editing mode, in which the Composer is a single window, marking a clip segment for slipping opens a two-up display in the Composer. The first frame shows the In frame of the clip segment you're slipping and the second frame shows the Out frame of the clip segment you're slipping. Both frames change during a slip trim since they represent the changing In and Out point of the marked clip A segment ready for slipping has single rollers on its head and tail (**Figure 7.21**).

Lassoed segment

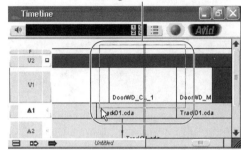

Figure 7.20 Drag a lasso from right to left around an entire segment to enter Trim mode and mark the segment for slipping.

PERFORMING A SLIP TRIM

In point of the clip segment

Out point of the clip segment

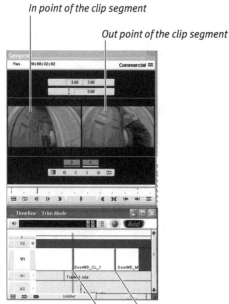

Out point of the clip segment
In point of the clip segment

New In point of the clip segment

New Out point of the clip segment

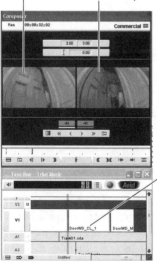

Nothing changes except the In and Out points of this segment.

Figure 7.21 Here, the length and position of the selected segment is good, but the segment needs to begin sooner—it needs a different source In point (above). Slipping a segment simultaneously moves the In and Out points to an earlier or later part of the clip (below).

In Source/Record mode, marking a clip segment for slipping opens a four-up display in the Composer:

◆ The first image shows the Out frame of the previous clip segment, which won't change with a slip trim. It's there only as a visual reference to help you make aesthetic judgments as you slip the next frame.

◆ The middle two frames show the In and Out frames of the clip segment you're slipping and will continuously update as you perform the slip trim.

◆ The last image shows the In frame of the next clip segment, which won't change. See **Figure 7.24** for an example of a four-up display.

PERFORMING A SLIP TRIM

To perform a slip trim:

1. *Do one of the following:*

   ▲ In normal editing mode, lasso the segments you want to slip by dragging from right to left around the entire segment. To lasso a track that is between other tracks, hold down Alt (Windows) or Control (Mac) while dragging (**Figure 7.22**).

   The Composer enters Trim mode and marks single rollers on the In and Out points of the clips you lassoed.

   ▲ In Trim mode, hold down the Shift key and click the head and tail of the clip segment you want to slip.

   Xpress Pro marks single rollers on the In and Out points of the segment to be slipped.

   If you're in dual-monitor Source/Record mode, the Composer displays four images, the middle two being the frames that will change during the slip. If you're in single-monitor Basic mode, the Composer displays only two images: the In and Out points of the marked clip you are slipping.

2. Trim to the left or right using the trim buttons or any other method described in "Performing Single- and Double-Roller Trims" earlier in this chapter.

   Slipping to the left moves the In and Out points of the segment earlier in the source clip. Slipping to the right moves the In and Out points of the segment later in the clip. The two segments on either side of the segment you're slipping do not change in length or position.

✔ Tips

■ You can slip multiple segments simultaneously. Select other segments on other tracks by holding down the Shift key and lassoing the segments from right to left.

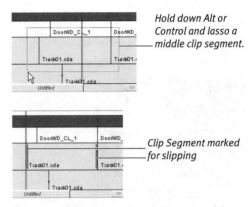

Hold down Alt or Control and lasso a middle clip segment.

Clip Segment marked for slipping

Figure 7.22 To lasso a segment that is on a track lower than the top one (above), hold down Alt (Windows) or Option (Mac) while you drag from right to left. Xpress Pro marks the segment for slipping (below).

■ If you lasso a segment by dragging left to right when you are in normal editing mode, you will enter Segment mode, not Trim mode.

■ When slipping by dragging, press Ctrl (Windows) or Command (Mac) to snap to edit points on other tracks.

PERFORMING A SLIP TRIM

Tail (Out point of preceding shot) Head (In point of following shot)

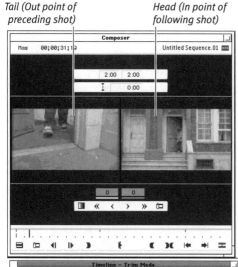

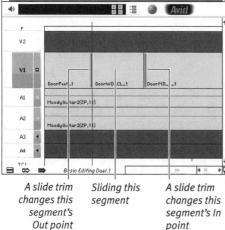

A slide trim   Sliding this   A slide trim
changes this   segment   changes this
segment's   segment's In
Out point   point

Figure 7.23 When you slide a clip, you change its position on a track. You also change the Out point of the preceding clip and the In point of the following clip.

Performing a Slide Trim

A slide trim uses two single rollers to move an entire clip segment to the left or right in a sequence, changing its position on a track but not its In or Out point. A slide trim can be thought of as the reverse of a slip trim in that it changes the Out point of the clip that precedes the clip that you slide, and the In point of the following clip (**Figure 7.23**).

continues on next page

In Source/Record mode, marking a clip segment for sliding opens a four-up display in the Composer, just as it does for a slip trim.

◆ The first image shows the Out frame of the previous clip segment. This image will change as you perform the slide trim.

◆ The middle two frames show the In and Out frames of the clip segment you're sliding. These two images do not change with a slide trim and are shown only as a visual reference.

◆ The last image shows the In frame of the clip segment following the one you are sliding. It will update continuously as you perform the slide trim (**Figure 7.24**).

You perform a slide trim using the same controls that you use for standard single-roller trims. See "Performing Single- and Double-Roller Trims" earlier in this chapter for more information on the four ways to perform trim operations.

To slide a segment:

1. *Do one of the following:*

▲ In normal editing mode, hold down Alt+Shift (Windows) or Option+Shift (Mac) and drag down and right to left, lassoing the entire segment.

Xpress Pro automatically enters Trim mode, with the segment prepared for sliding.

▲ In Trim mode, hold down the Shift key and click the tail of the preceding segment and the head of the following segment to add single rollers to each.

In frame of sliding segment (does not change)　*Out frame of sliding segment (does not change)*

Out frame of preceding segment　*In frame of following segment*

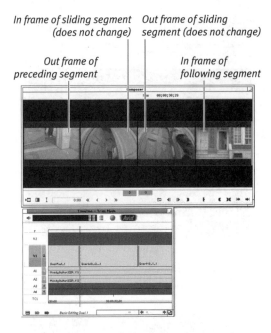

Sliding 20 frames to the right

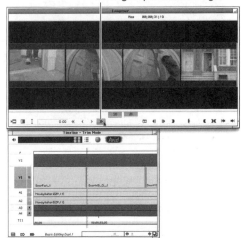

Figure 7.24 In Source/Record mode, the Composer displays four images during a slipping or sliding operation (above). Here, the marked segment slides 20 frames to the right (below).

Xpress Pro marks a single roller on the tail of the previous shot and the head of the following shot. If you're in dual-monitor Source/Record mode, the Composer displays four images, the first and last showing the frames that will change during the slide. If you're in single-monitor Basic mode, the Composer displays only two images: the In frame of the preceding clip and the Out frame of the following clip.

2. Slide the clip to the left or right using the trim buttons or any other method described in "Performing Single- and Double-Roller Trims" earlier in this chapter.

Sliding to the left shortens the tail of the preceding clip while extending the head of the following clip. Sliding to the right does the opposite. The In and Out points of the clip you are sliding do not change, but the clip's relative position in the Timeline does change.

✔ Tips

■ You can select multiple segments for slide trimming simultaneously by holding down Shift+Alt (Windows) or Shift+Option (Mac) and lassoing the segments from right to left.

■ When sliding by dragging, press Ctrl (Windows) or Command (Mac) to snap to edit points on other tracks.

■ An additional way to mark a clip for sliding is to enter Trim mode and Alt-double-click (Windows) or Option-double-click (Mac) a clip segment.

Adding Transition Effects in Trim Mode

You can add a transition effect to one or more edit points without leaving Trim mode, saving you the time of entering Effect mode or opening the Effect editor. Use the Quick Transition button to easily add one of six standard fades or dissolves, and use the Effect palette to add wipes. (For more information about transition effects, see Chapter 9, "Working with Video Effects.")

To add a fade or dissolve in Trim mode:

1. In Trim mode, with one or more edit points marked by pink rollers, go to the Composer monitor and press the Quick Transition button (**Figure 7.25**).

   The Quick Transition dialog box opens (**Figure 7.26**).

2. Choose the type of fade or dissolve and the alignment and rendering options.

3. Press Enter (Windows) or Return (Mac).

   Xpress Pro adds a dissolve or fade of the desired duration and alignment to all selected edit points.

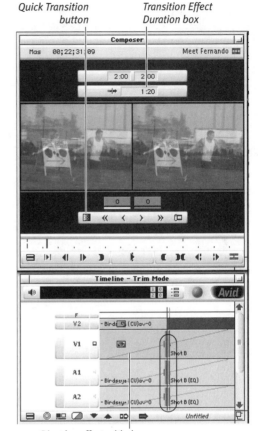

Quick Transition button   *Transition Effect Duration box*

Dissolve effect added to selected edit points

Figure 7.25 To quickly add a Dissolve effect to marked transitions, staying in Trim mode, enter a duration in the Composer's Transition Effect Duration box, and press Enter (Windows) or Return (Mac).

Choose transition type here. *Enter length of effect here.*

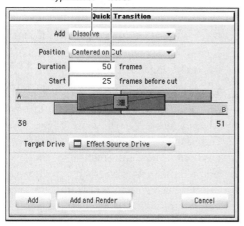

Figure 7.26 The Quick Transition dialog box allows you to quickly apply a common transition effect to one or more selected edit points in the Timeline.

Transition effect alignment options

Figure 7.27 You can determine the alignment (or centering) of your added Dissolve effects from the Transition Effect Alignment menu.

✔ Tips

- The fastest way to add your favorite dissolve is to simply type a transition duration in the Composer's Duration box. When you press Enter (Windows) or Return (Mac), the transition type that is currently selected in the Quick Transition dialog box is added, with a standard alignment of Centered on Cut.

- To change a transition alignment after you have added it, click the Transition Effect Alignment button (to the left of the Duration box) and choose a new alignment (**Figure 7.27**).

- To remove a transition effect, place the position indicator over the effect, select the track that contains the effect, and click the Remove Effect button (found by default on the Tool palette in the Composer Fast menu).

ADDING TRANSITION EFFECTS IN TRIM MODE

To add any transition effect in Trim mode:

1. In Trim mode, with one or more edit points marked by pink rollers, choose Tools > Effect Palette or click the Project window's Effect palette tab.

The Effect palette displays Xpress Pro's categorized effects. The first four—Blend, Box Wipe, Conceal, and Edge Wipe—are the transition effects.

2. Click an Effect palette category and double-click the transition effect you want to apply to the marked edit points (**Figure 7.28**).

Xpress Pro adds the same transition effect to all edit points that have pink rollers in the Timeline, giving them a default duration of 1 second and a default alignment of Centered on Cut.

3. To change the duration of the added effects, enter a new duration in the Composer's Effect Duration box and press Enter (Windows) or Return (Mac). Xpress Pro adjusts the duration of all of the transition effects you just applied.

4. To change the alignment of the added transitions, click the Transition Effect Alignment button (to the left of the Duration box) and choose a new alignment. (For more information on transition effect durations and alignments, see "Modifying Segment and Transition Effects" in Chapter 9.)

✔ Tip

■ If you want to continue working in Trim mode, keep the Effect editor closed while working in Trim mode. If the Effect editor is open, Xpress Pro will automatically close Trim mode and enter Effect mode after you apply any transition effect other than a dissolve.

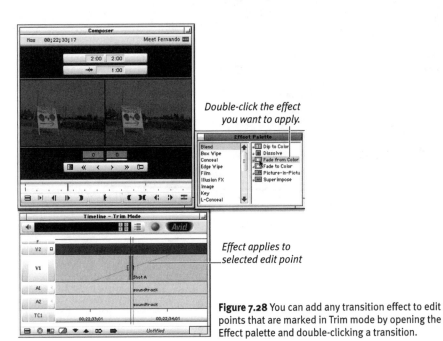

Double-click the effect you want to apply.

Effect applies to selected edit point

Figure 7.28 You can add any transition effect to edit points that are marked in Trim mode by opening the Effect palette and double-clicking a transition.

ADDING TRANSITION EFFECTS IN TRIM MODE

CREATING TITLES

Xpress Pro's prodigious Title tool is designed for high-volume production of attractive yet fairly simple titles.

What you create, format, layer, and arrange in the Title tool are *text objects* and *graphic objects*. Text objects are individual chunks of text that may contain one or more lines of letters and symbols. A graphic object can be a circle/oval, square/rectangle, or a line (with or without an arrowhead).

A saved title typically contains multiple objects, the formatting and style of which you can alter before or after you create them. If your productions tend to be heavy on titles that have common objects or object formatting, using custom styles and templates will help you avoid extra time and effort. Text-object formatting options include font, size, justification, kerning, leading, bold, and italic. Formatting options for both text and graphic objects include borders, blended colors, varied transparency, and drop and depth shadows.

Strategies for saving and rendering your titles depend on the project. For projects with tons of titles, you'll want to consider using Fast Save to send your titles to the bins unrendered and then batch-render them later. But once you render a title and edit it into the Timeline, it's still not set in stone; you can always modify it and save the changes to your bin.

One of the most advanced features of the Title tool lets you make moving video play inside your titles. For example, you could fill the title "Ocean" with a moving clip of crashing waves. With a little advance planning, you can have multiple titles stacked up in the Timeline, each with its own video fill layers.

Getting Started with the Title Tool

The Xpress Pro Title tool is a comfortably large layout window that contains all of the controls—with the exception of the Object and Alignment menus—that you need to create and format multiple text and graphic objects (**Figure 8.1**).

When you open the Title tool, Xpress Pro automatically loads the video image currently displayed in your Composer window as a background reference image to help you

position and color your title. However, it is merely a reference image and will not be saved with your title. Once you save your title, you can layer it over any video image you please in the Timeline.

As an alternative, you can give your title a solid background color within the Title tool; in that case, your saved title will include the background color.

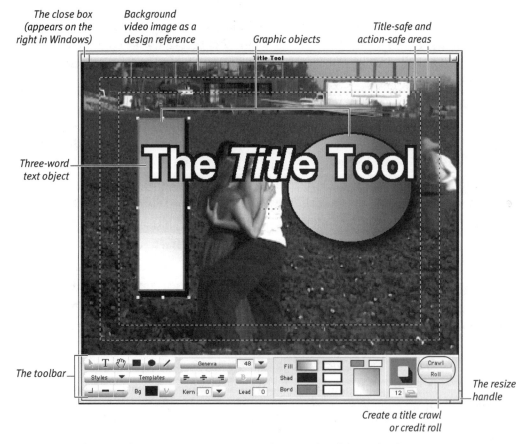

The close box (appears on the right in Windows)

Background video image as a design reference

Graphic objects

Title-safe and action-safe areas

Three-word text object

The toolbar

The resize handle

Create a title crawl or credit roll

Figure 8.1 The Title tool, starring Mr. Rectangle, Mr. Oval, and Mr. Bordered Text.

Video
Placement tool   The Title tool resized

Figure 8.2 To save space on your desktop, you can make the Title tool window smaller and use the Video Placement tool to move around the image. This approach is effective when you just need to alter individual objects and don't need to see the whole title layout.

To begin a new title:

Do one of the following:

◆ Choose Tools > Title Tool.

◆ Choose Clip > New Title.

◆ Click the Composer's Fast menu. When the tool palette appears, click the ⊥ Title tool button.

Xpress Pro opens the Title tool window, creates a blank title for you, and automatically selects the ⊥ Text tool, so you are ready to type away on your title background.

✔ Tips

■ Other windows often obscure the Title tool. To bring the Title tool to the front, choose Tools > Title Tool again.

■ If the Title tool window crowds your desktop, grab the lower-right corner of the Title tool and resize it smaller. You won't be able to see your entire title creation area, but you can use the 🖑 Video Placement tool (a hand tool) to move to a different part of the title image (**Figure 8.2**).

■ You can map the Title tool button to your keyboard or interface from the FX tab of the Command palette.

GETTING STARTED WITH THE TITLE TOOL

To change your video background reference frame:

1. Make sure the  Video Background button is highlighted green in the Title toolbar (**Figure 8.3**).

2. In the Timeline or Composer window, move the position indicator to the video frame you want to use as your new background reference.

3. Click the Title tool window again.

The Title tool now displays the same image that is in your Composer window.

To create a color background matte:

1. Deselect the Video Background button so that the button becomes gray (not green).

The video reference image disappears, replaced by black.

2. Click and hold the ■ Background Color (Bg) button.

The Title tool color picker appears (**Figure 8.4**).

3. To keep the color picker open, drag it upward and release the mouse. Using the color picker's controls, choose a color for your background. (For more information on choosing and manipulating colors, see "Coloring Your Text and Graphics" later in this chapter.)

Title tool now displays a colored background. Your saved title will not include an alpha channel; you cannot layer it over a background image in the Timeline. (For more information on alpha channels, see "Alpha Channels Explained" in Chapter 9.)

Video Background button

Figure 8.3 To enable the display of a background reference image, keep the Video Background button highlighted. To change the reference image, move the position indicator to a new location in the Composer or Timeline.

Figure 8.4 To choose a solid color matte for your title's background, click and hold the box next to Bg. Then choose a color from the color picker that appears.

✔ Tips

■ You can use the Title tool to create a dummy clip or slug, a placeholder for some yet-to-be edited footage. This approach can be more effective than using black filler as a slug, since a title segment is easier to see than filler.

■ To learn how to use the Title tool to create rolling credits, see "Creating Title Crawls and Rolls" later in this chapter.

GETTING STARTED WITH THE TITLE TOOL

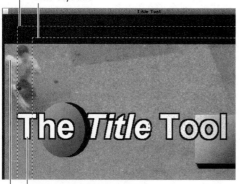

Action-safe line
Title-safe line

This letter may not be visible
on a broadcast monitor.

Part of this person may be cut
off on a broadcast monitor.

Figure 8.5 There may be a problem with one letter of this title, since it is outside the title-safe area.

To display title-safe and action-safe lines:

◆ Choose Object > Title Area/Global Grid, if necessary.

This setting is on by default, so you may not need to select it. Xpress Pro displays the dotted title-safe and action-safe lines. Keep all title objects within the inner, title-safe lines to make sure they appear on your television screen, without being clipped by the borders of the frame; keep all screen elements within the action-safe lines or they won't be seen at all on your broadcast TV (**Figure 8.5**).

✔ Tip

■ Remember that just because you can see a title on *your* television or studio monitor, this does not mean that it will show up on someone else's television. Trust the lines, not your screen.

To display safe colors:

◆ Choose Object > Safe Colors.

Xpress Pro will alter any colors that, according to current TV broadcast standards, contain unacceptable ("illegal") luminance or chrominance levels by altering them so they are legal.

Working with Text

To create text in the Title tool, you can use the Text tool to type characters, or you can copy and paste text from a word processing application.

After typing or pasting your text, you must convert it to an independent *text object*. A text object contains one or more characters confined by an invisible border, marked by eight small, square handles that you can use to resize the object (**Figure 8.6**).

You can move a text object wherever you want in the Title tool image area, and you can change a text object's formatting and color whenever you wish, using options in the Title toolbar (**Figure 8.7**).

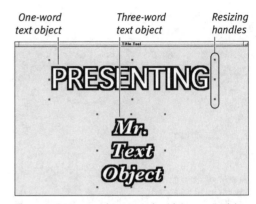

One-word text object   Three-word text object   Resizing handles

Figure 8.6 Two text objects, each with its own resizing handles. Drag one of the handles to resize the object.

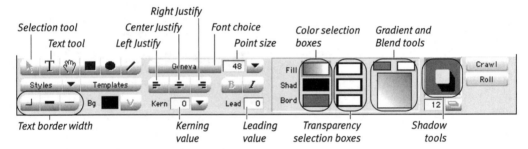

Selection tool   Text tool   Center Justify   Left Justify   Right Justify   Font choice   Point size   Color selection boxes   Gradient and Blend tools

Text border width   Kerning value   Leading value   Transparency selection boxes   Shadow tools

Figure 8.7 The Title toolbar contains many controls for formatting text objects and text within text objects.

Table 8.1

Text Formatting Options	
FOR INDIVIDUAL TEXT	FOR TEXT OBJECTS ONLY
Font	Leading
Point size	Color
Bold	Justification (left, center, right)
Italic	Border width
Kerning	Drop and depth shadows
	Transparency

- Increasing the point size of a text object often messes up its word wrapping. To fix that, resize the object by clicking and dragging one its handles.

- If you create text that is 128 points or larger, you must use a TrueType font.

- If you're pasting a lot of text, keep in mind that Xpress Pro limits the size of text objects. You may need to break a long text piece into multiple text objects.

Keep this in mind: Some formatting choices (such as font point size) can apply to individual text within a text object (a text object being group of words that can be moved as a whole); the first letter of a word can be very large while the rest of the letters are small. On the other hand, some formatting choices (like color) can apply only to a text object as a whole; all letters in one text object must be the same color (see **Table 8.1** for which formatting options can apply to individual text and which must apply to text objects as a whole).

To create a text object:

1. In the Title toolbar, select the Text tool.

2. Click in the image frame where you want your text to appear and *do one of the following:*
   - ▲ Type text, using Enter (Windows) or Return (Mac) for line breaks.
   - ▲ Open a word processing document, use Ctrl+C (Windows) or Command+C (Mac) to copy its text, return to Xpress Pro's Title tool, and press Ctrl+V (Windows) or Command+V (Mac) to paste the text.

3. To convert your text to a single text object, *do one of the following:*
   - ▲ Click the 🔖 Selection tool in the toolbar.
   - ▲ Alt-click (Windows) or Option-click (Mac) anywhere on the screen.

   Selection handles appear around the text, indicating that it is a text object. Xpress Pro formats the text according to the choices currently active on the toolbar.

✔ Tips

- Text borders, drop shadows, transparencies, and other formatting choices are not displayed until you convert the text into a text object by clicking the Selection tool.

WORKING WITH TEXT

Where Are My Fonts?

For Title tool text, Xpress Pro gives you access to most, if not all, of the fonts installed on your system.

On **Windows** systems, you can typically find your fonts in *drive:*\WINNT\Fonts. You can also open the Control Panel, open Appearance and Themes, and open Fonts.

On **Macintosh** systems, you can typically find OS X fonts in *drive*/Library/Fonts. In addition, Xpress Pro loads any fonts you have installed in the OS 9 system folder if it is located on the same drive as OS X.

If you transfer your project to a system that does not contain a font you used to create a title, or if you're missing a font for some other reason, Xpress Pro helps you find a substitute by opening the Font Replacement dialog box.

To manually find a substitute font at any time, select a text object or some text within a text object, choose Object > Font Replacement, and choose a replacement font in the Font Replacement dialog box (**Figure 8.8**).

A word of caution: Sometimes substituted fonts force undesirable line-wrapping changes, so you should always recheck each title when you substitute fonts. Of course, the best way to avoid font snafus is to bring your system fonts along with you whenever you switch workstations.

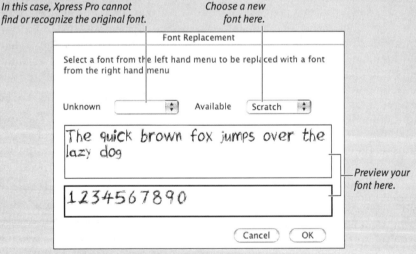

Figure 8.8 You can choose a replacement font in the Font Replacement dialog box. This is also a great way to quickly preview your font styles.

To edit text in a text object:

Do one of the following:

♦ Select the Text tool and click the text object.

♦ Alt-click (Windows) or Option-click (Mac) a text object.

The Text tool becomes highlighted, the text's formatting disappears, and the blinking cursor indicates that you can highlight and edit the text characters.

✔ Tips

■ You can select all of the text in a text object with the Text tool by double-clicking anywhere inside the object.

■ You can select multiple text objects by lassoing them or using Shift-click.

■ Once typed text becomes a text object, you can still go back and change the characters inside it at any time, even if the text is part of a template. (For more information, see "Using Title Styles and Templates" later in this chapter.)

■ After you use a tool in the toolbar, Xpress Pro automatically reverts to the Selection tool. To prevent this from happening, double-click a tool's icon when you first select it.

To reposition text or graphic objects:

1. Select one or more text or graphic objects. Select multiple objects by Shift-clicking or dragging a lasso around them.

2. *Do one of the following:*

   ▲ Drag the selected objects to a new location.

   ▲ Use the up, down, right, and left arrow keys on the keyboard to move the objects one pixel at a time.

   ▲ Use one of the Alignment menu commands. (For more information on aligning objects, see "Aligning and Distributing Objects" later in this chapter.)

WORKING WITH TEXT

To resize a text or graphic object:

1. Using the Selection tool from the Title toolbar, select a text or graphic object.

2. Drag one of the object's handles to resize it.

The text is reformatted to fill the new size of the text object.

✔ Tips

■ Use a text object's middle selection handles, on both the left and the right, to eliminate unused object space. Eliminating this space will help you align your text (**Figure 8.9**). (For information on using alignment tools, see "Aligning and Distributing Objects" later in this chapter.)

■ The quality of a title decreases when you resize it to a larger size. A better approach is to create a title larger than you need and scale it down than to create a small title and scale it up.

■ Here's a handy way to force a text object to fit snugly against the text it contains. Click the Kerning pop-up menu and select or deselect Pair Kerning; the text object's borders move flush against its text. (For more information on kerning, see "Using Leading and Kerning" later in this chapter).

Unnecessary space

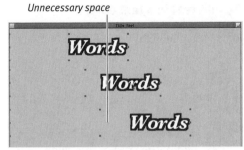

Figure 8.9 After you select all three objects and choose Alignment > Align to Frame Left, these text object aren't vertically aligned. Why? They're different sizes, and each includes a different amount of extra space. The lesson is this: Size your text objects so the boundaries fit the text exactly.

Jagged lines, sometimes called the jaggies—not good

Smooth lines, courtesy of anti-aliasing—very nice

Figure 8.10 After you choose Object > Preview, the jagged aliased edges (above) disappear (below). Don't worry; your final title will always be anti-aliased after rendering, so the Preview command is just that: a preview.

Previewing Titles

Normally, your title's text and objects will have rough, jaggy lines while you work on them. However, you can turn on the Preview feature on the Object menu to see your titles with fully anti-aliased edges and 8-bit alpha channels.

If you enter a previewed title object with the Text tool to edit it, Xpress Pro turns off the nice-looking preview. After you finish editing the text object and deselect it, however, Xpress Pro restores the smooth, anti-aliased preview (**Figure 8.10**).

To preview titles with anti-aliasing:

◆ Choose Object > Preview.

◆ Press Shift+Ctrl+P (Windows) or Shift+Command+P (Mac).

Your titles are now displayed in the layout window with smooth, anti-aliased edges—no jaggies—just as they will be rendered in your final output.

✔ Tip

■ You can modify your text objects and apply styles to them without affecting your anti-aliased preview.

WORKING WITH TEXT

Make Your Formatting Stick Around

When you'll be creating a long series of titles with the same basic font, shadows, and so on, you can set up your default formatting so that you don't have to keep selecting the same options. Open the Title tool, click the Selection tool, and then click the Text tool. *Do this before you type any text.*

Now make your formatting choices on the toolbar. Those choices are now your default settings for all of the text you create with the Text tool.

This method requires you to plan ahead, but it can save you much time in the long run when you need to create many titles in a row with identical or similar formatting.

Using Leading and Kerning

Kerning and leading allow you to fine-tune the exact spacing of your text after you've settled on a point size. **Leading** adjusts the amount of space between individual lines of text in an entire text object. **Kerning** adjusts the amount of space between individual letters. **Pair kerning** eliminates unneeded space between individual character pairs based on kerning tables that come with certain fonts. You generally use leading first to balance your overall graphic layout and then kerning second, to make stubborn text fit within a space that might seem just a little too small or too large at first.

The More Text Objects the Better

When creating text in the Title tool, properly positioning and wrapping words within a text object can be a frustrating endeavor. If you put all of your text in the same text object, all you have is the spacebar and the Enter (Windows) or Enter (Mac) key for word positioning and line breaks.

There's a better strategy: You can avoid awkward spacing and wrapping situations by planning ahead and breaking your text into multiple, independent text objects. This approach will afford you more freedom in laying out phrases, sentences, and paragraphs.

In addition, once you arrange your text as you like, you can select all of your text objects and choose Object > Group to make them what is essentially one giant object (which you can break up again later). (For more information, see "Working with Layers and Groups" later in this chapter.)

When you have multiple text objects, you can also take advantage of the Alignment menu's automatic object arrangement options. Because you can align the objects separately, you have more control over design than when you align just one big object.

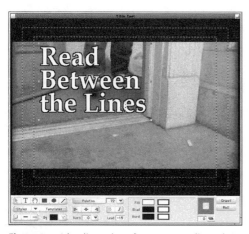

Figure 8.11 A leading value of –15 puts text lines close together.

Figure 8.12 The *K* and the *e* are too far apart (above). You can adjust the kerning between the two letters to make the letters fit together more closely (below).

To apply leading to a text object:

1. Select a text object.

2. In the Title toolbar, enter a leading value. Negative values create tight spacing, and positive values create loose spacing (**Figure 8.11**).

To apply kerning to text characters:

1. Select a text object or use the Text tool to highlight individual letters within an object.

2. On the Title toolbar, click the Kerning option and select Loose, Normal, or Tight from the list that appears, or enter your own value. Negative values create tight spacing, and positive values create loose spacing (**Figure 8.12**).

✔ Tips

- You can increase and decrease kerning by highlighting text with the Text tool, holding down Alt (Windows) or Option (Mac), and using the left and right arrow keys.

- Another way to adjust kerning is by selecting a text object, clicking the Kerning field on the toolbar, and using the up and down arrow keys.

- Sometimes changing the kerning value of a text object will automatically create unwanted cropping of the text or unwanted additional text lines. To fix this, resize the text object or adjust the leading of the text object.

To apply pair kerning to two text characters:

1. Using the Text tool, place the cursor between the two characters that you want to kern.

2. On the Title toolbar next to the Kerning field, open the pull-down menu and select Pair Kerning.

   The pair of characters are custom kerned, based on kerning tables that include the best match for every possible pairing of characters in the entire font set.

✔ Tip

■ If pair kerning appears to have no effect, your font may not support kerning tables. For example, Palatino supports kerning tables, but not all fonts do.

Using Symbols and Special Characters

You may occasionally need a symbol or special character not found on the standard keyboard (even by pressing Shift or Option). For example, the name of the composer Saint-Saëns requires a special symbol (an umlaut) over the *e*.

You can usually get a special character or diacritical mark from a word processing program. In Microsoft Word, for instance, you can choose Insert > Symbol and pick a special character from the character grid that appears (**Figure 8.13**). Insert the special character into your word processing document, copy it, and then paste it into Xpress Pro's Title tool. The symbol should carry over nicely.

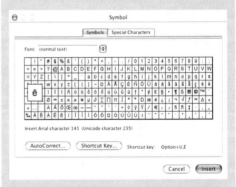

Figure 8.13 Microsoft Word has a dialog box that contains special characters and marks. You can insert what you need into a document and then copy the document and paste it into Xpress Pro's Title tool.

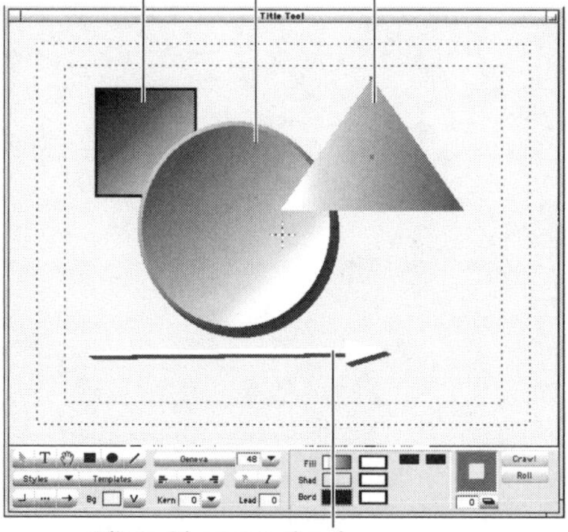

A circle with two blended border colors, two blended fill colors, and a drop shadow

A square with a solid border and two blended fill colors

Looks like a triangle, but it's actually a short line with a giant arrowhead

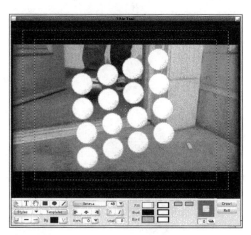

A line with an arrowhead and a drop shadow

Figure 8.14 You can format any of the three basic graphic shapes with many of the same formatting tools that you use on text and text objects. Hey wait— where did that triangle come from?

Figure 8.15 Here, one circle was copied and pasted to make two circles, then four circles, and so on, to quickly create 16 circles from one original.

Working with Graphic Objects

Xpress Pro titles can be more than just text. Using the Title toolbar, you can add the following simple vector-based shapes to your title: squares (or rectangles), circles (or ovals), and lines.

Because these graphic objects are vector based, you can make them any size or shape you want and later use the drag handles to resize them to fit your layout. The color and transparency formatting choices available to text objects can also be applied to graphic objects (**Figure 8.14**).

To draw a graphic object:

1. On the Title toolbar, click one of the three graphic object tools.

2. In the image area of the Title tool, drag the crosshair cursor to create the shape you want. Release the mouse when you like what you see.

3. Resize the shape if necessary by dragging one of the object's selection handles. Reposition the shape by clicking inside the shape and dragging.

   Xpress Pro automatically makes the shape a graphic object. With the object selected, you can color and format it as you wish.

✔ Tips

- You can constrain the shapes you draw to make perfect squares, circles, and straight lines by holding the Shift key as you drag.

- After you create one or more text or graphic objects, you can manipulate them using Cut, Copy, Paste, Select All, Delete, and Duplicate from the Edit menu (**Figure 8.15**).

WORKING WITH GRAPHIC OBJECTS

Creating Borders and Lines

Use the Border Width tool to add borders to text and graphic objects and adjust the thickness of lines. Xpress Pro considers a line to be a border, so you cannot add a border to a line, but you can adjust its width with the Border Width tool.

Choose the small dotted line at the top of the Border Width menu to give the selected object no border. Choose the bold dotted line at the bottom of the menu to open a custom width option in which you can type a value between 0 and 200 pixels for the border's width.

Drawing Rings and Triangles

Because the shapes you can draw in the Title tool are rather basic, drawing more than simple circles, squares, and lines requires some creativity.

For example, to draw a ring (an empty circle), you could first draw a circle, give it a solid border (Bord) color, and then set its fill color to a transparency level of 100. (For information on setting transparency, see "Setting Transparency Levels" later in this chapter.)

For a more subtle ring effect, you could make give the ring's border a gradient blend (see "Coloring Your Text and Graphics " later in this chapter). Then you could fade the second color of the border by setting its transparency level to 100 (**Figure 8.16**).

Here's another trick: You can approximate a triangle object by creating a short line with a giant arrowhead (see Figure 8.14 for an example). Use the Border Width tool menu and the custom arrowhead option on the Arrowhead tool menu to set the shape and orientation of the triangle.

(For more information about line attributes and rounded corners, see "Creating Borders and Lines" above.)

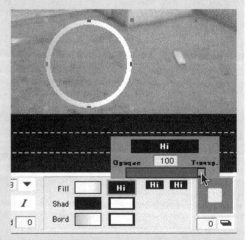

Figure 8.16 Careful use of color and transparency results in a ring. Here, a circle was drawn with a solid border, and a fill color with a transparency value of 100 was applied.

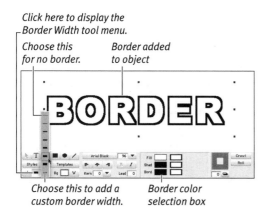

Click here to display the Border Width tool menu.

Choose this for no border.

Border added to object

Choose this to add a custom border width.

Border color selection box

Figure 8.17 To add a border to a text or graphic object, select the object, click the Border Width tool, and choose an option from the menu that appears.

To apply a border to a text or graphic object:

1. Select the text, text object, or graphic object with the Selection tool.

2. On the Title toolbar, click and hold on the Border Width tool ☰ and choose from the selection of border widths (**Figure 8.17**).

3. Click outside the selected object to make the new border width take effect.

   Your text or object displays a border based on the color that is active in the border color selection box.

✔ Tips

■ If your border does not seem to appear, check to make sure you have chosen a different color for your text and border. For instance, adding a small black border to black text will appear to have no effect.

■ You can make a border a solid color or give it a blended color gradient. You can also manipulate a border color's transparency. (See "Coloring Your Text and Graphics" and "Setting Transparency Levels" later in this chapter.)

WORKING WITH GRAPHIC OBJECTS

To round corners on squares and rectangles:

1. Select a square or rectangular graphic object with the Selection tool.

2. On the Title toolbar, click and hold on the ⌐ Box Corner tool, and choose from a selection of corner styles (**Figure 8.18**).

✔ Tip

The last choice on the Corner Styles menu opens a custom corner dialog box in which you can enter a maximum radius amount of 200 (**Figure 8.19**).

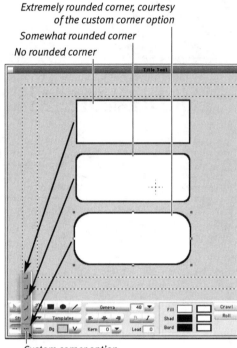

Extremely rounded corner, courtesy of the custom corner option

Somewhat rounded corner

No rounded corner

Custom corner option

Figure 8.18 The Box Corner menu contains five presets and one button for a custom corner.

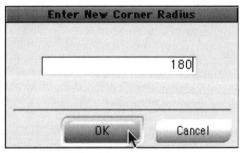

Figure 8.19 When you choose the custom border option in the Box Corner pop-up menu, a dialog box asks you to enter a numerical value for a new corner radius. You can enter a number as high as 200. The higher the value, the more rounded your rectangle.

Choose this to customize your arrowhead's shape.

Figure 8.20 When you click and hold on the Arrowhead tool, this pop-up menu appears. Choose the first option if you do not want any arrowhead attached to the line you create.

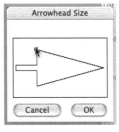

Figure 8.21 The The Arrowhead Size dialog box lets you design the shape of your arrowheads.

To add arrowheads to lines:

1. Select a graphic line object with the Selection tool.

2. On the Title toolbar, click and hold on the Arrowhead tool and choose from a selection of arrowhead styles (**Figure 8.20**).

✔ Tip

■ The last choice in the Arrowhead Style dialog box brings up the Arrowhead Size dialog box, which you can use to customize the arrowhead's shape (**Figure 8.21**).

To extend or rotate a line:

1. Click and hold on one of the selection boxes at either end of a line.

2. Drag the selection box to a new location; release the mouse when the line is positioned as you want it.

✔ Tip

■ Hold down the Shift key to constrain the angle of the line to 45-degree increments.

Coloring Your Text and Graphics

Using the controls on the right of the Title toolbar, you can give fill, shadow, and border colors to text objects, circles/ovals, and squares/rectangles. Lines never have borders, but they can have fill or shadow colors.

When you choose two colors for a fill, shadow, or border, the Title tool creates a gradient blend between the two choices and lets you choose the direction of the blend.

Often the best place to start when picking a color, especially when titles will appear over background images, is to sample from a reference image with the color picker's eyedropper. If you need to do careful color matching using print, Web, or other standardized color systems, click the color picker's radial dial button to open your system's color palette.

To choose a single color for an object:

1. Click the Selection tool and select a text or graphic object. Shift-click to select multiple objects.

2. Click the color selection box next to Fill (for the main color), Shad (for the color of the drop shadow), or Bord (for the color of the object's border).

   The Title tool color picker appears (**Figure 8.22**).

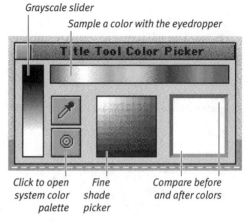

Grayscale slider

Sample a color with the eyedropper

Click to open system color palette   *Fine shade picker*   *Compare before and after colors*

Figure 8.22 The Xpress Pro color picker gives you an eyedropper, fine shade picker (which lets you choose a darker or lighter version of the chosen color), and a grayscale slider. You can also open your system color picker by clicking the radial dial button.

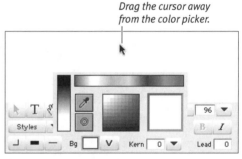

Drag the cursor away from the color picker.

Figure 8.23 When you click to display the color picker, you can keep the color picker open by dragging up before releasing the mouse button.

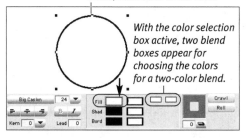

The circle is selected and the color selection box for its fill color is active, with white as the color.

With the color selection box active, two blend boxes appear for choosing the colors for a two-color blend.

Figure 8.24 Whenever a color or transparency box for either Fill or Border is active, two small blend boxes appear so you can create color or transparency gradients.

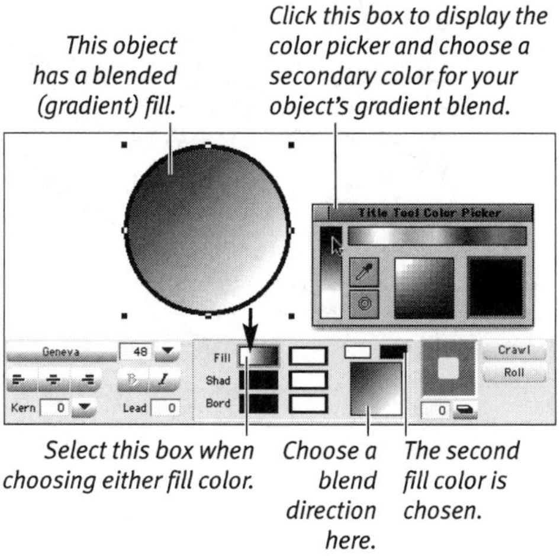

This object has a blended (gradient) fill.

Click this box to display the color picker and choose a secondary color for your object's gradient blend.

Select this box when choosing either fill color.

Choose a blend direction here.

The second fill color is chosen.

Figure 8.25 Here, a second color is chosen: black. Now the object will be a blend of colors from white to black.

3. In the color picker, *do one of the following:*

▲ Click the eyedropper and click somewhere on the Xpress Pro interface, such as within your video reference image, to sample its color.

▲ Choose a color or grayscale shade from one of the color picker's color choice panels.

▲ Click the radial dial button to open your system's color picker and choose a color.

The color choice immediately takes effect in the selected object. The box next to Fill, Shad, or Bord, as appropriate, displays the chosen color.

✔ Tip

■ To keep the color picker open after you click a color selection box, drag up before you release the mouse (**Figure 8.23**).

To create a two-color blended gradient:

1. Select either the Fill or Bord (border) color selection box.

Two small blend boxes appear at the right. At this point, the two blend boxes are the same color (**Figure 8.24**).

2. Drag in each of the two blend boxes to choose different colors for your gradient blend (**Figure 8.25**).

With two different colors chosen, the blend direction box appears.

continues on next page

3. Click in the blend direction box to choose a direction for the gradient, in increments of 45 degrees (**Figure 8.26**).

The color gradient appears on the selected object.

✔ Tip

■ You cannot blend two colors (create a gradient) for the shadow color.

Setting Transparency Levels

You can alter the transparency levels of an object's fill, shadow, or border color to create some shading and subtlety in your titles. Using a dual-color gradient for your fill or border, you can set independent transparency levels for each of colors in the gradient.

To set transparency for a single color:

1. With the Selection tool, select a text or graphic object. Shift-click to select multiple objects.

2. Click and hold on the transparency selection box for the Fill, Shad (shadow), or Bord (border) color.

3. Still holding the mouse button, move the cursor up to the Opaque/Transparency slider and choose a transparency value. Release the mouse.

A value of 0 means that the chosen color is entirely solid or opaque, and a value of 100 means that the color is entirely transparent (**Figure 8.27**).

✔ Tip

■ When you are adjusting the transparency of a color, the word *Hi* appears in the transparency box for that color to help you gauge the level visually. The word means, "Hi," as in "How are you doing out there?" and does not refer to a high numerical value, as opposed to a low value.

Click here.

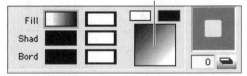

Figure 8.26 Click the blend direction box to choose a direction for your blended colors.

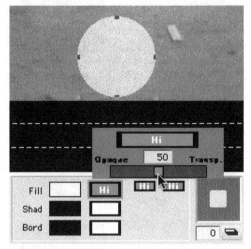

Figure 8.27 Here, the fill color transparency for the entire object is switched to 50 percent. The circle is semitransparent.

COLORING YOUR TEXT AND GRAPHICS

The left side of the
circle's gradient is
less transparent.

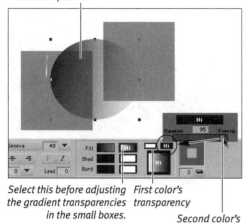

Select this before adjusting   First color's
the gradient transparencies   transparency
in the small boxes.
                                Second color's
                                transparency

Figure 8.28 Half of the circle has little transparency, and half is very transparent.

To set transparency for a dual-color gradient:

1. Select one or more objects with a dual-color gradient and click either the fill transparency selection box or the border transparency selection box (to the right of the similar-looking color selection boxes).

   The selected box becomes highlighted. Two smaller blend and transparency preview boxes appear to the right.

2. Drag in the small blend and transparency preview boxes and choose a transparency level for each.

   A large blend and transparency direction box opens below the small blend and transparency preview boxes.

3. Click in the large blend and transparency direction box to choose a direction for the gradient. Your choices come in increments of 45 degrees.

   The selected objects show you your transparency changes (**Figure 8.28**).

Don't Let Shadows Cloud Your Vision

When adjusting transparency for fill and border colors, you should turn off shadow and shadow softness, so it doesn't affect your judgment of your transparency levels. Click the shadow depth selection text box and enter *0* as the value. Do the same in the Soft Shadow dialog box (opened by choosing Object > Soften Shadow). (To learn more about shadows, see the next section, "Adding Drop and Depth Shadows.")

Adding Drop and Depth Shadows

A **drop shadow** is like a double of your object's image, positioned behind the object to mimic the effect of a shadow cast by light. A slight drop shadow often adds a little dimension to text (**Figure 8.29**).

A **depth shadow** looks very similar to a drop shadow, but it is not really a shadow at all. The subtle difference is that it graphically connects the shadow to the source object, creating the illusion of an extruded three-dimensional shape (**Figure 8.30**).

Table 8.2 lists shortcuts for shadow operation.

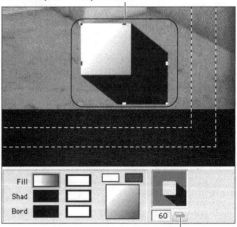

Drop shadow

Drop shadow position chosen here

Numerical value of shadow's distance from object

Toggle between drop and depth shadow here.

Figure 8.29 This square has a drop shadow, creating the illusion that there is a light source above the square, shining on it at an angle. It also suggests that the square is floating above the ground.

A drop shadow connected to its source object = a depth shadow.

To create a depth shadow, be sure the button is highlighted green.

Figure 8.30 The square has a depth shadow, creating the illusion that it is part of a three-dimensional object.

Table 8.2

Drop and Depth Shadow Shortcuts

OPERATION	COMMAND	
	WINDOWS	MAC OS
Increase shadow softness	Shift+Alt+ Up Arrow	Shift+Option+ Up Arrow
Decrease shadow softness	Shift+Alt+ Down Arrow	Shift+Option+ Down Arrow
Move shadow up	Shift+Up Arrow	Shift+Up Arrow
Move shadow down	Shift+ Down Arrow	Shift+Down Arrow
Move shadow left	Shift+Left Arrow	Shift+Left Arrow
Move shadow right	Shift+ Right Arrow	Shift+Right Arrow

ADDING DROP AND DEPTH SHADOWS

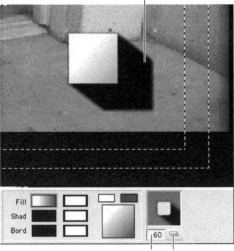

Values above about 20 create rather long shadows.

Shadow depth selection box   Highlighted green

Figure 8.31 The shadow depth selection box contains a value of 60, and Depth Shadow is turned on.

To add a drop or depth shadow to an object:

1. Select one or more objects with the Selection tool.

2. Click the shadow depth and direction box and drag the shadow representation to a new position.

3. Click the ⬛ Drop and Depth Shadow button to toggle between a drop shadow and a depth shadow. A green highlight indicates a depth shadow.

4. Click outside your selected objects to see the shadow take effect.

   A drop or depth shadow appears around your text or object. A number appears in the shadow depth selection box, indicating the distance between the shadow and the object.

✔ Tips

- If you want the shadow to appear farther from the object than clicking and dragging will allow, type a high number in the shadow depth selection box (**Figure 8.31**).

- You can adjust a shadow's color and transparency, but you cannot combine two colors in one shadow.

- To constrain a shadow's direction to 45-degree angles, hold down the Shift key as you drag in the shadow depth selection box.

- You can move the shadow to a new position from the keyboard by pressing the Shift key while using the up, down, left, and right arrow keys.

To soften a shadow:

1. Select one or more objects that have shadows.

2. *Do one of the following:*

   ▲ Choose Object > Soften Shadow.

   ▲ Press Shift+Ctrl+H (Windows) or Shift+Command+H (Mac).

3. In the Soft Shadow dialog box, enter a number between 0 and 40 for the degree of softness. The higher the number, the softer the edges. A value of 0 gives hard edges (**Figure 8.32**). The default softness is 4.

4. Click Apply to preview the result and click OK to close the dialog box.

✔ Tips

■ To create a glow effect, type *0* in the shadow depth selection box and type a high number in the Soft Shadow dialog box according to how soft you want the glow.

■ The shadow softness is represented visually in the shadow depth and direction box.

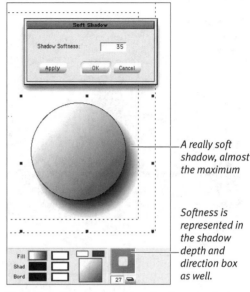

A really soft shadow, almost the maximum

Softness is represented in the shadow depth and direction box as well.

Figure 8.32 The minimum value of 4 gives a hard edge to the shadow. A value of 27 is near the maximum and adds a fuzzy glow underneath the object.

Using Title Styles and Templates

When you create a set of titles for any given project, you may want to establish a certain overall look for all of the titles using a carefully chosen configuration of standardized fonts, borders, colors, gradients, and so on. You can use Title Styles and Title Templates to quickly apply your desired look to any objects that you create in the Title tool.

The Styles menu: Click on the Titles tool's Styles menu to save only the specific parameters of the styles that you configure in the Title tool and not the actual text or graphic objects. You can use styles over and over again in your projects, or you can use any style as a starting point for creating a new variation on a favorite theme.

You can save the following title parameters as title styles:

◆ Font, style, size, justification, kerning, and leading

◆ Fill color and transparency

◆ Shadow color, transparency, depth, direction, softness, and type

◆ Border color, transparency, and width

The Templates menu: You can save any graphic and/or text arrangement in the Title tool as a template. Templates are helpful for creating recurring elements in multiple title sets. By default, once you save a template, the only aspect of a template that you can change is the particular lettering of a text object. (For how to reposition a template, see "Moveable Templates" in the following bullet list).

When you click on the Template menu in the Title tool, you can choose one of the following options:

◆ **Save Template:** Choose this option to save whatever is displayed in the Title tool as a template. A template contains the content, styles, and positioning of text and graphic objects.

◆ **Include Template:** Once you save a template you can add it to any future title you create by choosing this option.

◆ **Edit Template:** If you decide to include a template but realize that it has a flaw, you can select Edit Template to change any of its text or graphic elements.

◆ **Remove Template:** To completely delete a saved template that you've added to your current title, select this option and choose from the list of existing templates that appears.

◆ **Moveable Template:** Selecting a Template and Selecting a template and moving it allows you to break the template free from its frozen position, allowing you to move all the saved elements within the template as a whole.

To save a title style:

1. In the Title tool, use the Selection tool to select the object that will be the basis for the title style.

2. Click the arrow next to the Styles button.

3. In the pop-up menu that appears, choose Save As (**Figure 8.33**).

Click here to save the style.

Figure 8.33 To save a title style, first select the object that contains the style you want to save. Then click the down arrow button next to the world *Styles*. Choose Save As. After you configure and name the style, you can apply it to any text or graphic object you create in the future.

Templates in Action: An Example

Imagine that your opening credits feature a fixed word (such as *Starring*) that remains on the screen for 3 minutes while the cast names dissolve in and out below it. For each of those names, you need to create a separate title object in a separate title, but you don't need to re-create the word *Starring* every time.

If you save the fixed portion of your title as a template, then you can just include the template in every new title you create. In addition, you can create a template for the cast names so you can use the same format again; Xpress Pro allows you to alter the lettering of the text within templates, so you can simply enter the names of your new cast.

4. In the Title Style Sheet dialog box that appears, select the parameters you want to include in your title style (**Figure 8.34**). Usually, you can leave every parameter selected in the dialog, box, unless there are definitely parameters you do not want to include in the style.

5. Click Done.

Your title style is now listed in the Styles pop-up menu in the Title tool. It is also listed on the Settings tab of the Project window as a Title Style.

✔ Tip

■ You can assign a function key to a title style in the Function Key field of the Title Style Sheet dialog box. With a function key assigned, you can press just one key to make your selected object adopt your favorite style. However, check your Keyboard settings (on the Settings tab of the Project window) to make sure another function is not already mapped to a particular key.

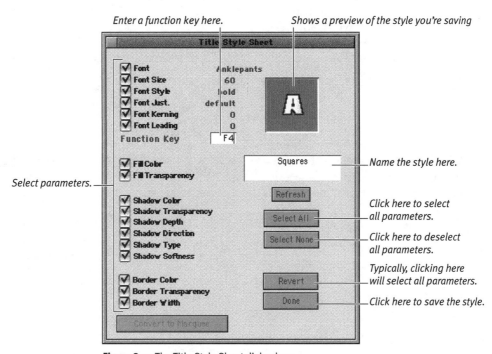

Figure 8.34 The Title Style Sheet dialog box.

To apply a title style to an existing object:

1. With the Selection tool, choose one or more objects.

2. *Do one of the following:*

   ▲ Click the triangle on the Styles pop-up menu and choose a style by name from the vertical scroll list (**Figure 8.35**).

   ▲ Click the oblong Styles button to display a visual Title Styles menu. Tear off the menu by dragging the pointer up above the menu and releasing it. Scroll through the window and choose an icon that represents a saved style (**Figure 8.36**). Use this method if you can't recognize your style by name alone.

   ▲ Press a function key to which you have mapped a style.

✔ Tips

■ To recall a style to apply to an object you haven't created yet, make sure that you have deselected all objects in the Title tool by clicking any blank area in the layout window before you load the style. After you load the style, any objects you create will take on those style parameters.

■ To see which function key a style is mapped to, open the Title Style Sheet dialog box from the Settings tab of the Project window.

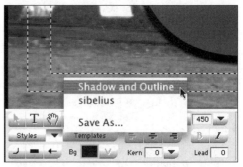

Figure 8.35 One way to call up a saved style is to click the small triangular button to the right of the word *Styles* in the toolbar and select a style name. Make sure you save each style with a name that tells you something about its function, so you can remember what the style does.

Move the pointer here to scroll left.
  Click to choose a style.
    Move the pointer here to scroll right.

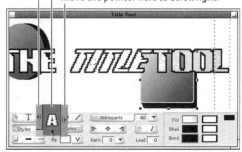

Figure 8.36 You can choose an icon of a style from the Styles pop-up menu. Move the pointer to the left or right arrow to scroll through the style icons; then click a style to choose it.

Every part of this title will be saved in the template. | *In a template, the only thing you can change is the text of text objects.*

Click here to save the template.

Figure 8.37 To save the current title as a template, choose Save Template from the Templates pop-up menu. Make sure you give your template a name that tells you what it is, and keep all of your templates in the same folder, so you know where to find them.

To save a title template:

1. Create your text and graphic objects in the Title tool. Be sure to delete any objects you don't want included in your template because the template is created from all objects in the layout window, not just the selected ones.

2. Click the Templates button and choose Save Template from the pop-up menu (**Figure 8.37**).

3. Give the template a descriptive name that you can easily remember.

4. Navigate to where you want to save the template on disk and click Save.

5. Close the Title tool window, choosing Don't Save when the dialog box appears.

   Your template is now saved as an independent file on disk, and you can reload it or move it to another system.

✔ Tips

- By default, Xpress Pro saves your title templates in Xpress Pro > Settings > Title_Templates. You can carry them with you when you move to a different workstation by saving them to disk, as e-mail attachments, or over any network.

- Templates do *not* include background color information.

USING TITLE STYLES AND TEMPLATES

To load a saved title template:

1. In the Title tool window, open a new title or an existing title into which you want to load the template.

2. Click the `Templates` Templates button and choose Include Template from the pop-up menu.

3. In the Open dialog box, navigate to the template you want to use and click Open.

    The template is now loaded in your current title, as if it were one single grouped object. You can edit any of the text or add other text and graphics to the same title. Save your title as you would any other title.

To reposition a template:

1. Load a template into your title, using the steps in the preceding task.

2. Click the Templates button and choose Moveable Templates.

    Xpress Pro places a check mark next to the Moveable Templates option, and you can now move any template you have loaded. Choose Moveable Templates again to remove the check mark, and Xpress Pro makes your templates fixed in stone again.

✔ Tip

■ If your title uses multiple templates, enabling Moveable Templates makes *all* of your templates moveable, so be careful.

To edit a template:

1. In the Title tool window, open a new title or an existing title into which you want to load and edit the template.

2. Click the Templates button and choose Edit Template from the pop-up menu.

3. Navigate to the template file you want to edit.

4. Choose Open.

    Your template is now loaded as a group of independent objects, and you can edit and modify all positions and parameters of every object, as if you had created them from scratch.

✔ Tip

■ Your original template remains unchanged on disk while you make your editing changes. If you want to save your changes, choose Save Template from the Templates pop-up menu. Save it with the same name as the older version to overwrite the original file, or with a new name to save the changed template as another independent template.

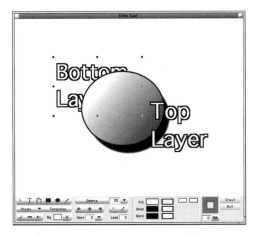

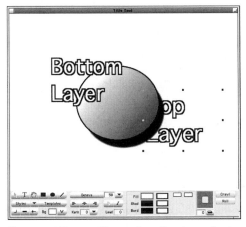

Figure 8.38 To move "Bottom Layer" to the top layer and "Top Layer" to the bottom layer, use Object > Send to Back and Object > Bring to Front.

Working with Layers and Groups

In the Title tool, layering objects on top of one another is challenging because there is no layer list, as there is in other graphic applications, to assist you. In Xpress Pro, you can manage your layers only by sending them to the back, to the front, or one increment in either direction.

The lack of a layer list in the Title tool makes repositioning, grouping, and locking objects an even trickier endeavor. When you are dealing with multiple objects, selecting the ones you need to move or group together may require some careful eyeballing and perhaps some temporary moving around of objects that you'd rather not touch.

To adjust the layer order of objects:

1. Select one or more objects with the Selection tool.

2. *Do one of the following:*
   ▲ Choose Object > Bring to Front or press Shift+Ctrl+L (Windows) or Shift+ Command+L (Mac) to move the object to the topmost layer (**Figure 8.38**).
   ▲ Choose Object > Send to Back to make the object the bottom layer.
   ▲ Choose Object > Bring Forward to move the object forward one layer.
   ▲ Choose Object > Send Backward to move the object back one layer.

Objects in the front will now obscure any objects they overlap that are one or more layers back.

To group and ungroup one or more objects:

1. Select the objects you want to group by Shift-clicking or lassoing them with the Selection tool on the toolbar.

2. Choose Object > Group or Object > UnGroup.

   A group of objects behaves just like a single object, and changes to one grouped object now affect all objects in the group.

To lock or unlock objects or groups:

1. With the Selection tool, select one or more objects or groups.

2. Choose Object > Lock.

   The small square handles around the locked object or group become square outlines, indicating that you cannot reposition or change the object until you unlock it.

3. To undo the lock, choose Object > Unlock.

✔ Tip

- Often it's a good idea to group a selection of objects before locking them, so that you can unlock the entire group at once.

It's Better to Travel in Groups

You can save time and keystrokes in a complex title by grouping objects together and making one change to the entire group instead of changing each object individually. Grouping is particularly useful when you want to make multiple mass changes to two or more objects. With grouped objects, you do not have to worry about lassoing and Shift-clicking each time want to change all of the objects in the group. They are always linked together and you can be formatted as if they were one massive object (**Figure 8.39**).

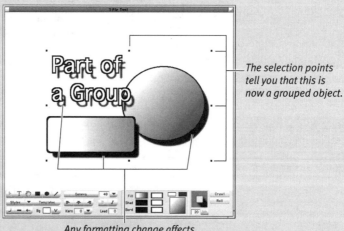

The selection points tell you that this is now a grouped object.

Any formatting change affects every object in the group.

Figure 8.39 A quick way to give all of these objects a drop shadow is to select the objects, group them, and then add the drop shadow.

Aligning and Distributing Objects

When you want to arrange title objects in a symmetrical formation, you can use the alignment grid to help you snap objects into place. You can also take advantage of the Alignment menu's automatic arrangement options to automatically distribute and power-align a long series of titles with a dozen or more objects in each title.

To align objects to the alignment grid:

1. Select one or more objects by clicking, Shift-clicking, or lassoing the objects. You can also press Ctrl+A (Windows) or Command+A (Mac) to select all objects in the title.

2. If you want to see the grid as your objects are aligned, choose Alignment > Show Alignment Grid.

   The grid is a visual reference that can help you position objects symmetrically.

3. Choose Alignment > Align to Grid.

   All selected objects snap to the grid.

ALIGNING AND DISTRIBUTING OBJECTS

To align or distribute objects automatically:

1. Select one or more objects by clicking, Shift-clicking, or lassoing the objects. You can also press Ctrl+A (Windows) or Command+A (Mac) to select all objects in the title.

   Note that the distribution/alignment choices behave differently, depending on the number of objects that are selected.

2. From the Alignment menu, *choose one of the following:*

   ▲ **Align to Frame Left, Right, Top, Bottom:** Moves one or more selected objects flush against the left, right, top, or bottom of the title-safe line or the nearest alignment grid line (**Figure 8.40**). See **Table 8.3** for the individual commands.

   ▲ **Center in Frame Horiz. Frame Vert.:** Centers one or more selected objects in relation to the title-safe lines.

Figure 8.40 When you choose Alignment > Align to Frame Left, all selected objects move to the far left and line up with the left title-safe line.

Table 8.3

Automatic Arrangement Shortcuts		
MENU FUNCTION	KEYBOARD COMMAND	
	WINDOWS	MAC OS
Align to Frame	Shift+Ctrl+Z	Shift+Command+Z
Center in Frame Horiz.	Shift+Ctrl+C	Shift+Command+C

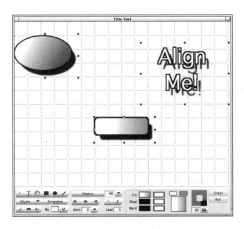

The objects align with
this (bottommost) object.

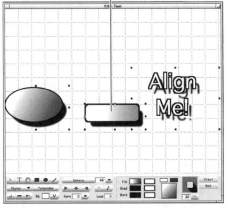

Figure 8.41 The result of choosing Alignment >
Align Objects Bottom depends on the position of
the bottommost object (above). The command
aligns the objects in a straight row, next to the
bottommost object (below).

▲ **Align Objects Left, Right, Top,
Bottom:** Uses one selected object as
an anchor to align two or more
selected objects. For example, Align
Objects Left uses the leftmost object
as a reference and aligns the remaining selected objects vertically under
the leftmost object (**Figure 8.41**).

ALIGNING AND DISTRIBUTING OBJECTS

▲ **Distribute Left to Right, Top to Bottom, First to Last:** Distributes three or more selected objects evenly between the first object you select and the last object you select (**Figure 8.42**).

The Title tool arranges your selected objects symmetrically.

See **Table 8.4** for a summary of the Alignment menu commands.

✔ Tips

■ Before you choose Align Objects Left (Right, Top, or Bottom), be sure to manually position your anchor object first. Then select the objects you want to align to it, then choose the Align menu option.

■ Distribute First to Last is especially useful for arranging items diagonally. Position your first and last objects manually first and then select the objects one by one, from first to last, using Shift-click. Do not select the objects you want to distribute by lassoing them together or pressing Ctrl+A (Windows) or Command+A (Mac) because then Xpress Pro won't know which is the first selected object and which is the last selected object.

First object selected   *Last object selected*

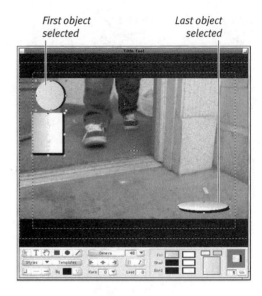

Only this object moves, to a position evenly spaced between the first and last objects selected.

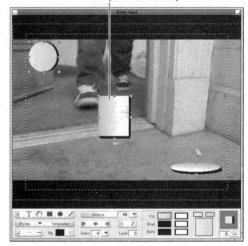

Figure 8.42 When you use Distribute First to Last, the first and last objects you select (above) remain stationary and the other selected objects evenly reposition themselves between the first and last objects (below).

Saving Titles

Xpress Pro gives you several workflow options for creating, modifying, and saving titles. If you are creating only a few titles, any option will work about as well as any other. If you are creating a long series of similar titles for a show or series, you'll want to consider the benefits of each option before you start work.

When you put the final polish on a single title and want to save it, you can use a simple File > Save operation; or, better yet, close the Title tool, click Save in the dialog that appears, and move on to your next task, such as editing the title into your sequence.

However, if you want to create a whole series of additional titles similar to the one you just made, you may want to use File > New Title to save the title you just created and leave the Title tool open, with all of its parameters set to match the new title to the title you just saved. In addition, you have a choice when saving one or more titles: You can render them individually as you go, or you can use Fast Save and render them later as one batch.

And just because you save a title to a bin doesn't mean you can't modify it later. In fact, you can open a title in a bin, change it, and save it under an identical or different name. (For more information, see "Modifying Saved Titles" later in this chapter.)

To save and render an individual title:

1. With the Title tool open and your title complete, make sure the bin into which you want to save your title is open.

2. *Do one of the following:*
    ▲ Choose File > Save Title or press Ctrl+S (Windows) or Command+S (Mac).
    ▲ Choose File > Save Title As or press Ctrl+Shift+S (Windows) or Command+Shift+S (Mac).

3. In the Save Title dialog box, give the title a name and select the bin where you want to save it, the media drive you want to save it to, and the resolution. Leave Fast Save (Unrendered) unchecked (**Figure 8.43**).

4. Click Save.

    The title's icon appears in your bin. You will see a progress box appear as Xpress Pro creates two media files for your title. The title will be loaded into the source monitor, ready to be edited into your sequence.

✔ Tips

■ If you want to leave the Title tool open and create more titles quickly, instead of choosing Save or Save As, simply choose File > New Title or press Ctrl+N (Windows) or Command+N (Mac). Xpress Pro will bring up the same Save Title dialog box and then, after you click Save, will automatically create a new, blank title for you to work on, in the Title tool.

Leave this unchecked to render the title when you save it.

Figure 8.43 The Save Title dialog box is where you name the title and send it to a particular bin and choose a drive for the title's media files.

SAVING TITLES

Title preview   *Generic title icon*

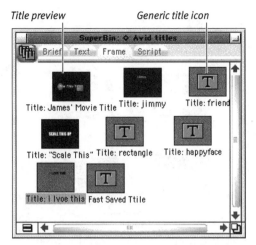

Figure 8.44 Selecting an icon in Frame or Script view and pressing the Home key gives you a preview of the actual title, instead of a generic title effect icon.

■ If you want to save just this one title and do something else, click the close box of the Title tool window, choose File > Close, or press Ctrl+W (Windows) or Command+W (Mac) instead of choosing Save Title from the menu. You get the same Save Title dialog box without having to choose File > Save.

■ To help keep your titles organized, create a separate bin specifically for Xpress Pro titles.

■ You can change your title's generic bin icon to a representative frame by selecting the title's icon and pressing the Home key (**Figure 8.44**).

The Fast Save Option

If you need to create a large number of titles, especially complicated titles that involve multiple text and graphic objects that take a while to render, use Fast Save. Fast Save saves the title to your bin without rendering or creating any title media, so you can bypass the burden of waiting through a lot of rendering every time you save an individual title. Instead, you can wait until after you create all of your titles and then render them all at once, while you take a break.

To save titles without rendering:

1. Choose File > New Title, File > Save, or File > Save As as you would normally when saving a title and keeping the Title tool open.

2. In the Save Title dialog box, give the title a name and designate a bin, drive, and resolution.

3. Check the Fast Save (Unrendered) box.

4. Click Save.

   Xpress Pro saves your title to your bin but does not render it, so it is marked "Unrendered' in the bin and "Media Offline" in the preview frame and in the source monitor (**Figure 8.45**).

✔ Tip

■ Remember to render your fast-saved titles before exporting an OMFI or AAF file or EDL from Xpress Pro.

(For information on rendering Fast Save titles, see "Rendering Titles" later in this chapter.)

Fast-saved title

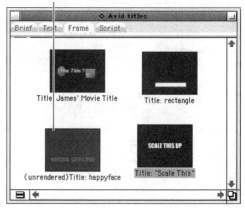

Figure 8.45 When you save a title with Fast Save checked, Xpress Pro saves it unrendered, and it is marked "Media Offline" in your bin.

Render Now Rather than Later

You can render offline titles in your bin or wait until you edit them into a sequence and then render the sequence. Waiting to render until the title is in a sequence may sound tempting, but remember that since the version in your bin has not been rendered, you'll have to re-render the title if you use it in multiple sequences or multiple versions of the same sequence. Rendering all of your titles in your bin before you edit them into a sequence can save you time in the long run, depending on your workflow.

SAVING TITLES

Editing Titles into a Sequence

Title clips get edited into sequences just like any other clip in your bin, except that they usually go on track V2 or higher if you want to layer them over video on a lower track.

The most common title editing procedure is as follows: You load a title into a source monitor, give it an In point, set In and Out points in the Timeline, and then perform an overwrite edit.

To edit a title into your sequence:

1. In the Timeline or Composer, set In and Out points where you want to place the title.

2. *Do one of the following:*
   ▲ Double-click the Title Effect icon in your bin to load it in a source pop-up window. Set an In point, select the appropriate track, and use any editing method, such as splice-in or overwrite, to edit it into your sequence
   ▲ Select the title's bin name on the Effect palette and drag the title from the palette to the space between the In and Out points in the Timeline.

   The title is edited into the sequence, just like any other clip. Unless you created a title with an opaque colored background, the image in the track beneath your title becomes the title's background.

✔ Tips

- When you set a title's In point in a source monitor, set the In point a few seconds into the clip. That way, if you ever need to add a transition effect or trim the head of your title backwards, you'll have enough media for the operation.

- By default, a title clip is 2 minutes long. If you need a longer title than 2 minutes, you will have to edit multiple versions of the same title into the sequence.

To drag and drop a title over video in the Timeline:

1. Place the position indicator on the video segment.

2. On the Composer or Timeline Fast menu, click Mark Clip to mark the segment's head and tail with In and Out points.

3. On the Track Selector panel, select the track above the video segment.

4. Drag a title from an open bin into the Timeline and hover the title between the In and Out points on the selected track.

5. When the ghost outline of the title matches the space between the Timeline In and Out points, release the mouse.

   The title appears in the Timeline, perfectly matching the length of the video segment beneath it.

To fade a title up or down:

1. Place the position indicator over the video segment.

2. On the Track Selector panel, select the track that contains your title.

3. Click the **E** Fade Effect button (on the FX tab of the Command palette). The Fade Effect dialog box appears.

4. Choose the number of frames for the head and/or tail fade.

5. Click OK.

   Xpress Pro automatically adds Foreground Level keyframes to your title effect, causing the title to Fade Up at the beginning of the effect and/or Fade Down at the end (**Figure 8.46**).

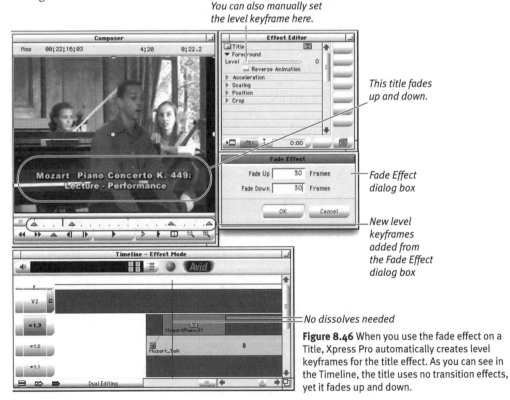

You can also manually set the level keyframe here.

This title fades up and down.

Fade Effect dialog box

New level keyframes added from the Fade Effect dialog box

No dissolves needed

Figure 8.46 When you use the fade effect on a Title, Xpress Pro automatically creates level keyframes for the title effect. As you can see in the Timeline, the title uses no transition effects, yet it fades up and down.

To view these level keyframes in the Composer/Effect editor, place the playhead over the title and click the Effect Mode button on the Timeline toolbar. (For more information about Effect mode and the Effect editor, see Chapter 9, "Working with Video Effects.")

✔ **Tip**

■ You can also add a transition dissolve effect, but dissolves are neither the most time- nor render-efficient way of fading titles into and out of a scene. (See Chapter 9 for more information.)

To delete a title from a sequence:

1. In the Timeline, place the position indicator on a title and select the track that contains the title.

2. On the Composer or Timeline Fast menu, click the ⊘ Remove Effect button once. Xpress Pro deletes the title icon and leaves behind the graphic fill segment.

3. Click the Remove Effect button again. Xpress Pro deletes the graphic fill segment, and the title is now fully deleted from your sequence.

✔ **Tip**

■ Instead of using Remove Effect, you can delete a title by entering Segment mode, selecting the title, and pressing Delete twice. Using Remove Effect is faster, however.

Solving Title Playback Problems

Xpress Pro plays all titles in real time, and playback problems can arise whenever the title is too complex for your particular system to play. Playback problems usually show up as background video jitter, image shifting, video and audio underrun, gray images, and other anomalies.

The solution to most title playback problems is to render the title in the Timeline. That way, Xpress Pro does not have to rely on real-time playback. If a Title icon in the Timeline has a green dot, then you know that the title is playing in real time and has not been rendered. A rendered title has no dot at all (**Figure 8.47**).

(For more information on rendering, see "Rendering Titles" later in this chapter, and Chapter 11, "Rendering and Real Time.")

Green dot means effect plays in realtime.

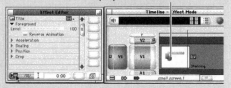

Figure 8.47 Even if a title is a real-time effect, playback problems may arise, requiring you to render the title.

Exactly What's in a Title Anyway?

Xpress Pro considers a title to be a *segment effect*. In fact, titles, along with the matte key effect, are the two most sophisticated segment effects in Xpress Pro because they are the only two that contain three nested layers. (For more information, see "Understanding Effects" and "Nesting Multiple Effects" in Chapter 9.)

To see the layers that are nested inside a title, find a title that is in the Timeline, click the Effect Mode button on the Other tab of the Command palette, and double-click the title. Xpress Pro opens the following three tracks that make up the title:

♦ **Alpha matte layer:** This track contains the alpha channel information for your title, which determines what part of your title is opaque and what part is transparent when you place your title over a background image. You can also think of the alpha channel as like a cookie cutter, determining the shape of the graphic fill layer right beneath it.

  (For more information on alpha channels, see "Alpha Channels Explained" in Chapter 9.)

♦ **Graphic fill layer:** This is a single bit-mapped still image that contains all of the color, gradient, and texture information for your title—everything that fills the shape of the alpha matte.

♦ **Empty background layer:** The bottom nested track of a title is reserved for whatever image you want as your title background. However, this track is usually left empty (though you can edit an image into it) because you can give your title a background by placing it on top of an image that's already on a regular Timeline track.

A side benefit of having a graphic fill layer that you can see and edit is that you can replace it with a moving video image. (For more information, see the next section, "Filling Titles with Video or Graphics.")

Of course, two of these hidden, nested tracks of your title—namely, the alpha matte and background layers—are irrelevant if you gave your title a solid-color background in the Title tool.

Figure 8.48 The text's normal fill layer has been filled with a video clip of water. The title was then layered over another video clip in the Timeline.

Filling Titles with Video or Graphics

Every title consists of a graphic fill layer and an alpha channel layer. You can replace the graphic fill layer with any video clip you want, filling your title text or graphics with moving images and making it seem to come alive (**Figure 8.48**).

You can also use this method to easily create custom picture-in-picture effects with various round or angled shapes and designs. Use graphic shapes such as rectangles, circles, and arrows to create the alpha channels and then fill them in with whatever video you want.

To replace a title's fill track with moving video:

1. Switch to Segment mode by pressing either the ⟱ Extract/Splice-In Segment Mode button, or ⟱ Lift/Overwrite Segment Mode button at the bottom left of the Timeline or on the Edit tab of the Command palette.

2. Double-click the title segment to step into the effect.

   (For more information on stepping into effects, see Chapter 9, "Working with Video Effects.")

3. Load the video or graphic you want to use to fill the text into the source monitor.

continues on next page

FILLING TITLES WITH VIDEO OR GRAPHICS

4. Patch the source clip's video track button (usually it's V1) to the record track button of the nested graphic fill track of the title (**Figure 8.49**). (For more information on patching tracks, see Chapter 6, "Making Edits.")

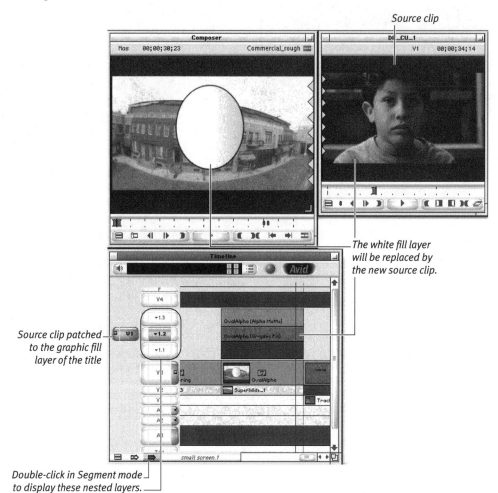

Source clip

The white fill layer will be replaced by the new source clip.

Source clip patched to the graphic fill layer of the title

Double-click in Segment mode to display these nested layers.

Figure 8.49 You can overwrite the title's graphic fill layer with another source clip. Just make sure you patch the V1 source track to the graphic fill track by clicking on the far-left V1 source button in the Timeline and dragging the arrow that appears to the appropriate record video track.

New filler segment overwrites the oval's graphic fill layer. *New filler image is composited into the oval's alpha channel.*

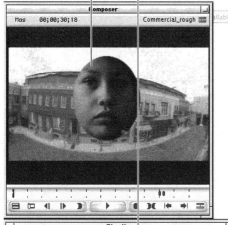

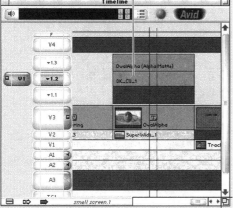

Figure 8.50 The video source clip has been overwritten on the title's graphic fill layer track to create a quick and easy picture-in-picture effect with an oval shape and a border.

5. Overwrite the graphic fill track with the new source track, using the Overwrite button or whatever editing technique you prefer (**Figure 8.50**).

✔ Tips

■ When you open a title with a video fill layer in the Title tool to modify it, the title reverts to the original graphic fill layer, and you must edit the video clip back into the fill layer again, so be careful to get the title's alpha channel set up the way you want it before you replace the graphic fill layer with video.

■ You can have multiple titles, each with its own fill layer, stacked on top of each other in the Timeline.

Want to Get Really Advanced with Your Animation? Promote Your Title to 3D!

If you want to be able to rotate your title along the X, Y, or Z axis or to add a funky object trail to it, load your title's parameters in the Effect editor and click the 3D button in the lower-right corner of the window.

The Effect editor changes into the 3D effect interface. You can now adjust your title using any of the displayed parameters, including the 3D tools (found on the 3D tab of the Command palette).

(For more information, see "Working with Xpress 3D Effects" and "The 3D Tools" in Chapter 9.)

FILLING TITLES WITH VIDEO OR GRAPHICS

Titles Like to Be Animated

You cannot use the Title tool to change the position or formatting of objects over time, since it has no animation capabilities besides crawl and roll.

However, once you edit a title into a sequence, it behaves just like any other clip; you can make your title fade, grow, shrink, and move from one point to another by animating its basic parameters in the Effect editor (**Figure 8.51**).

(For more information, see "Modifying Segment and Transition Effects" in Chapter 9.)

To load a title's parameters into the Effect editor, click the Effect Mode button on the Other tab of the Command palette and select the title you want to animate in the Timeline.

In the Effect editor, adjust the effect's Foreground, Acceleration, Scaling, Position, and Crop parameters while setting keyframes in the Composer monitor.

(For more information on keyframes, see "About Xpress Pro Keyframess" in Chapter 9.)

Animation parameters

Click this button to promote the title to a 3D effect so you can use 3D tools for animation.

Keyframes

Figure 8.51 Use a title's Effect Editor parameters to fly it, grow it, shrink it, crop it, fade it, and so on. Here, the Scaling and Position parameters have been set so that the title grows as it moves across the frame.

Scroll up and down through the roll.

Click to create a roll.

Skip to a page number here.

Figure 8.52 To create a credit roll, open the Title tool, click the Roll button, and type your text with the Text tool.

Table 8.5

Scroll Commands for Crawls and Rolls	
FUNCTION	BUTTON
Go to end of title	End
Go to beginning of title	Home
Go to next page (rolls only)	Page Down
Go to previous page (rolls only)	Page Up
Move to next title line (rolls only)	Down Arrow
Move to previous title line (rolls only)	Up Arrow

Creating Title Crawls and Rolls

Title crawls and rolls are two versions of the same idea: They involve text that moves in a straight line on the screen. In title crawls, the text moves horizontally across the screen, and in title rolls, the text moves vertically down the screen.

When you create a crawl or roll, you are creating one large text object; all formatting rules that apply to text objects apply to crawls and rolls.

To create a rolling title:

1. Open the Title tool and make sure the Text tool is selected.

2. Click the Roll button at the lower right of the tool.

   Xpress Pro configures the Title tool to create a rolling title. A page number box appears at the lower right of the tool.

3. Type your text, or paste it in from a word processor.

4. Use the scroll bar or scroll arrows to scroll through your text (**Figure 8.52**).

   See **Table 8.5** for other ways to scroll around your crawl or roll.

5. Save the title to a bin.

   You can now edit your rolling title into the Timeline like any other clip or title. However, do not mark any In or Out points for the title in the source monitor. The In-to-Out duration in the Timeline alone will determine the duration and pacing of your crawl or title. (See "Editing Titles into a Sequence" earlier in this chapter for more information.)

   Your title will roll down the screen as the Timeline plays.

   continues on next page

✔ Tips

- You can change the width of a rolling title by choosing the Selection tool in the Title tool and dragging the title's handles to resize the entire title.

- Your crawl or rolling title cannot contain a colored background. If you want your crawl or roll to appear over a solid color, create a solid-color title in the Title tool, export it as a PICT file, import the PICT file into Xpress Pro, and layer the color PICT file under your crawl or roll in the Timeline.

- To insert blank spaces into your rolling title (which you can leave blank or use for more text), choose Object > Insert Page and choose a page number from the dialog box that appears.

To create a crawling title:

1. Open the Title tool and make sure the Text tool is selected.

2. Click the Crawl button at the lower right of the tool.

   Xpress Pro configures the Title tool to create a crawling title. A page number box appears at the lower right of the tool. A scroll bar appears along the bottom of the image frame.

3. Type your text vertically, as if it were a rolling title (**Figure 8.53**).

4. If your text extends down beyond the area of one frame, choose the Selection tool, move the text object up, select the Text tool again, click at the end of the title, and continue typing.

5. When you have finished typing the text you need, choose Object > Make Crawl (**Figure 8.54**).

If you need more than one frame, use the Selection tool to move the text up.

Figure 8.53 To create a crawling title, open the Title tool, click the Crawl button, and begin typing your text vertically.

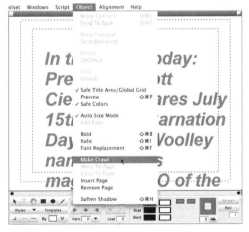

Figure 8.54 To convert your vertical text to a proper horizontal crawl, choose Object > Make Crawl.

Scroll through the crawl using these controls.

Figure 8.55 After you choose Object > Make Crawl, Xpress Pro converts your text to one horizontal line.

Resize the object.

Figure 8.56 To add text to an existing crawl, resize the crawl text object with the Selection tool, so you have room to type more text.

6. Save the title in a bin.

Xpress Pro converts your title to a one-line horizontal crawl (**Figure 8.55**). You can scroll to the end of it using the scroll bar at the bottom of the Title tool frame.

You can now edit your rolling title into the Timeline like any other clip or title. However, do not mark any In or Out points for the title in the source monitor. The In-to-Out duration in the Timeline alone will determine the duration and pacing of your crawl or title. (See "Editing Titles into a Sequence" earlier in this chapter for more information.)

Your title will roll down the screen as the Timeline plays.

✔ Tips

- In Xpress Pro, you cannot create a title roll or crawl longer than 66 video frames (for NTSC) or 56 video frames (for PAL).

- To add text to an existing horizontal crawl, choose the Selection tool, go to the end of the crawl, and resize the text object. Then select the Text tool and type more text (**Figure 8.56**).

- To insert blank spaces into your crawling title (which you can leave blank or use for more text), choose Object > Insert Page and choose a page number from the box that appears.

- Type your crawl text as a roll first. This way, you can read all of your text running vertically, which is much easier than reading it horizontally. Then later you can convert it to a crawl by selecting the Crawl button in the Title tool.

CREATING TITLE CRAWLS AND ROLLS

To add pages to your title:

Do one of the following:

◆ To automatically resize your crawl or roll page when you add or delete text, choose Object > Auto-size.

   Xpress Pro keeps this mode enabled by default.

◆ To add a page manually and turn off Auto-size mode, choose Object > Add Page.

To skip to a different page in your title:

1. Click in the page number box at the lower right of the Title tool.

2. Type a page number.

3. Press Enter (Windows) or Return (Mac).

   Xpress Pro takes you to the specified page in your crawl or roll.

✔ Tip

■ You can also skip to a different page by choosing Object > Move to Page.

Controlling the Pace of Your Crawl or Roll

How do you determine the speed at which your title crawls or rolls on the screen?

It all depends on the length of your title segment in the Timeline. It doesn't matter how many words are in your crawl or roll; if your Timeline In-to-Out duration is 2 seconds, then the crawl or roll will last 2 seconds. If the In-to-Out duration is 2 hours, the crawl or roll will last 2 hours.

Modifying Saved Titles

You can modify a title after you have created and saved it in a bin or in a sequence. The best method to use depends on several factors.

Often the cleanest way to modify a title is to modify it in a bin because you can save the new version and automatically overwrite the old one. If you modify a title from the Timeline, a new version of the title will be created and saved to a bin, which can get messy if you are modifying a ton of titles. That said, sometimes modifying a title straight from the Timeline is the fastest way to get the job done, without requiring any additional editing.

To modify a title saved in a bin:

1. *Do one of the following*

▲ Open the saved title in the Title tool by Ctrl-clicking (Windows) or Control+Command-clicking (Mac) the Title Effect icon in the bin.

▲ Open the Title tool and drag an existing title icon from a bin into the Title tool window.

2. In the Title tool, make your changes to the title.

3. Save your changes *by doing one of the following:*

▲ Close the Title tool window and click Save in the dialog box that appears.

This saves the revised title under the same name, overwriting the old version. This is the cleanest and fastest way to save a modified title you load from a bin.

▲ Choose File > Save Title and save the revised title under the same name, overwriting the old version.

With this method, you need to take an extra step to close the Title tool window after you save the title, so use Save Title only if you want to keep the Title tool open to modify another title.

To modify a title edited into a sequence:

1. Click the ⬛ Effect Mode button on the Composer Tool palette, the Timeline's top toolbar, or the Other tab of the Command palette.

2. Click the title in your sequence to load it into the Effect editor.

   In the upper-left corner of the Effect editor, the Other Options icon button is now labeled "Title" instead of "Other Options".

3. Click the ⬛ Title icon in the upper-left corner of the Effect editor (**Figure 8.57**).

4. In the Title tool, revise the title as necessary.

5. *Do one of the following:*

   ▲ Choose File > Save Title As to save the title with a new name and/or different media parameters.

   This is usually the best method, because you get to choose the bin in which to save the title.

   ▲ Choose File > Save Title and save the revised title with the same name to the bin containing your sequence.

   If a title in that bin has the same name, Xpress Pro adds a numbered extension (such as .01) to the name.

   ▲ Close the Title tool window and click Save in the dialog box that appears.

   Xpress Pro saves the title to your sequence bin. If a title in that bin has the same title, Xpress Pro adds a numbered extension (such as .01) to the name.

Figure 8.57 To modify a title that's in the Timeline, place the playhead over the title, select the track containing the title, click the Effect Mode button in the Timeline toolbar, go the Effect editor, and click the Other Options ("Title") button.

Rendering Titles

When you create and save Xpress Pro's vector-based titles one at a time, Xpress Pro renders them for you and creates the title media. You don't have to render them again, unless you add more effects to them in the Timeline.

However, in some instances, you may need to batch-render titles or re-create the title media:

◆ Perhaps you used Fast Save to create a series of unrendered titles and now you want to render them in one batch in your titles bin.

◆ Perhaps you erased the rendered media files for a project to make room for a rush job, and now you want to get back to work on your earlier project.

◆ Perhaps you've brought a rush job project to your workstation with titles already created and nicely edited inside a sequence, but they're all marked "Media Offline" because they have no media files to go with them.

Whatever the reason, **Create Unrendered Title Media** and **Re-create Title Media** are the two commands used to render or re-create one or more titles that are marked "Unrendered" in a bin or "Media Offline" in the Timeline.

To render or re-create an unrendered or offline title in a bin:

1. Select one or more unrendered or offline titles in a bin.

2. Choose Clip > Create Un-Rendered Title Media (**Figure 8.58**).

3. In the Create Unrendered Title Media dialog box, choose a drive for the effect's media files and choose a title resolution.

4. Click OK.

✔ Tips

■ To select all unrendered titles in a bin, use the bin's Fast menu to choose Select Unrendered Titles.

■ When you create unrendered offline media for a title in a bin, Xpress Pro adds a numbered extension to the end of the title's name.

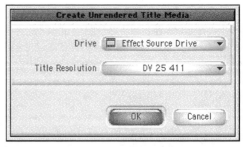

Figure 8.58 You can render titles in your bin at any time by selecting them (top) and choosing Clip > Create Unrendered Title Media (middle), and then telling Xpress Pro where to store the media files and what resolution to use (bottom).

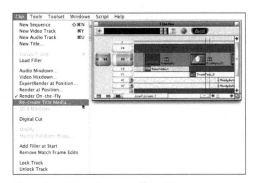

Figure 8.59 Do you have an offline title in your sequence? Place it online by choosing Clip > Re-create Title Media.

To re-create title media in a sequence:

1. Load a sequence containing the titles you want to re-create into the Timeline and Composer.

2. *Do one of the following:*
   ▲ Enter Segment mode and select the offline title you want to re-create.
   ▲ Mark In and Out points around the titles you want to re-create.

3. Select the tracks where the title or titles are located.

4. Choose Clip > Re-create Title Media (**Figure 8.59**).

5. In the Re-create Title Media dialog box, choose a drive for the re-created media.

6. Click OK.
   The title media files are regenerated.

✔ Tip

■ If you re-create title media using fonts not recognized by your system, Xpress Pro displays a dialog box that allows you to substitute fonts. (See the sidebar "Where Are My Fonts?" earlier in this chapter for more information.)

RENDERING TITLES

Exporting Titles

You can export Xpress Pro titles as graphic files for further manipulation in image-editing applications such as Photoshop or for other uses in video, DVD, Web, or print media. To export alpha channels with your titles, you must export from the Title tool. (See the sidebar "Exporting Titles with Alpha Channels and Soft Shadows" later in this chapter.)

To export a title from the Title tool:

1. With the Title tool open, choose File > Export Title.

2. In the dialog box that appears, choose the location to which you want to export the file. Type a name for the file in the File Name text box.

3. Click Save.

   Xpress Pro saves your title to disk as a PICT file in 720 x 486 nonsquare pixel format, with an alpha channel. Reminder: If your title contains any softened shadows, the export will contain undesirable blocky colors around the object; consider this a bug.

To export a title from a bin or sequence:

1. Highlight the title's icon in your bin or park the playhead over the title in a sequence.

2. Choose File > Export.

   Your system's Export As dialog box appears with a choice of standard export settings (**Figure 8.60**). To add to or configure any of these standard settings, use the export settings on the Settings tab of the Project window.

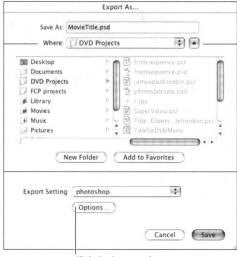

Click Options to alter your export settings.

Figure 8.60 After you choose File > Export, the Export As dialog box appears, allowing you to choose a location for your exported title.

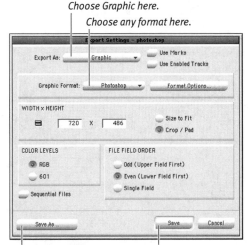

Choose Graphic here.

Choose any format here.

Click to save these
export settings
under a new name.

Click to replace the current
export settings with the
adjustments made here.

Figure 8.61 The Export Settings dialog box displays your current export settings. Adjust these settings and then click Save to return to the Export As dialog box.

3. *Do one of the following:*

▲ Choose one of your preset export settings from the Export Settings pop-up menu.

▲ Display the Export Settings dialog box by clicking the Options button that appears and then specify your custom export settings (**Figure 8.61**). Click Save or Save As when you have made your choices.

The Xpress Pro Export Settings dialog box closes, and the system Export As dialog box now uses your new settings as the standard export settings.

4. Back in the system Export As dialog box, designate a save folder and click Save.

Xpress Pro saves your title as a still image.

✔ Tips

■ Create export settings for your most common scenarios so you don't have to click the Options button each time you export a title. (For more information on configuring your export settings, see Chapter 3, "Customizing Your Workspace.")

■ JPEG is a common image format, but it uses a lossy compression scheme. Avoid using JPEG as an export file format unless you need to go directly to the web or CD, where the reduced file size of a JPEG image is a worthwhile trade-off for the loss of uncompressed-image quality.

Exporting Titles with Alpha Channels and Soft Shadows

Xpress Pro has a few limitations you should know about when exporting alpha channels with titles, particularly if you have any softened shadows in a title.

To export a title without an alpha channel, *do one of the following:*

◆ Select the title in your bin and choose File > Export.

The title's alpha channel is not included in the export, even if you export it as a PICT file or using some other image file format that usually carries an alpha channel, such as TIFF or TARGA.

◆ Place the position indicator over a title in the Timeline and choose File > Export.

As with the bin method, you cannot include an alpha channel using this method.

To include an alpha channel in your export, *you must do the following:*

◆ Load the title in the Title tool and choose File > Export Title.

With this method, you have no choice of format or size. All titles are exported from the Title tool as PICT files, at 720 x 486 pixels, with an alpha channel. Currently, this is the only way to export your title and include its alpha channel information.

But beware: If your title contains a softened shadow of any kind, the PICT file's alpha channel will not be displayed properly.

WORKING WITH VIDEO EFFECTS

Xpress Pro's effects capabilities extend further than the eye can see, especially when you consider all the third-party AVX plug-ins you can install and use within the Xpress Pro interface.

While the results you can achieve are seemingly limitless in variety, all effects break down into three basic categories: *segment effects, transition effects,* and *motion effects.* Segment effects apply to edited segments, transition effects apply to edit points, and motion effects can speed, slow, reverse, strobe, or freeze your footage.

This chapter provides the basic information you need to apply, create, and manipulate each of the effect types. It also describes how to layer and combine effects with *nesting* and how to animate them with both standard and advanced *keyframes.*

However, this chapter does not pretend to cover the details of every possible kind of Xpress Pro eye candy; for example, you can discover the subtleties of each Sawtooth Wipe transition on your own. What's more important is that you learn the fastest and most efficient way to fine-tune and shape effects to suit your specific artistic vision. This aim includes knowing how to apply multiple effects at once, how to use QuickTransition, how to create your own effect templates, how to copy and paste keyframes, and how to take advantage of Xpress Pro's advanced keyframes.

As you learn how to create effects, keep in mind that this chapter goes hand in hand with Chapter 11, which discusses how to render your effects and preview them in real time. Most Xpress Pro effects are real-time preview effects, meaning that you can play them in your Composer monitor without rendering. With the Mojo, you play effects out to your external monitor in real time. So let the visual razzle-dazzle commence . . .

Understanding Effects

Xpress Pro has three types of effects:

- **Segment effects:** Found on the Effect palette and edited in the Effect editor, these effects apply to entire Timeline clip segments. For example, if you drop a Color Correction effect on a clip segment in your Timeline, it affects the hue, saturation, brightness/contrast, and so on of every frame in that image.

- **Transition effects:** Also found on the Effect palette and edited in the Effect editor, these effect apply to the edit points between clip segments. Transition effects include dissolves, wipes, and any effect that creates a transition from shot A (the segment before the cut) to shot B (the segment after the cut).

  (For more information on segment and transition effects, see "Applying Segment and Transition Effects" later in this chapter).

- **Motion effects:** Usually created in the Motion Effect dialog box, these effects apply to source clips and result in the creation of new motion effect clips. Motion effects include fast motion, slow motion, reverse motion, strobe motion, and freeze frames.

  (For more information on motion effects, see "Using Motion Effects," and "Creating Freeze Frames" later in this chapter).

(For an overview of the entire effect creation process, see **Figure 9.1**).

✔ Tips

- If you plan to work in Effect mode for a while, you can choose Toolset > Effects Editing to display a window layout that is optimized for effects work.

- A title counts as a segment effect, although you edit it into the Timeline like a clip (see Chapter 8, "Creating Titles").

The Xpress Pro Effects Process in a Nutshell

If you're looking for a *quick* version of the Xpress Pro effects creation process, here is the procedure in three simple steps:

1. **Apply the effect.** Using the Effect palette, you can apply a segment effect to a Timeline clip segment or a transition effect to a Timeline edit point, or you can apply a motion effect to a clip in a bin by loading the clip into a source monitor and clicking the Motion Effect button. (For more information, see "Applying Segment and Transition Effects" and "Using Motion Effects" later in this chapter.)

2. *Do one of the following:*

   - **Adjust the segment or transition effect.** You use the Effect editor to manipulate the parameters of your segment or transition effects. (For more information, see "Modifying Segment and Transition Effects" later in this chapter.)

   - **Add the motion effect clip.** After you apply a motion effect to a source clip, Xpress Pro creates a new motion effect clip in your bin, which you can edit it into your sequence just like any other clip.

3. **Render the effect.** Unless you're working with a real-time effect, you must render your effects to make them play on your Composer or external client monitor. Eventually, you'll need to render *all* of your effects. (For more information on rendering, see Chapter 11, "Rendering and Real-Time.")

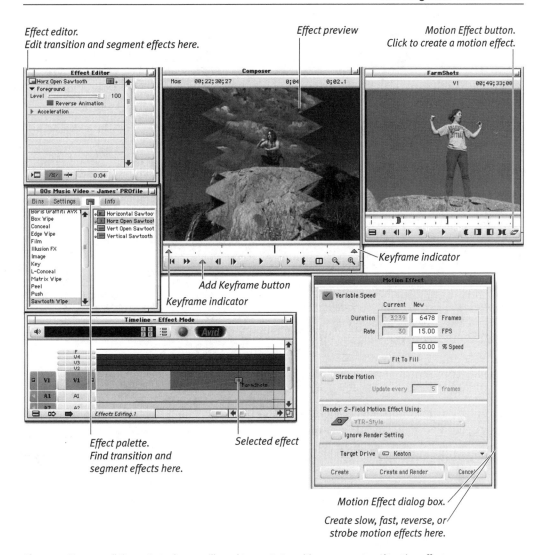

Effect editor.
Edit transition and segment effects here.

Effect preview

Motion Effect button.
Click to create a motion effect.

Keyframe indicator

Add Keyframe button

Keyframe indicator

Effect palette.
Find transition and
segment effects here.

Selected effect

Motion Effect dialog box.
Create slow, fast, reverse, or
strobe motion effects here.

Figure 9.1 Here are all the main tools you will need to create transition, segment, and motion effects.

Applying Segment and Transition Effects

Segment and transition effects are found on the Effects palette and include third party effect plug-ins like BorisFX and IllusionFX as well as all those that come with the basic Xpress Pro application (**Figure 9.2**).

There are no labels that distinguish segment effects from transition effects; knowing which is which comes with experience. (For the categories that contain each type, see **Table 9.1**).

To apply a segment or transition effect:

1. Open the Effect palette by choosing Tools > Effect palette or by going to the Project window and clicking the Effect palette icon.

   The Effect palette displays all available segment and transition effects.

2. To find the effect you need, click a category name on the left side of the palette.

   On the right, the Effect palette displays the effects that the selected category contains.

3. To apply an effect, *do one of the following:*

   ▲ Drag a segment effect icon from the Effect palette to a Timeline clip segment. When the clip segment becomes highlighted, release the mouse (**Figure 9.3**).

   ▲ Drag a transition effect icon from the Effect palette to a Timeline edit (transition) point. When the edit point becomes highlighted, release the mouse.

Effect categories   *Individual effects*

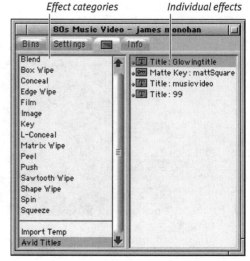

Figure 9.2 The Effect palette organizes effects by category. The Image category, for example, contains several of Xpress Pro's most powerful segment effects, including Color Correction.

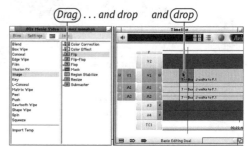

Figure 9.3 You'll know which segment gets the effect because Xpress Pro will highlight it before the drop. Keep the Timeline close to the Effect palette so your dragging is not an epic journey.

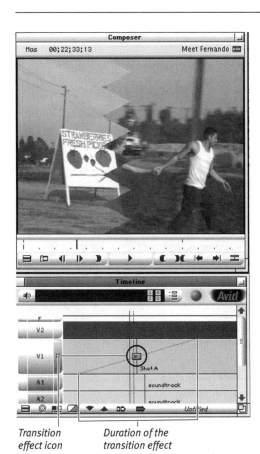

| Composer |
| Mas   00;22;33;13   Meet Fernando |

Transition effect icon — *Duration of the transition effect*

Figure 9.4 After you apply a transition effect to a Timeline edit (transition) point, a transition effect icon appears at the selected edit point, and a diagonal line spans the duration of the effect.

Table 9.1

Effect Palette Categories for the Three Effect Types

EFFECT TYPE	CATEGORIES THAT CONTAIN THE EFFECT TYPE
Segment effects	Blend, Film, Image, Key, Xpress 3D Effect
Transition effects	Blend, Box Wipe, Conceal, Edge Wipe, Film, L-Conceal, Matrix Wipe, Peel, Push, Sawtooth Wipe, Shape Wipe, Spin, Squeeze
Motion effects	Timewarp (presets only)

If you applied a segment effect, its icon appears in the middle of the selected Timeline clip segment. If you applied a transition effect, its icon appears at the selected edit point (**Figure 9.4**).

The Composer displays a preview of the effect.

4. To adjust the parameters of the effect, open the Effect editor by clicking the Effect mode button or by choosing Tools > Effect Editor.

(For more information on using the Effect editor, see "Modifying Segment and Transition Effects" later in this chapter.)

✔ Tips

- To use After Effect plug-ins in Xpress Pro, you need the application called Elastic Gasket. (For more information, see Appendix B, "Post Production Extras".)

- You can create an audio cross-dissolve by applying any video transition effect to an audio edit point.

- You can create your own customized segment or transition effect templates, which are personally configured favorites. (For more information, see "Creating Favorite Effect Templates" later in this chapter.)

- If you applied an effect that is not a real-time effect, then you need to render the effect for it to play in your Composer or external monitor. Even if it is a real-time effect, you'll need the Mojo box to play it on your external monitor without rendering. (For more information, see Chapter 11, "Rendering and Real-Time").

APPLYING SEGMENT AND TRANSITION EFFECTS

To apply an effect to multiple clip segments:

1. Enter a Segment mode by clicking the ⬦ Extract/Splice-in or ➡ Lift/Overwrite Segment mode button (the buttons appear by default at the bottom left of the Timeline).

2. In the Timeline, click a clip segment to select it. Shift-click to add other clip segments to your selection (**Figure 9.5**).

3. To apply the same effect to all selected clip segments, go to the Effect palette and double-click the icon of a segment effect.

   The effect applies to all selected clip segments (**Figure 9.6**).

To apply a transition effect to multiple edit points:

1. Enter Trim mode by clicking the ▣ Trim mode button (located by default in the Composer and on the Timeline toolbar).

   When you enter Trim mode, the edit point nearest the position indicator displays pink rollers.

2. Shift-click to add either one or two pink rollers to the edit points you want to affect. (To deselect a pink roller at an existing edit point, you also use Shift-click.)

   The edit points that will receive your transition effect now display either one or two pink rollers.

Selected clip segments

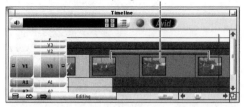

Figure 9.5 To apply the same effect to multiple segments, first Shift-click to select the clip segments in the Timeline.

Same effect applied to all clip segments

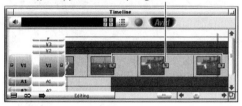

Figure 9.6 Here, the Flop effect was applied to all selected segments.

Double-click the effect to apply it.

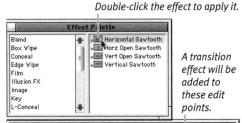

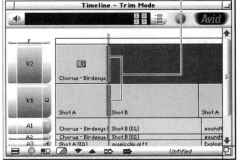

A transition effect will be added to these edit points.

Figure 9.7 To add a transition effect to multiple edit points, enter Trim mode, mark the edit points you want to affect with pink rollers, and double-click a transition effect on the Effect palette.

Not selected
Selected

Will not be deleted
Will be deleted

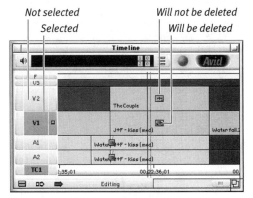

Figure 9.8 To delete the effects under your position indicator, click Remove Effect. Careful! Select only tracks that contain the effects you want to delete.

3. On the Effect palette, double-click a transition effect (**Figure 9.7**).

The transition effect is applied to all selected edit points. Xpress Pro switches from Trim mode to Effect mode.

✔ Tips

- Entering Trim mode is the only way to apply effects to multiple edit points. (For more information on Trim mode, see Chapter 7, "Fine-Tuning Your Edits.")

- Although you can apply transition effects to several edit points simultaneously, you can apply only one transition effect per track.

To delete a segment or transition effect:

1. In the Timeline, park the position indicator over the effect you want to delete.

2. If there are multiple effects under your position indicator, click the record track buttons to select only the tracks containing the effects you want to delete (**Figure 9.8**).

3. Click ⃠ Remove Effect (located by default on the Timeline tool bar and on the Composer's Fast menu).

Xpress Pro deletes all effects under the position indicator on the selected tracks.

continues on next page

APPLYING SEGMENT AND TRANSITION EFFECTS

✔ Tips

- You can map the Remove Effect button to your keyboard or interface from the FX tab of the Command palette.

- When you try to delete a title or matte key effect, clicking Remove Effect will eliminate the alpha channel layer but leave behind the effect's fill clip segment. To delete that remaining segment, enter a Segment mode, select the segment in question, and press Delete (**Figure 9.9**).

Title

Remaining fill layer

Figure 9.9 Park the position indicator over a title and click Remove Effect (left). What happens? Only half of the effect is erased; the fill layer remains (right). To delete the remainder, enter Lift/Overwrite Segment mode, select the segment, and press Delete.

Selected transitions

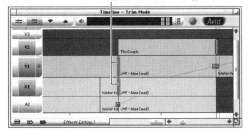

Deleted transition effects

Figure 9.10: To delete a transition effect in Trim mode, select the transitions you want to eliminate (above) and click Remove Effect (below).

- You can delete a transition effect while in Trim mode. Mark the transition point in question with one or two pink rollers and click Remove Effect (**Figure 9.10**).

To delete multiple effects at once:

1. Enter Effect mode by clicking the ⏭ Effect mode button (located by default on the Timeline toolbar).

2. In the Timeline, Shift-click to select multiple segment or transition effects.

   Note that you can select only one type of effect.

3. Click Remove Effect.

   Xpress Pro deletes all of the effects on the selected segments or edit points.

✔ Tips

- You can map the Effect mode button to your keyboard or interface from the Other tab of the Command palette.

- For more information on working in Effect mode, see "Modifying Segment and Transition Effects" later in this chapter.

Remove Effect Versus Delete

To completely get rid of an effect, your best bet is to park the position indicator over the effect and click Remove Effect (located by default on the Timeline toolbar): Most editors prefer this method because it does not require switching to Effect mode.

You can also use the Delete key to remove an effect, but not without first switching to either Effect mode or a Segment mode. If you accidentally press Delete while in regular editing mode, Xpress Pro thinks you want to erase entire tracks. So forget that key! Use Remove Effect.

Deleting Both Segment and Transition Effects in a Segment

If a segment contains both a segment effect and a transition effect, clicking Remove Effect deletes the transition effect first. To delete the segment effect as well, you need to click Remove Effect again.

However, if you want to delete the segment effect but keep the transition effect, you need to click the Effect mode button (or open the Effect editor), go to the Timeline and select the segment effect, and click Remove Effect.

To replace an effect:

◆ Drag a new effect from the Effect palette and drop the new effect on top of an existing effect in the Timeline.

Xpress Pro replaces the old effect with the new effect.

To replace multiple effects at once:

1. Enter Effect mode by clicking the Effect mode button (located by default on the Timeline toolbar).

2. In the Timeline, Shift-click to select either a group of segment effects or a group of transition effects.

You can select only one effect type.

3. On the Effect palette, double-click the new effect you want (**Figure 9.11**).

Xpress Pro replaces the selected effects with the new effect.

✔ Tip

■ When replacing a segment effect with another segment effect, you don't have to enter Effect mode. Just enter a Segment mode by clicking the Extract/Splice-in or Lift/Overwrite button (found at the bottom left of the Timeline). Select one or more segment effects, go to the Effect palette, and double-click the new segment effect.

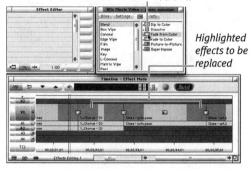

Double-click to apply effect.

Highlighted effects to be replaced

Figure 9.11 Your dissolves are too cliché? Enter Effect mode, select them, and double-click something more original on the Effect palette.

Don't Erase It—Replace It

If you want to apply a Flip instead of a Flop or eschew Color Effect for Color Correction, don't waste your time by deleting the effect you don't like. Instead, replace it by simply dropping a new effect icon on top of the old one.

And don't fret about redoing your transition parameters. Xpress Pro is smarter than you think: When it replaces a transition effect, the new effect keeps the length and positioning of the original.

Using QuickTransition

If you find yourself using the same transition effect over and over again, you don't need to apply it from the Effect palette. Instead, you can apply the effect with the QuickTransition button (located by default on the Timeline toolbar and on the Composer Fast menu).

QuickTransition can do the following:

◆ Quickly apply one of four common effects: Dissolve, Fade to Color, Fade from Color, and Dip to Color.

◆ Apply one of your own customized transition effect templates (see the sidebar "Applying Favorites with QuickTransition" later in this chapter).

◆ Apply effects to every edit point between In and Out points on the Timeline.

To apply a QuickTransition effect:

1. In the Timeline, place the position indicator near an edit point that needs a transition effect.

2. Select the Record Track button for the track that contains the edit point. (If the edit point aligns vertically through multiple tracks, you can select multiple track buttons to apply the effect on those tracks.)

3. Click the QuickTransition button (located by default on the Timeline toolbar and the Composer Fast menu).

   Xpress Pro highlights the edit points on the selected tracks and opens the Quick Transition dialog box (**Figure 9.12**).

   continues on next page

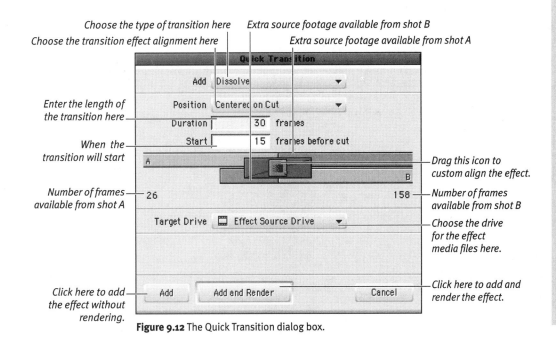

Figure 9.12 The Quick Transition dialog box.

4. In the dialog box, click the Add pull-down menu and choose a transition effect type.

5. Click the Position pull-down menu and choose an alignment for the effect. If you choose Custom, you can set a custom transition by dragging the effect graphic to the left or right.

6. Click the Target Drive pull-down menu and choose a target drive for your effect's media files.

7. Click Add to apply the effect without rendering or Add and Render to apply the effect and render it.

Xpress Pro applies the chosen transition effect to the selected edit points in the Timeline.

✔ Tips

■ You can map the QuickTransition button to your keyboard or interface from the FX tab of the Command palette.

■ If you lack sufficient source footage for your QuickTransition on either shot A or shot B, Xpress Pro will position the effect as close as possible to your desired alignment. For example, a transition effect for which you specify Centered on Cut may not end up exactly centered, but Xpress Pro will center it is as much as possible.

USING QUICKTRANSITION

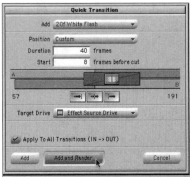

All of these edit points will receive a transition effect.

Figure 9.13 To use QuickTransition to apply the same effect to multiple edit points, you mark a region of your Timeline with In and Out points, select the track, and then click the QuickTransition button.

To apply QuickTransition effects to multiple edit points:

1. Set In and Out points in the Timeline, marking a region that contains all of the edit points in question.

2. Click to select the record track buttons for the tracks that contain the edit points in question.

3. Click the QuickTransition button and set your transition effect parameters in the Quick Transition dialog box that appears (see "To apply a QuickTransition effect" earlier in this chapter).

4. In the dialog box, select Apply to All Transitions.

5. If you do not want to render real-time effects, select Skip Real-Time Effects.

   (This option appears only when you are applying multiple effects.)

6. Click Add to apply the effects without rendering or Add and Render to apply the effects and render them (**Figure 9.13**).

   Xpress Pro applies the effect to every transition between the Timeline In and Out points on the selected tracks.

USING QUICKTRANSITION

Creating Quick Fades with Fade Effect

Clicking the Fade Effect button (located by default on the Composer Fast menu) is the fast way to fade the opacity level of most segment effects up or down by a custom number of frames. This approach is ideal for quickly fading titles and any of the Key effects.

The Fade Effect function works by automatically creating Level keyframes for the existing effect. These quick fades save you from having to apply an additional transition effect, such as a Dissolve or Fade-to-Color. So if you want to fade an image in or out, don't reach for the Dissolve transition effect!

The Fade Effect button commonly applies to segment effects like Superimpose, Chroma Key, Luma Key, Matte key, Picture-in-Picture, titles, and all of the Xpress 3D effects.

To fade one or more effects using Fade Effect:

1. In the Timeline, place the playhead on the effects you want to fade. Make sure the tracks containing the effects are selected.

2. If you want to fade multiple effects at once, click either the Extra/Splice-In or Lift/Overwrite Segment button and Shift-click the effects in question.

3. Click the 🖅 Fade Effect button.

   The Fade Effect dialog box appears (**Figure 9.14**).

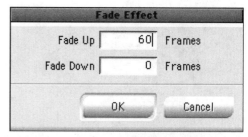

Figure 9.14 The Fade Effect dialog box. Enter the number of frames for the fade up and the fade down. The fade amounts do not have to be identical.

Fade Effect adds this keyframe   *The title fades up without the need for a transition effect*

Figure 9.15 When you apply Fade Effect to an effect, Xpress Pro adds a keyframe in the Composer window. For a fade up, the first keyframe has a Level parameter value of 0, and the second keyframe has a value of 100. The opposite applies to a fade down.

4. In the Fade Effect dialog box, enter the number of frames to fade up or down.

5. Click OK.

Xpress Pro creates a Fade Effect keyframe for the effect (**Figure 9.15**).

✔ Tips

■ If you try to apply Fade Effect to a segment effect that does not allow it, Xpress Pro presents a dialog box with the message "The effect doesn't allow the fade."

■ You can adjust the frame on which the fade begins or ends in the Composer monitor by first clicking the Effect mode button and then Alt-clicking (Windows) or Option-clicking (Mac) the keyframe and dragging it to the left or right.

CREATING QUICK FADES WITH FADE EFFECT

Modifying Segment and Transition Effects

After applying an effect, you can modify the parameters and transition alignments by entering Effect mode. In Effect mode, the Effect editor displays the parameters for a selected effect in parameter groups (**Figure 9.16**). The Composer transforms into an effect preview monitor and represents parameter keyframes as pink triangles on the Composer playbar. (For more information on keyframes, see "About Xpress Pro Keyframes" later in this chapter.)

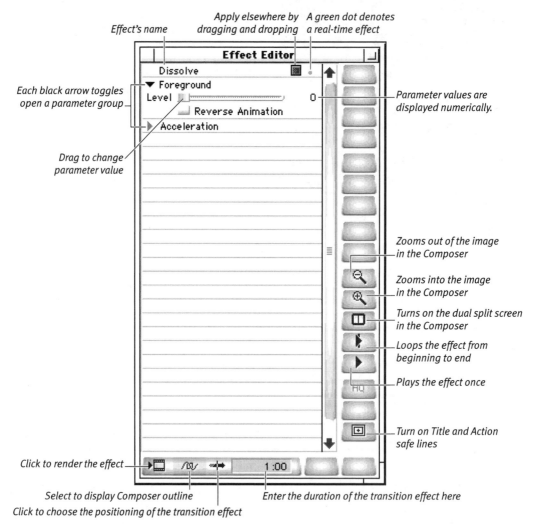

Effect's name — *Apply elsewhere by dragging and dropping* — *A green dot denotes a real-time effect*

Each black arrow toggles open a parameter group

Parameter values are displayed numerically.

Drag to change parameter value

Zooms out of the image in the Composer

Zooms into the image in the Composer

Turns on the dual split screen in the Composer

Loops the effect from beginning to end

Plays the effect once

Turn on Title and Action safe lines

Click to render the effect

Select to display Composer outline

Click to choose the positioning of the transition effect

Enter the duration of the transition effect here

Figure 9.16 The Effect editor in action for a transition effect. It currently displays the parameters for a Dissolve effect.

Parameters in parameter group

Parameter group name

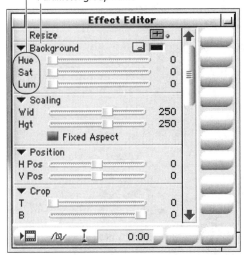

Figure 9.17 To display the parameters within parameter groups, click the black arrow to the left of a group's name. To keep the Effect editor small, you should open only the parameter groups you need to adjust in the effect.

- You don't need to click the Effect mode button to enter Effect mode. Another way is to open the Effect editor, park the position indicator over a Timeline effect, and click the Effect Editor window.

- To leave Effect mode and return to normal editing, click the Effect mode button or click the Timeline away from any effects.

To modify an effect's parameters:

1. Position the Timeline position indicator over the effect you want to modify and enter Effect mode by clicking the Effect mode button (located by default on the Timeline toolbar).

   Xpress Pro enters Effect mode and opens the Effect editor, which displays the parameters of the effect underneath the Timeline position indicator.

2. If there are multiple effects under the position indicator and the Effect editor does not display the effect you want to edit, go to the Timeline and select the effect you want to edit.

   The Effect editor displays the parameters of the selected effect.

3. In the Effect editor, click the black triangle next to a parameter group name to display the parameters in the parameter group (**Figure 9.17**).

4. To adjust a parameter that has a numerical value, *do one of the following*:
   - ▲ Drag a parameter slider to the left or right.
   - ▲ Click to select a parameter slider and then type a new parameter value from the keyboard.

   The parameter change applies to the selected keyframe indicator in the Composer monitor. The Composer's effect preview updates to reflect the parameter changes.

   (For more information on keyframes, see "About Xpress Pro Keyframes" later in this chapter.)

✔ Tips

- You can map the Effect mode button to your keyboard or interface from the Other tab of the Command palette.

MODIFYING SEGMENT AND TRANSITION EFFECTS

To edit the duration of a transition effect:

1. Enter Effect mode by clicking the Effect mode button (located on the Timeline toolbar).

   Xpress Pro opens the Effect editor.

2. In the Timeline, select the transition effect you want to edit.

   The Effect editor displays the parameters for the selected transition effect.

3. In the input field at the bottom right of the Effect editor, type a timecode number for the duration of the transition and press the Tab key.

   Xpress Pro adjusts the duration of the transition in the Timeline.

✔ Tip

- When adjusting a transition duration, you may get an insufficient source warning if you lack sufficient source clip footage to accommodate the new duration. (For more information, see the sidebar "Insufficient Source Warnings" later in this chapter.)

To edit the alignment of a transition effect:

1. In Effect mode, go to the Timeline and select the transition effect you want to align with the cut.

   The Effect editor displays the parameters for the selected transition effect.

2. At the bottom of the Effect editor, click the Transition Effect Alignment button and choose *one of the following* (**Figure 9.18**):

   ▲ **Centered on Cut:** For example, a 1-second transition will begin half a second before the cut and half a second after the cut (**Figure 9.19**).

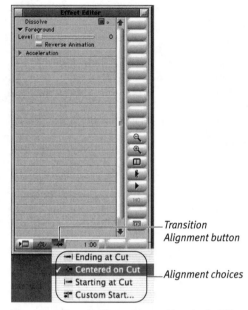

Transition Alignment button

Alignment choices

Figure 9.18 You can align your transitions in the Effect editor with the Transition Alignment button.

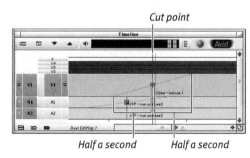

Cut point

Half a second *Half a second*

Figure 9.19 A 1-second Centered on Cut dissolve begins half a second before the cut point and ends half a second after the cut point.

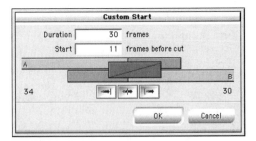

Figure 9.20 In the Custom Start dialog box, you can create nonstandard effect alignments. For example, you can have a 30-frame dissolve start 11 frames before the cut (meaning that it ends 19 frames after the cut).

▲ **Ending at Cut:** A 1-second transition begins 1 second before the cut and ends at the cut.

▲ **Starting at Cut:** A 1-second transition begins at the cut and ends 1 second after the cut.

▲ **Custom Start:** Use this option to create a nonstandard, nonsymmetrical alignment. For example, you can make a 30-second Dissolve start 11 frames before the cut and end 19 frames after the cut (**Figure 9.20**).

Xpress Pro aligns your effect in the Timeline.

✔ Tips

■ The Custom Start dialog box also has three buttons—Ending at Cut, Centered on Cut, and Starting at Cut—in case you change your mind and want to return to a standard alignment.

■ The Custom Start dialog box is also an alternative place for setting your transition effect's duration regardless of whether the effect has standard alignment.

Insufficient Source Warnings

Transition effects require extra source material beyond what you see in the Timeline. For example, if you create a 4-second transition effect and choose Centered on Cut, then shot A's master clip must have 2 seconds of extra footage at its tail, and shot B's master clip must have 2 seconds of extra footage at its head.

If a clip lacks sufficient source material, the Insufficient Source dialog box appears and informs you of one of the following problems:

◆ *Your transition length extends beyond the length of one of the two segments involved in the transition point.* The dialog box reports either "Past Head A" (not enough footage on the first shot) or "Past Tail B" (not enough footage on the second shot; see **Figure 9.21**).

◆ *The first shot's (shot A's) master clip does not contain sufficient tail footage.* The Insufficient Source dialog box reports "Off Media A."

◆ *The second shot's (shot B's) master clip does not contain sufficient head footage.* The Insufficient Source dialog box reports "Off Media B" (**Figure 9.22**).

To fix an insufficient source problem, you'll need to click on the Size to Fit button in the warning dialog to automatically shorten the effect, use the Effect editor to shorten the effect's duration manually, choose a different transition effect alignment, or use a different segment in the Timeline for the cut from a master clip that has more source material.

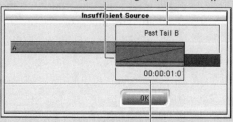

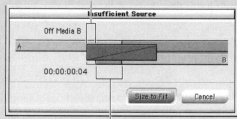

Cut point   Length of transition effect   Amount of extra source footage needed

Length of the segment   Available source footage

Figure 9.21 In this case, the chosen length of the transition effect is longer than the segment itself. The effect goes past the end of shot B by 1 second and 1 frame. To fix this problem, click OK and then shorten the length of the transition effect.

Figure 9.22 In this case, the transition effect is not possible because there is not sufficient source footage for shot B. The head of shot B's master clip has four too few frames. To fix the problem, click Size to Fit; Xpress Pro shortens the length of the transition effect.

Applying an Effect with the Effect Editor

The Effect editor isn't just for editing an effect. You can also use it to copy one effect elsewhere in your sequence. After you load the effect you want to copy in the Effect editor, just drag the effect icon from the upper right of the Effect editor to a new transition point or segment in the Timeline (**Figure 9.23**).

Figure 9.23 To apply an effect from one segment to another, load the segment in the Effect editor and then drag the effect icon (at the upper right of the window) to the other segment in the Timeline. This saves you from having to re-create the effect parameters.

The Other Options Button

When working with effects in the Effect editor, you may occasionally encounter the ⬛ Other Options button. Typically, clicking this button opens another window that is relevant to your effect.

For example, any effect that requires a color choice, such as Fade to Color, uses the Other Options button to open your system's color palette (**Figure 9.24**).

✔ Tip

■ To modify a title that is already in your Timeline, load the title in the Effect editor and click the Other Options button. The Title tool automatically opens, and you can make and save any changes you want.

The Split Screen Button

The Split Screen button (located on the right side of the Effect editor and on the Other tab of the command palette) is very useful when editing any effect that changes your image significantly.

Selecting Split Screen displays a before-and-after view in your Composer window. The left side of the Composer window displays your image unaffected, and the right side displays your image with the effect applied (**Figure 9.25**).

This view is especially helpful when performing color correction, allowing you to see just how much you've altered your image.

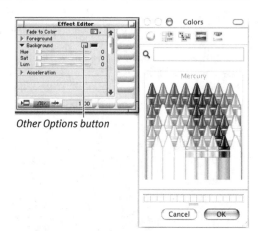

Other Options button

Figure 9.24 To choose a background color for Fade to Color, you can click the Other Options button to bring up your operating system's color palette.

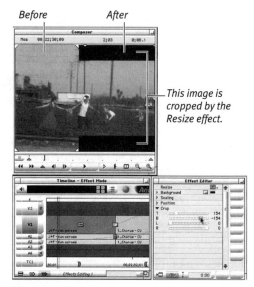

Before   After

This image is cropped by the Resize effect.

Figure 9.25 To see the before-and-after view for the effect, click the Split Screen button. This view is great for seeing the difference made by a Color Correction effect or checking how much an image is cropped.

Split-screen resize handles

Figure 9.26 With Split Screen turned on, drag one of the corners of the "before" image to resize it.

Origin point   Destination point

Path of movement

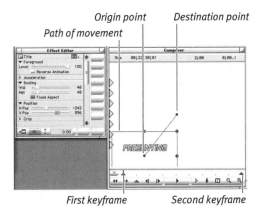

First keyframe   Second keyframe

By the second keyframe, the image is full size

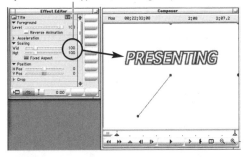

Figure 9.27: The image—a title (above)—moves up the frame and becomes larger from one keyframe to the next (below). The black line represents the path of its movement

✔ Tip

- You do not have to settle for the Split Screen's default display. There are four white triangles on the corners of the "before" image. You can drag them to resize the display (**Figure 9.26**).

The Outline/Path Button

When resizing and moving images from one location in the frame to another, you can use the ⚯ Outline/Path button (located at the right side of the Effect editor) to help you see and control the motion path you want the image to follow. This feature is especially useful for the following procedures:

♦ **Moving an image.** The path displayed by the button is a movement path. If, during a certain period of time, an object must move from point A to point B, Xpress Pro shows you the path it travels with a black line and two black dots that represent the image's origin and destination, respectively (**Figure 9.27**).

continues on next page

MODIFYING SEGMENT AND TRANSITION EFFECTS

- **Resizing or distorting an image.** The outline displayed by the Outline/Path button consists of lines that show the boundaries of your image. Three black dots appear on the outline; you can use these to resize the image or change its aspect ratio (**Figure 9.28**). (For more information, see "Resizing Images" later in this chapter.)

Transition Effects Make Great Image Masks

If you treat a transition effect as you would a segment effect, by applying it to a segment instead of a transition point, you can quickly create an image mask with a funky shape. The transition effect acts like a mask, blacking out part of the image (**Figure 9.29**).

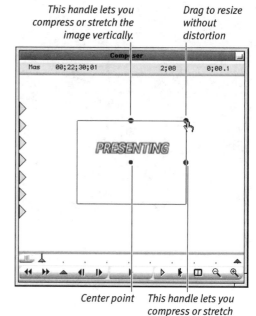

This handle lets you compress or stretch the image vertically.

Drag to resize without distortion

Center point

This handle lets you compress or stretch the image horizontally.

Figure 9.28: The outline displayed by the Outline/Path button represents the borders of your image. Use the dot in the upper-right corner of the image to resize the image. Use the dots on the top and right of the image to change the aspect ratio.

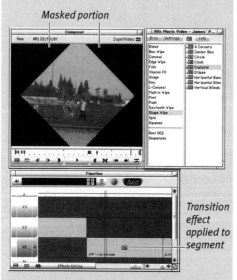

Masked portion

Transition effect applied to segment

Figure 9.29 An effect like Diamond is supposed to be a transition effect, but if you apply it to a segment, it acts as a mask. This effect switcheroo is helpful for making quick mask shapes that you cannot create simply by cropping.

Color Sampling Controls

When an effect requires you to choose a color, you have two options, both available in the Effect editor:

◆ You can click the Other Options button and choose a color from the operating system color palettes that appear.

◆ You can use the eyedropper to sample a color from the image in your Composer or source monitor (see the following task for the steps to do this).

Both methods are equally sound, but you will probably want to use the eyedropper method when you want your chosen color to match or complement a color in your movie.

To sample a color with the eyedropper:

1. In the Effect editor, position the pointer over the color preview box (next to the Other Options button).

2. When the eyedropper appears, click the mouse and drag the eyedropper to the pixel you want to sample (usually, you sample a color in the Composer monitor).

3. Release the mouse.

The sampled color appears in the color preview box (**Figure 9.30**).

Eyedropper

Color preview box

Figure 9.30 To choose a color using the eyedropper, first click and hold the mouse on the color preview box. Then drag the eyedropper to a pixel you want to sample. When you find the color, release the mouse. The new color appears in the color preview box.

Effects Editing: The Shortcuts

Here are some keyboard-centric shortcuts to enhance your control over effect editing:

◆ In Effect mode, tap the **Tab** key with your left hand to jump from parameter slider to parameter slider. With your right hand, use the **numeric keypad** on your keyboard to enter the parameter values for highlighted sliders. Remember to use the minus sign for negative coordinates.

(The catch is that Xpress Pro jumps only to the next visible parameter slider, so when you first open the Effect editor, toggle open the disclosure triangles for all of the parameter groups you want to affect.)

◆ To set a transition's duration, you can also use **Tab** and the **numeric keypad.** In the Effect editor, tapping Tab eventually highlights the transition effect Duration box. Here, you can type in a duration using Xpress Pro's shorthand. Typing *.23* provides a 23-frame duration, typing *123* provides a duration of 1 second and 23 frames, and so on. Press Enter to officially set the duration.

You can further increase your speed by using the following buttons, especially if you map them to the keyboard:

◆ **Step Forward** and **Step Backward** (located by default in the Composer): In Effect mode, these buttons move the position indicator one field forward or backward in the Composer monitor.

◆ **Add Keyframe** (located by default in the Composer): To keep your hands flying on the keyboard, map this button to the keyboard, not the mouse.

◆ **Fast Forward** and **Rewind** (located on the Move tab of the Command palette): In Effect mode, these buttons jump from keyframe to keyframe. Once you land on a keyframe, use Tab and the numeric keypad to set its values.

◆ **Go to Next Edit** and **Go to Previous Edit** (located by default in the Composer): These load the next or previous effect into the Effect editor. The cool thing is, if you can add the Add Option button (located on the More tab of the Command palette) to these mappings, you don't have to worry about which tracks are selected.

With some clever keyboard mapping that splits tasks between your two hands, the mouse will become less tempting after awhile. Now create a special keyboard setting, name it "Effects Editing," and link it to your Effects Editing toolset.

Using Motion Effects

You can make speed change, reverse motion, strobe motion, and fit-to-fill effects using the Motion Effect dialog box (**Figure 9.31**). Freeze frames are unique because you create them via the Clip menu (See "Creating Freeze Frames" later in this chapter). When you apply a motion effect to a source clip, the result is an entirely new clip that you can use anytime or anywhere in your sequence.

The subtle visual qualities of many motion effects with field-based video depend on how you ask Xpress Pro to render them. For more information on your motion effect rendering options, see the sidebar "The Four Motion Effect Render Options" later in this chapter.

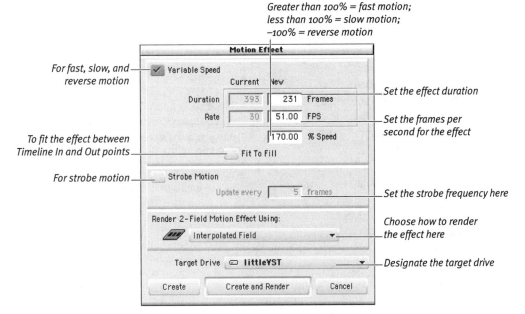

Greater than 100% = fast motion; less than 100% = slow motion; –100% = reverse motion

For fast, slow, and reverse motion

Set the effect duration

Set the frames per second for the effect

To fit the effect between Timeline In and Out points

For strobe motion

Set the strobe frequency here

Choose how to render the effect here

Designate the target drive

Figure 9.31: The Motion Effect dialog box, where you can create fast, slow, reverse, or strobe motion.

To speed up, slow down, or reverse a clip:

1. In a bin, double-click a clip to load it into a source monitor.

2. In the clip's source monitor, set In and Out points for the portion of the clip to which you want to apply the motion effect.

3. Click the ✍ Motion Effect button (located by default at the lower right of the source monitor).

   The Motion Effect dialog box opens.

4. In the Motion Effect dialog box, select the Variable Speed box (**Figure 9.32**).

5. *Enter a value for one of the following:*

   ▲ **New Duration: Frames:** Enter a new number of frames for the clip. A value higher than the current number will slow down the clip. A lower value will speed up the clip.

   ▲ **New Rate: FPS:** Frames per second. An FPS value higher than the current FPS rate will speed up the clip. A lower value will slow down the clip.

   ▲ **%Speed:** Normal speed is 100%. A higher percentage speeds up the clip. A lower percentage slows down the clip. A negative percentage reverses the clip.

6. Open the Render 2-Field Motion Effect Using pop-up menu and choose a rendering option.

   (For more information on the rendering options, see the sidebars "The Four Motion Effect Render Options" and "A Render Option Preset Makes Life Easier" later in this chapter).

7. Click Create and Render to create the motion effect clip and render it, or click Create to create the clip without rendering.

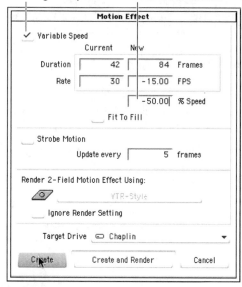

Select this box to change the speed

In this case, the clip will run half as fast as normal and in revers

Figure 9.32 In the Motion Effect dialog box, check the Variable Speed box to change the speed of a clip. Enter a speed percentage: lower than 100% for slow motion; higher than 100% for fast motion. A negative percentage makes the clip move backward.

USING MOTION EFFECTS

Motion effect
clip icon   *New speed of clip*

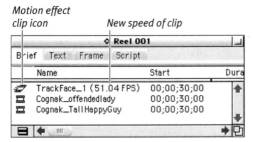

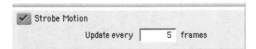

Figure 9.33: A motion effect has a unique icon and when it involves a speed change. Xpress Pro lists the new number of frames per second (FPS) next to the clip's name in the bin.

Figure 9.34 You need to do two things in the Motion Effect dialog box to create strobe motion: check the Strobe Motion option and enter a numerical strobe frequency in the box next to it. With the setting shown here, the clip will momentarily stop every five frames.

8. In the dialog box that opens, select the target bin to which you want to send the new motion effect clip. Then click OK.

Xpress Pro creates a new motion effect clip and places it in your target bin. You can edit it into your sequence, just like any other source clip (**Figure 9.33**).

✔ Tips

- You can map the Motion Effect button to your keyboard or interface from the FX tab of the Command palette.

- The Select dialog box (for selecting motion effect target bins) lists only open bins.

- You can preset a target drive for motion effects on the Motion Effects tab of the Media Creation settings dialog box.

- You can combine strobe motion and reverse motion with either fast or slow motion.

To create strobe motion:

1. In a bin, double-click a clip to load it into a source monitor.

2. In the clip's source monitor, set In and Out points for the portion of the clip to which you want to apply the motion effect.

3. Click the Motion Effect button (located on the FX tab of the Command palette).

4. In the Motion Effect dialog box, select the Strobe Motion option (**Figure 9.34**).

5. To determine the rate of the strobe, enter a number in the Update Every *x* Frames box.

A rate of 3, for example, causes every third frame to be held for three frames before updating.

continues on next page

USING MOTION EFFECTS

6. Choose a rendering method from the Render 2-Field Motion Effect Using pop-up menu. (For more information, see the sidebar "The Four Motion Effect Render Options" later in this chapter.)

7. Click Create or Create and Render.

8. In the dialog box that opens, select the target bin for the effect. Then click OK. Xpress Pro creates the motion effect and places it in your target bin.

✔ Tip

■ Editors often use strobe motion with fast motion for comic effect; they often use strobe motion with slow motion to emphasize a dramatic moment.

A Render Option Preset Makes Life Easier

If you don't want to worry about how to render a motion effect each time you create a new one, you can preset your rendering choice in the render settings.

On the Settings tab of the Project window, double-click your active render settings. In the Render Setting dialog box, open the Motion Effects Render Using pop-up menu and choose one of the four render options.

After you choose a render preset, the Render 2-Field Motion Effect Using menu will be dimmed in the Motion Effect dialog box when you create the motion effect.

If you want to return to setting rendering options in the Motion Effect dialog box, open your Render Setting dialog box again, open the Motion Effects Render Using menu, and select Original Preference (**Figure 9.35**).

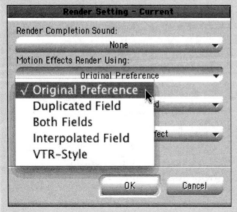

Figure 9.35 If you like rendering your motion effects the same way all the time, make a preset choice in the Render Setting dialog box. If you do this, the Render 2-Field Motion Effect Using pop-up menu will be dimmed in the Motion Effect dialog box unless you click Ignore Render Setting.

Timewarp Motion Effect Presets

If you need to quickly create a 50% speed or reverse speed motion effect, you can avoid the Motion Effect dialog box altogether by applying a Timewarp effect from the Effect palette to a Timeline clip segment.

The Timewarp effects—which are noncustomizable motion effect presets—also include the following four preset speed ramps:

◆ **0% to 100%:** This effect makes a clip start as a freeze frame and gradually increase speed until it reaches full speed at the end of the clip.

◆ **100% to 0%:** This effect (the opposite of the 0% to 100% effect) makes a clip start at full speed and gradually slow down until it comes to a freeze frame at the end of the clip.

◆ **Speed Boost:** This effect makes the clip start at slower than normal speed. Then it ramps up to faster than normal speed in the middle of the clip, only to return to slower than normal speed at the end of the clip.

◆ **Speed Bump:** This effect (the opposite of Speed Boost) makes the clip start at faster than normal speed. Then it ramps down to slower than normal speed in the middle of the clip, returning to faster than normal speed at the end of the clip.

The Four Motion Effect Render Options

When you apply a motion effect in the Motion Effect dialog box, you have four options for rendering the result. From worst to best quality, the options are as follows:

◆ **Duplicated Field:** Xpress Pro creates the effect using one field. Use this option only when working with single-field media. Do not use it with your DV media (which involves two fields) because the resulting image will be low in quality.

◆ **Both Fields:** Xpress Pro uses two fields from each frame to create the effect. Use this option for clips that are from film-to-tape transfers, clips that have interfield motion, or still shots. This option is also a good (and fast) choice for reverse motion. When using Both Fields to render a motion effect, you will get the best results if you use evenly divisible frame rates (like 60 FPS).

◆ **VTR-Style:** Xpress Pro creates the effect by shifting the selected video fields of the original media by a full scan line. Use this option if you favor a sharp image over a smooth one. The image will be less blurry than that produced by the Interpolated Fields option, but it may also seem jittery. This is the most popular option for strobe motion. When applying fast motion, the render choice is a real toss-up between VTR-Style and Interpolated Fields. Experiment and see what you like.

◆ **Interpolated Fields:** Xpress Pro creates a second field by combining scan-line pairs from the first field. Use this option if you favor a smooth image over a sharp one. This option is most popular choice for slow motion, but it also takes the longest time to render.

To apply a Timewarp motion effect:

1. Open the effect palette by choosing Tools > Effect palette; or go to the Project window and click the Effect palette icon.

2. In the Effect palette categories on the left, click the Timewarp category.

   The Timewarp motion effect presets appear on the right.

3. Drag a Timewarp effect on top of a Timeline clip segment.

   Xpress Pro changes the speed of the clip segment (**Figure 9.36**).

✔ Tip

- When you apply a Timewarp effect to a Timeline clip segment, Xpress Pro does not create a motion effect clip in your bin.

Creating a Fit-to-Fill Motion Effect

Fit-to-Fill fits a specified amount of source material into a specified amount of space in the Timeline, creating a speed-adjusted motion effect clip. You can add a Fit-to-Fill effect in two ways: by using the Motion Effect button and by performing a Fit-to-Fill edit.

The advantage of using the Motion Effect button over performing a Fit-to-Fill edit is that the motion effect approach allows you to double-check your render setting and add strobe or reverse motion to the speed-adjusted clip. (For more information on Fit-To-Fill edits, see "Performing Fit to Fill Edits" in Chapter 6.)

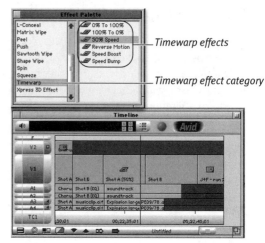

Timewarp effects

Timewarp effect category

Figure 9.36 With the 50% Timewarp effect dragged on top of a clip segment, the clip runs at half speed.

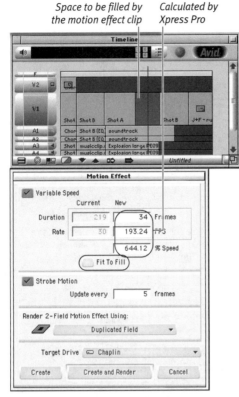

Space to be filled by the motion effect clip   *Calculated by Xpress Pro*

Figure 9.37 To perform a Fit-to-Fill edit, check the Fit to Fill box in the Motion Effect dialog box.

To create a Fit-to-Fill motion effect:

1. Mark In and Out points in the Timeline.

The duration spanned by these two points will be the duration of your speed-adjusted clip.

2. Load a clip into a source monitor and set In and Out points for it.

3. Click the Motion Effect button (located by default at the lower right of the source monitor).

4. In the Motion Effect dialog box, select the Variable Speed box.

5. Select the Fit to Fill option (**Figure 9.37**). Xpress Pro automatically sets the frame duration, FPS rate, and speed percentage for the effect.

6. (Optional) You can add strobe motion to the effect by clicking the Strobe motion box. You can reverse the motion of the clip by adding a minus sign in the % Speed box.

7. Choose a rendering method from the Render 2-Field Motion Effect Using pop-up menu. (For more information, see the sidebar "The Four Motion Effect Render Options" earlier in this chapter.)

8. Click Create and Render to create the motion effect clip and render it, or click Create to create the clip without rendering.

9. In the dialog that opens, select the target bin for the effect. Then click OK.

Xpress Pro fits the source clip in between the In and Out points in the Timeline, in the process creating a motion effect clip.

Creating Freeze Frames

Freeze frames qualify as motion effects, but you create them using the Clip Menu Freeze Frame option rather than the Motion Effect dialog box.

You need to make two significant choices when creating a freeze frame:

- **Duration:** The clip menu provides preset durations as well as an Other choice for setting a custom duration.

- **Rendering option:** Xpress Pro gives you three choices for two-field freeze frames: Duplicated Field, Both Fields, and Interpolated Fields. In most DV situations, it's hard to see any difference among these choices, but you may want to experiment.

To create a freeze frame:

1. Load a clip into a source monitor.

2. Park you position indicator on the frame you want to freeze.

3. Choose Clip > Freeze Frame > 2 Field Freeze Frames and choose a rendering option from the list that appears.

4. Choose Clip > Freeze Frame again and *do one of the following*:

   ▲ Choose a preset duration such as 1 Second or 5 Seconds (**Figure 9.38**).

   ▲ Choose Other. This opens the Freeze Frame dialog box in which you can type a timecode duration for the effect.

Xpress Pro creates the freeze frame and stores it as a motion effect clip in your bin. The application opens the freeze frame clip in a source monitor. You can now edit it into your sequence.

Pick a duration from the list that appears

Put the position indicator on the source clip frame that you want to freeze

Figure 9.38 To create a freeze frame, open a clip in a source monitor, park the position indicator on the frame you want to freeze, and choose Clip > Freeze Frame.

Freezing the End of Shot: The Strategy

Often you need to freeze a frame toward the end of a Timeline clip segment (to create an effect similar to the end of many 1970s TV shows).

To create this effect quickly, match-frame a Timeline clip segment. When Xpress Pro opens the match-framed master clip in a source monitor, create your freeze frame from the displayed frame. Once the freeze frame clip is created, you can edit it into your sequence, at the end of the related Timeline clip segment.

(For more information on using the Match Frame feature, see "Using Match Frame" in Chapter 6.)

The key to success is not to move the position indicator in the Timeline and the master clip source monitor during this whole process; otherwise, you may not freeze the correct frame or edit the freeze frame into the correct place in your sequence.

Always keep effects bins loaded (or open) in the SuperBin

To customize the effect, drag this to a bin

Give the effect templates descriptive names

Figure 9.39 To create an effect template, drag an effect's icon from the Effect editor to an open bin.

Creating Favorite Effect Templates

Effect templates—customized effects that contain your favorite parameter values—can save you from creating similar effects over and over again. For example, if you think your 10-minute music video will use at least 10 eight-frame white flashes (Dip to Color effects), then it's definitely worthwhile to make an eight-frame Dip to Color effect template.

To create an effect template:

1. Click the Effect mode button (located by default on the Timeline toolbar) to open the Effect editor.

2. In the Timeline, click to select the effect you want to save as a template.

   The Effect editor displays the parameters for the selected effect.

3. In the Effect editor, set the parameters for the effect according to your preferences.

4. Open the bin into which you want to place the effect template.

5. In the Effect editor, click the effect's icon and drag it to the bin (**Figure 9.39**).

6. Click the effect's name. When the name becomes highlighted, type a new name that will remind you what the effect does.

   You can now apply your effect template using the Effect palette or by dragging the effect icon from the bin into the Timeline.

✔ Tips

- It's also a good idea to create a bin specifically for effect templates and keep that bin loaded in the SuperBin; then you can apply your templates directly from the Effect palette.

- If you really go crazy with effect templates, just remember to give your effect templates unique names to remind you what they do.

Applying Favorites with QuickTransition

Besides using QuickTransition to quickly apply a generic Dissolve, Dip to Color, or other effect, you can use it to apply a favorite effect template. In other words, you can use QuickTransition to apply your own custom transition effects.

To make a favorite effect available in QuickTransition:

1. On the Bin tab of the Project window, create a bin and name it Quick Transitions.

2. Place one or more custom transition effect templates in the Quick Transitions bin.

   Any effect templates in this bin will be accessible from the Add pop-up menu. (**Figure 9.40**).

   (For more information, see "Creating Favorite Effect Templates" earlier in this chapter.)

✔ Tip

■ An added bonus is that you can apply the first-listed effect template in your Quick Transitions bin by pressing Ctrl+R (Windows) or Command+R (Mac). This applies the effect, but skips the Quick Transition dialog box altogether.

Custom effect templates

Figure 9.40 Maybe you can't get enough of eight-frame white flash transitions. If so, make a Dip to Color effect template that uses white and lasts eight frames and put it in a bin labeled "Quick Transitions." Whenever you want to add the effect, click the QuickTransition button and choose the effect from the Add pop-up menu.

CREATING FAVORITE EFFECT TEMPLATES

Getting the Effect Palette to List Your Bin Effects

Xpress Pro requires that you store titles, effect templates, and imported matte effects in bins. You can apply these bin effects by dragging them directly from the bin to the Timeline. However, this is not the simplest nor the fastest way to apply an effect from a bin (except for the instances when you need to load a title in a source window).

Here's how to make your life simpler: The Effect palette, being the sophisticated window that it is, has the ability to list all bin effects from open bins. Once you load a bin into the SuperBin, the palette lists bin names underneath the standard effect categories. When you click a bin name in the palette, the window conveniently lists all of the effects that bin contains. Now you can drag a title effect template or imported matte effect directly from the Effect palette to the Timeline (**Figure 9.41**).

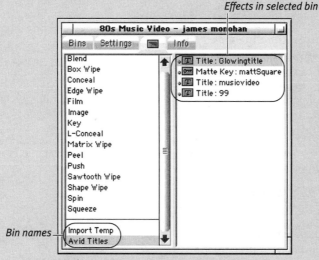

Figure 9.41 The Effect palette provides the fastest way to access effects that are in bins. Instead of hunting for titles in bins, apply them directly from the palette. Just make sure you keep the effect bins loaded at all times.

Nesting Multiple Effects

Once you start playing around with effects in Xpress Pro, you will eventually arrive at a point where adding only one effect per clip or manipulating only one layer of video at a time is not enough. Don't fret. Xpress Pro can take you to an advanced level of effects creation when you start using nests. Nests enable you to do the following:

◆ **Add multiple effects to the same segment.** If you want to add a Resize, Color Effect, and Flop effect to the same segment, creating a nest makes it possible.

◆ **Collapse multiple Timeline video layers into one layer.** If you want to apply the same effect to multiple layers of video, first you need to collapse all of those layers into one nest. Collapsed layers are always marked by the ▦ Submaster effect icon. Then you add an effect that applies to everything that's been collapsed.

To add multiple effects to the same segment:

◆ Alt-drag (Windows) or Option-drag (Mac) an effect from the Effect palette on top of an existing segment effect icon.

Xpress Pro nests the old effect together with the new one. The new segment icon appears on the segment, but the other effect is there, too, within the nest. To open the nest, double-click the segment.

✔ Tip

■ The nesting procedure works only for segment effects, not transition effects. You can't nest transition effects.

Layers to be collapsed into a nest

Figure 9.42 To collapse multiple layers of video into one layer that you can treat like one segment, first target the tracks containing the layers and set In and Out points around the area in question.

To collapse multiple video layers into one layer:

1. In the Timeline, select the tracks that contain the segments you want to collapse into a nest (**Figure 9.42**).

2. In the Timeline, mark an In point and an Out point around the area you want to collapse into a nest.

continues on next page

3. Click  Collapse (located on the Other tab of the Command palette).

Xpress Pro collapses the selected Timeline area or selected segment into a one-track nest and marks it with the Submaster icon. You can now add another effect to the nest and that effect will apply to every layer in the nest (**Figure 9.43**).

✔ Tips

- You can also use the ▼ Submaster effect (found in the Image category on the Effect palette) to render multiple video layers as one effect, without collapsing layers. (See "The Submaster Effect and Rendering" in Chapter 11.)

- You can nest whole sections of your Timeline, including sections with segment and transition effects.

Now this collage can be treated as one layer

Five layers in one nest

Submaster icon

Figure 9.43 After you click Collapse, Xpress Pro combines the selected section of your Timeline into a one-track nest.

To add multiple effects to a nested Submaster effect:

1. Apply a new effect to the nest that is marked by the Submaster effect.

   The Submaster effect icon changes to the icon of the new effect (**Figure 9.44**). The new effect is applied to every track in the nest.

2. Hold down Alt (Windows) or Option (Mac) and drag another effect icon onto the segment.

   The new effect is applied to the entire nest. You can keep doing this over and over again, adding effect upon effect to the nest.

✔ Tips

- You can have nests within nests. See "Modifying Nested Effects" later in this chapter to learn how to get inside nests.

- You can even apply advanced effects like Picture-in-Picture, 3D PIP, Superimpose, Chroma Key, Luma Key, and Matte Key to nests. Just hold down Alt (Windows) or Option (Mac) and drag the new effect onto the nested effect.

- To erase an effect that has been applied to a nest, do not use the ⊘ Remove Effect button. That will erase the entire nest. Instead, drag a Submaster effect to the nest; it will replace the current top effect, but it won't affect what's inside the nest.

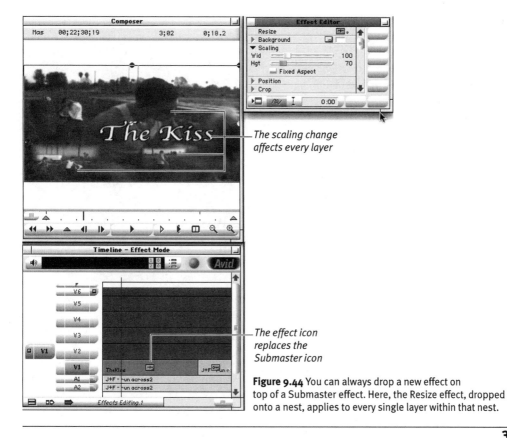

The scaling change affects every layer

The effect icon replaces the Submaster icon

Figure 9.44 You can always drop a new effect on top of a Submaster effect. Here, the Resize effect, dropped onto a nest, applies to every single layer within that nest.

NESTING MULTIPLE EFFECTS

Modifying Nested Effects

After you create a nest, you may want to access the layers within it. For example, you may want to edit or replace one of the nested layers or create a nest within the nest.

There are two ways to view and modify the hidden tracks within a nested effect:

◆ **Expand or close the nest.** In the Timeline, expanding or closing the nest allows you to view the nested tracks amid all of the other tracks in your sequence.

◆ **Step in or out of the nest.** Stepping in or out of a nest allows you to view the nested tracks alone, in their own sequence Timeline. This method is best if you don't have much viewing room in your Timeline. It also offers the least confusing way to create nests within nests.

To expand or close a nested effect:

◆ Click the Effect mode button (located on the Other tab of the Command palette) to enter Effect mode. In the Timeline, double-click the nested effect to expand it. If it is already expanded, double-click the nested effect again to close it.

Xpress Pro opens the nested tracks, labeled 1.1, 1.2, 1.3, and so on. If there is another nest within that nest, double-click it to open its tracks. Xpress Pro labels the next level of tracks 2.1, 2.2, 2.3, and so on (**Figure 9.45**).

Second-level nested tracks
First-level nested track

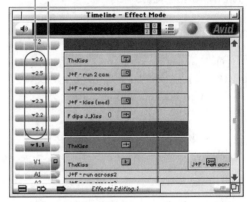

Figure 9.45 Double-click a nest to view the tracks within it. Do the same with any nests within the nest. Here, the first level nest has only one track, but the second level has five (plus one background layer).

NESTING MULTIPLE EFFECTS

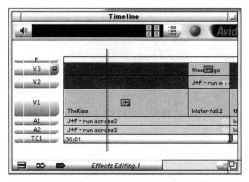

Figure 9.46 To step into a nest, park the position indicator on the nest in the Timeline and click the Step In button. Xpress Pro displays the nested tracks within their own Timeline. To get back to your sequence Timeline, click the Step Out button.

To step into and out of a nested effect:

1. In the Timeline, place the position indicator over the nested effect. If there is more than one nested effect at that position, select the track containing the effect.

2. Click the ▼ Step In button or the ▲ Step Out button (located on the FX tab of the Command palette).

   When you step in, the Timeline displays only the tracks within the nested effect (**Figure 9.46**). When you step out, Xpress Pro switches to a normal display of the Timeline, and you do not see any nested tracks.

✔ Tips

- If there are multiple nests on top of one another in the Timeline and you select more than one track, Xpress Pro steps into the uppermost nest.

- Segment effects technically are nested effects. Most contain one nested track, but the Picture-in-Picture, 3D PIP, Superimpose, Chroma Key, and Luma Key effects each contain two nested tracks. The Matte Key effect and titles are special because they contain three nested tracks.

NESTING MULTIPLE EFFECTS

About Xpress Pro Keyframes

Whenever you want to change an effect over time—dissolving from one image to another, flying an image across the screen, zooming into a still, and so on—you need to use keyframes (**Figure 9.47**).

A keyframe determines the value of an effect parameter at a particular point in time. To use a simple keyframing example, if you applied the Resize effect to a Timeline clip and wanted to use the effect to make your image shrink down to nothing through the duration of the clip, you would put a keyframe at the beginning of the effect and a keyframe at the end of the effect. Then you would select the first keyframe and give the effect's Scale parameter a value of 100 (for full size). Finally, you would select the last keyframe and give the Scale parameter a value of 0 (for no size). Thus, from first keyframe to last keyframe, the image would shrink from full size to nothing.

First keyframe   Second keyframe

Figure 9.47 Here, a Push transition uses two keyframes. At the first keyframe, shot A is full screen. At the second keyframe, shot B is full screen.

The Origin of Keyframes

Keyframes come from the old world of hand-drawn animation, in which principal artists draw the most important frames of an action (the keyframes) and then let other artists fill in the frames between the keyframes. In a simple example, if a character expression changes from a frown to a smile, one keyframe marks point A (the initial frown) and the second one marks point B (the final smile); in between are the transitional frames (the interpolation) needed to go from point A to point B.

Some Effects Always Use Keyframes

Since transition effects inherently involve a change in the image, these effects always use keyframes. (Segment effects, do not always use keyframes because they can be static.)

For example, in a Dissolve effect, the first keyframe marks the start of the dissolve (when shot A is at 100% opacity), and the second keyframe marks the end of the dissolve (when shot B is at 100% opacity).

One keyframe contains all parameter values

Figure 9.48 One keyframe contains the values for every parameter in the Effect editor for that point in time. You probably won't complain about this—until you learn about advanced keyframes and the freedom of independent keyframes.

Xpress Pro offers you two ways to work with keyframes: using standard keyframes and advanced keyframes. The standard keyframing method is simple to use; the advanced keyframing method approaches the sophistication of a powerful compositing tool like After Effects:

◆ **Standard keyframes:** Every segment and transition effect in Xpress Pro can use standard keyframes. When you're in Effect mode—with the parameters of the effect you want to adjust displayed in the Effect editor—the positions of standard keyframes are represented in the Composer monitor by pink triangles (called keyframe indicators).

A distinguishing limitation of standard keyframes is that one keyframe indicator includes the value for every effect parameter at a particular frame in time; you cannot assign a different standard keyframe to each individual effect parameter (**Figure 9.48**).

◆ **Advanced keyframes:** As of Xpress Pro 4.0, the standard keyframes for three segment effects—Resize, Picture-in-Picture, and 3D PIP—can be promoted to advanced keyframes.

Unlike when you work with standard keyframes, every effect parameter is assigned its own advanced keyframe. In addition, each advanced keyframe has its own keyframe graph, which provides sophisticated ways of positioning keyframes and manipulating their values.

(For more information on the advantages and use of advanced keyframes, see "Working with Advanced Keyframes" later in this chapter.)

ABOUT XPRESS PRO KEYFRAMES

Working with Standard Keyframes

Although standard keyframes are not as sophisticated as advanced keyframes, they are adequate for most of the effect animation you'll do in Xpress Pro (after all, really fancy keyframing is best reserved for a designated compositing application).

By default, every transition and segment effect is assigned two keyframes: one at the beginning of the effect, and one at the end.

While in Effect mode, you can manipulate effect parameters by adjusting Composer monitor keyframe indicators in the following ways: You can add a keyframe, change a keyframe's parameter value, move a keyframe to new position in time, and copy a parameter value from one keyframe to another. (See **Table 9.2** for keyframe shortcuts.)

To create a standard keyframe:

1. Click the 🔲 Effect mode button (located by default at the upper left of the Timeline toolbar) to enter Effect mode.

2. In the Timeline, click a segment or transition effect to display its parameters in the Effect editor.

3. In the Composer, put the position indicator where you want to create a keyframe.

Table 9.2

Shortcuts for Keyframes	
PROCEDURE	COMMAND
Go to Next Keyframe	▶▶
Go to Previous Keyframe	◀◀
Select Current and Next Keyframe	Shift+ ▶▶
Select Current and Previous Keyframe	Shift+ ◀◀
Nudge Keyframe Forward 1 Frame	❯
Nudge Keyframe Backward 1 Frame	❮
Nudge Keyframe Forward 10 Frames	❯❯
Nudge Keyframe Backward 10 Frames	❮❮

4. Click the  Add Keyframe button (located on the FX tab of the Command palette; **Figure 9.49**).

In the Composer monitor, Xpress Pro adds a keyframe indicator at the position of the playhead.

✔ Tip

■ If you position the playhead on an existing keyframe and click Add Keyframe, nothing happens. There can be only one standard keyframe per frame. (For other options, see "Working with Advanced Keyframes" later in this chapter.)

To delete one or more keyframes:

1. In Effect mode in the Composer window, select the keyframe you want to delete. If you want to delete multiple keyframes, use the Shift key to select the other keyframes.

2. Press the Delete key.

The selected keyframes disappear from the Composer.

✔ Tip

■ Just as you cannot move a starting or ending keyframe, you cannot delete a keyframe at the beginning or ending of an effect, so don't even think about it.

Add Keyframe button — New keyframe

Figure 9.49 To create a new keyframe, position the playhead in the Composer and click Add Keyframe. Xpress Pro adds a keyframe indicator. Add Keyframe is a great button to map to your keyboard.

WORKING WITH STANDARD KEYFRAMES

To move a keyframe:

◆ In Effect mode in the Composer monitor, Alt-click (Windows) or Option-click (Mac) the keyframe indicator you want to move; the cursor arrow changes to a pointing hand. Still holding the mouse, drag it to a new location (**Figure 9.50**).

✔ Tips

■ You can use ⎗ Trim Left 1 Frame, ⎘ Trim Right 1 Frame, ⎗ Trim Left 10 Frames, and ⎘ Trim Right 10 Frames to move keyframes 1 or 10 frames backward or forward. (All of these buttons are located on the Trim tab of the Command palette.)

■ You cannot change the position of standard keyframes that rest at the beginning or ending of an effect, but with advanced keyframes you can. (For more information about standard and advanced keyframes, see "About Xpress Pro Keyframes" earlier in this chapter.)

■ You cannot move a group of standard keyframes at once.

To modify the parameters of a standard keyframe:

1. In the Composer monitor, click the keyframe whose parameters you want to change.

   The selected keyframe turns pink.

2. In the Effect editor, change the value of one or more parameter sliders (**Figure 9.51**).

✔ Tip

■ For parameters such as Scaling and Position, you can select a keyframe and change its value by dragging the image or image handles in the Composer monitor.

Pointing hand

Figure 9.50 To move a keyframe indicator using the mouse, Alt-click (Windows) or Option-click (Mac) and drag the indicator to its new location. When you do this, the cursor changes to a pointing hand.

Selected keyframe

The V Pos value applies to the selected keyframe.

Figure 9.51 To change a parameter value at a keyframe, first select the keyframe in the Composer. Then go to the Effect editor and change the value of one or more parameters. Remember that you can also use the keyboard to set your parameters. (See the sidebar "Effects Editing: The Shortcuts" earlier in this chapter).

Figure 9.52 The first and fourth keyframes have normal Scaling values, and the second and third keyframes have zoom-in Scaling values. To create a momentary zoom into an image, copy the first value to the fourth and the second to the third.

Ease In, Ease Out with the Acceleration Control

Displayed in the Effect editor for many effects, the Acceleration parameter provides the only way to control the smoothness by which Xpress Pro moves from one standard keyframe to the next. The Acceleration parameter slider affects keyframe interpolation—the automatic filling in of the frames between keyframes. By dragging the Acceleration slider to the right, toward the curved line, you increase the amount of easing in and easing out of keyframes in your effect.

For more advanced easing in and easing out control, you need to use advanced keyframes. (For more information see "Working with Advanced Keyframe Interpolation Curves" later in this chapter.)

To copy and paste a keyframe's parameters:

1. In the Composer monitor, select the keyframe you want to copy.

2. Choose Edit > Copy.

3. *Do one of the following:*
   ▲ Select another keyframe in the Composer. To select multiple keyframes, Shift-click.
   ▲ While still in Effect mode, select a different segment in the Timeline that has the same effect. Select one or more keyframes from that effect.

4. Choose Edit > Paste.
   Xpress Pro copies all of the parameters from one keyframe to the one or more keyframes that you select (**Figure 9.52**).

✔ Tips

■ Here's a cool trick: You can apply a single parameter value from an effect template to an effect that is loaded in the Effect editor. To do this, Alt-drag (Windows) or Option-drag (Mac) an effect template to a parameter slider of an identical type of effect in the Effect editor. The parameter adopts the same value as your effect template.

■ You cannot copy more than one keyframe at a time. However, you can paste a keyframe parameter onto multiple selected keyframes.

■ You can paste a keyframe parameter value from one effect to the same type of parameter value of another effect. For example, you can paste the Scaling parameter of one Resize effect to the Scaling parameter of a different Resize effect.

■ When selecting keyframes, you can choose Edit > All to select all of the keyframes in the Composer.

To select or deselect multiple keyframes:

◆ In the Composer monitor, Shift-click multiple keyframes to select them. Shift-click keyframes again to deselect them.

✔ Tips

■ Hold down Shift and click [▶▶] Fast Forward to select the current selected keyframe as well as the keyframe to the right of the current keyframe; hold down Shift and click [◀◀] Rewind to select the current selected keyframe as well as the keyframe to the left of the current keyframe (**Figure 9.53**).

■ You cannot deselect every keyframe. Xpress Pro always keeps one keyframe selected.

Shift+Fast Forward selects this keyframe (the active one) and the next one.

Figure 9.53 To keep the current keyframe selected and select the next keyframe as well, hold down Shift and click the Fast Forward button. Using this approach, you avoid a lot of mouse clicking.

What's Reverse Animation?

Many Xpress Pro effects include a parameter option called Reverse Animation.

When you select Reverse Animation, Xpress Pro takes all of your keyframes and flops them, creating a mirror image of their initial positions in the Composer. The starting keyframe becomes the ending keyframe, and the ending keyframe becomes the starting keyframe. What happens at the beginning of the shot, happens at the end, and vice versa.

Suppose you have a title that fades in from black. In addition, the title starts out large and scales down to normal size by the time the fade ends. If you load such a title's parameters in the Effect editor and select Reverse Animation, you get the following result (see **Figure 9.54**):

- The title no longer fades in at the beginning of the shot. Instead, it fades out at the end of the shot.

- The title no longer shrinks at the beginning of the shot. Instead, it grows at the end of the shot.

The best way to visualize the effect of Reverse Animation is to imagine your keyframes marked on a transparent page in a book. Selecting Reverse Animation is like flopping over that page.

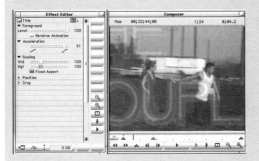

This keyframe moved from the beginning to the end.

Figure 9.54: (left) Before the animation on this effect is reversed, the title shrinks and fades in at the beginning of the effect. (right) After the animation is reversed, the title grows and fades out at the end of the shot.

Working with Advanced Keyframes

As of the current version of Xpress Pro, the effects that employ advanced keyframes are Resize (found in the Image category), Picture-in-Picture (found in the Blend category), and 3D PIP (found in the Xpress 3D category).

Advanced keyframes have the following advantages over standard keyframes:

◆ In the Effect editor, every parameter has an individual keyframe with its own keyframe track (**Figure 9.55**).

◆ Each advanced keyframe track can open a keyframe graph, which you can use to adjust keyframe values when applying advanced Interpolation options such as Bézier curves (**Figure 9.56**).

◆ You can simultaneously add, delete, or change the value of keyframes in multiple keyframe graphs at once.

◆ In keyframe graphs, you can move groups of keyframes at once, and with the Aligning and Slipping commands, you can even move keyframes beyond the normal boundaries of an effect.

◆ You can specify whether the positions of advanced keyframes are automatically adjusted after you change the length of a segment, by choosing either Fixed or Elastic keyframe behavior.

Keyframe tracks

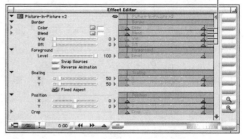

Figure 9.55 In the Effect editor, every parameter has an individual keyframe with its own keyframe track.

Figure 9.56 You can use keyframe graphs to adjust keyframe interpolation in advanced ways. Here, Bézier handles alter the interpolation curve of the first keyframe.

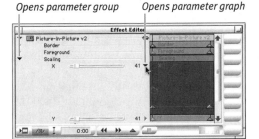

Opens parameter group   *Opens parameter graph*

Figure 9.57 Every parameter in advanced keyframes has its own keyframe graph. The length of each keyframe timeline and graph depends on how you size the Effect editor window.

To promote standard keyframes to advanced keyframes:

1. Apply the Resize, Picture-in-Picture, or 3D PIP effect to a segment and click the Effect mode button to enter Effect mode.

   The Effect editor opens, displaying the parameters for the effect.

2. At the lower right of the Effect Editor window, click the 🖼 Promote to Advanced Keyframes button.

   Xpress Pro changes the Effect editor's parameter display to Advanced Keyframe mode, in which each parameter has its own keyframe track and graph. The name of the effect changes to *Effect Name* v2.

To view an advanced keyframe graph:

1. In the Effect editor's advanced keyframe display, click an arrow to the left of one of the parameter group names.

   The arrow turns down, revealing the parameters within the parameter group.

2. To view a parameter's graph, click the arrow to the right of one of the individual parameter names.

   The arrow turns down, revealing the keyframe graph for that parameter (**Figure 9.57**).

To adjust the advanced keyframe graph view:

◆ To zoom into and out of the graph, move the zoom slider at the bottom right of the keyframe graph.

◆ To scroll horizontally to the left and right, click and hold down the mouse on the thumbwheel at the bottom left.

◆ To adjust the vertical size of the graph, hold the cursor at the base of a keyframe graph until it becomes an up-and-down arrow; then drag up or down (**Figure 9.58**).

✔ Tips

■ If you cannot see all of your keyframes in the keyframe graph due to scrolling, you can recenter the graph's view: right-click (Windows) or Ctrl+Shift-click (Mac) and select Reset Graph View from the menu that appears.

■ To increase the length of a keyframe graph, resize the Effect Editor window.

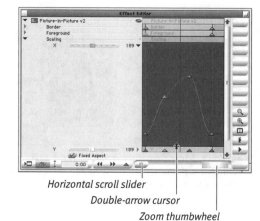

Horizontal scroll slider

Double-arrow cursor

Zoom thumbwheel

Figure 9.58 You can adjust the view of your keyframe graph with the zoom and scroll controls.

Playing Peak-a-Boo with Keyframes

Sometimes you can't see keyframes at the very top or very bottom of your keyframe graph.

The solution is to scroll up or down a keyframe graph by selecting two or more keyframe indicators (by Shift-clicking) and then pressing Alt+Shift (Windows) or Option +Shift (Mac) on one of the keyframe indicators and dragging directly up or down. This exposes either the top or the bottom of the keyframe graph (**Figure 9.59**).

Make sure you press the keys before you click to drag or you will move the keyframe, not the graph.

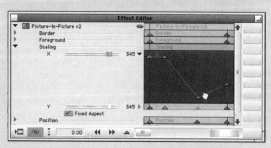

Figure 9.59 To scroll a keyframe graph vertically, select more than one keyframe; then press Alt+Shift (Window) or Option+Shift (Mac) and drag up or down. This is a better approach than using the scroll bar.

Figure 9.60 If you want to add a keyframe to only one parameter, right-click (Windows) or Ctrl+Shift-click (Mac) the parameter's timeline and choose Add Keyframe. Don't bother with the Add Keyframe button (at the bottom of the screen) for such a simple operation.

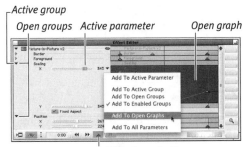

Figure 9.61 In contrast to the similar button in the standard keyframe interface, the Add Keyframe button in the advanced keyframe interface gives you plenty of options for adding keyframes.

✔ Tip

■ You should know what you want to do before you open the advanced keyframe add/delete menu; otherwise, you'll spend a lot of time staring at the screen, overwhelmed by those choices.

To add one or more advanced keyframes:

1. In the Effect editor, move the position indicator to the point in an advanced keyframe parameter track where you want to add a keyframe.

2. To quickly add a keyframe, right-click (Windows) or Ctrl+Shift-click (Mac) on the keyframe Timeline. In the shortcut menu that appears, choose Add Keyframe (**Figure 9.60**). This is the simple technique. To add a keyframe to more than one parameter, click the ▲ Add Keyframe button at the bottom of the Effect editor. In the menu that appears (**Figure 9.61**), *select one of the following*:

▲ **Add to Active Parameter:** Xpress Pro adds a keyframe to the active parameter only (for example, a highlighted slider).

▲ **Add to Active Group:** Xpress Pro adds a keyframe to the active parameter as well as to all of the parameters in the active parameter's group (an example of a parameter group is Scaling).

▲ **Add to Open Groups:** Xpress Pro adds a keyframe to any open parameter group (you open a parameter group by clicking the arrow next to a parameter group name).

▲ **Add to Enabled Groups:** This is the same as Add to All Parameters (all groups are enabled at all times. Ignore this option.

▲ **Add to Open Graphs:** Xpress Pro adds a keyframe to any open keyframe graph.

▲ **Add to All Parameters:** Xpress Pro adds a keyframe to every keyframe track.

Xpress Pro adds one or more keyframes, according to your selection.

To delete an advanced keyframe in a keyframe graph:

1. In the Effect editor, click to select the keyframe you want to delete.

2. *Do one of the following:*

   ▲ Press the Delete key. This is the simplest way to delete one keyframe.

   ▲ Alt-click (Windows) or Option-click (Mac) the ▲ Add Keyframe button (at the bottom of the Effect editor) and choose a delete command from the pop-up menu that appears. (See the preceding task "To add one or more advanced keyframes" and Figure 9.61 to understand the options).

   Xpress Pro deletes all selected keyframes, according to the menu command you pick.

✔ Tips

■ For the Scaling parameter, if you select Fixed Aspect and adjust the X coordinate, the Y coordinate matches the value (and vice versa). However, if you delete an X-coordinate keyframe, the Y-coordinate keyframe value remains the same (and vice versa).

■ When you delete a keyframe using the Delete key, you delete every selected keyframe in the effect. If you just want to delete only the keyframe that you're clicking, right-click (Windows) or Ctrl+Shift-click (Mac) and choose Delete Keyframe from the pop-up menu.

To copy and paste advanced keyframe parameters:

1. In the Effect editor, click to select the keyframe you want to copy. To select multiple keyframes, Shift-click.

2. Choose Edit > Copy.

3. Select the keyframes to which you want to paste. Shift-click to select multiple keyframes.

4. Choose Edit > Paste.

   Xpress Pro pastes the value of the copied keyframe to all of the selected keyframes in the keyframe track.

✔ Tip

■ Copying and pasting advanced keyframe values works exactly as it does for standard keyframes, except that advanced keyframes allow you to paste values to different parameter tracks.

Repositioning Advanced Keyframes

There are three ways you can move an advanced keyframe in its graph: vertically, horizontally, or any direction. Moving it vertically changes the keyframe's value, but not its position. Moving it horizontally changes its position, but not its value. Moving a keyframe in any direction means that you can change its value and position at the same time.

So how do you do it? As you'll see, moving a keyframe one way or another depends on which keys you hold down while you drag.

To move an advanced keyframe vertically:

1. Open the keyframe's graph.

2. Click the keyframe indicator; drag up to increase the parameter's value and down to decrease it.

   This changes the keyframe value, but not its position.

✔ Tips

- When a keyframe graph is closed, you can use the Trim buttons to increase a parameter's value by increments of 1 or 10. (While in Effect mode, you can access these buttons by opening the Command palette, clicking Active Palette, and clicking the Trim tab.)

- You can also use the up and down arrows on your keyboard to increase or decrease a keyframe's value.

To move an advanced keyframe horizontally:

Do one of the following:

◆ With the keyframe graph closed, Alt-click (Windows) or Option-click (Mac) the keyframe indicator and drag it to the left or right (**Figure 9.62**).

◆ With the keyframe graph open, Alt+Shift-click (Windows) or Option+Shift-click (Mac) the keyframe indicator and drag it to the left or right.

✔ Tip

■ You cannot move a keyframe past the position of another keyframe. Keyframes constrain each other.

To move a keyframe in any direction:

1. Open the keyframe's graph.

2. Alt-click (Windows) or Option-click (Mac) the keyframe and drag it left, right, up, or down (**Figure 9.63**).

   This changes both the keyframe's value and position. You cannot change a keyframe in this way with the keyframe graph closed.

✔ Tip

■ As you drag, Xpress Pro displays the changing parameter value next to the slider and at the top of the keyframe graph.

To move multiple advanced keyframes at once:

1. Shift-click to select two or more keyframe indicators in the keyframe graph.

2. Click one of the keyframes; then press Alt+Shift (Windows) or Option+Shift (Mac) and drag left or right.

   The selected keyframes move together.

Drag left or right

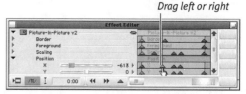

Figure 9.62 You don't have to have the keyframe graph open when you move the keyframe horizontally (to change its position). Just Alt-click (Windows) or Option-click (Mac) and drag the keyframe indicator to the left or right.

Drag up, down, left, or right

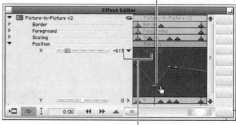

Updated keyframe values

Figure 9.63: Moving an advanced keyframe up and sideways simultaneously requires holding down a modifier key (Alt or Option) while you drag. You can only do this with the keyframe graph open.

✔ Tips

■ Make sure you click before you press the keys, or you will merely scroll the graph up and down.

■ For other ways to move keyframes together, see "The Aligning and Slipping Functions," next.

The Aligning and Slipping Functions

It's a real pain to move a whole bunch of keyframes by dragging them one by one. That's why the Aligning and Slipping options are available for advanced keyframes:

◆ **Aligning:** This command allows you to quickly move one or more keyframes to the position of the playhead in the advanced keyframe graph. Only selected keyframes will move.

◆ **Slipping:** This command also allows you to quickly move one or more keyframes to the position of the playhead. The difference between this option and Aligning is that all keyframes follow along regardless of whether they are selected.

The key concept to understand before delving into these tasks is the *reference keyframe*. This is the last keyframe that you select on a track. When you align a keyframe with the playhead, it is the reference that jumps to the playhead position while the rest of the keyframes follow along like obedient children.

To align one or more keyframes to the position indicator:

1. Select one or more keyframes on one or more tracks. Make sure the last keyframe that you select on each track (the *references)* are the ones you want to align with the position indicator.

   Xpress Pro brightly highlights the reference keyframes and slightly dims the other selected keyframes.

2. Place the position indicator where you want to move the reference keyframes (other keyframes will follow).

continues on next page

3. *Do one of the following:*

▲ To move keyframes on only one track, right-click (Windows) or Ctrl+Shift-click (Mac) the keyframe track.

▲ To move keyframes for the entire parameter group, right-click (Windows) or Ctrl+Shift-click (Mac) the top track of the parameter group.

▲ To move keyframes for the entire effect, right-click (Windows) or Ctrl+Shift-click (Mac) the top track in the Effect editor, above the topmost keyframe track.

4. From the pop-up menu, choose Align Keyframes.

The reference keyframes jump to the position of the playhead. Other selected keyframes follow along symmetrically (**Figure 9.64**).

✔ Tips

■ Here's one limitation: Xpress Pro does not let you align a reference keyframe beyond the position of another keyframe. The closest it can get is one frame away from the next or previous keyframe.

■ Aligning with all keyframes in a track selected usually has an effect similar to that of slipping keyframes (see the next task, "To slip one or more keyframes to the position indicator").

*Click here to align   Click here to align the
the entire effect   Crop parameter group*

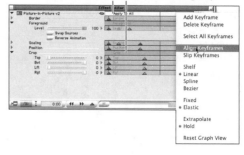

*Keyframes cannot move past or before
other keyframes on the same track*

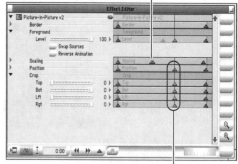

*Reference keyframes move to
the position of the playhead*

Figure 9.64 Here, all reference keyframes for the entire effect (above) are aligned with the position of the playhead (below).

We Now Return to an Effect Already in Progress

The Align Keyframes command lets you position keyframes outside the boundaries of the effect. In other words, you can position keyframes before the start of the shot and after the end of the shot. This feature is useful when you want to start a shot with an effect already in progress, or when you want an effect to seem to be continuing even when your shot ends.

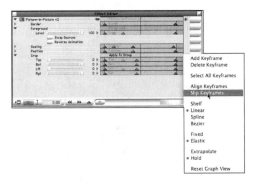

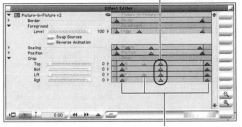

*Reference keyframes move to
the position of the playhead*

*All other keyframes move along, some
moving beyond the boundaries of the effect*

Figure 9.65 Here, all reference keyframes for the Crop parameter group (above) are slipped to the position of the playhead (below). In contrast with Align Keyframes, Slip Keyframes moves all keyframes on the tracks, whether or not they are selected.

To slip one or more keyframes to the position indicator:

1. Select the reference keyframes that you want to move to the location of the position indicator. Select one per track. If you have more than one selected, make sure that the one you want to move to the position indicator is the last one you select: the reference.

2. Place the position indicator where you want to move the reference keyframe (other keyframes will follow).

3. *Do one of the following:*

    ▲ To slip keyframes on only one track, right-click (Windows) or Ctrl+Shift-click (Mac) the track.

    ▲ To move keyframes for the entire parameter group, right-click (Windows) or Ctrl+Shift-click (Mac) the top name track in the parameter group.

    ▲ To move keyframes for the entire effect, right-click (Windows) or Ctrl+Shift-click (Mac) the top track in the Effect editor, above the topmost keyframe track.

4. From the pop-up menu that appears, choose Slip Keyframes.

    Xpress Pro moves all reference keyframes to the position indicator. All other keyframes, selected or not, are pushed or pulled relative to the references. (**Figure 9.65**).

✔ Tips

■ When performing slipping for the entire effect, you do not need to select a reference keyframe on every single track.

■ As when you align keyframes, a slip may move keyframes beyond the boundaries of the effect.

Extrapolate and Hold: Advanced Keyframe Esoterica

For the most part, you don't have to worry about whether your keyframes are set for Extrapolate or Hold, unless you align or slip advanced keyframes. The default is Hold, and this setting is usually the one you want. But if you want to switch to Extrapolate, right-click (Windows) or Ctrl+Shift-click (Mac) a keyframe track and choose the option from the pop-up menu.

Here are the circumstances in which whether you choose Extrapolate or Hold becomes important:

◆ You align or slip your keyframes so that the first keyframe of the effect moves to the right, beyond the beginning of the effect.

◆ You align or slip your keyframes so that the last keyframe of the effect moves to the left, in front of the end of the effect.

Say you align or slip your keyframes to the right: you need to decide whether you want your parameter's value to remain the same for the beginning of the effect. If the answer is yes, then you want to choose Hold for that parameter (**Figure 9.66**). On other hand, if you want Xpress Pro to guess that your parameter values are increasing or decreasing up until the position of the moved keyframe, then choose Extrapolate.

Here's how Extrapolate works: If the effect parameter values are increasing after your first keyframe, then Extrapolate makes the effect parameter values increase up until the repositioned first keyframe (**Figure 9.67**). If effect parameters values are decreasing after the first keyframe, then Extrapolate makes the parameter values decrease up until the repositioned first keyframe.

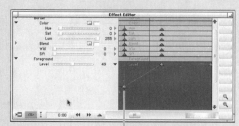

Beginning of effect

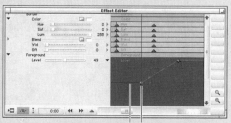

First keyframe   First keyframe is value holds steady   slipped here

Figure 9.66 Here, the Foreground parameter keyframes (above) are slipped to the right (below). This means that the first keyframe gets moved to the right of the effect's beginning. So, now what are the parameter values before that keyframe? If you choose Hold (the default), then the answer is that the value of the first keyframe remains constant during the beginning of the effect.

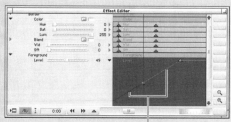

Xpress Pro follows the trend and calculates increasing values before the first keyframe

Figure 9.67 With Extrapolate selected, Xpress Pro calculates parameter values before the repositioned first keyframe. The values go up or down based on the direction of values between the first two keyframes.

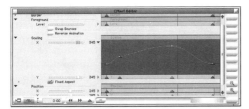

Figure 9.68 Shelf interpolation is rarely used. It holds your keyframe value constant until the very last frame before the next keyframe, when it suddenly jumps to the next value.

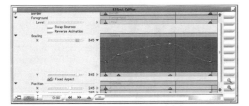

Figure 9.69 Spline interpolation involves curves that ease in and out of keyframes. In this Spline interpolation, the Acceleration slider is pulled all the way to the right in standard keyframing.

Working with Advanced Keyframe Interpolation Curves

Your choice of interpolation curve determines how Xpress Pro automatically animates or transitions from keyframe to keyframe, which, in turn, affects the feel of your animation. Xpress Pro gives you the following interpolation options:

◆ **Shelf:** This option holds a keyframe's value until the very last frame before the next keyframe. The result is that there is no smooth transition between keyframes. Instead, one keyframe suddenly jumps to the next keyframe (**Figure 9.68**).

◆ **Linear:** This is Xpress Pro's default interpolation option. The interpolation between keyframes is a straight line. There is no easing in or easing out of keyframes. There is no acceleration or deceleration between keyframes.

◆ **Spline:** With this option, the interpolation between keyframes is a curved line, similar to the effect of the Bézier option (but without the handles). This interpolation provides general easing in and easing out of keyframes (**Figure 9.69**).

◆ **Bézier:** This option adds curved Bézier lines between keyframes (similar to the effect of the Spline option), but with the added bonus of are Bézier handles that allow you to fine-tune the shape of the Bézier curves. (For more information, see "Bézier Handles" later in this chapter.)

The most advanced choice is, of course, the Bézier option, mainly because it allows you to manually shape the curves between keyframes. Before jumping right to the Bézier option, try using Spline, to see what a generic easing in and easing out of keyframes feels like. Then switch to the Bézier option and customize your curves.

To choose an interpolation option for one keyframe track:

1. *Do one of the following:*

    ▲ To choose interpolation for one graph, right-click (Windows) or Ctrl+Shift-click (Mac) the keyframe track.

    ▲ To choose interpolation for an entire parameter group, right-click (Windows) or Ctrl+Shift-click (Mac) the top parameter name track of the parameter group, above the topmost keyframe track of the group.

    ▲ To choose interpolation for the entire effect, right-click (Windows) or Ctrl+Shift-click (Mac) the top effect name track, above the topmost track in the effect.

2. From the pop-up menu that appears, choose Shelf, Linear, Splint. or Bézier.

    Xpress Pro changes the keyframe inter-polation curves in the keyframe graph.

Bézier Handles

Choosing the Bézier option for selected keyframes does two things: It adds a smooth Bézier interpolation curve between keyframes, and it displays two interpolation handles on each selected keyframe. You use the handles to shape your interpolation curves using one of three methods; however, you need to keep track of which method you are using because Xpress Pro does not give you any explicit sign.

*You have more control
over this handle*

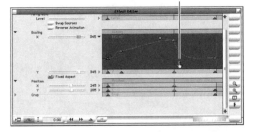

Figure 9.70 The asymmetrical manipulation of Bézier handles.

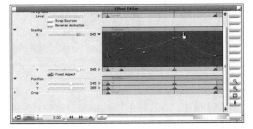

Figure 9.71 The independent manipulation of one Bézier handle.

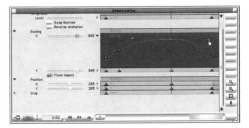

Figure 9.72 The symmetrical manipulation of Bézier curves.

The three Bézier handle options are as follows:

◆ **Asymmetrical:** This is the default selection after you choose Bézier interpolation. Both handles make changes as you drag the selected handle. However, you have more obvious control over the handle that you drag; the other handle and the other curve do not match your movement with the selected handle and curve (**Figure 9.70**).

◆ **Independently:** Dragging a direction handle changes both the length and rotation of the handle you drag. However, the opposite handles and curve do not change. This is one of the easier techniques to follow visually and is good for isolating one side of a keyframe (**Figure 9.71**).

◆ **Symmetrical:** Dragging a Bézier direction handle changes the length and shape of both handles symmetrically. Both the length of the handle and curve of the line mirror the handle and curve you are dragging (**Figure 9.72**).

To change to a different Bézier adjustment method:

1. While adjusting a Bézier curve, release the mouse.

2. Hold down the Alt (Windows) or Option (Mac) key and drag a Bézier handle.

   Xpress Pro switches to the next adjustment option and adjusts the Bézier curve accordingly. For example, if you were using a symmetrical adjustment, holding Alt (or Option) switches to asymmetrical adjustment.

To maintain the same Bézier adjustment method:

◆ After switching to the adjustment method you need, continue to drag the Bézier handles. Do *not* hold down the Alt (Windows) or Option (Mac) key again.

Making Advanced Keyframes Fixed or Elastic

When you trim a clip segment that has an effect on it, Xpress Pro can either adjust the effect's keyframe relative to the new size of the clip (the keyframes are *elastic*) or keep the keyframes where they are despite the segment size change (the keyframes stay *fixed*).

Standard keyframes always use Elastic keyframes. With advanced keyframes, however, each keyframe graph can be either Elastic or Fixed (see **Figure 9.73**).

To make advanced keyframes Elastic or Fixed:

Do one of the following:

◆ To change the keyframes for one parameter, Alt-click (Windows) or Ctrl+Shift-click (Mac) a keyframe track or keyframe graph. From the pop-up menu that appears, choose Elastic or Fixed.

◆ To change the keyframes for one parameter group, Alt-click (Windows) or Ctrl+Shift-click (Mac) the top name track of the parameter group. From the pop-up menu that appears, choose Elastic or Fixed.

◆ To change the keyframes for an entire effect, Alt-click (Windows) or Ctrl+Shift-click (Mac) the topmost track of the effect. From the pop-up menu that appears, choose Elastic or Fixed.

If you change keyframes to Fixed, the shape of the keyframes change so you can distinguish them from Elastic keyframes.

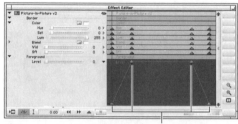

Fixed keyframe icons

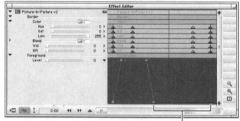

The segment was lengthened, but the keyframes remain in their fixed positions

Figure 9.73 Here, a segment has Level keyframes that fade a segment up and down (above). However, they are *Fixed* keyframes, so they don't change when the segment is lengthened or shortened (below). Fixed keyframes are especially useful when you need an effect to maintain sync with dialogue or music.

Working with Individual Effects

There is not enough room in this book to cover the intricacies of every single effect in Xpress Pro. However, there are some segment effects that deserve some coverage here because of their complexity.

The following sections cover tricky issues related to Resize, Picture-in-Picture, 3D PIP, Chroma Key, Luma Key, Matte Key, and Xpress 3D effects.

Resizing Images

Scaling an image up or down, with or without maintaining its aspect ratio, is a common image manipulation. In Xpress Pro, the Resize, Picture-in-Picture, and 3D PIP effects all allow you to scale an image, with the 3D PIP effect offering the most advanced control. (For more information on these effects, see "Resize Versus Picture-in-Picture Versus 3D PIP" later in this chapter.)

To resize an image:

1. Apply the Resize, Picture-in-Picture, or 3D PIP effect (found in the Image, Blend, and Xpress 3D categories, respectively) to a Timeline clip segment.

2. Click the Effect mode button (located by default on the Timeline tool bar) to enter Effect mode.

   The Composer displays your clip (at half size if it's a PIP effect) surrounded by an image outline.

continues on next page

3. To scale the image without distorting it, *do one of the following*:

▲ In the Composer window, click the upper-right corner outline handle and drag up or down to resize the image while maintaining its aspect ratio.

▲ In the Effect editor, toggle down the Scaling parameter group arrow and select the Fixed Aspect box. Move the X or Y scaling handles to resize the image while maintaining its aspect ratio (**Figure 9.74**).

4. If you want to squish or expand the image vertically (distorting the image), go to the Composer and drag the top selection hand up or down.

The image squishes or expands vertically.

5. If you want to squish or expand the image horizontally, go to the Composer and drag the rightmost selection handle to the left or right.

The image squishes or expands horizontally.

✔ Tips

■ When making an image bigger by dragging the outline handles in the Composer monitor, the task is easier if you first click the Zoom Out button so you can always see the handles in the Composer window (**Figure 9.75**).

■ When dragging outline handles to resize an image, hold down the Shift key to resize in large increments.

Figure 9.74 To resize an image and maintain its aspect ratio (avoiding distortion), drag the upper-right corner handle in the Composer monitor.

You can now see these handles while you resize the image

Click this button to shrink the Composer monitor display in 25% increments

Figure 9.75 Before making an image larger by dragging handles in the Composer monitor, click the Zoom Out button, so you can see the handles as you drag them.

Select Swap Sources to
interchange the foreground
with the background

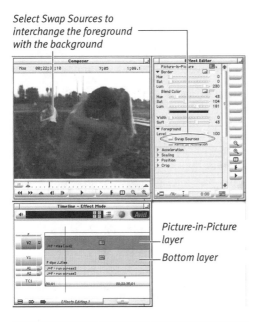

Picture-in-Picture
layer

Bottom layer

Figure 9.76 The bottom layer already has a segment effect on it (above). If you want to make the bottom layer the Picture-in-Picture layer, without nesting or changing anything in the Timeline, click Swap Sources (below). This is the easy way to switch your foreground and background image.

■ When you use the Picture-in-Picture effect, you can switch the foreground and background images by selecting Swap Sources in the Foreground parameter group. This procedure is especially handy when the segment you want to make into a Picture-in-Picture effect already has an effect on it; when you use Swap Sources, you avoid having to do any nesting (**Figure 9.76**).

Resize Versus Picture-in-Picture Versus 3D PIP

Resize, Picture-in-Picture, and 3D PIP, all effects that enable the resizing of images, differ as follows:

◆ **Resize:** This effect provides a quick way to shrink, grow, move, and crop an image if all you need is one image plus a background color. However, this effect does not create an alpha channel. You cannot layer it over another video image!

◆ **Picture-in-Picture:** This effect can do everything the Resize effect can, and in addition, it can create an alpha channel, so you can layer a PIP effect over a background image in the Timeline.

◆ **3D PIP:** This effect can do everything the Picture-in-Picture effect can do, and in addition, it is a 3D effect, so you can use any of the 3D tools (found on the 3D tab of the Command palette) to rotate your image around the X, Y, and Z axes.

(For more information, see "Working with Xpress 3D Effects" and "The 3D Tools" later in this chapter.)

All three of these effects can be promoted to advanced keyframes. (For more information, see "Working with Advanced Keyframes" earlier in this chapter.)

Alpha Channels Explained

A tricky concept to grasp in the world of video effects, motion graphics, and still graphics is the invisible, but powerful, alpha channel.

Simply described, an alpha channel contains invisible information in a moving or still image that governs which pixels are transparent and which are opaque.

For the most part, you won't have to worry about alpha channels when working in Xpress Pro. Most images you'll work with do not use them; they simply use the three visible channels that determine the images' basic color and luminance.

However, Xpress Pro does include a few effects that create alpha channels, including the following:

- **Titles:** A title is made up of an alpha channel layer and a graphic fill layer. The alpha channel layer is like a cookie cutter, determining the shape of the title, and the graphic fill layer determines what's inside the shape.

- **Matte Key:** Similar to a title, this effect turns a high-contrast image (usually a black-and-white image) into an alpha channel. That image becomes the cookie cutter, and the background image beneath it is like the fill layer of a title; it fills up the transparent part of the alpha channel.

- **Chroma Key:** In this effect, you create an alpha channel by sampling a specific color in your image. The alpha channel makes pixels that share the sampled color transparent.

- **Luma Key:** Similar to the Chroma Key effect, Luma Key creates an alpha channel after you sample a specific luminance value in your image. The alpha channel makes pixels that share the sampled luminance value transparent.

Using the Chroma Key Effect

The Chroma Key effect—traditionally used with clips that feature a subject shot against bluescreen or greenscreen—enables you to sample a color in an image and make every pixel of that color transparent. After applying the effect, you can layer the keyed clip on top of a background clip in your sequence.

To apply the Chroma Key effect:

1. Edit the clip segment that will be your background image onto track V1 (or whichever track will be your background track).

2. Edit your foreground image (one that preferably features a subject shot against bluescreen or greenscreen) on track V2 or one track above the background image.

3. Drag the Chroma Key effect (located in the Key category of the Effect palette) onto the V2 clip segment.

4. Click the Effect mode button (located by default on the Timeline toolbar) to enter Effect mode.

   The Effect editor opens, displaying the Chroma Key effect parameters.

5. To sample the color value that you want to make transparent, go to the Effect editor and click and hold on the Color Choice box. Drag the eyedropper to the Composer. Hover over the part of the image that has the color you want to key; then release the mouse.

   The keyed color appears in the Effect editor's Color Choice box. In the Composer, pixels of the same color as the keyed color become transparent.

continues on next page

How Do I Know What an Alpha Channel Looks Like?

After you edit any of the effects described in the preceding sidebar, you can click a button in the Effects editor called Show Alpha. If you do so, the Composer displays a grayscale image. The white parts of the image represent the transparent pixels of the alpha channel. The black parts of the image represent the opaque pixels of the alpha channel. Any gray parts are in between transparent and opaque (**Figure 9.77**).

Opaque   Transparent

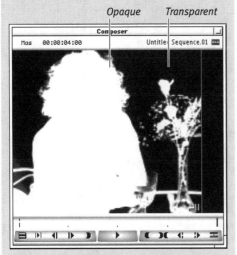

Figure 9.77 This is the kind of black-and-white image you see when you select Show Alpha in the Effect editor. This image is from a Chroma Key effect; the effect treated a shot of a girl against a solid greenscreen. The effect made all of the green pixels transparent. What remains is the shape of the girl.

6. To fine-tune your results, manipulate *one or more of the following*:

▲ **Gain** and **Soft:** You can find these controls in the Key, Secondary Key, and Spill Suppression parameter groups. You should play with these controls in the Key parameter group before moving to Secondary Key and Spill Suppression. These controls often achieve satisfactory results by themselves.

▲ **Secondary Key:** If your bluescreen or greenscreen background does not key out entirely, there may be slightly different shades of the background color not covered by the primary Key color choice. Use the Secondary Key parameter group to key out the varying shades of your Key color.

▲ **Spill Suppression:** If, after using the Gain, Soft, and Secondary Key controls, you still have residual greenscreen or bluescreen color around the edges of your foreground image, use Spill Suppression to further reduce the residual color as much as possible (**Figure 9.78**).

▲ **Show Alpha:** To find out what pixels you have and haven't keyed (made transparent), click this box. The Composer will display a black-and-white image in which the white is what you made transparent and the black is the image that remains. (For more information on alpha channels, see the sidebar "Alpha Channels Explained" earlier in this chapter.)

✔ Tip

■ When playing with the Soft controls, be careful that your subject (foreground image) doesn't become overly transparent.

Foreground

Background

Greenscreen keyed out (made transparent)

Figure 9.78 The greenscreen image is on track V2, and the background is on track V1 (above). Achieving a proper key of the green required an initial key as well as some spill suppression and fiddling with the Gain and Soft controls (below).

Figure 9.79 Here is the background image for the Luma Key effect, placed on the lower track in the Timeline.

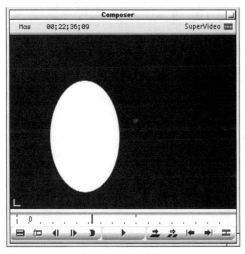

Figure 9.80 Here is the foreground image for the Luma Key effect, placed one track above the background image. This is a simple image of a white oval against black. In this case, the white will be keyed.

Using the Luma Key Effect

The Luma Key effect is similar to the Chroma Key effect; the difference is that instead of keying out pixels based on their color, it keys out pixels based on their luminance values (relative lightness and darkness). Colors do not matter with the Luma Key effect.

To apply the Luma Key effect:

1. Edit the clip segment that will be your background image onto track V1, or whichever track will be your background track (**Figure 9.79**).

2. Edit your foreground image (one that preferably has contrasting luminance values) onto track V2, or one track above the background image.

3. Drag the Luma Key effect (located in the Key category of the Effect palette) onto the V2 clip segment (**Figure 9.80**).

4. Click the Effect mode button (located by default on the Timeline toolbar) to enter Effect mode.

   The Effect editor opens displaying the Luma Key effect parameters.

continues on next page

5. To sample the luminance value you want to make transparent, go to the Effect editor and click and hold on the Color Choice box. Drag the eyedropper to the Composer. Hover over the part of the image that has the luminance you want to key; then release the mouse (**Figure 9.81**).

The keyed color (which contains the keyed luminance) appears in the Effect editor's Color Choice box. In the Composer, pixels that share the same value as the keyed luminance become transparent.

6. To fine-tune your key, *adjust one or both of the following controls:*

▲ **Gain:** Use this control to finely select the pixels that will be keyed (made transparent).

▲ **Soft:** This control is especially useful when you have gradient images with shades of gray. Pushing the slider to the right adds fuzziness to the effect's luminance calculations.

The pixels in your image that have the sampled luminance value are now transparent.

✔ Tips

■ You can use the Luma Key effect to blend images in a way that is often much more interesting than a simple Superimpose.

■ To find out what is transparent and what is opaque after you apply the Luma Key effect, go to the Effect editor and click the Show Alpha button. The white portions of the alpha channel display show you what is transparent; the black portions show you want is opaque. (For more information, see the sidebar "Alpha Channels Explained" earlier in this chapter.)

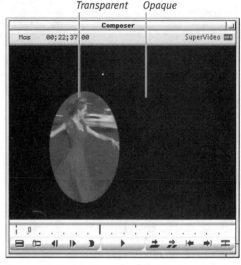

Transparent   *Opaque*

Figure 9.81 Here is the end result of the Luma key effect. After the white (the bright color) of the foreground image is keyed out, the white oval becomes transparent.

Getting Luma Key to Appreciate the Gray Area

How does Luma Key work with images that are not so black and white (literally speaking)? What about gradient images in which there are many different luminance values, including various shades of gray (**Figure 9.82**)? The Luma Key effect *can* work with these images, but you need to adjust the effect's Gain and Soft controls in the Effect editor. Usually, a Gain value of 1 and a maximum Soft value will best maintain the various luminance tones of a gradient image (**Figure 9.83**).

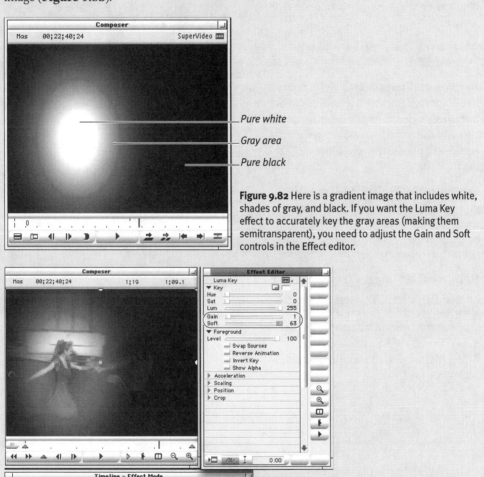

Pure white

Gray area

Pure black

Figure 9.82 Here is a gradient image that includes white, shades of gray, and black. If you want the Luma Key effect to accurately key the gray areas (making them semitransparent), you need to adjust the Gain and Soft controls in the Effect editor.

Figure 9.83 Giving Gain a value of 1 and increasing the Soft value makes the Luma Key effect work accurately. Grays in the alpha image translate into soft, feathered edges.

Using the Matte Key Effect

The Matte Key effect is one of the more complex effects in Xpress Pro, as it is one of only two effects that contains three nested layers (the other is a title). However, if you already know how titles work (see Chapter 8, "Creating Titles"), then the Matte Key effect should be easy to grasp since it operates the same way.

The three layers that constitute a Matte Key effect are as follows:

- **Background image:** This is the bottom layer of the effect. The Matte Key effect punches a hole through this image in the shape of the high-contrast image. It's the equivalent of any image you put underneath a title.

- **Foreground (fill) image:** This is the middle layer of the effect and is the image that fills the shape of the high-contrast image. It's the equivalent of a title's Graphic Fill layer.

- **High-contrast image:** This belongs on the top track of the effect. It serves as the effect's alpha channel and controls the shape of the foreground image (**Figure 9.84**). This is the equivalent of a title's Alpha Matte layer and is usually a black-and-white image.

High-contrast image for the alpha channel

Foreground fill

Background

Figure 9.84 Put the background on the low track (V1), the foreground (fill) on the middle track (V2), and the high-contrast image on the top track (V3).

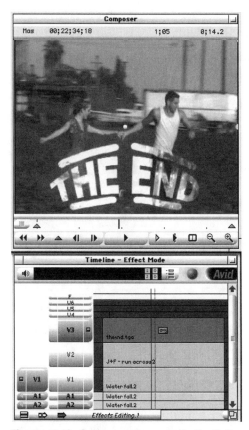

Figure 9.85 The final composite created by the Matte Key effect.

To apply the Matte Key effect:

Do one of the following:

◆ In the Timeline, edit the following three layers are on top of each other: a high contrast (alpha) image on the top track, a fill layer on the middle track, and a background image on the bottom track. Apply the Matte Key effect to the top layer (**Figure 9.85**).

◆ In the Timeline, edit in only one segment: the high-contrast (alpha) image. Apply the Matte Key effect to this segment. Click the Effect mode button and double-click the effect to open its nested tracks. Edit the foreground (fill) image onto the middle nested track and the background image onto the bottom track.

✔ Tips

■ If you are familiar with how to fill titles with video, or if you want to conserve tracks in the Timeline, the second method in the preceding task is the one to use.

■ There is often confusion about which layer to call the background image and which to call the foreground. At the end of the day, it doesn't matter because you can always select Swap Sources in the Matte Key parameter to switch the foreground and background images.

■ The Matte Key effect can be promoted to 3D. (See "Working with Xpress 3D Effects" later in this chapter.)

■ If your high-contrast image is not contrasty enough, you can use Color Effect to raise its contrast. Then to nest Color Effect within the Matte Key effect, apply the Matte Key effect to the image by holding down Alt (Windows) or Option (Mac) when you drag the Matte Key icon to the segment to which Color Effect is applied.

Importing, Panning, and Scaling Large Still Images

Xpress Pro normally imports still images at your project's resolution; for DV, that's DV 25 411 or 15:1s. However, you can import and manipulate a still image that is higher than your project's resolution by using the Avid Pan & Zoom effect (located in the Image category of the Effect palette).

The advantage of importing a high-resolution still is that you can scale it up without noticeable pixelation (**Figure 9.86**).

Unfortunately, using the Avid Pan & Zoom effect is not a straightforward process. To use the effect, you need to first create a placeholder segment of the same length as the still image that you want to manipulate and edit that placeholder into the Timeline. Then you need to apply the Avid Pan & Zoom effect to the placeholder and point Xpress Pro to the large-resolution still image on disk.

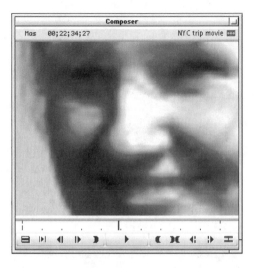

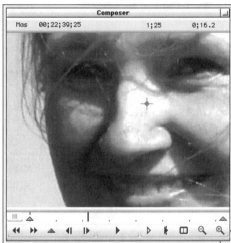

Figure 9.86 (above) Here's a still image imported normally (at DV res) and scaled 8x with the Resize effect. Note the pixelation and blurriness. (below) Here's the same still image imported at its original (high) resolution and resized 8x using the Avid Pan & Zoom effect.

To be replaced by a large-resolution still

Figure 9.87 When you want to use a large-resolution still in your sequence, the first step is to edit any video segment into the Timeline to serve as the image's placeholder. If you want, you can use a low-resolution version of the image.

Click here

Figure 9.88 To replace your placeholder image with the large-resolution still, click the Other Options button in the Effect editor and navigate to the still on your computer.

- You can tell Xpress Pro what color values to use (601 or RGB) and what pixel aspect ratio your large still image has (square or nonsquare) in Avid Pan & Zoom's Advanced parameter group.

- When you replace your placeholder with the large still, the placeholder's segment name does not change.

- If you already imported a version of the large still at DV (or 15:1s) resolution, it makes sense to use that low-res image as your placeholder.

To import and use a high-resolution still image:

1. Edit any video segment into the Timeline to serve as a placeholder, making it the length of whichever still you want to import and manipulate in your sequence (**Figure 9.87**).

   Make sure that your video segment comes from a master clip with significant head and tail material, in case you want to change the length of the segment later.

2. On the Effect palette, click the Image category and drag the Avid Pan & Zoom effect onto the segment placeholder in the Timeline.

3. Click the Effect mode button to enter Effect mode and open the Effect editor.

4. In the Effect editor, click the Avid Pan and Zoom Other Options button in the upper-left corner of the window (**Figure 9.88**).

   Xpress Pro opens a finder window, asking you to find the high-res still image that you want to import.

5. Select the still image that you want to import and click Choose.

   The still image replaces the placeholder segment, and the image appears in the Composer monitor.

✔ Tips

- If your placeholder is a little too short or too long, enter Trim mode and perform a double-roller trim to shorten or lengthen the placeholder. (For more information, see the sidebar "Performing Single- and Double-Roller Trims" in Chapter 7.)

To pan and zoom a large still image:

1. If you are not already in Effect mode, go to the Timeline and place your position indicator over an Avid Pan & Zoom effect and click the Effect mode button.

   The Effect editor displays the Avid Pan & Zoom parameters.

2. To see the effects of your panning and zooming, go to the top of the Effect editor, click the Display Fast menu, and select Target.

   As you manipulate the Size and Position parameters, the Composer will show your image zooming and panning.

3. In the Effect editor, manipulate the zoom parameter to zoom in and out of your image and the Position parameter group to pan to different parts of your image (**Figure 9.89**).

4. To animate your panning and zooming, create keyframes in the Composer monitor and give the keyframes different parameter values. (For more information on keyframes, see "Working with Standard Keyframes" earlier in this chapter.)

5. In the Effect editor, choose the image render quality from the Filter In Fast menu. See **Table 9.3** for the options.

6. (Optional) In the Effect editor, use the choices in the Velocity parameter group to control the smoothness and feel of your pans and zooms from keyframe to keyframe.

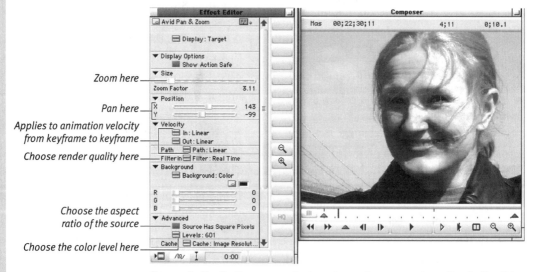

Figure 9.89 Use the Zoom parameter to scale your image up or down. Use the X and Y parameters to pan around your image.

Table 9.3

Avid Pan and Zoom Render Options (the Filter In Parameter)	
OPTION	FUNCTION
Real-Time	Has the fastest render time, but low quality.
Triangle	Yields soft image results.
Quadratic	Creates a soft image, but not as soft as Triangle.
Cubic	Creates a soft image, but not as soft as Quadratic.
B-Spline Catmull	Popular; similar to Cubic, but better for little to no zooming or extreme zooming in.
Gaussian	Produces a popular soft look.
Avid Hi Qual	Creates a sharp image, especially when you zoom out.
Avid Ultra Qual	Creates an extremely sharp image, especially when you zoom out.

✔ Tips

- If you zoom or pan your image in such a way that the background is revealed, you can choose a background color in the Background parameter group of the Avid Pan & Zoom effect.

- Using Pan & Zoom, you can also pan an image manually by doing the following: In the Effect editor, select Source in the Display Fast menu. Then, in the Composer monitor, drag the crosshairs in the middle of the image outline (**Figure 9.90**).

- The most popular render quality on the Effect editor's Filter In Fast menu is B-spline Catmull, but you should experiment with the others to see what you like. Note that Avid Hi Qual and Avid Ultra Qual require the longest render times.

Choose Source   *Pan by moving the crosshairs*

Figure 9.90 You can also pan your image by dragging the crosshairs in the Composer monitor. While you do this, keep Source selected in the Effect editor's Display Fast menu.

Working with Xpress 3D Effects

There are a few Xpress Pro effects that qualify as 3D effects, not because they enable true 3D object creation, but because they use the 3D tools (found on the 3D tab of the Command palette); these tools allow you to move and rotate images along the X, Y, and Z axes. In addition, 3D effect parameters (**Figure 9.91**) enable you to add extra eye candy such as motion trails and shadows to images.

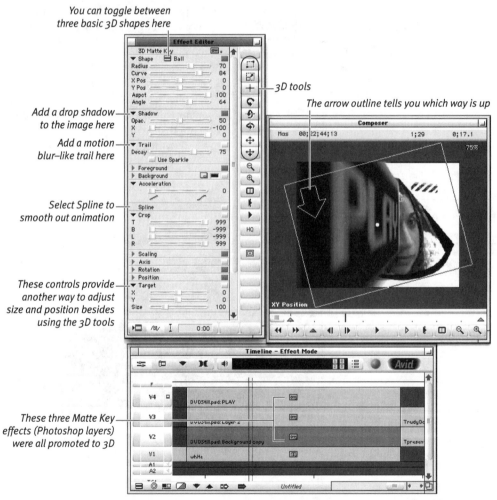

You can toggle between three basic 3D shapes here

3D tools

The arrow outline tells you which way is up

Add a drop shadow to the image here

Add a motion blur–like trail here

Select Spline to smooth out animation

These controls provide another way to adjust size and position besides using the 3D tools

These three Matte Key effects (Photoshop layers) were all promoted to 3D

Figure 9.91 All of the 3D-enabled effects include similar parameters, with the 3D tools accessible on the right side of the Effect editor.

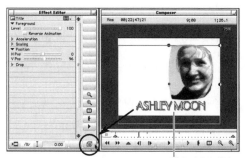

This title will be promoted to 3D

Figure 9.92 To promote a title or Matte Key effect to 3D—enabling you to manipulate the effect with 3D parameters—click the 3D button at the lower right of the Effect editor.

The standard 3D effects are located on the Effect palette, in the Xpress 3D category. They include the following:

◆ **3D Ball:** This effect can curve and sphere an image.

◆ **3D PIP:** This effect is similar to the normal Picture-in-Picture effect and is the only 3D effect that also allows the use of advanced keyframes.

◆ **3D Page Fold:** This effect creates the illusion of an image folding over itself.

◆ **3D Slats:** This effect breaks an image into multiple pieces.

In addition to the effects listed here, Xpress Pro allows you to promote the Matte Key effect or any title to 3D, meaning that you can use the 3D tools to manipulate and animate those effects, too.

To promote titles or the Matte Key effect to 3D:

1. Edit a title into the Timeline or apply the Matte Key effect to a Timeline segment.

2. Open the Effect editor and make sure it displays the parameters for the title or Matte Key effect.

3. At the lower right of the Effect editor, click the 3D button (**Figure 9.92**).

   Xpress Pro now displays 3D parameters and 3D tools in the Effect editor, which you can use to manipulate the title or Matte Key effect.

The 3D Tools

The Scale, Crop, and XY Pos tools are nothing spectacular; they allow you to scale, crop, and move an image, respectively. However, the XZ Pos, X Rot, Y Rot, Z Rot, and Axis tools are very cool because they allow you to simulate 3D behavior in ways not possible with non-3D effects. Here is a description of each of these unique tools:

◆ **XZ Pos:** This tool allows to you reposition an image along the X axis, moving it left to right, while simultaneously repositioning the image along the Z axis (**Figure 9.93**).

◆ **X Rot:** This tool visually pulls the top of an image toward you or pushes the top of an image away from you, resulting to a perspective change similar to the opening titles in *Star Wars*.

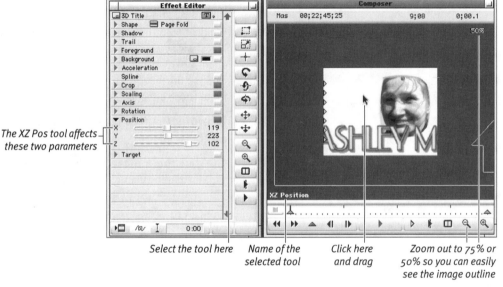

The XZ Pos tool affects these two parameters

Select the tool here   Name of the selected tool   Click here and drag   Zoom out to 75% or 50% so you can easily see the image outline

Figure 9.93 To make an image larger with the XZ Pos tool, click the image and drag down. To make it smaller, drag up. Move the pointer to the left or right to simultaneously position the image left or right.

- ◆ **Y Rot:** Use this tool to make the left or right of the image appear closer to you and the other side appear farther away (**Figure 9.94**).

- ◆ **Z Rot;** Use this tool to rotate or spin an image.

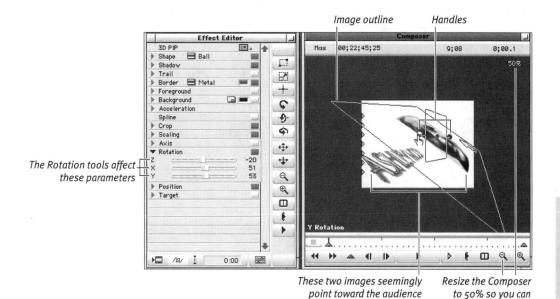

Image outline   Handles

The Rotation tools affect these parameters

These two images seemingly point toward the audience

Resize the Composer to 50% so you can see the image outline

Figure 9.94 The Y Rot tool is the coolest of the three Rotation tools, allowing you to make an image visually point out toward the audience. To use it, just drag one of the image handles and follow the shape of the image outline.

◆ **Axis:** If you want to rotate an image around a point other than the image's center, select this tool, go to the composer, and drag the axis (or anchor point) to a different location (**Figure 9.95**).

To use the XZ Pos tool:

While working with a 3D effect, select the XZ Pos tool at the right of the Effect editor and *do one of the following*:

◆ To make an image smaller (or farther away), go to the Composer, click the image, and drag up, positioning the image to the left or right as desired.

◆ To make an image larger (or closer), go to the Composer, click the image, and drag down, moving the image to the left or right as desired.

The image grows bigger or smaller while moving left or right.

To move the rotation axis (anchor point):

1. While working with a 3D effect, go to the Effect editor and select the ⊞ Axis tool.

A cross appear on your image, in the center of which is a handle point.

2. To move the axis point, click the handle point in the center of the cross and drag it to a new location.

When you use the X Rot, Y Rot, or Z Rot tool, the image will rotate around the axis point.

Repositioned axis (or anchor point)

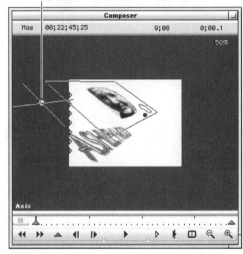

Figure 9.95 Use the Axis tool to reposition the point around which an image rotates.

To use the X Rot tool:

1. While working with a 3D effect, at the right side of the Effect editor select the ⟳ X Rot tool.

   An outline appears around the image in the Composer, with handles on the top and bottom of the image.

2. *Do one of the following:*

   ▲ To make the top of the image appear closer to you while the bottom appears farther away, click the top handle and drag down. If you drag far enough, you'll flip the image.

   ▲ To make the bottom of the image appear closer to you while the top appears farther away, click the bottom handle and drag up. If you drag far enough, you'll flip the image.

✔ Tip

■ You can reposition an image with the X Rot tool by clicking the middle of the image and dragging.

To use the Y Rot tool:

1. While working with a 3D effect, go to the Effect editor and select the 💠 Y Rot tool.

    An outline appears around the image in the Composer, with handles on the left and right of the image.

2. *Do one of the following:*

    ▲ To make the left side of the image appear closer to you, click the left handle and drag to the right. If you drag far enough, you'll flip the image.

    ▲ To make the right side of the image appear closer to you, click the right handle and drag to the left. If you drag far enough, you'll flip the image.

✔ Tip

■ You can reposition an image with the Y Rot tool by clicking the middle of the image and dragging.

To use the Z Rot tool:

1. While working with a 3D effect, at the right side of the Effect editor select the 🔄 Z Rot tool.

    An outline appears around the image in the Composer, with handles on the lower left and lower right of the image.

2. Click one of the image handles up or down to rotate the image in one direction or the other.

✔ Tip

■ You can reposition an image with the Z Rot tool by clicking the middle of the image and dragging.

Aim for the Target Parameter Last

You can use the Target parameter, located in the Effect editor for all 3D effects, to reposition and resize your 3D creation along the X and Y axes.

However, since this parameter is at the top of the 3D effect hierarchy, it treats all of your other 3D parameters as if they were inside a nest. The advantage of this behavior is that you can use Target to resize and reposition your 3D effect without disturbing the relationships among your other parameter settings.

So the short of it is this: You should use Target after setting every other parameter for your 3D effect, to nudge or tweak the size or position of the effect as a whole.

COLOR CORRECTION

10

Color correction typically has two goals: to represent colors realistically and consistently and/or to stylize colors to meet the artistic aims of your project.

Xpress Pro's Color Correction mode features the multi-tab Color Correction tool and the three-up Composer monitor and can help you fix problems that undermine the realism of your project. For example, you can make what's supposed to be white appear white, and what's supposed to be black appear black. Or you can make sure that every person in every shot has a realistic skin tone. Furthermore, you can use Color Correction to achieve hue, saturation, and luminance consistency across all of your shots.

The Color Correction tools also allow you to do things out of the ordinary, such as radically change your movie's contrast, or turn a color movie into a black-and-white piece, or add a greenish tint to make your scenes all look like *The Matrix*.

The special features that will increase your workflow efficiency include the ability to create and apply Color Correction templates and the Match Color button, which enables shot-to-shot consistency in color and luminance.

About Color Correcting

Color theory and color correction are topics that can take up a whole book by themselves; hence, this chapter focuses on just the basics of how to achieve realism, consistency, and artistic stylization by manipulating the following two basic elements of a video image:

♦ **Chrominance:** Chrominance refers to the color of a pixel—its hue—and the intensity of that color—its saturation.

One of the most common correction procedures related to chrominance is *color balancing* your image, the process of manipulating red, green, and blue values to achieve a realistic look across the dark parts (shadows), midtones, and bright parts (highlights) of an image.

(To learn how to color balance your image in Xpress Pro, see "Color Balancing Your Shots" later in this chapter. To learn how to match color between shots, see "Using the Match Color Button" later in this chapter.)

♦ **Luminance:** Separate from the color information in a video clip, luminance refers to the amount of light emitted by any particular pixel (its brightness).

A common luminance-related procedure is increasing the tonal range of your image, which involves increasing the range of luminance values in an image.

(To learn how to maximize tonal range and adjust luminance in Xpress Pro, see "Adjusting Tonal Values" later in this chapter.)

Keep in mind that some color correction controls affect both chrominance and luminance at once. For example, raising the gain of an image increases the overall perceived brightness of an image, but it also increases the intensity of the image's color.

How Color Correction Works in Xpress Pro

Xpress Pro's Color Correction effect (located on the Image tab of the Effect palette) is a unique segment effect because 95 percent of the time you apply it not by dragging the effect from the Effect palette, as you do with most effects, but by opening the Color Correction toolset and manipulating specialized controls while in Color Correction mode.

Opening the Color Correction toolset transforms the Composer into a three-up window, which features a long Color Correction tool window containing every correction parameter control (**Figure 10.1**).

This is the clip segment you will correct if you manipulate the Color Correction tool.

The clip segment at the location of the position indicator

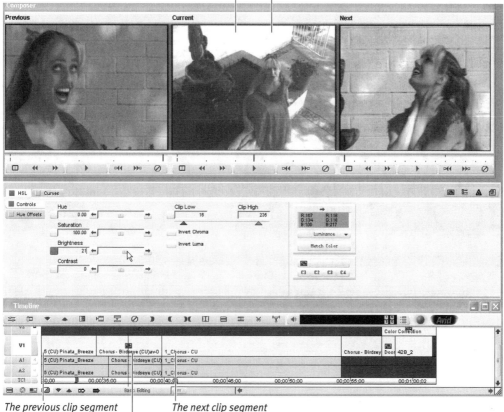

The previous clip segment

The next clip segment

Xpress Pro adds the Color Correction effect icon to the clip you are correcting.

Figure 10.1 Color Correction mode features a unique Composer monitor display and the large Color Correction tool. These windows and the Timeline are all you need to begin color correcting.

The Color Correction toolset by default displays the current clip you're correcting (the clip under the playhead on the topmost monitored Timeline track; see **Figure 10.2**) as well as the clips before and after the current clip (displayed in the Previous and Next windows).

The most common operations performed with the Color Correction toolset are as follows:

◆ **Correcting clip by clip:** You can apply unique correction to every clip in your sequence, one clip at a time. Remember: because of the way Xpress Pro handles effects, your correction affects the clip on the topmost monitored track (the current clip) as well as every clip beneath it at the position of the playhead (**Figure 10.3**).

Select this track button to correct clip segments on the lower track.

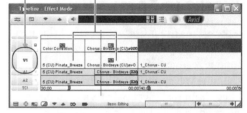

Figure 10.2 The Composer monitor displays the clip segments on the topmost selected track, so if you want to color correct a lower track but not the track above it, select only the button for the lower track.

Select this track to apply correction to the V2 and V1 clip segments.   *Both images will change.*

Figure 10.3 If you apply color correction to the clip segment on the top track, the correction also affects every clip segment below it.

If, for example, you have two video layers (a Picture-in-Picture, or PIP, effect, for instance) and you want to correct each layer individually, you need to use the Step In button to step into the top nest. (To learn how to step into a nest to perform color correction, see the sidebar "Color Correcting Single Layers: Step Around the Traps" later in this chapter.)

◆ **Applying one clip's correction to other clips:** To avoid having to re-create the same color correction for similar clips, the Color Correction tool window allows you to save up to four corrections as templates and then, with one click, apply a template to any other clip in your sequence. Or you can save a correction template the old-fashioned way: by dragging the correction icon to an open bin.

You can also use the Match Color button to match the hue, saturation, RGB curves, and so on of two shots. (See "Using the Match Color Button" later in this chapter.)

◆ **Correcting the entire sequence as a whole:** After you've corrected your shots individually, you can apply a final color correction tweak to the entire sequence by creating a black filler layer above the sequence top track and applying a Color Correction effect to that black filler. A common application of this technique is to turn a color movie into a black-and-white piece.

To color correct clip by clip:

1. In the Timeline, select and monitor the topmost track containing the video clip segment that you want to color correct.

2. *Do one of the following:*
   ▲ Choose Toolset > Color Correction (for the default correction tool layout).
   ▲ Choose Tools > Command Palette, select the palette's CC tab, choose Active Palette, and click the [▥] Color Correction mode button.

   Xpress Pro transforms the Composer monitor into a three-up window and opens the dual-tab Color Correction tool.

   By default, the Composer displays the previous, current, and next video clip segments on the topmost selected track. The position indicator rests on the head frame of the current image.

3. After entering Color Correction mode, manipulate one or more of the controls in the Color Correction tool to alter the current image in the Composer.

   As you manipulate the Color Correction controls, your adjustments are applied to the current (center) Composer image. In the Timeline, a Color Correction effect icon appears on the corrected clip segment.

continues on next page

4. To correct other clips on the topmost monitored track, *do one or more of the following:*

   ▲ To color correct the image in the Previous window—the previous clip segment on the topmost selected track—click the ◀◀ Previous

Uncorrected button (located by default in the Composer window) and manipulate the correction controls **(Figure 10.4)**. Or click ◀◀ Rewind to jump to the previous image, even if it has already been corrected; you can now recorrect the image **(Figure 10.5)**.

Click to load this clip segment as the current image.

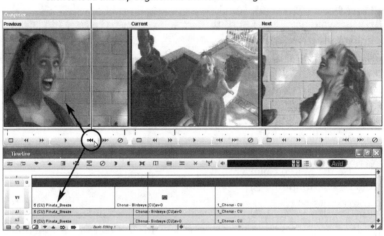

Figure 10.4 Click the Previous Uncorrected button to correct an uncorrected clip segment directly behind the current Timeline clip segment.

Use these buttons to load clip segments that are already corrected.

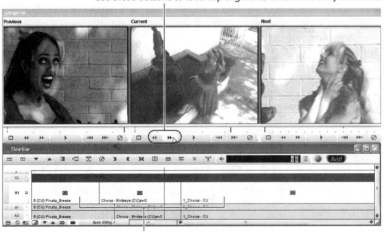

The Color Correction icons indicate that these shots have already been corrected.

Figure 10.5 To recorrect a shot you've already corrected, use the Fast Forward or Rewind button to jump to the Timeline clip segment that you want to adjust.

▲ To color correct the image in the Next window—the next clip segment on the topmost selected track—click the ▶▶□ Next Uncorrected button (located by default in the Composer window) and manipulate the correction controls. Or click ▶▶ Fast Forward to jump to the next image, even if it has already been corrected; you can now recorrect the image.

5. To exit Color Correction mode, click the Color Correction mode button again or choose a different toolset from the Toolset menu.

✔ Tips

■ If you add color correction to a clip that already has an effect applied to it (for instance, a PIP), Xpress Pro creates a nested effect, combining the old effect with the Color Correction effect. (For more information on nests, see Chapter 9, "Working with Video Effects.")

■ To delete a Color Correction effect, place the position indicator over the effect in the Timeline, select the track containing the effect, and press ⊘ Remove Effect (located by default at the bottom of the Composer window).

■ If you double-click a source clip in a bin while in Color Correction mode, Xpress Pro will close the Color Correction windows and put you back in normal editing mode.

To apply one correction to another clip using a template:

1. Be sure to first display the clip segment that has the color correction you want to save as a template in the Current window in the Composer.

2. Turn off any parameters that you don't want to include in the correction template by deselecting the purple button next to the unwanted parameter controls.

3. At the right of the Color Correction control window, Alt-click (Windows) or Option-click (Mac) one of the correction buttons (C1, C2, C3, or C4).

   A Color Correction effect icon appears above the correction button (in a bucket), indicating that your Color Correction template has been saved (**Figure 10.6**).

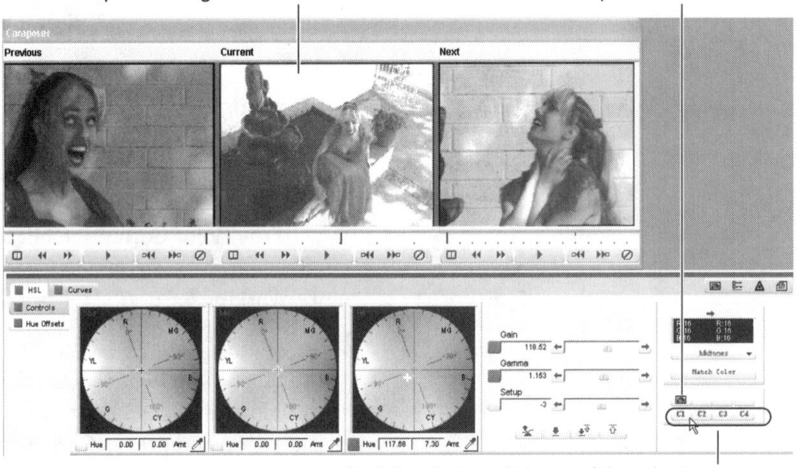

The color correction for this image is saved.   *Saved template icon*

Alt-click or Option-click one of these buttons.

Figure 10.6 To save a Color Correction effect as a template, Alt-click (Windows) or Option-click (Mac) one of the four template buckets in the Color Correction tool.

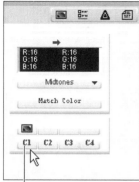

Figure 10.7 To apply a Color Correction template to the current clip segment, click C1, C2, C3, or C4, depending on which template you want to apply.

Click to apply a template.

4. Use the Rewind or Fast Forward button (located by default in the Composer monitor) to make sure that the clip segment to which you want to apply the correction template is displayed as the current image in the Composer.

5. On the right side of the Color Correction control window, click C1, C2, C3, or C4 to apply one of your saved templates to the current clip (**Figure 10.7**).

   Xpress Pro applies the saved color correction effect and its parameters to the current image.

✔ Tips

- You can map the C1, C2, C3, and C4 buttons to your keyboard or interface from the CC tab of the Command palette.

- If you already have four templates saved (an effect icon in all four correction buckets), then saving a new Color Correction template will overwrite the existing template.

- Xpress Pro does not retain your Color Correction tool templates after you quit the application. To save a Color Correction template permanently, you need to save the template to one of your bins.

To save a Color Correction template to a bin:

Do one of the following:

◆ After applying color correction to an image, choose Tools > Command Palette to open the Command palette, click the CC tab, select the Active Palette radio button, and click the Save Correction button.

◆ Drag a Color Correction effect icon (above C1, C2, C3, or C4) from the Color Correction control window to an open bin.

Xpress Pro displays your Color Correction effect template in the bin. Give the saved Color Correction effect a unique name that hints at what it does (**Figure 10.8**).

Xpress Pro keeps the custom Color Correction effect in the bin; you can now apply it to any Timeline clip segment.

(For more information on custom effect templates, see "Creating Favorite Effect Templates" in Chapter 9.)

✔ Tip

■ You can set the default naming scheme for saved Color Correction effects by using the Safe Color Label pop-up menu on the Features tab of the Color Correction Mode Settings dialog box. (To access the dialog box, click the Color Correction Mode Settings button at the upper right of the CC tool.)

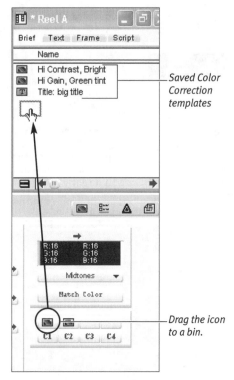

Figure 10.8 To save a Color Correction template to a bin—saving the effect permanently—drag a template icon from the Color Correction tool to an open bin. Then give the effect a unique name.

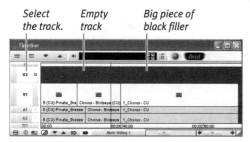

Select   Empty   Big piece of
the track.   track   black filler

Figure 10.9 To color correct every shot in your sequence, first create a new video track and select its track button.

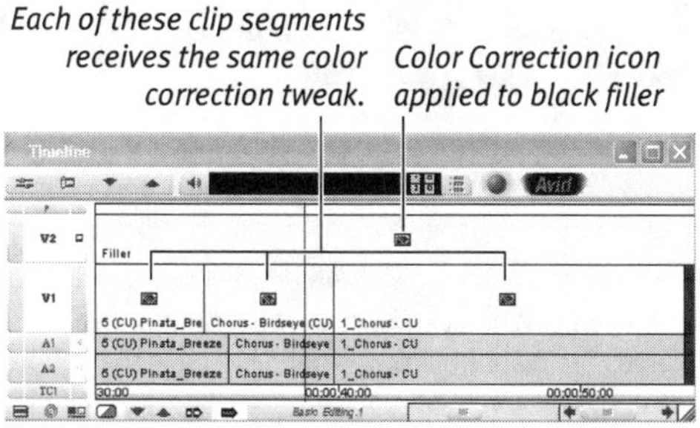

Each of these clip segments
receives the same color   Color Correction icon
correction tweak.   applied to black filler

Figure 10.10 When you start manipulating the Color Correction tool controls with the top empty track selected, Xpress Pro applies your correction to every single shot underneath the top track's black filler.

To color correct your entire sequence at once:

1. After color correcting each shot in your sequence, right-click (Windows) or Ctrl+Shift-click (Mac) and choose Add New Video Track from the context menu.

    A new track, containing a black filler layer, appears above your original tracks (**Figure 10.9**).

2. Select the topmost track button (the empty track).

3. In the Color Correction tool, manipulate any of the controls.

    Xpress Pro applies your color correction to the black filler segment, affecting every shot under the black filler segment in the top track. The black filler turns into a visible clip segment with a Color Correction icon on it (**Figure 10.10**).

✔ Tips

■ As with all buttons, you can map the Color Correction mode button from the Command palette to your keyboard or interface.

■ If the image in the Previous, Current, or Next window in the Composer is black, most likely the clip on the topmost selected Timeline track is a black filler segment.

Comparing "Before" and "After" Versions

In the Composer window of the Color Correction toolset, you can use the Dual Split option to keep track of your color correction progress by comparing your corrections with the uncorrected version of the same image.

By using this split-screen feature, you'll know whether you've made an improvement in the image or just made things worse.

To display "before" and "after" images:

◆ At the bottom of the Composer window, beneath the current image (or the previous or next image, depending on which image you want to view), click the Dual Split button.

Xpress Pro displays a split image (**Figure 10.11**). On the left is your shot without any color correction. On the right is the shot with the color correction applied. You can turn off the dual display by clicking the Dual Split button again.

✔ Tips

■ You can map the Dual Split button to the keyboard or interface from the Other tab of the Command palette.

■ You can change the shape of your split image display by dragging one of the white triangles in the Composer monitor.

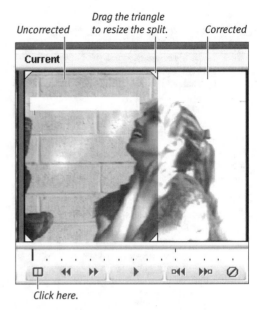

Uncorrected   *Drag the triangle to resize the split.*   *Corrected*

Click here.

Figure 10.11 When you click the Dual Split button, Xpress Pro displays a split-screen image in the Composer monitor. This shows you uncorrected and corrected versions of the image.

Color Correcting Single Layers: Step Around the Traps

Watch out! If you color correct a bottom video layer and then color correct a video layer above it (such as a clip segment with the PIP effect applied to it), the top color correction will compound the correction on the bottom layer: your bottom layer will receive unwanted extra correction! This result is due to the funky way that Xpress Pro handles the layering of effects; you can't simply color correct (or add any effect to) each layer individually.

The workaround is to use the Step In button (located by default on the Timeline toolbar). Park the position indicator on the top (PIP) video layer, select its track, and click Step In. Then add the Color Correction effect to the clip segment that appears in the Timeline. This is like going back in time, color correcting the top layer before you add the PIP effect.

Using this method, you won't unintentionally color correct the clip segment on the track beneath the PIP.

Now click the Step Out button (located by default on the Timeline toolbar). The nest closes, and your lower or top layers can have different color corrections that don't affect one another.

(For more information about nests, see Chapter 9, "Working with Video Effects.")

Switching from the Composer's Default Display

The Color Correction Composer's default three-window display of Timeline clip segments—Previous, Current, and Next—is adequate for most color correction situations.

However, you can switch from this default setting by clicking a source menu above one of the Composer images and choosing a different display option from the list that appears (**Figure 10.12**).

For example, if you want to show the image *after* the next clip segment, you can choose Second Next. Or if want to be able to view and play your whole sequence in one of the Composer monitors, you can choose Sequence. Or if you want to keep the current image displayed as the reference image as you start correcting other shots, you can choose Reference.

However, know this: When you are color correcting, one of the Composer image monitors always must display the current clip segment. Otherwise, how will you know the result of your correction?

Choose a different display from this list.

Figure 10.12 To change the sequence clip segment displayed in any of the Composer image monitors, click the menu above one of the images and choose from the options that appear.

Safe-Color Warnings

If you plan to show your movie on broadcast television, then your color saturation and luminance levels will probably have to meet certain broadcast standards to be considered broadcast legal.

You can configure Xpress Pro to warn you about colors and levels that exceed certain preset limits, and are therefore are not considered safe or legal by broadcast engineers, while you color correct your project. Using these warnings as a guide, you can bring down illegal levels before outputting your project to tape.

The Color Correction tool indicates whether safe-color warnings are enabled by the color of the safe-color triangle—orange if safe-color warnings are active, and black if they are not. Next to the triangle are five black rectangles that warn you about illegal colors using the following system:

◆ If all of your colors and luminance levels are legal, then colored bars appears in the middle of all the black rectangles.

◆ If levels exceed one or more of your preset safe-color ranges, then colored bars appear at the top of one or more of the black rectangles (**Figure 10.13**).

◆ If levels are lower than one or more of your preset safe-color ranges, then colored bars appear at the bottom of one or more of the black rectangles.

See **Table 10.1** for the meaning of the colors in each safe-color black rectangle.

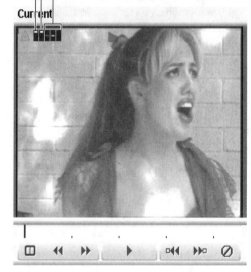

Composite video color values are too high.
Luminance levels are too high.
RGB gamut levels are legal.

Figure 10.13 Here, the image contains colors that exceed the preset range specified for Composite in the Safe Color Settings dialog box, as well as the preset range set for Luminance. However, all three RGB gamut levels are fine.

Table 10.1

Safe-Color Rectangle Color Bars	
COLOR OF BAR	MEANING
Yellow	Composite video signal warnings
White	Luminance level warnings
Red	RGB gamut warnings for the color red
Green	RGB gamut warnings for the color green
Blue	RGB gamut warnings for the color blue

Action buttons

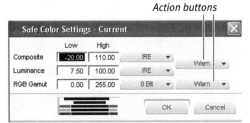

Figure 10.14 To turn on safe-color warnings for composite video colors and luminance levels, switch the top action button to Warn. To turn on safe-color warnings for the set range of red, green, and blue colors, switch the bottom action button to Warn as well.

- You can also use waveform monitors and vectorscopes to get warnings about illegal colors, as you will see in the next section.

To enable safe-color warnings:

1. At the upper right of the Color Correction tool, click the black safe-color triangle.

   The Safe Color Settings dialog box appears.

2. To turn on warnings for both illegal colors in the composite video signal and illegal luminance levels, click the action button on the upper right and switch its display from Ignore to Warn (**Figure 10.14**).

   Xpress Pro will warn you when pixels in your image exceed the level numbers set in the Low and High boxes for Composite and Luminance.

3. To turn on warnings for illegal colors that are outside the preset color range, click the lower-right action button and change the setting from Ignore to Warn.

   Xpress Pro will now also warn you if any color falls outside the range set in the RBG Gamut Low and High boxes.

4. (Optional) If you must meet broadcast standards different from Xpress Pro's default presets, adjust the Low and High values for Composite (the legal colors within the composite video signal), Luminance (the legal brightness levels), and RGB Gamut (the legal color range).

5. Click OK.

   In each Composer image monitor, Xpress Pro will now display an orange rectangle and five black rectangles that will warn you about pixels in each image that exceed or dip beneath the Composite, Luminance, and Red, Green, and Blue Gamut preset ranges.

✔ Tips

- If you're producing your project for broadcast television, check first with the broadcast engineers in charge for your delivery specifications so you can set your safe-color warnings correctly.

Using Waveforms and Vectorscopes

When color correcting, you may want to trust waveforms and vectorscope displays more than your eyes when checking an image's exact color and luminance information.

Waveform and vectorscope information can be helpful when you want match color corrections between shots (for example, to make sure that the amount of red displayed in one image's vectorscope matches the amount of red displayed in another image's vectorscope). Waveform and vectorscope information can also provide warnings about illegal color and luminance levels.

To display waveform and vectorscope information:

1. In the Composer monitor, in Color Correction mode, click the image for which you want to display waveform or vectorscope information.

2. Open the source menu above another Composer image and choose a waveform or vectorscope display from the list that appears. (**Table 10.2** provides a brief description of each option.)

Table 10.2

Waveform and Vectorscope Options	
DISPLAY	FUNCTION
Quad Display	Shows YC Waveform, Vectorscope, RGB Histogram, and RGB Parade displays. (See other options in this table for descriptions.)
RBG Histogram	Shows the red, green, and blue values that appear most frequently in your image.
RGB Parade	Displays red, green, and blue waveforms side by side. Any white pixels represent illegal colors that fall outside the RGB gamut range set in the Safe Color Settings dialog box. (For more information, see "Safe-Color Warnings" earlier in this chapter.)
Vectorscope	Displays chroma information on a circular graph, analogous to the color wheels displayed on the Hue Offsets tab of the Color Correction tool.
Y Waveform	Displays luma information for your image. White pixels indicate luminance levels that fall outside the Luminance range set in the Safe Color Settings dialog box.
YC Waveform	Displays both luma and composite video signal information. White pixels indicate luminance or composite video levels that fall outside the ranges set in the Safe Color Settings dialog box.
YCrCb Histogram	Displays luma information on top and indicates the variety of colors in your image in the ChromaRed and ChromaBlue graphs. Too wide a spread in the lower graphs indicates too much saturation.
YCrCb Parade	Displays waveforms for luma, ChromaRed, and ChromaBlue information side by side. If the ChromaRed and ChromaBlue information is not near the center of the graph, your image may have an unwanted color cast.

Xpress Pro displays waveform and vectorscope information for the image selected in the Composer. It will keep displaying this information until you choose a different display option from the source menu (**Figure 10.15**).

The waveform or vectorscope displays information about the image you selected.

Choose the waveform or vectorscope display here.

Figure 10.15 Display waveform or vectorscope information for an image in the Composer and then go to another image and choose a waveform or vectorscope display from its source menu.

Color Correction Workflow Strategies

Rob Gonsalves, Avid's color correction engineer, recommends that to achieve the most naturalistic colors in your images, especially skin tones, you should color balance your image first before applying Auto-Contrast or some other tonal range procedure.

Experiment and see what strategy works best for your situation.

Color Balancing Your Shots

Color balancing is about adjusting the levels (hue, saturation, and luminance) of red, green, and blue (the colors that comprise the digital video pixel) in your image. One of the most common uses for color balancing is to correct an outdoor scene shot with an indoor white balance setting or vice versa.

For example, an outdoor snow scene might appear blue if shot with an indoor white balance setting. You can use Xpress Pro's Auto-Balance buttons to correct such a mistake and make the snow look white.

In Xpress Pro, you can use the following tools to perform color balancing:

◆ **Auto-Balance buttons:** Xpress Pro can automatically color balance your images when you click the Auto-Balance button on either the Hue Offsets tab of the HSL tab or the Curves tab. The Auto-Balance buttons on the two tabs produce slightly different results; the button that is most effective depends on the nature of the shot you're correcting.

Avid color correction engineer Robert Gonsalves says an advantage of the Curves Auto-Balance button over the HSL button is that the Curves button corrects your shot and preserves color-safe values, whereas the HSL button does not.

◆ **Hue Offsets wheels:** You can use all three Hue Offsets wheels to color balance the shadows (pixels on the dark side of the luminance range), midtones, and highlights (pixels on the bright side of the luminance range), respectively.

These wheels are especially useful if you shot a reference chip cart during production containing pure black, pure white, and neutral gray. Using the Remove Color Cast eyedropper for each wheel, you can tell Xpress Pro what's supposed to be black in your image (using the Shadow wheel), what's supposed to be neutral gray (the Midtone wheel), and what's supposed to be white (the Highlight wheel).

◆ **RGB curves:** The most specific (hence, advanced) way to color balance your image is to use the Red, Green, and Blue graphs on the Curves tab. These graphs allow you to adjust the values of red, green, and blue (and hence, the amount of cyan, green, and yellow) in your image by creating and dragging control points on the graph lines. Curves allow finer control over your color values than the Hue Offsets wheels.

The Curves tab also includes a Remove Color Cast eyedropper, which you can use to sample parts of your image that are supposed to be black (shadow), white (highlight), and neutral gray (midtone); the tool is smart enough to figure out which kind of tone it's sampling.

To automatically color balance an image:

Do one of the following:

◆ On the Hue Offsets tab, found on the HSL tab of the Color Correction tool, click the Auto-Balance button.

Xpress Pro balances the image designated as Current by manipulating the hue and saturation amount values of the Shadow, Midrange, and Highlight color wheels (**Figure 10.16**).

◆ On the Curves tab, click the Auto-Balance button.

Xpress Pro balances the image designated as Current by adjusting the levels of red, green, and blue in the Red, Blue, and Green graph curves (**Figure 10.17**).

Anything that's supposed to look white is white.

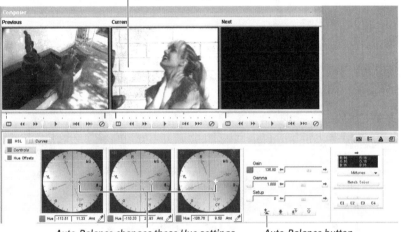

Auto-Balance changes these Hue settings. *Auto-Balance button*

Figure 10.16 If you click Auto-Balance on the Hue Offsets tab, Xpress Pro guesses what's supposed to be white, black, and neutral gray in your image and manipulates the three color wheels.

Auto-Balance changes these Curves settings. *Auto-Balance button*

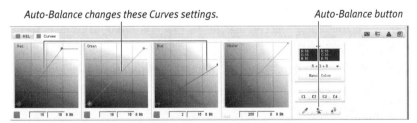

Figure 10.17 After you click the Auto-Balance button on the Curves tab, Xpress Pro manipulates the Red, Green, and Blue graphs so that white looks white, gray looks gray, and so on.

To manually color balance an image using Hue Offsets:

1. On the Hue Offsets tab of the HSL tab, click the Remove Color Cast eyedropper underneath the Midtone color wheel and, in the current image, sample what's supposed to be neutral gray.

2. Click the eyedropper underneath the Shad (Shadow) color wheel and sample what's supposed to be black in the current image.

Xpress Pro treats the sampled part of the image as black and changes the position of the crosshairs in the Shadow color wheel (**Figure 10.18**).

3. Click the eyedropper underneath the Hlt (Highlight) color wheel and sample what's supposed to be white in the current image.

Xpress Pro treats the sample area as white and changes the position of the crosshairs in the Highlight color wheel.

Sample this part of the image if you want this to be black.

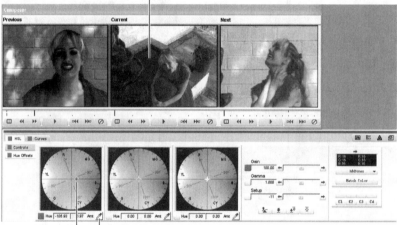

After you use the eyedropper, this crosshair's position changes

Click here to change your cursor to an eyedropper (for sampling).

Figure 10.18 To manually balance the shadows, you need to know what part of the image is supposed to be black. Then you can sample that part of the image with the Shadow eyedropper.

To manually color balance an image using Curves:

1. On the Curves tab of the Color Correction tool, click the Remove color cast eyedropper and sample what's supposed to be neutral gray.

2. Repeat step 1, sampling what's supposed to be black and then what's supposed to be white.

   Xpress Pro adjusts the curve lines in the Red, Green, and Blue graphs to color balance your image.

✔ Tips

- Ideally, you should sample your black from an image that contains a chip chart shot on the set during production and illuminated with the same lighting as your primary subject.

- You do not have to sample black, white, or gray from the image in the Current window in the Composer monitor. You can also sample colors from any image on your computer monitor or from your system's color palette.

- You can use the Hue Offsets wheels to create coloring that doesn't look natural. They don't have to be strictly used for realistic color balancing (**Figure 10.19**).

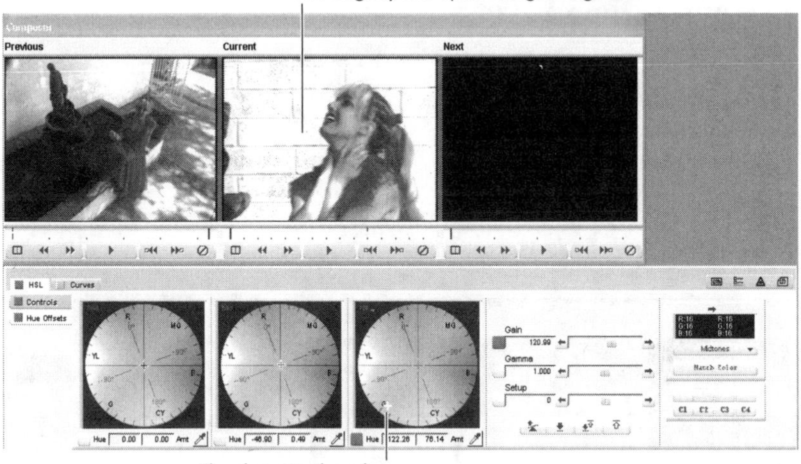

The bright parts of the image are green.

The closer to the edge, the higher the saturation

Figure 10.19 In this case, all the highlights of the image have a saturated green tint.

COLOR BALANCING YOUR SHOTS

Don't Delete It—Just Reset or Disable It

If you make a mistake while color correcting a shot, there is no need to delete the effect and start over. Instead, you can reset one or more Color Correction parameter controls back to the default, or you can temporarily disable a Color Correction parameter control. The advantage of disabling a control is that Xpress Pro remembers the setting of the parameter or tab setting, so you can turn on the correction setting again later.

To reset a Color Correction control, all you have to do is hold down Alt (Windows) or Option (Mac) and click the highlighted button next to a parameter or tab. Xpress Pro resets the parameter (or group of parameters) to the application's default value (**Figure 10.20**). To return the parameters to their previous values, choose Edit > Undo.

To disable a Color Correction control, you can do one of the following:

♦ Click a purple highlighted parameter button to disable a particular parameter (such as Gain).

♦ Click a purple highlighted button on a tab (HSL or Curves, or Controls or Hue Offsets) to disable all controls for that particular tab (**Figure 10.21**).

One word of caution: After you disable a Color Correction parameter, that parameter's setting is not included in the final rendered effect. Xpress Pro renders only enabled parameters.

Resetting the Brightness parameter returns the setting to its default value of 0.

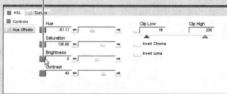

Figure 10.20 To return a color correction parameter to its default setting, Alt-click (Windows) or Option-click (Mac) the purple button next to it.

Click here to disable the Hue Offsets settings.

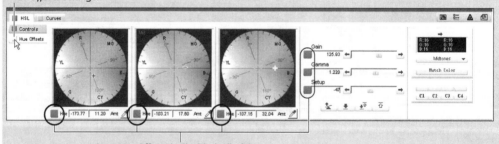

Once Hue Offsets is disabled, all of these settings no longer apply to the effect.

Figure 10.21 To disable every parameter control on a tab, click the purple button next to the tab name.

Eyedropper Settings

Before sampling colors with the eyedropper—used when manually correcting shots with the Hue Offsets color wheels or when sampling colors with the Match Color button—you should check your eyedropper settings to configure the tool's behavior.

On the Features tab of the Correction Mode Settings dialog box, you have the following eyedropper options:

◆ **Eyedropper 3x3 Averaging:** If you select this option, then Xpress Pro does not sample an exact pixel at the position of your eyedropper. Instead, it takes the average of nine pixels around the position of your eyedropper. In most cases, you should keep this option selected because a general reading of color or luminance is better than a reading of just one pixel.

◆ **Show Eyedropper Info:** When using the eyedropper to sample colors for use with the Match Color feature, select this option to display red, green, and blue information (represented by numbers between 0 and 255) above the Match Color button after you hold down the mouse on one of the two Match Color sampling boxes. This color information changes in real time as you drag the eyedropper around different parts of an image, which can help you quickly assess the color information in your image, for comparison with other images (**Figure 10.22**).

(For more information about the Match Color button, see "Using the Match Color Button" later in this chapter.)

◆ **Eyedropper Picks from Anywhere in Application:** With this setting enabled, you aren't limited to sampling from the Composer. You can sample colors from anywhere in the Xpress Pro application, including your system's color palette.

This color information is updated as you drag the eyedropper.

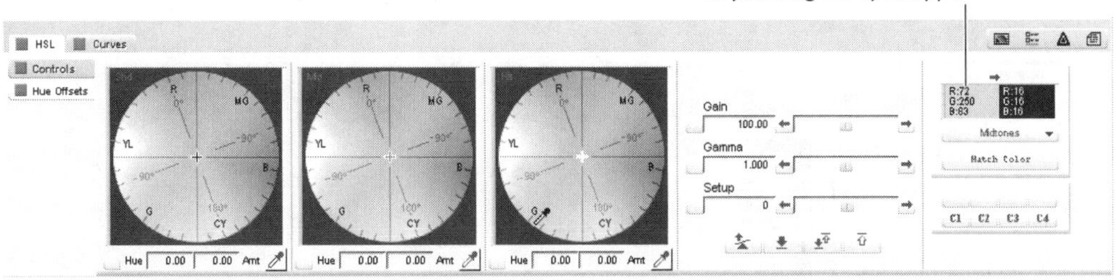

Figure 10.22 With Show Eyedropper Info enabled in the Correction Mode Settings dialog box, hold down one of the two Match Color sampling boxes and drag the eyedropper; the RGB information updates in real time.

To configure your eyedropper settings:

1. Click the Correction Mode Settings button, at the upper right of the Color Correction tool.

2. In the Correction Mode dialog box, enable or disable the listed eyedropper options.

   In general, the default configuration (all eyedropper settings enabled) is the optimal configuration for color correction.

✔ Tip

- You can also access your Correction Mode settings by going to the Settings tab of the Effect palette and double-clicking the Correction Settings listing.

Adjusting Tonal Values

Adjusting a shot's tonal values involves the following:

- **Optimizing the contrast automatically:** You can automatically optimize the contrast—maximizing the range of dark pixels to bright pixels—by clicking the Auto-Contrast button on either the Hue Offsets tab of the HSL tab or the Curves tab (both buttons achieve similar results).

  The Auto-Contrast button optimizes your black point and white point simultaneously, but if you want to optimize just one or the other, you can use Auto-Black or Auto-White.

- **Adjusting contrast manually:** You can also manually adjust the contrast by using the Controls tab of the HSL tab, but you'll typically use this control for darkening dark pixels and brightening bright pixels beyond simple optimization (increasing contrast beyond normal is often something people do to video to give it more of a film look).

  In a similar fashion, you can use the Gain and Setup sliders (on the Hue Offsets tab) to adjust your white point and black points, respectively.

  Finally, you can use Master Curve on the Curves tab to make sophisticated adjustments to tonal values in the shadows, midtones, and highlights of your image.

- **Adjusting the gray point:** Best left for the final stages of tonal range adjustments, adjusting the gray point using the Gamma slider on the Hue Offsets tab will generally brighten or darken the midtones of the image without affecting the highlights and shadows. Specifically, adjusting the gray point determines whether most pixels have a tonal range between middle gray and white or between middle gray and black.

To automatically optimize contrast (maximizing tonal range):

Do one of the following:

◆ On the Hue Offsets tab of the HSL tab, click the Auto-Contrast button.

◆ On the Curves tab, click the Auto-Contrast button.

If you click Auto-Contrast on the HSL tab, Xpress Pro manipulates the Gain, Gamma, and Setup controls to optimize your tonal range. If you click Auto-Contrast on the Curves tab, Xpress Pro manipulates the Master graph to optimize the tonal range (**Figure 10.23**).

You now have a broad range of luminance values; your black pixels are as black as they can be, and your white pixels are as white as they can be.

To automatically optimize the black level:

◆ On the Hue Offsets tab of the HSL tab, click the Auto-Black button.

Xpress Pro manipulates the Setup parameter so that the darkest part of your image has the darkest pixels possible, while still maintaining a broad tonal range.

✔ Tip

■ Clicking Auto-Black usually reduces the Setup value, but it might raise Setup instead if some of your dark pixels are too dark.

Control points and curve shape created by Auto-Contrast   *Auto-Contrast button*

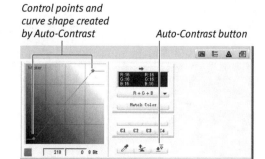

Figure 10.23 When you click the Auto-Contrast button on the Curves tab, Xpress Pro manipulates the Master graph to optimize the tonal range.

To automatically optimize the white level:

◆ On the Hue Offsets tab of the HSL tab, click the Auto-White button.

Xpress Pro manipulates the Gain parameter so that the brightest parts of your image have the brightest pixels possible (**Figure 10.24**).

✔ Tip

■ Clicking Auto-White usually raises the Gain value, but it might lower Gain instead if some of your bright pixels are too bright; Auto-White's main goal is to increase the tonal range across your bright pixels (highlights).

The brightest pixels are as bright as they can be. Auto-White changes this setting.

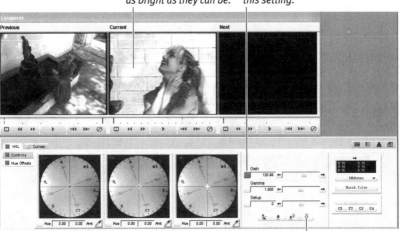

Auto-White button

Figure 10.24 When you click Auto-White on the Hue Offsets tab, Xpress Pro manipulates the Gain parameter to optimize the tonal range in the highlights.

To manually increase or decrease contrast:

Do one of the following:

◆ On the Controls tab of the HSL tab, drag the Contrast slider to the left or right. For finer control, click the left and right arrows on either end of the slider to decrease or increase the contrast value incrementally.

 If you move the slider to the left, Xpress Pro evens out the difference between the dark and bright parts of your image (**Figure 10.25**). If you move the slider to the right, Xpress Pro increases the difference between the dark and bright parts of your image; the blacks become blacker, and the whites become whiter.

◆ To manually decrease or increase the white point of your image, adjust the Gain value on the Hue Offsets tab. To manually decrease or increase the black point of your image, adjust the Setup value on the Hue Offsets tab.

◆ In the Master graph on the Curves tab, set a control point at the lower left of the curve line to adjust shadow levels, at the middle of the curve line to adjust the midrange levels, and at the upper right of the line to adjust highlight levels.

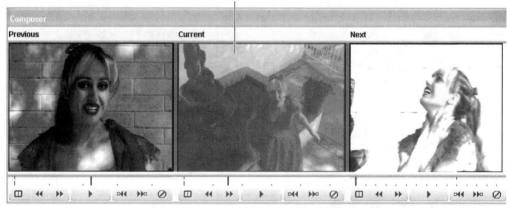

Washed out

Figure 10.25 When you decrease an image's contrast, you generally create a washed-out look; every pixel in the image approaches the same middle tone (gray).

If you lower the curve line on the left end, the darkest pixels in your image (the shadows) become darker (**Figure 10.26**). If you raise the curve line, the darkest pixels in your image become brighter.

If you lower the curve line on the right end, the brightest pixels in your image (the highlights) become darker based on your manipulations. If you raise the curve line, the brightest pixels in your image become brighter (**Figure 10.27**).

(For more information on graphs, see "Manipulating Graphs on the Curves Tab" later in this chapter.)

Darkest pixels are now really dark.

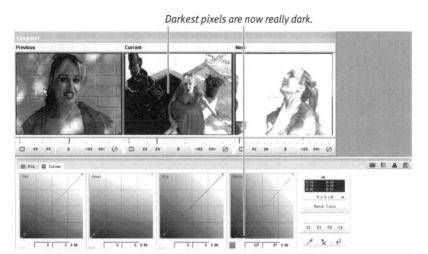

Figure 10.26 If you lower the left end of the curve line in the Master graph, the darkest pixels become darker.

Brightest pixels are not really bright.

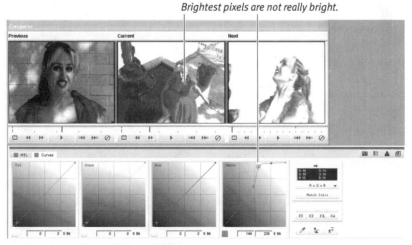

Figure 10.27 If you raise the right end of the Master graph curve line, the brightest pixels become even brighter.

✔ Tips

■ To brighten your shadow tones, you can also use the Clip Low/High parameter on the Controls tab of the HSL tab. Drag the far-left (Clip Low) triangle a few degrees to the right to brighten your shadows.

■ To increase your image's highlight tones, you can also increase the Gain value on the Hue Offsets tab of the HSL tab.

■ To decrease your image's highlight tones, you can also use the Clip Low/High parameter on the Controls tab of the HSL tab. Drag the far-right (Clip High) triangle a few degrees to the left to lower your highlights.

■ The button adjacent to any parameter control turns purple when you adjust the value. (To find out how to use the purple button to reset or disable the parameter, see the sidebar "Don't Delete It—Just Reset or Disable It" earlier in this chapter.)

To adjust a clip's gray point:

◆ On the Hue Offsets tab of the HSL tab, increase or decrease the Gamma value (**Figure 10.28**).

In general, your image brightens or darkens according to your manipulations.

✔ Tip

■ To brighten an image, you can also try adjusting the Brightness slider on the Controls tab of the HSL tab.

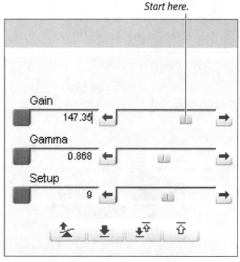

Start here.

Figure 10.28 Gain, Setup, and Gamma all affect the perceived brightness of your image. Gain adjusts the white point, Setup changes the black point, and Gamma adjusts the middle tones.

Don't Be Redundant with Your Corrections

Since each control interacts best with other controls in its own set, you should focus on adjusting your shot with one set of controls at a time, rather than jumping back and forth between different sets that essentially have the same function.

For example, to adjust brightness and contrast, you should stick to one of the following sets of controls: Brightness/Contrast, Gain/Gamma/Setup, or the Master graph, rather than jumping among them.

If necessary, after making broad and general adjustments using one set of controls, you can jump to another set of controls for fine-tuning.

ADJUSTING TONAL VALUES

Auto-Correct Settings

If you know that you need to correct the color balance or contrast for several shots in your sequence, you can save time with the Auto-Correct settings, which make Xpress Pro perform basic automatic corrections each time you initially apply the Color Correction effect to a clip segment. For example, you can tell Xpress Pro to automatically apply Auto-Contrast and Auto-Balance from the HSL tab each time you apply the Color Correction effect to a video clip segment.

Xpress Pro allows you to configure up to three automatic operations on the Auto-Correct tab.

To configure Auto-Correct operations:

1. In the Color Correction tool, click the Correction Mode Settings button at the upper right of the tool.

   The Color Correction Mode settings dialog box appears.

2. Click the Auto-Correct tab and choose an Auto-Correct operation from the first pop-up menu.

   If you choose one Auto-Correct operation, another pop-up menu appears (up to three total) so that you can choose an additional Auto-Correct operation (**Figure 10.29**).

   Now whenever you first manipulate Color Correction controls for an image (or apply the Color Correction effect from the Image tab of the Effect palette), Xpress Pro will automatically perform the operations set on the Auto-Correct tab.

✔ Tip

■ You can also access the Correction Mode Settings dialog box by going to the Settings tab of the Project window and double-clicking the Correction settings.

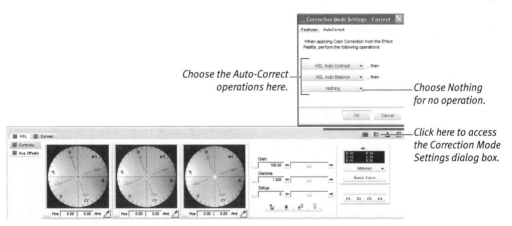

Choose the Auto-Correct operations here.

Choose Nothing for no operation.

Click here to access the Correction Mode Settings dialog box.

Figure 10.29 You can choose up to three Auto-Correct operations on the Auto-Correct tab of the Correction Mode Settings dialog box. These operations are applied the first time that you add a Color Correction effect to a video clip segment.

ADJUSTING TONAL VALUES

Using the Match Color Button

When you want shot elements to look consistent from shot to shot, you can use the Color Correction tool's Match Color button to apply color and luminance information from one shot to another. **Table 10.3** summarizes the Match Color operations that you can apply to another shot on each of the tabs.

For example, if you want a person's skin tone to remain consistent from shot to shot—which is often a priority in many correction situations—you can sample the person's skin in one shot and then apply the skin's HSL or RGB levels to the shot.

On the Curves tab, a bonus Match Color option is Natural Match; you enable Natural Match if you need to match a hue or saturation level but want to compensate for differences in shadowing that occurred on the set (for example, a person was shaded by a tree in one shot and away from the tree in another shot).

To match skin tone from one shot to another using Match Color:

1. Click the Curves tab of the Color Correction tool.

2. Make sure the image that has the skin tone that you want to use is displayed in the Previous, Current, or Next window in the Composer monitor.

Table 10.3

Match Color Applications on Each Color Correction Tab	
COLOR CORRECTION TAB	WHAT YOU CAN MATCH
HSL > Controls	Hue+Saturation+Luminance or Hue only, Saturation only, or Luminance only
HSL > Hue Offsets	Shadow, or Midtone, or Highlight (Hue/Saturation)
Curves	Master graph, Red+Green+Blue graphs, with Natural Match turned on

3. Hold down the mouse on the Select a Reference Color box (the right box above the Match Color button) and drag the eyedropper to the part of the image that you want to sample. Release the mouse to sample the skin tone color.

Xpress Pro will use this color as the reference skin tone to match (**Figure 10.30**).

4. Load the image that you want to correct in the Current window in the Composer monitor.

continues on next page

You want skin in every shot
to match this skin color.

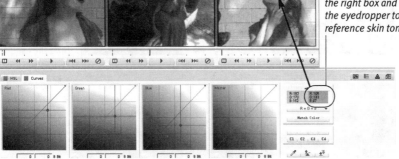

Hold down the mouse on
the right box and drag
the eyedropper to the
reference skin tone.

Figure 10.30 The first step in keeping a person's skin tone consistent in every shot is to use the Match Color eyedropper to sample the skin tone that you want to use as your reference.

USING THE MATCH COLOR BUTTON

5. Hold down the mouse on the Select a Color to Be Changed box in the Current Monitor box (the box on the left above the Match Color button) and drag the eyedropper to the part of the image (the skin tone) that you want to change. Release the mouse to sample the skin tone color (**Figure 10.31**).

6. Choose R+G+B from the Match Type pull-down menu (above the Match Color button).

7. (Optional) If the skin tone you're changing is in shadow and the reference tone is not (or vice versa), you may want to select R+G+B (Nat) from the Match Type pull-down menu (**Figure 10.32**).

Natural Match will compensate for any lighting differences between the two skin tones you're trying to match.

8. In the Color Correction tool, click the Match Color button.

Xpress Pro changes the current image so that the sample skin tone matches the skin tone of your reference image. All other colors in the image also change in relation to the new skin tone color.

Sample the skin tone that you want to change.

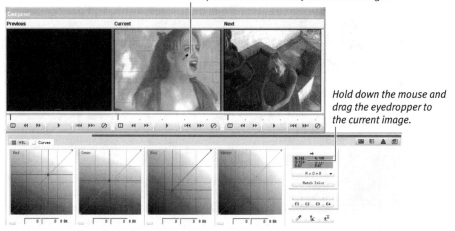

Hold down the mouse and drag the eyedropper to the current image.

Figure 10.31 After sampling a reference skin tone, load the image you want to change and sample the skin tone you want to change by clicking the left Match Color box and dragging the eyedropper to the skin tone that you want to change.

Figure 10.32 If there were differences in shading on the set, select Natural Match from the pull-down menu above the Match Color button.

✔ Tips

- You can also match skin tone on the Controls tab of the HSL tab by selecting H+S+L from the Match Type pull-down menu before clicking Match Color.

- Your reference color does not have to come from an image. You can use the eyedropper to sample a color from your system's color palette.

To apply one shot's brightness to another shot using Match Color:

1. Click the Curves tab of the Color Correction tool.

2. Load the image that you want to match in the Previous, Current, or Next window in the Composer monitor.

3. Hold down the mouse on the Select a Reference Color box (the right box above the Match Color button) and drag the eyedropper to the part of the image that has the brightness that you want to sample. Release the mouse to sample the skin tone color.

   Xpress Pro will use the luminance of your reference image as the brightness to match (**Figure 10.33**).

4. Load the image that you want to correct in the Current window in the Composer monitor.

   Usually, the image that you want to change will contain the same object that you sampled as the reference image. (For example, two shots might contain a wall, and you want the wall's brightness to be consistent in all shots.)

continues on next page

The reference wall

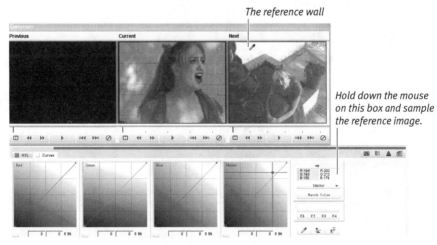

Hold down the mouse on this box and sample the reference image.

Figure 10.33 In this case, the luminance of the white wall needs to be consistent in every shot. The first step is to sample the correct white wall as the reference image.

5. Hold down the mouse on the Select a Color to Be Changed box in the Current Monitor box (the box on the left above the Match Color button) and drag the eyedropper to the part of the image that you want to change. Release the mouse to sample the part of the image that has the brightness value that you want to change (**Figure 10.34**).

6. Choose Master from the Match Type pull-down menu (above the Match Color button).

7. In the Color Correction tool, click the Match Color button.

Xpress Pro updates the current image so that the area that you sampled increases or decreases in luminance to match the luminance of the reference image sample.

✔ Tips

- Performing a color correction with the Match Color button applies a color correction to an image as a whole. It does not create an alpha channel that isolates only particular pixels in the image.

- You can also match luminance on the Controls tab of the HSL tab by choosing luminance from the Match Type pull-down menu.

This wall's luminance will be changed to match the reference.

Click here and sample the image to be changed.

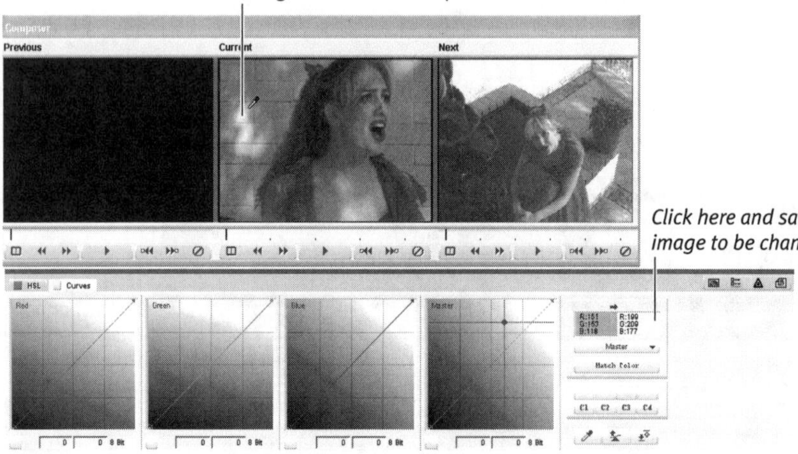

Figure 10.34 After sampling the reference wall, you can sample the wall that needs its luminance changed, in the Current window.

Manipulating Graphs on the Curves Tab

The trickiest controls to master in the Color Correction tool are the Red, Green, Blue, and Master graphs on the Curves group tab.

By using control points to manipulate the curve of a graph line, you can control an image's color levels (in the Red, Green, and Blue graphs) or luminance levels (in the Master graph) across the shadow, midrange, and highlights of your image.

The graphs indicate shadow levels on the left, midrange tones in the middle, and highlight tones on the right. So, for example, if you want to reduce the amount of red in your highlights, you can use control points to drag the far right of the Red curve line below its default position (**Figure 10.35**).

(For information on adjusting luminance with the Master graph, see "Adjusting Tonal Values" earlier in this chapter.)

Control points   The amount of red in the highlight tone has been reduced.

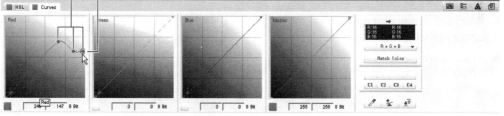

Figure 10.35 Graphs represent shadows and midrange and highlight tones from left to right, and levels up and down. So, for example, if you want to decrease the amount of red in your highlights, you need to use control points to drag the right side of the Red curve down.

To manipulate a graph line:

1. Click anywhere on the line to create a new control point or click an existing control point to select it.

   Xpress Pro puts a circle around the selected control point (**Figure 10.36**).

2. Drag the control point to a new position. Xpress Pro modifies the shape of the curve line.

✔ Tips

- By default, there is already one control point on the far left of a curve line and one on the far right.

- You can add multiple control points to any one curve line. The number you add depends on how you want to adjust the line. Generally, the more control points you add, the more you can isolate one part of the curve line for adjustment. (See "To isolate one part of the curve for adjustment" on the next page.)

- As you adjust a control point's position, the curve line—that is, the portion of the curve line between adjacent control points—adjusts its shape in a Bézier fashion. The image in the Current window in the Composer updates as you change the shape of the curve line.

- You can also position a control point by typing what are essentially X and Y coordinates in the Input and Output boxes below each curve (corresponding to RGB values). The minimum value is 0 and maximum is 255 (**Figure 10.37**).

- You can nudge a control point to the left by selecting it and tapping the Up arrow key. You can nudge a control point to the right by selecting it and tapping the Down arrow key.

- You cannot drag a control point to the left or right past the position of an adjacent control point (**Figure 10.38**).

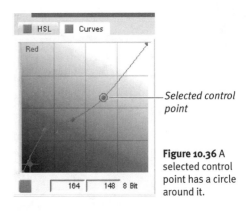

Selected control point

Figure 10.36 A selected control point has a circle around it.

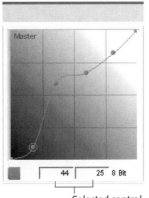

Figure 10.37 The selected control point is positioned 44 points across and 25 points up from the bottom of the graph.

Selected control point coordinates

The selected point can't move to the left of this point.   *The selected point can't move to the right of this point.*

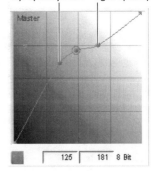

Figure 10.38 Xpress Pro doesn't allow you to move a control point past the horizontal position of an adjacent control point.

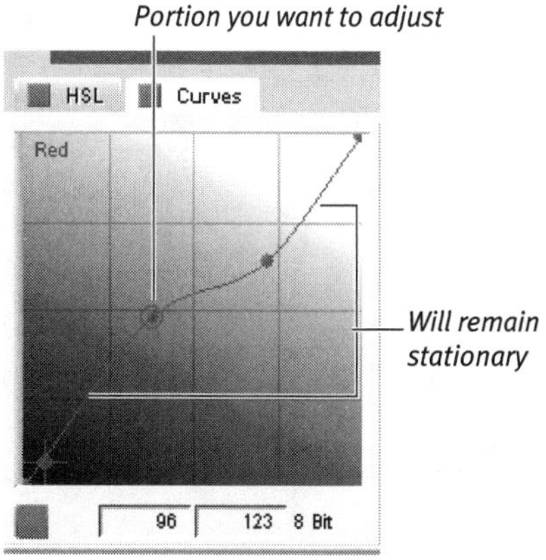

Portion you want to adjust

Figure 10.39 To isolate a portion of a curve for adjustment, first set two control points around the portion that you want to adjust. The part of the curve not between these points will remain fixed.

To delete a control point:

1. Click a control point to select it.

2. Hover the cursor over the selected control point and press Delete.

 The control point disappears, and Xpress Pro modifies the shape of the curve line.

To isolate one part of the curve for adjustment:

1. Create two control points around the portion of the curve line that you want to isolate.

 The portion of the curve line between these two points is what you will move; the rest of the line will remain stationary (**Figure 10.39**).

continues on next page

When You Lower One Color, You Raise Another

In the Red, Green, and Blue graphs on the Curves tab, you can reduce the amount of red, blue, and green in different tones of your image by moving parts of the curve line below its default position. However, when you lower the level of one color, you raise the level of another:

◆ If you lower a red level, then you raise the cyan level.

◆ If you lower the green level, then you raise the magenta level.

◆ If you lower the blue level, then you raise the yellow level.

MANIPULATING GRAPHS ON THE CURVES TAB

2. Create a third control point in between the first two points, near the part that you want to isolate (**Figure 10.40**).

This third point further narrows the portion of the curve that you want to adjust and ensures that other control points will not move during the adjustment.

3. Create a fourth control point exactly on the portion of the curve line that you want to isolate.

4. Move the fourth control point to a new position.

As you manipulate the fourth control point, the other parts of the graph do not move; they are anchored in their position (**Figure 10.41**).

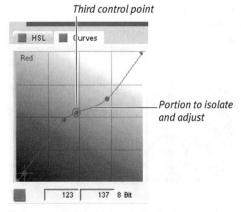

Third control point

Portion to isolate and adjust

Figure 10.40 Add a third control point between the first two control points, near the part that you want to isolate.

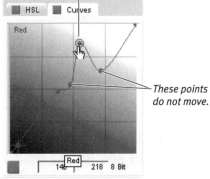

Isolated control point dragged to a new position

These points do not move.

Figure 10.41 After you add a fourth point to the exact part of the curve line that you want to isolate and adjust, you can drag the point to a new position. Meanwhile, the other portions of the curve line remain stationary.

Rendering
and Real-Time

Real-time effects are effects that can play instantly without any rendering (effect processing) time. In a perfect world, everything would be real time; video editing and compositing would be like painting: instant creation, instant results.

Xpress Pro features more than a hundred real-time effects that can play instantly on your external monitor via the Mojo box. However, without the Mojo box, these effects are preview only; they can play back on your desktop but not on your external monitor without rendering. That said, expert with or without Mojo, you can preview an effect frame by frame on your external monitor using Render-on-the-Fly.

When it comes to rendering, you have a few options: you can render one effect at time, render many effects at once, or use ExpertRender to render only those effects needed for smooth playback.

Whether or not you enable real-time effect playback during the edit, you'll need to render every effect in your sequence at the end of your project, to ensure smooth output.

(For more information on the Mojo box and its real-time capabilities, see Appendix B, "Post-Production Extras.")

About Rendering and Real-Time

When you apply an effect to a video or audio clip, Xpress Pro requires processing (rendering) time to play back that effect at full quality. Ultimately, before you output your project to tape, you will need to render all effects in your sequence to ensure the highest performance. Whenever you render an audio and video effect in Xpress Pro, the application creates additional source media files on your hard drive, which are represented by precompute clips in your bins (you can choose to display precomputes by configuring your Bin Display settings).

During editing, however, Xpress Pro's real-time capabilities can help you save the time it usually takes to render effects. Software-only versions of Xpress Pro let you preview more than a hundred effects on the Composer monitor in real time, without waiting for rendering to complete; Xpress Pro systems that have the Mojo box let you preview effects on an external monitor as well.

The rest of this chapter is about how to configure your real-time effects options and how to render effects either during or at the end of the editing process.

✔ Tip

■ At the end of your project, when you're ready for output, you should make sure that your media drives have room for the media files that the application needs to create during the final render.

Real-Time Modes

If you are using Xpress Pro software only (without the Mojo box), then you will always work in one of the following two modes, which determine real-time playback:

◆ **Green-dot mode (non-Mojo only):** When the Timeline's round Real-Time toggle button is green, every Effect palette effect that has a green dot next to its icon can play back on your Composer monitor without the need for rendering.

The downside to green-dot mode is that playback on your external monitor is disabled. (The ability to use your external monitor is a big reason to buy the Mojo.)

◆ **Blue-dot mode (non-Mojo only):** When the Real-Time toggle button is blue, your movie can play back, through FireWire, to your external broadcast monitor.

The downside to blue-dot mode is that none of the Effect palette effects can play in real time on either your Composer or external monitor.

In both green- and blue-dot modes, you can affect playback quality by choosing from the following Video Quality settings at the bottom left of the Timeline:

◆ **Best Quality:** This video-quality option enables real-time effects to play back at the best quality possible on software-only (non-Mojo) systems (1/4, single-field resolution).

However, sometimes this playback mode taxes the Xpress Pro system to the extent that real-time playback stutters.

◆ **Best Performance:** This video-quality option reduces real-time playback to 1/16, single-field resolution. In general, the image looks very blurry.

Enable this option when real-time playback problems occur in Best Quality mode.

Real-Time toggle button

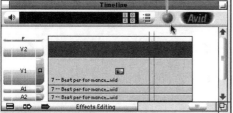

Figure 11.1 To turn on real-time effects playback, click the big button to the left of the Avid icon on the Timeline toolbar.

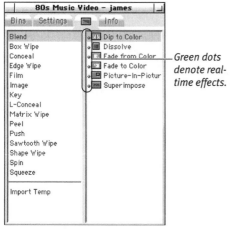

Green dots denote real-time effects.

Figure 11.2 If real-time effects are turned on in the Timeline, green dots appear next to effect icons on the Effects palette. If real-time effects are disabled, these dots disappear.

Is this dot green or blue?

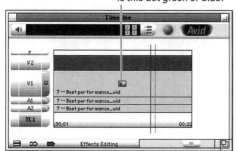

Figure 11.3 If the icon of an applied effect in the Timeline has a green dot, then the effect should play in real time. If real-time effects are disabled, the dot is blue.

If you own the Mojo box, you have an additional video-quality option available:

◆ **Full Quality:** This option offers the highest resolution available (two-field resolution). Playback likely will suffer in this mode once your effects go beyond minimal complexity.

On Mojo systems, Best Quality is called Draft Quality. (For more information about Mojo, see Appendix B, "Post-Production Extras.")

To enable software-only real-time preview (non-Mojo):

◆ In the Timeline, click the Real-Time toggle button (the round button) at the top right of the Timeline toolbar so that it turns green (**Figure 11.1**).

Xpress Pro enables real-time playback. Green dots appear next to real-time effects on the Effects palette. You can now preview those real-time effects on your Composer monitor without rendering.

✔ Tips

■ With real-time playback enabled, all real-time effects have a green dot to the left of their icons (**Figure 11.2**). If an effect is not real-time capable, or if real-time playback is disabled, the dot is blue. A blue dot on an effect in the Timeline means that effects need to be rendered to play (**Figure 11.3**).

■ As long as Render-on-the-Fly is selected, you can preview any effect frame by frame on your external monitor. (For more information, see "Using Render-on-the-Fly" later in this chapter.)

To disable software-only real-time playback and enable external playback (non-Mojo):

1. In the Timeline, click to remove the green highlight from the Real-Time toggle button.

   The Real-Time toggle button turns blue.

2. Choose Special > Enable Digital Video Out.

   You can now play your sequence on your external monitor via FireWire, but you cannot preview your real-time effects.

✔ Tip

- On software-only systems, you need to enable Digital Video Out before outputting your sequence to tape. (For more information, see Chapter 14, "Outputting and Exporting.")

To choose video playback quality (software-only and Mojo systems):

Do one of the following:

◆ At the bottom left of the Timeline, click the Video Res toggle button to choose Best Quality, Best Performance, or (for Mojo systems) Highest Quality.

◆ Right-click (Windows) or Control+Shift-click (Mac) the Video Res toggle button and choose your video quality setting from the list that appears (**Figure 11.4**).

   The appearance of your video in the Composer and on your external monitor changes based on your setting. If you chose a low setting such as Best Performance, the image will appear blurry.

   The advantage of Best Performance is that complicated effects or multiple layers will play back more smoothly.

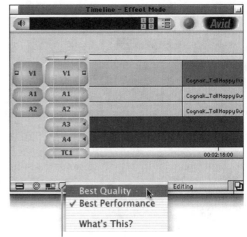

Right-click (Windows) or Control+Shift-click (Mac) here.

Figure 11.4 To set video quality, right-click (Windows) or Control+Shift-click (Mac) the Video Res toggle button and choose from the list that appears.

How Good Is Xpress Pro's Real-Time?

Measuring an NLE's real-time performance is not just about counting the number of effects it can play back in real time. Also important is the number of real-time effects and video layers you stack on top of each other—that is, the number of real-time streams that Xpress Pro can play.

With or without Mojo, Xpress Pro offers four real-time streams, or five streams on a really fast computer (such as a 2-Mhz G5). For example, you can stack a video segment (as a background) and three titles on top of each other, and they will all play in real time.

Configuring Real-Time Settings

Whether you own the Mojo or are running the software-only setup, you need to address the following settings to help address real-time performance lapses:

◆ **Video prefill:** In the Video Display Settings dialog box, you can enter a number for Seconds of Video to Pre-Fill.

The video prefill amount delays the playback of real-time effects by up to 10 seconds so that Xpress Pro can preprocess effects. This is like giving a runner a head start in a race and increases the likelihood that Xpress Pro will be able to play back all real-time effects successfully and without any hiccups.

◆ **Stream limit:** In the Video Display Settings dialog box, you can also reduce the real-time stream limit below the default maximum of 5; but try other options for improving real-time playback first, because lowering the stream limit reduces your real-time capabilities.

(For more information on addressing real-time playback problems, see the sidebar "Handling Real-Time Playback Problems" later in this chapter.)

◆ **Real-time playback bars:** You can turn on color-coded real-time playback bars in the Timeline Settings dialog box; these warn you about effects that were difficult for Xpress Pro to play.

Red bars denote the frames that the system was unable to play. Yellow bars denote the frames that the system had difficulty playing. Blue bars denote the frames that did not play successfully due to disk speed limitations.

To adjust Video Display settings:

1. On the Settings tab of the Project window, double-click your current Video Display settings.

   The Video Display Settings dialog box opens.

2. In the Video Display Settings dialog box, enter a number of seconds in the Seconds of Video to Pre-Fill box; the default is 0, and the maximum is 10 (**Figure 11.5**).

   The higher the number, the longer Xpress Pro will have to preprocess frames before playing your sequence, but the better the chances of smooth playback.

3. In the Video Display Settings dialog box, change the Stream Limit value if necessary; the maximum is 5.

   The number you enter here sets the maximum number of video streams that Xpress Pro can play back in real time. A PIP effect, for example, takes three streams: an alpha channel layer, a foreground layer, and a background layer.

   (For more information, see the sidebar "How Good Is Xpress Pro's Real Time?" earlier in this chapter.)

4. Click OK.

   Xpress Pro plays back real-time effects according to your settings.

✔ Tips

■ The Enable Confidence View option is unrelated to real-time effects. If you select this option, Xpress Pro plays video in the Composer and on the external monitor when capturing or outputting to tape.

■ If your system does not have sufficient memory (RAM), then Xpress Pro may not be capable of using the full amount of time you enter for prefill seconds. As a result, the wait may be shorter than expected.

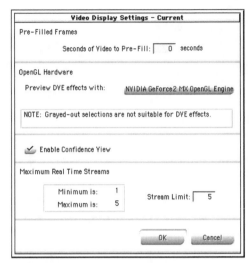

Figure 11.5 Here, Seconds of Video to Pre-fill is set to 0 seconds; after you click Play, playback will begin immediately. But if real-time effects give you problems, you may want to enter a number in this box. You can specify up to 10 seconds of prefill.

Figure 11.6 To turn on color-coded real-time playback bars, select Highlight Suggested Render Areas after Playback in the Timeline Settings dialog box.

Playback bars

Figure 11.7 Playback bars appear on the timecode track, underneath your video and audio tracks.

To turn on real-time playback bars:

1. On the Settings tab of the Project window, double-click your Timeline settings.

2. On the Display tab of the Timeline Settings dialog box, select Highlight Suggested Render Areas After Playback (**Figure 11.6**).

   After playback, Xpress Pro displays playback bars along the Timecode track in the Timeline (**Figure 11.7**). You'll get the best playback results if you render those sections marked with red or yellow bars. (See the sidebar "Handling Real-Time Playback Problems" on the next page.)

✔ Tip

■ By default, real-time effects are turned on in the Timeline, and color bar warnings are enabled in the Timeline settings.

Handling Real-Time Playback Problems

If Xpress Pro displays red, yellow, or blue color bars in the Timeline, or if you see problems with real-time playback, you can use a number of strategies to deal with the problem:

- ◆ **Choose a lower video quality.** At the bottom left of the Timeline, choose a lower quality option from the Video Res toggle button. (For more information, see "Real-Time Modes" earlier in this chapter.)

- ◆ **Use ExpertRender.** ExpertRender will save you from having to render every real-time effect in order to fix your problem. (For more information, see "Using ExpertRender" later in this chapter.)

- ◆ **Move the playhead earlier in the sequence and click Play.** Starting playback before the troublesome effect often increases performance, especially if you have set a video prefill amount in the Video Display Settings dialog box.

- ◆ **Adjust your Video Display settings.** Change your video prefill amount or real-time stream limit. (For more information, see the previous section, "Configuring Real-Time Settings".)

- ◆ **Get faster drives.** If Xpress Pro marks the Timeline with any blue playback bars, the problem lies with the media drives. Possible solutions include reformatting your hard drives (they may be fragmented) or obtaining faster drives.

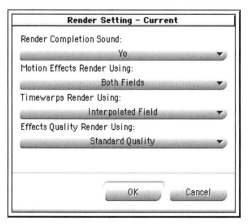

Figure 11.8 The Render Setting dialog box.

Configuring Render-Related Settings

Before rendering any effects in your sequence, including motion effects and the Timewarp effect, you should configure the render-related settings found in the Render Setting dialog box and on the Timeline Fast menu.

The Render Setting dialog box (**Figure 11.8**) contains the following options:

◆ **Render Completion Sound:** After a render is complete, you will hear the sound that you select here. This sound allows you to walk away from your computer while rendering and do other chores. Select None if you do not want an alert sound.

◆ **Motion Effects Render Using:** This setting determines how Xpress Pro renders motion effects by default. Choose Original Preference if you always want to set this option in the Motion Effect dialog box when you create a motion effect.

(For more information on these render options, see "The Four Motion Effect Render Options" in Chapter 9.)

◆ **Timewarps Render Using:** This setting determines how Xpress Pro renders Timewarp motion effects. These options are the same as for motion effects, plus there are two Timewarp-only options: Blended Interpolated and Blended VTR (for explanations of these options, see the Xpress Pro help system).

(For more information about the Timewarp motion effects, see "Timewarp Motion Effect Presets" in Chapter 9.)

continues on next page

◆ **Effects Quality Render Using:**
Regardless of whether you own the Mojo box, you can switch a number of Xpress Pro video effects (but not all) from Standard Quality to High Quality rendering. Switching an effect to High Quality typically smoothes out jagged edges in effects such as 3D PIP and 3D Ball.

You can set a default rendering quality or choose Quality Set in Each Effect to configure the setting for each effect individually using the Effect editor.

You can also set the following render-related display option on the Timeline Fast menu:

◆ **Render Range:** This option determines how specific Xpress Pro is when alerting you to effects (or parts of effects) that need rendering.

To configure your render settings:

1. On the Settings tab of the Project window, double-click the active Render settings.

2. In the dialog box that appears, choose options for Render Completion Sound, Motion Effects Render Using, Timewarps Render Using, and Effects Quality Render Using.

3. Click OK to close the dialog box.

   The next time you render an effect, Xpress Pro will use your currently configured settings. (These settings do not affect effects that are already rendered.)

This part is already rendered.   *The red line marks the part that needs rendering.*

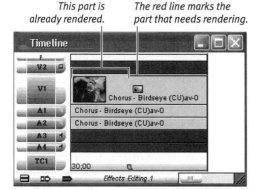

Figure 11.9 Here, a red line marks a portion of a segment that needs rendering.

To choose a Timeline render range display:

1. Open the Timeline Fast menu.

2. Click Render Ranges and *choose one of the following:*

   ▲ **Partially Only:** This option marks the unrendered part of a partially rendered segment with a red line. Segments containing effects that are entirely unrendered are not marked at all (**Figure 11.9**).

   ▲ **None:** Choose this option if you don't care whether an effect is partially or wholly rendered.

   ▲ **All:** This option uses a red line to mark the unrendered part of a partially rendered effect as well as effects that are completely unrendered.

   When an effect is partially rendered, you can use Render In/Out or Expert Render In/Out to render the unrendered portion and not waste time re-rendering the portion that is already rendered.

To tell Xpress Pro how to render motion effects:

1. On the Settings tab of the Project window, double-click your Render settings.

2. In the Render Setting dialog box that opens, click Motion Effects Render Using and *choose one of the following:*

   ▲ **Original Preference:** Xpress Pro creates the motion effect using the Render Effect w-Field Motion Effect Using choice that was selected in the Motion Effect dialog box when the effect was created (**Figure 11.10**).

   ▲ **Duplicated Field:** Xpress Pro creates the effect using one field.

   ▲ **Both Fields:** Xpress Pro uses two fields from each frame to create the effect.

   ▲ **Interpolated Fields:** Xpress Pro creates the effect by combining scan line pairs from the first field to create the second field.

   ▲ **VTR-Style:** Xpress Pro creates a second field by shifting selected video fields of the original media by a full scan line.

   The next time you create a motion effect, Xpress Pro will render it according to your settings here, unless you override them in the Motion Effect dialog box.

   (For more information on the Motion Effects Render Using option, see "Using Motion Effects" in Chapter 9.)

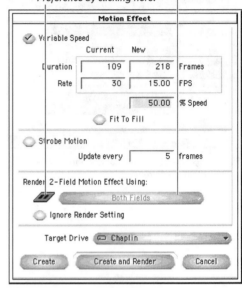

Original Preference respects this choice.
But you can override Original Preference by clicking here.

Figure 11.10 Choosing Original Preference in the Render Setting dialog box tells Xpress Pro to obey whatever option was selected in the Motion Effect dialog box when the motion effect was created.

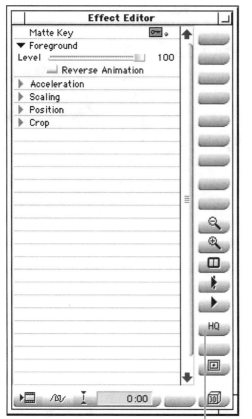

High Quality button

Figure 11.11 To promote an effect from Standard Quality to High Quality, open the Effect editor for the effect and click the HQ button at the lower right of the window.

To promote an effect from Standard Quality to High Quality:

1. In the Timeline, park the playhead over the effect that you want to promote to High Quality.

2. In the Timeline, select the track that contains the effect and click the Effect Mode button (located by default on the Timeline toolbar).

   The Effect editor opens, displaying the parameters for your effect.

   If the effect is enabled for High Quality, then an HQ button appears at the lower right of the Effect editor.

3. To promote the effect to High Quality, click the HQ button (**Figure 11.11**).

   The video image improves on both your Composer and external monitor. Most noticeably, striated edges become smooth. The effect will render at the highest quality.

✔ Tip

- You can set High Quality as the default for all High Quality–capable effects in the render settings. (For more information, see the previous section, "Configuring Real-Time Settings.")

Rendering One or More Effects

When rendering effects in the Timeline, regardless of whether they're real-time or non-real-time effects, you have the following options:

◆ **Render a single effect.** You can render a single effect in either the Timeline or the Effect editor.

◆ **Render effect layers.** Using the Render At Position command, you can render multiple video track effect layers at the position of the playhead.

◆ **Render multiple effects at once.** By either selecting multiple effects or using Timeline In or Out points, you can render a range of effects simultaneously.

To render a single effect:

1. In the Timeline, place the position indicator over the clip that contains the effect to be rendered.

2. Select the track containing the effect.

3. *Do one of the following:*

   ▲ Click the ⬛ Render Effect button (located by default on the Timeline toolbar).

   ▲ Click the Effect Editor button (located by default on the Timeline toolbar). When the Effect editor opens displaying the parameters of the effect in question, click the Render Effect button at the bottom left the Effect editor (**Figure 11.12**).

   (For more information about the Effect editor, see Chapter 9, "Working with Video Effects.")

This effect is currently loaded in the Effect editor.

Render Effect button

Figure 11.12 One way to render an effect is by clicking the Render Effect button in the Effect editor, provided that the effect you want to render is loaded in the window.

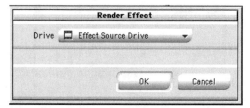

Figure 11.13 The Render Effect dialog box.

Figure 11.14 Select Effect Source Drive if you want Xpress Pro to create the render file on the same drive as the clip you're affecting (for a transition, the outgoing clip).

4. In the Render Effect dialog box, select the drive where you want the rendered media saved (**Figure 11.13**).

5. Click OK.

Xpress Pro renders the effects and creates a precompute clip (a rendered effect file) on the selected drive. The colored dot on the effect icon in the Timeline disappears.

✔ Tips

- The Effect Source Drive is the drive that contains the source media for the outgoing shot of a transition (**Figure 11.14**). If you are not rendering a transition, this drive is the drive that contains the media files for the segment to which the effect is applied.

- If your media drive does not have enough room to store the effect, a dialog box asks if you want to stop the rendering process or continue on the chance that there may be enough room.

- To avoid having to choose a render drive each time you render an effect, hold down Alt (Windows) or Option (Mac) when you click the Render Effect button. This makes Xpress Pro use the last drive you selected.

- When rendering nested effects, you have to render only the top layer of the nest for all of the effect to play.

RENDERING ONE OR MORE EFFECTS

To display the render status:

◆ *Do one of the following:*

▲ To display the render status in hours, minutes, and seconds, press the T key. To hide the display, press the T key again (**Figure 11.15**).

▲ To display the render status as the percent rendered, press the P key (**Figure 11.16**). To hide the display, press the P key again.

Depending on your choice, Xpress Pro displays a time estimate for your render or the percentage already rendered.

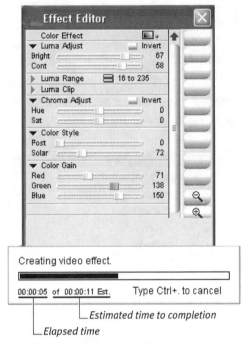

Creating video effect.

00:00:05 of 00:00:11 Est.   Type Ctrl+. to cancel

└Estimated time to completion
└Elapsed time

Figure 11.15 Press T to display rendering time.

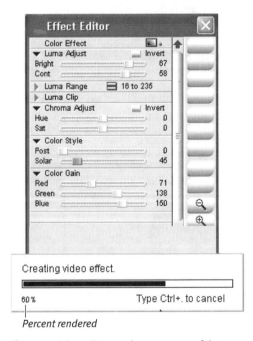

Creating video effect.

60%   Type Ctrl+. to cancel

Percent rendered

Figure 11.16 Press P to see the percentage of the render that has been completed.

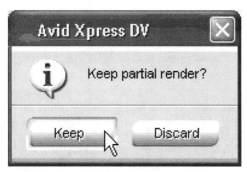

Figure 11.17 You can choose to keep or discard the rendered part of a partially rendered effect.

These effects can be rendered using Render at Position.

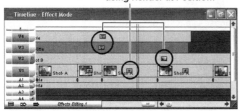

Figure 11.18 To render effects that are vertically stacked in the Timeline, first place the playhead over the effects and select the tracks that contain the effects.

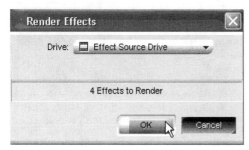

Figure 11.19 The Render Effects pop-up menu lists the number of effects that are selected for the render. Choose your media drive here.

To interrupt a render:

1. Press Ctrl+. (period) (Windows) or Command+. (period) (Mac).

2. *Do one of the following:*
   - ▲ In the dialog box that appears, click Keep to save the portion of the effect that has been rendered (**Figure 11.17**).
   - ▲ In the dialog box that appears, click Discard to end the render and erase anything that was rendered.

   Xpress Pro stops rendering and returns you to normal editing mode.

To render layers of effects at the playhead position:

1. In the Timeline, place the position indicator on top of the effects in the Timeline.

2. Select all of the track buttons for the tracks that contain the effects (**Figure 11.18**).

3. Choose Clip > Render at Position.

4. In the Render Effects pop-up menu, choose a drive for the render files (**Figure 11.19**).

5. If you do not want to render real-time effects, select Skip Real-Time Effects.

6. Click OK.

   Xpress Pro renders all effects underneath the position indicator on the selected tracks.

✔ Tips

- ■ The Effect Source Drive is the drive that contains the outgoing clip of a transition. If you render an effect that applies to just one segment, the source drive is the drive that contains the master clip.

- ■ If your selected drive doesn't have enough space to render the effect, Xpress Pro displays a dialog box asking whether you want to stop the render or continue on the chance that there is enough room.

To render a range of effects between In and Out points:

1. Select (target) all of the tracks containing the effects you want to render.

2. Mark an In point before the start of the first effect to be rendered.

3. Mark an Out point after the last effect to be rendered.

4. Choose Clip > Render In/Out (**Figure 11.20**).

5. In the pop-up menu that appears, select a drive for the render files.

6. Select Skip Real-Time Effects if you do not want to render real-time effects.

7. Click OK.

   Xpress Pro renders all effects that are entirely or partially marked by In and Out points on the selected tracks.

✔ Tips

- Timeline In and Out points do not need to completely enclose an effect for it to be rendered. As long as the In and Out points partially mark an effect, the entire effect will be rendered.

- If you apply the Submaster effect to the track above layered effects, you can render all effects underneath the Submaster effect just by rendering the Submaster effect (**Figure 11.21**).

   (For more information on using Submaster effects, see "Nesting Multiple Effects" in Chapter 9.)

Rendering One or More Effects

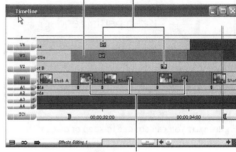

This entire title will be rendered, even though it is only partially marked.   *These effects will not be rendered.*

These effects will be rendered.

Figure 11.20 In the Timeline, set In and Out points around the effects that you want to render. Then choose Clip > Render In/Out.

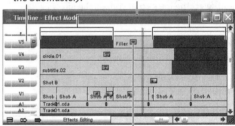

To render all of the effects under the Submaster effect, you have to select only the top track (the one containing the Submaster).   *These portions of the effects will not be rendered by rendering the Submaster effect because they don't fall beneath the Submaster segment.*

Render this Submaster segment, and Xpress Pro renders all effects that are directly beneath it

Figure 11.21 If you create a Submaster effect above other layered effects, all you have to do is render the Submaster effect to render all of the effects below it.

This effect is the only one that ExpertRender suggests rendering.

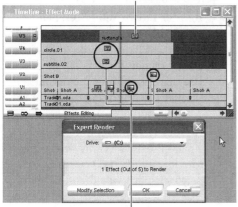

ExpertRender does not think that these effects need to be rendered to achieve smooth playback.

Figure 11.22 Even though there are multiple effects layered on top of each other, ExpertRender suggests rendering only 1 of 5 effects (the top title).

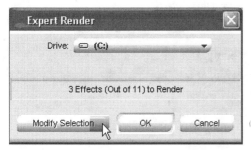

Figure 11.23 To modify ExpertRender's recommendations (and highlight more or fewer effects for rendering), choose Modify Selection in the Expert Render dialog box.

✔ Tip

◆ When it comes to rendering nests, ExpertRender always renders the effect outside the nest rather than any effects inside the nest. If you want to render anything inside the nest, you need to modify ExpertRender's recommendations.

Using ExpertRender

When rendering effects to fix playback problems, you usually don't need to render every effect in the problematic area. Instead, you can use ExpertRender to find out which effects should be rendered to ensure smooth playback, saving you from a lot of unnecessary rendering.

ExpertRender commands correspond to those for normal render operations: you can choose either ExpertRender at Position (to render at the position of the playhead) or ExpertRender In/Out (to render between Timeline In and Out points).

Rendering at the playhead position with ExpertRender:

1. Select the tracks that contain the effects you want to render. (Select All Tracks is a good choice when using ExpertRender.)

2. Move the playhead to the position of the effects you want to render.

3. Choose Clip > ExpertRender at Position. ExpertRender highlights the effects that need rendering. The Expert Render dialog box tells you how many effects out of the total need rendering (**Figure 11.22**).

4. In the Expert Render dialog box, choose a drive for the render (precompute) files.

5. *Click one of the following:*
   ▲ **Cancel:** Nothing is rendered.
   ▲ **Modify Selection:** Clicking this button closes the Expert dialog box and allows you to Shift-click in the Timeline to add to or subtract from the effects that ExpertRender recommends rendering. Then you can click the normal Render button to render the selected effects (**Figure 11.23**).
   ▲ **OK:** Xpress Pro renders the highlighted effects.

To render effects between In and Out points using ExpertRender:

1. Select all the tracks that contain the effects you want to render. (Select All Tracks is a good choice when using ExpertRender.)

2. Mark an In point before the start of the first effect to be rendered.

3. Mark an Out point after the last effect to be rendered.

4. Choose Clip > ExpertRender In/Out. ExpertRender highlights those effects between the In and Out points that should be rendered to achieve smooth playback (**Figure 11.24**).

5. In the Expert Render dialog box, select a drive for the render files.

6. If you are rendering effects after real-time playback, the dialog box also asks you to choose one of the following:

   ▲ **Render Entire Selection:** Render everything between your In and Out points that ExpertRender says you should render (the highlighted effects). Use this option if you are outputting through DV (FireWire) to tape or your external monitor.

   ▲ **Render Recommended Ranges:** Xpress Pro renders only what is necessary for smooth real-time preview playback (what would normally be marked red or yellow by the real-time playback bars). Use this option if you don't care about external monitor playback and you just want a smooth real-time preview.

ExpertRender recommends rendering these effects.

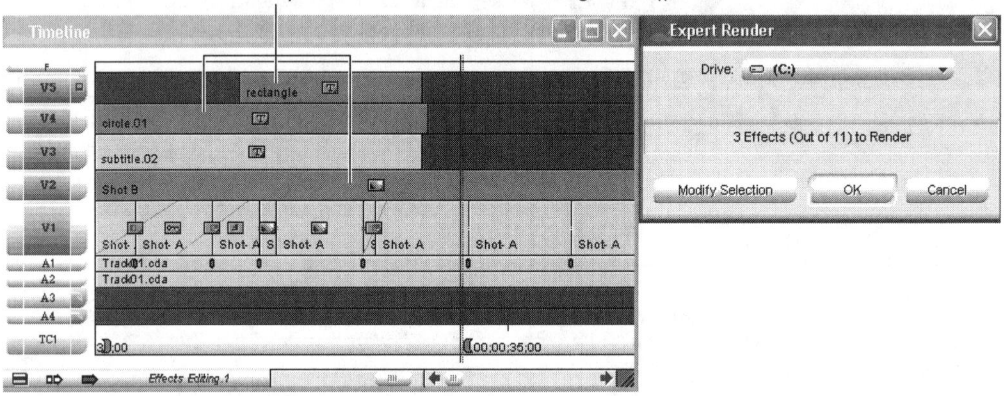

Figure 11.24 In this case, ExpertRender In/Out recommends rendering 3 out of the 11 effects between the Timeline In and Out points.

7. *Click one of the following:*

▲ **Cancel:** Nothing is rendered.

▲ **Modify Selection:** Clicking this button closes the Expert Render dialog box and allows to you Shift-click in the Timeline to add to or subtract from the effects that ExpertRender recommends rendering. Then you can click the normal Render button to render the selected effects.

▲ **OK:** Xpress Pro renders the highlighted effects.

Your selected effects are rendered.

To interrupt an ExpertRender render operation:

◆ *Do one of the following:*

▲ Click the timecode track in the Timeline to move the position indicator.

▲ Double-click either the ➡ Lift/ Overwrite or ⬛ Extract/Splice-in mode button.

▲ Choose Clip > ExpertRender. In the Expert Render dialog box, click Cancel.

When to Modify ExpertRender's Recommendations

You don't always have to follow ExpertRender's advise exactly.

Here are three scenarios in which you might want to modify ExpertRender's recommendations by clicking Modify Selection in the Expert Render dialog box:

◆ You forgot to target (select) a track that contains an effect that you need to render.

◆ You want to render an effect inside a nest and not the effect outside a nest as ExpertRender can render only effects outside a nest.

◆ ExpertRender highlights an entire segment for rendering when you know that only a transition effect on that segment needs rendering. (Sometimes ExpertRender incorrectly highlights an entire segment instead of just a transition.)

Eventually, Render Everything

When you eventually prepare to output your DV movie, to be on the safe side you generally should render all effects in your sequence, or you should at least use ExpertRender In/Out after marking In and Out points around the entire sequence.

USING EXPERTRENDER

Using Render-on-the-Fly

Selecting Render-on-the-Fly does not render entire effects; it renders one frame of an effect at the position of the playhead.

Hence, Render-on-the-Fly is a great tool for previewing, on both your external monitor and computer screen, how an effect will look after you render it (**Figure 11.25**).

In fact, if you start playback when the playhead is over an unrendered effect, Xpress Pro uses Render-on-the-Fly to play the sequence on your external monitor. You will see a slow, frame-by-frame preview of your rendered effect at approximately one or two frames per second. That's better than nothing.

Turn off Render-on-the-Fly only if you want to limit the small pauses that result from the processing required.

To turn Render-on-the-Fly on or off:

◆ Choose Clip > Render-on-the-Fly.

Now when you click the Play button over an unrendered effect, Xpress Pro renders the effect frame by frame.

✔ Tip

■ You can interrupt a Render-on-the-Fly operation by simply moving or dragging the position indicator to a different point in the Timeline. Of course, when you stop dragging, Xpress Pro will start rendering the frame on which you land.

These effects are not rendered, but you can preview them using Render-on-the-Fly.

Preview image displayed on the Composer monitor

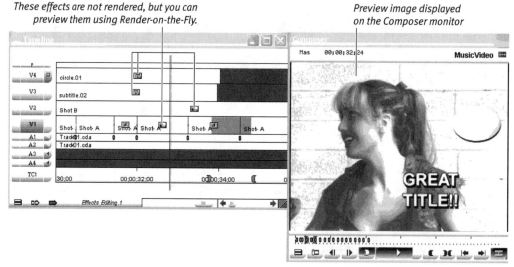

Figure 11.25 Although the effects are not rendered, Render On-the-Fly displays a one-frame preview of what the final image will look like after rendering.

The Submaster Effect and Rendering

The Submaster effect icon may be familiar to you as the icon that marks nested layers. (See "Nesting Multiple Effects" in Chapter 9.) But you can also use Submaster effects to save you rendering time. If you have multiple effects on top of one another in the Timeline, you can use a Submaster effect to combine them into one render file.

The procedure works as follows: You place the Submaster effect above a group of segments that contain effects. Then you render only the Submaster effect, which makes Xpress Pro render all of the effects below it (**Figure 11.26**).

Submaster effect   *The Submaster effect combines all of these effects into one render file.*

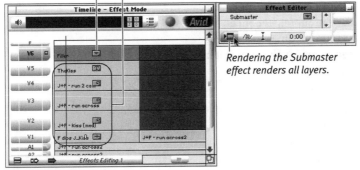

Rendering the Submaster effect renders all layers.

Figure 11.26 In this example, after applying the Submaster effect to black filler on V6, you can render V1 to V6 as one file.

Playing Rendered and Unrendered Effects

Warning: The way in which Xpress Pro plays your effects depends on the position of the playhead when you click Play.

If playback begins on a rendered frame, Xpress Pro attempts to play everything in real time. You see the rendered portion in real time, but the unrendered portion does not play.

If you start playback on an unrendered frame, then Xpress Pro uses Render-on-the-Fly to play the entire effect.

To render with a Submaster effect:

1. Drag the Submaster effect (located in the Image category on the Effect palette) to the top layer of a group of effects that you want to render as one.

   You can apply the Submaster effect to a video segment or a black filler segment.

2. Click the ▣ Render Effect button (located on the FX tab of the Command palette) to render the Submaster effect.

   Xpress Pro renders all of the effects below the Submaster effect.

✔ Tips

- Once you make a change to one of the effects under the Submaster effect, the Submaster group becomes unrendered, and you need to render the Submaster effect again.

- To create a black filler segment that matches the length of the effects below it, use the Add Edit button (located on the Edit tab of the Command palette) to force edits on the filler.

Render File Management Strategies

When Xpress Pro renders your effects (including titles and motion effects), the program creates one or both of the following types of effect:

- **Rendered effects (also called precompute clips):** These can be displayed in a bin, using the Set Bin Display command in a bin's Fast menu (**Figure 11.27**).

- **Associated source media files:** These are miscellaneous data files created by your renders. Conveniently, when you render an effect more than once, older effect files are overwritten or deleted. You cannot display these files in your bin, however.

(For more information about precompute files and source media files, see Chapter 5, "Preparing to Edit.")

You can also display render-related precompute clips and source media files by using the following:

- **Files > Reveal File:** This command points you directly to the source media files associated with a particular precompute clip. Just select the precompute clip in your bin and choose File > Reveal File.

  (For more information about the Reveal File command, see Chapter 13, "Media and Project Management.")

- **Media tool display:** You can use the Media tool to display precompute clips and source media files that are associated with a particular project or hard drive.

  (For more information about using the Media tool, see Chapter 13.)

After you reveal or display precompute clips or associated source media files, you can delete them if you don't think they're needed.

Select this to display precompute files.

Figure 11.27 To see the precompute files in your bin, choose Set Bin Display from the bin Fast menu and select Rendered Effects from the Set Bin Display dialog box.

Working with Audio

Xpress Pro provides several audio tools that enable you to mix levels and apply sound effects without relying on another application. You can make broad track-level adjustments with the Audio Mix tool's virtual sliders, or detailed adjustments using audio keyframes, also known as rubber bands.

You can also do audio effect work in Xpress Pro, applying EQ or any of a variety of Digidesign or third-party AudioSuite plug-ins, all the while using audio effect templates to decrease unnecessary repetition.

Of course, getting the knack for how Xpress Pro handles audio requires knowing the program's limitations as well as the relevant workarounds. Sure, you can monitor only eight tracks at a time and apply only one AudioSuite plug-in effect per audio segment. But if you're willing to do some extra grunt work, like performing multiple audio mixdowns, you can stretch Xpress Pro's audio abilities a greater distance than you might expect.

Keep in mind that if you plan to hand your audio tracks off to a sound designer who will mix and sweeten everything in ProTools (or a similar application), then you may not want to be overzealous in manipulating levels, pans, and effects in Xpress Pro when it's all going to be redone by someone else anyway.

About Audio Workflow

The key to understanding Xpress Pro's audio tools is to forget what they're named and focus on what they do.

Xpress Pro's audio tools—which are often redundant with one another—won't seem as daunting when you realize that their functions boil down to one or more of the following: monitoring your audio, adjusting audio levels, adjusting audio pan values, and applying and manipulating audio effects.

Simplified further, the function of audio editing is to monitor your sound and fix any problems you hear.

Monitoring Your Sound

Monitoring your audio—a task that involves your ears as well as your eyes—allows you catch sound problems such as distortion, peaking, inaudibility, hiss, and hum.

Using the Xpress Pro audio meter—displayed in the Audio tool and on the Timeline toolbar—you can visually monitor your output (and input) levels to make sure your sound is audible without any distortion (**Figure 12.1**).

Furthermore, by using Timeline monitor buttons, the Audio Loop button, and In and Out points, you can isolate particular audio tracks or sequence sections and play them out to your headphones or speakers through either your computer's sound card or another connected device (such as Mojo or your DV camera).

(The tasks in this chapter related to monitoring sound include "Displaying Audio Waveforms," "Monitoring Peak Levels," "Turning Audio Tracks On and Off," "Using Audio Loop Play to Isolate Audio Sections," and "Scrubbing Audio.")

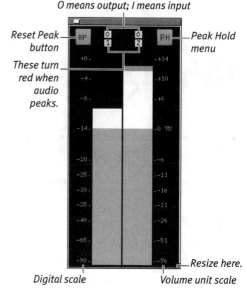

O means output; I means input

Reset Peak button — Peak Hold menu

These turn red when audio peaks.

Digital scale — Volume unit scale

Resize here.

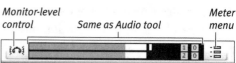

Monitor-level control — Same as Audio tool — Meter menu

Figure 12.1 You can visually monitor your output levels in one of two places: the Audio tool (above) or the Timeline toolbar (below).

✔ Tip

- Another way to visually track your audio is to turn on Timeline audio waveform display by selecting Sample Plot in the Timeline Fast menu. (See "Displaying Audio Waveforms" later in this chapter.)

Apply changes to multiple
segments using the Fast menu.

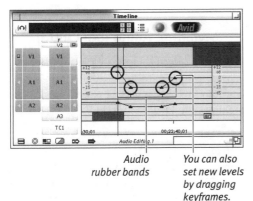

Set pan   Set level   Or set   Or set
here.   here.   pan here.   level here.

Audio   You can also
rubber bands   set new levels
                 by dragging
                 keyframes.

Figure 12.2 You can raise or lower the overall level for
one or more segments, as well as adjust audio pan
levels, using either the Audio Mix tool or the Automation Gain tool. You can create audio rubber bands
in the Automation Gain tool or directly in the Timeline.

Fixing Your Sound

Once you pinpoint the particular audio that
needs improvement, you can adjust it in one
or more of the following ways:

◆ You can adjust audio levels using either
the Audio Mix tool or the Automation
Gain tool. You can also create audio
rubber bands (graphical audio-level
keyframes) directly in the Timeline. This
allows you to boost your audio in some
areas and lower it in others.

(For tasks related to audio-level adjustment, see "Adjusting Audio Levels" later
in this chapter.)

◆ You can adjust audio pan values by
manipulating each track's pan setting
in either the Audio Mix tool or the
Automation Gain tool. You can send
each track to the left speaker, right
speaker, or somewhere in between the
two speakers.

Figure 12.2 illustrates Xpress Pro's level
and pan controls.

continues on next page

Use the Timeline!

Since many of the Timeline's capabilities
and features are redundant with those
of other audio tools, you can usually
perform audio functions faster in the
Timeline than anywhere else.

In the Timeline toolbar, you can see
almost everything that the Audio tool
displays, plus you can perform any level
adjustments in the Timeline without the
use of the Audio Mix or Automation Gain
tool. (See the sidebar "When You Don't
Need the Audio Mix and Automation
Gain Tools" later in this chapter.)

◆ You can apply an audio effect using either the EQ tool (to adjust frequency range levels) or the AudioSuite window (to apply a Digidesign plug-in). You can also drag and drop the audio effects listed on the Effect palette.

Audio effects can cut out unwanted sounds or alter sounds in specialized ways (**Figure 12.3**).

(For more information, see "Applying AudioSuite Plug-in Effects" later in this chapter.)

✔ Tips

■ To activate the Audio Mix tool level sliders, you must first select Audio Clip Gain from the Timeline Fast menu. To activate the Automation Gain tool level sliders and rubber banding, you must first select Auto Clip Gain from the Timeline Fast menu.

■ To create an audio-level keyframe on a Timeline audio segment (the first step in creating rubber bands), select a Timeline track and click Add Keyframe on the FX tab of the Command palette.

■ The Timeline, Audio Mix tool, Automation Gain tool, and AudioSuite tool all have track monitor buttons that enable you to listen to particular tracks (and mute others) while you use the tools.

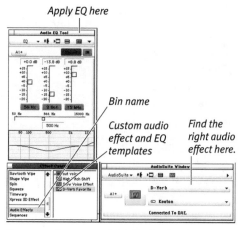

Apply EQ here

Bin name

Custom audio effect and EQ templates

Find the right audio effect here.

Figure 12.3 You can apply audio plug-ins from the AudioSuite window or the Effect palette. You can apply EQ effects from the EQ tool or the Effect palette.

Avoiding Audio Tool Clutter

You don't need to open all four of the principle audio tools—Automation Gain, Audio Mix, EQ, and AudioSuite—in Xpress Pro at the same time.

Rather, to save monitor space, you can toggle between all four of these tools from within the same window. Just click the upper-left corner of the open audio tool and choose a different tool from the list that appears (**Figure 12.4**).

Figure 12.4 To toggle from one audio tool to another, click the Effect Mode Selector menu of a tool and choose from the list that appears.

Changing Capture-Related Audio Project Settings

In Chapter 4, you learned how to configure the audio project settings (**Figure 12.5**) related to capturing and importing audio source media. (For a full explanation of audio project settings, see "Configuring Your Audio Settings for Capture or Recording" in Chapter 4.)

However, when you begin to edit your project, after capturing and importing, your audio project settings take on a different significance.

If special circumstances arise, you may change audio project settings in the middle of a project. Such changes will not affect media files that Xpress Prohas already created; they affect only media files created after your settings change.

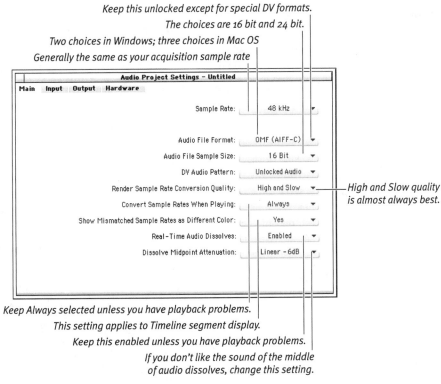

Keep this unlocked except for special DV formats.
The choices are 16 bit and 24 bit.
Two choices in Windows; three choices in Mac OS
Generally the same as your acquisition sample rate

High and Slow quality is almost always best.

Keep Always selected unless you have playback problems.
This setting applies to Timeline segment display.
Keep this enabled unless you have playback problems.
If you don't like the sound of the middle of audio dissolves, change this setting.

Figure 12.5 The most important choices you make in the Audio Project Settings dialog box are the audio file format and audio sample rate.

This section describes audio project settings as they pertain to editing and working with existing audio, rather than capturing or importing.

♦ **Audio File Format:** This setting governs the format of mixdown files and new audio master clips created by the AudioSuite tool. (For an explanation of audio file formats, see "Configuring Your Audio Settings for Capture or Recording" in Chapter 4.)

(For reasons why you might change the audio file format setting, see the sidebar "Changing Your Audio File Format in Midproject" on the next page.)

♦ **Sample Rate:** This setting governs the sample rate—32, 44.1, or 48 kHz—at which your sequence plays audio. If your sequence contains a mixture of segments with different sample rates, Xpress Pro can play them at one sample rate in real time.

(For an explanation of sample rates, see "Configuring Your Audio Settings for Capture or Recording" in Chapter 4.)

You might change this setting if a different sample rate becomes more prevalent in your sequence. (For more information, see "Converting the Sample Rate" later in this chapter.)

♦ **Audio File Sample Size:** You should not change this setting after capture and import unless you want to recapture your audio at a different sound quality (the choices are 16 bit to 24 bit).

(For an explanation of audio sample size, see "Configuring Your Audio Settings for Capture or Recording" in Chapter 4.)

♦ **Render Sample Rate Conversion Quality:** This setting governs the quality of any sample rate conversion you may perform during your project, and you should keep High and Slow selected. That said, you might choose Low and Fast when you have hundreds of files to convert and the clock is ticking.

(For more information, see "Converting the Sample Rate" later in this chapter.)

✔ Tips

■ Other audio project settings covered in Chapter 4 include DV Audio Pattern (on the Main tab) and Input Gain and Input Source (on the Input tab).

■ The level choice made for the Master (monitor) Volume Output setting will override your computer's output volume setting. Since this can be annoying while jumping between Xpress Pro and other applications, try adjusting your computer's output level so it matches Xpress Pro's setting.

■ All of the output settings depend on your particular audio hardware.

Don't Touch That Slider

The Output tab of your Audio Project Settings dialog box has a slider for output gain: This slider controls the overall volume output. For DV projects, always keep this slider at 0 dB, since Xpress Pro is pre-calibrated for a level optimal with most consumer DV gear.

In analog projects, you should also keep this slider at 0 dB except in very special circumstances, such as when you need to boost the level of your entire sequence for output to tape.

Changing Your Audio File Format in Midproject

Unless absolutely necessary, you usually won't need to switch your audio format—be it WAVE, AIFF, or SDII—in the middle of a project, because you want your movie's audio to be all the same format eventually.

Hence, editors start with audio source clips that are all the same format before beginning to edit.

That said, in special circumstances—you just received a whole bunch of new audio material in a different format and you don't have the time or space to convert it, for instance—you may need to switch formats.

Switching formats means that any new audio you import or capture will have the same format. The switch does not convert the old audio already in your sequence.

Xpress Pro can play a mixture of formats within the same sequence while you edit, but at the end of the project, you'll probably want to convert all of your audio to the same format. To do this, select the sequence in your bin and choose File > Export. Then choose Audio from the Export As pull-down menu and choose your final audio file format.

If you try to export a sequence containing mixed sample rates as an OMF file, Xpress Pro warns you that your OMF file may not work. Do not take that chance (**Figure 12.6**).

(For more information on OMF export, see Chapter 14, "Outputting and Exporting".)

Figure 12.6 If you try to export a sequence that contains mixed sample rates, Xpress Pro will display a warning.

Converting the Sample Rate

When you set your project's audio sample rate in the Audio Project Settings dialog box—to 32, 44.1, or 48 kHz—you determine the sample rate at which Xpress Pro plays your sequence. This setting does not, however, alter the sample rate of any existing source clip or segment in your project.

To actually convert existing clips to a different sample rate, you need to do so specifically. You can convert clips in two ways:

◆ **Select and convert individual clips.** You can select clips in your bin and then convert their sample rates, keeping or deleting the original clips.

◆ **Select and convert sequences.** If you select and convert a sequence in your bin, then Xpress Pro converts every source clip that relates to every segment within that sequence.

(For more information on audio sample rates, see "Configuring your Audio Settings for Capture or Recording" in Chapter 4.)

✔ Tip

■ To find your clips' audio sample rate, click the Text tab in a bin window and look at the Audio column (**Figure 12.7**).

48 kHz   44.1 kHz

Figure 12.7 Check a clip's audio sample rate by checking the Audio column on the Text tab of a bin. Audio sample rates are not listed for sequences (since they may contain a variety).

Checking Sample Rates by Color

If you want to know whether or not audio segments in your Timeline have different sample rates, open the Audio Project Settings dialog box and select Yes from the Show Mismatched Sample Rates as Different Color pull-down menu (it's selected by default).

With this choice selected, a 32 kHz Timeline segment (to use an example) appears in a different color than a 48 kHz segment.

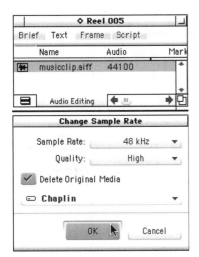

Figure 12.8 Here, a 44.1 kHz clip is about to be converted to 48 kHz, with the original media deleted.

Convert Your Sample Rate at the Right Time

If you're working with one sample rate but know you eventually want to finish in a different rate, just wait until the end of your project.

For example, if you're editing a project from source clips recorded at 32 kHz (also called 12-bit sound) and need to convert everything to 48 kHz (also called 16-bit sound) to meet some broadcast standard, wait until you've finished with the project. At that point, all you have to do is convert your sequence audio and not every single source clip in your bins.

(For more information on sample rates, see "Configuring Your Audio Settings for Capture or Recording" in Chapter 4.)

To change the audio sample rate of a clip or sequence:

1. Select a sequence or clip in a bin. Shift-click to select multiple sequences or clips.

2. Choose Bin > Change Sample Rate.

3. In the dialog box that appears, choose 32 kHz, 44.1 kHz, or 48 kHz as the sample rate.

4. Choose Low, Medium, or High quality.

5. If you want to delete the master clips that have the old sample rate, select Delete Original Media.

6. Choose a drive for the new source files.

7. Click OK (**Figure 12.8**).

   Xpress Pro converts your selected clips or sequences to the new sample rate. If you selected Delete Original Media, old versions of the clips are kept in their bins, but Xpress Pro deletes their source media files (the clips play silence).

   Xpress Pro adds a .new extension to the newly created clips.

✔ Tip

■ Choose High quality for your new sample rate unless you have a huge batch of clips to convert in a short period of time. A low-quality conversion is faster, but usually not worth the result.

Configuring Editing and FX-Related Settings

Before starting to manipulate source clips or Timeline audio, you need to configure some other general audio settings in the Audio and Audio Project Settings dialog boxes. You can change these at any time during your project. These settings include the following:

◆ **Monitor Volume (also called Master Volume):** Found on the Output tab of the Audio Project Settings dialog box and on the Timeline toolbar. This setting governs the volume of your project's audio on your speakers or headphones during editing or output.

Do not confuse this setting with the Output Gain setting, which should be kept at 0 dB except for special analog output scenarios (**Figure 12.9**). (See the sidebar "Don't Touch That Slider" earlier in this chapter.)

◆ **Audio Tools Response:** Found in the Audio Settings dialog box. This setting governs how quickly adjustments made with the Audio Mix, Automation Gain, and AudioSuite tools take effect. Usually, this selection should remain set to Default (**Figure 12.10**). If you adjust a level, however, and there's an intolerable delay before the change takes effect, then you can select a faster setting, provided that your computer is fast enough to handle it.

◆ **Convert Sample Rates When Playing:** Found on the Main tab of the Audio Project Settings dialog box. If you start to have playback problems and your Timeline contains audio of different rates, disable this setting. Xpress Pro has the ability to play a sequence that contains a mixture of different audio sample rates, but doing so taxes the system. If your system works fine with this setting selected, then always keep it enabled.

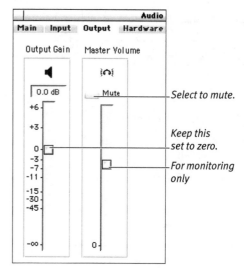

Figure 12.9 The monitor volume (or master volume) is the volume of what you hear through your headphones or external speakers while editing. This is different from the output gain, which should be kept at 0 dB unless you need to raise the level of your entire project for output to tape.

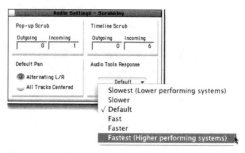

Figure 12.10 If it takes too long hear a level or EQ change, you may want to increase the Audio Tools Response setting if you have a system that can handle the speed.

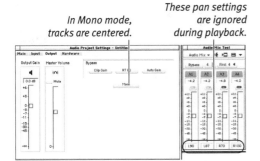

In Mono mode, tracks are centered.

These pan settings are ignored during playback.

Figure 12.11 If you choose Mono as your Mix mode, then Xpress Pro ignores all pan settings in the Audio Mix or Automation Gain tool.

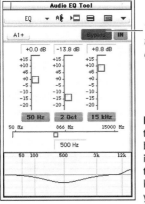

This temporarily turns off Audio EQ adjustments.

Figure 12.12 It's best to use the Bypass button provided by individual audio tools. That way, you know exactly what you're turning off.

◆ **Mix Mode Selection:** Found on the Output tab of the Audio Project Settings dialog box. Keep Stereo selected for this setting unless you absolutely know that you want a monaural project. Stereo, the default, mixes your audio tracks as stereo pairs; this enables you to pan tracks to either the left or right speaker.

Choosing Mono here mixes every track to the center and disables panning (**Figure 12.11**).

◆ **Bypass (Clip Gain/RT EQ/Auto Gain):** Found on the Output tab of the Audio Project Settings dialog box. Selecting one of the three Bypass buttons turns off any level adjustments made with the Audio Mix tool, EQ tool, or Automation Gain tool, respectively.

(Note: Bypassing Automation Gain turns off all rubber-band level adjustment.)

You never really need to bother with the Bypass buttons here, because you can always use the Bypass button available on individual audio tools (**Figure 12.12**).

✔ Tips

■ The two dissolve-related audio project settings are covered in "The Two Dissolve Settings" later in this chapter.

■ For the audio settings related to digital scrubbing, see "Scrubbing Audio" later in this chapter.

■ For the audio settings related to panning, see "Panning Audio Tracks and Segments" later in this chapter.

CONFIGURING EDITING AND FX-RELATED SETTINGS

Displaying Audio Waveforms

Audio waveforms are graphical representations of your audio that can help you make precise audio edits as well as gauge the relative loudness or softness of an audio recording.

The only problem with audio waveforms is that Xpress Pro takes a long time to draw them on your screen, especially if your computer monitor is very large and you have several audio tracks. To cut down on Xpress Pro's screen-drawing time, you can tell the program to display only those waveforms between Timeline In and Out points.

To turn on audio waveform display:

◆ In the Timeline Fast menu, select Sample Plot.

Xpress Pro draws waveforms over your Timeline audio segments (**Figure 12.13**).

To display only waveforms between In and Out points:

◆ Open your Timeline settings, select Show Marked Waveforms, and click OK.

All Timeline waveforms disappear except those between Timeline In and Out points.

✔ Tips

■ To see the waveforms for a source clip, click the Toggle Source/Record button at the left of the Timeline. This button displays your source tracks like a sequence in the Timeline window.

■ If your audio is so loud that the waveform blacks out the Timeline, press Ctrl+Alt+K (Windows) or Command+Option+K (Mac) to reduce the size of the waveform without reducing the size of the track.

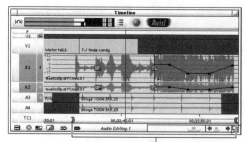

Xpress Pro displays waveforms between In and Out points.

Figure 12.13 To save audio waveform screen drawing time, select Show Marked Waveforms in the Timeline settings.

■ If your audio is so soft that you cannot see the waveforms, press Ctrl+Alt+L (Windows) or Command+Option+L (Mac) to enlarge the size of the waveform without enlarging the size of the track.

■ You can halt the redrawing of audio waveforms by pressing Ctrl+. (period) (Windows) or Command+. (Mac).

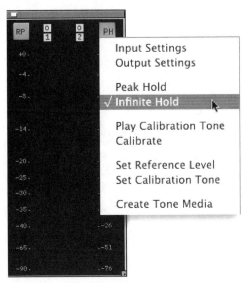

Figure 12.14 Click the PH (Peak Hold) button to select the behavior of Audio tool peak warnings. If you choose Peak Hold, then an audio peak warning will light up for only a couple of seconds. If you choose Infinite Hold, then the peak warning remains lighted until you click RP (Reset Peak).

Monitoring Peak Levels

By default, the Audio tool (and its miniature version in the Timeline) displays your output levels: the levels of the sound that will eventually go out to recording devices such as decks or cameras via FireWire or the Mojo box.

The most important output-level problem to watch out for in the Audio tool is audio peaking: extremely high audio levels that may result in perceivable audio distortion.

When you are outputting a digital signal (as you do when working with DV), audio peaking is unforgivable. Any levels above 0 dB on the digital scale will result in distortion. You should eliminate all audio peaks in your project before you output to tape.

If an audio channel peaks, its channel number turns red in the Audio tool to warn you that you need to lower levels to avoid audio distortion.

The Peak Hold menu (and the Timeline's Meter menu) have two options that determine how the Audio tool warns you about peaks (**Figure 12.14**):

◆ **Peak Hold:** With this selected, the Audio tool lights up a peaked audio channel number (in red) for a couple of seconds and then continues to monitor levels as usual.

Select this option if you are in the middle of editing and don't need to fix every audio problem immediately. Xpress Pro will then inform you of the location of multiple audio peak problems in your sequence as you play your movie.

continues on next page

◆ **Infinite Hold:** With this option selected, the Audio tool lights up a peaked audio channel number (in red) and keeps it lighted until you either click the RP (Reset Peak) button or select Reset Peak in the Timeline Meter menu.

Select this option if you want to address any audio peak problems when they arise.

✔ Tips

- The number of channels displayed in the Audio tool (between 2 and 8) depends on the configuration of your system.

- To create an audio tone that you can edit into the Timeline, select Create Tone Media from either the Peak Hold (PH) or Timeline Meter menu. (For more information, see "Preparing for Output to Tape" in Chapter 14.)

- You know that the Audio tool displays output levels (as opposed to input levels) when it displays a little O button above the channel numbers. If it displays I (for input), click the button to change it to O.

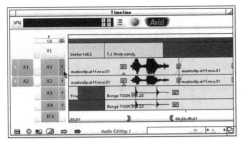

Figure 12.15 Here, to listen to track A1 alone (soloing it), you would Ctrl-click (Windows) or Command-click (Mac) its monitor button. The soloed button will turn green. Another click will unsole the track.

Pro Advice: Use Designated Audio Tracks

If you plan to give your project's audio to a sound designer, you need to consider that most audio professionals prefer you to assign certain sounds to certain tracks, to make their editing lives a lot easier.

Typically, your final edit in Xpress should have eight tracks (since that's the maximum you can hear at any one time). You might break those tracks down as follows:

◆ **Tracks A1–A2:** Dialogue

◆ **Tracks A3–A4:** Sound effects

◆ **Tracks A5–A6:** Music

◆ **Tracks A7–A8:** Voice -over

This is just an example, but the point is that you should separate different types of sounds onto different tracks. Your sound designer will love you for it.

Turning Audio Tracks On and Off

For the most part, turning audio tracks on and off in the Timeline is a straightforward enterprise using the Timeline's audio monitor buttons:

◆ **To hear an audio track:** Click its monitor button so that a monitor icon appears.

◆ **To solo an audio track (hearing that track and only that track):** Ctrl-click (Windows) or Command-click (Mac) a monitor button so that it turns green (**Figure 12.15**).

◆ **To give two audio tracks digital scrubbing priority:** Make sure those track have gold speaker icons. (See "Scrubbing Audio" later in this chapter.)

However, there is one important limitation: in Xpress Pro, you can hear only eight tracks at once. If you have more than eight tracks of audio and you want to hear all of the audio play at the same time, you may need to perform an audio mixdown of two or more tracks. (For more information, see "Mixing Down Audio Tracks" later in this chapter.)

(For more information on monitor buttons, see "Monitoring Tracks" in Chapter 6.)

✔ Tip

■ If your project is set for stereo, odd-numbered tracks play from the left speaker and even-numbered tracks play from the right. (For information on panning tracks, see "Panning Audio Tracks and Segments" later in this chapter.)

Using Audio Loop Play to Isolate Audio Sections

When listening to audio adjustments made in an Audio Mix, Automation Gain, Audio EQ, or AudioSuite window, you will usually want to hear only a specific part of your Timeline on selected tracks.

To listen to selected portions of your Timeline, use the 🔲 Audio Loop Play button on the Play tab of the Command palette. The resulting looped playback follows one of the following In and Out point configurations:

- **If you do not mark any In or Out points in the Timeline or Composer:** Audio Loop Play plays the shortest segment at the location of the position indicator on selected tracks.

- **With an In and an Out point marked in the Timeline:** Audio Loop Play keeps playing the section between the points until you press the spacebar (the Play button) to stop playback (**Figure 12.16**).

- **With only an Out point marked in the Timeline:** Audio Loop Play uses the position indicator as your In point.

- **With only an In point marked in the Timeline:** Audio Loop Play uses the position indicator as your Out point.

Audio Loop button

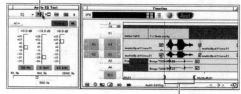

Xpress Pro loops A1 and A2 between the In and Out points.

Figure 12.16 Here, to monitor changes made with the EQ tool for a selected area, you set In and Out points in the Timeline, monitor the appropriate tracks, and click Audio Loop.

Scrubbing Audio

Scrubbing audio means playing your audio at different speeds in order to locate a specific frame in your source clip or sequence based on what you hear.

Xpress Pro offers two types of audio scrubbing:

◆ **Smooth Audio Scrubbing:** This is the type of scrubbing you do when you use the J-K-L keys—Play Reverse, Pause, and Play Forward—to play a clip or sequence in slow motion, in reverse, or up to 5X normal speed. (At 8X normal speed, Xpress Pro does not play the audio.)

(For more information on using the J-K-L keys to play clips and sequences, see the sidebar "The Power of the J-K-L Keys" in Chapter 6.)

◆ **Digital Audio Scrubbing:** A more precise way of scrubbing through your audio, digital scrubbing involves manually dragging the position indicator through your clip or sequence while holding the Shift key. The way it works depends on your digital scrub settings, although the default settings are best for most circumstances.

When you digitally scrub in the Timeline or Composer, the tracks that have the gold speaker monitor icons have priority. If Xpress has trouble digitally scrubbing all of your tracks, you will hear the priority tracks, but not the others.

To digitally scrub through audio:

Do one of the following:

◆ In a source monitor, Composer window, or Timeline, Shift-drag the position indicator to the left or right. The speed of the audio depends on how quickly or slowly you drag (**Figure 12.17**).

◆ Shift-click the Step Forward or Step Backward button on the Move tab of the Command palette.

✔ Tip

■ To give an audio track a gold speaker monitor icon—that is, to give it digital scrubbing priority—Alt-click (Windows) or Option-click (Mac) the track's monitor button.

To configure your digital scrub settings:

1. On the Settings tab of your Project window, double-click the active (checkmarked) Audio settings.

2. In the dialog box that appears, enter the number of frames of audio before and after the position indicator that you want to hear whenever you perform a digital scrub. The left two boxes pertain to scrubbing in a source monitor, and the right box pertains to the Composer or Timeline.

   To avoid confusion about where your position indicator is, always enter *0* in the left or right box. That way, you'll know you're hearing frames either in back of the position indicator or in front of it (**Figure 12.18**).

✔ Tip

■ The default digital scrub settings (0 and 1) are adequate for most situations, though sometimes it's helpful to enter a higher number than 1 if you want to hear chunks of audio at a time.

Figure 12.17 You can digitally scrub in a source monitor, the Composer, the clipboard monitor, or the Timeline. However, the Timeline is usually the best place to scrub because you can match the sound to the audio waveform (Sample Plot) display.

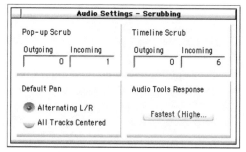

Figure 12.18 With these settings, when you digitally scrub in the Timeline, you will hear six frames of audio at a time in front of the position indicator.

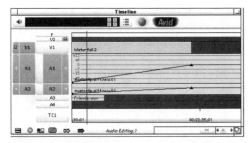

Figure 12.19 Here the beginning of an audio segment fades up, an effect created either by dropping the Dissolve effect onto the segment or clicking the Head Fade button.

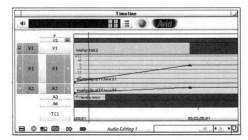

Figure 12.20 Here, the beginning of an audio segment fades up, an effect created by clicking Add Keyframe in two different spots on the segments and dragging the first keyframe down to silence. The result is similar to Figure 12.19.

Don't Drag the Dissolve Effect

Adding a fade or dissolve by dragging and dropping the Dissolve effect from the Effect palette is a pain because Xpress Pro does not automatically apply it to all selected tracks; you have to drop it on each individual audio cut point. But usually you'll need to affect two tracks at once. That's why QuickTransition is better for adding a dissolve to audio cut points.

Fading or Dissolving Audio

The most common audio manipulations you'll perform are likely audio fades and dissolves. Fades and dissolves allow you to smooth out hard audio cut points that would otherwise jar the listener.

Xpress Pro gives you two principle ways to create fades or dissolves:

♦ **Dissolve effect:** The fastest way to fade audio is to apply the Dissolve effect to audio cut points by clicking the Head Fade or Tale Fade button. For dissolves, the fastest method is to click Quick-Transition and use it to add a dissolve to the audio cut point (**Figure 12.19**). (For more information on QuickTransition, see "Using QuickTransition" in Chapter 9.)

♦ **Automation gain keyframes:** You can manually create audio fades by creating and dragging audio keyframes (also called rubber bands; see **Figure 12.20**). (For more information on this method, see "Creating and Manipulating Audio-Level Keyframes" later in this chapter. For more advice about audio fades, see the sidebar "How to Fade Audio: Avid Tradition vs. Rubber Bands vs. the Fade Buttons" later in this chapter.)

✔ Tip

■ To create automation gain keyframes (audio rubber bands), you need to have Auto Clip Gain selected in the Timeline Fast menu.

To create an audio fade with Head Fade or Tail Fade:

1. Park the position indicator either where the fade up will end or the fade down will begin (**Figure 12.21**).

2. Select the audio tracks that you want to affect.

3. *Do one of the following:*

   ▲ To add a fade up that starts at the beginning of the segment and ends where the position indicator is, click the Head Fade button.

   ▲ To add a fade down that starts where the position indicator is and ends at the end of the segment, click the Tail Fade button (**Figure 12.22**).

   A Dissolve effect icon appears on the audio segment. Play back the fade to make sure it sounds as expected.

✔ Tip

■ For more information on adjusting dissolves, see "Modifying Segment and Transition Effects" in Chapter 9.

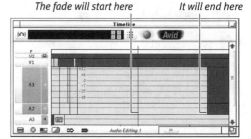

The fade will start here   *It will end here*

Figure 12.21 Before clicking the Tail Fade button, place the position indicator where the fade will start on the segment.

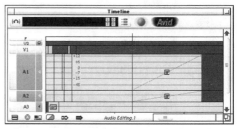

Figure 12.22 Clicking Tail Fade adds a dissolve ending at the cut point on selected tracks. In this case, the dissolve fades to silence because the audio segment is next to black filler.

What Is an Audio Fade, Really?

In the world of Xpress editing, an audio fade is actually a dissolve.

Fade is just a term for a Dissolve effect aligned to start at a cut point (if it's a fade up) or end at a cut point (if it's a fade down).

Hence, if you fade an audio segment that is flush against another audio segment, you will hear the adjacent segment fading down or up while your segment fades up or down. It sounds like a dissolve.

So what if you want to hear a more traditional head or tail fade?

If you want a an audio segment to fade up from nothing or fade down to nothing, then you need to place that segment next to a black filler segment.

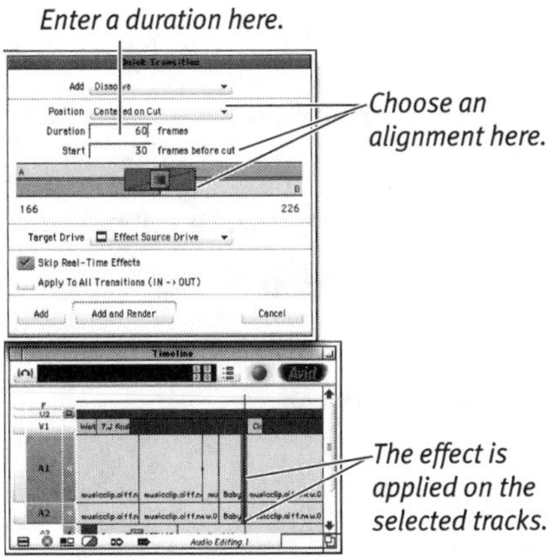

Enter a duration here.

Choose an alignment here.

The effect is applied on the selected tracks.

Figure 12.23 Here, QuickTransition will add a two-second audio dissolve that is centered on the cut.

The Two Dissolve Settings

Two parameters in the Audio Project Settings dialog box affect the behavior of audio dissolves:

◆ **Real-Time Audio Dissolves:** You should always keep this setting enabled, unless real-time audio dissolves start posing playback problems.

◆ **Dissolve Midpoint Attenuation:** If you create an audio dissolve and right in the middle the level takes a dip down, then you might want to change this setting.

Your two choices are Constant and Linear. Constant maintains a consistent sound level through the cut point during a dissolve, and Linear maintains a consistent amplitude.

The effect of each choice should be judged on a case-by-case basis. Change this setting only when what you hear in the middle of a dissolve doesn't sound right.

To create an audio dissolve with the Dissolve effect:

1. Place the position indicator near the audio edit point that you want to affect.

2. Select the tracks containing the edit point that you want to affect.

3. Click ▦ QuickTransition. In the dialog box that appears, choose Dissolve (or a custom effect template) as the effect type, enter a duration, choose an alignment, and click Add and Render (**Figure 12.23**).

   The Dissolve icon appears on the selected audio transition points. If you play the edit point now, you'll hear a smooth transition between the two audio segments.

   (For information on using custom effect templates with QuickTransition, see "Applying Favorites with QuickTransition" in Chapter 9.)

How to Fade Audio: Avid Tradition vs. Rubber Bands vs. the Fade Buttons

Before Avid added audio keyframe capabilities (rubber bands) to its software, editors created fades in the following manner:

1. Use Add Edit to split a segment where the fade up ends as well as where the fade down begins.

2. Use the Audio Mix tool to lower the levels of the first and third segments.

3. At the two new cut points, add cross-dissolves.

4. For the alignment of the first cross-dissolve, select Ending at Cut.

5. For the alignment of the second cross-dissolve, select Starting at Cut.

Editors who still create fades this way mainly do so because of tradition (**Figure 12.24**).

(For more information on adjusting dissolves, see "Modifying Segment and Transition Effects" in Chapter 9.)

However, rubber bands usually provide a faster method for creating these kinds of fades. Here's all you have to do:

1. Press Add Keyframe where you want the fade up to begin and end, as well as where you want the fade down to begin and end (a total of four keyframes).

2. Alt-drag (Windows) or Option-drag (Mac) the first and last keyframes to the lowest level.

    (See "Creating and Manipulating Audio-Level Keyframes" later in this chapter.)

This method may feel especially comfortable if you're used to programs like Premiere, Final Cut Pro, and ProTools (**Figure 12.25**).

However, for simple audio fades like these, an even faster method is to use the Head Fade and Tail Fade buttons on the FX tab of the Command palette. (See "Fading or Dissolving Audio" earlier in this chapter.)

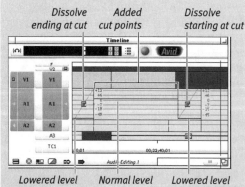

Figure 12.24 The old, traditional way of creating fades in Xpress Pro is to create two cut points on a segment with Add Edit, lower the level on the first and third piece, and add dissolves to the cut points.

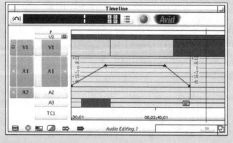

Figure 12.25 Head and tail fades were created using four audio keyframes.

FADING OR DISSOLVING AUDIO

Adjusting Audio Levels

Xpress Pro provides you with two tools—the Audio Mix tool and the Automation Gain tool—to adjust levels on source audio tracks and Timeline audio tracks.

◆ **Audio Mix tool:** Use this tool to make overall level adjustments to one or more audio segments. To enable the tool, you must select Audio Clip Gain in the Timeline Fast menu.

◆ **Automation Gain tool:** Use this tool to create detailed, keyframed level adjustments (also called rubber bands—graphical Timeline representations of audio levels that you can drag up and down). You can also use this tool to make record-level adjustments in real time. To enable the tool, you must select Auto Clip Gain in the Timeline Fast menu.

Before reading about how to use Audio Mix or Automation Gain, you might as well know Xpress Pro's dirty secret: editors can make most level adjustments they need without opening either of these tools!

(For more information, see the sidebar "When You Don't Need the Audio Mix and Automation Gain Tools" later in this chapter.)

✔ Tips

■ As for recording level adjustments with the Automation Gain too, only those with digital mixers hooked up to Xpress Pro via MIDI can take advantage of this feature.

■ The Audio Mix tool displays only monitored audio tracks.

■ If you plan to add audio rubber bands to a segment, you should not also adjust the segment's overall level with the Audio Mix tool, or things can get very confusing. (See the sidebar "Audio Mix Versus Automation Gain: Use One or the Other" on the next page.)

Audio Mix vs. Automation Gain: Use One or the Other

You should avoid applying both Audio Mix and Automation Gain adjustments to the same segment.

The reason is that Audio Mix level adjustments and rubber bands are additive. Thus, if you raise a segment 2 dB with the Audio Mix tool and also raise it 5 dB with the Automation Gain tool, then what you're really doing is raising the segment 7 dB.

You can then become confused, especially since Xpress Pro does not graphically represent the cumulative level adjustment (in the preceding example, it would simply display an audio mix level of 2 and an Automation Gain level of 5) (**Figure 12.26**).

Therefore, use one tool or the other. Either make broad level adjustments to chunks of your Timeline or create detailed, keyframed adjustments (rubber bands).

But also remember this: Every level change you can make in the Audio Mix tool can also be accomplished with the Automation Gain tool (as long as you add audio keyframes to the segments you're adjusting).

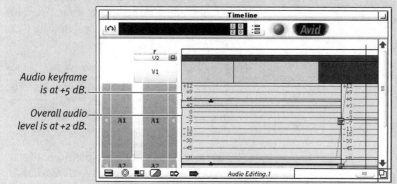

Audio keyframe is at +5 dB.

Overall audio level is at +2 dB.

Figure 12.26 The Audio Mix and Automation Gain tools are additive, which is why it's best to use one or the other. For example, here the overall level is +2 dB, and the audio rubber-band level is at +5 dB, for a total +7 dB raise.

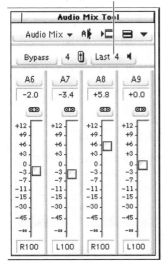

Which Set of Tracks to Display button

Figure 12.27 If you're working with more than four tracks of audio, you can click the Which Set of Tracks to Display button to display the last four tracks in your audio tool without having to display all of your tracks.

Audio Mix and Automation Gain Tool Buttons

Both the Audio Mix and Automation Gain tools have the following important button in common:

◆ **Bypass:** If you select this button in any particular audio tool, Xpress Pro turns off any level adjustment you've made with the tool. You can use this button to compare your segments before and after your level adjustments.

To determine what tracks to display in these tools, use the following two buttons:

◆ **Number of Mix Panes:** This button determines whether the tool displays four or eight tracks. Usually, you should keep the button for four tracks active.

◆ **Which Set of Tracks to Display:** This button toggles between display of the first four tracks in your Timeline and display of the last four tracks in your Timeline. You can use this button as an alternative to displaying a full eight tracks in the window (**Figure 12.27**).

ADJUSTING AUDIO LEVELS

To adjust the global level of one audio segment:

1. From the Timeline Fast menu, select Audio Clip Gain and click the monitor buttons for the tracks that you want to hear.

2. Choose Tools > Audio Mix Tool to open the Audio Mix tool.

3. To adjust the level of the segment at the location of the position indicator, *do one of the following*:

   ▲ Drag the level slider under the appropriate track button.

   ▲ Click the level value box under the track number button and type a positive or negative number for the track level.

   A black level line appears on the segment in the Timeline, indicating the track's new volume.

✔ Tip

■ To simultaneously adjust levels on more than one track, click the gang buttons for the tracks that you want to adjust (**Figure 12.28**).

To apply your global-level adjustment to other segments:

1. Place the position indicator over the segment whose level you want to copy elsewhere and *do one of the following*:

   ▲ To apply your level change to an entire track, erase your Timeline In and Out points.

   ▲ To apply your level change to a group of segments across the Timeline, use Mark In and Mark Out to mark all or part of the segment that you want to affect.

2. In the Audio Mix tool (or the Timeline), select the tracks that you want to affect. To select multiple tracks, in the Audio Mix tool hold down Shift.

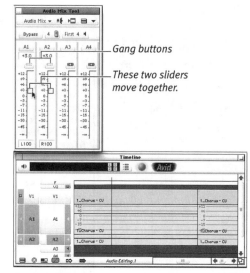

Gang buttons

These two sliders move together.

Figure 12.28 To adjust the audio levels of more than one segment at the location of the position indicator, turn on the gang buttons in the Audio Mix tool for the track that you want to lock together.

3. To paste your level change to all marked segments on selected tracks, click the Audio Mix tool Fast menu and *choose one of the following:*

▲ **Set Level on Track - Global (or Set Level on Track - In/Out):** Choose this option to give every segment on every selected track the same audio level (**Figure 12.29**). If you marked In and Out points, this choice affects only marked segments (**Figure 12.30**).

▲ **Adjust Pan/Vols on Track - Global (or Adjust Pan/Vols on Track - In/Out):** Choose this option to increase or decrease every level on every selected track by the same amount. In the dialog box that appears, type a positive or negative number in the Gain Adjustment in dB box and click OK. If you marked In and Out points, this choice affects only marked segments.

A black level line appears on all marked audio segments on selected tracks, indicating that all marked segments now have the same audio level.

continues on next page

Select the track that contains the segment with the desired audio level.   *Click here.*

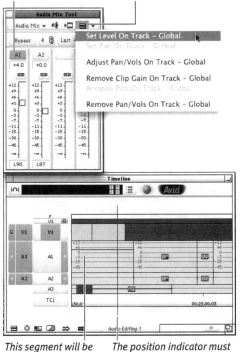

This segment will be applied to every segment on A1.   *The position indicator must be over the segment with the desired audio level.*

Figure 12.29 To apply a segment level change to every other segment on the same track, select that track in the Audio Mix tool and choose Set Level on Track - Global from the Audio Tool's Fast menu.

Make sure to select the appropriate track buttons.

These In and Out points affect four Timeline segments.

Figure 12.30 Any segments that are partially marked by In and/or Out points in the Timeline will be affected when you choose Set Level on Track - In/Out.

✔ Tips

- To return a level value to zero, Alt-click (Windows) or Option-click (Mac) the level slider.

- If you adjust the audio level for a segment that contains a rendered audio effect, that effect becomes unrendered. You can click the Render Effect button in the Audio Mix tool to render it again.

- When adjusting a group of segments, you can get away with setting just an In or just an Out point. Click Mark In if you want to affect every segment from the In point through the end of the sequence. Click Mark Out if you want to affect every segment up to the Out point.

- To choose the correct track button in the Audio Mix tool (step 2 in the preceding task), you can also Alt-click (Windows) or Option-click (Mac) any track button and choose from the list that appears (**Figure 12.31**).

To adjust the audio levels for source clip tracks:

1. Load a source clip into a source monitor and make sure the monitor is active.

2. Open the Audio Mix tool and adjust the tracks as you would for Timeline segments. (See the task "To adjust the global level of one audio segment," earlier in this section.)

✔ Tip

- To help you visualize your source clip level adjustment, you can display your source clip's tracks in the Timeline. To do this, select the 🖭 Toggle Source/Record in Timeline button (**Figure 12.32**).

Alt-click or Option-click here.

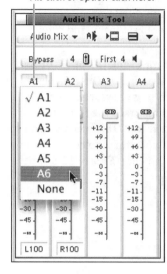

Figure 12.31 If not all track buttons are visible in the Audio Mix tool, you can Alt-click (Windows) or Option-click (Mac) a button and choose from the list that appears.

Timeline record buttons

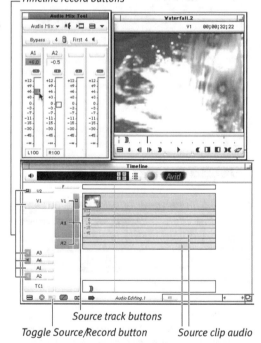

Source track buttons

Toggle Source/Record button

Source clip audio

Figure 12.32 When adjusting a source clip's audio level, before you edit it into the Timeline you may want to use the Toggle Source/Record in Timeline button to display its tracks in the Timeline.

ADJUSTING AUDIO LEVELS

To reset any level adjustments on one or more segments:

1. Depending on what segments you want to affect, *do one of the following:*

▲ To delete level adjustments for either an entire source clip or every segment on one or more tracks, select the appropriate track buttons in the Audio Mix tool but do not mark any In or Out points in the Timeline.

▲ To delete level adjustments for a group of segments across the Timeline on one or more tracks, select the appropriate track buttons in the Audio Mix tool and use Mark In and/or Mark Out to mark a region of segments in the Timeline.

2. In the Audio Mix tool, *choose one of the following:*

▲ **Remove Clip Gain on Track - Global:** This option eliminates level information for the entire selected tracks.

▲ **Remove Clip Gain on Track - In/Out:** This option appears if you marked more than one segment using In and/or Out points. Levels are erased on all marked segments on the selected tracks.

The black level lines disappear from the segments in question. The segment levels return to 0 dB.

✔ Tips

■ See the sidebar, "When You Don't Need the Audio Mix and Automation Gain Tools" later in this chapter for an easier way to create and delete global level adjustments.

■ To mark a segment in the Timeline, your In or Out point must at least partially encompass the segment.

Creating and Manipulating Audio-Level Keyframes

Manipulated audio-level keyframes are also called rubber bands. Rubber bands provide an easy, graphical way to dip or raise audio within a segment.

You can use the Automation Gain tool to create rubber bands. However, the tool isn't absolutely necessary. In fact, you can create and manipulate rubber bands without leaving the Timeline. (See the sidebar "When You Don't Need the Audio Mix and Automation Gain Tools" later in this chapter.)

To create an audio level keyframe:

1. In the Timeline, place the position indicator on the frame where you want to add the audio keyframe.

2. Make sure you select Auto Clip Gain in the Timeline Fast menu.

3. Select the record track containing the segments that you want to adjust.

4. (Optional) Choose Tools > Automation Gain to open the Automation Gain tool. Do this if you prefer setting by entering numbers or by dragging sliders. Otherwise, you do not need to open the tool to set Auto Gain keyframes. (See the sidebar, "When You Don't Need the Audio Mix and Automation Gain tools" later in this chapter.)

5. Click ▲ Add Keyframe.

   Xpress Pro adds a keyframe point (a black dot) to every segment on the selected tracks at the location of the position indicator (**Figure 12.33**).

✔ Tip

- You can add an audio keyframe to a source clip track if you first select the Toggle Source/Record in Timeline button at the bottom left of the Timeline window.

Audio keyframe indicators

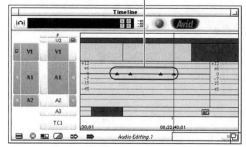

Figure 12.33 To create an audio keyframe, place the position indicator on the right frame and click Add Keyframe. Make sure you select the appropriate track first.

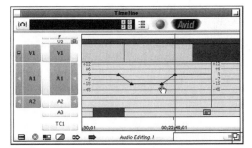

Figure 12.34 To change keyframe's value, drag the audio keyframe indicator up or down.

All in the Gang

To adjust keyframes on multiple tracks with the Automation Gain tool, select gang buttons to lock the relevant tracks together. You don't need to do this when dragging in the Timeline (**Figure 12.35**); there, just select the relevant tracks.

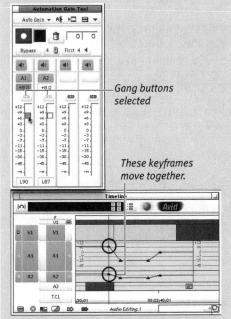

Gang buttons selected

These keyframes move together.

Figure 12.35 When adjusting audio keyframe levels with the Automation Gain tool, you need to gang together tracks if you want to adjust keyframes on the same frame on other tracks.

To adjust a keyframe's value:

Do one of the following:

◆ Select the Timeline tracks that contain the keyframes that you want to adjust. Hold the arrow over a keyframe until it changes to a pointing hand. Drag the keyframe up or down to increase or decrease the keyframe's value (**Figure 12.34**).

◆ In the Automation Gain tool, drag the level slider to increase or decrease the keyframe's level.

Xpress Pro reflects the keyframe's new level in all selected tracks in the Timeline as well as in the Automation Gain tool.

✔ Tips

■ As you drag a keyframe up or down, you can snap its value to audio-level reference lines by holding down Ctrl (Windows) or Command (Mac).

■ As you manually change a keyframe's level in the Timeline, the new level value is displayed at the bottom of the Timeline.

■ When adjusting a keyframe in the Automation Gain tool, you can set the keyframe's value by manually typing a positive or negative level number in the Volume Level box.

■ Clicking ◀◀ Rewind or ▶▶ Fast Forward with the Automation Gain tool active will snap the position indicator to the previous or next keyframe in the Timeline.

When You Don't Need the Audio Mix and Automation Gain Tools

If all you need to do is either adjust or delete audio levels within a segment or across a section segments, you don't even need to open the Audio Mix or Automation Gain tool.

You can manipulate levels within the Timeline in one or more of the following ways:

◆ To create an audio keyframe, click the Add Keyframe button.

◆ To adjust a group of keyframes at once across multiple segments, mark In and Out points around the audio keyframes, select the appropriate tracks, and drag one of the keyframes up or down. The rest will follow (**Figure 12.36**).

    In fact, you can use this technique to raise or lower an entire track, as long as each segment on the track has at least one audio keyframe on it.

◆ To delete one keyframe, hold the pointer over a keyframe and press Delete.

◆ To delete a group of audio-level adjustments, mark In and Out points around the audio keyframes, hold the pointer over one of the keyframes, and press Delete.

Drag any keyframe
between In and Out points.

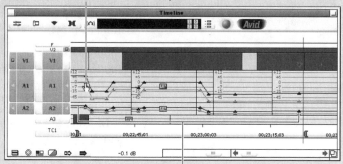

All of these rubber bands move
up or down by the same amount.

Figure 12.36 To raise or lower rubber bands on Timeline segments, mark the segments (at least part of them) by setting In and Out points, select the appropriate tracks, and drag the rubber band up or down.

Press Delete.

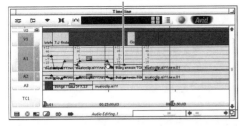

All of the rubber bands were deleted.

Figure 12.37 To eliminate rubber bands on a group of segments (above), select the appropriate tracks, mark In and Out points around the keyframes, hold the pointer over one of the keyframe points, and press Delete (below).

To adjust the value of multiple keyframes across the Timeline:

1. In the Timeline, mark In and Out points around the keyframes that you want to adjust.

2. Select the tracks that contain the keyframes that you want to adjust.

3. Drag one of the keyframes up or down. All of the keyframes between In and Out points on selected tracks move together.

✔ Tip

- When dragging a keyframe up or down, you can snap it to a reference dB line by pressing Ctrl (Windows) or Command (Mac) while you drag.

To delete one audio-level keyframe:

- In the Timeline, move the pointer over a keyframe dot. When the pointer changes to a pointing hand, press the Delete key. The keyframe dot disappears. If it was the last keyframe on the audio segment, then the segment's level returns to 0 dB.

To delete multiple audio-level keyframes:

Do one of the following:

- To delete keyframes between Timeline In and Out points, use Mark In and Mark Out to at least partially mark segments that have rubber bands. Hold the pointer over a keyframe until it turns into a pointing hand and press the Delete key (**Figure 12.37**).

- To delete keyframes on an entire *track*, select the appropriate track buttons in the Automation Gain tool. Then open the Fast menu and choose Remove Automation Gain on Track - Global. The keyframes disappear, and the Auto Gain levels go back to 0 dB.

✔ Tip

- You can delete keyframes between In and Out points using the Automation Gain tool and choosing Remove Automation Gain on Track - In/Out. But why bother? Pressing the Delete key in the Timeline is a lot faster.

To move an audio-level keyframe horizontally:

1. Hold the cursor over a keyframe until it changes into a pointing hand.

2. Press Alt (Windows) or Option (Mac) and drag the keyframe dot to the left or right.

   The keyframe moves to a new position.

✔ Tips

■ If there is a keyframe at an identical position on another selected track, it will follow the keyframe you're moving (**Figure 12.38**).

■ If you do not select Audio Auto Gain from the Timeline Fast menu, the system displays a pink triangle on Timeline segments. This tells you that the segments have adjusted levels even though you can't see them.

Hold down Alt or Option and drag.

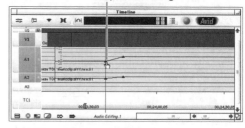

Both keyframes were moved.

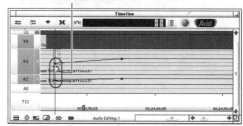

Figure 12.38 In the Timeline, Alt-dragging (Windows) or Option-dragging (Mac) a keyframe (above) enables you to move it to the left or right. Keyframes on the same frame on other selected tracks will move simultaneously (below).

ADJUSTING AUDIO LEVELS

Recording a Live Mix with the Automation Gain Tool

The Record button on the Automation Gain tool is there for a reason: It enables you to play a section of your Timeline and mix audio levels in real time while Xpress Pro memorizes your actions. For some sound mixers, this is a more natural way of mixing levels: by responding directly to the real-time flow of the soundtrack.

Remember that the Automation Gain Record button only records audio-level keyframes. The tool does not record any audio.

✔ Tips

- Usually editors use this feature only with an external digital mixer connected to Xpress Pro via MIDI, because no one is fast enough with a mouse to record a real-time mix using the virtual sliders in the Automation Gain tool.

- You may occasionally record level adjustments using the Automation Gain tool sliders, but only when you don't have many tracks to adjust.

- For mixers compatible with Xpress Pro, visit the Avid Web site (www.avid.com).

To record level adjustments in real time:

1. Mark In and/or Out points in the Timeline around the section of your sequence that you want to adjust and select the relevant Timeline track buttons.

2. Choose Tools > Automation Gain.

3. Using the Automation Gain tool monitor buttons, turn on one or more tracks according to what you want hear during playback. Turn on gang buttons for tracks that you want to lock together.

4. Type a number of seconds for preroll and postroll (the part of your Timeline that you want to hear before or after recording) in the boxes next to the trash can in the Automation Gain tool.

5. To start recording, *do one of the following:*
   ▲ Click the Record button in the Automation Gain tool.
   ▲ Press the B key.

   Xpress Pro starts playback, and the indicator box next to the Record button starts flashing red (**Figure 12.39**).

6. Make level adjustments by dragging level sliders up and down or by manipulating your external mixer.

   When Xpress Pro gets to your Timeline Out point or the end of the sequence, playback stops. Depending on your level changes, your Timeline may now contain several audio keyframes (**Figure 12.40**).

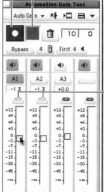

Click here to start recording
This indicator flashes as you record

Gang tracks together if you want.

Xpress Pro plays between In and Out points.

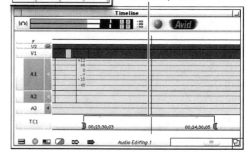

Figure 12.39 To record your Automation Gain tool adjustments, mark In and Out points in the Timeline and click the Record button.

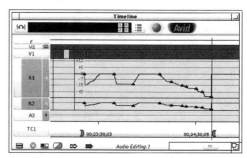

Figure 12.40 When Automation Gain tool recording stops, audio keyframes appear in the Timeline, reflecting your live mixing choices.

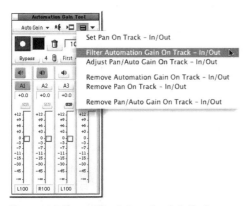

Figure 12.41 Choose Filter Automation Gain Keyframes if you think some of the recorded keyframes are redundant. This filtering cleans up your rubber banding.

7. (Optional) You can get rid of some of the keyframes that Xpress Pro created by choosing Filter Automation Gain on Track - In/Out or Filter Automation Automation Gain tool Fast menu (**Figure 12.41**).

Repeat step 7 until you are left with only the essential keyframes you need in the Timeline. This filtering decreases the visual mess in your Timeline and simplifies your options for fine-tuning the keyframe levels.

✔ Tips

- A few seconds of preroll can help you mentally prepare your level adjustments before the Automation Gain tool starts recording your actions. Postroll will tell you whether your adjustment will blend well with the following audio section.

- To cancel recording, click the trash can in the Automation Gain tool window. To erase a recording after recording finishes, choose File > Undo.

- If you hear any audio crackles or drops while recording, select a slower Audio Tools Response setting in the Audio Settings dialog box and start recording over again.

RECORDING A LIVE MIX WITH THE AUTOMATION GAIN TOOL

Panning Audio Tracks and Segments

By default, Xpress Pro projects are in stereo, and odd-numbered tracks play from the left speakers and even-numbered tracks play from the right speakers. (You can change a project to monaural—centering everything—in the Audio Project Settings dialog box.)

For stereo projects, you can adjust pan settings for any segment or group of segments by using either the Audio Mix tool or the Automation Gain tool. Which tool you use does not matter.

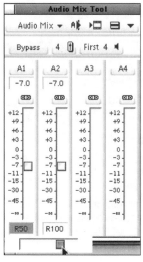

Figure 12.42 When you pan a segment's audio, hold down the Pan button and drag to the left or right. In this case, the segment on track A1 is panned halfway to the right.

✔ Tips

■ A pan value applies to an entire segment; you cannot keyframe a pan value in the middle of a segment.

■ To take advantage of pan and level adjustments, you must have Stereo selected as the Audio Mix mode in the Audio Project Settings dialog box.

To adjust an audio segment's pan value:

1. In the Timeline, place the position indicator over the segment that you want to adjust.

2. Choose Tools > Audio Mix Tool or Tools > Automation Gain to open either the Audio Mix or Automation Gain tool.

3. In the Audio Mix or Automation Gain tool, adjust the pan values *by doing one of the following*:

   ▲ Drag the pan box underneath the level slider to the left or right (**Figure 12.42**).

   ▲ Type a negative (for left) or positive (for right) number in the pan box. Press Enter (Windows) or Return (Mac).

   The pan box displays left pan values as L*n* and right values as R*n* (where *n* is a number between 0 and 200). A centered pan value is designated "MID."

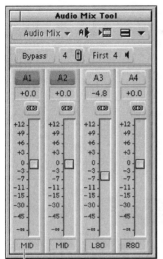

Figure 12.43 To center tracks, equally balancing them between the left and right speakers, Alt-click or Option-click the pan value box.

The track is centered.

✔ Tips

- To simultaneously adjust multiple segments at the same position on other tracks, click the gang buttons in the Audio Mix or Automation Gain tool for the tracks that you want to lock together.

- If you adjust the pan value for a segment that contains a rendered audio effect, that effect becomes unrendered. To render it again, you can click the Render Effect button in the Audio Mix tool.

- To center the pan value, Alt-click (Windows) or Option-click (Mac) the pan box (**Figure 12.43**).

To apply your pan adjustment to other audio segments:

1. Place the position indicator over the segment whose pan you want to copy elsewhere and *do one of the following:*

   ▲ To apply your pan value to an entire track, erase your Timeline In and Out points.

   ▲ To apply your pan value to a group of segments across the Timeline, use Mark In and Mark Out to mark all or parts of the segment that you want to affect.

2. In the Audio Mix tool (or the Timeline), select the tracks that you want to affect. In the Audio Mix tool, hold down Shift to select multiple tracks.

continues on next page

3. To paste your pan value to all marked segments on selected tracks, click on the Audio Mix tool Fast menu and *choose one of the following:*

▲ **Set Pan on Track - Global (or Set Pan on Track - In/Out):** Choose this option to give every segment on every selected track the same pan value. If you marked In and Out points, this choice affects only marked segments.

▲ **Adjust Pan/Vols on Track - Global (or Adjust Pan/Vols on Track - In/Out):** Choose this option to adjust every pan value on every selected track by the same amount. In the dialog box that appears, type a positive or negative number in the Gain Adjustment in dB box and click OK. If you marked In and Out points, this choice affects only marked segments.

Xpress Pro applies the pan value at the location of the position indicator to all other marked segments on selected tracks. The pan boxes display left pan values as L# and right pan values as R#. A centered pan value is designated "MID."

✔ Tips

■ To center the pan value, Alt-click (Windows) or Option-click (Mac) the pan box so that it displays "MID."

■ When adjusting a group of segments, you can get away with setting *either* an In *or* an Out point. Set an In point and choose "Set Pan On Track -from In" from the tool Fast menu if you want to affect every segment from the In point through the end of the sequence. Or set an Out point and choose "Set Pan on Track - To Out" if you want to affect every segment up until the Out point (**Figure 12.44**).

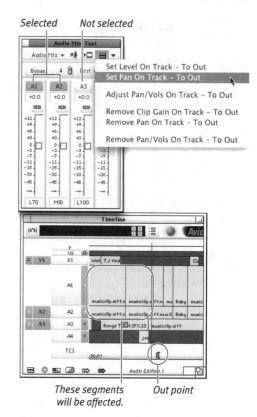

Selected   Not selected

These segments will be affected.   Out point

Figure 12.44 Here, every segment on A1 up until the Out mark will be assigned a pan value of L70. Every segment on A2 up until the Out mark will be assigned a pan value of MID. A3 and A4 will not be affected because they are not selected in the Audio Mix tool.

PANNING AUDIO TRACKS AND SEGMENTS

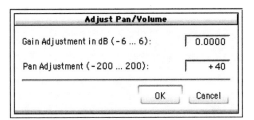

Figure 12.45 in the Adjust Pan/Volume dialog box, you can adjust the pan values (of marked segments on selected tracks) by a specified amount. A positive number pans to the right speaker, and a negative number pans to the left speaker.

■ Choose Adjust Pan/Vols on Track from the Audio Mix tool or Automation Gain tool Fast menu to adjust pan values by the same amount. You can specify your settings in the Adjust Pan/Volume dialog box that appears (**Figure 12.45**).

To adjust the pan values for source clip tracks:

1. Load a source clip into a source monitor and make sure the monitor is active.

2. Open the Audio Mix tool and adjust the pan values as you would with Timeline segments. See the task "To adjust an audio segment's pan value" earlier in this section.)

To delete any pan adjustments on one or more segments:

1. Prepare to delete pan values *by doing one of the following:*

   ▲ To delete pan adjustments on every segment on one or more tracks, eliminate Timeline In and Out points.

   ▲ To delete pan adjustments on a group of segments across the Timeline, click Mark In and/or Mark Out to mark a region of segments in the Timeline.

2. In the Audio Mix tool, *choose one of the following:*

   ▲ **Remove Pan on Track - Global:** This option eliminates pan information on entire selected tracks.

   ▲ **Remove Pan on Track - In/Out:** This option appears if you marked more than one segment using In and/or Out points. Pan adjustments disappear on all marked segments on the selected tracks.

   The pan values return to the Xpress Pro default: odd-numbered tracks return to L100, and even-numbered tracks return to R100.

PANNING AUDIO TRACKS AND SEGMENTS

About Xpress Pro's Audio Effects

There are two types of audio effects—each with a different icon—that you can apply to your audio in the Xpress Pro Timeline:

◆ **EQ effect:** Adjusting a segment's equalization, or EQ, with the EQ tool raises or lowers certain frequencies within your audio. For example, if you think the bass guitar in a piece of music is too overwhelming, you can use the EQ tool to lower the frequencies between, say, 20 and 120 Hz.

◆ **AudioSuite plug-ins:** Several plug-in effects are available in the AudioSuite window. Typically, they can eliminate unwanted sounds from your audio or create special effects such as reverberation or pitch shifts.

✔ Tip

■ You can apply one EQ effect and one AudioSuite plug-in to any particular audio segment, but no more than that. Unfortunately, you cannot nest multiple audio effects in one segment. (For the workaround, see "Mixing Down Audio Tracks" later in this chapter.)

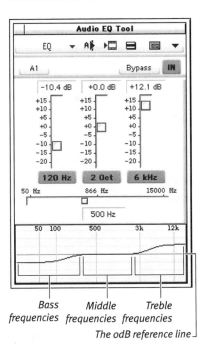

Bass   Middle   Treble
frequencies frequencies frequencies

The 0dB reference line ⌐

Figure 12.46 You can see from the graph that the base frequencies are below 0 dB and the treble frequencies are above 0 dB. The middle frequencies remain at a normal level, at 0 dB.

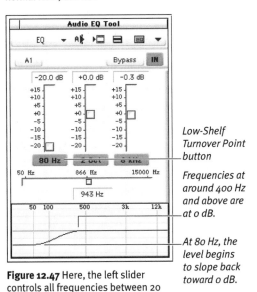

Low-Shelf Turnover Point button

Frequencies at around 400 Hz and above are at 0 dB.

At 80 Hz, the level begins to slope back toward 0 dB.

Figure 12.47 Here, the left slider controls all frequencies between 20 Hz and 80 Hz. At 80 Hz, the frequency level begins to slope up toward 0 dB.

Applying EQ Effects to Audio

What really makes EQ adjustments in the Audio EQ tool easy to understand is the graph at the bottom of the window. From left to right, it displays a spectrum of audio frequencies. When you make EQ slider adjustments, you can graphically see where the level dips below the 0-dB reference line and where it rises above it (**Figure 12.46**).

The functions of the EQ tool's four sliders are summarized here:

♦ **The far-left slider:** When you adjust what's called the low-shelf slider, you affect all frequencies between 20 Hz and whatever you choose from the Low-Shelf Turnover Point button (**Figure 12.47**). This slider controls the low, bass sounds.

If you want to affect a large range of bass sounds, choose 240 Hz as your turnover point (the frequency at which the level returns to 0 dB). If you want to affect only the very lowest of the low sounds, choose 50 Hz here.

♦ **The far-right slider:** This, the high-shelf slider, is the opposite of the low-shelf slider. Use this slider to adjust the high, treble frequencies. To affect the broadest range of frequencies, choose 6 kHz as your turnover point by clicking the High-Shelf Turnover Point button. If you want to affect just the highest notes, choose 15 kHz.

continues on next page

- **The middle slider and the small horizontal slider:** The middle slider is called the Parametric Midrange slider, and it works hand in hand with the horizontal slider below it, which is called the EQ Range slider.

Use these sliders to determine the range and location of either a level dip or level raise in audio. If you select 2 Oct for the Bandwidth Around Center Point button, then you can use the Parametric Midrange slider to create a level dip or level raise that covers a broad range of frequencies (**Figure 12.48**).

In contrast, 1/4 Oct for Bandwidth Around Center Point is ideal for isolating a particular frequency because the range of frequencies that it covers is very narrow. (For some tips on using this range, see "Isolating Frequencies" later in this chapter.)

Drag the EQ Range slider to the left or right to specify the frequencies that you want to affect.

✔ Tips

- All of these sliders can be disabled by clicking the orange buttons and choosing Disable.

- You can apply equalization to a source clip or a Timeline audio segment.

To adjust a clip or segment's EQ:

1. *Do one of the following:*
   - ▲ In the Timeline, select the tracks that contain the segments that you want to adjust.
   - ▲ In the EQ tool, click the track selection button and select the track that you want to adjust. To adjust multiple tracks, hold down the Shift key when selecting tracks.

Bandwidth Around Center Point button

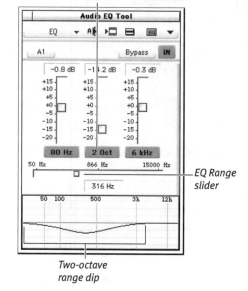

Figure 12.48 With 2 Oct chosen for Bandwidth Around Center Point, raising or lowering the middle slider affects a broad range of frequencies. Meanwhile, the EQ Range slider determines the position of the midrange hump or dip.

2. Adjust the EQ values *by doing one of the following:*

   ▲ Click and drag a slider.

   ▲ Select a slider button or an EQ value box and type a positive or negative number. Press Enter (Windows) or Return (Mac) to apply the change.

✔ Tips

- To apply an EQ effect to only part of a segment, you must use Add Edit to split the segment into two. You cannot use In and Out points.

- Alt-click (Windows) or Option-click (Mac) an EQ slider to snap it to 0 dB.

To apply an Xpress Pro preset EQ value:

1. In the Timeline, park the position indicator over the segment to which you want apply the effect.

2. In the Timeline or the Audio EQ tool, select the tracks that you want to affect.

3. Open the Audio EQ tool Fast menu and choose from one of the many preset options that appear (such as the Tape Hiss Filter).

✔ Tips

- You can create your own EQ preset templates and make them available in the Audio EQ tool. (See "Creating Custom EQ Effect Templates" later in this chapter.)

- You can add an EQ effect to an audio segment that already has an AudioSuite plug-in applied to it. However, an audio segment can have no more than one EQ effect and one AudioSuite effect.

Adjusting EQ During Playback

You can adjust EQ sliders while Xpress Pro loops the portion of your Timeline between In and Out points. However, the EQ change will not be instantly apparent; depending on your system, it will take a moment for you to hear the new frequency level values.

If want to try to improve the response time of your EQ adjustments, open your Audio Settings dialog box and make a different choice from the Audio Response pull-down menu.

At any rate, it's a good idea to use audio looping while making EQ adjustments so you don't have to keep clicking Play or Play In to Out over and over again. Just mark In and Out points to mark the segment that you want to adjust and click the Audio Loop Play button.

Furthermore, to increase response time, monitor as few audio tracks as possible.

APPLYING EQ EFFECTS TO AUDIO

To apply one EQ effect to other segments:

1. Park the position indicator over the segment that has the EQ that you want to apply elsewhere.

2. Mark the segments to which you want to apply the EQ effect using In and Out points.

   Any segment at least partially marked by In and Out points on selected tracks will be affected.

3. In the Audio EQ tool, open the Fast menu and choose Set EQ In/Out, Set EQ from In, or Set EQ to Out.

   The EQ effect applies to all marked segments on the selected tracks.

✔ Tip

■ Selecting Show Marked Region in your Timeline settings and marking both In and Out points will help you specify which segments receive the EQ effects.

To delete one or more EQ effects:

1. Set In and/or Out points in the Timeline, around the effects that you want to delete.

   Any effect partially marked by an In or Out point can be deleted.

2. (Optional) If you need to delete effects on more than one track, select the tracks in either the Timeline or the Audio EQ tool.

3. Open the Audio EQ tool Fast menu and *choose one of the following:*

   ▲ **Remove EQ Effects on Track:** This option deletes effects on only one track, no matter which tracks are selected. Check the Track Selection Menu button to see the number of the selected track (if the button says A2+, then you're deleting effects on track A2).

EQ Presets That You Can't Edit

You may notice that Xpress Pro does not allow you to adjust certain preset templates that you can apply from the EQ tool Fast menu. This is just a fact of life. You have to trust the preset template.

What you can do, if you like having more control, is use the standard EQ sliders to try to mimic the line curve of the EQ parameter graph.

Isolating Frequencies

If you need to remove a hum or sound from your audio that you think is limited to (or at least strongest at) a particular frequency, click the Bandwidth Around Center button underneath the middle slider and choose 1/4 Oct.

Then lower the middle slider (the Parametric Midrange slider) all the way down to –20 dB. Finally, move the EQ Range slider to the left or right until you think you have isolated and decreased the annoying frequency in question (**Figure 12.49**).

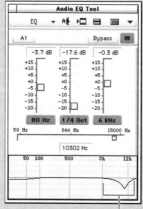

Figure 12.49 Here, frequencies around 10 kHz have been isolated and lowered.

One-quarter octave range

APPLYING EQ EFFECTS TO AUDIO

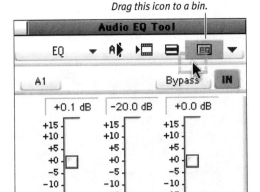

Drag this icon to a bin.

Figure 12.50 To save an EQ setting as a custom effect template, drag the small EQ icon from the EQ tool to an open bin.

▲ **Remove EQ Effect on Enabled Tracks:** This option deletes all marked EQ effects on the selected tracks.

✔ Tip

■ Since an EQ effect is an effect like any other, you can delete one by parking the position indicator over it in the Timeline and pressing the Remove Effect button. (For more information, see Chapter 9, "Working with Video Effects.")

Creating Custom EQ Effect Templates

If you create an effective EQ setup by manipulating the four sliders in the EQ tool, and you want to save your settings for future use, you can create your own custom EQ template.

Once you create an EQ template, you can apply it to another segment from the bin, or with some extra effort, you can make all of your personal EQ templates available on the EQ tool Fast menu along with the other presets.

To save an EQ effect as a template:

1. In the Timeline, park the position indicator over the segment that contains the effect that you want to save.

2. In the Timeline or the Audio EQ tool, select the track that contains the effect that you want to save.

3. From the Audio EQ tool, drag the EQ icon to a bin (**Figure 12.50**).

4. Give the template a unique name so you can remember its function.

✔ Tip

■ You should create a bin specifically for EQ effects and keep it open so that the Effect palette displays them.

APPLYING EQ EFFECTS TO AUDIO

To list your custom EQ templates in the EQ tool Fast menu:

1. *Do one of the following:*

   ▲ In Windows, press Ctrl+O and open the bin called Site_EQs_Bin.avb (found in *drive* > Program Files > Avid > Avid Xpress > Supporting Files > Site_Effects).

   ▲ In Mac OS, press Command+O and open the bin called Site_EQs_Bin.avb (found in Avid Xpress Pro > Supporting Files > Site_Effects).

2. Drag your custom EQ effect template from its current bin into Site_EQs_Bin (**Figure 12.51**).

3. Close Site_EQs_Bin.

   From now on, you can access your EQ effect template from the EQ tool Fast menu.

To apply an EQ effect template to a clip or segment:

Do one of the following:

◆ Drag an EQ effect template from a bin to a segment in the Timeline.

◆ If you saved your template in Site_EQs_Bin, you can choose the template from the EQ tool Fast menu (**Figure 12.52**).

✔ Tip

■ EQ templates are also available on the Effect palette if their bins are open. (For more information on the Effect palette, see Chapter 9, "Working with Video Effects.")

Custom EQ effect template

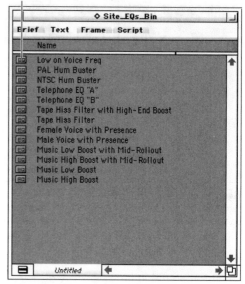

Figure 12.51 After saving a custom EQ template in a bin, open Site_EQs_Bin (in the Site_Effects folder) and drag your template into it.

Custom effect template

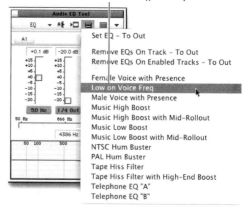

Figure 12.52 After you drag a custom EQ effect template to Site_EQs_Bin and close the bin, your custom effect becomes available on the EQ tool Fast menu.

Table 12.1

AudioSuite Plug-in Buttons	
BUTTON	**PURPOSE**
OK	Saves the effect and closes the dialog box.
Cancel:	Closes the dialog box and does not save the effect.
Preview	Plays back a portion of the clip with effect processing. (Some effects can preview without rendering and some cannot.)
Render	Renders the effect and creates a new audio media file.
Bypass	Plays the selected audio without effect processing. Use this button to compare the audio clip with and without the plug-in.
Find Peak	Performs a peak-analysis pass on the effect. Most plug-ins perform this analysis automatically.

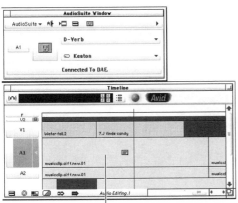

This segment has EQ as well as the plug-in D-Verb applied to it.

Figure 12.53 Xpress Pro allows to you apply both an EQ adjustment (using the EQ tool) and an AudioSuite plug-in to the same audio segment. The EQ effect is always on top, so clicking Remove Effect will delete the EQ effect but leave the plug-in behind.

Applying AudioSuite Plug-in Effects

Whereas you apply video effects from the Effect palette, you apply audio effects from the AudioSuite tool. The included audio effects are courtesy of Digidesign, the maker of ProTools and a division of Avid.

When you apply an audio plug-in, you must click the large plug icon in the AudioSuite window to open the effect's parameters. (**Table 12.1** lists the buttons common to all effect parameter dialog boxes.) Keep in mind that audio plug-ins are not keyframeable, and you cannot alter parameters over the course of one segment as you can with video effects.

✔ Tips

■ As mentioned earlier—but worth repeating—the bad news about AudioSuite plug-ins is that you can apply only one plug-in to any particular audio segment, so you cannot nest audio effects as you can video effects. (For the workaround, see the sidebar "When You Really Need More than One Audio Effect" later in this chapter.)

■ Although you can't apply multiple plug-ins to the same audio segment, you can apply an AudioSuite plug-in plus an EQ adjustment to the same segment (**Figure 12.53**).

APPLYING AUDIOSUITE PLUG-IN EFFECTS

How Can I Get More Audio Plug-ins?

You can go to the Digidesign Web site (www.digidesign.com) and buy plug-ins, such as Maxim and Focusrite d3, that aren't included with your Xpress Pro installer.

At the Digidesign site, click Products, then click Online Catalog, and then click Plug-ins.

Not all of the plug-ins listed are compatible with Avid Xpress software. For a clue as to which ones are compatible, open the Goodies folder included with your Xpress Pro install disc. In the AudioSuite_Demo_Plugins folder, you'll find an installer that will install a series of extra plug-ins. After installing these demos, match the names to the prices and descriptions listed at the Digidesign Web site.

Where Do New Plug-ins Go?

When you install a new audio plug-in from a third-party application, the plug-in should come with instructions as to where to install it.

Sometimes you may have to manually drag the new plug-in to the Plug-In folder; this is in the DAE folder application folder.

The Engine Behind the AudioSuite

A separate application, called DAE, actually is required to run the AudioSuite's plug-in effects. Whenever you launch Xpress Pro, DAE automatically launches.

But if you don't need this application, you can turn it off by Ctrl-clicking (Windows) or Command-clicking (Mac) the status display bar (**Figure 12.54**).

Turn off DAE only if you have multiple applications open and need the extra RAM; once you turn off the DAE application, you have to relaunch Xpress Pro to turn it on again.

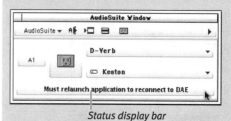

Status display bar

Figure 12.54 You can turn off the DAE application, to save your system resources, by holding down Ctrl (Windows) or Command (Mac) and clicking the status display bar.

Shift-click here.

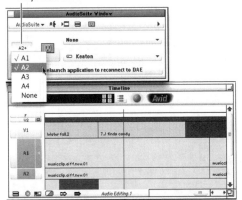

Figure 12.55 To apply a plug-in to multiple segments at the location of the position indicator, Shift-click the track selector button in the AudioSuite window.

To apply an AudioSuite plug-in effect:

1. Choose Tools > AudioSuite to open the AudioSuite window.

2. Park the position indicator on the Timeline segment that you want to affect.

3. In the Timeline or the AudioSuite window, select the tracks that you want to affect. To select multiple tracks in the AudioSuite window, Shift-click the Track Selection Menu button (**Figure 12.55**).

4. From the Plug-in Selection pop-up menu, choose a plug-in to apply (**Figure 12.56**).

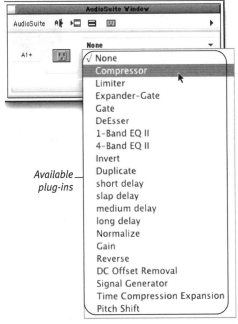

Available plug-ins

Figure 12.56 The AudioSuite window lists the plug-ins installed on your system.

APPLYING AUDIOSUITE PLUG-IN EFFECTS

continues on next page

5. From the Target Drive pop-up menu, choose a target drive for the effect media files.

6. Click the Activate Current Plug-in button (the big plug).

A dialog box appears that allows you to adjust the parameters of the chosen effect (**Figure 12.57**). After you adjust the parameters, you can click Preview to hear the result, click Render to render

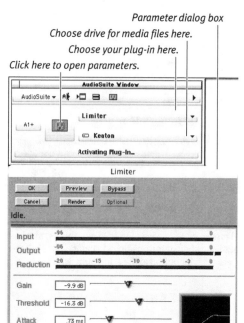

Parameter dialog box
Choose drive for media files here.
Choose your plug-in here.
Click here to open parameters.

Figure 12.57 To open the parameter dialog box for a plug-in you just applied, click the large plug icon.

When You Really Need More than One Audio Effect

The only way to apply more than one effect to an audio segment (or an audio segment pair) is to perform an audio mixdown. (See "Mixing Down Audio Tracks" later in this chapter.)

The problem with this workaround is that it's rather time consuming, plus mixdown tracks cannot be batch recaptured and do not contain usable timecode for an EDL (Edit Decision List).

However, if you know that you will be outputting your final movie to tape from Xpress Pro , then this is a viable workaround for a frustrating limitation.

APPLYING AUDIOSUITE PLUG-IN EFFECTS

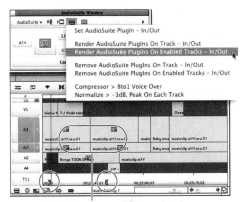

These effects will be rendered.

Figure 12.58 One way to render all audio effects between Timeline In and Out points is to choose Render AudioSuite Plugins on Enabled Tracks - In/Out from the AudioSuite Fast menu. (You can also choose Clip > Render In/Out.)

the effect, and click OK close the parameter dialog box.

To render one or more plug-in effects:

To select the effects that you want to render, *do one of the following:*

◆ To render only effects at the location of the position indicator, select the tracks that contain the effects and click the Render Effect button or choose Render AudioSuite Plugins on Enabled Tracks - Global from the AudioSuite Fast menu.

◆ To render all effects marked by Timeline In and Out points, select the tracks that contain the effects and mark In and Out points around them. Choose Clip > Render In/Out and open the AudioSuite Fast menu and choose Render AudioSuite Plugins on Enabled Tracks - In/Out (**Figure 12.58**).

Xpress Pro renders the audio effects, and the orange dots on their icons disappear.

(For more information on rendering, see Chapter 11, "Rendering and Real-Time.")

✔ Tips

■ You must render all audio effects before you output to tape.

■ To cancel a render operation, press Ctrl+period (Windows) or Command+period (Mac).

To modify an effect's parameters:

1. Park the position indicator over the effect in the Timeline. Make sure that its track is selected.

2. In the AudioSuite window, click the large plug (the Activate Current Plug-in button). The effect's parameter window appears.

3. Modify the effect and render it again.

Working with Audio Effect Templates

As with other Xpress Pro effects, if you like the parameters you've set for a particular audio effect, you can save it as an audio effect template for future use.

In addition, if you're willing to take a couple of extra steps, you can have AudioSuite list your effect template in its effect pull-down menu; then you can apply your effect directly from the AudioSuite window.

To save an audio plug-in custom template:

1. In the Timeline, park the position indicator on the effect that you want to save as a template and select the track that contains it.

2. In the AudioSuite plug-in window, drag the small plug icon (the effect icon) to an open bin (**Figure 12.59**). Give the effect a unique name.

   In the future, you can apply the effect by dragging it from the bin to an audio segment.

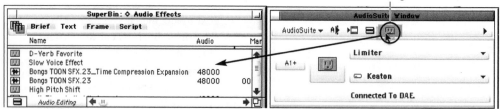

Figure 12.59 To save your effect's settings as a custom effect template, drag the small effect icon from the AudioSuite window to an open bin.

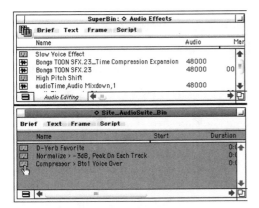

Figure 12.60 To make your custom effect template available in the AudioSuite window, open Site_AudioSuite_Bin (found in the Site-Effects folder), drag the effect into it, and close the bin.

To make your custom audio template available in the AudioSuite window:

1. *Do one of the following:*

   ▲ In Windows, press Ctrl+O and open the bin called AudioSuite_Bin.avb (found in *drive:*\Program Files\Avid\Avid Xpress\ Supporting Files\Site_Effects).

   ▲ In Mac OS, press Command+O and open the bin called Site_AudioSuite_Bin (found in *drive*/Avid Xpress Pro/ Supporting Files/Site_Effects).

2. Drag your custom AudioSuite effect template from its current bin into Site_AudioSuite_Bin (**Figure 12.60**).

3. Close Site_AudioSuite_Bin.

   You can now load your custom template from the AudioSuite plug-in selection menu.

Applying AudioSuite Plug-ins to Source Clips

You may need to apply an AudioSuite plug-in to a source clip in the following types of situations:

♦ You want to manipulate the speed of an audio segment by using the Time Compression Expansion effect, which is the audio equivalent of a motion effect. Depending on your parameter settings, the effect creates a new audio master clip either shorter or longer than the original.

♦ You may need to apply some kind of delay or reverb effect (such as D-Verb) to a Timeline segment. Often, reverb effects require extra frames beyond the original Timeline segment, to make the echo trail away, and it's best to load the audio segment's original master clip to create this effect.

continues on next page

APPLYING AUDIOSUITE PLUG-IN EFFECTS

Slowing Down or Speeding Up an Audio or Video Clip

Some tricky steps are required if you want to speed up or a slow down a Timeline audio segment (or stereo pair) and also do the same to its corresponding video segment. The key is to make sure that the resultant speed-changed clips are the same length.

Applying a speed change to the video track requires that you apply a Motion effect, whereas an audio speed change requires a Time Compression Expansion effect. Both effects create new master clips in your bin.

First, to adjust the speed of the audio segment pair in your Timeline, do the following (note that this procedure works well only for a clip that has audio and video of the same length in the Timeline):

1. Select the Timeline tracks that contain the video and audio of the clip.

2. Click Previous Edit to jump to the first frame of the segment.

3. Click Match Frame to load the video and audio segments into a source monitor. (An In point marks the first frame.)

4. Go slightly beyond where you think the clip will end and click Mark Out (**Figure 12.61**).

2. Mark an Out point.

1. Place the position indicator on the first frame and click Match Frame.

Figure 12.61 To prepare to change the speed of an audio segment pair to make it match its corresponding video, go to the beginning of the segment and click Match Frame. Then mark an Out point in the source monitor.

Slowing Down or Speeding Up an Audio or Video Clip *(continued)*

5. Go to the bin where the master clip is (the one currently displayed in the source monitor) and drag that to the AudioSuite window.

6. Apply the Time Compression Expansion effect.

7. After rendering the effect a new time adjusted audio clip will appear in your bin. Make a note of its duration (**Figure 12.62**).

continues on next page

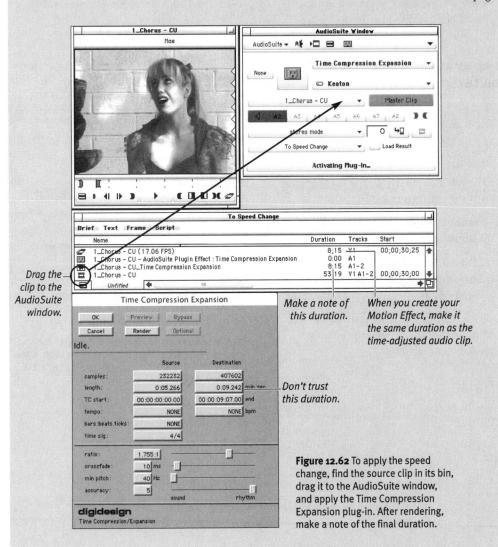

Drag the clip to the AudioSuite window.

Make a note of this duration.

When you create your Motion Effect, make it the same duration as the time-adjusted audio clip.

Don't trust this duration.

Figure 12.62 To apply the speed change, find the source clip in its bin, drag it to the AudioSuite window, and apply the Time Compression Expansion plug-in. After rendering, make a note of the final duration.

Slowing Down or Speeding Up an Audio or Video Clip *(continued)*

Now change the speed of the corresponding video segment and match the length of the new audio segment:

1. Go back to the source monitor and click Motion Effect.

2. In the Motion Effect dialog box, type a duration that matches the duration of the audio clip.

3. Render the effect.

Now when you edit the new audio and video speed-adjusted clips into your Timeline, they will match in length.

To apply an audio plug-in to a source clip:

1. Drag a source clip from the bin to the AudioSuite window.

2. Click the track numbers for the tracks that you want to include in the new effect.

The track number with the speaker icon is the monitored track.

3. Choose a plug-in from the Plug-In Selection pop-up menu.

4. Choose a target bin for the new master clip from the target bin pull-down menu (**Figure 12.63**).

5. Click the big plug (the Activate Current Plug-in button) to open the effect's parameter dialog box.

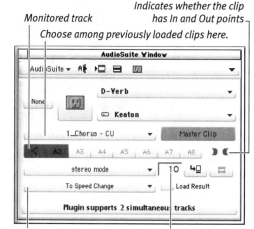

Monitored track
Choose among previously loaded clips here.
Indicates whether the clip has In and Out points

Choose the bin for the rendered effect here.
Add a handle if you want an extra head and tail added to the clip.

Figure 12.63 When you drag a master clip to the AudioSuite window, the window expands to show the master clip settings. Now you can apply an effect to the loaded clip.

6. Render the effect.

After you render the effect, Xpress Pro creates a new master clip in the target bin. It also places the effect icon in the same bin; this is essentially a new effect template that you can apply to other clips.

The system names the new master clip by combining the original clip name with the effect name.

Now you can edit that new master clip into your Timeline.

✔ Tips

- To change the monitored track when applying a plug-in to a master clip, Alt-click (Windows) or Option-click (Mac) the button of the track that you want to monitor in the AudioSuite window.

- If you want to add extra frames to a new master clip created by the AudioSuite window, type a value in the Handle Length for End of Master Clip text box to lengthen the clip by a specific amount. Use this approach for any plug-in except the Time Compression Expansion effect.

- If you dropped more than one master clip in the AudioSuite window, you can choose a clip to work on from the Clip Selection pop-up menu.

- If you want to return to applying effects to Timeline segments (and not source clips), click the Master Clip button in the AudioSuite window again to remove the highlight.

APPLYING AUDIOSUITE PLUG-IN EFFECTS

Mixing Down Audio Tracks

Audio track mixdown is the audio equivalent of nesting, except that you can't nest audio effects within audio mixdowns.

You may need to mix down (or combine) multiple Timeline audio tracks for one of the following reasons:

♦ You have more than eight tracks of audio in your Timeline, but Xpress Pro can monitor only eight tracks at a time, so to hear them all, you need to mix down some of them.

♦ You want to apply more than one AudioSuite effect to an audio segment (or to two segments, if it's a stereo pair). To do this, you apply the first effect and then mix it down before applying the second effect. (See the sidebar "When You Really Need More than One Audio Effect" earlier in this chapter.)

To mix down several audio tracks to one or two audio tracks:

1. In the Timeline, select the tracks that you want to combine.

2. Mark the section of your Timeline that you want to mix using Mark In and Mark Out.

3. Choose Clip > Audio Mixdown.

4. In the Audio Mixdown dialog box, select Mono if you want to mix everything down to one track or Stereo if you want to mix everything down to two stereo tracks.

5. Choose a target track for the new mixdown segments.

6. Choose a destination drive and a destination bin.

7. If you want to save your sequence as it is (before the mixdown), select Save Premix Sequence.

The Audio Mixdown Downside

Because audio mixdown files do not include usable timecode tracks, do not include any mixdown tracks in your final sequence if you plan to do one of the following:

♦ Batch recapture your audio source material.

♦ Export an Edit Decision List (EDL) of your sequence.

You also should not include mixdown tracks in a sequence that you want to export as an OMF for import into ProTools. Your sound designer will probably want to work with original, separated tracks rather than some mix of your own devising.

8. Click OK (**Figure 12.64**).

Xpress Pro creates a new track in your sequence and places the newly combined audio segment on that track. It also creates a new master clip out of the mixdown and places it in the designated bin (**Figure 12.65**).

continues on next page

New master clip

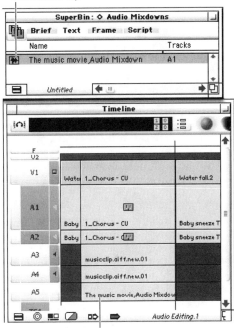

Figure 12.65 After mixing down your audio, Xpress Pro places a new mixdown master clip in the designated bin and adds the mixdown segment on a new track in the Timeline.

New audio segment

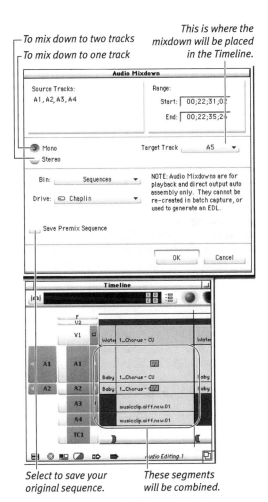

To mix down to two tracks

To mix down to one track

This is where the mixdown will be placed in the Timeline.

Select to save your original sequence.

These segments will be combined.

Figure 12.64 In the Audio Mixdown dialog box, you can choose to combine tracks into either one mono track or two stereo tracks.

MIXING DOWN AUDIO TRACKS

✔ Tip

■ After mixing down your audio, you will want to turn off the monitor buttons for the old audio segments. If you mix down entire tracks and save the premix sequence as a backup, then you may want to delete the old tracks altogether (**Figure 12.66**).

Old version of sequence

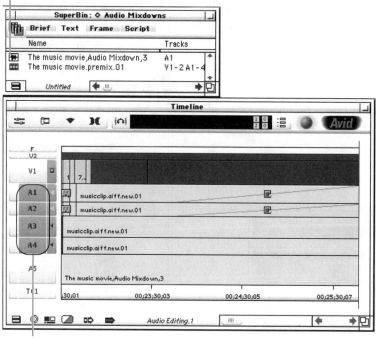

You may want to delete these tracks to simplify the Timeline.

Figure 12.66 If you plan to delete old tracks after an audio mixdown, make sure that you select Save Premix Sequence in the Audio Mixdown dialog box. That way, you can always go back to the old version of the sequence if necessary.

MEDIA AND PROJECT MANAGEMENT | 13

While you edit away in Xpress Pro, the actual media files behind your movie remain mostly invisible; what you actually work with in the application are the references to the media files: clips and sequences.

But sometimes, especially when problems arise such as clips being marked "Media Offline," you have to go behind the scenes and, like a public figure caught in a scandal, face the media.

This chapter looks at how to peek behind the curtain and solve Media Offline problems. It also looks at media management tasks that are often needed near the end of your project, when you're ready to trim the project down to its essentials, switch from an offline to an online resolution, or move everything to, say, Avid Symphony.

About Managing Your Media

Managing your project and its media involves keeping track of the source media files (usually OMF files) that Xpress Pro creates whenever you capture a master clip, import a clip, render an effect, or mix down tracks.

(For more information about source media files see the sidebar "Avid's Source Media File Formats" on the next page.)

Media and project management typically employ at least one of the following commands:

◆ File > Load Media Directories, File > Refresh Media Directories, or File > Reveal File

◆ Bin > Batch Import, Bin > Relink, Bin > Consolidate/Transcode, or Bin > Decompose

At least one of these commands applies to each of the following situations and tasks:

◆ **Finding source media behind your clips and effects:** If you want to find out exactly where Xpress Pro keeps the source media files behind particular clips in your project, you can use the Reveal File command and the Media tool to display the source media files.

Once you know where the source media files are located, you can move, copy, or delete them.

◆ **Reconnecting media for clips marked "Offline":** When either a source monitor or the Composer displays the message "Media Offline," the clip you're playing is no longer connected to its source media file; Xpress Pro thinks the media is no longer available on your computer system.

However, if you know that your source media *is* on your computer, you can use the Load Media Database, Refresh Media Database, Relink, or Batch Import command to reconnect media to clips and sequences.

◆ **Transferring a project to another computer system:** Maybe you want to finish your project in Avid Symphony, or maybe you simply want to transfer your project to Xpress Pro on another computer. To do so efficiently, use the Media tool to display all the media files for your project and then choose the Consolidate command to copy the source media to another hard drive (say, an attached FireWire drive). Those media files, along with your project file, are what you need to bring to the other workstation.

◆ **Trimming away unneeded media:** Say you created a 10-minute movie from 2 hours of footage. You can use the Consolidate command to trim away and erase the 1 hour and 50 minutes of unneeded source media and keep just the 10 minutes of various media files you need for the finished project.

◆ **Converting your project to a different resolution:** This task is common when you need to switch your project from an online (high) resolution to an offline (low) resolution. For example, you may need to edit a DV project on your main computer, but you want to first edit a 15:1s (low res) version of the project on your laptop during a plane trip. Using the Transcode command, you can convert your DV project to a 15:1s project, keeping the original DV media on your main computer.

◆ **Recapturing your project at a different resolution:** This task is common when you need to switch your project from an offline (low) resolution to an online (high) resolution. For example, you may have edited your project using 15:1s media to save drive space. When the movie is finished, you need to recapture all your media at full-resolution DV. You can use the Decompose command to intentionally bump your low-res media offline so you can recapture at a different (higher) resolution.

Avid's Source Media File Formats

For most projects, you'll capture and import files using OMFI as your source media file format. You select this format in the Capture tool before capturing or in the Media Creation settings for other tasks (such as importing).

Open Media Format Interchange (OMFI) format is the result of collaboration between Avid and other companies to create a format that can be easily transferred between different applications.

(For more information, see Chapter 4, "Capturing and Importing Media.")

The other source media file option is Material Exchange Format (MXF). This format allows exchange between file servers, tape streamers, and digital archives. Applications such as Avid|DS and ProTools support MXF files.

When you capture source footage, import footage, render effects, and so on, Xpress Pro creates source media files in the OMF file format. (For more information about video and audio format choices, see Chapter 4, "Capturing and Importing Media.")

Source media files are the video and audio data files that take up large amounts of space on your hard drives. A typical clip that has one video and two audio tracks has three source media files: one for each track.

Your clips and sequences, on the other hand, are merely references to those source media files. (For more information about clips, sequences, and other media objects, see "About Media Objects" in Chapter 5.)

If you delete a source media file from your computer, you can't retrieve that image or sound unless you recapture or reimport the media from an external source.

But if you delete every instance of a particular clip in your project, you can still retrieve the clip by reimporting the clip's source media file (or opening an old version of the bin that used to contain the clip).

Finding Source Media Files

Xpress Pro keeps your OMF source media files in a folder called OMFI MediaFiles—there's one on each of the target media drives you designate in your Media Creation settings.

(For more information about OMF files, see the sidebar "Avid's Source Media File Formats" earlier in this chapter.)

Although you may feel confident enough in your desktop skills to hunt down your source media files outside of Xpress Pro so you can move, copy, or delete them, such a strategy is unwise since source media files have long, technical names, and it can take a while to figure what's what.

Instead, you should first use one of the two following features to locate your source media files from within the Xpress Pro application:

♦ **Reveal File:** Use this File menu command if you want Xpress Pro to take you outside the application, to the OS desktop/Finder level, and spotlight exactly which source file or files are linked to a selected bin media object.

(For more information on bin media objects, see "About Media Objects" in Chapter 5.)

♦ **Media tool:** Use this tool to remain within the Xpress Pro application and list, in one window, all of the master clips, precompute clips (rendered effects), and source media files associated with one or all of your projects. You can then delete the displayed bin objects or, with master clips, use Transcode or Consolidate and move them to a chosen drive.

(For more information on Transcode and Consolidate see "Transferring and Trimming Your Sequence and Media" later in this chapter.)

To reveal source media files on the desktop/Finder:

1. In a bin, click to select a master clip, effect, or precompute (rendered effect) clip.

2. Choose File > Reveal File.

   Xpress Pro opens an OMFI folder from your desktop and highlights the source media file associated with the selected bin item (**Figure 13.1**).

If the selected bin object has more than one associated source media file, the Reveal Next File dialog box appears.

3. (Optional) If you want to reveal the next source media file associated with the selected bin object, go to the Reveal Next File dialog box and click OK (**Figure 13.2**).

   Xpress Pro opens a desktop/Finder folder and highlights the next media file (if there is another one) associated with the selected bin object.

   You can do what you want with the revealed source media file, such as delete or move it from your media drive.

continues on next page

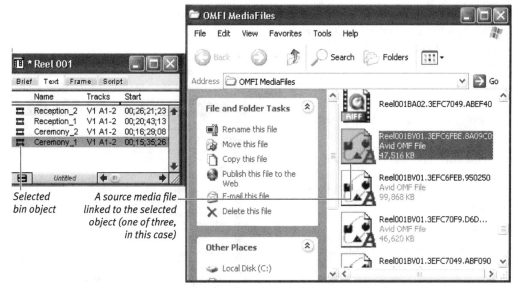

Selected bin object

A source media file linked to the selected object (one of three, in this case)

Figure 13.1 To reveal a bin object's source media, select the object and choose File > Reveal File.

Click to see the next associated source media file.

Figure 13.2 If more than one source media file is linked to the selected bin object, Xpress Pro displays the Reveal Next File dialog box.

FINDING SOURCE MEDIA FILES

✔ Tips

- Remember: You may have visibility turned off for some bin media objects (like Rendered Effects). To make bin objects visible or invisible, open your bin's Fast menu and choose Set Bin Display.

- The Reveal File command does not work for sequences, subclips, source files, or group clips.

- You can use the Reveal File command with only one bin object at a time.

To find source media files with the Media tool:

1. Choose Tools > Media Tool.

   The Media Tool dialog box appears, listing your drives on the left and your project titles on the right (**Figure 13.3**).

2. Click to select the media drive you want to search, or click the All Drives button to select all of your drives.

3. On the right side of the Media tool, select the names of the projects you want to search, or click the All Projects button to search all of your projects.

4. At the bottom of the window, select Media Files, Precompute Clips, and/or Master Clips, depending on what you want to find.

5. Click OK.

   All source media files, precompute clips, and master clips associated with the selected projects appear in one bin-like Media Tool window (**Figure 13.4**).

✔ Tips

- In the Media tool, you can annotate the information columns of listed master clips, but you cannot change the source media file or precompute information columns.

Select the drives you want to search.   Select the projects you want to search.

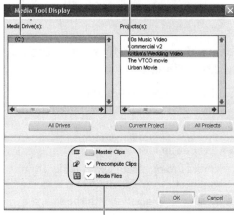

Select the types of files you want to find.

Figure 13.3 The Media tool lists your drives on the left and projects on the right. You can use the tool to search one or more drives at a time and one or more projects at a time for source media files.

Rendered effect (precompute)
Source media file
You can view the listed items on any of these tabs.

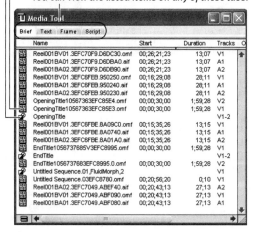

Figure 13.4 In this case, the Media tool lists all source media files and precomputes linked to the current open project.

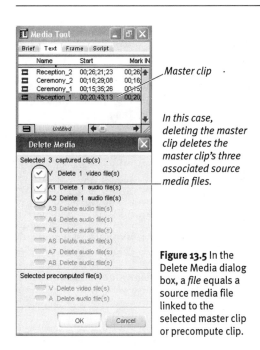

Master clip

In this case, deleting the master clip deletes the master clip's three associated source media files.

Figure 13.5 In the Delete Media dialog box, a *file* equals a source media file linked to the selected master clip or precompute clip.

- From the Media tool, you can drag master clips into project bins.

- To find out what your precompute clip video image looks like, click the Frame tab of the Media tool. You can even play a precompute clip by selecting its frame and using the J-K-L keys.

- One advantage of displaying source media files is that you can then delete individual tracks from a master clip (each source media files represents an individual master clip track).

To delete source media files with the Media tool:

1. Select the objects listed in the Media tool—master clips, precompute clips, and media source files—that you want to delete. Ctrl-click (Windows) or Shift-click (Mac) to select multiple items.

2. Press the Delete key.

   The Delete Media dialog box appears. Keep the items you want to delete selected (**Figure 13.5**).

3. Click OK.

   Xpress Pro deletes the selected source media files. If you choose to delete a master clip, Xpress Pro deletes that master clip's source media.

Warnings about Manual Media Management

If you don't use Xpress Pro's media management tools to manage your source media files and prefer sorting through media files yourself by opening desktop OMFI folders, you should keep the following pitfalls in mind:

♦ Do not manually duplicate or move source media files from your desktop with the Xpress Pro application open or your project could become corrupted.

♦ Do not keep duplicate source media files on the same computer; if you must do so, store the duplicates in a folder named something other than OMFI Files.

Since Xpress Pro keeps a media database that tells the application which source media files are associated with which master clips and sequences in open bins, disturbing the files in the OMFI folders will confuse Xpress Pro.

(For more information about Xpress Pro's media database, see "Relinking Offline Clips to Online Source Media" later in this chapter.)

Why the Media Tool Window Is and Isn't Like a Bin

After you display master clips, precompute clips, and media files in the Media Tool window, you can sift, sort, annotate, delete, or duplicate any clips or files listed in any of the window's four tabs, just as you can in a normal bin window.

(For more information on organizing and annotating items in bin windows, see "Working with Bins and Folders" in Chapter 5.)

Generally, you can do most everything in the Media Tool window that you can do in a bin window, except for the following:

♦ You cannot perform a batch capture, batch import, or relink operation.

♦ You cannot display subclips or sequences.

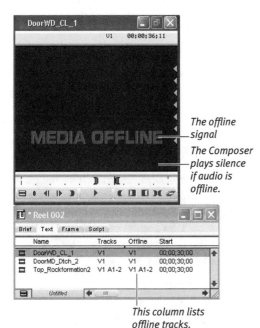

The offline signal

The Composer plays silence if audio is offline.

This column lists offline tracks.

Figure 13.6: If a track's source media file is offline, the Composer displays "Media Offline," and the track is listed as offline in the bin.

Relinking Offline Clips to Online Source Media

If you try to play a clip or title in a source monitor or sequence and the Composer monitor displays "Media Offline" (**Figure 13.6**), then Xpress Pro has lost the link between the clip and its video source media file (or, if the Composer plays silence, then the audio media file is missing).

A clip or effect may be marked "Media Offline" for several reasons:

◆ You recaptured or relinked clips to source media while the sequence bin was closed, making the sequence offline. (For more information on recapturing, see "Decomposing and Recapturing a Sequence" later in this chapter.)

◆ You moved your source media files to a different media drive or to a folder other than the OMFI folder.

(For more information on the OMFI folder, see the sidebars "Avid's Media File Formats" and "Warnings About Manual Media Management" earlier in this chapter.

◆ You erased your source media files from your hard drive (either accidentally or intentionally).

◆ You purposely made your clip offline by choosing Bin > Unlink. (For more information, see "Breaking the Link Between Master Clips and Source Media" later in this chapter.)

continues on next page

◆ You used Consolidate or Decompose to make your sequence offline and want to either relink your project to different source media files or recapture your source media at a different resolution. (For more information, see "Transferring and Trimming Your Sequence and Media" and "Decomposing and Recapturing a Sequence" later in this chapter.)

If you know that your source media files are on your computer even though your clips are marked "Media Offline," you can fix the problem by doing one or more of the following:

◆ **Refresh the media database.** If your clips are possibly offline because you temporarily removed a hard drive from your system or moved your OMFI folder to a different hard drive, you can refresh the database to have Xpress Pro automatically look through your media drives and relink the appropriate files to offline clips.

(For more information about the media database, see the sidebar "The Hidden Media Database.")

◆ **Load the media database.** If your sequence is offline because you relinked or recaptured master clips while the sequence bin was closed, load the database.

◆ **Use the Relink command.** The Relink command attempts to automatically relink source media and master clips. (Relink can also reconnect subclips and clips to related sequences.)

◆ **Use the Batch Import command.** This command offers probably the most reliable method of pointing Xpress Pro directly to a source media file that's supposed to be linked to a selected offline clip.

◆ **Move source files into the proper folder.** Do this when the Xpress Pro application is closed.

The Hidden Media Database

While you edit, Xpress Pro keeps a database (or catalog) of the source media files connected to your clips, precompute files, and so on. However, to conserve memory, it builds only a partial database for the clips that are in open bins.

Because of this memory-saving strategy, you may have to load the media database if you recaptured or relinked clips to source files while their associated sequence was in a closed bin.

Or you may have to refresh the media database if your clips and sequences are offline because you temporarily disconnected your media drive from the computer.

How Can You Tell That a Clip or Sequence Is Offline?

In addition to the obvious clues—the Composer displays "Media Offline" or plays silence when there should be sound—you can also check your bin to see if any clip or effect tracks are offline.

The Brief and Text tabs of your bin display the Offline column, which lists tracks that are offline (tracks that typically might be offline are V1, A1, and A2).

If you don't see the Offline column, click your bin's Fast menu and choose Headings to display the info column heading selection dialog box.

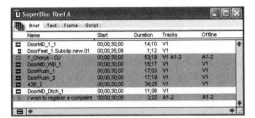

Figure 13.7: Ctrl-click (Windows) or Shift-click (Mac) to select all offline clips that need to be relinked to source media files.

Select this option to relink your selected master clips to their source media files. | *Choose which drives to search here.*

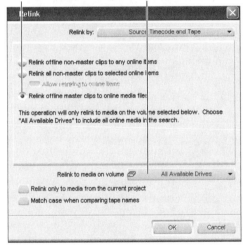

Figure 13.8: In the Relink dialog box, you can tell Xpress Pro what kinds of objects you want to relink to source media and which drives to search.

To load or refresh the media database:

Do one of the following:

◆ If a sequence is offline because you recaptured master clips while the associated sequence was in a closed bin or you used the Consolidate feature to move source media files to a different drive and relinked the files to clips while the sequence bin was closed, choose File > Load Media Database.

With luck, your offline sequence will be online again, after Xpress Pro loads the database.

◆ If anything is offline after you take a media drive on and off the computer or move your media files to a different drive, choose File > Refresh Media Database.

Xpress Pro searches your drives and relinks source media files to offline clips, sequences, and so on.

✔ Tip

■ Since Xpress Pro remembers the media database until you quit the application, you need to load the media database only once per editing session.

To link offline master clips to online source media using Relink:

1. In a bin, select a group of offline master clips. Ctrl-click (Windows) or Shift-click (Mac) to select multiple items (**Figure 13.7**).

2. Choose Bin > Relink.

The Relink dialog box appears (**Figure 13.8**).

3. If you are relinking master clips to source media, select Relink Offline Master Clips to Online Media Files.

continues on next page

4. At the bottom right of the window, click the Relink to Media on Volume button and choose the drives that contain your media files (or click All Available Drives).

5. Click OK.

With luck, Xpress Pro will match your offline clips to their associated source media files. Your clips will no longer be marked "Media Offline."

If this procedure does not work (which is common), use the Batch Import command (see the next task).

✔ Tips

- By default, Xpress Pro relinks offline master clips using source timecode and tape information. But for film projects, you open the Relink By pop-up menu (in the Relink dialog box) and choose Key Number.

- When a title is offline, you don't have to bother relinking its media. Just select the title and choose Clip > Create Unrendered Title Media. (See Chapter 8, "Creating Titles," for details.)

- If a subclip is offline, you need to first relink its parent master clip. Usually, Xpress Pro automatically relinks your subclip to the online master clip. However, if the subclip is still offline after you relink its master clip, select the subclip, choose File > Relink, and select Relink Offline Non-master Clips to Any Online Items.

These offline clips need to be relinked to source media.

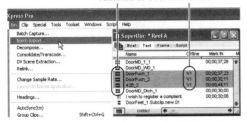

Figure 13.9 The most reliable way to relink offline master clips is to select them and choose Bin > Batch Import.

If Xpress Pro cannot guess a location, the listing is highlighted in red and contains a question mark.

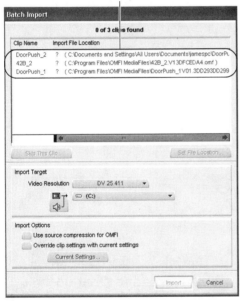

Figure 13.10 At the top of the Batch Import dialog box, Xpress Pro lists the locations where it guesses that the source media files for the offline clips can be found.

To link offline bin objects to online source media using Batch Import:

1. Select one or more offline master clips (or rendered effect clips) in a bin.

2. Choose Bin > Batch Import (**Figure 13.9**).

3. In the dialog box that appears, click Offline Only.

   The Batch Import dialog box appears. At the top of the window Xpress Pro lists in black any source media files it finds that it guesses are related to one or more of your selected bin objects. The dialog box lists source media files it cannot find in red (**Figure 13.10**).

continues on next page

RELINKING OFFLINE CLIPS TO ONLINE SOURCE MEDIA

4. To point Xpress Pro directly to a source media file, select a red or black clip listing at the top of the Batch Import dialog box and click Set File Location.

A system window opens, allowing you to point Xpress Pro directly to the relevant source media file (**Figure 13.11**).

5. Navigate to the relevant source media file, select it, and click Open.

6. Repeat steps 4 and 5 for all the items listed at the top of the Batch Import dialog box.

7. In the Batch Import dialog box, click Import.

Xpress Pro imports the selected source media, relinking it with the selected offline bin objects. The selected clips and so on are now online in your bin.

Breaking the Link Between Master Clips and Source Media

In some cases—such as when you want to go from offline to online quality by relinking your master clips to different source media files—you may want to intentionally break the link between a master clip and its source media.

For example, you might break the link between your clips and 15:1s resolution media files so that you can relink your clips to full-resolution DV media files.

Select the clip to relink here.   Find the source media file here.

Click here.

Figure 13.11 To point Xpress Pro directly to the location of a source media file, select a clip listing at the top of the Batch Import window and click Set File Location.

Relink vs. Batch Import: What Works and What Doesn't

For relinking offline master clips that were unintentionally thrown offline, most editors have more success with Bin > Batch Import than Bin > Relink.

Bin > Relink is actually best used after you *intentionally* unlink master clips to their source files, which you might do if you want to then relink those master clips to different (higher-resolution) source media files that are on a different drive.

These clips will be bumped offline.

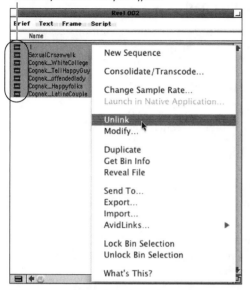

Figure 13.12 To break the link between master clips and their source media files, select the clips and then choose Bin > Unlink.

To unlink a master clip and its source media:

1. Select one or more online master clips you want to unlink. Shift-click to select multiple items.

2. Right-click (Windows) or Ctrl+Shift (Mac) and choose Unlink (**Figure 13.12**). Xpress Pro breaks the link between the selected master clip and its source media files. The master clip is now marked "Media Offline."

Relinking Master Clips to Subclips and Sequences

In addition to linking master clips to source media files, you can use Bin > Relink to make sure that master clips are linked to their related subclips and sequences (a procedure that does not directly involve source media files).

If your master clips are online, but related subclips or sequences (those that contain instances of the master clip) are marked as offline, you can use one of two commands in the Relink dialog box to relink master clips to their related subclips or sequences.

If your master clips are offline, you can use the Relink dialog box to make sure that related subclips and sequences are linked to them.

Want to Edit on the Road?

Xpress Pro makes it easy to transcode a high-resolution project to a low-resolution version so you can easily edit on a laptop on the road or edit on another computer that doesn't have access to fast hard drives.

Generally, the workflow for converting your project to a lower resolution is as follows:

1. Open a final-resolution project (for example, it might use DV or uncompressed video) and use Bin > Consolidate to transcode it to a low resolution (such as Photo-JPEG).

(For information on transcoding, see "Converting Your Project to a Different Resolution" later in this chapter.)

2. Copy the low-res media and your Avid User and Avid Project folders onto your laptop.

You can now edit your movie on the road with ease.

3. Return your project file folder to your main workstation, the one that has both your final-resolution media and low-res media versions. Continue to work in offline resolution on your main workstation.

You can find the project folder in *drive*:\Program Files\Avid\Avid Xpress Pro\Avid Projects*CPU system user name* (Windows) or *drive*/Users/Shared/Avid Projects/*CPU system user name* (Mac).

4. When you want to convert your project from an offline (low) resolution to an online (high) resolution, use Bin > Unlink to break the link between your master clips and the low-res media.

5. Choose Bin > Relink to relink your master clips to the drive that contains the high-resolution version of the source media.

Now you're ready to output to tape.

To connect subclips and sequences to online master clips:

1. Move the offline subclips and sequences into the same bin as the online master clips to which they're related.

2. Select the offline subclips and sequences.

3. Choose File > Relink.

4. In the Relink dialog box that appears, select Relink Offline Non-master Clips to Any Online Items.

5. Click OK.

   Xpress Pro makes your offline subclips and sequences online again.

To link related subclips and sequences to a selected master clip:

1. Move the subclips and sequences into the same bin as the online master clips to which they're related.

2. Select the master clip that you want to link to the related subclips and sequences.

3. Choose File > Relink.

4. In the Relink dialog box that appears, select Relink All Non-master Clips to Selected Online Items.

5. (Optional) Select Allow Relinking to Offline Items to allow Xpress Pro to link the selected master clip to subclips and sequences even if all the objects are offline.

6. Click OK.

   Xpress Pro relinks the subclips and sequences to the selected master clip.

Transferring and Trimming Your Sequence and Media

The Consolidate command (actually called Consolidate/Transcode) is used for two very important operations: to transfer your sequence and all of its media to a different computer, and to trim the source media of your sequence to its essentials.

When you consolidate all of the media files associated with your project, copying them to a single (preferably removable) drive, you can take that drive along with your project file to another computer and continue editing.

When you reach a stage in your project where you no longer need all the raw media not used in your final sequence, you can consolidate just that sequence, which copies only the portions of the media files that you need for that sequence. In other words, Xpress Pro trims your source media, saving the essential parts; this procedure has obvious space-saving benefits.

To transfer all of your project's media files to another computer:

1. Choose Tools > Media Tool.

   The Media Tool window opens.

2. Click All Drives to select your system's hard drives (or select only the drives that contain your project's media, if you know which they are).

   All drives listed in the left pane of the window become highlighted.

3. In the right pane of the window, select the name of your project.

4. In the bottom part of the window click source files and deselect master clips and precomputes.

*The Media tool can display all
of your project's source files.*

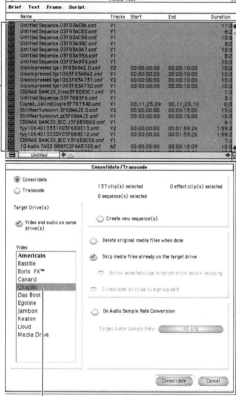

*Select one (removable) drive for all of
your project's media for easy transport.*

Figure 13.13 To copy your project's entire media files
to one or more selected drives without trimming, use
the Media tool to display the project's source media
and choose Bin > Consolidate/Transcode.

- Instead of using the Media tool to perform a consolidation operation, you can just drag all of the master clips, precompute files, effects, subclips, and sequences that you need into the same bin, select them all, and choose Consolidate.

5. Click OK.

The Media tool searches the selected
drives and opens a window containing all
of the source files associated with your
project.

6. In the Media tool, press Ctrl+A
(Windows) or Command+A (Mac)
to select all of the source media files.

7. Choose Bin > Consolidate/Transcode.

The Consolidate/Transcode dialog box
opens. At the top of the dialog box, the
number of clips selected indicates the
number of source media files selected
in the Media tool.

8. On the left side of the dialog box, select
the drive, preferably one that's removable, to which you want to copy all of
your project media.

9. (Optional) To be on the safe side, select
Skip Media Files Already on the Target
Drive if you know that some of the
media files in question are already on
the selected hard drive. Deselect Create
New Sequence(s) and Delete Original
Media Files When Done (**Figure 13.13**).

10. Click Consolidate.

Xpress Pro copies all of your project's
source media to the selected drive. Now
you can carry that drive, along with a
copy of your Xpress Pro project folder,
to another computer.

✔ Tips

- Your project folders are located at
  drive:\Program Files\Avid\Avid Xpress
  Pro\Avid Projects*CPU system user
  name* (Windows) and *drive*/Users/
  Shared/ Avid Projects/*CPU system
  user name* (Mac).

To transfer and trim your finished sequence:

1. In a bin, select the sequence that you want to consolidate.

2. Choose Bin > Consolidate/Transcode (**Figure 13.14**).

   The Consolidate/Transcode dialog box opens (**Figure 13.15**).

3. In the upper-left corner of the dialog box, select Consolidate.

4. In the Target Drive(s) area, select one or more drives on which you want to store the consolidated source media files.

5. In the Handle Length box, enter the number of frames to add before and after the consolidated media files.

6. Select Create New Sequence(s) to create a new, consolidated version of the selected sequence.

7. If you want to keep just the consolidated, trimmed media and dump the old, full-length media, select Delete Original Media Files When Done.

8. If your target drive may already contain some of the necessary media files, select Skip Media Files Already on the Target Drive.

9. To make sure that Xpress Pro links to those files on your target drive and not to equivalent files on another drive, select Relink Selected Clips to Target Drive Before Skipping.

10. If you have group edit clips, select Consolidate All Clips in a Group Edit.

    (For more information on group edits and Xpress Pro's multicamera features, see "Grouping Clips and Multicamera Editing" in Chapter 6.)

The source media files linked to these selected items will be consolidated on the same hard drive so they can be easily moved to another computer.

Figure 13.14 You can put all of the bin objects you want to consolidate into the same bin and in one swoop consolidate their media files by selecting them all and choosing Bin > Consolidate/Transcode.

Select a target drive. *Select this option to keep only those media files that are used in the selected bin items.*

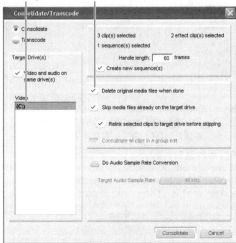

Figure 13.15 To consolidate selected bin items, select Consolidate at the upper left of the Consolidate/Transcode dialog box and select a target drive for the consolidated media files.

11. If you want to convert all of your audio to the same sample rate, select Do Audio Sample Rate Conversion.

12. Click Consolidate.

Xpress Pro creates a new sequence in your bin with the word *Consolidated* added to its title.

Xpress Pro creates new master clips and places them in the same bin as the sequence with the extension .new plus an incremental number (.01, .02, and so on) added to each name.

Xpress Pro also creates new source media files on your target drive containing only the portions of your original media necessary to play your sequence and selected clips.

✔ Tips

■ If you choose to consolidate only a sequence, then Xpress Pro consolidates only those source media files (plus handles) contained within your sequence.

■ You can use Consolidate to create a subclip so you can turn a subclip into a new master clip with its own source media files.

■ Before consolidating a sequence, create a duplicate of it as a backup, to make sure you have one copy of the sequence linked to the original (nonconsolidated) source media files.

■ For more information on group clips see Chapter 6, "Making Edits."

Moving Your Entire Project to a Different Computer: The Checklist

When you want to move your entire Xpress Pro project to another computer, make sure you bring along the following after you consolidate your sequence:

◆ **Your project folder:** You can find your project folder in *drive:*\Program Files\Avid\Avid Xpress Pro\Avid Projects*CPU system user name* (Windows) or *drive*/Users/Shared/ Avid Projects/*CPU system user name* (Mac).

◆ **Your OMFI (source media) drive or folder:** Bring the drive to which you consolidated your source media or, if it's small enough, copy the OMFI folder you need to a DVD or CD.

◆ **Your User profile folder:** This folder, which contains your important user settings, can be found in *drive:*\Program Files\Avid\Avid Xpress Pro\Avid Users*CPU system user name* (Windows) or *drive*/Users/Shared/ Avid Users/*CPU system user name* (Mac).

Converting Your Project to a Different Resolution

If you want to convert your project to a different resolution—for example, an offline resolution such as 15:1s—you need to transcode your project.

You can transcode either the entire project (transcoding all of the source media for your master clips and effects) or only the source media needed for a selected sequence (trimming the media).

To transcode your project or sequence:

1. *Do one of the following:*

   ▲ To transcode the entire project, open the Media tool, select All Drives, and display all of the source media for your project (the same procedure for consolidation described in the task "To transfer all of your project's media files to another computer" earlier in this chapter).

   ▲ To transcode the entire project, drag the sequences, master clips, and effect clips (namely, titles) that you want to transcode into the same bin and press Ctrl+A (Windows) or Command+A (Mac) to select all files.

   ▲ To transcode just the media needed for a sequence, click to select the sequence in your bin.

2. Choose Bin > Consolidate/Transcode (**Figure 13.16**).

3. At the upper left of the Consolidate/Transcode dialog box that opens, select Transcode.

4. Open the Target Video Resolution pop-up menu and choose a new resolution (**Figure 13.17**).

The source media linked to each of these clips will be transcoded.

The source media of every clip in this sequence will be transcoded.

The source media linked to these titles will be transcoded.

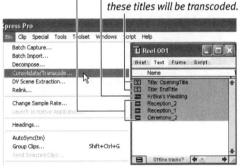

Figure 13.16 To transcode the source media linked to selected bin objects, select the objects in the same bin and choose Bin > Consolidate/Transcode.

Select the drive for the new files here.

Choose the new resolution here.

Add handles to sequence clip media here.

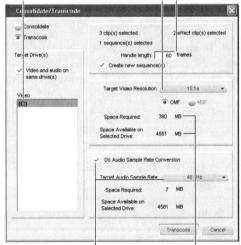

If necessary, convert all of your audio to the same sample rate here.

Check to see if you have enough drive space for the new files.

Figure 13.17 After selecting Transcode in the Consolidate/Transcode dialog box, you need to choose your new source media file resolution.

5. If you want to transcode all of your audio to a certain sampling rate, select Do Audio Sample Rate Conversion, open the Target Audio Sample Rate pop-up menu, and choose a sampling rate.

6. If you want audio and video source media files to go to the same drive, on the left side of the dialog box select Video and Audio on Same Drive(s).

7. On the left side of the dialog box, select the drive to which you want to send your transcoded project.

8. At the top of the window, in the Handle Length box, enter a number of frames to add before and after the clips in the selected sequence.

9. If you want Xpress Pro to create new versions of the selected sequences during the transcode operation, select Create New Sequence(s).

10. Click Transcode.

   Xpress Pro transcodes the source media behind your selected items. You can now edit your selected sequence using the new resolution. Since you know the drive on which the transcoded files reside, you can easily move them to another computer.

✔ Tip

■ If you choose to transcode only a sequence, then you will transcode only the source media behind the clips (plus handles) within the selected sequence.

Taking Your Project from Offline to Online Quality: The Strategy

Typically, taking a project from an offline resolution (such as 15:1s) to full resolution for final output requires recapturing only the media you need for your final sequence (plus clip handles). You don't need to recapture all of your master clips; that will take up loads of space and defeats the purpose of editing in an offline resolution in the first place.

So just select your final sequence, not your master clips, when you choose Bin > Batch Capture to recapture your media.

Decomposing and Recapturing a Sequence

If you initially edited your project at a low resolution (such as 15:1s) and have now finished editing and want to finalize your project at full (say, DV) resolution, you need to recapture your finished sequence at DV resolution.

You can recapture your sequence at a different resolution in two ways: either decompose your sequence and recapture it or choose Bin > Batch Capture.

Decomposing your sequence intentionally unlinks your sequence from its source media, creating an offline version of your sequence and new versions of every master clip needed for the sequence. The decompose procedure also organizes all of the new decomposed items in the same bin. You can then select the offline sequence and recapture it.

Most editors choose this method because it gives them peace of mind; since the Decompose feature organizes all the clips and effects included in the sequence in the same bin, it's easy to grasp what is and isn't going to be recaptured.

You can also recapture a sequence at a different resolution by bypassing the Decompose command altogether. Just select the sequence and choose Batch Capture. This method is the faster of the two, but it may not give you the peace of mind that decomposing does.

Recapturing a sequence captures only the source media needed for the sequence, not your original full-length master clips, so make sure you save a backup version of your sequence before performing a batch-recapture operation.

Sequence to decompose

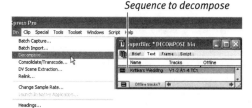

Figure 13.18 You'll need a new bin for the items that Xpress Pro creates after a decompose operation. Place the sequence in the bin and choose Bin > Decompose.

Deselect this option if you don't want imported media bumped offline.

Deselect this option too if you want to recapture all master clips in your sequence.

Decompose

- Offline media only
- ✓ Digitized clips
- Imported clips
- All clips in a group edit

1 sequence(s) selected

Handle Length: 60 frames

Extend handles beyond Master Clip edges

OK   Cancel

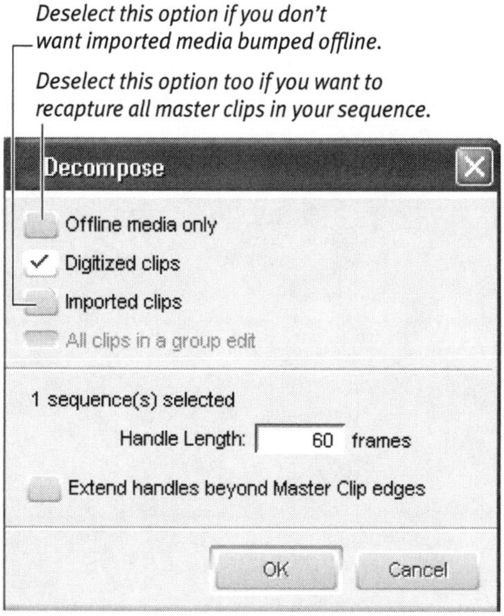

Figure 13.19 In the Decompose dialog box, you can configure Xpress Pro to place only your digitized clips offline and keep your imported clips (such as Photoshop files and CD audio), so that you won't have to re-import the imported items.

To decompose a sequence for recapturing:

1. Create a new bin for your decomposed sequence and drop the sequence that you want to decompose and recapture in the bin.

2. Select the sequence and choose Bin > Decompose (**Figure 13.18**).

   The Decompose dialog box appears (**Figure 13.19**).

3. If you plan to decompose and recapture the entire sequence (to take the project from offline to online quality), deselect the Offline Media Only option.

4. If you want to decompose (place offline) all clips in your sequence that were captured from tape, select Digitized Clips.

5. If you want to preserve imported clips such as imported CD audio or imported Photoshop files, deselect Imported Clips.

6. Enter a handle length to add extra frames (for transitions) to the master clips you will recapture after the decompose operation.

continues on next page

DECOMPOSING AND RECAPTURING A SEQUENCE

7. Click OK. When the warning dialog box appears, click OK again.

Xpress Pro places offline every clip in the sequence that you selected to decompose (in the Decompose dialog box).

In addition, Xpress Pro creates new offline master clips in the same bin as the selected sequence, adding the extension .new plus a sequential number to their names (**Figure 13.20**).

✔ Tips

- When you decompose a sequence, all of the clips it contains are marked "Media Offline." However, the original source media files remain intact on your drives; they're just no longer linked to your sequence.

- If there might be timecode breaks on your source tapes beyond the beginning and ending of your current master clips, do not select Extend Handles Beyond Master Clip Edges in the Decompose dialog box.

- If you have any group clips in your sequence, you can decompose them by selecting All Clips in a Group Edit in the Decompose dialog box. (For more information on group clips, see Chapter 6, "Making Edits.")

New master clips

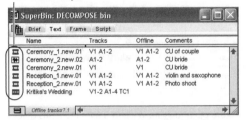

Figure 13.20 After a decompose operation, Xpress Pro creates new master clips that have the durations necessary for your decomposed sequence.

The Alternative to Recapturing

There's another way to link an offline sequence (created by Decompose) to new source media: Instead of recapturing an offline decomposed sequence, you can transfer already-captured online-quality source media files to your computer, select the sequence, choose Bin > Relink, and select the drive with the high-res source media files as the target drive in the Relink dialog box.

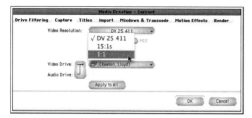

Figure 13.21 In this case, the new capture resolution will be 1:1 (uncompressed) video.

Figure 13.22 To recapture a sequence—whether it's a decomposed sequence or still has media files attached to it—select the sequence and choose Bin > Batch Capture.

Figure 13.23 To recapture a decomposed sequence, select Offline Media Only in the Batch Capture dialog box.

To recapture a sequence:

1. Prepare your deck or camera and source tape for capturing, as explained in Chapter 4, "Capturing and Importing Media."

2. Choose the new resolution to capture *by doing one of the following:*
   - ▲ On the Settings tab of the Project window, double-click your Media Creation settings, click the Capture tab of the Media Creation dialog box, and choose a new video resolution from the pop-up menu. Choose a target drive for the new media files from the pop-up menu (**Figure 13.21**).
   - ▲ Choose Tools > Capture to open the Capture tool and choose a new video resolution from the pop-up menu; choose a target drive for the new media files from the pop-up menu.

3. Select the sequence you want recapture, whether it be a decomposed offline sequence or a sequence that is still linked to low-res media files.

4. Choose Bin > Batch Capture (**Figure 13.22**).
   The Batch Capture dialog box appears, along with the Capture tool.

5. *Do one of the following:*
   - ▲ If you're recapturing a decomposed, offline sequence, in the Batch Capture dialog select Offline Media Only (**Figure 13.23**).
   - ▲ If you're recapturing a sequence that is not decomposed, deselect Offline Media Only.

6. In the Handle Length box, enter a number of frames to add to the head and tail of new master clips.

continues on next page

DECOMPOSING AND RECAPTURING A SEQUENCE

7. To add more footage to new media files than was included in the original master clips, select Extend Handles Beyond Master Clip Edges.

8. Click OK.

   Xpress Pro cues your source tape to the beginning of the first master clip to capture and begins capturing.

   After capturing, your sequence is online with media at the newly selected resolution.

✔ Tips

- If your footage contains timecode breaks, you should not select Extend Handles Beyond Master Clip Edges in the Batch Capture dialog.

- Before recapturing a decomposed sequence, you can select the decomposed offline clips as well as the sequence, but this is not necessary. Xpress Pro automatically relinks those offline master clips after relinking the sequence that contains them.

DECOMPOSING AND RECAPTURING A SEQUENCE

OUTPUTTING AND EXPORTING

At the end of the editing process, you can output your final sequence to tape or export it to disk for use in another medium, such as a DVD or Web stream.

Exporting material to disk isn't relegated to the end process, however. You can also export QuickTime movies as self-contained videos or as reference movies, still images, audio tracks, and so on to be manipulated and altered in other applications and optionally brought back into your Xpress Pro Timeline.

In addition, you can export shot logs and edit decision lists (EDLs) to recapture your footage and re-create your edited movie automatically in another editing application.

Preparing for Output to Tape

When your movie is finished and ready to show to the world, the usual final step is to output (or record) your final sequence to a tape inserted into a connected deck or camera.

You can output directly from FireWire to a DV deck or camera. And if you have the Mojo box, which acts as a digital-analog converter, you can output your digital signal to an analog recorder via component (YcrCb), composite, or S-Video connections.

(To find out about inputting and outputting component signals with the Mojo, see the section, "Xpress Pro with Mojo" in Appendix B.)

Outputting to tape is different than exporting your movie to disk, which creates a digital file on your hard drive.

(For more information on exporting material to disk, see "Exporting Material to Disk" later in this chapter.)

Before you output to tape, you can take the following steps to ensure smooth and professional output:

◆ **Add bars and tone.** Color bars and an audio reference tone at the beginning of your sequence help whomever screens your project to set video and audio levels before your movie begins.

◆ **Back up your sequence.** Duplicate your final sequence and perform any video or audio mixdown operations on the duplicate; this way, you leave the tracks of the backup uncollapsed, in case you need to make further changes later.

◆ **Mix down your video and audio.** Before outputting your finished sequence to tape, you can mix down your video and audio tracks to ensure smoother and more synchronized playback.

A video mixdown takes all of your video tracks and combines them into one video master clip (creating a new source media file) to be placed on one video track.

An audio mixdown takes all of your audio tracks and combines them into either a one-track clip (for mono projects) or a two-track clip (for stereo projects).

◆ **Set audio output.** You usually don't have to touch this setting if you're outputting a digital sequence via a digital channel (such as DV over FireWire, with or without Mojo).

However, if you have a software-only (non-Mojo) system and are outputting from an analog sound card, you may need to adjust your audio output level depending on the performance of your sound card.

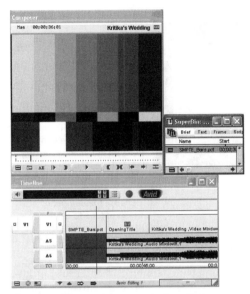

Figure 14.1 After you import a color bar still from Xpress Pro's Supporting Files folder, you can splice in the color bars at the beginning of your sequence.

To add color bars to your sequence:

1. On the Settings tab of the Project window, double-click your active Import settings and make sure the settings are configured to import 601 color.

2. Select a bin and choose File > Import. The Import dialog box appears.

3. Using the File to Import dialog box, import Avid's SMPTE_Bars.pict file (or one of the other color bar files) *from one of the following locations:*
   - ▲ *drive*:\Program Files\Avid\Avid Xpress Pro\Supporting Files\Test_Patterns (Windows)
   - ▲ *drive*/Applications/Avid Xpress Pro/ SupportingFiles/TestPatterns (Mac)

   After import, the color bars appear as a master clip in the selected bin.

4. Insert edit the color bars into the beginning of your sequence (**Figure 14.1**). The color bars will help people who play your movie configure their monitor's video settings.

✔ Tips

- SMPTE stands for the Society of Motion Picture and Television Engineers, an organization that establishes professional standards for film and television.

- When people watch your movie on a television monitor, they can adjust the color and brightness levels using the color bars for reference.

- According to Avid, SMPTE_Bars patterns are not 100 percent accurate. If you need completely accurate bars, you'll have to record SMPTE bars from a signal generator. (For more information, consult the Xpress Pro Help.)

To add an audio tone to your sequence:

1. Choose Tools > Audio Tool.

   The Audio tool opens.

2. Click the PH (Peak Hold) button and choose Create Tone Media from the menu that appears (**Figure 14.2**).

3. In the Create Tone Media dialog box that opens (**Figure 14.3**), enter the level, frequency, and duration (if you want settings different than the defaults) for the new audio master clip.

4. From the Number of Tracks pop-up menu, choose the number of tracks of audio tone that you want to create.

5. From the Target Bin pop-up menu, choose the bin in which you want Xpress Pro to store the new audio tone master clip.

6. From the Target Drive pop-up menu, choose the target drive for the new audio media file.

7. Click OK.

   Xpress Pro creates an audio tone master clip in the target bin. You can now edit the audio tone clip into your sequence, directly underneath the SMPTE color bars (**Figure 14.4**).

   When people play your movie on a television monitor, they can now set the volume level according to how they hear the audio tone.

✔ Tip

- Usually you'll want to add a few seconds of black filler after your color bars and tone, before your main sequence begins. (For information on loading and adding filler, see "Editing Filler into Your Sequence" in Chapter 6.)

Click here.

Figure 14.2 You can create an audio tone to go with your color bars by opening the Audio tool's PH menu and selecting Create Tone Media.

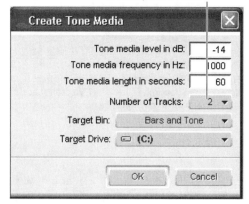

Choose the number of tracks of tone to create.

Figure 14.3 In the Create Tone Media dialog box, you choose the duration of your audio tone master clip as well as its level and frequency.

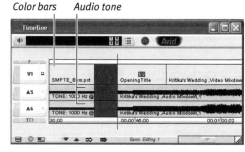

Color bars   Audio tone

Figure 14.4 Typically, you will use an overwrite edit to edit your audio tone directly underneath your color bars.

Video to mix down

Figure 14.5 To mix down video tracks, mark In and Out points around the video that you want to mix down, monitor the topmost track, and choose Clip > Video Mixdown.

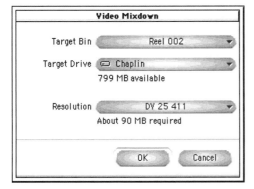

Figure 14.6 In the Video Mixdown dialog box, you tell Xpress Pro where to put your new mixdown sequence and master clips and on which drive to store your mixdown media files.

To mix down video tracks:

1. Duplicate your current sequence as a backup.

2. Render every effect in your sequence.

   (For information on rendering, see Chapter 11, "Rendering and Real Time.")

3. Monitor the topmost video track that you want to mix down.

4. Select the track buttons for the video tracks that you want to mix down.

5. In the Timeline, use Mark In and Mark Out to mark the area that you want to mix down.

6. Choose Clip > Video Mixdown (**Figure 14.5**).

7. In the Video Mixdown dialog box that appears, choose a target bin for your new mixdown sequence and master clips, and a target drive and resolution for the new mixdown source media file (**Figure 14.6**).

8. Click OK.

   Xpress Pro performs a video mixdown, creating a new video mixdown master clip in the target bin, which you can now edit into the Timeline in place of the pre-mixed video tracks.

To replace your video layers with the video mixdown clip:

1. Double-click the new mixdown master clip to load it into a source monitor.

2. Click the Mark Clip button (located by default at the bottom of the source monitor) to mark an In point at the beginning of the clip and an Out point at the end of the clip.

3. In the Timeline, mark an In point at the beginning of the video layers that you used to create the mixdown clip.

4. In the Timeline, select all the video tracks you're replacing,

5. Patch your source video track to the lowest selected record track.

6. Perform the edit by clicking the Overwrite Edit button (located by default on the Composer Fast menu).

   Xpress Pro performs an overwrite edit, replacing your video layers with the one-track video mixdown clip (**Figure 14.7**). Your sequence will now have a better chance of playing back smoothly.

✔ Tips

- Since a video mixdown combines video tracks so that you cannot separate them again, don't perform video mixdown until the last stage of the editing process.

- You can map the Overwrite Edit button from the Edit tab of the Command palette.

Video mixdown clip

Figure 14.7 Replace your video layers with the new video mixdown clip by loading the mixdown clip into a source monitor, selecting all the video tracks in the Timeline, patching the source track to V1, and using an overwrite edit in the mixdown clip.

Audio tracks to mix down

Figure 10.8 To mix down your audio tracks, first mark In and Out points around the audio you want to mix down and choose Clip > Audio Mixdown.

In this case, the audio will mix down to two tracks.   *The new audio mixdown master clip will be mixed down to this bin.*

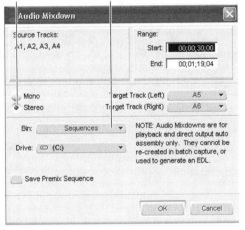

Figure 10.9 The most important decision to make in the Audio Mixdown dialog box is whether to mix to one or two tracks.

To mix down audio tracks to one or two tracks:

1. Open the same sequence that contains your video mixdown.

2. Select the audio track buttons for the tracks that you want to mix down.

3. In the Timeline, mark In and Out points around the audio that you want to mix down (**Figure 14.8**).

4. Choose Clip > Audio Mixdown (**Figure 14.9**).
   The Audio Mixdown dialog box opens.

5. *Do one of the following:*
   - ▲ If you want to mix down your audio to one track, choose Mono and select a target track from the first Target Track pop-up menu.
   - ▲ If you want to mix down your audio to two tracks, choose Stereo and select two target tracks from the Target Track pop-up menus.

6. (Optional) In the Audio Mixdown dialog box, adjust the start and end timecode (In and Out points) for the range of audio you're mixing down.

7. In the Audio Mixdown dialog box, choose a target bin for your new sequence and mixdown master clip and a target drive for the new mixdown source media file.

8. (Optional) If you want Xpress Pro to save a copy of your sequence as it is before the mixdown, choose Save Premix Sequence.

continues on next page

9. Click OK.

Xpress Pro performs an audio mixdown, creating a new audio mixdown master clip in the target bin and placing the clip below the lowest audio track in the Timeline.

The mixdown also creates a new audio source media file on your target drive, as well as a premix sequence (if you selected Save Premix Sequence in the Audio Mixdown dialog box).

Xpress Pro selects the layered audio tracks in the Timeline.

10. In the Timeline, select the tracks you just mixed down and press Delete to eliminate them.

Now the only audio remaining in your Timeline is the audio mixdown clip (**Figure 14.10**). You're ready for output.

✔ Tips

■ Although Xpress Pro can support 24 audio tracks in the Timeline, it can play back only 8 audio tracks at a time. So before output, to make sure that all your audio plays out to tape, you should consolidate your audio down to 8 tracks.

■ If you do not mark In and Out points in the Timeline, then Xpress Pro mixes down all audio in the sequence, which might be fine if the mixdown is for final output.

New master clip
Premix sequence
Audio mixdown clips

Figure 14.10 After you perform an audio mixdown and delete the old audio layers from your sequence, you have a simplified Timeline.

Figure 14.11 To play a calibration tone, open the PH menu in the Audio tool and select Play Calibration Tone.

Adjust the output level here

Set to 0, for Output

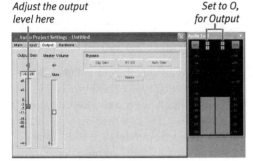

Figure 14.12 To adjust the audio output level, click the Output tab of the Audio Project Settings dialog box, play a calibration tone in the Audio tool, and adjust the output level.

To adjust the audio output level:

1. On the Settings tab of the Project window, double-click your Audio Project settings.

2. In the Audio Project Settings dialog box, click the Output tab.

   The Audio Output controls appear, including the level slider for the global output level.

3. Choose Tools > Audio Tool to open the Audio tool.

4. At the top of the Audio tool, click the two small In/Out toggle buttons so they display the letter O, for Output.

5. In the Audio tool, click the PH (Peak Hold) button and choose Play Calibration Tone from the choices that appear (**Figure 14.11**).

6. In the Audio Project Settings dialog box, adjust the Output Gain level slider until the audio level in the Audio tool reaches the desired output level (**Figure 14.12**).

✔ Tip

■ You should rarely, if ever, need to adjust your audio output level in the Audio Output Settings dialog box when outputting a digital sequence, because your levels should usually be set in the Xpress Pro Timeline for best results. However, you can use this control as a quick and dirty way to raise or lower your overall audio level right before output, in a pinch.

PREPARING FOR OUTPUT TO TAPE

609

Outputting to Tape

When outputting to tape from Xpress Pro, you have the following four options, though the last two are not available unless you control your deck or camera with an RS-422 serial connection:

- **Crash-record:** Crash recording involves pressing Record on your deck or camera and clicking the Preview Digital Cut button in Xpress Pro's Digital Cut window. It is the most common output method for editors using DV cameras or decks for output.

    (According to Avid, crash recording by simply clicking Play in the Timeline and pressing Record on your camera or deck may not be as safe as using the Preview Digital Cut button to play your sequence; the click Play method may produce audio-video sync problems.)

    However, the crash-record method does not allow you to perform an assemble edit or insert edit. You cannot control exactly where your movie will begin on your recording tape, nor the timecode of your sequence on tape.

    If your client demands particular timecode for your outputted sequence, you need to perform a digital cut insert or assemble edit using an RS-422 serial connection, as DV decks and cameras do not respond completely accurately to FireWire device control, making timecode-accurate device control over FireWire unreliable.

- **Digital cut controlled by 1394 (FireWire):** A digital cut allows you to set the In point on your recording tape where you want the output to begin. It also allows you to determine the portion of your Timeline that you output to tape.

    If you're outputting a DV sequence to a DV deck or camera controlled by 1394

(FireWire), you can perform a digital cut, but it may not be precisely frame accurate.

Hence, the Insert Edit and Assemble Edit options normally displayed in the Digital Cut tool do not appear when you're controlling your deck with 1394 (FireWire).

- **Digital cut (insert edit):** This method—which requires reliable RS-422 control of your deck or camera—is a frame-accurate output method that requires you to stripe your recording tape before output (record black with timecode on the entire tape).

    An insert edit digital cut is the most sophisticated type of output to tape because it allows you to insert material anywhere on your recording tape without disrupting timecode, even if the tape already has material recorded on it. In addition, an insert edit digital cut allows you to choose which tracks of your sequence you want to output, allowing you to, for example, lay video from your sequence over audio that's already on the tape.

    (For more information on controlling your deck or camera with RS-422, see the sidebar "Reading Timecode Accurately" in Chapter 4.)

- **Digital cut (assemble edit):** This type of digital cut—which is possible only with RS-422 serial deck or camera control— is more limited than a digital cut with an insert edit. You cannot select tracks to output; you must output every track in your sequence.

    However, the advantage of the assemble edit method over the insert edit method is that it's faster; you need to prestripe only 10 to 20 seconds of the recording tape rather than the whole thing.

Deselect this option to output only the portion marked by In and Out points. *Click this button after you press Record on your deck or camera.* *Enter the duration of added black filler here.*

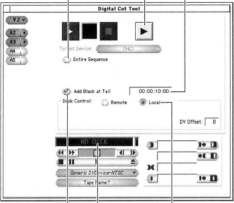

Select this option to add black filler at the end of your output sequence. *Xpress Pro does not need to recognize your deck to perform crash recording.* *You must be in Local mode to perform crash recording.*

Figure 14.13 To crash-record, press Record on your deck or camera and click the yellow Preview Digital Cut button in the Digital Cut tool.

Click here to override the default offset and enter a new value. *Enter a value here.*

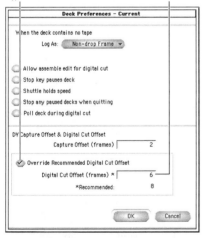

Figure 14.14 If you want to override the recommended DV Offset setting (which is eight frames), you can do so in the Deck Preferences dialog box.

To crash-record to tape:

1. If your deck has a serial control switch, switch it to Local mode and insert a recording tape.

2. (Optional) If you do not want to output your entire sequence, go to the Timeline and mark In and Out points around the portion of your sequence that you want to output to tape.

3. Click the monitor button for the topmost video track that you want to output and monitor all the audio tracks that you want to output.

4. Choose Clip > Digital Cut. The Digital Cut tool opens.

5. If you are not outputting your entire sequence, deselect the Entire Sequence option.

6. If you want to add some black filler at the end of your sequence, click the Add Black at Tail option and enter a duration in the adjacent box.

7. In the Deck Control area of the window, select Local (**Figure 14.13**).

8. (Optional) If you're outputting DV and want to change the DV offset from the recommended eight frames, go the Settings tab of the Project window and double-click the Deck Preferences. Select Override Recommended Digital Cut Offset and enter a new DV Offset value (**Figure 14.14**).

9. Press Record on your deck or camera.

continues on next page

OUTPUTTING TO TAPE

10. In the Digital Cut tool, click the yellow Preview Digital Cut button.

The sequence plays from your Timeline In point (or the whole sequence plays, if you selected Entire Sequence in the Digital Cut tool).

11. When your sequence or sequence selection is finished playing, click OK in the dialog box that appears.

The recording is complete. You can press Stop on your deck or camera.

To perform a digital cut via FireWire:

1. Render all effects in your sequence. (For more information on rendering, see Chapter 11, "Rendering and Real Time.")

2. In a bin, select the sequence you want to output to tape.

3. Choose Clip > Digital Cut.
The Digital Cut dialog box opens.

4. *Do one of the following:*
- ▲ Select the Entire Sequence option if you want to output your entire sequence without any regard for Timeline In and Out points.
- ▲ Deselect the Entire Sequence option if you want to output the portion of your sequence between Timeline In and Out points.

5. In the Digital Cut tool, select Remote to control your deck or camera with the deck controls.

6. To tell Xpress Pro where to start recording on your record tape, open the Deck Control pop-up menu and *select one of the following options:*
- ▲ **Mark In Time:** This option (the most popular when outputting a typical DV sequence) requires you to use the Digital Cut controls to cue your recording tape to where you want to start the recording and mark an In point. Use this method to be precise about where the digital cut will begin on your recording tape.
- ▲ **Record Deck:** This option ignores the sequence timecode and begins recording wherever the recording tape is currently cued.
- ▲ **Select Sequence:** This option starts recording at the timecode number on your recording tape that matches the starting timecode of your sequence.

7. If you selected Mark In Time from the Deck Control pop-up menu, use the deck controls to play your tape to where you want to begin recording and then click the Mark In button on the bottom right of the Digital Cut tool.

8. To have Xpress Pro automatically add black filler to the end of your sequence, select Add Black at Tail and add a duration in the adjacent box.

9. (Optional) To preview your digital cut, click the yellow Preview Digital Cut button.

Xpress Pro plays a preview of the configured digital cut without actually recording to tape.

10. Click the Play Digital Cut button.

Xpress Pro cues your deck or camera to the starting point and plays your sequence, recording to tape. Playback video appears in your Composer and external video monitor.

✔ **Tip**

- When controlling a DV deck or camera through 1394 (FireWire), you cannot pick individual tracks to output to tape; Xpress Pro must output all of your tracks.

To perform a digital cut insert edit:

1. Record black with timecode on your entire recording tape (prestriping it).

2. Choose Clip > Digital Cut.

3. In the Digital Cut dialog box that opens, select Insert Edit.

4. Follow the steps in "To perform a digital cut via FireWire" on the previous page and perform an insert edit.

✔ **Tips**

- Some decks have functions that facilitate the prestriping of your recording tape. For DV consumer cameras, however, one low-budget method is to put the lens cap on your camera, put the camera in Camera Record mode, and press Record.

- If you are outputting a DV sequence to DV tape using 1394 (FireWire) to control your deck or camera, the Assemble Edit option is disabled. You instead need to use RS-422 or RS-232 to control your deck.

FireWire Deck Control Allows a "Backspace Edit" but Not an Insert Edit

If you are controlling your DV deck or camera using a reliable control interface such as RS-422 or RS-232, you can choose between an insert or assemble edit digital cut, but if you're controlling your deck or camera via 1394 (FireWire), you cannot perform an insert edit. You can, however, mark an In point to indicate where to begin recording on your recording tape, though not an Out point, performing a "backspace edit." This edit is essentially identical to an assemble edit.

OUTPUTTING TO TAPE

To perform a digital cut assemble edit:

1. Record black with timecode for at least 11 seconds on the recording tape (partially prestriping the tape).

2. On the Settings tab of the Project window, double-click your Deck Preferences.

3. In the Deck Preferences dialog box, select Allow Assemble Edit for Digital Cut (**Figure 14.15**). Then close the Deck Preferences dialog box.

4. Choose Clip > Digital Cut.

5. In the Digital Cut dialog box that opens, select Assemble Edit.

6. If possible, set your deck's External/Internal sync switch to Internal and set the internal timecode to Regen(erate) or Slave Lock (not Preset).

7. Set your deck's Remote/Local mode switch to Remote mode.

8. Perform an assemble edit digital cut as outlined in "To perform a digital cut via FireWire:" earlier in this chapter.

✔ Tip

- If you are outputting a DV sequence to DV tape using 1394 (FireWire) to control your deck or camera, the Assemble Edit option is disabled. You instead need to use RS-422 or RS-232 to control your deck.

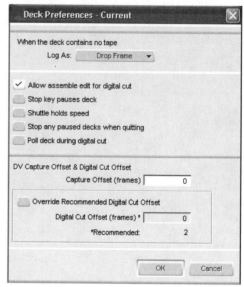

Figure 14.15 Before performing a digital cut assemble edit, you must select Allow Assemble Edit for Digital Cut in the Deck Preferences dialog box.

XPress Pro Bin (Drag) and (drop) Desktop folder

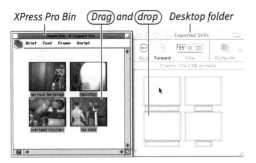

Figure 14.16 After marking In points in your clips and sequences and selecting Use Marks in the Export Settings dialog box, you can drag and drop the clips and sequences to an open folder, exporting still frames.

Exporting Material to Disk

When exporting files from Xpress Pro to one of your hard drives, you have myriad choices: You can export one or more clips at a time, one or more sequences at a time, or one or more still frames at a time; you can export to any of a variety of file formats; and you can export entire clips and sequences or just the portions between In and Out points.

To quickly export multiple clips or sequences using drag and drop:

1. Make sure that you set In and Out points on clips and sequences (if you want to export only portions) and select only the tracks that you want to export (unless you want to export all tracks).

2. To export multiple clips or sequences quickly, go to the Settings tab of the Project window and select an Export settings preset.

3. Either lasso or Ctrl-click (Windows) or Shift-click (Mac) multiple bin items and drag them to an open folder on your OS desktop (Windows) or Finder (Mac) (**Figure 14.16**).

   Xpress Pro export all clips or sequences to the open desktop folder, following the currently selected Export settings.

✔ Tip

■ When drag-and-drop exporting in Windows, minimize your desktop folder to a taskbar button at the bottom of the screen. Drag the selected files to the folder's taskbar button; Windows will automatically open the folder.

To export one or more clips or sequences:

1. Make sure that you set In and Out points on clips and sequences (if you want to export only portions) and select only the tracks that you want to export (unless you want to export all tracks).

2. *Do one of the following:*

    ▲ To set your Export settings as you go, go to a bin, select one or more clips or sequences to export, and choose File > Export.

    ▲ To export the sequence displayed in your Timeline, go to the Composer and right-click (Windows) or Ctrl-Shift+click (Mac). From the menu that appears, choose Export.

3. At the lower right of the Export As dialog box, click Options.

4. In the Export Settings dialog box that appears (**Figure 14.17**), click the Export As pop-up menu and choose an export format from the list that appears.

    The options in the Export Settings dialog box change according to the format that you choose.

5. To export only the material between Timeline In and Out points, at the top of the Export Settings dialog box, select Use Marks.

6. To export only selected tracks, select Use Enabled Tracks.

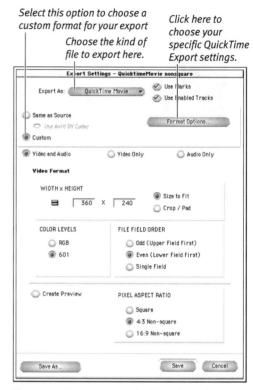

Select this option to choose a custom format for your export

Choose the kind of file to export here.

Click here to choose your specific QuickTime Export settings.

Figure 14.17 To export a movie with a size and compression different from that of the source movie, choose QuickTime Movie from the Export As menu and select Custom.

Figure 14.18 If you click Format Options in the Export Settings dialog box, the Movie Settings dialog box appears, allowing you to configure the specifics of your QuickTime export.

Access custom export presets here.

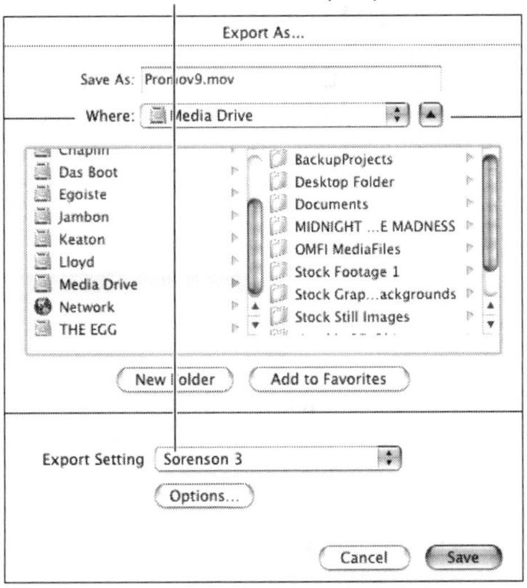

Figure 14.19 If you click Save As in the Export Settings dialog box, you can save your settings as a custom export preset, which you can then access from the Export Setting pull-down menu in the Export As dialog box.

7. If you want to export in a format other than the source format, select Custom, click the Format Options button, and configure your settings in the Movie Settings dialog box; then click OK (**Figure 14.18**).

8. After finalizing your settings in the Export Settings dialog box, you can click Save As to save your settings as a custom preset (**Figure 14.19**). Click Save to return to the Export As dialog box. The Export Settings dialog box disappears.

9. In the Export As dialog box, navigate to the folder in which you want to save your exported file.

10. Click Save.

Xpress Pro exports your selected clip and places it in the designated folder.

✔ Tips

■ To export a still image from a frame in a video clip, choose Graphic from the Export As menu in the Export Settings dialog box and choose one of the file formats listed in the Graphic Format pull-down menu. Select Use Marks to export the frame at the In point (otherwise, Xpress Pro exports the image at the playhead position).

■ Depending on the settings you choose in the Export Settings dialog box, you can export video and audio, video only, or audio only.

■ If you want to export sequential still images—one image for every frame between In and Out points in a selected clip—select Use Marks and Sequential File in the Export Settings dialog box.

EXPORTING MATERIAL TO DISK

617

Reference Movies and the Send To Feature

To work on a piece of your Xpress Pro Timeline in another application (such as After Effects), often the first step is to export a reference movie from Xpress Pro and import that reference movie into the third-party application.

A reference QuickTime movie is better than a normal QuickTime movie because it is not a recompression of your DV media; it is not a new media file. Rather, a reference movie is a file that merely refers to the Avid source media already on your computer. Hence, exporting a reference movie is a great way of exporting a sequence or clip without any duplicate recompression having to take place.

Reference movies are especially useful when you want to do the following:

◆ **Import an Xpress Pro clip or sequence into another application:** After you export the reference movie, you can treat it like any audio-video file, bring it into a third-party application (such as After Effects), make changes, and render a new movie, preferably using the Avid codec.

Importing a reference movie into the third party application avoids one recompression that could potentially produce artifacts.

(For more information on the Avid codec, see the sidebar "Make Sure Third-Party Applications Have the Avid Codec" later in this chapter.)

◆ **Prepare to create a DVD:** You can export a reference movie to be encoded in MPEG2 format; you can then bring this movie into your DVD authoring application.

(For more information, see the sidebar "Creating a DVD?" on the next page.)

There are two ways to export a reference movie from Xpress Pro: Choose File > Export and set Reference Movie as the type of file in the Export dialog box, or select what you want to export in a bin and choose File > Send To to display a more automated reference movie export dialog box.

The File > Send To option is the faster way to export a reference movie because it can automatically open the third-party application to which you want to send the reference movie. And with some applications, it can automatically load your reference movie into the third-party interface!

Self-Contained Movies vs. Reference Movies

When you configure your Export settings to export a QuickTime movie, the result is much different than when you export a QuickTime reference movie.

A QuickTime movie is a self-contained, independent piece of media. It can exist outside of your computer, away from your Xpress Pro media files.

A QuickTime reference movie, on the other hand, is just a small, text-based reference file that points to other self-contained QuickTime media files. Since a QuickTime reference movie contains just pointers to the real media files, it works only if the media files it points to are on the same system or network as the reference movie. If you copy a reference movie onto a CD and try to play it somewhere else, nothing will happen.

*Select the sequence
to export from a bin.*

Figure 14.20 To export a reference movie and open a third-party application, select a clip or sequence in a bin and choose File > Send To. In the Send To dialog box, pick an application from the Send To menu.

Creating a DVD?

If you want to create a DVD from your sequence, select the sequence, choose File > Send To, and export a reference movie; you can then encode the reference movie in MPEG2 format and import it into a DVD authoring application.

One popular encoding application (especially among Windows users) is Sorenson Squeeze.

If you're on a Mac and have DVD Studio Pro, Xpress Pro includes a bonus feature: Choose File > Send To > DVD Studio Pro, and your sequence will automatically be set up for MPEG2 encoding.

To export a reference movie using Send To:

1. Use Mark In and Mark Out to mark the portion of the sequence or clip that you want to export.

2. In your bin, select the sequence or clip to export.

3. Choose File > Send To.

4. In the Send To dialog box that appears, *do one of the following:*
   - ▲ Click the Send To pop-up menu and choose an application from the list that appears (**Figure 14.20**).
   - ▲ If the application you need is not listed, click the pop-up menu and select Add Item. In the dialog box that appears, navigate to the application you want to use and click Open.

   The name of the application you chose appears in the Send To pop-up menu.

5. To automatically launch the third-party application when you export the reference movie, select Auto Launch Application.

6. Click the Browse button and choose a destination folder for the exported movie.

7. Select Use Enabled Tracks to export only selected tracks and Use Marks to export only the portion of the clip or sequence between In and Out points.

8. Configure your desired pixel aspect ratio and other settings in the four pop-up menus.

continues on next page

REFERENCE MOVIES AND THE SEND TO FEATURE

9. Click OK.

Xpress Pro exports your clip or sequence as a reference movie. If you selected Auto Launch Application in the Send To dialog box, then the third-party application automatically launches and imports your reference movie.

Or the third-party application launches and reveals your file in the Finder or Desktop, so you can easily drag it into the application (**Figure 14.21**).

✔ Tips

- You can use File > Send To to trigger scripts that automatically launch designated applications and perform particular functions. Check the Avid Goodies folder that came with your installer for sample scripts.

- A reference movie export should take very little time since no additional compression is involved.

- If the third-party application does not successfully load or reveal your exported reference movie, you'll need to manually open the reference movie from within the third-party application.

- ◆ To export the sequence displayed in your Timeline, go to the Composer and right-click (Windows) or Ctrl+Shift-click (Mac) and choose Export from the menu that appears. Then choose QuickTime Reference Movie from the Export As pop-up menu.

Third-party application window   *Revealed reference movies*

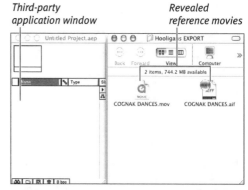

Figure 14.21 Xpress Pro automatically launched After Effects and revealed the exported reference movies in their destination folder.

Make Sure Third-Party Applications Have the Avid Codec

When you create an effect or movie in a third-party application (such as After Effects) and want to render it for import back into Xpress Pro, make sure that you render the movie using the Avid codec. If you're working with DV, you should render with the Avid DV codec.

You can download both the Windows and the Mac QuickTime Avid DV codec from the Avid Web site.

Always keep these codecs handy so you can send them to others (for instance, to a Combustion effects artist) working on the same project.

Exporting OMFI and AAF Files with AvidLinks

OMF Interchange (OMFI) and AAF files are platform-independent file formats that can include both digital media files (audio, video, and so on) and the instructions that describe how the media has been edited together to form a sequence (together referred to as an OMF or AAF composition).

One instance where you can use OMF files is when exporting your audio to ProTools, another program that uses OMF files. Your audio OMF export to ProTools will contain not only your audio media, but also your editing decisions and level information.

In addition, you can use AvidLinks to quickly export OMF files to other Avid applications such as ProTools and Avid | DS.

(For more information about OMF export and ProTools, see Appendix B, "Post-production Extras.")

To export an OMF or AAF composition:

1. In a bin, right-click (Windows) or Ctrl+Shift-click (Mac) a clip or sequence and choose Export.

2. In the Export As dialog box that opens, click the Options button.

3. In the Export Settings dialog box that opens, choose OMF 1.0, OMF 2.0, or AAF from the Export As pull-down menu (consult the application in which you're importing these files to find out which choice is best).

4. Specify whether to include all video tracks and all audio tracks.

5. In the Export Method pull-down menu, *choose one of the following:*

▲ **Link to Current Media:** Choosing this option is like creating a reference movie. The OMF or AAF files merely refer to the Xpress Pro source media already on your drives. Use this option if you do not need to bring the files outside of your computer system.

(For more information about reference movies, see the sidebar "Self-Contained Movies vs. Reference Movies" earlier in this chapter.)

▲ **Copy Media and Link to Copied Media:** This option creates reference OMF or AAF files but copies the linked source media to the destination drive of your choice. This option requires a lot of extra drive space but allows you to copy your media onto an attached drive that you can then bring to another system.

This option is similar to consolidating your project without trimming source media.

(For more information about consolidation, see "Transferring and Trimming Your Sequence and Media" in Chapter 13.)

▲ **Consolidate and Link to Consolidated Media:** This option creates reference OMF or AAF files, trims your source media down to only what is needed for your exported sequence or clip, copies that trimmed media onto the drive of your choice, and links your OMF or AAF files to that media.

continues on next page

EXPORTING OMFI AND AAF FILES WITH AVIDLINKS

Use this option if you want to export only the media contained in your sequence and don't need to export all of your source media. This option is similar to performing consolidation and trimming all of your source media.

(For more information about the consolidation operation, see "Transferring and Trimming Your Sequence and Media" in Chapter 13.)

▲ **Embed Media:** This option (**Figure 14.22**) creates self-contained OMF or AAF files, not reference files, upon export. Your edit decisions are carried over, along with untrimmed master clips.

Use this option rather than Consolidate and Embed Media if you may need to do some re-editing in another application and need to have full source media files (for the original master clips) rather than just the media used in your sequence.

▲ **Consolidate and Embed Media:** This option also produces self-contained OMF and AAF files, but trims your media to include only what you need to re-create your sequence in another application.

(For more information about consolidation, see "Transferring and Trimming Your Sequence and Media" in Chapter 13.)

6. Specify a destination folder (**Figure 14.23**).

7. Click Save.

The Export Settings dialog box closes.

8. In the Export As dialog box, navigate to the location of your export and choose Save.

The clip or sequence is exported as an OMF (or AAF) file, and you can now import that file into a compatible application.

Choose between AIFF-C and WAV.

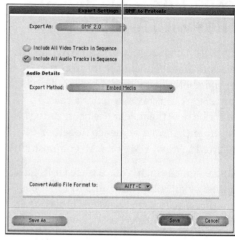

Figure 14.22 A common way that TV editors get the audio from a finished sequence to a ProTools editor is by consolidating their entire audio-video sequence and then exporting an OMF file of the audio with embedded media (no extra consolidation necessary).

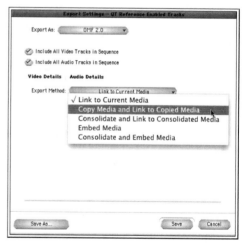

Figure 14.23 When you choose to export an OMF or AAF file, click the Export Method pop-up button to choose exactly what to export.

Figure 14.24 To export an OMF or AAF file to another Avid application, select a clip or sequence in your bin and choose File > AvidLinks.

To export an OMF file using AvidLinks:

1. In a bin, select the clip or sequence to export and choose File > AvidLinks.

2. The AvidLinks menu appears, listing a few Avid applications (including ProTools).

3. Choose the Avid application to which you want to export your clip or sequence (**Figure 14.24**).

4. In the AvidLinks Export To dialog box that appears, change the name of the file if necessary and select a destination folder for the export.

5. Click Save.

   Avid exports the selected clip or sequence as an OMF or AAF file, ready for the designated application.

✔ Tip

■ The advice from professional Avid editors is that an AvidLinks export to ProTools is more limited in options than an OMF export using the basic File > Export command.

Exporting Shot Logs and EDLs

When you want to re-create your Xpress Pro project in another application (for example, Final Cut Pro), you traditionally need to do the following:

◆ **Export a shot log.** A shot log is a set of instructions on how to log and capture your source media. Remember when you first logged your source clips for capture? Those logged clips comprise a shot log.

◆ **Export an EDL.** An EDL, or edit decision list, contains the instructions that tell a third-party application how you cut together your clips into a sequence in Xpress Pro. Using an EDL, you can re-create your edit in, say, Final Cut Pro, after using the exported shot log to recapture your source media.

Increasingly, however, recapturing clips from shot logs and re-creating edits with EDLs are becoming old-fashioned means of transferring sequences to another application.

Sebsky Tools allows you to convert an Avid Log Exchange shot log into a Final Cut Pro batch list and to add timecode and reel names to QuickTime files exported from Avid, so you can recapture the clips in FCP. (For more information on Sebsky Tools, see Appendix B, "Postproduction Extras," and www.dharmafilms.com/sebskytools.)

Another application, Automatic Duck, allows you to export your Xpress Timeline as an OMF file and import it into Adobe After Effects or Boris RED 3GL. (For more information, see Appendix B and www.automaticduck.com.)

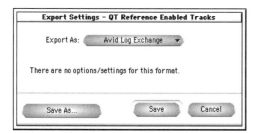

Figure 14.25 To export a shot log from Xpress Pro, choose Avid Log Exchange in the Export Settings dialog box.

To export a shot log:

1. Put all the master clips that you want to export as a shot log in the same bin and select the bin's Text tab.

2. Select the clips that you want to export in the shot log. Use Ctrl-click (Windows) or Shift-click (Mac) to select multiple items.

3. Choose File > Export.

4. In the Export As dialog box that opens, click the Options button.

5. In the Export Settings dialog box that opens, click the Export As pop-up menu and *choose one of the following*:
   ▲ **Avid Log Exchange:** Your shot log will comply with Avid Log Exchange (ALE) specifications (**Figure 14.25**). (For more information on ALE, see Chapter 15, "Special Features and Bundled Applications.")
   ▲ **Tab Delimited:** Your shot log will be a tab-delimited ASCII text file.

6. Click OK.

7. In the Export As dialog box, click Save. Xpress Pro exports the shot log to the designated folder. You can now use the shot log to recapture your media with matching timecode in another application.

✔ Tip

■ To save your shot log export settings, click Save As in the Export Settings dialog box.

To export an EDL:

1. If you have EDL Manager installed on your computer, select a sequence in a bin and choose Tools > EDL.

   The EDL Manager application opens.

2. In the EDL Manager, choose File > Get Current Sequence.

   EDL Manager loads the EDL information for your currently selected Xpress Pro sequence. You can now save the EDL in the format of your choice.

   (For more information, see "Using EDL Manager" in Chapter 15.)

EXPORTING SHOT LOGS AND EDLS

SPECIAL FEATURES AND BUNDLED APPLICATIONS

This book's page limit cannot accommodate in-depth discussions of everything that ships with the Xpress Pro application. Herein can be found introductory explanations of Script Integration, EDL Manager, Avid Log Exchange (ALE), FilmScribe, and MetaSync Manager, plus tasks to help you get started with each. For more details, consult the Xpress Pro manual and the manuals for Avid Log Exchange, FilmScribe, and MetaSync Manager.

Using Script Integration

Script Integration is a feature within Xpress Pro that allows you to import your shooting script and use it as a road map for editing your movie.

For narrative film and video projects, the Script Integration workflow might proceed as follows:

1. During production, your script supervisor lines the script, marking the shots and takes that correspond to particular action and dialogue in the script. After production, a hard copy of this script is given to the editor.

2. As the editor, you can import a text file of the script into Xpress Pro and, using the marked hard copy as a reference, drag and drop clips (creating slates) onto the script, associating each with particular action and dialogue.

   In addition to visually outlining the basic shot ordering for you, this process should help you determine whether any coverage is missing and whether additional shots need to be filmed.

3. You can drag another take (another master clip or subclip) to each slate and then play each take in the Script Integration window, listening and watching and adding marks in the script that correspond to what happens in the take.

4. Then you can double-click to load each preferred take directly from the Script window and edit all of the takes in order into your Timeline, creating a rough cut.

   Here's a sample scenario: You may prefer the cut in take 1 for the entire scene, but then realize that a character says a particular line well in take 2. So in the Script window, you click the script mark next to that preferred line in take 2, and the slate window (a mini-source window) jumps to that frame, and you can set an In and Out point and overwrite what you want from take 2 into the Timeline.

   (For an additional workflow idea, see the sidebar "A Storyboarding Strategy Using Script Integration" later in this chapter.)

   (For more information on using the Script Integration controls, consult the Xpress Pro Help.)

To import a script into Xpress Pro:

1. In a third-party word processing application, save your script in Text with Layout or Text Only with Line Breaks format.

2. In Xpress Pro, click the Bins tab in the Project window.

3. Choose File > New Script.

   The imported script appears on the Bins tab along with the bin icons. Your script opens in Xpress Pro's Script window (**Figure 15.1**).

✔ Tip

■ File > New Script is dimmed unless you select the Bins tab in the Project window.

The imported script

Each slate can contain multiple takes.

Click a script mark to play a particular line of dialogue.

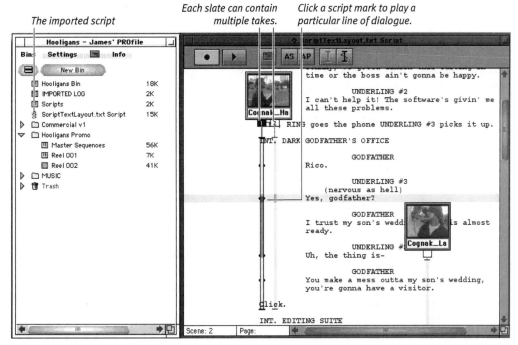

Figure 15.1 When you choose File > New Script, Xpress Pro imports the script into the Script Integration window and places the script among the bin icons in the Project window.

USING SCRIPT INTEGRATION

To associate a clip with a portion of the script:

1. In the Script window, drag to highlight the portion of the script that you want to associate with a clip.

2. Go to an open bin and drag and drop a clip onto the highlighted portion of the script in the Script window.

   The clip icon appears on the script, and a line extends down from the icon, marking the part of the script that the clip covers.

Special Concerns for Editing Film

Editing a project for film in Xpress Pro is very different than editing a video project. For one thing, you can't use any effects or transitions from the Effect palette except those found in the Film category of the Effect palette (unless you have the budget to create digital effects).

In addition, you have to look out for duplicate frames, which is not as much of a worry in video. Duplicate frames in your sequence (frames that appear more than once) will mess up the cut list. Your negative cutter obviously can't create a duplicate frame from the negative (except using an optical effect, which would be impractical for just one duped frame here and there). In Xpress Pro, you can catch duplicate frames by turning on Dupe Detection in the Timeline Fast menu.

(For more information about film editing, see the Xpress Pro and FilmScribe help.)

A Storyboarding Strategy Using Script Integration

To enhance preproduction and post-production workflow, you can begin using Script Integration even before anything is shot in production:

You can import stills of hand-drawn storyboards and or moving QuickTime movies exported from storyboarding software such as ZebraDevelopment's recently released Storyboard Pro and then use the storyboard to pre-line your script in Xpress Pro.

Optionally, you can then use Xpress Pro's editing, audio, and effects features to create what is essentially an animatic: a moving storyboard presentation that will help you plan your production shoot.

When production is finished and you've captured all your takes, you can then replace the storyboard versions of each scene with the actual footage, both in the Script Integration window and in the Timeline.

(For more information on ZebraDevelopment's Storyboard Pro, a 3D storyboard interface creation program, see www.zebradevelopment.com.)

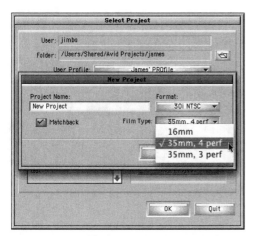

Figure 15.2 Selecting Matchback and a film type in the New Project window tells Xpress Pro to expect footage that has been tranferred from film to video (telecined).

Cutting Film Projects in Xpress Pro

The common procedure for cutting an actual film project (16mm or 35mm) in a nonlinear editing system is to transfer the 24 fps film to 29.97 fps (NTSC) or 25 fps (PAL) video, which is then captured and edited in the application.

After editing is complete, the editing decisions of the 29.97 fps or 25 fps edit must be translated back into 24 fps terms. Then a cut list can be generated that will be handed to a negative cutter, who will use the list as a guide for cutting the actual film negative for printing.

Without getting too technical, Xpress Pro's Matchback option (selected in the Select Project dialog box), along with the included FilmScribe application and film-related settings in Xpress Pro, help you create an accurate 24 fps film cut list from your 29.97 or 25 fps video edit.

To start an Xpress Pro film project:

1. When you first launch Xpress Pro, select New Project in the Select Project dialog box.

2. In the New Project dialog box that appears, select the Matchback option.

3. From the Film Type pop-up menu, choose the type of film in which your project was shot.

4. From the Format pop-up menu, choose the video format that you'll be capturing (**Figure 15.2**).

5. Click OK.
   Xpress Pro opens, and you're ready to begin editing the film project.

✔ Tip

- When you create a film or 24p project, a setting called Film and 24p appears on the Settings tab. The dialog box for this setting controls the way that ink numbers and auxiliary ink numbers are formatted and displayed (ink numbers are the timecode equivalents for film).

Using Avid Log Exchange

The Avid Log Exchange (ALE) application, included with Xpress Pro, is usually used only for film projects. When film is transferred to video, a shot log is often created; ALE can convert those shot logs to logged clips in your bin, which you then use to capture the video transfer (**Figure 15.3**).

(For more information, see the Avid Log Exchange help.)

(To learn about another use for Avid Log Exchange, see the sidebar "Moving a Project from Xpress Pro to FCP or FCP to Xpress Pro.")

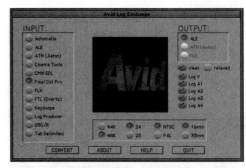

Figure 15.3 You can convert outside log files to ALE log files for import into your Xpress Pro bins.

Moving a Project from Xpress Pro to FCP or FCP to Xpress Pro

You may want to move an Xpress Pro project into Final Cut Pro to take advantage of a particular feature in that application. Or you might want to move a Final Cut Pro project into Xpress Pro take advantage of a feature in Xpress Pro.

Whichever direction you're going, moving a project across applications requires the following:

◆ **Instructions for re-creating your sequence in another application:** Traditionally, these instructions come in the form of an edit decision list (EDL), which you can export from your original editing application.

 If you want to export your Final Cut Pro Timeline into Xpress Pro, you can alternatively buy Automatic Duck Sequence Export, which translates your FCP Timeline into Xpress Pro. (For more information see "OMF Interchange via Automatic Duck" in Appendix B.)

◆ **Source media that has timecode and reel number information:** You need to carry over not just your source media, but the timecode numbers and reel numbers of the clips; otherwise, you can't re-create your sequence from the instructions.

There are two traditional ways to carry over source media with proper information: export a batch list or shot log from the original application and use that log to recapture your clips in the other NLE application; or export actual QuickTime files from the original application, import them into the other application, and somehow reattach timecode and reel number information to the imported clips (this information won't carry over automatically).

If you want to carry over your source media clips from Final Cut Pro to Xpress Pro, the best bet is to use Automatic Duck to transfer your Timeline from FCP to Xpress Pro, or use the free utility Sebsky Tools (www.dharmafilms.com/sebsky tools) to convert an FCP batch list into an Xpress Pro shot log and use that shot log to recapture your clips in Xpress Pro.

If you want to carry over source media from Xpress Pro to Final Cut Pro, you can use Sebsky Tools. Using the exported Avid QuickTime files plus ALE file exports of each Xpress Pro bin, Sebsky Tools can add correct timecode and reel numbers to each file you bring into Final Cut Pro. This makes re-creating your Xpress Pro cut in FCP easy, provided you also export an EDL from Xpress Pro.

(For more information about EDLs, see the next section, "Using EDL Manager.")

Using EDL Manager

An edit decision list, or EDL, is a set of instructions describing how to take a sequence edited on one editing system and re-create it on another system. The EDL represents the edit decisions using clip timecode and reel numbers; this is one reason why it's so important to accurately capture timecode and log reel numbers when you initially start editing.

So if you want to re-create your Xpress Pro edit on a tape-to-tape editor or another NLE (perhaps with higher-resolution material—a common practice when creating an online edit from an offline edit), you can export an EDL from the application and import it into the other system.

The reverse applies as well: you can import an EDL to re-create a sequence edited on another system.

(For more options on how to move projects between systems, see the sidebar "Moving a Project from Xpress Pro to FCP or FCP to Xpress Pro" on the previous page.)

To export an EDL from Xpress Pro:

1. In a bin, highlight the sequence that you want to re-create somewhere else using an EDL.

2. Choose Tools > EDL.

   EDL Manager launches, and the EDL Manager window opens.

3. Click the right arrow next to the Avid icon (the one pointing to the Update icon).

   EDL Manager displays your sequence's EDL in the window.

4. To set your EDL format and other options, choose Windows > Options, make changes, and click Apply.

5. Save your EDL to disk.

   You can now use the EDL on another system to re-create your edited sequence.

To re-create an edited sequence in Xpress Pro by importing an EDL:

1. Make sure that you capture (or import) the clips you need for the sequence you want to re-create. Also make sure that the clips have timecode and reel numbers that match the information in the EDL.

   If the clips do not have the correct timecode or reel number information, you may have to select the clips one by one, choose Clip > Modify, and change the timecode and reel numbers (source) manually.

Figure 15.4 If your master clips do not have the correct reel numbers or timecode, before you use Bin > Relink, you can modify them by choosing Clip > Modify and setting the correct source (reel number) and starting timecode.

2. Bring an EDL file (which could be just a text document) onto your computer.

3. Launch Xpress Pro and choose Tools > EDL. EDL Manager opens.

4. Choose File > Open and choose the EDL file that you want to import.

   A window will appear that asks you the frame rate of the EDL.

5. Click the frame rate button to indicate the frame rate of the incoming EDL.

   The EDL text appears in the EDL Manager window.

6. If necessary, make adjustments to the EDL and then click the left-pointing arrow (the one pointing from the Update icon to the Avid icon).

   Xpress Pro appears, and a Select dialog box opens, asking you to choose or create a bin for the imported EDL sequence.

7. Choose a bin or create a new one and click OK.

   A new offline sequence appears in your chosen bin.

8. Select the sequence and choose Bin > Relink (**Figure 15.4**). In the dialog box that appears, choose Relink Offline Non-master Clips to Any Online Items and click OK.

   Xpress Pro links the offline sequence to the master clips that you already have in bins, provided they have the correct timecode and reel numbers. Your sequence is re-created.

USING EDL MANAGER

Importing an EDL Weirdness

When you re-create a sequence from an EDL exported from FCP, Xpress Pro creates an offline sequence as well as a series of 24-hour offline master clips, each representing a different reel from your EDL (**Figure 15.5**). This seems very strange, and it is.

The clips you see in the offline sequence reference the 24-hour clips, which do not reference anything. What you have to do is select each 24-hour clip, one at a time, choose Clip > Modify, and give each clip the correct reel number (using the Set Source pull-down menu).

When all of the clips are modified, select the offline sequence (*not* the 24-hour clips) and choose Bin > Relink. Keep the Relink Offline Master Clips to Online Media Files radio button selected and choose Relink.

The offline sequence, created from the imported EDL, links to your master clips; your sequence is re-created in Xpress Pro.

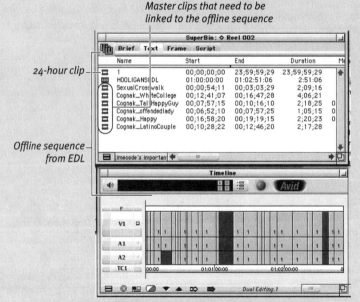

Figure 15.5 When you import an EDL exported from FCP, an offline sequence will appear in your bin along with one 24-hour master clip for each reel used in the EDL. Select each 24-hour clip and use Clip > Modify to confirm the reel number for each clip (in the Set Source pull-down menu).

Using MetaSync Manager

MetaSync Manager and MetaSync Publisher are tools useful only for the niche field of interactive television.

In Xpress Pro, you can import what are generally called interactive enhancements (or interactive triggers) and edit them into the meta track of your Xpress Pro Timeline (**Figure 15.6**).

(For more information on MetaSync Manager and interactive enhancements, see http://avidbeta.goldpocket.com.)

✔ Tip

■ To create a meta track in Xpress Pro, right-click (Windows) or Ctrl+Shift-click (Mac) the Timeline and choose New Meta Track. To display a meta track, open the Timeline Fast menu and choose Show Track > M1 (or M2).

Imported enhancements

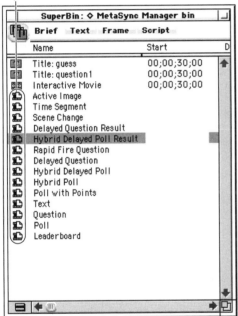

Meta track   *Enhancement*

Figure 15.6 MetaSync enhancements can be imported into your bin (left) and then edited into the meta track of your Timeline (right).

USING METASYNC MANAGER

Xpress Pro Help Resources

If you have a question and encounter an issue in Xpress Pro that isn't addressed in either this book, Xpress Pro Help, or the Xpress Pro manual, you can always turn to the number-one source of free help: your fellow Xpress Pro users and digital filmmakers.

This appendix profiles the top online and onsite resources that will keep you informed and in tune with the ever-evolving world of Xpress Pro and digital media creation.

Avid Xpress Pro Web Forums

The most immediate way to discuss Xpress Pro conundrums and possible solutions is to jump on any of the myriad of Xpress Pro-related bulletin boards on the Web. Since Xpress DV is so similar to Xpress Pro, boards devoted to that application should often prove just as helpful.

◆ **Avid.com/forums:** Though modest in traffic during the first few weeks of Xpress Pro's public life, Avid's own Xpress Pro (and Xpress DV and Xpress) boards load quickly and should gain momentum and gather crowds as the software matures. A further attraction of the Avid boards is that they're split into PC and Mac groups.

◆ **DMNforums.com:** On Digital Media Net's endless list of forums is one devoted to both Xpress DV and Xpress Pro. Look for "Avid Xpress DV/Xpress Pro". There are a lot of users on this forum; too bad the DMN site takes so long to load.

◆ **CreativeCow.net > Avid Editing:** Creative Cow forums have become the hippest place to network with fellow digital artists and give and receive tips and tricks. For Xpress Pro users, there is only a general "Avid Editing" forum, but it is highly populated and full of Xpress Pro users.

◆ **2-pop.com > Forums:** When you get to 2-pop, click on the Forums link, and you'll be taken to a whole slew of mostly FCP-related bulletin boards. Scroll down to see the Avid-related boards. As of this writing, 2-pop has only an Xpress DV board but that should change in the near future.

The Avid-L (E-mail List)

The Avid-L is an old e-mail list, mostly populated by hardcore Avid professionals who cut for a living on higher-end systems. Many of these seasoned veterans have been trying out Xpress Pro and are excellent resource for answers to advanced questions.

(To find out more about Avid-L, visit www.avid.com/community/maillist.)

To subscribe to Avid-L:

◆ Send an e-mail request to subscribe-Avid-L@Avid.com. To unsubscribe, send an e-mail request to unsubscribe-Avid-L@Avid.com.

Avid User Groups

If you're the type who likes to communicate with real people rather than screen names and emoticons, joining a local Avid user group may be more rewarding than life as a bulletin board rat.

User groups typically meet once a month to talk about tips and tricks, and the latest new toys.

Avid's Web site conveniently posts the names, locations, and e-mail contacts for Avid groups both within the U.S./Canada region and outside the U.S./Canada region (internationally).

To find the Avid user group nearest you:

1. Go to Avid.com, click on Community, and click on Avid User Groups.
   The Avid Communities page loads.

2. Under the Avid User Groups heading, click on either U.S./Canada or International.
   A page loads displaying the user groups for the chosen region.

Avid Classes and Education Centers

You can supplement your Visual QuickPro training with skills taught in a live classroom by checking out one of the many Avid education centers scattered throughout the world.

Avid's Web site lets you select the course you want to take and then displays the times and locations of classes taught throughout the world.

To find an Avid education center:

1. Go to Avid.com, click Training, and click Centers on from the Training page that appears.

   The Centers page appears listing Avid Authorized Education Centers.

2. At the top of the page, you can choose a geographical region that you want to display.

To find a specific Avid education course near you:

1. Go to Avid.com and click on Training.

2. On the Courses + Schedules page that appears, choose either a course title from the Select a Course menu or an Avid product from the Select a Product menu.

The next page will display a list of courses from which to choose, perhaps first asking you to choose a region to search.

POST-PRODUCTION EXTRAS

Plan to invest in editing suite add-ons that maximize what you can provide to a client, if you're serious about the Pro part of your Xpress Pro system. These days, there are almost as many people calling themselves editors as there are people calling themselves writers. Suffice it to say that the editors who get hired these days are expected to be multitaskers—skilled not just in straight cutting, but also in music, sound editing, special effects, and motion graphics.

Of course, at the top of the Xpress Pro must-have list is the magical Mojo box, which allows you to play back real-time effects on your external monitor as well as input and output uncompressed video. In addition, there are some very powerful AVX plug-ins (video effects that work with Avid applications), AudioSuite plug-ins (audio effects that work with Xpress Pro), After Effects plug-ins that work with Xpress Pro via Elastic Gasket, and sound editing applications (including Avid's ProTools) that are definitely worth a stretch in your budget.

In addition, your author has spent much effort scouting for stock music, sound effects, and motion-graphic resources that provide the best bang for the buck for the low-budget, post-production suite, because these, days, especially with the job market as competitive as it is for editors, clients often expect to find an editing, graphics, sound, and music solution in one post-productive superhero.

Xpress Pro with Mojo

The Mojo box is an external hardware device that connects to your computer via a six-pin FireWire (1394) cable. Additional In and Out options include a four-pin FireWire connection (for connecting a DV deck or camera), S-Video In and Out, composite (RCA) video In and Out, stereo (RCA) audio In and Out, and a connection for a black-burst generator (also known as a house sync generator, commonly used in professional post-production suites to provide gen-lock synchronization for the timing of all equipment in a studio).

For an additional charge, you can purchase a special BNC-to-S-Video/composite video cable for Mojo that allows you to input and capture a true YRyBy component signal, which is higher end than a composite signal. (To purchase this cable, go to Avid's online store at digidesign.store.com, enter the keyword *component*, and look for *Avid Mojo Component Video I/O Option*.)

The Mojo box facilitates the following operations:

◆ **Digital-analog conversion, with multiple inputs and outputs:** You can capture DV video and audio with Mojo, just as you can without Mojo. However, the Mojo box also serves as an analog-to-digital converter. For example, you can capture Hi-8, VHS, and S-VHS footage through either Mojo's composite or S-Video connection, converting those analog formats into a digital signal.

Even better, you can hook up a BetaSP or DigiBeta deck, and capture a true component (YRyBy) signal using Mojo's optional component cable option, as described earlier.

When to Capture DV Footage as Uncompressed Standard-Definition Analog Video

If you are creating a video piece with intensive still and motion graphics, greenscreen or bluescreen shots, and the need for clean mattes, you should capture your DV footage uncompressed (preferably via the optional component connection cable available at the Avid online store.

With DV footage, effects artists have an especially hard time applying chroma keys (removing greenscreen and bluescreen), rotoscoping, and generally producing clean mattes. So many editors concerned with the limitations of DV footage play their DV source tapes on a deck with component outputs; they capture DV via a component signal, rather than through FireWire.

The result of capturing DV as component video? The DV footage coming through component video uncompressed, as opposed to video captured via FireWire, has finer, more interpolated edges where one color meets another—which will, for example, help you separate a foreground subject from a background greenscreen or bluescreen. You will be able to remove bluescreen and greenscreen more cleanly and perform more successful color-related and matte-related operations; overall, the graphics in your final piece will look better.

During playback and output to tape, your digital video travels back through FireWire to the Mojo box, where it is converted from all-digital back to an analog signal and can play out to an analog deck through the box's analog composite, S-Video, or component connection. Simultaneously, the digital signal can remain true digital and play through FireWire to a DV deck or camera.

- **Real-time FX playback to tape and external monitor:** On software-only systems, Xpress Pro can preview more than a hundred real-time effects on the computer monitor only. With Mojo, these real-time effects play out through FireWire in real time.

By hooking up your external monitor to the analog outputs on Mojo, you can simultaneously watch real-time effects on the monitor as they play through FireWire to your DV camera or deck, all without rendering.

continues on next page

XPRESS PRO WITH MOJO

◆ **Uncompressed video capture and editing:** With a Mojo-enabled system, you can capture, import, render, and edit 601 standard-definition (SD) analog video or graphics at 1:1 compression, which is much higher-quality video than DV (which has an inherent 5:1 compression).

Without Mojo, your available video resolutions in the Capture tool and Media Creation settings are only DV 25 411 and 15:1s (a low-quality resolution). With Mojo, you will have the additional option of selecting 1:1 for your video resolution (**Figure B.1**).

Hence, you can use Xpress Pro as an offline and online solution for standard-definition video. For example, you might want to edit BetaSP footage at best quality and eventually output at full quality (uncompressed resolution). You can initially capture from the BetaSP deck through Mojo at 15:1s or DV 25 411 resolution, to save space during the edit and take advantage of real-time effects. Then at the end of your project, you can batch recapture your edit at 1:1 resolution and output to the BetaSP deck via Mojo's component connections.

(For the advantages of capturing DV as uncompressed video, see the sidebar "When to Capture DV Footage as Uncompressed Standard-Definition Analog Video" on the previous page.)

Figure B.1 When you launch Xpress Pro with the Mojo box connected, you can choose 1:1 as your resolution for Capture, Titles, Import, Mixdown and Transcode, and Render in the Media Creation settings. You can also choose 1:1 resolution in the Capture tool.

◆ **Mixing different resolutions in the same Timeline:** Xpress Pro's ability to mix uncompressed standard-definition and DV resolution material in the same Timeline is an advantage if your final project will be in uncompressed resolution. However you will want to edit in DV resolution to take advantage of Mojo's real-time playback capabilities.

In applications that don't support a mix of DV and uncompressed resolutions in the same Timeline (such as software-only Xpress Pro), the uncompressed motion graphics you create in programs like After Effects must be down-converted to your offline DV resolution for offline editing.

But with Xpress Pro and Mojo, you can use the same uncompressed graphics in your offline edit (DV resolution) as you do in your online edit (uncompressed resolution). All you have to recapture and replace then are the DV clips in your sequence. Plus, with Xpress Pro and Mojo, your uncompressed graphics will play in real time, along with the DV material, through FireWire to your external monitor while you edit.

✔ **Tips**

■ To learn how to build your own component cable for the Mojo box, go to support01.avid.com/support, enter *Mojo* in the search engine, and find the article titled *Avid Mojo Component Cable Wiring Diagram*.

■ If you want to capture an SDI signal through the Mojo component connections, but your SDI deck does not have component outputs, then you need to buy an SDI-to-component analog converter like the one sold by AJA (aja.com).

Drive Bandwidth for Uncompressed Video

As of the writing of this book, it is unknown what drive products and configuration produce the bandwidth required for Xpress Pro uncompressed editing. Unfortunately, Avid tests only its own drives, so users will have to try out third-party options themselves. But if you do use non-Avid drives, remember to go to the Drive Filtering tab of the Media Creation dialog box and deselect Filter Based on Resolution. Otherwise, Avid filters all drives but its own, because it can qualify only its own drives.

RS-422 Serial Adapter

If you want to use Xpress Pro and Mojo for professional work, having a serial connection for a nine-pin RS-422 cable on your computer is a must for timecode-accurate device control of your capture or recording deck.

Many PCs come with a serial connection, but if you're a Mac user the best bet for adding an RS-422 connection is getting Keyspan's twin serial adapter (keyspan.com), which plugs into a USB port. No need to open up your tower and replace the modem as Mac editors were forced to do in the past with other serial port products.

In fact, the Keyspan adapter is the only serial adapter that Avid tests and supports for use with an Xpress Pro editing system.

Third-Party AVX Plug-ins

Avid Visual Extension (AVX) plug-ins are third-party visual plug-ins that you can purchase from other companies and use within Xpress Pro. Once installed in your AVX Plug-Ins folder (within the Xpress Pro folder), they appear on the Effect palette just like any other segment or transition effect.

Avid keeps a list of AVX partners on its Web site at www.avid.com/partners/avx/displayPartners.html, but make sure you check the manufacturer's Web site to check for Xpress Pro compatibility before taking a plunge.

The following are brief descriptions of those AVX products known to work with Xpress Pro at the time of this book's release (or expected to work soon), starting with your author's five favorite third-party plug-ins (marked with asterisks) and then continuing alphabetically:

*Gen Arts' *Sapphire* (genarts.com)

The Sapphire plug-ins (almost 200 are available in one package) are at the top end of third-party AVX offerings in terms of quality, as well as price. Still, they're more affordable for use in Xpress Pro and Xpress DV than for any other Avid application.

These plug-ins are among the easiest to use, with default settings that pack a significant "Wow" factor. The glow and blur effects resemble (and may in fact be) a lot of the flashy effects you see on TV these days. Since there's no room here to go into each effect individually, the best way to check them out is to download the free demo from the GenArts Web site; you'll probably see ways to manipulate video images that you never imagined before.

✔ Tip

- At the time of this writing, GenArts sells a package of 99 of the most popular Sapphire plug-ins.

*Boris (borisfx.com)

Boris recently has made great leaps forward in improving the power of its plug-ins and applications, though they could benefit from better default settings on a par with Sapphire's (especially for the Boris RED and Continuum effects).

◆ **Boris RED 3GL:** RED is a compositing program of the same species as After Effects and Commotion and at the top end of Boris' product line. As of this book's writing, RED's advantage over its counterparts is its high level of integration with Xpress Pro and Xpress DV; for Avid editors, it may now be the package to buy rather than After Effects.

You can port Xpress Pro Timeline layers into Boris RED by dropping a Boris RED layer effect from the Effect palette onto a black filler clip above the layers you want to export.

Click the Other Options button on the Effect palette, and the Boris interface opens. After doing whatever you want in RED, choose Quit, and you will automatically go back to Xpress Pro. Render your top Boris RED layer, and you're done. And you can always go back later to tweak your work.

◆ **Boris Continuum:** For editors who want to remain in the Avid interface for effects work, Boris offers the Continuum set of effects, all found in the Boris RED 3GL application, as AVX plug-ins that work with Xpress Pro. You manipulate these effects in the Effect Editor, not in the Boris RED interface.

◆ **Boris Graffiti:** Graffiti is for those who want to mainly focus on Boris' 2D and 3D title creation and animation capabili-

ties, and the package includes many customizable presets.

◆ **Boris FX:** These plug-ins include effects such as particle generators, color correction, keying, and large-image panning and zooming, with many customizable presets.

✔ Tips

■ A limited version of Boris Graffiti ships with Xpress Pro.

■ Buying Boris RED is like buying a combination of Continuum, Graffiti, FX—and then some.

■ Boris RED, Graffiti, and FX also support several After Effects plug-ins like the popular Re:Vision Effects' Twixtor and Trapcode's Shine. See the Boris FX Web site for the complete list.

*Digital Film Tools (digitalfilmtools.com)

Helmed by LA-based special effects expert Marco Paolini, Digital Film tools sells four different AVX plug-in packages for Xpress Pro that encompass a wide variety of very popular types of effects that rival the "Wow" factor and ease of use of the Sapphire plug-ins.

◆ **Digital Film Lab:** These plug-ins simulate the looks of film lenses and film lab processes in very convincing ways. They include trendy color correction presets such as Bleach Bypass.

◆ **Composite Suite:** This motley bunch of 28 plug-ins includes compositing effects, film effects, blur and defocus effects, and the especially impressive Light!, which can spice up plain-looking shots with natural lighting effects.

- **55mm:** These plug-ins focus on the optics, film grain, and color produced by film lenses and trendy filmic looks. There's some overlap between 55mm and Digital Film Lab, with 55mm offering additional options that mimic more lens filters.

- **zMatte:** For those who want to do expert bluescreen and greenscreen keying but can't afford Ultimatte, this may be the way to go.

*StageTools' *Moving Picture* (www.stagetools.com)

If you're creating a documentary-style project and need to pan and zoom a lot of high-resolution images (Ken Burns style), Moving Picture gives you a very speedy tool. The plug-in's claim to fame is its ease of use.

In addition, unlike Avid Pan and Zoom, Moving Picture can handle alpha channels, so you can use it to animate images over a background layer. In addition, the tool lets you distort and rotate your images, which Profound Effects' similar Move plug-in does not do.

*Profound Effects' *Elastic Gasket* (profoundeffects.com):

Let's face it: After Effects (AE) is still probably the top choice for compositing, though Boris RED is right on its heels. Profound Effects' very popular Elastic Gasket enables you to use several AE plug-ins from within the Xpress Pro interface. Check the company's Web site to see the current list see table B1. Keep in mind that Boris RED also accepts many AE plug-ins; combine RED with Elastic Gasket, and you can get a lot of compositing done using familiar AE plug-ins without ever having to leave Xpress Pro.

THIRD-PARTY AVX PLUG-INS

Table B.1

Elastic Gasket–Compatible After Effects Plug-Ins

Plug-in Name	Description	Web Site
BigFX's FilmFX	Film look plug-in	bigfx.com
Conoa's 3D Effects	3D creation, object creation	conoa.com
Digital Anarchy: Text Anarchy	Text animation	digitalanarchy.com
Digital Anarchy: Gradient!	gradient creation	digitalanarchy.com
Digital Anarchy: Psunami 1.0	Photorealistic water	digitalanarchy.com
Digital Anarchy: Aurora Sky	Sky and star creation	digitalanarchy.com
Trapcode: Shine	Popular text lighting effect	trapcode.com
Trapcode: Starglow	Star-shaped glow creation	trapcode.com

Note: These were the plug-ins available as of October 2003.

3 Prong Effects (3.prong.com)

Whereas some plug-ins try to reproduce grungy film problems, these plug-ins aim to fix them:

♦ **ColorFiX:** The main selling point of this color correction program is its feature that lets you select one color and make everything else black and white (something Xpress Pro's Color Correction tools can't do).

♦ **DirtFiX:** This plug-in provides an easy (and cost-saving) way to paint over film dirt and defects with clone patches (a feature that usually requires an advanced program like Commotion). You can also use DirtFiX to hide unwanted elements in a shot.

♦ **FlickerFiX:** This repair-oriented plug-in helps remove unwanted flicker from film or video caused by changing lighting, auto-iris problems, and so on. It also includes Twitter-FX to cut interlace flicker from computer images (very handy!).

♦ **SpeedRamP:** This plug-in, along with Boris RED/Continuum's Velocity Remapping and Re:Vision Twixtor (which you can use with Boris RED), are probably the best options for creating customizable speed ramps in Xpress Pro. The Speed Ramp plug-in features FilmSim, which adds a 3:2 pulldown to video to make it look more like film.

dTective from Avid and Ocean Systems (oceansystems.com)

The dTective group of plug-ins is used mainly by law enforcement for forensic purposes, to enhance surveillance video and audio to bring out details that are initially too dark, blurry, or muffled to detect.

Inscriber TitleMotion, TitleMotion Pro, and Texture Pak (Windows only) (inscriber.com)

The Inscriber plug-ins cover all things title-related, including 3D text, and provide numerous templates and logo design tools. The Texture Pak offers animated texture mappings for text.

Pixelan Spicemaster (Windows only) (pixelan.com)

The Spicemaster plug-ins are best known for their transitions and their prodigious number of preset effects. For those who prefer subtlety over overt "cheese," their directional dissolves are especially interesting as alternatives to Avid's standard fare.

Profound Effects' *Swim and Move*

◆ **Move:** This plug-in, meant for panning and zooming around high-resolution stills, is similar to Avid's Pan and Zoom and StageTools' Moving Picture. One of the best things about this effect is that it handles alpha channels, which Avid Pan and Zoom does not; this makes it possible to pan and zoom oddly shaped company icons, for instance.

The main drawback of Move is that you can't rotate your image from side to side (as in VH-1's *Behind the Music* documentaries). (If you need this rotating capability, see "StageTools' Moving Picture" earlier in this chapter.)

◆ **Swim:** This distortion/refraction effect is good for creating liquid-like, rippling effects. Before biting, you may want to compare Swim to similar effects in bundles like Sapphire and the Boris products.

Ultimatte's *AdvantEdge* (ultimatte.com)

Ultimatte's AdvantEdge is considered the hands-down winner for software-based bluescreen and greenscreen work, with advanced spill suppression, matte clean-up, and roto screen correction (an automatic process that eases the potential tedium of rotoscoping). AdvantEdge is especially good for applying chroma keys on notoriously difficult DV footage.

You can go to Ultimatte's Web site, download a demo, and also download some sample bluescreen and greenscreen images to test this plug-in's matte creation and matte fix-it capabilities.

OMF Interchange via Automatic Duck (automaticduck.com)

At the writing of this book, Automatic Duck's Pro Import and Automatic Sequence Export Pro are much-hyped, celebrity plug-ins among Avid and Final Cut Pro editors that may spell the death of EDLs.

◆ **Automatic Duck Pro Import:** This plug-in allows you to translate an Xpress Pro Timeline into Adobe After Effects and Boris RED 3GL (**Figure B.2**). This capability isn't so dazzling if you're working with Boris RED, since RED so tightly integrates with Xpress Pro, but it's a big time saver if you're working with AE.

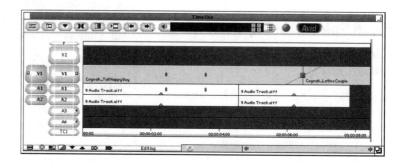

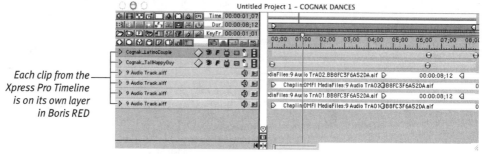

Each clip from the Xpress Pro Timeline is on its own layer in Boris RED

Figure B.2 When you export an Xpress Pro Timeline as an OMF file (above), you can import it into Boris RED (below) or Adobe After effects using the Automatic Duck Import plug-in.

You install the plug-in in Boris RED 3GL and Adobe After Effects, not Xpress Pro. Then you select your Xpress Pro sequence, choose File> Export, and export an OMF 2.0 (or AAF) file of the sequence. In RED or AE, Automatic Duck import is a menu option.

All of your Xpress Pro Timeline video and audio clips line up on separate tracks of the RED or AE Timeline. You can then do what you want with the Xpress Pro sequence, render to the Avid codec, and drag and drop the sequence back into Xpress Pro.

♦ **Automatic Sequence Export Pro:** This plug-in can translate the Final Cut Pro Timeline to any Avid system. It is often used by those who edit their offline (low resolution) project in Final Cut Pro but then want to online (finish at high resolution) in Avid Symphony. Conceivably, you can use Xpress Pro plus Mojo as a good online solution as well, since Mojo handles uncompressed video.

As of this writing, Automatic Duck for exporting from Xpress Pro to FCP (the opposite) has yet to be released. But to learn how to perform such a transfer (with the help of Sebsky Tools), see the sidebar "Moving a Project from Xpress Pro to FCP or FCP to Xpress Pro" in Chapter 15.

THIRD-PARTY AVX PLUG-INS

Stock Motion Graphics

Stock motion graphics are typically premade moving backgrounds created by 2D and 3D motion-graphic artists. When you buy these collections, you buy a license to use them in your productions. These stock animations can serve as backgrounds or textures in promos, network identities, corporate videos, DVD menus, educational videos, and so on. Typically, they are loopable, meaning that you can duplicate them back to back without visual jumps in the image at the cut point.

Most editors don't use stock motion backgrounds raw; rather, they use transfer modes (blend modes) in combination with alpha mattes to create customized looks. (To find out how to get a virtually free plug-in that enables transfer modes in Xpress Pro, see the sidebar, "Using Transfer (Composite/Blend) Modes in Xpress Pro" below.)

Your author investigated several stock motion-graphic packages and recommends the following as the top five resources in terms of quality and budget.

DV Footage Source (DVFootageSource.com)

DVFootageSource.com (your author's number-one recommendation) may be a small operation, but the quality of its motion-graphic backgrounds, animations, and textures rivals the eye candy of the more-established, higher-end sources.

At the time of this writing, each 20-movie collection of background loops sells for $40. The company also offers collections of animations, animated loops, textured backgrounds, and customizable text animations in the form of After Effects projects. Quality, variety, and price considered, these animations are a top choice for the budget-conscious editor or producer.

Using Transfer (Composite/Blend) Modes in Xpress Pro

As of this book's writing, if you become a member of DMN's ultra-affordable digital stock resources service (digitalstockresources.com), you can freely download the Profound Effects plug-in Transfer from the DMN Web site. Transfer enables you to blend video layers together using modes such as Screen, Add, and Multiply. Transfer is a must-have for anyone who wants to do basic compositing work in Xpress Pro.

DMN's *Digital Stock Resources* (digitalstockresources.com)

Digital Media Net features a great, affordable community resource for not just stock motion backgrounds, but stock videos, music, 3D objects, and still images. Different companies and members of the DV community upload their stock materials, which you can download for a membership fee of $1.54 a week.

Admittedly, DMN needs to get more content on the site; as of this writing, you can probably download everything they have in two or three weeks. So upload your own goodies, and that will encourage others to follow suit.

Digital Juice (digitaljuice.com)

Digital Juice is a popular, established provider of both animated and still stock backgrounds. What have made editors especially happy are the following:

◆ **Editor's Toolkit:** The Editor's Toolkit is excellent because of its variety: the multiple DVD bundle includes fancy animated backgrounds as well as lower-third templates, still objects, fonts, and black-and white mattes (for alpha channels).

◆ **Jump backs:** Jump backs are loopable motion backgrounds that can be easily speed adjusted using the included Juicer utility.

✔ Tip

■ Digital Juice also sells a collection of stock footage. It lacks the film quality of footage from a company like ArtBeats, but it offers decent quality for the budget-conscious producer.

12-Inch Design's *Production Blox* (12inchdesign.com)

12-Inch Design, which releases a new stock package every three months, is the high-end of stock motion-graphic purveyors in terms of slickness and price. The company's animated backgrounds come bundled with matching static elements (including lower thirds, for documentary name tags) that you can animate yourself. In addition, its DVDs are packaged with animated (black-and-white) mattes for creating alpha channels.

3D Backgrounds (3dbackgrounds.com)

3D Backgrounds' Corporate Animation collection is an affordable batch of animated backgrounds similar to what you find at DvFootageSource, Digital Juice, and 12-Inch Design. The company's Nature's Motion collection features stock footage of moving clouds, fire, and water. 3D Backgrounds also sells a cheesy (though apparently very popular) collection of wedding animations.

Adding Music to Your Xpress Pro Project

If you want to use music in your Xpress Pro movie, usually you will follow either of two routes:

- **Compose music or hire a composer:** If you have musical skills, you can create an original musical score yourself; even if you can't play an instrument, you can use one of the powerful loop-oriented soundtrack creation applications available that make creating an impressive track very easy.

  (For more information on loop-oriented applications, see "Creating Soundtracks with Loop Software" later in this chapter.)

  Hiring a composer isn't as expensive as you might think. A good place to start is the bulletin board at a film school; you'll probably be amazed at how much talent you can sign on for a relatively small fee.

- **License prerecorded music:** Cutting music from your personal CD collection into your Xpress Pro projects can be fun, but ultimately you have to come to terms with the world of music licenses if you plan to broadcast, perform, or distribute your movie (including at film festivals and over the Internet) with someone else's music.

  The cheapest way to license prerecorded music is to buy a music collection with a buy-out license. (For more information, see the next section, "Buy-Out License Music Collections.")

  Licensing higher-quality music, however, usually entails purchasing needle-drop and production blanket licenses from higher-end companies. (For more information, see "Needle-Drop and Production-Blanket Music Licenses" later in this chapter.)

Buy-Out License Music Collections

A buy-out music collection typically offers the most affordable music licensing route you can take. When you buy a buy-out license music collection, you buy the rights to use the music whenever and however you want forever (certain restrictions may apply). Usually, the only additional requirement is that, if your project is broadcast, you must submit a cue sheet to the broadcast network. (For more information on cue sheets, see the sidebar "Cue Sheets Explained" later in this chapter.)

Unfortunately, most buy-out collections have tracks that most people consider rather cheesy. Synthesized sounds are not bad in themselves, but what disgruntles many video and film producers are inappropriate synth instrumentations, such as violins and trumpets that sound electronic.

Luckily, your dutiful author has sampled 30 to 35 buy-out music collections and lists his top five recommendations for quality and price here. Of course, as music is a matter of taste, sample tracks on company Web sites when possible.

Studio Cutz (studiocutz.com)

High up on my list of buy-out music library recommendations is a company called Mediatone Music, Inc. Its multistyle Studio Cutz Collection was composed by a sizable group of production music composers, many of whom compose for high-end needle-drop and blanket-production license libraries. Studio Cutz CDs offer, in this author's opinion, the best production values and instrument quality for the price. None of the sampled tracks contained anything generic, cheesy, or inappropriately synthy, and most of the tracks are subtle enough for under-scoring purposes.

Depending on how many CDs you buy, you can purchase buy-out licenses for Studio Cutz music for $37 per disc, a deal that will make any friend who signed up with a needle-drop or production-blanket service extremely jealous. Especially impressive are the rock, Latin, jazz and electronica-oriented tracks.

UniqueTracks (uniquetracks.com)

Another excellent group of collections are UniqueTracks' buy-out collections. These include full-length themes, remixes, backgrounds, transitions, and loops—all helpful for crafting correctly timed underscores. Your author especially likes the Classical Master Series (classical music with real instruments, categorized by mood), Pianoscapes (solo piano pieces), and the entire Project 2 Series (vintage rock and jazz).

Granted, there are a few cheesy tracks here and there, but overall, there's an impressive amount of compositional skill and scoring expertise behind what is one of the best-quality collections for the money. You can sample tracks on the Web site to judge for yourself

In addition, you can order UniqueTracks collections as regular CDs or as drag-and-drop-friendly digital files (WAV or AIFF). You can also buy UniqueTracks' music on a track-by-track basis and download the tracks directly from the Web site.

Crank City Music (crankcity.com)

Crank City's specialty is variety. Its four AMU (atmospheres, moods, and underscores) and two world music volumes include a vast array of musical styles; such variety is especially useful if you edit commercials, comedy sketch pieces, or other short-form material.

Crank City also has a classical music collection on a par with Unique Tracks'; again, you'll hear real orchestras. Especially helpful to the editor is the Transitions collection, which contain 5- to 25-second bumpers, stingers, segues, and hits to help your scenes flow from one to the next.

CSS Music and Redi-Loops (CssMusic.com) (Redi-loops.com)

It's easy to be overwhelmed by the sheer number of collections produced by CSS Music as its Web site features over 20 multi-CD collections. Admittedly, some of the tracks feature instruments that sound inappropriately synthesized, but if you're willing to invest some time hunting and pecking through samples, you can find many diamonds in the rough. Start with SuperThemes, which is the company's top-quality product and a good collection to consider buying as a whole. Or check out Target Trax, which, considering its budget-friendly price, has some well-conceived compositions and a lot of variety.

At CssMusic.com, follow the Free $40 Download link; you can search the collections and download any track that CSS Music sells, including full-length, 60-second, and 30-second versions. And if you do buy one of the collections on disc, it will come with a search utility (for finding the style you need quickly) and use MP4 compression, a near CD-quality format that will save you much hard drive space.

Redi-loops, a site run by the same people who run CSS, features some decent loop music collections, best manipulated in loop applications like Apple's Soundtracks or Ableton Live. (For other music loop sources, see **Table B.2**.)

(For more information on loop applications, see "Creating Soundtracks with Loop Software later in this chapter.)

Table B.2

Music Loop Sources	
WEB SITE ADDRESS	**FEATURES**
Mediasoftware.sonypictures.com/Loop_Libraries/	Loops for Acid Loop Library
Shockwave-Sound	Downloadable loops and tracks
KillerSound	Downloadable loops

Needle-Drop and Production-Blanket Music Licenses

High-end production music companies, like FirstCom.com and PremiereTracks.com, generally do not offer buy-out licenses. Instead, you pay for tracks per use (with a needle-drop license), or you pay for unlimited use of tracks over a certain number of productions or a certain period of time (with a production-blanket license).

Each company does business differently, and license costs often depend on your movie's distribution. For example, the Valentino Evergreen Music Collection (tvmusic.com), a collection of vintage orchestral music from the 40s, 50s, and 60s, has different needle-drop fees depending on the length of your project; whether the project is for broadcast; whether the broadcast distribution is local, regional, or national; and so on. Talk to representatives and look over Web sites carefully to nail down exactly what deals a company offers, and don't be afraid to negotiate.

That said, one per-use licensing service, Cuepop.com, doesn't charge you a fee. Composers upload their tracks at Cuepop to promote their work, and all you have to do is download what you need and submit a cue sheet when you use the music in a production. (For more information on cue sheets, see the sidebar "Cue Sheets Explained" later in this chapter.)

Know Your Rights

When it comes to music licensing, video and film producers typically need to consider four types of rights. When you purchase a buy-out music license or license music on a per-use (needle-drop) basis, make sure that you have the following rights, as necessary:

◆ **Synchronization right:** Very important for film and video producers, this is the right to synchronize a musical composition to visual images on film or video.

◆ **Public performance right:** This is the right a creator of a musical work has to authorize the use of a work in public. Anytime you screen your movie on cable or on a television station or in any public arena, the authorization of the copyright holder is required.

◆ **Mechanical right:** Mechanical rights give you the right to record and distribute a musical work. This right applies to a popular song that you record yourself or get a composer to duplicate.

◆ **Reproduction right:** This is the exclusive right of the music copyright owner to authorize the mechanical reproduction of a musical work on a record, CD, and so on. For film producers, this right is especially important if you want to release a soundtrack of your film that contains copyrighted material.

Cue Sheets Explained

If you license music and use it in a broadcast production, you are usually required to submit a cue sheet to the broadcast network, which then submits the information to the local performance royalty organization.

A cue sheet details the nature of your project and lists all tracks used in your video or film, including duration information.

The performance royalty (or public performance) organization to which a cue sheet is submitted varies by country; in the United States, the two big organizations are BMI and ASCAP.

The benefit of cue sheets is that the composers and producers of the music you use in your project are financially compensated by funds set aside by the networks (HBO, for instance) as prepaid blanket music licenses to be distributed to composers.

For more information, visit the BMI (bmi.com) and ASCAP (ascap.com) Web sites.

ProTools and the DV Toolkit

In their current state, Xpress Pro's audio editing capabilities are not very formidable, especially since you cannot apply more than one AudioSuite plug-in to an audio clip at a time. So if you'll be sound designing your DV projects and creating soundtracks, you may want to consider getting a sound editing application such as ProTools (Digidesign.com). Owned by Avid, ProTools is an obvious favorite for Xpress Pro editors because of its easy file interchange capabilities.

For sound editing, ProTools LE with the Mbox (a USB-connected audio In/Out device) is the entry-level product and very popular among current Xpress DV and Xpress Pro editors. However, to import Xpress Pro OMF files into ProTools LE, you need to buy the DV Toolkit option, which facilitates OMF/AAF transfer and comes with additional film-related plug-ins. (See the next section, "AudioSuite Plug-ins.")

(For more information on exporting OMF files to ProTools, see Chapter 14, "Outputting and Exporting.")

AudioSuite Plug-ins

Since the engine behind Xpress Pro's AudioSuite is essentially a Digidesign product, you can install and use Digidesign's ProTools and third-party audio plug-ins and use them in your Xpress Pro Timeline; hence, you can apply these cool sound effects without ever touching ProTools.

Plug-ins helpful in film and video post-production include the following:

♦ **Synchro Arts' VocAlign:** Use this plug-in for dialogue replacement (or dubbing), a common need in most video and film productions to fix bad or unintelligible dialogue. It can be installed directly in Xpress Pro's AudioSuite or in ProTools.

♦ **GRM Tools:** GRM's myriad plug-ins include Doppler, which can widen perceived audio channel separation to an extreme degree and manipulate channel placement to create the Doppler effect for objects traveling across the screen at high speeds. Shuffling is a granular delay plug-in that can garble a sound as if it were playing over a bad radio or turn one voice into a crowd of voices.

Creating Soundtracks with Loop Software

Since Apple's release of Soundtrack, a stand-alone application that uses loops to create soundtracks for video projects, the loop manipulation method of creating soundtracks has been gaining attention. Suffice it to say that looping software is a cost-effective alternative to licensing music or hiring composers.

Loop-oriented applications make soundtrack creation easy even for nonmusical people, allowing you to layer and manipulate loops (from one to four second segments of music) in a variety of ways without ever having to play an instrument or know how to read music.

Apple's Soundtrack is impressive mainly for its ease of use, though much more powerful applications are available, such as Ableton Live (Mac and Windows), which includes MIDI recording capabilities, and the popular Acid Pro.

Finding Sound Effects

There are a lot of buy-out license sound effects collections out there, but if you're a budget-conscious editor or producer, why not look for free sound effects first?

Here are some Web sites that offer links to free sound effects:

◆ **TheFreeSite.com/Free_Sounds:** This site features a master list of Web sites that offer free sound effects as well as free music clips and loops.

◆ **FindSounds.com:** This site searches the entire Internet for sound effects by keyword. It lets you filter your search by file format, number of channels, resolution (bit rate), and sample rate.

✔ Tip

■ Of course, free sound effects still may require licensing. Check free sites for copyright information.

The iPod of Sound Effects and the Need for Speed

There are obvious advantages to buying an actual sound effects collection. For one thing, it can save you from the arduous task of searching endlessly through Web sites. Unfortunately, many collections come with a lot of unlabeled CD tracks and an accompanying track title booklet (something else to search through).

Some collections, however, do come with pre-labeled tracks and search applications. For example, Valentino music (tvmusic.com) produces Pocket Studio, a portable 20-GB iPod-like USB device that comes loaded with thousands of prelabeled sound effects and music clips.

You can bring such a plug-and-play device to any onsite editing job without much hassle—very impressive to a client on a tight deadline when you perform a keyword search on your desktop, instantly display the effect you need, and

INDEX

INDEX